TELEVISION

Fp THE FREE PRESS · NEW YORK

COLLIER-MACMILLAN LIMITED · LONDON

TELEVISION

Selection of Readings from TV Guide® Magazine

Edited by Barry G. Cole

The Free Press
A DIVISION OF THE MACMILLAN COMPANY
866 Third Avenue, New York, New York 10022

Collier-Macmillan Canada Ltd., Toronto, Ontario

Library of Congress Catalog Card Number: 72-111373

printing number
1 2 3 4 5 6 7 8 9 10

PREFACE

Despite an increase in the number of books and articles concerning commercial television, there has been no single collection of readings designed to provide an overview of today's medium: that is, the content of television, how information about the audience is obtained and used, television's role and its significance in society, and its regulation and control. This consideration, along with my conviction, shared by many of my colleagues, that much of the most significant material about television has appeared in TV GUIDE, provided the impetus for this volume.

This book, therefore, has a dual purpose. First, to make readily available some of the important writing about contemporary commercial television from TV GUIDE; second, to at least partially fulfill the need for a basic reader in television which will be of benefit to both the layman and the college student of broadcasting and communications.

Throughout, I have attempted to keep editing to a minimum. I have updated information in footnotes and in the introductions when I thought it useful. It has occasionally been advisable to delete material from individual articles when the material was dated or when the subject was covered in greater detail and more appropriately placed in other portions of the book. These deletions are formally noted.

Some of the more lengthy articles included in this collection were originally published as separate parts in two or more issues of TV GUIDE. In some cases these divisions were eliminated while in other instances material reviewing earlier parts of the article were deleted and the divisions were kept intact.

The articles are not reproduced in chronological order and thus there are many apparent inconsistencies in the titles of industry personnel. The references to executives and personnel are so numerous, however, that in most instances I felt it inadvisable to tamper with these titles and risk interfering with the reader's concentration.

I wish to acknowledge my gratitude to Professor Robert Schenkken, Mrs. Martha Budd, Miss Clara Gebauer and Mrs. Irene Layton for obtaining resource materials; and to Mrs. Carlene Delameter, Miss Pam Leming, Mrs. Ann Grubbs and Miss Judy Gates for typing the manuscript. The Research Department of TV GUIDE was a valuable aid in obtaining information for the editor's notes.

I am obligated to all fifty-three contributors, and to Professor Stanley Donner, Joseph Osbourne and a number of my former students at the University of Texas who read portions of the manuscript. Charles Clift III, a Ph.D. candidate in the Department of Mass Communications at Indiana University and my research assistant for 1969-70 was especially helpful in checking the entire manuscript for inaccuracies and omissions. My special thanks to my wife, Fran, for her professional assistance and encouragement.

To Merrill Panitt, editor of TV GUIDE, my sincere appreciation for his full cooperation and help whenever it was requested.

B.G.C.

CONTENTS

PREFACE   v

CONTRIBUTORS   xiii

I NEWS

QUALITY OF NEWS   3

How Well Does Television Keep America Informed?   11
NEIL HICKEY

Okay, You're for Motherhood, but What About Vietnam?   20
JOEL H. COHEN

TV News Bulletins: Too Many and Too Soon?   25
NEIL HICKEY

A Creed for Television Newsmen   30
JAMES C. HAGERTY

VIETNAM   33

The Vietnam War: Is Television Giving Us the Picture?   36
NEIL HICKEY

Does TV Confuse Americans About Vietnam?   55
MARTIN MALONEY

CIVIL DISORDERS AND URBAN COVERAGE   60

A Look at TV's Coverage of Violence   63
NEIL HICKEY

Detroit: Television on Trial   70
NEIL HICKEY

POLITICAL CONVENTIONS · 78

Television's Role in Politics · 81
WILLIAM S. WHITE

Television in Turmoil · 87
NEIL HICKEY

Chicago: A Post-Mortem · 106
REUVEN FRANK

2 PROGRAMMING

GETTING ON THE AIR · 119

Why Shows Are Canceled · 122
RICHARD K. DOAN

The Man on the 34th Floor · 127
RICHARD WARREN LEWIS

How Did THAT Show Ever Get a Sponsor? · 135
ROBERT LEONARD

How TV Shows Are Sold · 138
NEIL HICKEY
JOSEPH FINNIGAN

The Show That Died After One Night · 147
RICHARD K. DOAN
JOSEPH FINNIGAN

DAYTIME PROGRAMMING · 153

The Soaps—Anything but 99-44/100 Percent Pure · 156
EDITH EFRON

Everything's Up-to-Date in Soap Operas · 163
MARYA MANNES

America's Great Spectator Sport · 169
EDITH EFRON

DRAMA · 174

Can TV Drama Survive? · 176
EDITH EFRON

TV's Disastrous Brain Drain · 183
DICK HOBSON

Is Drama the Thing? · 188
RICHARD K. DOAN

COMEDY 192

The Hollywood Sphinx and His Laff Box 194
DICK HOBSON

When Comedy Writers Hunt Jobs, It's Not Very Funny 201
BILL O'HALLAREN

Why Do You Laugh? 204
SHELDON LEONARD

SPORTS 208

Greed Is the Name of the Game 210
STANLEY FRANK

What TV Has Done to Sports 216
STANLEY FRANK

TV and Sports: A Rebuttal 223
WILLIAM DAVEY

When Will Sportscasters Be Allowed to Speak Up? 226
MELVIN DURSLAG

ADVERTISING 230

The Commercial's the Thing 233
PETER ANDREWS

Commercials and Our Changing Times 236
PATRICK WALSH

Does TV Advertising Make You Buy? 239
MARTIN MAYER

A Word About Commercials 246
RICHARD K. DOAN

Why Color Commercials Are Successful 249
JUDY JOBIN

BLACKS ON THE SCREEN 252

Black is the Color of Our New TV 255
MARTIN MALONEY

What the Negro Wants From TV 259
ART PETERS

WOMEN ON THE SCREEN 265

Television and the Feminine Mystique 267
BETTY FRIEDAN

Should Women Only Be Seen and Not Heard?   276
MARYA MANNES

3 CENSORSHIP AND CONTROL

CENSORSHIP AND CONTROL   285

The FCC   290
MARTIN MAYER

Is Speech on Television Really Free?   303
EDITH EFRON

Is Speech on Television Really Free?   310
DEAN EDWARD BARRETT
SENATOR JOHN O. PASTORE

Is Speech on Television Really Free?   316
WILLIAM F. BUCKLEY, JR.
ARTHUR M. SCHLESINGER, JR.

The Silent Screen   322
NICHOLAS JOHNSON

He Has Exercised His Right to Be Wrong   330
RICHARD SALANT

"PERMISSIVENESS"   338

Senator John O. Pastore's Campaign to "Clean Up" Television   340
SENATOR JOHN O. PASTORE
RICHARD K. DOAN

A Conversation With Television's Chief Censor   345
STOCKTON HELFFRICH
RICHARD K. DOAN

How Will TV Handle Sexy Movies?   350
PEGGY HUDSON

The New Movie Code   356

VIOLENCE   359

How Much Violence Is There on Television?   364

Television Violence Is Harmful   371
SENATOR CLAIBORNE PELL

Television Violence Is Not Harmful   376
MARTIN MALONEY

4 AUDIENCE

RATINGS   385

The Ratings, How Can They Be True?   388
RICHARD K. DOAN

Nielsen Defends His Rating Service   398
ARTHUR C. NIELSEN, JR.
THEODORE BERLAND

Who Watches What?   403
DICK HOBSON

OTHER AUDIENCE FEEDBACK   409

The Steiner Report: The People Look at Television   411
GARY STEINER
ROGER YOUMAN

What They Do With Your Letters   419
EDITH EFRON

A Station Just Can't Win   424
RICHARD F. AHLES

Who Speaks for the Viewer?   427
RICHARD K. DOAN

SHOULD THE AUDIENCE REIGN SUPREME?   432

Don't Give Viewers What They Want   434
HARRY J. SKORNIA

Television: The Lion That Squeaks   437
ARNOLD J. TOYNBEE

The Petulant Highbrow and TV   442
GILBERT SELDES

5 EFFECTS

TELEVISION'S ROLE   451

There Need Be No Apology, No Lament   453
LEE LOEVINGER

Television—The Comforting Presence   458
KARL MENNINGER
JEAN MENNINGER

The Electronic Express   461
RUSSELL LYNES

Pippa Passes, Ky., Joins the Nation   465
EDWARD MORRIS

Television's Contribution to the Senior Citizen   469
ELEANOR ROOSEVELT

POLITICS   472

Politics and Television   477
ARTHUR SCHLESINGER, JR.

CONTENTS

How TV Has Raised Campaign Costs   484
NEIL HICKEY

A Proposal for Unshackling Television   488
NEWTON N. MINOW
LAWRENCE LAURENT

Political Leaders, Broadcasters Debate the Minow Plan   494

CHILDREN   498

What Is TV Doing to Them?   501
NEIL HICKEY
EDITH EFRON

OTHER EFFECTS   536

Is Television Killing the English Language?   538
JESS STEIN

Does Television Tip the Scales of Justice?   541
LOUIS NIZER

It Has Battered Its Rivals Out of Shape   545
MARTIN MAYER

Television's Impact On Our Civilization   550
LOUIS KRONENBERGER

The Effect of Television   554
MARTIN MALONEY

6 THE FUTURE

THE FUTURE   563

Here Come the '70s   565
NEIL HICKEY
RICHARD K. DOAN
DAVID LACHENBRUCH

CATV—The Wave of TV's Future   581
RICHARD K. DOAN

Global Television—When?   586
RICHARD K. DOAN

INDEX

CONTRIBUTORS

RICHARD F. AHLES is Information Director for WTIC-TV, Hartford, Connecticut.

PETER ANDREWS is a freelance writer and the author of *A Tragedy of History*. He has been on the staff of *Readers Digest, Newsweek* magazine, and the Hearst Headline Service.

EDWARD W. BARRETT is the former Dean of the Graduate School of Journalism, Columbia University and now Director of the Communications Institute at the Academy for Educational Development. Mr. Barrett was Director of Overseas Operations for the office of War Information during World War II and was Assistant Secretary of State for Public Affairs from 1950 to 1952.

THEODORE BERLAND is a freelance writer. One of the magazines he writes for is TV GUIDE.

WILLIAM F. BUCKLEY, JR. is Editor-in-Chief of the *National Review*. One of the nation's best known political observers, Mr. Buckley has authored and contributed to a number of books and writes a syndicated newspaper column.

JOEL H. COHEN is a freelance writer and an occasional contributor to TV GUIDE.

WILLIAM DAVEY is an account executive for Colle & McVoy Advertising Agency in Minneapolis. When he wrote the article included here he was Promotion Manager for KSTP, a Minneapolis television station.

RICHARD K. DOAN is the writer of "The Doan Report," a weekly feature of TV GUIDE which reviews important industry developments. He was formerly a television observer for the New York Herald Tribune.

MELVIN DURSLAG is a frequent contributor to TV GUIDE, especially about television sports. He is the author of a newspaper column syndicated by King Features.

EDITH EFRON is a staff writer for TV GUIDE. She was formerly a *Time-Life* correspondent, Assistant Woman's Editor for *Look* magazine, and on the staff of the *New York Times* (Sunday) *Magazine*.

JOSEPH FINNIGAN is a writer and reporter for TV GUIDE's Los Angeles Bureau. He has worked on newspapers, magazines and a national wire service.

REUVEN FRANK is President of NBC News. Associated with that news organization since 1950 and producer of the *Huntley-Brinkley Report* from 1956 to 1962, Mr. Frank has received numerous Emmy awards for the news and documentary programs he has produced for NBC.

STANLEY FRANK is a freelance writer. He is a frequent contributor to TV GUIDE.

BETTY FRIEDAN is the author of *The Feminine Mystique*. Since writing that book in 1964, she has elaborated on her theories of the female's role in American society through lectures and articles.

JAMES C. HAGERTY is Vice President for Corporate Relations at ABC. Mr. Hagerty came to ABC in 1961 as Vice President for News, following an eight-year tenure as Press Secretary to President Eisenhower and earlier assignments with Governor Thomas Dewey of New York and *The New York Times*.

STOCKTON HELFFRICH is Director of the NAB Code Authority. He was previously Chief Censor at NBC.

NEIL HICKEY is Chief of TV GUIDE's New York Bureau. A former newspaperman and magazine writer, he is co-author of *Adam Clayton Powell and the Politics of Race*.

DICK HOBSON is a staff writer for TV GUIDE. He was formerly associated with various television film companies.

PEGGY HUDSON is the Radio-TV Editor for *Scholastic* magazine. She is an occasional contributor to TV GUIDE.

JUDY JOBIN is a member of TV GUIDE's New York Bureau. She occasionally does articles for the magazine.

NICHOLAS JOHNSON has been a member of the Federal Communications Commission since 1966. A former law professor at the University of California at Berkeley, Commissioner Johnson was Chairman of the Maritime Administration in the Department of Commerce at the time of his appointment to the F.C.C.

LOUIS KRONENBERGER is Professor of Theatre Arts at Brandeis University and a staff contributor to *Atlantic Monthly*. A former drama critic for *Time* magazine and the author and editor of numerous books, he has taught at Harvard, Columbia, Stanford and Oxford Universities.

DAVID LACHENBRUCH is Editorial Director of *Television Digest*, an industry newsletter. He is a frequent contributor to TV GUIDE on the technological aspects of television.

LAWRENCE LAURENT is the television critic for the *Washington Post* and Chairman of the Editorial Board of the *Television Quarterly*. He edited *Equal Time: The Private Broadcaster and the Public Interest* by Newton Minow and was a contributing author to *The Eighth Art* and *Television's Impact on American Culture*.

ROBERT LEONARD is a pseudonym for a retired Vice President in charge of Television at one of Madison Avenue's largest advertising agencies.

SHELDON LEONARD is an executive of several television production companies and a trustee of the Academy of Television Arts and Sciences. A former film and radio actor, Mr. Leonard has produced numerous successful television shows including *The Andy Griffith Show*, *The Dick Van Dyke Show*, *The Danny Thomas Show*, *Gomer Pyle, U.S.M.C.*, *I Spy* and *My World and Welcome to It*.

RICHARD WARREN LEWIS is a frequent contributor to major magazines. He was formerly an editor of *Show Business Illustrated*.

LEE LOEVINGER was an F.C.C. Commissioner from 1963 to 1968 and is now an attorney in Washington. He has been an Associate Justice on the Minnesota Supreme Court, Assistant United States Attorney-General in charge of the Antitrust Division of the Department of Justice, and a professor at the University of Minnesota.

RUSSELL LYNES was Managing Editor of *Harpers* magazine from 1947 to 1967 and since then has been a contributing editor to that magazine. He is the author of eight books, including *Highbrow, Lowbrow and Middlebrow*, *Tastemakers*, and *A Surfeit of Honey*.

MARTIN J. MALONEY is Professor of Radio and Television at Northwestern University. A frequent contributor to professional journals and the author of hundreds of radio and television scripts, Professor Maloney has written chapters in several books on broadcasting and is currently writing a book on mass media and society.

MARYA MANNES is a magazine writer and author. A former feature editor for *Vogue* magazine and *Glamour* magazine, Miss Mannes was a regular contributor to *The Reporter* magazine.

MARTIN MAYER is a well-known freelance writer and the author of six books, including *Madison Avenue USA*. A former associate editor of *Esquire* magazine, Mr. Mayer has done extensive writing, research and consulting in the field of education since 1961.

JENETTA (JEAN) L. MENNINGER is a psychiatrist and the wife of Karl Menninger. She has co-authored some of her husband's works and has been active at the Menninger Foundation.

KARL A. MENNINGER is one of the nation's foremost psychiatrists and is Chairman of the Board of the Menninger Foundation, Topeka, Kansas. The author of numerous books and articles on psychiatry, Dr. Menninger is on the advisory councils of many important medical and research bodies.

NEWTON N. MINOW, Chairman of the Federal Communications Commission from 1961 to 1963, is now a member of a Chicago law firm. A collection of Mr. Minow's speeches as F.C.C. Chairman may be found in *Equal Time: The Private Broadcaster and the Public Interest.*

EDWARD MORRIS was Assistant Professor of English at Alice Lloyd College, Pippa Passes, Kentucky when he wrote the article included here.

ARTHUR C. NIELSEN, JR. has been President of A. C. Nielsen Company since 1957. He is a director of several companies and President of the Management Executives Society.

LOUIS NIZER is a noted lawyer and is General Counsel for the Motion Picture Association of America. A frequent counselor for actors and writers, Mr. Nizer is also the author of six books, including *My Life in Court* and *The Jury Returns.*

BILL O'HALLAREN is a freelance television comedy writer. His credits include some of television's most successful comedy shows.

JOHN O. PASTORE has been United States Senator (Democrat) from Rhode Island since 1950. As Chairman of the Communications Subcommittee of the Senate Commerce Committee, Senator Pastore is closely involved in matters relating to governmental regulation of broadcasting.

CLAIBORNE PELL has been United States Senator (Democrat) from Rhode Island since 1961. Senator Pell was the former Director of the International Rescue Commission, and he received the Legion of Honor from France, the Knight Crown of Italy and the Red Cross of Merit from Portugal for his work prior to his election to the Senate.

ART PETERS is City Editor of *The Philadelphia Tribune*, a Negro newspaper. He is a frequent contributor to magazines.

ANNA ELEANOR (MRS. FRANKLIN D.) ROOSEVELT was the wife of thirty-second President of the United States. She was the author of eleven books, was active in educational and political affairs and, at one time, had her own television show.

RICHARD S. SALANT has been President of CBS News since 1966. Before becoming a director of CBS in 1961, Mr. Salant was an attorney for the United States Government and a Vice President of CBS Incorporated.

ARTHUR M. SCHLESINGER, JR. is Schweitzer Professor of Humanities at City University of New York and was a special assistant to the President from 1961 to 1964. Professor Schlesinger was awarded the Pulitzer Prize for History in 1945 for *The Age of Jackson*, and the Pulitzer Prize for Biography in 1965 for *A Thousand Days: John F. Kennedy in the White House*.

GILBERT SELDES has been a pioneer critic and practitioner in television; he was the first Director of Television Programs for CBS from 1937 to 1945, the first Dean of the Annenberg School of Communications at the University of Pennsylvania and a former television critic for TV GUIDE. He is the author of *The Seven Lively Arts, The Great Audience,* and *The Public Arts*.

HARRY J. SKORNIA is Professor of Radio and Television at the University of Illinois, Chicago campus. The former President of the National Association of Educational Broadcasters, Professor Skornia is the author of several books on television, including *Television and Society* and *Television and the News: A Critical Appraisal*.

JESS STEIN is a Vice President of Random House and the Editor of the *Random House Dictionary*, the *American College Dictio-*

nary, American Everyday Dictionary and the *Basic Everyday Dictionary*. He was formerly the head of the Random House college reference department.

GARY A. STEINER was a social psychologist at the University of Chicago. Dr. Steiner was the author of *The People Look at Television* and co-author of *Human Behavior: An Index of Scientific Findings*.

ARNOLD J. TOYNBEE is Professor Emeritus of Byzantine and Modern Greek Language, Literature and History at the University of London. The distinguished British historian has written numerous books since 1915 and is the author of the thirteen-volume *A Study of History*.

PATRICK WALSH is a freelance writer. He was formerly Associate Editor of TV GUIDE.

WILLIAM S. WHITE has been a nationally syndicated political columnist and has written a number of books on politics. A former Senate correspondent for *The New York Times* and Washington correspondent for *Harpers* magazine, Mr. White received the Pulitzer Prize in Letters in 1955, the year he wrote *The Taft Story*.

ROGER J. YOUMAN is Assistant Managing Editor of TV GUIDE. He is co-author of the book *How Sweet It Was: Television—A Pictorial Commentary*.

NEWS

Chapter I

Quality
of News

William Paley, who has directed CBS since 1928, contends that "at no point in our history has the function of news and public affairs broadcasting been so critical and important to our national life." Fred Friendly, CBS news president until 1966, states "every day there is more for the people of the world to know and every day what we don't know can kill us."

News has been called the *raison d'être* of local stations. It is one of the few remaining vestiges of creative programming, and the quality of news coverage differentiates good from bad stations. Former FCC Commissioner Lee Loevinger (a contributor to this collection, pp. 453-457) seems to support this contention with his statement: "Since it is the journalistic function which gives the principle social value to broadcasting, I would measure performance principally by the degree to which it performs this function."

According to the Roper survey, commissioned by the broadcasting industry, television is the primary source of news for approximately six out of ten Americans over the age of twenty-one. The Roper survey, first conducted in 1959, indicates also that television is considered by American adults to be the most believable of all the news media. The sixth and most recent survey, taken shortly after the 1968 elections, indicated that even the controversial coverage of the 1968 Democratic Convention in Chicago (a subject which is discussed at some length on pp. 87-115) failed to reduce the public's reliance on and the belief in television news. When asked, for example, which news media source they would be most likely to believe in the case of conflicting news stories, 44 percent of the respondents indicated television. Newspapers, which ranked second on this question, were cited by 21 percent of the respondents. This finding was reinforced by the 1969 Louis Harris study for *Time* magazine. When asked to imagine "only one source of news," nearly one-half

3

4 of the respondents preferred television while one-third preferred newspapers.

Public reliance on television news is a cause for concern in various quarters. Harry Skornia, author of *Television News: A Critical Appraisal* (and a contributor to this volume, pp. 434-436), has criticized television news for too much "rip and read" reporting— from the teletype machine, continual plagarism from other media, selection of the visual over the significant, overemphasis on firstness or fastness, preference for conflict or violence, use of quantity and expense as the criteria for excellence, fragmentation and discontinuity, preoccupation with gadgetry, consideration of profit and meekness in the face of industry censorship and taboos. Skornia feels that a great deal of research needs to be conducted with regard to broadcast news. Some of his concerns include: How much and what kind of news do people really absorb and retain? Do commercials impede absorption or comprehension and to what degree? Do all people always prefer the visual story to a straight talk presentation?

Robert McNeil, former NBC newsman now working for the British Broadcasting Corporation and author of *The People Machine,* is another outspoken critic of television journalism. McNeil claims that television news is suffused with show business values, disregards researching for facts as a primary function, subordinates the reporter's role and concentrates on recording action rather than probing for its significance. McNeil's particular concerns are what he considers the superficiality of coverage—the average wordage on a half-hour newscast could fit on the front page of most newspapers— and the lack of adequate analysis and interpretation.

McNeil suggests that television as a journalistic medium is not highly esteemed by print journalists who contend that TV journalism has drunk from the same well and then has been influenced by businessmen, entertainers and advertisers. Walter Cronkite, in his 1969 William Allan White Memorial Lecture at the University of Kansas, defended TV news from this kind of criticism by newspapermen and drew some relevant comparisons between electronic journalism and the press. He argued that while television is criticized by newspapers for interrupting news with commercials, papers continually break-up their stories and force readers to chase through numerous pages of advertising to pick up the story on a later page. The press criticizes television sensationalism, yet the papers cover the same stories, often with front page photographs. Television news has been said to be too concerned with competitive ratings, but the newspapers had vicious circulation battles in earlier days of com-

petition between several owners in one locality. Although television 5
has been accused of blandness in many interviews, the same bland
interviews are quoted in the papers the next day. There are rigid time
limits in television news broadcasting; however, the number of columns in newspapers is determined, not by the news events of the day,
but by the amount of advertising obtained. Cronkite further pointed
out that while station owners are inspired by profits, the same can
also be said of newspaper owners.

Cronkite emphasized that the viewer of the TV newscast receives
essential information as a guide to the events of the world for that day,
even though only about twenty items are included in an average half-
hour nightly newscast and the script read by the news reporters could
fit on the front page of the newspaper. The television news audience
is introduced to the people and places making news in a way that is
not possible in other media with graphics enabling television to communicate a great deal of information in a few seconds. Cronkite acknowledged, however, that there is still not enough investigative
reporting and analysis being aired.

Eric Sevareid, who is probably TV's best known commentator
and, like Cronkite, a former newspaperman, supports Cronkite's defense against criticisms from the press. Sevareid contended in a
December 1967 TV GUIDE article that "1. The press covers TV and
not vice versa. 2. The press accepts the TV system of predicting
elections, not vice versa. 3. The movement of aspiring journalists
is from the press to TV, far more than vice versa. 4. Newspaper
salaries have risen in the direction of TV salaries, not vice versa."

Two conflicting criticisms of television news were made within
three days of each other in November 1969. On November 10, a
survey supported by the Alfred O. du Pont Foundation and Columbia University, published as *Survey of Broadcast Journalism 1968-69,*
was released. The jurors for the survey were Sir William Haley,
former director-general of the BBC and former editor of the London
Times, author-critics Marya Mannes and Michael Arlen, Richard
Baker, acting dean of the Columbia Graduate School of Journalism,
and his predecessor, Dean Edward Barrett (Mannes and Barrett are
both contributors to this volume, see pp. 163-168, 276-280, and
pp. 310-312).

The jurors concluded that when television covered major news
events as they happened in 1968-69, it was "fascinating, beautiful,
exciting, devastating, illuminating, or whatever other adjective of
admiration one wished to apply," but in the "no less essential and
challenging chores of covering day-to-day news and public affairs . . .

6 the picture was somewhat less dazzling." According to the jurors, "investigative efforts by news departments of commercial networks were disappointing . . . and few appeared especially notable for the amount of subsurface probing required." Moreover, documentary programming hit a new low: of twelve major categories of documentaries, only three, race and minorities, politics, and crime and youth received adequate coverage.

The survey suggested that the drama and violence of the assassinations of Dr. Martin Luther King and Senator Robert Kennedy and the two political conventions seemed to give the industry "a new sense of dignity, an increased awareness of the import of its journalistic functions," but in the months that followed "good intentions have been deplored and ridiculed where special interests were threatened, dedication has flagged in favor of profits, nerves have failed when stockholders have grown restive." The jurors found that television could often be accused of reluctance to undertake hardhitting exposés, particularly where these might be expected to arouse major controversy. "Broadcasting must be enlisted to challenge and inspire rather than indulge and enervate the public," the report stated. "Broadcasters must pursue an expanding view of life and insist upon presenting it as it is."

On November 13, 1969, three days after the du Pont-Columbia survey was released criticizing television for avoiding controversy, Vice President Agnew made a speech in Des Moines, Iowa, in which he accused the networks of undertaking an "endless pursuit of controversy." Agnew's speech was triggered by the "instant analysis and querulous criticism" of President Nixon's Vietnam speech of November 3 by network commentators and their "expert" guests. The Vice President's address was carried live by all three networks and his remarks caused a controversy of their own.

Mr. Agnew's major emphasis was directed at "A small group of men, numbering perhaps no more than a dozen anchormen, commentators and executive producers" who "not only enjoy a right of instant rebuttal to every Presidential address, but, more importantly, wield a free hand in selecting, presenting and interpreting the great issues in our nation." The Vice President stated that these men "can create national issues overnight" and "can elevate men from obscurity to national prominence within a week . . . can reward some politicians with national exposure and ignore others." "For millions of Americans," Agnew continued, "the network reporter who covers a continuing issue like the ABM or civil rights, becomes, in effect, the presiding judge in a national trial by jury." According to the Vice

President, this power is not confined to the substantive. A raised 7
eyebrow, an inflection of the voice, a caustic remark about the veracity
of a public official or the wisdom of a Government policy can carry
great influence.

This "small and unelected elite . . . a tiny enclosed fraternity
of privileged men elected by no one and enjoying a monopoly sanc-
tioned and licensed by Government" represents to Agnew "a concentration of power over American public opinion unknown in history,
a power which we would never give to an elected Government."
While some people might argue that this power presents no danger
in the hands of those who have used it responsibly, the Vice President
indicated that there was real question whether the "small elite" had
used their power responsibly. "Gresham's Law seems to be operating
in the network news" said the Vice President. "Bad news drives out
good news. The irrational is more controversial than the rational . . .
normality has become the nemesis of the network news." Agnew
maintained that "a narrow and distorted picture of America" often
emerges from televised news with violence and lawlessness being
portrayed as the rule rather than the exception. According to Agnew,
the networks had "compensated with a vengeance" for what Fred
Friendly in *Due to Circumstances Beyond Our Control* considered
the missing ingredients in network news, conviction, controversy
and a point of view.

The Vice President claimed that "The views of the majority of
this fraternity do not . . . represent the views of America." He suggested that the "small and unelected elite" all live in either New York
City or Washington, D.C., all read the same newspaper, draw their
political and social views from the same sources and "talk constantly
to one another, thereby providing artificial reinforcement to their
shared viewpoints." "Perhaps it was time," declared Mr. Agnew,
"that the networks were made more responsive to the views of the
nation and the people they serve." He indicated that he was raising
questions and was making "no attempt to suggest the answers. The
answers must come from the media men. They are challenged to turn
their critical powers on themselves, to direct their energy, their talent
and their conviction toward improving the quality and objectivity of
news presentation." Meanwhile the people could "let the networks
know they want their news straight and objective."

The three networks heads inferred government intimidation from
Agnew's speech and voiced strong objections. CBS president Dr. Frank
Stanton, for example, called it an "ominous attempt" to intimidate a
media licensed by the government. Stanton also criticized the speech

8 as being "replete with misinformation, inaccuracies and contradictions." Stanton wondered how the Vice President could reconcile his comments concerning the "profound influence" of television over public opinion with those suggestions that television news executives do not represent the views of the American public.

More objections to Agnew's comments soon followed. Howard K. Smith agreed that television newsmen must try harder to be fair, to welcome criticism and to exercise self-discipline, but they must also insist that things stop "well short of intimidation." Smith's colleague at ABC, Edward P. Morgan, called the speech "sinister" and a "perfect gauge" of the administration's attempt to manage the news. NBC president Julian Goodman commented that "Evidently he [Agnew] would prefer a different kind of . . . reporting, one that would be subservient to whatever political group was in authority at the time." Many newsmen and executives resented the implication that their criticism of President Nixon's speech was "instant," since they had seen the speech an hour or two before and there had been a news briefing by Mr. Nixon's Foreign Policy Adviser, Henry Kissinger, prior to the speech. Newsmen also objected to Agnew's assumption that the networks should allow the President to have the right to deliver a carefully prepared speech and command the air waves for as long as he required them, without anyone else having the opportunity to comment upon the President's remarks. Eric Sevareid thought the networks should reconsider their policy of simultaneously carrying a presidential speech because "Perhaps this is a kind of monopoly position given to a political leader that he ought not to have."

Agnew's characterization of "a tiny enclosed fraternity" talking constantly to one another to reinforce shared viewpoints brought quick reactions. Avram (Av) Westin, executive producer of the *ABC Evening News*, commented, "I'll be damned if I'll compare notes with anyone. My job is to beat the hell out of the other networks." Westin's counterparts at the other networks, Les Midgley at CBS and Wally Westfeldt at NBC, reportedly had never met each other prior to the Vice President's speech. Similarly, Agnew's suggestion that the networks be made responsive to the views of the nation was faulted. Eric Sevareid noted that "not only do majority moods change but the public mood of the moment is not necessarily in the long range public interest."

The Vice President's charge that a "narrow and distorted picture of America" which over-emphasizes violence and lawlessness was characterized by NBC News president Reuven Frank (a contributor to this volume, see pp. 106-115) as just another example of the mes-

senger's being blamed for the message. "If we hurt them with our
coverage," declared Frank, "they say we say too much. If we hurt
them by not covering, they say we say too little." Mr. Agnew's call for
more objectivity in news caused David Brinkley to suggest that "the
word objectivity is acquiring a new meaning: to report the news the
way I want to hear it is objective. To report it any other way is biased. . . ." Brinkley has indicated on occasion that he considers true
objectivity incompatible with normal behavior, an attitude which
Agnew specifically noted in his speech when he suggested that news
commentators allowed their biases to influence the selection and presentation of the news. Brinkley contends an objective man "would
have to be put away in an institution because he's some sort of
vegetable." It is fairness, according to Brinkley, which is a realistic
goal, not objectivity.

Agnew had said that "the people can let the network know that
they want their news straight and objective." Thousands of people
did make their views known to the networks, by telephone as well as
by mail and telegram. While the split between calls supporting the
Vice-President and calls supporting the network was closely divided
at all three networks (at ABC it was almost exactly 50-50), the letters
and telegrams received showed overwhelming support for the Vice-
President's position, with ratios from 6-1 to 10-1 depending upon
the network.

One immediate change that followed the speech and the audience feedback was ABC's decision to retain the word "Commentary" on the screen for the duration of the closing comment on the
ABC Evening News. Previously the word "Commentary" had been
shown for only a few seconds at the beginning of the closing comment.
The Vice President had called for a greater distinction between news
and commentary. ABC maintained that this change would enable
the viewer who tuned in during the middle of the commentary to
know that he was hearing commentary, not news.

One major criticism of Agnew's speech was his failure to recognize that the networks are not the only source of TV news. In fact,
local stations produce three to four times as much (in terms of hours)
news and public affairs programming as do the networks. This coverage is out of the hands of Agnew's "small elite on the east Coast."
Neil Hickey (pp. 11-19) discusses the quality of local television news
and the attitudes of television news directors, newsmen, executives
and critics about criticism of local television journalists. In the first
part of his article (pp. 11-16) Hickey explores the reactions of TV

10 newsmen to the public's increasing reliance upon television as a source of news, and the major problems faced by television news departments: lack of money, staff, air time and properly trained interviewers. The second part of Hickey's article (pp. 16-19) comments on the superficiality of television news coverage, the varied qualities of local news and local TV reporters, and some suggestions by James Reston relating to the improvement of television journalism.

Joel Cohen (pp. 20-24) considers editorializing by local television stations. He maintains that increased editorializing on local issues, caused mainly by newspaper monopoly and inaction, has met with favorable response from both the public and sponsors. Cohen explains why the networks rarely editorialize and suggests the difficulties of presenting local editorials on national and international affairs.

Neil Hickey (pp. 25-29) describes the abuses of news bulletin interruptions resulting from the intense rivalry among the networks. He summarizes each network's official policy for the presentation of special news bulletins, but contends that in actual practice official policy is often disregarded. Hickey presents reactions of the three network vice-presidents for news on the overuse of bulletins, and comments on some possible solutions which the networks 'are attempting to institute.

James Hagerty (pp. 30-32) outlines the major challenges that television news reporting must meet if television journalism is to truly come of age. These include the need for factual, impartial, fearless reporting; the need for analysis of why an event occurred and what it might lead to; the importance of not overlooking or neglecting local and regional news; the need to anticipate trouble spots and educate audiences to their potential danger; the need for the camera to have access to news events; and the need for reporters to earn trust from the public.

Hagerty wrote this article in 1961, shortly after he became ABC vice-president for news. In responding to a letter from the editor informing him that his article was to be included in this collection, Hagerty wrote: "I am convinced that what I said then is just as applicable—indeed maybe more applicable—to the present as it was in 1961."

How Well Does Television Keep America Informed?

By Neil Hickey

MARCH 9 AND 16, 1968

As revolutions go, the one being fought over how America gets its news is a deceptively bloodless one—a shift of public habit having great and subtle ramifications for the country's future conduct of its affairs. The central fact of this revolution is: 64 percent of Americans now get most of their news from television, instead of from newspapers or radio.[1]

Hardly anybody, including TV newsmen, claims that this reversal of form is a fortuitous one, since television news—as currently constituted—is a medium of headlines and short feature stories, and has neither the time nor the capacity to describe a day's worth of world and local events in the fullness of their detail and meaning.

As a result, many Americans are now thinking and voting their prejudices—and even shaping their lives—based on television's skeletal version of what's really going on in an increasingly complex and incomprehensible world. The question, then, of how conscientious the Nation's 600 [690] television stations are about conveying even this shorthand journalism to their viewers becomes a matter of some moment—especially since ignorance is regularly transmuted into public policy via the opinion polls which lawmakers lately have held so close to their hearts.

"I certainly hope we're not taking readers away from the newspapers," says Jay Crouse, president of the Radio and Television News Directors Association. "We can't replace newspapers; that's not our aim or intention. Our two media are complementary. We can break a big story and whet the viewer's appetite for more information, but we can't give the full background which newspapers can."

This opinion is widespread among TV newsmen. Time-Life Broadcast executive Sheldon Peterson says it another way: "Television journalists have never argued that their medium ought to provide the ultimate and sole source of news. We encourage the public to

11

12 go to the newspapers to be fully informed, and I don't think any serious TV newsman claims otherwise. Broadcast news complements newspaper news. No broadcaster says people should get their news exclusively from TV."

Unfortunately, as we know, *most* people are getting *most* of their news from television. Newspapers in the U.S. are the products—sometimes the all too imperfect products—of 250 years of journalistic tradition; television news, as practiced in the newsrooms of those 600 [690] television stations as well as at the network level, is barely 20 years old.

It's a precocious adolescent, to be sure, and learning fast; but it is thus far too unformed—and may always be—to support the full weight of the public's "right to know" about what's going on in its own community and elsewhere.

We recently interviewed TV news directors, reporters, executives, TV critics, college professors and private citizens in more than 20 cities across the United States to construct a profile of TV news at the grass-roots, and to find out, if possible, the nature of its biggest problems.

No generalization suffices, we discover, to describe the spectrum of TV news quality, which ranges from the most abject and melancholy amateurism to dedicated and energetic investigative probing. No news director claimed to have enough money, staff, or air time to do the job he'd like to do; all claimed to be highly sensitive to the "awesome responsibility" which the public's shift in loyalty from newsprint to the TV tube has placed upon them.

. . . .

Ray Miller, news director of KPRC-TV in Houston, has strong thoughts on how TV news departments fill their air time: "All of us, and some more than others, are bound to the newspapers. I often see on afternoon news shows something that came right out of that morning's newspapers. And the television treatment of it adds nothing to what was in the paper. It is simply a television version of something that's already appeared in print. . . . It's a poor practice, but it's a fairly general practice—in order to have *something* on the air. That, I think, is poor television reporting, but it's pretty generally done."

Percy Shain, TV critic of the *Boston Globe*, thinks that news coverage in his area is "generally terrible," that it's too fragmented, too sketchy; and the stations feel that "since it is impossible to give full and complete stories in the allotted time, they don't try." Gabe Pressman, New York's scrappy reporter for WNBC-TV (by all odds the city's dean of local TV newsmen), says: "I can count on the fingers of one hand the TV reporters in New York City whom I'd consider pros." But he adds, "I also realize in more sober moments that we've come a hell of a long way in 10 years; that we have the beginnings of competent middle-layer supervision; that while we're still very much behind the newspapers in quality of coverage, we're healthy, thriving and moving fast, while newspapers are declining."

This shift toward dependence on TV news is bound to accelerate in the years ahead as we move further into a McLuhanesque world of visual passivity, and the "cool" medium of TV overpowers the old-fashioned mystique of print. "That's the way it is," says Professor William A. Wood of the Columbia University Graduate School of Journalism, author of *Electronic Journalism*.[2] "I'm not surprised, but it worries me a little. TV is such an interesting medium that it attracts people who like their news that way."

But Professor Wood is quick to add that "the job the best local stations are doing today . . . has earned them extraordinary loyalty and trust from their audiences." It didn't happen overnight, says Wood, and it couldn't come out of a shoddy product or abuse of responsibility. "It represents, I believe, one of the most exciting and positive developments in the story of commercial television in the United States."

All true. Still, a sampling of TV news-reporting techniques around the U.S. leaves one with the impression that, much too frequently, the reporters hand over their medium to public figures and special pleaders who are "on the make"; that interviewees frequently are given a platform for the unchallenged dissemination of half-baked opinions; that reporters are either not sufficiently prepared or not competent to ask the sort of digging, probing question which will produce the real truth of the matter; and that TV news is all too frequently a conduit for, and not a processor of, the events which take place before its cameras and microphones.

A reporter for KMBC-TV in Kansas City, Missouri, Jim Overbay, says this: "The television interviewer has the toughest 'go' of any reporter. A newspaperman can sit down, interview his subject, get to know him quite well, discuss things with him informally for an hour. He then takes from this hour's worth of notes what he wants to use, perhaps only a few sentences. In our case, we have to accomplish much of this editing before the camera rolls."

The hardest thing about this process, says Overbay, is to decide whether or not his role should be that of debater. What posture does the TV reporter take to offer a contrast to the interviewee's opinion?

14   "If a newsman takes the Joe Pyne approach, he's stepped beyond the realm of a newsman. But an interviewer who can be the devil's advocate and still not join the battle himself—that's the ideal. It's a thin line one must be careful not to cross."

The trouble is, however, that far too many TV newsmen never even get near that invisible line. Consider a few examples:

When Mrs. Louise Day Hicks was running for mayor of Boston in the November 1967 election (which she lost), one of the principal issues was white backlash. The network TV news shows gave the matter its proper attention. At the local level, however, hardly any TV reporter—either out of embarrassment or from some misplaced sense of propriety—put the issue squarely to the candidates, and as a result Bostonians had a decidedly imperfect notion of who stood for what.

When Mrs. Shirley Temple Black announced for Congress in California, she was asked by newsmen why she should be considered qualified for the office. Why not? she wanted to know. A "Haberdasher was elected President." Nobody thought to challenge her—on behalf of teen-agers who might not recall the fact that Harry S. Truman was a U.S. Senator and Vice President of the United States subsequent to his brief career in the clothing business.

At a press conference on October 31, 1967, in Sacramento, California, Governor Ronald Reagan called columnist Drew Pearson "a liar" for having suggested that homosexuals had been uncovered on Reagan's staff. The governor went on to say that three Presidents had also called Pearson a liar, and that "to my knowledge none of them have ever seen fit to retract that opinion and I certainly have never seen anything that would justify my disagreeing with those three Presidents on that score."

Not one newsman asked Reagan for the names of the "three Presidents" and at a news conference of his own on November 4, Pearson confessed he could only remember two (Roosevelt and Truman) and that he had in his possession a communication form James Roosevelt, FDR's son, stating that his father's remark was "in jest." Truman and he, said the columnist, "are old friends now, with that remark ancient history along with a few others he called me."

TV news partisans can surely point to as many examples of shrewd questioning of public figures as these inept ones. But the fact remains that even a little shoddy journalism on TV news programs is too much, and there appears to be far more than a little. "Plain bad questions" is most often the problem, says Millie Budd, TV editor of the *Houston Post*. "Part of it is a lack of training in basic reporting."

Allan Moll, former news director of station KHJ in Los Angeles, 15
agrees that perceptive interviewing is the name of the game, but that
"there aren't enough newsmen capable of doing it."

Tom Powell, news director of WDAU in Scranton, Pennsylvania,
puts it another way: "The interview is one of television journalism's
most powerful tools and the conduct of an interview generally reflects
the station's over-all approach to news. A station that digs hard for
enterprising material and wades fearlessly into controversy will have
more than its share of exciting interviews. A station that treats news
in perfunctory fashion and shrinks from controversy is likely to have
perfunctory, noncontroversial and hence pretty dull interviews."

Like these, perhaps?

*In New Orleans, a TV reporter asked the head of a teacher's
union if he thought teachers should unionize.

*Also in New Orleans, Congressman Edwin E. Willis (D., La.),
chairman of the House Un-American Activities Committee, was asked
if he thought the press gave fair coverage to his committee.

*In Chicago, a sports reporter asked a subject: "Is good physical
condition important to success in sports?"

*In Santa Monica, California, a TV newsman approached a family
friend of the late President Kennedy as she emerged from the home of
Pat Lawford, the President's sister, shortly after the assassination. He
inquired, "Does this shock you?"

A classic parody of inept television reporting was composed by
journalist George Scott for the *Guardian* of Great Britain, where television reporting techniques are far more free-swinging and even mischievous than almost anything we know here. A returning diplomat
is being questioned:

"'Sir, would you say that your visit to Timbuktu had been worthwhile?'

"'Oh, yes, I would definitely say my visit had been worth-while.
Yes, certainly.'

"'Ah, good, well, could you say what topics you discussed, sir?'

"'No, I'm afraid I couldn't do that. These talks were of a highly
confidential nature, you understand, and you wouldn't expect me to
reveal anything that might prejudice our future relations.'

"'No, of course not, sir. Well, sir, you must be very tired after
your talks and your journey—may I ask, sir, are you going to take it
easy for a while now—a holiday, perhaps?'

"'Ah, if only one could. But you know a Minister in Her Majesty's
Government can never take it easy, never rest, not really, you know.
They're waiting for me now.'

16   " 'Well, thank you very much, sir.'

" 'Thank *you* very much.' "

Perhaps the last word on TV interviewing belongs to NBC News executive [president] Reuven Frank, who—upon the occasion of the *Huntley-Brinkley Show* going from 15 to 30 minutes—composed a now-celebrated treatise on broadcast journalism for distribution to the program's staff. He had this to say about interviewing:

"An interviewer is not an individual human in conversation. He is the representative of the curiosity of an audience, presumably its legitimate curiosity. His supposed good manners are often the means of denying information to his fellow citizens. An interview which is not more than a conversation is less than an interview. You are wasting our time, and we are invading the dullness and superficiality of your privacy."

Among TV journalists it is a truism scarcely worth restatement that television news programs simply aren't spacious enough to give definitive coverage to many of the major news stories; nor is there an audience—in the numbers required for economic good health—of sufficient toleration and inquisitiveness to demand longer, fuller news shows.

. . . .

One of our respondents, Bill Henry, news director of WFLA in Tampa, Florida, said this: "The fact is, people just aren't that interested in being informed. I would like a two-hour newscast, but it must be made palatable to the public. Perhaps if we were't worried constantly about the ratings, we could do it."

. . . .

Ralph Renick, vice president of news at WTVJ, Miami, says: "Television is all front page. There is not time or room for the insignificant. . . . Daily television news is . . . a surface medium. We can only go into depth in our documentaries and special features." (The minimal audiences who watch documentaries and special features, many observers suspect, are customarily the same people who are heavy newspaper readers anyway.) Ray Dantzler, news director of WTVT, Tampa, says: "TV news creates newspaper readers because at best we scrape the news off the top."

When newspaper reporters and TV newsmen get together, they frequently debate just how different is the news-dissemination process, now that television is so central a part of it; how well are Americans served by this new presence; and how informed are they now as against that Pleistocene, pre-television era which fewer and

fewer Americans remember. This last is a question of such delectable *17*
impenetrability as to keep a gaggle or two of sociologists busy and off
the streets for years—and it probably will, since no formal study of
the matter exists.

Meantime, an adventurous guesser might conclude that collectively we do in fact know more about our world than the citizens
of, say, 1940; but that since the planet has so shrunk in size and grown
in complexity in the interim, a stern partisan of TV news is in danger
of deluding himself that he does, indeed, have a workable grasp of
what's going on when he almost certainly does not.

Still, in many parts of the U.S., television is the *only* window on
the world for people with a yen for news; hundreds of towns and cities
have only one newspaper, or perhaps two (New York, incredibly
enough, has only three), and these are frequently so inadequate that
the reader gets a diet of truncated wire-service dispatches and badly
written and edited reports of PTA meetings and weddings.

Only a small percentage has easy access to the better journals,
and that fact creates a wondrous opportunity for the three big networks, who package and promulgate an assortment of brief news programs each day, as well as live coverage of the more portentous
events; and the 600 [690] local TV news departments, which have
undertaken to report on matters of interest in their own communities.

As Walter Cronkite pointed out recently, the interdependence
between network and affiliate is almost complete in the area of news;
the Huntley-Brinkleys, [Smiths] and Cronkites achieve large audiences or small ones in a particular city depending on how well or
badly the local news show is received and vice versa.

So the efforts of local television news departments achieve
heightened importance in light of all these circumstances. A sampling
of opinion about their effectiveness, however, turns up considerable
disagreement.

"The viewing audience is being cheated and confused as well
as not being informed," says Joe Nevens, a news writer for station
KTLA in Los Angeles. "As long as there is sufficient news to satisfy
the FCC and separate the time between commercials, many station
managers are more concerned with minimum bodies on the payroll
than with quality in the newscasts."

Woody Klein, a newspaperman in New York for 10 years before
becoming an investigative reporter for WCBS-TV—and subsequently
press secretary to Mayor John V. Lindsay—says this: "The potential
for covering news better than ever before is there. I used to write
10 news stories to accomplish the same minor reform which later I

18 could do with one TV report. Many good newsmen are looking to television as the future of the news business. Newspapers, with few exceptions, are losing the race for attention."

Ray Miller, news director of KPRC in Houston: "We can convey to the public a lucid report of an event, but we have not learned how to convey understanding. . . . A good example of that is the Vietnam war."

. . . .

Harry Sonneborn, managing editor of the *Milwaukee Sentinel*, says: "TV's main job is to entertain, causing news reporting to be secondary. A newspaper's main job is news reporting, with entertainment as a side light."

John Corporon, vice president of news for the Metromedia chain of stations, says: "It's becoming more common for a TV reporter to spend a week developing a story; if he's done his work properly, he'll end up with something better than the newspapers have. TV reporting is getting more sophisticated, although the art of TV journalism is still in its infancy. Newspapers don't change much; they've reached a plateau. But TV journalism is still growing."

Perhaps the most elemental concern of the truly aware TV journalist is his medium's unfaltering preoccupation with pictures, frequently at the expense of fine, tight, explicatory news writing. Richard Pack, senior vice president of programming and production for the Westinghouse stations, says: "We've been misled by that old Chinese axiom about one picture being worth a thousand words. Unfortunately, many television newsmen feel that any picture story is better than any spoken story."

Gabe Pressman, of New York's WNBC, expresses it even more strongly: "We became camera slaves," he says. "In the coverage of government and politics, especially, the camera perpetuates oversimplifications, outright distortions, and lies. . . . Off-camera, an official frequently will tell you the straight story which he can't tell you on-camera. It's our responsibility to recognize that film is two-dimensional, and the third dimension is the reporter providing a context. The camera can lie, make no mistake about it. It cannot substitute for a reporter's brain, nor his ability to sift fact from fiction."

The larger questions of how television journalism is to fulfill its manifest destiny have engaged the thoughts of newsmen like James Reston of *The New York Times*, who, in his book *The Artillery of the Press*,[3] suggests that the networks should set aside an hour each weekend in prime time to "review the important news of the week and put it into some historical perspective."

He also thinks that, ideally, the United States should have a   *19*
television and radio service of special news and cultural events
available on all sets and in all areas of the country. "Much more could
also be done, through a nation-wide educational-television network
and other ways, in the field of adult education on foreign affairs."
The problem, he says, is to "present the great issues as a series of
practical choices: Let the people look at the alternatives as the
President has to look at them and try to decide among the hard and
dangerous courses."

But one must conclude, more in sorrow than in anger, that
commercial television news, as currently constituted, is far too imperfect a vessel to contain the letter and spirit of our world; but that
this condition is not so chronic that it cannot be improved by broadcasting's entrepreneurs.

It needs also TV journalists of sufficient stature and perspicacity
to lead the public taste, not follow it, by contriving news programs
rich enough and spacious enough to engage the public imagination
and, by the same act, providing the firmest, truest footing for Americans eager to confront their Nation and their world.

Okay, You're for Motherhood, but What About Vietnam?

By Joel H. Cohen

FEBRUARY 4, 1967

The issue may be only as controversial as motherhood or curbing your dog, but a sizable number of the Nation's television stations are letting viewers know where they stand on matters of public concern. For the most part, though, whether the TV editorials treat something as general as sin (they're usually against it), as innocuous as conservation or as specific and debatable as Sunday closings, the focus is local or regional.

If the stations so limit themselves, and if the TV networks are reluctant to editorialize [as opposed to commentary], who's going to take an editorial position on what former CBS News chieftain Fred W. Friendly calls the questions "that will determine whether this planet is here 50 years from now"? Whether they should take up this slack or concentrate on the subjects (local and regional) about which they're better informed and thus better equipped to form reasoned judgements is one of the dilemmas confronting broadcasters who editorialize on a regular basis.

. . . .

The question—of what priority TV stations should assign to national and international issues in their editorials—was posed at a recent conference on broadcast editorializing, cosponsored in New York by one of Friendly's new employers, Columbia University's Graduate School of Journalism (the other is the Ford Foundation), and by the Radio-Television News Directors Association.

"Get smart or get out" was Friendly's impassioned admonition to broadcasters who side-step editorials about national and international issues on the grounds that they aren't sufficiently informed. His advice: Get smart enough or hire someone smart (that is, educated, in the broad sense) enough to develop and present opinions on the Big Issues.

"Does your local newspaper say there are only some subjects

it can deal with? Or does it take the whole world as its beat?" Friendly *21* demanded. To help give local broadcasters a better appreciation of international questions, he suggested that the networks include affiliates in a daily closed-circuit briefing.

. . . .

Reuven Frank, NBC News vice president, who also addressed the fourth annual National Broadcast Editorial Conference, said NBC doesn't editorialize on its TV network because "NBC feels this would be an imposition on several hundred stations which might not subscribe to the editorial position expressed." A spokesman for ABC offered a similar explanation for the absence of network editorials.

Apropos of this, one of Friendly's suggestions was that the TV networks present 55-minute rather than hour-long documentaries, with local stations having the option of using that last remaining three- or five-minute period for an editorial provided by the network or developed at local level.

Frank said that while a plan exists to permit NBC owned-and-operated stations to present editorials in their cities, "we have not yet found [until September, 1969][4] the need; we see no one waiting for our editorials, no problems demanding that we speak out, no conditions of newspaper editorial monopoly in a metropolitan area compelling us to offer an alternative voice."

Despite NBC's experience, several stations either began or intensified their editorializing *because* of newspaper monopoly or inaction. A. Louis Read, for example, whose New Orleans radio and TV stations, WDSU, scorn Mother's Day and Smokey the Bear as suitable editorial subjects and devote 72 percent of their editorials to local or state issues "because it is here that we can be most effective," reports they started editorializing in 1958, concurrent with the beginnings of monopoly press in New Orleans.

According to Read, the sale of the opposition newspaper to the *Times-Picayune* gave WDSU "the final push" into editorializing. Emphasizing that WDSU's sole purpose was *not* to react to the newspapers, Read did specify that the broadcasting editorials launch into areas the newspapers won't even touch. "We did a series of editorials criticizing the Ku Klux Klan when the papers chose to remain silent," Read said. "We have exposed conflict-of-interest cases in state government involving a previous governor, and the paper would not speak out."

Dean Edward W. Barrett of the Columbia Graduate School of Journalism, who admits he once opposed broadcast editorials on grounds they might constitute abuse of a public franchise but has

22   since changed his view, said, "The somnolence of some of our highly
profitable newspapers provides a particular opportunity—and challenge—for alert broadcasters."

Noting that 94 percent of American newspapers are monopolies,
Barrett said, "Many are alert and vigorous, but a minority—too big
a minority—are fat, smug, complacent and reluctant to offend local
powers-that-be." He cited Jacksonville, Florida, "where the newspapers have been inordinately sleepy and timid, and where WJXT
has been conducting an esposé that has just led to the indictment of
three city officials."

The indictments to which Dean Barrett referred involved two
city councilmen and a third official, who were charged with billing
a city department for such personal household articles as television
sets. All in all, indictments were returned against eight officials—
these two councilmen and two others, to city commissioners, the city
auditor, and the head of the city's sports complex, which includes
the Gator Bowl. More indictments may be forthcoming. The grand-
jury investigation of WJXT's allegations of corruption and waste in
the city has gone beyond the six-month period originally set. Alleged
politicking and inefficiency in the city police department and large
purchases by the city from friends of politicians without bidding have
been among the targets of WJXT's three-year crusade to clean up
Jacksonville. The crusade was undertaken by the TV station, according to Bill Grove, director of news and public affairs, because "somebody needed to do the job of informing the people of exactly what
was going on. . . . We wanted to add the ingredient of real journalism
to TV news.

The impact of local editorials may account, in part, for the reluctance of some broadcasters to become involved with international issues. KOGO in San Diego, California, in a 25-month period,
claims to have played a key role in eight grand-jury investigations,
four major exposés, seven bills in the state legislature, two city
ordinances, one state attorney-general's investigation and the possibility of a U.S. Attorney-General's investigation, as well as being responsible, either directly or indirectly, for the arrest of 12
persons.

According to Clayton H. Brace, KOGO general manager and a
vice president of Time-Life Broadcasting, who broadcasts the editorials; and Gene Fuson, former research director and now news
director, who develops them, the city's civic leadership now frequently comes to KOGO to seek out its attitude on a proposed course
of action or other community matter, as it does with publishers. "We

wanted to deal ourselves into the game" (of the city's power structure), 23
Fuson commented, and KOGO apparently has succeeded. Of 80
editorials on a wide range of subjects from fire insurance to alleged
conflict of interest involving lawyers on the city council, 70 accomplished their purpose, Fuson said.

How much attention the general public pays to broadcast editorials is a moot point, but indications are that the public supports the
idea of the editorials, although it opposes those recommending political candidates. Issues, yes; candidates, no.[5]

Surprisingly, there are also indications that sponsors like the
idea of TV and radio stations editorializing. Although they may not
agree with what's said, they won't pull out. Eldon Campbell, vice
president and general manager of the WFBM stations in Indianapolis,
found that the stations' willingness to stand for something won advertiser support. One letter threatening removal of advertising notwithstanding, Campbell feels editorializing is good business. "Today,"
he said, "some of our best friends are those who were angered by our
stand on Sunday closings" (his stations' first editorial theme).

On the same subject, Read said, "We know that now and then
there are sponsors who don't like what we say, but in nearly all
instances I believe they respect us because we attempt to base our
editorial conclusions on fact and upon reason. . . . I don't believe we
have ever lost a sponsor because of an unpopular editorial. Nor have
we ever aired an editorial just to placate or play up to a sponsor." At
the national level, where sponsors worry about the impact of, say, a
strong pro-integration stand in the South, the effect may be quite
different. But in local markets some broadcasters find their editorials
even may help sell time.

Some TV stations that editorialize gauge the success of their
editorials by the amount of adverse reaction stirred up. Prompted
in part, at least, by the Federal Communications Commission's "Fairness Doctrine" (which requires a broadcaster who has presented one
side of an issue to provide reasonable opportunity for the presentation
of the opposing views of substantial and responsible groups in the
community—see pp. 303-321), several TV outlets seem to go to great
lengths to help responsible opposition spokesmen formulate rebuttal,
even to the extent of providing a film crew.

Several make a point of giving prior notification of an editorial
to interested parties, including likely opponents of the editorial stand
being taken. WCBS-TV in New York provides a booklet with tips
("No need to memorize your script." . . . "Use simple direct sentences." . . . "Men should wear dark suits and off-white shirts") to

24   help an acceptable representative of the opposition present rebuttal. WABC, New York, whose radio-TV editorial director, Layhmond Robinson, says, "We go out of our way" to help an opposition spokesman polish rebuttal, will provide the rebutter with as much studio time as necessary.

WDSU makes use of an editorial cartoonist to illustrate its position. How do you rebut a cartoon? The station gives equal time, said Read, but won't lend the opposition its own cartoonist. Illustrated or only verbal, static or dramatic, TV editorials are emerging as an opinion-molding force, a force to be reckoned with by the Establishment in some cities, at least.

The question remains, what should the scope of the editorials be? Friendly, who emphasized he was not advocating national and international editorials *at the expense of local and regional themes,* sees a great need for stations to go beyond pollution and corruption. He deplores the attitude that says, in effect, "What would I in Des Moines know about the UN and De Gaulle and the World Court?"

Challenging local broadcasters not to abdicate to the newspapers the responsibility for sharing informed opinion on these subjects, Friendly pointed out that "raw facts are not news . . . analysis is part of journalism." He commented: "If we were umpires, we'd be wearing striped shirts and carrying whistles."

TV News Bulletins:
Too Many and Too Soon?

By Neil Hickey

MAY 8, 1965

You are seated in front of your television set intent on a drama. The hero is approaching a crisis. The story is rushing onward to a conclusion. You are immersed in the lives and problems of the characters.

Suddenly the actors disappear and on the screen flashes the word BULLETIN. You blink with reflex dismay at the abrupt wrench from your concentration. In the few seconds of silence that ensue, you regroup your mental forces and bring them to focus on the single word which, by now, is growing more ominous by the moment. Your heartbeat quickens. "We interrupt this program to bring you a special news bulletin from. . . . "

Has it finally happened, you think? Is this really the voice of doom telling me that a larger drama—the atomic one—has reached its logical denouement? In the next instant, you reflect, I may discover that everything I am, and know, and hope to be is about to crumble. Or perhaps it's not that bad. Maybe it's only that the Chinese have entered the war in Vietnam and are pushing our forces into the South China Sea. That wouldn't be quite so bad. Or perhaps it's simply that some near-by missile site has had an accidental explosion and the atmosphere is being polluted with radioactive gases.

" . . . to bring you a special news bulletin from . . . " A pause, and the announcer says: "President Johnson's cold has improved slightly, his physicians reported a moment ago, and he is expected to leave Bethesda Naval Hospital and return to the White House within the next 12 hours. This has been a special bulletin from . . . "

You slump in the chair, relieved. Your heart returns to its normal pace, your scalp loosens, and you breathe out heavily. The actors return to view, and you discover them engaged in a heated colloquy, the motivations for which you will have to guess.

Vignettes such as this one happened frequently in late January 1965, when President Johnson suffered a flu attack and had to be taken

25

26 to the hospital. A second outbreak of news bulletins accompanied the United States' retaliatory air strikes in North Vietnam, and the apparent escalation of that guerrilla war.

Those two breaking stories, coming close together as they did, returned public attention to a subject which has been argued hotly both by viewers and TV news officials for a long time now: the matter of news-bulletin interruptions and the abuses to which that practice is susceptible, especially in the atmosphere of intense rivalry in which the network news departments find themselves.

On February 11, 1965, as the Vietnam crisis was enlarging, Elmer W. Lower, ABC's News boss, memoed his staff: "We will interrupt regular programming with bulletins . . . as our own judgment dictates. We will try earnestly to avoid an air of alarm or crisis when one does not exist. . . . Let's keep our feet on the ground and inform—not frighten—our viewers. . . ."

Next day, Fred Friendly told his CBS News staff in a privately circulated note: "The news 'interrupt' bulletin . . . if used with judgment and discretion, is the best tool we have for getting vital news to the public quickly. But its indiscriminate use for competitive reasons or for promoting one's own image as a news organization is a disservice. . . ." Responsibility means restraint and wisdom, as well as alertness and energy, Friendly wrote. "We are in the news—not the panicbutton—business.

A standing order in NBC's procedure manual says: "Only in the case of bulletins of transcending importance should the existing program be interrupted at once and without question and, even in such cases, the bulletin should be subjected to the tests of good taste in handling."

Thus, in the abstract, each of the networks has only the most public-spirited intentions about bulletins. They agree solemnly that to "cry wolf" by rushing helter-skelter to the air waves with these jarring and sometimes frightening intrusions is to perform a colossal disservice both to viewers and to themselves.

But in practice, there are no rules, no hidebound criteria guaranteed to protect from error a news editor confronted with a hot story and the even hotter breath of the competition on his neck.

One day last year, for example, CBS went on the air with a bulletin that Nikita Khrushchev was reported dead. Their information was based on an unconfirmed Reuters dispatch which proved to be in error. A moderate delay would have spared CBS the embarrassment of having to point out later that the Reuters report was, indeed, false.

A too-eager news editor at ABC interrupted programming to award viewers the intelligence that Elizabeth Taylor and Richard Burton had just been married in Montreal. An ABC news official, watching at home, said later, "I could have died a million deaths when I saw that one."

A "peak of irritation"—in the words of one New York TV critic— was reached on February 21, 1965, when ABC's New York outlet broke in on a performance of the Bolshoi Ballet to report that Malcolm X, the Black Nationalist leader, had been murdered in Harlem as he was about to give a speech. That news could have waited, insisted the aggrieved critic, until the end of "Swan Lake," a matter of perhaps 10 minutes.

Traditionally, one of the most irritating aspects of news bulletining to viewers has been television's handling of airline disasters. Many local stations have been in the habit of breaking into their schedule at the first notification of a plane crash without waiting for fuller details, thereby worrying every viewer who had a relative or friend traveling that day. More responsible news editors are careful to get better information before interrupting: name of the airline, destination and flight number of the plane, time of departure, and so forth.

Recently, TV GUIDE interviewed top network news officials to find out exactly how they feel about news bulletins, their use and abuse. "There's only one real criterion," Fred Friendly told us: "The public interest." Three guidelines assist CBS to a decision on whether or not to interrupt, Friendly said: "is it a service that the people need at this moment, such as an alarm? Is the news of such great importance that the viewer would want to be interrupted? What program is in progress, and will the content of the bulletin fit tastefully into the context of the program?"

In his role as a news chief, Friendly says, "I have immediate access to every living room in the United States, and I must use that power with restraint. Even after all this time in TV news, I'm still awed by that responsibility. When I'm at home and see a news bulletin come on CBS, I think, 'This better be important.'"

Julian Goodman, NBC's vice president of News [now NBC President], says he's had "innumerable discussions" on the subject of bulletins with his staff, and has decided that the key element is the experience and judgment of the news editor on duty. "We tend to support the decisions of these editors, one of whom is on duty 24 hours a day. Of course, they can't afford to make many mistakes."

Goodman maintains that NBC's procedure for getting a bulletin

28 on the air is slower but surer than its competitors'. "We go through a few extra steps, one of which is contacting our broadcast-operations co-ordinator to find out the best spot in a program to insert the bulletin. You can't announce the death of an important figure in the middle of a comedy, and then come back to laughter. If we have to wait 10 minutes in the interests of good taste, we do so."

Jesse Zousmer, ABC's [late] vice president and director of TV News, says "The criterion is your reflex. If you try to draw up a document, you're lost. Therefore, one must countenance errors. Briefly, it's a matter of using the best news judgment available and worrying about it later. There's no doubt that bulletins shock one out of one's reverie. But what's the alternative? Should we come on and say, 'In a half hour we're going to tell you something unpleasant'? The harshest critics of news bulletins are the same TV reviewers who are always saying we need more documentaries and public affairs shows. You can't satisfy everybody."

A few cynical observers have claimed to discern the ugly face of economics peering through the fragrant rose garden of public service. How come commercials never seem to get pre-empted, they ask? Why do bulletins always seem to come in the middle of a program—where there's no financial sacrifice—rather than bumping a sponsor message? Nonsense, say the networks' news chiefs in unanimous chorus. Money has nothing to do with it, they insist: it's the nature of the news which determines when and how a bulletin gets aired. Julian Goodman, voicing the consensus, says: "On many, many occasions we've pre-empted a commercial for news bulletins. If it's the sort of story which must go on right now, we put it on whether it pre-empts a commercial or not. There's certainly no internal policy which advises us to leave commercials alone."

Speaking to the New York State Broadcasters Association in Albany on March 2, 1965, James C. Hagerty, former press secretary to President Eisenhower and now a vice president of ABC's parent company, advised TV newsmen "to take corrective action on our own" with regard to bulletins, lest "we be forced to do so by outside pressure of public condemnation."

Hagerty called into question the networks' decision to "flood the air with special programs and breathless bulletins" during President Johnson's flu attack, when his life obviously was not in danger. "Admittedly, the President is the most important person in the free world. But honestly, didn't we all overdo it just a little?"

It appears at last that the networks are, in fact, realizing that they've been overdoing it a little; that viewers are painfully sensitive to the volatile potential in a number of international situations: to the confrontation of two world powers in Vietnam; to the proliferation of nuclear arms and the enlargement of the "nuclear family"; to the shifting policies and uncertain aspirations of a new leadership bloc in the Soviet Union. TV newsmen are the first to agree that such a time needs only the coolest and most responsible news reporting.

Solutions are forthcoming. One network has in preparation a "million dollar piece of equipment" which would allow news editors to display bulletins instantly in a strip of lettering designed to travel across the bottom of a viewer's screen and thus not interrupt the show in progress. (Such a display is already in existence, but is not nearly fast enough for use with bulletins.)

Another network is investigating the chances of confining all but the most urgent bulletins (such as a national alarm) to the few moments when the credits are on view at the end of a show. Those seconds frequently are used for no better purpose than to promote the program next in view.[6]

The object of any solution is to preserve us all from skipped heartbeats and mounting blood pressure and perhaps to guarantee our right to sit through such shows as *World War I, Combat!,* and *12 O'Clock High* in some sort of peace and quiet.

A Creed for Television Newsmen

By James C. Hagerty

FEBRUARY 25, 1961

Television news reporting must prepare itself now to take advantage of an age of science which is just beginning. Mankind, through the collective genius of its scientists, is reaching for the stars and is going to get there one day. As our scientists continue to probe space and the far reaches of the universe, one important by-product of their research is that communications systems, especially those for television, are going to be constantly expanded until they are truly world-wide in operation. . . . That is when television news reporting will truly come of age. As television works toward that day, it must begin now to train itself for the responsibility that comes with adulthood.

Here, as I see it, are a few challenges that television news reporting must meet now and in the future as it prepares itself to become a world-wide partner with radio and the other mass communication media.

1. TV news reporting must be factual, impartial, free and fearless. It cannot permit itself to be dominated or even remotely to be associated with any group or faction of special interest, any political party or any government. It must expand further its world-wide staff of trained professional reporters so that they will be able to present news developments wherever they occur accurately and without bias or personal opinion. In reporting news, television must do just that—report what is happening in the world, what is being done, what is being said. TV reporters must be trained in the use of the most modern TV tools. They must be able not only to write their news reports, but to speak them, with ease.

2. TV news reporting must also try to analyze news developments, explain the reason why an event occurred and what it might lead to. But, and this is a big but, it must not confuse news reporting with personal opinion of a commentator who, after all, is expressing

only his own thoughts and analysis. News must be reported as news— straight and to the point. Commentary is an important and integral part of TV news reporting, but it must be labeled as opinion, apart and aside from straight news reporting. The American public can— and will—then form its own opinion, based on factual reporting and the additional commentary.

3. Local regional and national news will always be of commanding interest and must never be neglected or overlooked. I firmly believe that TV news reporting has not taken full advantage of the tremendous potential that exists on the staffs of local affiliated stations. These reporters are experts in their own right and are completely familiar with the problems and events of their own localities. They should be used more on national networks.

4. Expanding communication systems will bring with that expansion inevitable emphasis on news reporting from all sections of the world. This, I think, is good. All too often reporting of some faraway trouble spot is ignored until it is catapulted into prominence when disaster finally occurs. TV news reporting must look ahead, try to anticipate these trouble spots and educate audiences to their potential danger. I have often wondered what would happen if the people of the United States, and of the world, had continuing reports before trouble, which was developing, exploded on the world scene. Such reporting, I am sure, could have been extremely helpful, for example, in making the people of the world more aware of the rise to power, and the threat to world peace, of an Adolf Hitler—or any dictator who seeks to subvert and control human freedoms. Public opinion is a potent force for good in this world—but it must be an informed public opinion. Responsible TV news reporting can contribute to that end by supplying visual evidence of the truth.

This, of course, will take a larger staff of trained reporters—more than television has now. But that's part of television's growing-up process. And, incidentally, American television will have to start now to train reporters who speak languages other than their own. As worldwide television comes into being—as it inevitably will—knowledge of foreign languages will be an essential of that operation.

5. The television camera must have the right to cover news wherever it happens, here at home or overseas. Right now television cameras are barred from many events that are open to reporters. In Congress, television can cover Senate hearings but not those of the House of Representatives. Across our country and abroad, some public officials refuse to permit camera coverage of their press conferences. And, of course, the judiciary has long declined to

32 permit cameras, in many instances, to cover the courts of the land.

I believe that the camera must be recognized as the same kind of equipment as a pencil in the hand of a newspaper reporter. This will take some doing. There are many prejudices to overcome from those who will be reported by the camera lens, not the least of which is from the newspaper profession itself. But free coverage of the news and the basic principle of freedom of the press demand no less. Television must insist on equal treatment. It is entitled to the same standing and privileges accorded other free communication media.

6. The camera, like the pencil, is no better or no worse than the individuals who operate or direct it. A good reporter does not seek to fake or exaggerate his story. He gets the news as it happens and reports the truth, the whole truth. That is his job.

There have been ugly instances where television reporters and cameramen have deliberately stirred up trouble or tried to keep a story going by interviewing or urging partisans to demonstrate just for the sake of "getting crowd shots on film" or to "keep a story going." This practice is not only unethical, it is betrayal of the responsibility that rests with a free press. By prearranging news stories, newsmen are deliberately becoming participants in a story which they were assigned to cover impartially. They are not reporting news as it happens; they are manufacturing it. It's bad business, and it must not be allowed to continue. If the television camera is to become accepted along with the reporter's pencil, the camera and individuals who operate or direct it must become trusted and responsible representatives of the free press.

These, then, are a few of the challenges that face TV news reporting as it enters the scientific age. The scope of such reporting is going to increase greatly in the years that lie ahead. I am firmly convinced that TV news reporting can contribute to the fund of common knowledge that will be so necessary in the future. I am sure also that TV news reporting can—and will—meet the challenges that confront it and will measure up to its responsibility of keeping its viewers intelligently informed of the great issues and problems of our times.

Vietnam

Although the Korean conflict was given very limited coverage by the then infant medium of television, Vietnam is considered to be television's first war. For the first time, American television news has brought military conflict, sight and sound together, into the American living room without the need for extensive reconstruction of events by words.

CBS president Frank Stanton has defined the duty of television; "to bring the face of this war—the human face on the battlefield and the issues behind it—to all the people so that they can witness it and understand it." Stanton has pointed out that the Vietnam fighting, as well as having a baffling intrinsic nature, has frustrated TV newsmen and cameramen who operate on their own in a war of no fixed position and "have had to use ingenuity, persistence and sheer guts to bring the harsh reality of this agonizing war to us back home."

Sophocles said, "None loves the messenger who brings bad news." And not surprisingly, the networks and their newsmen who spend between five and six million dollars a year to cover events in Vietnam receive more criticism than praise. The networks receive a great many protesting letters: the networks are bringing the horrors of war too forcefully and are reporting facts too unpleasant for the public to know; they are showing too much or not enough of the fighting; they devote too much attention to the draft-card burning; they are propagandists for the war or against it; they are the Administration's mouthpiece or its bugbear. These letters support sociologist Morris Janowitz's contention that television has hardened and polarized public sentiment regarding the war. Jack Gould and others have urged more analysis and commentary about Vietnam by the networks; however, Frank McGee has suggested that in this case the same polarization would still occur, with the viewer favoring and listening to the commentator who reinforces his or her view.

Some of the major criticisms of the Vietnam coverage relate to the amount of battle footage aired. Most critics claim that television shows too much footage and does not devote the requisite time to back-

34 ground stories. Robert Northshield, executive producer of *The Huntley-Brinkley Report*, defends existing coverage. He maintains that there is no alternative to what the networks are doing: "Something over one hundred guys a week are getting killed and it seems to me that by any standard, that's news." Northshield emphasizes that the networks cannot give complete coverage to the whole Vietnam situation any more than they can to the whole American story.

Conversely, Robert McNeil, former NBC newsman and author of *The People Machine,* criticizes the networks for not giving enough coverage to the fighting. He contends that when two hundred Americans were being killed a month, during 1967, the viewer had no indication of how badly the war was going and received no suggestion of crisis or emergency. Consequently, the public became conditioned to the war and lost interest in the few regular programs devoted to Vietnam—such as NBC's *Vietnam Weekly Review*—which no longer appeared by the end of 1967. According to McNeil, only after the Tet offensive in February, 1968, did battle coverage increase and the public receive some indication that the war was not going well.

Neil Hickey, during a ten-week trip to Washington, New York and South Vietnam, interviewed military officials and network executives; he also observed war correspondents in Saigon and in the jungle war zones. His purpose was to "measure, count and catalog" the problems relating to television's presence in Vietnam and, further, to describe and evaluate television coverage of the war. In his detailed article (pp. 36-54), which was published in four parts, Hickey presents the results of his investigation. He first concentrates his attention on the correspondents in the field (pp. 36-41). He discusses their credentials, backgrounds, their reasons for coming to Vietnam, and some of the dangers and frustrations of their work.

While in Saigon, Hickey interviewed the network bureau chiefs. In the second part of his article (pp. 41-46), he sketches their daily routines and discusses some of their problems. The network chief, in his position as a liaison between New York and the correspondents, has the responsibility of determining which stories are sent home. Hickey reports the opinions of the chiefs about the shortcomings of existing television coverage.

Hickey then lists the Pentagon's criticisms of television coverage of the war and the responses of television newsmen in Vietnam to these criticisms (pp. 46-49). He outlines the difficulties of doing background reporting and the reluctance of the networks to let young correspondents do political analysis. The Pentagon especially criti-

cized the use of foreign cameramen and technicians to aid Americans
in covering the war; the foreign technicians were felt to be a source of
biased coverage. Without exception, the people interviewed felt this
criticism to be unfounded.

In part four (pp. 49-54), Hickey describes the nature and extent of
censorship of news going out of Vietnam. Although the Saigon
Government exercises no censorship, Hickey notes that the relationship between government press officers and newsmen is strained and
a credibility gap exists. Control of information is accomplished largely
through gentlemen's agreements, press agents and various impromptu
ground rules. Among the most serious obstacles to obtaining accurate
and complete news are the rivalry between the armed services for
television exposure and the massive public relations establishments
of both the Saigon Government and the United States Military.
Hickey concludes with his observations regarding the extent of
television coverage in Vietnam and the objectivity and honesty of
the reporting.

Martin Maloney (pp. 55-59) submits that some of the problems of
television coverage of Vietnam and public reaction to it are inherent
in the medium. He coins the phrase "TVietnam" to illustrate what he
feels is the basic difference between the coverage of this war and, say,
World War II: that is, television is presenting the war to us as it
happens, in bits and pieces. Earlier, before television, war was presented to the public after the fact and in a well rationalized, digested
form. According to Professor Maloney, the need of people to make
sense of what is happening around them is being continually frustrated by their being presented with pieces of an endless puzzle
which they feel they must solve and cannot.

The Vietnam War: Is Television Giving Us the Picture?

By Neil Hickey

OCTOBER 1, 8, 15 AND 22, 1966

At first light, the three helicopters climbed from the camp at Dak To in South Vietnam's jungled highlands and curved north, flying low under a gray ceiling of monsoonal cloud. Far overhead and out of sight were B-52 bombers, their bays yawning upon a regiment of surrounded North Vietnamese soldiers dug in along a ridge line.

In the helicopters were American television correspondents and their two-man crews: CBS's Bill Stout, NBC's Howard Tuckner and ABC's David Snell. The choppers swung lazily along beside the ridge and soon the great fireballs blinked through the morning haze as sheets of 750-pound bombs crashed into the high ground. In one of the open-sided helicopters a 35-year-old Vietnamese cameraman named Vo Huynh swung his NBC camera outward toward the explosions; the wind flattened his black hair and he squinted hard to find the bursts flashing where the ridge line broke the clouds.

The other choppers lolled nearby, and Vo Huynh could see the snouts of two cameras pointed at the churning devastation which was opening raw sores in the jungle tree line. Now the last bombs were falling, and U. S. troops of the 101st Airborne Division were poised on the ground to rush inside the bombed sector and engage the North Vietnamese at close range.

The three helicopters slid downward sharply and landed where the attacking battalions were mustered; the TV crews leaped out and hurried into other choppers which were ferrying troops by sixes inside the North Vietnamese perimeter. It was time now for a re-enactment of the central experience of a TV crew's life in Vietnam: the helicopter assault landing in hostile terrain.

Ron Headford, ABC's 30-year-old Australian cameraman, cradled his camera between his knees during the helicopter's brief, parabolic leap, and then he was jumping outward with it, and Snell and the soundman were behind him. They ran in a low crouch away from the chopper's violent downdraft, across a clearing, and threw themselves into a ditch at the edge of a bamboo thicket.

Machine-gun fire rattled somewhere, and they heard the snap of North Vietnamese rifles. Hurriedly, Headford shouldered his camera, stood straight up and began filming other helicopters wheeling in, disgorging troops and then mounting past the tree tops. Soon all the attackers were on the ground, and the march upward began, over a narrow jungle trail and under whispering artillery fire which smashed into the hillside ahead. Thick monsoon showers fell, leaving the trail muddy and awash.

In the ensuing several hours, ABC's trio—bearing 25-pound camera, sound gear, film cans, tape recorder, canteens, ponchos, jungle blankets and C-rations—climbed toward the high ground, waded through streams and muddy, waist-deep sinkholes, huddled against the rains and filmed the troop column's tortuous advance. Nearby, the two other network crews were engaged in similar business.

It was a day like hundreds of others in Vietnam; a few North Vietnamese were killed, and a few Americans wounded. At the end of it the three correspondents hurried to ship their film off to Saigon, where it would be transferred quickly to cargo planes heading for the United States. Twenty-four hours later those battle films would be visible on the Huntley-Brinkley and Walter Cronkite and Frank Reynolds and Howard K. Smith network news programs.

TV GUIDE had come to Vietnam to live such days, to observe television crews at work in the field; to listen to the problems of the bureau chiefs in Saigon; and to assess the adequacy and honesty of television's handling of this strange and complex war. Two factors had prompted the undertaking: 1) Vietnam is television's first war, and 2) almost 60 percent of Americans now get most of their news about the conflict from television's network news.

Here are some of the men covering Vietnam for TV:

Roger Peterson, 29, ABC: "A major frustration is that there are so many stories to be done in Vietnam and so little television time available for them. Many of a correspondent's best pieces just never get on, but we go ahead and do them anyway for our own satisfaction."

John Flynn, 33, CBS: "Vietnam is where the big story is. This is where it's happening, and I see no reason to be anywhere else."

Howard Tuckner, 35, NBC: "Correspondents are always saying to field commanders, 'Just tell me where the heaviest fighting is going

38 to be. That's all I ask.' Then we go there and try to film it. I'm grateful for the chance to cover this war. If I were married, my wife would have to understand what this story means to me."

Lou Cioffi, 40, ABC: "You begin wondering when the law of averages will catch up with you. I'm scared all the time, but I'm more scared now than when I first came out here. TV has nothing in its history to prepare it for this kind of story."

David Burrington, 35, NBC: "There are so many imponderables and ironies here that it's sometimes difficult, if not downright impossible, to explain what's happening in terms that an American audience will understand."

Peter Kalischer, 51, CBS: "Once you commit yourself to a company during a military action, you're with them. You can't jump in a jeep and look someplace else for a battle; there are no jeeps in the jungle. You're hoping to get shot at; otherwise you don't have a story."

Ray Maloney, 38, ABC: "The soldiers in the field are enormously pleased to have TV crews around. To them, it means somebody really cares about what they're doing. They'll share their last C-ration with you, and tie down your poncho tent properly so it doesn't blow away. I have never felt more appreciated, nor more humble."

These men and their colleagues—technicians and bureau chiefs— are volunteers; none are sent to Vietnam. They've asked for the assignment or heeded a call. The correspondents are indeed a special breed, a new kind of newsman, a glomeration of special traits: ambition, competitiveness, muscle power, adventurousness, perseverance, ingenuity and pridefulness—tinged in some cases with harmless vanity, for TV newsmen are, after all, part performer.

Some are hellbent for personal glory and the big payoff that awaits those whose reputations flourish in these jungles. "Let's be truthful," one of the younger ones said. "We're all war profiteers. We know that if we prove ourselves here we can short-cut our careers by five to 10 years. Here in Vietnam you can get your face on the network news three or four times a week. That's more than you can do in the United States. It's risky, but it's money in the bank. A lot of us realized that reputations were being made out here, and that we'd better get in on it. For TV newsmen of a certain age group, you've got to have Vietnam on your record if you want to succeed. It's like being knighted into full correspondent status."

The reasons for their coming are as varied as the correspondents themselves, but they all share the same dangers, which are considerable. Remarkably, no TV crew member has yet been killed in Vietnam, although a number have been wounded seriously. One of the most astonishing episodes of the coverage occurred at Qui Nhon, on the coastal lowlands, in March, 1966.

John Laurence, a 26-year-old CBS newsman, was marching with an American unit when a South Vietnamese armored column—mistaking the Americans for North Vietnamese—opened fire on them. Laurence's Danish cameraman, Carl Sorensen, hurriedly commenced filming the armored column's belching guns, the nearby explosions, and panning his camera to an American officer who was shouting into a field telephone: "For God's sake, stop it! We're Americans!"

In the next instant CBS's soundman—a 22-year-old Thai named Vallop Rodboon—was struck in the abdomen by shrapnel and fell to the ground. Laurence, microphone in hand, turned quickly to interview Rodboon where he lay; Sorensen's camera, still rolling, captured the scene. But, most remarkable of all, Rodboon, in his seriously wounded state, continued to operate the sound equipment for his own interview—one of the most poignant of the Vietnam war.

Young correspondents learn survival fast in the jungles and rice paddies. On an operation with the 1st Air Cavalry Division north of An Khe, NBC's David Burrington was standing near two soldiers when a burst of Vietcong machine-gun fire killed one of them and wounded another. His cameraman, Vo Huynh, said later: "I thought Burrington was dead. I saw the bullets kicking up dirt, then all three of them crumbled to the ground." The newsman, however, was unhurt and hugging the ground behind a shrub. Vo Huynh shouted and waved for the correspondent to find sturdier cover, but Burrington only waved back reassuringly until he perceived his colleague's meaning, and leaped behind a rock. "Shrubs don't stop bullets," the veteran cameraman reminded Burrington later, and of such small lessons is survival in Vietnam made. TV crews soon learn not to stand near soldiers carrying maps or radio equipment because snipers often choose those men as targets.

During nine days last May, when the northern town of Danang was the scene of bitter fighting between Buddhist-led rebel troops and loyalist forces from Saigon, ABC's Roger Peterson—revolted and angered by the senseless bloodshed all around him—ad-libbed to his camera: "The only sane thing I've seen since arriving in this town is a dog chasing a cat." When a loyalist attack to crush the rebels was imminent, Buddhist leaders called a press conference at their pagoda headquarters—a corner of which was filled with 35 bodies dragged inside during the week—for a group of newsmen including Peterson, NBC's Ron Nessen, and CBS's Dan Rather and Bill Stout.

When all were gathered and waiting, it soon became apparent that no conference would be held and that the reporters were wanted

40   as hostages against the loyalist attack which already was mustering outside in the darkening courtyard. A few newsmen walked from the pagoda hurriedly, and in a cross fire which erupted at that moment four of them were badly wounded. Some of the TV men came out shouting *"Bao Chi!"* ("Press!") and shining television lights in their faces to establish that they were noncombatants. Through scattered fire, they made it safely down the broad steps of the pagoda, across the courtyard and past the loyalist troops. "It was the scariest evening of my life," said one of them later.

Two months later, on July 12—and only five weeks before his year-long tour in Vietnam was to end—Ron Nessen was wounded in the chest by grenade fragments while covering a reconnaissance patrol in the central highlands.

But far more typical of a TV crew's life in Vietnam is something the correspondents call the "walk in the sun" story. Three CBS newsmen described it: "We helicoptered to a peak 2300 feet over a Vietcong-controlled valley," said Peter Kalischer. "For the next seven hours we slid down the steep incline, hanging on to trees and struggling to protect our equipment. It was the most grueling physical exertion I've ever encountered on a story. At the bottom, we discovered the Vietcong had vanished. There was no contact, and we exposed not one usable foot of film."

Murray Fromson: "Near Chu Lai, I walked for six hours in 130-degree heat. Sixty Marines fell of heat prostration, but there was no significant contact with unfriendly forces. No story."

Dan Rather: "For four days we walked with the Marines near Danang without finding Vietcong. A major apologized for the lack of action, but said, 'Tomorrow the chances are quite good.' We were up at 3 A.M., moved out before dawn, walked 17 kilometers and reached a South Vietnamese army outpost which already had been wiped out. So all I got was one hundred feet of an aftermath story. No battle footage."

For TV men, as well as soldiers, this is the walking war, the jungle life of malaria, amoebic dysentery and hepatitis; of ambush, land mines and booby traps; of sleeping on the ground, washing from upturned helmets and drinking warm water from canteens; of scrounging helicopter rides to the roughest action; of shouting into field telephones that barely work, and—as one correspondent put it—"pushing the cause of journalistic profanity to new horizons."

There is indeed nothing in television's past to prepare it for this kind of endeavor, and so the rules are being written, day by day, one at a time. World War II was reported by precocious young correspondents of courage and durability—Edward R. Murrow, Howard K. Smith, Eric Sevareid, Charles Collingwood, William L. Shirer, Robert Trout, Winston Burdett, Richard C. Hottelet and many others. Vietnam is producing a new roster of candidates for a similar canonization.

It is certain, however, that the Vietnam war is exorbitantly more demanding, both mentally and physically, than anything those earlier newsmen faced in Europe or the Pacific. Television news—like many other American teen-agers—is growing up in the rice paddies and rain forests of Asia.

Saigon is the war capital, the mottled "pearl of the Orient"; a city fashioned by the French for a half-million people and now crowded with four times that number; a haven for profiteers and adventurers, home to history's most active black market, and focus, currently, for the world's biggest news story.

Out of Saigon's airport, the world's busiest, flows newsfilm aimed at America's 70,000,000 television sets, many of them in the homes of troubled parents and wives of the 300,000 military men now in Vietnam. Three years ago, fewer than a dozen newsmen covered the Vietnam war for all news media. A recent press list showed the names of 400 men and women accredited as journalists in Vietnam—82 of them employed by the three American television networks.

This is the "television presence" in Vietnam: something new in warfare; a kind of Cyclops in the rain forests—a one-eyed, adolescent giant whose footfall is loud and whose shadow is long. Television's coverage of a war, it is now apparent, carries the highest emotional—if not cerebral—impact of any reporting medium. Three men here in Saigon—the network bureau chiefs—have the responsibility for managing this new brand of coverage in a new kind of war:

Jack O'Grady, 39, ABC: "We must be highly selective about the stories we send out of here every day. New York can't look at great quantities of film in the short time available to the news editors there to decide what goes on the air. The competition between the networks is fierce here in Saigon, and the bureau chiefs are always gambling that the other fellow doesn't have a story you've missed. It's a game of guts, timing, talent and luck."

Peter Herford, 30, CBS: "This is the toughest story I've ever had to handle—geographically, technically and humanly. Sending people out on combat stories day after day is a tremendously wearing thing. I've known most of these guys for years. So you sit in Saigon and worry. The greatest job we can do is get everybody back alive."

42   Ron Steinman, 32, NBC: "It's a constant game of nerves; you try to deploy your available forces to the best advantage. Each network bureau chief has his own set of confidential contacts in Saigon who he hopes will tip him off to the next big military operation or civil demonstration."

These are young men, as important journalists go. Another, 33-year-old Elliot Bernstein, recently succeeded O'Grady as head of ABC's bureau. Jack Fern, a well-seasoned news hand who preceded Steinman in the NBC job, sat in the alfresco, French-style La Pagoda cafe on Saigon's Tu Do Street one summer afternoon, and talked about the life of television newsmen in Vietnam: "If you don't want to go into combat, there's nothing wrong with you; in fact, it's probably a sign of high intelligence. But if you come to this party, you've got to dance; you've got to go into the fighting day after day in order to cover this story. When I have youngsters in the field and I learn there's been heavy contact, I start waiting for the phone to ring to see if everybody is OK—and, secondarily, if they've gotten the battle on film and have managed to ship it.

"Sometimes crew members crack under this," Fern continued. "I've had men come to me and say, 'I can't go out any more. I'm scared.' That's when I take them off duty and send them home. These guys push themselves. You can see it happening. Maybe some have a need to test themselves. Whatever the reason, the fear and fatigue eventually catch up with them. Sometimes a man's friend will be wounded seriously, or a soldier is killed near him; and all the stuff goes out of him, and after that he's no good at this any more."

In Saigon the work week is seven days and the working day usually exceeds 12 hours. Nobody is ever quite sure what day it is, and the main conversation topic is always the war. "I've never seen anything like it," says CBS's Bill Stout. "In World War II the main subject was women. Here it's the war. You talk about it and hash it over all your waking hours."

To counteract a peculiar form of Asian distemper which afflicts many newsmen who remain in Vietnam overlong, the networks all have compulsory "R & R" programs affording bureau members regular periods of rest and rehabilitation in near-by Taipei, Hong Kong, Singapore, Bangkok and Manila. Still, the numbing effects of the work load, the long hours, the heat, and the general impenetrability and waywardness of Vietnamese politics combine to erode the professional resources of even the best television newsmen.

Some become cranky, withdrawn and start counting the days until their Vietnam tour ends. One of them said: "A few weeks ago, I suddenly realized I had to get out of here for a while, or go nuts. So I went up to Hong Kong and just sat around for a few days. Maybe it's the changelessness of the story that gets you, the feeling that it seems to have no end; or perhaps it's the frustration of never being able to get on top of the story and stay there."

A Saigon bureau chief's daily routine is itself a study in sameness: He's at his office around 8 A.M., and pouring over the night's accumulation of wire-service dispatches and cables from New York. By midmorning he and a camera crew have decided what local stories need covering in Saigon (he has two or three other crews searching for battles in the central and northern provinces).

Tips for these stories come in mysterious Oriental ways. At least one network has a paid informer in Premier Nguyen Cao Ky's office; but more frequently, leads on breaking news come from friends and relatives of Vietnamese employed by the networks. A typical scene: The telephone rings at Bureau X—the bureau chief answers, but there's silence at the other end—that's the signal—he hangs up, and 30 seconds later it rings again—this time, he motions his Vietnamese office manager to respond—the man listens, then speaks in rapid, polyphonic Vietnamese—he hangs up, and says to the bureau chief: "A Buddhist immolation will take place at the Secular Institute at 2 P.M."—the bureau chief musters a camera crew and hurries to cover the story.

In the afternoons the bureau chief frequently telephones his own contacts among Public Information Officers in the armed services, in the U.S. Embassy or among the few South Vietnamese officials who speak English. He also assures that film from his correspondents in the field is met at the Saigon airport and hustled aboard the first outgoing plane for the United States.

At 5 P.M. there occurs daily in Saigon a military and political briefing—called by the newsmen, with bemused disrespect, "The Five O'Clock Follies"—attended by 75 to 100 of the Saigon press corps in a small theater built for the purpose at the Joint United States Public Affairs office. The bare bones of the day's ground, air and sea actions—plus a few words about the U.S. Embassy's activities —are handed the correspondents to be used as the basis for their own dispatches. An adjectival description of American casualties—"light," "moderate" or "heavy"—is included, but without any guidance as to whether the description relates to a platoon, a battalion, or a brigade.

Most of the newsmen feel these briefings are far too peremptory. "You can't possibly rely on them" says ABC's Roger Peterson. "I

44   don't feel any animosity to the briefers; they're doing what they're told, and often they'll level with you if you approach them privately." Says CBS's Peter Herford: "My attitude toward the briefings is that any time one of our men comes up with a story on his own, we give priority to that because it will always top the briefing stuff. The briefing material is frequently fairly old, incomplete and not always accurate. Actually they give you leads by what they don't say, and if a correspondent has the proper cynicism, he can figure out what to go after."

Herford adds: "I've never in my life seen such a profusion of Public Information Officers. There's a PIO war going on here. One can't argue with the natural tendency of PIO's to make their particular service look good, and to get as much good publicity for it as possible. But it's detracting from their main mission, which is to inform the press about the military situation. There are too many flacks and not enough information officers."

After the briefing, the final act in the day's routine is to contact New York on a live radio circuit. This occurs around 7 P.M. in Saigon, which is 12 hours earlier in New York. The newsmen chat with their editors halfway around the world, describe film footage which is en route, and record a few radio spots and TV voice-overs. Thus, the day ends around 8 P.M.

So fiercely competitive are the network bureaus in Saigon, however, that correspondents and bureau chiefs rarely fraternize with the opposition in their off hours, fearful of dropping some hard-fought-for bit of information about an upcoming military action or political turn. Even within bureaus, socializing is in short supply.

Said one bureau chief: "I've created a life of my own in Saigon, independent of the correspondents. I can't let myself get too close to them, because I have to make tremendous demands on them. They're all ambitious; some are better than others. But one of these days, one of them will be killed or wounded seriously, and if I know him too well, my reaction to it might be more than I can handle."

Most TV crewmen would rather cover a jungle battle than a street riot in Saigon. Says ABC's Ron Headford: "You have no protection while filming a civil demonstration. You can get hit from any side." Two NBC newsmen had such troubles: David Burrington was pushed into a police wagon during a riot, and his camera smashed; Dean Brelis was ordered away from the scene of a riot at gun point.

Another young correspondent says: "I'd much rather be in the field than in Saigon; there's more truth out there. Anyway, I don't consider myself a political expert, and in Saigon you have to do stories

NEIL HICKEY
THE VIETNAM WAR: IS TELEVISION GIVING US THE PICTURE?

45

on the murky and mercurial political situation. You're treading on
eggs when you try to describe it. I'll take a nice simple battle any
day."

Battles are indeed at the hard core of television's Vietnam coverage. This fact amuses some of the Saigon TV newsmen and angers
others. One correspondent said: "New York will send us a cable
saying, 'Need more background stories on political and social angles.'
So we send filmed pieces on the inflation in Saigon, on the rice
harvest, or the black market. Then New York cables back: 'Your piece
on inflation excellent. However we note that Network X had terrific
Marine battle near Danang.' The only way you can get a blast from
New York is to get beaten by the opposition on a combat story."

Another says: "Battle films have a way of becoming clichés.
As a result, each time you go out, you've got to get something better
and hotter than last time to satisfy New York. It's like a narcotics
addiction, where you need increasingly larger dosages to have an
effect. It's too bad, really, because so many of these military actions
are meaningless in the long view. They're just tiny pieces of an
immense jig-saw puzzle. But we're caught up in this competitive
bind, and have convinced ourselves it's what the audiences want
to see."

The necessity of living like a soldier—with all the concomitant
dangers, discomforts and exposure to disease—is a principal cause of
all three networks' difficulty in getting seasoned and knowledgeable
newsmen in good supply to come to Vietnam. A bureau chief said:
"Let's be brutally frank: There are no long lines forming in New York
of people volunteering to come out here—not correspondents,
cameramen, soundmen or potential bureau chiefs."

TV newsmen and technicians, generally, are not responding in
sufficient numbers. Some have attempted to stipulate (without
success) that if they did come, they would not leave Saigon to go into
combat; others simply have refused to come here under any circumstances. This vacuum has created enormous opportunities for the
young and ambitious. "Some great new talent has been discovered
here," says Jack Fern, "and they're bringing honor to broadcasting."

But some of the older TV hands are fearful that the general lack
of experience is hurting television's coverage. "I'm disappointed in
the over-all quality of the reporting," says one of them. "New York
has, on occasion, sent misfits, people whose jobs were in jeopardy
at home, and who were told to volunteer to come here—or else.
They're untrained, or undertrained. They're an odd assortment of
many nationalities—adventurers from all over the world."

46   Says another: "I'm appalled that some correspondents are
allowed to come here for as little as three months. They have no interest in Asian affairs. They're here to make a quick name for themselves and get out. Two years from now I—and a few others like me—
will still be working in Asia, and that gives continuity to the reporting. Covering a battle is the simplest thing in the world. But to
make sense out of what you've seen, both in the field and in Saigon—
that's what these young hotshots can't do."

TV's "young hotshots" and old hands alike, however, are among
the war's most mobile, courageous and resourceful journalists: Out
of 400 accredited newsmen in Vietnam fewer than 100 venture
regularly into the battle zones, and at least half of those work for television. That's the way it's been ever since that electronic Cyclops
became a war correspondent.

Pentagon officials offered a list of particulars relating to television's presence in Vietnam. The consensus:

That TV is far too engrossed with the picturization of battle
scenes, air strikes and civil mayhem—at the expense of the duller but
more significant stories of Vietnamese politics, inflation, pacification,
education, and the construction of harbors, schools and hospitals.

That the camera's eye is all too myopic and its angle of vision too
narrow to convey the full truth of a military action involving large
forces, and the cameraman thus becomes an "editor" as he chooses
to record the action's more violent and dramatic aspects.

That TV crews too often move with the smaller units—platoons
and even squads—although what happens at that level has only
minimal significance in the larger picture. Viewers thus receive a
partial, out-of-context story.

That many of television's correspondents are too young and inexperienced to convey fully the nuances of this complex Asian war.

That TV bureaus in Vietnam, perhaps out of pecuniary motives,
employ far too many foreign nationals—Vietnamese, French, Scandi-
navian, British, Korean, Australian—and that many of these are in
such strong disagreement with U.S. policies that their opinions
infect the quality of the news.

That TV has, on occasion, broadcast pictures of wounded soldiers
before their next-of-kin were notified, thereby causing anguish to
relatives in the United States; and that correspondents have interviewed wounded who were under sedation and not fully in control
of their thoughts.

TV men in Vietnam admit a validity to some of these plaints, and

are contemptuous of others. NBC's Jack Fern said: "All of us here   *47*
worry about achieving a proper balance between combat and background stories. But let's fact it, there's nothing more exciting than
actual violence. The very fact that a camera is recording some fascinating event brings that event an importance it otherwise wouldn't
have and maybe doesn't deserve."

Another newsman said: "No cameraman in his right mind can
resist pointing his camera at violence going on right before his
eyes—and no producer in New York can resist running it. But still,
we go out of our way to attempt some of the things which newspapers
are able to do incomparably better. Television will never replace
The New York Times."

Colonel Rodger R. Bankson, Chief of Information in Vietnam,
told TV GUIDE: "I haven't seen a TV newsman yet who'll show
something gruesome just for the shock value of it."

It is a fact that the biggest battles of the war go on in the minds
of Vietnamese and U.S. Officials who are searching for answers to
some of the thorniest problems any young nation has faced in the post-
World War II period. But those battles are not visual. They cannot
be made into pictures—and pictures are television's special business.
So the U.S. networks opt too often for the battles they can cover—
jungle gun fights, artillery bombardments, air strikes, the slogging,
day-to-day life of soldiers: a face of the war recognizable to every
American who grew up watching John Wayne action movies.

It is a valid face, to be sure, and the one which is of most interest
to American viewers having sons and husbands in the fighting.
But television's trickiest problem in Vietnam is to achieve balance
betwen the seductive and the significant; to submerge the conviction
that a scene of violence is important merely because a camera is recording it; to find the substance behind the shadow.

A single camera cannot encompass the movements of a battalion
or brigade, and therefore must narrow in on, or "sample," the battle
action of platoons and even squads. This sample often proves far too
random to please the Pentagon. But the correspondents, instinctively
aware of their camera's limitations, attempt to use their narrations as
a framework for the battle's larger aspects.

Peter Kalischer recalls that he was once ordered out of Korea by
General Douglas MacArthur over a disagreement about some close-in
coverage of the fighting. When MacArthur finally relented and let
Kalischer return, he told the reporter: "But don't report the war from
the platoon level any more." Kalischer says: "So this is a very old
complaint. Wars always look better from division headquarters than
they do in the foxholes."

48   American authorities in Vietnam often are more responsive to television's special problems than their counterparts and superiors in Washington. Colonel Bankson said: "I think that TV newsmen out in the field are doing a tremendous job. Even though there may be more information available at brigade headquarters, the TV teams can't cover a military operation from there alone. They have to be where the action is."

In New York CBS's Charles Collingwood—a frequent visitor to Vietnam—had told us: "Vietnam is the most physically demanding role that reporters have ever been asked to take. So it's a young man's war, and the coverage has all the failings and strengths of young men: It's more passionate, more colorful, and perhaps more erratic."

TV's war correspondents in Vietnam must have the stamina of youth and the wisdom of age—an anomalous combination. The younger newsmen are out of their depth on the wilder shores of Vietnamese politics—and they admit it. Kalischer says: "We're reluctant to let a young correspondent do a stand-up, look-in-the-eye piece on some aspect of Vietnamese politics, and to try to make some sense out of it for an American audience. I consider it very dangerous to try. I'm supposed to be the grand old man around here, and I'm reluctant to do it myself. Short-range political prognostication in Vietnam is very, very risky."

The responsibility for solid background reporting is thus left to the occasional visits of cruising pundits like Eric Sevareid, Howard K. Smith and Chet Huntley; and to the Asian regulars—newsmen like CBS's Kalischer and Murray Fromson, ABC's Lou Cioffi and Sam Jaffe and NBC's John Rich—who come to Vietnam on short-term assignment from bases in Bangkok, Tokyo and Hong Kong.

The sellers' market in TV talent for Vietnam duty extends to cameramen and soundmen, who are in continual short supply—a fact which necessitates the recruitment of nonunion technicians from many parts of the world other than the U.S. Highly trained union technicians in the United States are almost invariably too old for jungle marches in 130-degree heat, and too affluent to want to bother with them.

Their union wage scales—even with the waiving of overtime provisions—are enough to make them the highest paid members by far of their respective Saigon bureaus, including correspondents and bureau chiefs. The effect on morale of such an imbalance has been found to be destructive to a bureau's efficiency.

The claim of some Government officials that many of these foreign nationals are unfriendly to American goals in Vietnam—and

that their hostile sentiments are prejudicing the coverage seems more **49**
than a little paranoid when viewed at ground level both in combat and
in Saigon. It is less a cameraman's politics than his primal professional
instincts—and sometimes the shouted orders of the correspondent
under whose direction he is working—which urge him to film a scene
of violence or tragedy happening before his eyes.

English-speaking Vietnamese, as cameramen and soundmen, are
vital to TV crews for purposes of interpreting and interrogating.
CBS's Dan Rather says: "We almost feel an obligation to hire Vietnamese for our staffs. It's their country, isn't it?"

The problem of television's photographing and interviewing
wounded men is less an issue today than it was six months ago. The
networks are sensitized to their responsibility to the worried relatives
of fighting men, and to the need for restraint in the handling of
pictures which might cause those relatives needless anguish. On
April 25, 1966, the Military Assistance Command in Vietnam issued
a memorandum—not, they emphasize, a "directive"—inviting
television's cooperation in respecting the privacy of wounded men,
and suggesting that a soldier who has been injured has a right to
suffer in private.

Since then Assistant Secretary of Defense Sylvester—the Pentagon's spokesman to the press—has met in New York with leading network news executives to appeal the matter further. In Saigon Colonel
Bankson indicated: "We're meeting with nothing but understanding
from all the TV people [on the matter of films of the wounded]. We
said, 'This is the problem,' and they said, 'We'll help.'" Bankson
added: "We have no problem out here which men of good will can't
solve." There are times in Vietnam, however—in the skirmishing
between television and the U.S. Government's public relations
legions—when that appraisal appears far too optimistic.

War and censorship have been amiable bedfellows in the conflicts
of recent memory. Correspondents routinely have submitted their
dispatches for the excision of facts which might aid or comfort the
enemy; and this process has been, historically, a foregone condition
of their presence in the battle zones.

That thrifty situation, for better or worse, does not exist in Vietnam. There is no formal censorship of outgoing news here. The lines
of external communication are owned or licensed by the Vietnamese
government and produce revenue for it. Newsmen are free to travel
anywhere in the country they wish; free to send off their dispatches

50   by radio, cable, air mail, telephone or teletype; free to ship newsfilm straight from the battlefield to their home offices without soliciting the advice or consent of any American or Vietnamese official.

This condition is less a beneficence than a categorical imperative: Formal censorship is technically impossible in Vietnam, although—for differing reasons—many newsmen and Government press officers alike are hotly in favor of it. But the machinery for such formal censorship would be so ponderous as to be altogether unmanageable.

The South Vietnamese government—whose responsibility it would be to administer the censorship, since Americans are merely "guests" of the nation—would require hundreds of expert linguists to review dispatches in scores of languages and screen vast amounts of newsfilm. In addition the South Vietnamese are concerned that their "image" as an emerging democratic nation not suffer injury through association with any such oppressive and unpopular action.

The newsmen in Saigon who favor formal censorship—and they are a minority—feel that a change in U.S. policy to "total and uncompromising candor," combined with censorship, would end the shouted accusations of "News management!" on the one hand, and "Shoddy reporting!" on the other. A peculiar tension exists between Government press officers (both civilian and military) and newsmen in Vietnam, growing out of the total absence of formal censorship here.

There is in Saigon to this day a formidable "credibility gap"—part of it justified and part an unfortunate hangover from the Ngo Dinh Diem regime and the period after, when the press was indeed misled and even lied to by both Vietnamese and American officials about the war's progress and prospects. With the American troop build-up that began in the fall of 1965—and the concomitant press corps expansion—any similar misrepresentations became perilous at the least.

In this vacuum has been constructed a massive public-relations establishment whose purpose is to convey the bare bones of U.S. activity in Vietnam, as well as what many newsmen call a "sanitized" description of the war's gorier and more inhumane aspects. It is this bumpy road of press agentry which the TV newsmen—and they are the most courted among Vietnam journalists—must travel on their journey to the unvarnished truth.

ABC's Lou Cioffi says: "For the armed sercices, Vietnam is the most beautiful public-relations opportunity that exists. It's a chance to show their stuff. That's what a military man needs; without it, he atrophies." The rivalry for TV exposure among the armed services is intense in Vietnam; it's their chance to "play the Palace," with *51* TV as the proscenium.

NBC's Jack Fern says: "Some of the Public Information Officers here have no idea of the function of a free press. They consider you a petty traitor when you try to tell the truth. But lots of us who come out here to Saigon are not irresponsible oafs. I personally have a lifetime invested in broadcast news and I don't intend to spend my time here playing piano in a sporting house.

"The arts of public relations, packaging, publicity and image-building have all grown up in the last 20 years," Fern added, "and now, for the first time, they're being applied to war; there are unnumbered people here whose sole job is to put American military efforts, no matter how grisly, in a good light. The number of PIO's in Vietnam is fantastic, all cranking out a party line, or trying to get their unit its share of publicity." Fern added: "My job is not to put anybody in a good light. I'm not a flack for any group. My responsibility is to the American public, or to some private theory of truth."

We asked a high-ranking civilian press officer to comment on these notions: "The briefing officers do indeed try to put the military in a good light," he said. "Do you expect them to put their friends, who are dying on the field, in a bad light? The press must count this a part of the rules of the game. These officers are representing their colleagues, who would raise hell if their efforts were criticized in public. . . . The press must distinguish between a briefing officer's natural desire to call attention to his service's successes in Vietnam, and a deliberate attempt to lie. I admit that sometimes those lines are obscure. But the policy here is indeed candor. We will not lie. This is a matter of pure self-interest, because we're fighting this war in a glass bowl."

He regretted that a "bad tradition" had grown up in Vietnam between press and official spokesmen and that this tradition was proving "extremely hard to live down." Its basis, he claimed—buried in past public-relations mistakes of South Vietnamese governments and their American advisors—is no longer valid.

More recently, the Saigon press corps' chief complaints have attached to reported statements of Assistant Defense Secretary Arthur Sylvester that newsmen should "get on the team," and perhaps even be the "handmaidens of government" in a posture of united purpose before the American people and the world.

Such words have been a red flag to Saigon's newsmen, who deeply resent having their patriotism confused with current U.S. policies in Southeast Asia—whether or not they agree with them, and

52   many do. As a result, much of the press corps has over-reacted to what it perceives to be Mr. Sylvester's (and by extension, the White House's) desire for a laundered reporting of the Vietnamese war. Many have gone far out of their way to establish—before their colleagues, their news editors and the Government—that they are of independent mind; that in this complex, undeclared war their first duty is to inform the public well and truthfully; and that they cannot be "had" by any official line.

Another Saigon press officer said: "There is no precedent for the condition here. In World War II correspondents wore Army uniforms and were indeed 'on the team.' They felt part of the military effort. But this is a contested war within our own ranks; Americans are in disagreement about it. Other wars didn't allow for dissent; there was such a thing as treason. The criticism was directed at the ways and means of prosecuting the war, and not at the very principle underlying it."

At least one network forbids its correspondents to use expressions such as "our forces" or "we attacked"—anything that would suggest a complicity. "You must remember," said the press officer, "that the U.S. Government is the avowed advocate here, and that having assumed such a posture—rightly or wrongly—we want our efforts to have the best possible press. Still—and it's almost paradoxical— we help the press in every conceivable way."

There's an arcane sanity in all this. The dog-cat relationship of the press and the political-military Establishment in Vietnam is a predictable corollary of the absence of formal censorship: guidelines, ground rules, gentlemen's agreements and press agentry have replaced the censor's scissors and blue pencils. And in spite of the flying sparks and occasional shouted recriminations, it works—not ideally, but it works.

The strongest lever in the hands of U.S. and Vietnamese officials is their power to suspend or cancel a correspondent's accreditation. So far it has not been used against any television newsman. There's little doubt that some U.S. authorities, both in Saigon and Washington, wish that television would depart the field and leave the war coverage to men with pads and pencils; their jobs would be simpler if TV eschewed the filming of jungle battles, weeping civilians, burned villages, and conveying the color of blood to America's living rooms. But in Vietnam, television journalism has become a fully accredited presence in warfare for the first time, and that status will never be reversed.

In certain kinds of news reporting—such as national political

conventions, elections and space shots—TV's coverage is incom- 53
parable, dominant, and practically pre-emptive. But in an important
sense Vietnam is not television's meat; it only appears to be. The
basic story defies visualization, and for too many Americans the two-
minute reports on the Huntley-Brinkley, Walter Cronkite, and Peter
Jennings [Reynolds-Smith] programs are the whole war.

Television is not essentially a news-disseminating creature, as are
newspapers, wire services and some magazines. As a franchised
medium, it absolves part of its responsibility to the public by a characteristically objective brand of news reporting and a reluctance to
take sides. Its half-hour weekly digests of the war news, its costly
pre-emptions, and its panel discussions (even though such programs
win disturbingly meager audiences) are a clue to the television industry's determination that everything possible be done to illuminate the
war's darker corners for America's television watchers.

But the ultimate questions remain: Is television's coverage of
Vietnam adequate? It is not. One must range farther for an understanding of Vietnam—before hardening one's convictions about it or
before committing so important a prize as one's vote.

Is television's coverage honest? It is—given the complexities of
the conflict, the limitations of the medium and the normal fallibility
of newsmen. In spite of some official fears, there is nothing sinister
nor conspiratorial about television's effort in Vietnam.

Is it objective? The better question is: "Is total objectivity
possible in so argumentative an atmosphere?" It appears not. Most
newsmen either are in favor of continued prosecution of the war or
against it; the ground between is narrow indeed.

It is Washington's uncomfortable—and not altogether unfounded
—suspicion that more than half of TV newsmen in Saigon and New
York are liberals and thus opposed to America's course in Vietnam,
and that this opinion is reflected subtly in the coverage more often
than its opposite. As a result, network newsmen are sometimes the
objects of excited telephone calls from the White House, the Pentagon and the State Department at the instant some supposed injury
to the truth about Vietnam is detected on the Huntley-Brinkley,
Cronkite, or Jennings [Reynolds-Smith] news programs.

At such times the television people weigh the complaint before
responding that wars are ugly, that this one is uglier than most and
that television's mission is to pictorialize the truth in its many facets.
Thus, total objectivity in Vietnam reporting is as elusive a quality as
total candor among American and South Vietnamese officialdom on
the war's prospects. This standoff is built-in and not likely to relax.

54   Soon stationary satellites will hang like moons over the Pacific Ocean, bringing the promise of live television coverage of jungle battles and civil disorders from the world's other side (see pp. 586-590). When that chapter begins, television's role in Vietnam will be even more central, and its responsibilities to Americans even weightier.

Does TV Confuse Americans About Vietnam?

By Martin Maloney

DECEMBER 2, 1967

Like millions of other Americans, I am disturbed by the war in Vietnam. I am not a pacifist, although I think that war in this day and age may prove to be the ultimate disaster. I did spend some time in uniform 20 odd years ago, and in 1950 I thought that Harry Truman was probably right when he decided that North Korea had to be stopped.

But Vietnam is something else again. It's pretty hard to visualize the embattled citizen taking his old rifle down from the mantelpiece and going off to keep Ho Chi Minh's Asian legions from eating Texas chile in the White House. It's even pretty hard to see anyone resembling the old-fashioned conscientious objector in those mobs of demonstrators who occasionally heckle Hubert Humphrey and hiss Dean Rusk. I suspect that the demonstrators, along with many others, are people like me: namely, confused, upset—or, in the current lingo, bugged. I have begun to wonder whether I , at least, am not reacting to a combination quite new in human experience: something which I think of as TVietnam, the big war in the little box, the war brought to me by courtesy of pain-relievers, deodorants and low-cal beverages.

Let me make myself clear. In the first place, I think that TV coverage of the Vietnam war, in the United States, has been professional and conscientious. Given the war, the medium and a special way of handling news, the network news teams seem to me to have done an honest job.

In the second place, I don't mean to suggest that TV has created Vietnam out of whole cloth. The medium is not entirely the message in this case. Still, there may be a kind of fatality in the fact that the first TV war is also the war best—or worst—adapted to TV coverage.

There can be no question that Vietnam is the TV war. The Arab-Israeli conflict, of recent memory, was not really covered at all while it lasted—partly because the Arabs didn't know what was going on,

55

56 partly because the Israelis were busy and anyway preferred to leave
the event to history. When Korea was fought, the coaxial cable was
hardly settled all snug in its bed. The European war of 1939-1945
was the first and last of the radio wars, and the Pacific-Asian conflict of that period was so remote that it was covered by the press
only with difficulty and had to wait on the postwar histories and
memoirs for full reporting. But the Vietnam war came along in an age
of television, of supersonic jets and satellite transmissions, and so
is the first—and so far, the only—true TV war. It may persist into a
period when, as someone has noted, American parents may sit comfortably before the box in the living room and watch their sons being
killed and wounded, 10,000 miles away, precisely while the event is
taking place.

If that time comes, I venture to suggest that the parents so blessed
by modern technology may react in a peculiar way, simply because
the experience is utterly new. They may take these instantaneous
images of terror, shock and death as we take so many other images of
the TV world—with a sort of nagging, tortured, inward concern
which may force them to become participants in the agony of the
times. Previous wars were presented to us in the press, on film, in
books, even on radio—always well-rationalized, and always after the
fact. But a war processed through TV approaches simultaneity; it
comes to us now as a kind of daily puzzle which we must ourselves
piece out and understand. This is a frustrating experience. How does
it work?

TVietnam is like all TV news: fragmented and repetitious. Any
TV news broadcast segments the day into a certain number of items,
each presenting a more-or-less dramatic and exciting high point in
the diurnal history. Where the event is particularly dramatic, and/or
film footage is available, the news broadcaster's narrative account
will be followed by a film sequence which presents the event in the
most concrete dramatic terms. Naturally, where a given crisis continues, or where a series of similar events occurs, the TV version
tends to be highly repetitive. As a fairly consistent viewer on TV news
programs, I sometimes get the nightmarish feeling that I have been
trapped in a 6 o'clock treadmill: There is nothing new about the news.

The Vietnamese war has been processed through the TV news
machinery, and it has gone on for a long time. As a result, it continues,
over and over, and over again, in a series of vignettes, each one barely
meaningful in itself, each one echoing a hundred similar news items
past, and perhaps a thousand to come. And then there are the pictures,
which effectively reduce the war to the dimensions of a horrid Punch-
and-Judy show.

Visually, TVietnam is a small, dim war, fought by puppet-like 57 figures. GI doll images appear in gray-on-gray, struggling through swamps, riding atop toy tanks, firing automatic weapons which go pop-pop-pop. Then there are the omnipresent helicopters, strictly out of Disneyland. Occasionally, we see the figure of the enemy, a willowy, starved-looking mite; occasionally, too, the figures of the dead or wounded, also small and usually sacked up in stretchers or blankets. These scenes occur again and again; the fight goes on forever, seemingly in the same terms; the living, the dead and the wounded are always caught in the same terrifying, miniaturized drama, and they are always very small.

Unless my memory of a similar war, now 20 years past, has betrayed me utterly, TVietnam differs from the realities of combat as much as it does from the earlier press, film, radio presentations of war. To the best of my recollection, a major battle, if you are in it but not immediately involved, gives a feeling of enormous size—the thud and shock of explosions, the roar of engines, stabs of flame, smoke— which reduces you, the observer, to a minute scale. You are a midget in a huge universe of stink and shock and blast. When you become involved—being bombed, shelled, strafed, shot at, trying to find cover, trying to fight back, or hoping that somebody will fight back—this universe contracts into an absolute hell of noise and haze.

The response you make to it is frequently one of wild exhilaration and excitement, and sometimes of absolutely paralyzing fear; the experience of battle is a shocking, shaking experience which cannot ever be forgotten. TV reduces this experience to doll-scale and detaches the viewer from it; the information is all there, but in a faint, weak form, like the signal from a remote statellite. The watcher needs a special scanner to pick up the information at all, and a special amplifier to bring the signal up to understandable strength.

There are other profoundly disturbing aspects of TVietnam. For one thing the war is almost inaccessible to the human intellect. It appears to be the first multivalued war in American history. In previous conflicts, one could always describe what was happening as a war between Us and Them. But in Vietnam, We were not engaged in warfare at all for a long time (We simply had sent military advisors to the Good Guys), and even today it is hard to tell whether We are at war or not, or with Whom.

. . . .

There is also no geographical logic to TVietnam. In World War II the British, Americans, Canadians and others made beachheads at Normandy in 1944 and pressed eastward, toward Berlin. At the same time, the Russians came thundering westward, toward Berlin. Be-

58 tween the two assaults Germany and her allies were crushed, Hitler shot himself, and the war ended. It was a nice, linear, well-oriented war, which made a lot of sense. TVietnam is something else again. In the country proper, there are of course a North and a South, and what is jokingly called a Demilitarized Zone between; but if the war has actually progressed from North to South, or South to North, or in any other discoverable direction, you would never know it from TV. The news broadcasters seem almost to have given up on maps, and may be about to give up on place names. (A mention of "Pleiku," for instance, even reinforced with a map, doesn't tell you how or where the war is going.)

The final solution to the tangle seems to be to reduce the whole war to simple numbers, and to report it rather like a series of baseball games in an endless hot summer. Old Walter, or Chet, or Harry, or somebody, comes on and says: "This was an average fighting week in Vietnam. Opposition casualties: 2473. South Vietnamese: 417. Americans: 201." But the numbers don't mean anything, really; they're like the scores in a game so remote and incomprehensible that you hardly know whether the stake is matchsticks, or home runs, or human lives.

Maybe this explains some of the hypnotic fascination which the war seems to exert on the American imagination, as well as the re-vulsion and horror. The war inside the box is a monstrosity which every viewer must invent for himself. M. R. James once wrote a short story about a wealthy collector who bought an antique doll's house, elaborately decorated and furnished, which turned out to be haunted in a strange way. Each night the new owner would awaken from sleep and find himself forced to gaze on his new possession, in which the dolls had come to life and were acting out a gruesome drama of greed, murder and spectral revenge. The happy fact about James's doll house was that, once the drama had run its course, the restless spirits which haunted it were appeased, and the device lost its power to fascinate and terrify.

But the war inside the box is never acted out in full; *this* drama continues, night after night, world without end. Who can seriously believe, watching TVietnam, that the war will actually end? The numbers keep coming in, but nobody knows what numbers, if any, will signal the end of the game.

Somehow, it does not surprise me that people exposed to the big war in the little box protest, complain, demonstrate, cry out. They are suffering the ultimate human discomfort; they need desperately to make sense out of one of the crucial events of the time, an event which

eats at them—at their secure existence, at their children, at their sense 59
of what is decent and proper, at the whole fabric of their lives. And
the sense is not given them. It simply is not there.

Meanwhile, the news broadcasters, caught between necessity and
habit, will continue to produce their box scores. Meanwhile, the discomfort will become more and more painful. The end is not in sight.

Civil Disorders and Urban Coverage

Television has been referred to as the "great addiction of the ghetto, far more extensive than booze, heroin or cocaine" and the "universal appliance of the ghetto." The National Advisory Commission on Civil Disorders—the Kerner Commission—stated that television is the ghetto's most relied upon formal source of news. Television has also been called the "chosen instrument" of the Civil Rights Revolution in the United States, mainly because "when the Negroes got ready for their revolution, TV was there . . . ," as William Monroe, Chief of NBC's Washington News Bureau has said. According to Monroe, television has "conveyed the emotional values of a basically emotional contest with a richness and fidelity never before achieved in mass communication."

Many observers go so far as to claim that without television the Negro Revolution of the 1960's could not have occurred. Others, more moderate, contend that the Civil Rights Bill passed when it did because of the television coverage it received. An assistant to former Attorney General Nicholas Katzenback has supported this latter contention with his statement, "Southern Negroes used TV to appeal over the heads of their local editors and politicians to congressmen and senators in other districts around the country."

Prior to 1965, television was generally considered to be highly beneficial to the civil rights movement. During the years immediately following, however, television coverage of civil disorders and of the movement was increasingly criticized and, especially after the Detroit riots, television was on the defensive. The charges against the medium's coverage were varied.

One very common charge was that television spurred participation and inflamed the riots because of its presence at the scene. One writer charged that television transformed the riots into a sort of Roman spectacle, the police playing the lions and the Negroes play-

60

ing the Christians, but here the Christians were winning. It was *61*
charged that television was a participant in the riots rather than
merely an observer, and thereby affected the outcome of the real
events. The medium was accused of staging incidents, referred to by
David Boorstin as "Pseudo events," and examples were cited from
the Watts and Newark riots. Television was also accused of interfering with attempts to restore order. Critics contended that, as well as
creating events, television created violent Negro leaders, like Malcolm X or Stokely Carmichael. These men, the critics said, became
national figures because they were able to talk face to face with millions via the medium.

Television defended itself against these charges in three ways.
The premise that television coverage can create events, or anything
for that matter, was denied, as illustrated by Frank Stanton's remark
that broadcasting sees exactly what happens and does not create
spectacles or circuses. Second, the premise was accepted, but not the
critics' assumption that the outcome was bad; for example, Walter
Cronkite maintained that, although the presence of television is
obtrusive, an awareness on the part of the participants that the whole
world is watching may well have positive rather than negative results.
The third defense was that even though the charges may well be true,
the alternative of a virtual news blackout would be far worse.

Other charges against television's coverage of the civil rights
movement and civil disorders were that the medium did not fully and
fairly report the riots, that negative stories were given more coverage
than positive ones, that the medium lacked technically trained specialists who were knowledgeable about the origins of the riots and the
nature and extent of the civil rights struggle.

The Kerner Commission Report indicated that neither a black
nor a white case could be made for or against TV. The Report also
declared that, in the opinion of the Commission, TV made a real
effort to provide balanced and factual reporting, although it did not
focus sufficiently on underlying grievances and tensions and it tended
to emphasize the problems of law enforcement. Defending the broadcaster's position before the Kerner Commission, Leonard Goldenson,
President of ABC, stated that television was "reaping the harvest
of having laid it on a line" and that many people were unwilling to
accept "the mirror we have held up to our society." In this vein, the
National Association of Broadcasters passed a resolution: "Along with
other media TV must continue to present the world as it is, not as we
might like it to be."

As in the case of the Vietnam War, television is faced with the

62 major challenge of establishing a precedent for creative, analytical, exploratory journalism. Perhaps an accurate evaluation of the performance of the medium regarding civil disorders and civil rights movements was made by John Dunne in the *New Republic*. He suggested that to tell newsmen to "cool it" is "too glib" an answer. Objectivity is perhaps not humanly possible when dealing with a riot situation. Dunne pointed out that the deficiencies of broadcasters are the same deficiencies that exist among our citizens. We as a nation are "not profound enough, sensitive enough or even educated enough" to understand the facts and ramifications of the racial issues of our times, and broadcasters as a group are no exception.

The two articles on television coverage of civil disorders and urban life included here were written by Neil Hickey. His first article (pp. 63-69) is concerned primarily with the debate about whether or not television shapes events. Hickey explores the nature and extent of the camera's effect on potentially violent situations. The question of television's news-making effects resulted from criticisms of the coverage during the riots of the summer in 1967 and Hickey summarizes the reactions of network executives and correspondents to these charges. Although, as he maintains, no established code can replace the dispassion and detachment of a seasoned TV newsman, Hickey outlines attempts being made by television stations in cooperation with police officials to establish voluntary guidelines for the reporting of civil disorders.

Detroit exemplifies the typical problems faced by large cities and their news media, and was one of the fifteen cities studied by the Kerner Commission. In his second, two-part, article (pp. 70-77) Hickey presents a lengthy discussion of the problems relating to television coverage in a large, racially-troubled city. Hickey feels that Detroit illustrates (particularly before the summer of 1968 when its newspapers were on strike) the inability of television news to provide white people with a real sense of what is going on in the black ghetto. He also finds that the resentment of many inner-city Negroes against television is, in many instances, justified. Hickey notes that the city leaders he interviewed confirm grievances against television noted by the Kerner Commission Report. He reviews the Commission's recommendations that would enable television to make an "inestimable" contribution to the improvement of race relations in the United States.

A Look at TV's Coverage of Violence

SEPTEMBER 16, 1967

A new law of television journalism is emerging in the atmosphere of civil protest, picketing, parades, demonstrations, labor strikes and the broad spectrum of public expression of discontent which has become a central aspect of American life in the last several years, and—more immediately—in the violent summer we have just weathered. Stated most starkly, the law is: "Television, by its very presence, creates news."

Never before today has the law been more operative. Only in recent months have legislators, police officials and TV newsmen come to a suspicion of the full impact of television upon the news it is covering; of TV's power to shape events it chooses to record; of the medium's rather frightening capability of creating a cause, a public figure or a newsstory where—but for the cameras—none might otherwise exist. The charge sheet against TV news is shaping up this way:

1. That the presence of cameras frequently transmutes a potentially violent situation into an actually violent one, and that mischief-makers often show their most troublesome selves at the sight of television crews.

2. That TV pictures of looting, destruction and mayhem create a contagion—far more so than radio or newspaper reports—which causes riots to feed upon themselves.

3. That TV stations and networks give too much time to the flashier and more vocal extremists—such as Stokely Carmichael and H. Rap Brown—whose words foster violence, and not enough to the less theatrical but saner voices of moderation.

4. That pressure groups of all types have become extremely "savvy" in manipulating television by staging protests and parades specifically for the cameras and thereby achieving an inflated importance for their private, special pleading.

63

64   These are only a few of the complaints—some of which have been denied by broadcasting executives—being aimed at TV news in the current controversy. TV GUIDE asked Detroit police commissioner Ray Girardin about the effects of television's presence in his city during the summer's terrible strife in which 43 people died. His response was firm and unequivocal: "The showing of films of scenes from riot-torn areas seemed to arouse the curiosity of hundreds of people who wanted to see for themselves what was happening. Almost immediately, the streets were crowded with curiosity-seekers hampering law-enforcement offiicers.

"TV could have performed a civic duty," Girardin added, "by informing people to stay away from the dangerous sections. Many innocent people were injured and some killed by snipers because they wandered into the troubled areas to see the action."

Police officials in Newark, another scene of recent strife, are similarly disturbed about TV's riot coverage: "We were very disappointed by the behavior of TV crews," a spokesman says. "Doubly so since we had called a meeting as far back as June 23 and invited about 20 news organizations—both local and national—to discuss an informal 'code of ethics' for reporting trouble, should any arise. Three attended the meeting."

Senator John McClellan (D., Ark.) plans to include testimony on TV's riot coverage in hearings currently in progress before his Permanent Subcommittee on Investigations. Congressman Torbert Macdonald (D., Mass.), chairman of the Communications Subcommittee, also is eager to call TV industry executives to Washington for hearings on the medium's capacity for exacerbating troublesome situations and creating new ones. Congressman Macdonald told us: "I'm not saying that Congress should interfere, but I wonder about the wisdom of what TV does in this area. Is it really news if one Negro gets up and shouts, 'Burn Whitey!'? I'd like to find out if the networks and stations have policies on these matters and what instructions they give their reporters."

The disturbances in the streets amount to rebellion, Macdonald added. "I'd like to know if this rebellion is being fed by television and radio. Television may have to take a share of the blame for spreading dangerous doctrines. I'd like to find out what steps they're taking to live up to their responsibility to their audiences."

Senator Hugh Scott (R., Pa.) entered the controversy on August 2, 1967, with a statement that he was "greatly concerned about the newspaper and radio and television coverage of the recent riots and civil disturbances throughout the country. I believe that the news media, in many instances, inadvertently contributed to the turmoil."   65

That salvo elicited return fire from all three networks. Dr. Frank Stanton, president of CBS, insisted that "so far as the news presented over our radio and television networks . . . goes, I can find no evidence that this is true. On the contrary, there is considerable evidence that the exact opposite is the case." At the same time Stanton admitted that "serious problems" attend television's handling of civil disorder and that his own news officials had been duly warned of the "unsettling effect on a stimulated crowd that the presence of cameras may have."

NBC president Julian Goodman echoed Stanton's disfavor of any "code of emergency procedure" (as suggested by Scott) that might impinge upon TV's freedom to cover the news as it sees fit. ". . . A code cannot exercise judgment," said Goodman. "It cannot foresee all the variables in the fast-breaking events with which newsmen must deal."

Another quick response to Scott's statement came from James C. Hagerty, vice president of American Broadcasting Companies. In a "Dear Hugh" letter, Hagerty defended his network's news practices while adding that the whole subject has "been a matter of continuing concern to all us us here. . . .The danger that news coverage can influence or inflame an event is foremost in our thoughts."

Other criticism of TV news has come from pundits and private-interest groups. Columnist Max Lerner says: "Americans seem to have struck a Faustian bargain with the big media, by which they have received total and instant coverage and have in turn handed themselves over the vulnerable chances of crowd psychology and of instant infection." Henry Lee Moon, public relations chief of the National Association for the Advancement of Colored People told us: "Negroes have generally been unhappy about the way television has played their affairs. It's damaging to the cause of civil rights to give a forum to somebody shouting 'Kill Whitey' and cast him as a Negro leader when he represents no substantial part of the Negro population."

TV newsmen are as sensitive as anybody else to such dangers. ABC News executive William Sheehan says that he thinks "it's no coincidence that the flourishing of the civil-rights movement has occurred at the same time that television news has reached the point where every evening it literally saturates the country with reports on world happenings." Another TV executive recalls that during the AFTRA strike of March, 1966, when TV reporters were idle for two weeks, a sharp diminution in protests and picketing for peace and

66 other causes was apparent. "Nothing seemed to be happening," he says. Then the TV news directors realized that—in the absence of cameras—the protestors had concluded it was pointless to mount a protest.

TV people become aware of their own influence in a variety of ways. Cindy Adams, a glamorous reporter for WABC-TV in New York, recalls the time she accepted a telephone call in her newsroom and was informed that a private group planned a demonstration at the Dominican Republic's UN mission headquarters to protest U. S. involvement in that country's affairs. "Can you cover it?" asked the lady caller. "Well, I'm not sure," Cindy said. "How many of you will there be?" "How many do you need?" the woman answered. A bit startled, Cindy replied that it wasn't exactly her place to say. "What time will you be demonstrating?" the reporter then asked. "Maybe right away. That suit you?" "Well, we have no crews here right now," said Cindy. "We'll have as many marchers as you want out there any time you say," the caller assured her. WABC did indeed cover the demonstration, moving Cindy Adams to recall recently: "That woman knew what she was doing; she was savvy in the ways of TV news." An increasing number of social and political activists are learning that it is possible to manipulate TV news to their own interests.

Similarly, TV people have been known to attempt the manipulation of an incipient news story to their own interests. When James Meredith was testing the University of Mississippi's exclusion policy, a potentially volatile stiuation grew out of the studen body's tension and anger over his presence. A TV reporter from a Southwestern station drove onto the campus one day, hoping for some exciting newsfilm, and was disappointed that the students' mood seemed taut but controlled. He leaned from his car and shouted to a group of them: "Hey! Where's the action? I heard there was action going on around here!" That triggered them. First, they turned the newsman's car over and burned it, sending him scrambling; the violence spread from there. At the end of it, two men were dead.

Many observers are sure that TV news (as well as newspapers) fanned the embers which erupted into the bitter riots of the Harlem and Bedford-Stuyvesant section of New York in the summer of 1964. During spring and early summer, almost daily interviews with "Negro leaders" predicting a holocaust were visible on television. Many of these men were spokesmen without a following, ambitious activists eager for exposure. But their words created an air of tension and expectancy, convincing the ghetto dwellers that violence was indeed imminent. Nobody was surprised when it came.

In Los Angeles in 1965, mobile TV vans moved into riot areas of 67 Watts and showed live pictures of looting even before the police had arrived. A police official remembers: "Television served as a terrific guide for potential looters who wanted to know where to go for some action."

Still, there's no gainsaying that TV reporters as a class are well aware of the effect of their presence on an evolving story. We asked a number of network correspondents—experienced in coverage of street demonstrations—for their thoughts:

Tom Jarriel, ABC: "There's no doubt that a camera causes pickets to act up more vigorously. They know the power of TV exposure; all these people want their story told. The camera is an attraction. The problem is to keep it from becoming a bigger story than the one you're covering. "We often leave our cameras on the seat of the car and stand to one side while a situation is developing. When something actually happens, we film it."

Jarriel feels that the TV presence also can have a moderating influence. "I doubt that James Meredith would have completed his most recent march in Mississippi unmolested if the cameras hadn't been there. People didn't heckle him; they stayed away so as not to cause a major incident on nation-wide TV."

John Laurence, CBS: "More trouble is caused by young and inexperienced wire service reporters than by TV men. They can make a quick phone call and in minutes a bulletin is going out on their wires. The presence of a TV camera often tends more to keep a situation honest than to aggravate it. If a camera is on a policeman and his prisoner, chances are the policeman won't beat the prisoner and the prisoner won't attack the policeman."

Don Oliver, NBC: "Once a public disturbance has begun, cameras have very little effect on its progress, but in the early stages— where the possibility for violence exists—the sight of a TV crew can have a bad effect. Police and TV people work well together most of the time; but as a riot goes into its third or fourth day, the police get edgy and angry and start feeling that the cameras are drawing attention to them."

Bill Matney, NBC: "Cameras have very little effect while a disturbance is actually going on. In Detroit, I interviewed two fellows while they were actually looting, and later filmed their arrest. On one day, while whole sections of the city were going up in smoke, the TV people refrained from reporting it so as not to make it worse. That was an independently-arrived-at decision by the local stations."

CBS's Midwest bureau manager, Dan Bloom, had the job of set-

68   ting up that network's riot coverage in a number of cities during the summer. "It boils down to the fact that the equipment is sometimes a magnet," he says. "But our policy is simple. If a reporter has any suspicion that a performance is going on just for the camera, we immediately pack up and move away. This is rigidly enforced. On the other hand, if you have a peaceful demonstration that goes on for 60 minutes and a bomb is thrown in the last two minutes, where is the story? We'd be remiss if we didn't put that part of the action on the air. We make a very deliberate attempt at setting the proper balance."

Before this past summer, many TV newsmen were understandably reluctant to admit television's influence on evolving news, but the proliferation of protests and riots, as well as the thoughtful criticism of lawmakers and private citizens, are forcing the subject onto center stage, where it must now be examined in full public view, and some firm conclusions arrived at. CBS News president Richard S. Salant, for example, admits, "It is certainly true that a great many events—almost all except tornadoes—are, at least to some degree, designed in time or in place or even in nature for all of the mass media. . . . But our job is to report news, not to shape it."

And there are no easy, self-executing rules applicable to all situations, Salant adds. "We know that one cannot simply ignore these events because indeed they are news. And we have come to the conclusion, then, that the wise policy is a policy of restraint and awareness of what the problems are."

For the last several years, the U. S. Justice Department's Community Relations Service has been working quietly in cities across the country getting TV people together with police officials and helping them agree on voluntary guidelines for the reporting of civil disorders. Together, they've come up with solid recommendations aimed at keeping good order in the streets while not raising the ugly specter of censorship. Scores of TV stations have agreed to: a.Hold off reporting mass violence until police establish some modicum of control. b.Use unmarked cars, hand-held cameras, no bright lights, and expose the cameras to public view only when there's something to film. c.Avoid reporting rumors, trivia and wild statements. d.Use command posts set up by police in strife areas as clearinghouses for news breaks, and not cruise about the streets aimlessly. e.Refrain from using the word "riot" unless there's simply no other word to describe what's happening.

The networks and many local stations try to do many of these things out of common sense, and not from official nudging. But it's apparent that no guidelines nor agreements can replace the dispassion and detachment of a seasoned TV newsman who is determined to convey—soberly and untheatrically—the full sense of a public disorder; whose eye is not upon competing newsmen nor on the aggrandizement of his own reputation; and who is sensitive to the effect of his words upon an anxious audience.

A part of television's difficulty in this area is inherent in the nature of the medium and will never be absolved altogether. But the opinion is now abroad that networks and stations must do a great deal more than they're doing to ensure that the medium does not alter the shape of events it touches and does not let itself be manipulated by the show-business appeal of special pleaders.

It is apparent that the adaptation of rigid "codes" is not the answer. But if, indeed, television's self-generating potential for news is an operative unwritten "law" of broadcast journalism, it is a law in need of prompt and drastic—unwritten but nonetheless effective—amendment.

Detroit: Television on Trial

By Neil Hickey

JUNE 1 AND 8, 1968

Scarcely a dozen hours had passed since the death of the Rev. Dr. Martin Luther King Jr. in Memphis, Tennessee; and now in Detroit, Mayor Jerome Cavanagh lounged in his 11th-floor office in the slab-like City-County Building overlooking the Detroit River, and wondered what this new catastrophe meant to his city, which was tense and brittle enough already in the dour expectation of another summer of civil strife.

Moments earlier, in an adjoining room, the mayor had told a press conference of television and radio reporters (Detroit's two daily newspapers had been strike-bound for months, in the longest newspaper blackout the city had ever suffered) that he hoped Dr. King's death would not fan to flame the embers of rage that had left 43 dead and miles of the city in ruins during 1967's violence, the worst in U. S. history.

And now the mayor was rubbing his eyes and telling a visitor he wished there were newspapers in operation to help him stay in better touch with the people, to lance any incipient boils of disorder, because television—no matter how well-intentioned—doesn't fill the vacuum. Without newspapers, "things aren't known," said the mayor earnestly, "and people need the reassurance of knowing that the administration is doing things, is affirmatively engaged." But Detroit's television stations "hadn't done enough to take up the slack" caused by the newspaper shut-down, he said, and Detroiters were more in the dark than they should be, and more edgy about the approaching summer than was healthy, and more vulnerable to wild rumors.

But Detroit was, in fact, that day a near-perfect laboratory case for any passing social scientist who might have wondered what happens in a great American city which has: no newspaper; 40 per cent of its population, much of it disaffected, living in a ghetto, and

70

therefore imagined by whites to be forever on the edge of violence; and a terrible unanimity of opinion among its black leaders that—even in the best of circumstances—the black community receives shoddy, shallow, misinformed and wrong-headed treatment from the press, and that television is even worse than the newspapers.

To cast a little light on those questions, we searched out both white and black spokesmen who could describe concretely how Detroit is typical of many urban centers having large minority populations, and make some worthwhile judgment about whether, from television news, white people are getting a real sense about what's really going on in the black ghettos of the United States.

The answer to that last question—on the unlikely chance you're still in suspense—is a resounding "They are not!" It is that logjam on the river of understanding that is of such deep concern to knowledgeable activists of both races; for practical purposes, they say, the lines are down, the bridges are washed out.

One day a few weeks ago, the managing editor of the *Michigan Chronicle*—Detroit's well-read weekly Negro newspaper—leaned across an incredibly cluttered desk and complained that the only time most Negroes see a television crew is when one comes to the ghetto to film rioting, looting and mayhem. At all other times, he claimed, there's a marked scarcity of TV reporters inquiring about the run-of-the-mill, day-to-day civic-action life of the black community—the sort of thing which gets routine coverage among the whites.

As a result—Al Dunmore added—Negroes are as likely to throw a brick at a television camerman as they are at a policeman, because he's just one more facet of a white establishment that's insensitive to the root aspirations of black people. "Television is deeply resented by many inner-city Negroes," Dunmore says. "Whenever something big happens in the ghetto, I get calls from TV news directors and reporters, asking, 'What does it mean?' I don't mind helping them out once in a while, but they should know what it means. They should have in their news departments the kind of specialists who would tell them what it means. TV lives in a dream world, because 90 percent of its editors have been brought up ignorant of what's going on."

It's that same brand of near-invincible ignorance—on the part of both local stations and network operatives—which disturbs such other Detroit leaders as the Rev. Roy Allen, president of the Detroit Council of Organizations and pastor of the Chapel Hill Baptist Church. "I once asked a TV reporter why we only saw him around the neighborhood when there was violence. He said, 'Reverend, I'm sorry to have

72   to say it, but bad news is good news.' It does, in fact, seem to be what white audiences want and expect. And it's the sort of news which keeps the TV reporters in business. . . . If a black man steals, rapes, or kills, the story gets top coverage. But the duller—and more important —stories usually aren't good enough for TV. They're not exciting or visual. Somehow, society will have to use its influence to change this—soon."

Detroit's TV stations have, however, demonstrated a readiness, when called upon, to help foster good order and discipline. All of them gave free prime time to Mayor Cavanagh last March 6 for an appeal to Detroiters to stop buying guns. They did it again on April 18 when the New Detroit Committee—a group formed by the mayor and Governor George Romney after last July's riots—released its report on the causes of the city's disharmony.

But many activists continue to express bleak views on TV's treatment of Negroes. One of them is Dr. Karl T. Gregory, an economist at Wayne State University in Detroit and a frequent spokesman for black causes in that area. The mass media of television, radio and newspapers become "vehicles for preserving the status quo," says Gregory. "They propagandize for existing bureaucracies and thus preclude social change."

The reality of ghetto life projected by television is "not representative," and is even "farcical" at times, Gregory maintains. "White reporters have their own social habits. Through existing social arrangements, they have a set of contacts among black poeple whom they depend upon for information and interpretation. They go to these 'authentic' sources for interviews and get these people to say what they want them to say. Meanwhile, everybody in the black community is laughing." However, says Gregory, the very fact that these Negro "spokesmen" are known at all to reporters of the mass media is a fair indication that they're not the leaders genuinely influential with the ghetto-dwellers.

A dramatization of that fact may be contained in the following incident. Three times in a single day of interviewing, this reporter was warned about a local Detroit character who had come to the city and purposefully set himself up as a Negro spokesman by the simple means of having stationery printed indicating himself as "chairman" of a high-sounding and largely nonexistent civic committee, and volunteering opinions to any press people who would listen.

"He's a pleasant guy," said one Negro informant, "an amiable and harmless charlatan, and something of a publicity-seeker. But he represents absolutely nobody but himself." That same evening, on two separate television newscasts, that same would-be spokesman was quoted respectfully and at length by the anchor men on an important issue relating to Negro aspirations.

Gregory also claims that television as presently constituted is a "racist apparatus." His special scorn is reserved for TV "scandal-mongers" among reporters, and interview-show emcees, who "cater to the worst instincts in the white community" by bringing together on the same program militant whites and blacks and then simply standing aside while they claw at each other in a rancorously unpleasant display having more value for the station's ratings than for the cause of civil rights.

Some of these grievances were, in fact, noted in the recently released Report of the National Advisory Commission on Civil Disorders[7] (called the Kerner Commission Report after its chairman, Governor Otto Kerner of Illinois), which President Johnson constituted to get some answers about why the summer of 1967 was so riotous.

Television is the news source most relied upon in the ghetto, according to the Commission (which did its work in Detroit and 14 other cities). It quoted a study which indicated that 75 percent of ghetto-dwellers turned to television for national and international news, and that 86 percent regularly watched television from 5 to 7 P.M.—the dinner-hour news period. It also noted that 87.7 percent of nonwhite households own television sets.

In view of this overwhelming dependence upon TV by ghetto-dwellers, the Commission regretted that broadcast news (and newspapers as well) had "failed to analyze and report adequately on racial problems in the United States and, as a related matter, to meet the Negro's legitimate expectations in journalism." The news organizations also have "failed to communicate to both their black and white audiences a sense of the problems America faces and the sources of potential solutions. The media report and write from the standpoint of a white man's world. The ills of the ghetto, the difficulties of life there, the Negro's burning sense of grievance, are seldom conveyed."

The white press, said the Commission, repeatedly although perhaps unconsciously reflects the biases and paternalism—and at times the indifference—of white America: a condition which is understandable but not excusable, since news agencies "have the mission to inform and educate the whole of our society."

The Commission's strongest words on the matter are these: "The world that television and newspapers offer to their black audience is almost totally white, in both appearance and attitude. . . . [The white

74   press] is at best mistrusted and at worst held in contempt by many black Americans. Far too often, the press acts and talks about Negroes as if Negroes do not read the newspapers or watch television, give birth, marry, die, or go to PTA meetings."

The percipience of the Kerner report's findings is confirmed by a number of knowledgeable whites in the Detroit area, among them Richard Marks, who is secretary-director of the City's Commission on Community Relations and so vocal a partisan that he has been hanged and burned in effigy in downtown Detroit by white extremists.

Marks says that television news is an easy mark for any activist—white or black—who has a propaganda idea, a mimeograph machine and a good media sense. Into that category he places a Detroit organization called Breakthrough, which saw fit recently to disrupt a civil-rights rally at Ford Auditorium conducted by Father James Groppi, the angry young Catholic priest who has led many activist protests in the Midwest. Marks claims that the local television stations gave only a fraction of a minute of air time to Groppi's speech and many times that amount to Breakthrough's disruptive tactics. News judgments like that are commonplace not only in Detroit but elsewhere, he says.

TV stations have three basic, stereotype Negro news stories, according to Marks: the 101-year-old ex-slave interview, which he lumps in with other "tinker-toy" nonevents, such as coverage of Boy Scout meetings; interviews with flashy and vocal but essentially unimportant ghetto characters ("They've always loved Prophet Jones," Mark says, referring to a Detroit preacher famed for his threatricality); and the riot, arson and looting story.

"As a result, the Negro community has no respect for this medium," Marks claims. "A hundred separatists have a meeting and it gets plenty of local coverage, because these fellows are sophisticated propagandists. The fault is somewhere in those news departments." There's no need to manufacture black leaders for the cameras, Marks says, because the real ones are there, but many TV people "don't have the right kind of seeing-eye dogs to find them—a savvy Negro cameraman, perhaps, who could steer them off phony stories and onto solid ones."

One interviewer employed by the Kerner Commission reported that: "The average black person couldn't give less of a damn about what the media say. The intelligent black person is resentful at what he considers to be a totally false portrayal of what goes on in the ghetto."

Why is the treatment of blacks by TV news of such central importance at this particular time? Consider: Since World War II, millions of Negroes have migrated from rural areas to the big cities. By 1970 it's likely that 50 of the largest U. S. cities will have majorities of black inhabitants, and by 1975 the country's 14 largest cities will have black majorities of 60 to 80 percent.

This inevitable process of imagined "upward mobility" sees blacks flowing into the big cities and whites flowing outward—in a mad, centrifugal hegira—to the suburbs. W. H. Ferry, writing in *The Center Magazine,* a publication of the Center for the Study of Democratic Institutions, points out that our cities, for the most part, are laid out in rough concentric circles from a core of official and mercantile buildings, expanding "until they bump into that green and leafy ring closing the circle on all sides, the suburbs. This is a barrier that is virtually unpassable, except to a few blacks, a they-shall-not-pass miles thick and getting thicker. . . .Thus, the growing blackness of our central cities is a result ordained by whites, like all major matters affecting blacks."

To this premise must be applied the fact that the country's 650 [690] television stations have their signals clustered over these dense population centers, the same inner cities where 86 percent of the black citizens peruse their TV screens nightly during the news programs for some image of themselves and their affairs. What they're seeing—according to every indicator—frequently angers them.

In Detroit, the news directors of the three VHF commercial TV stations are not insensitive to the problem. "We'd like our lines into the Negro community to be better," says Bob McBride of WJBK. "Still, we've found out that the Negro leaders aren't always in touch with the Negro masses. Who are the clearly defined spokesmen? Our motives are good, but it's sometimes difficult to pin down where the action is.

"We have a Negro reporter on our staff," McBride says, "and she's been spat upon by Negroes. The Kerner Report says we should hire more Negroes, and when you do, that's what happens." WWJ's Jim Clark says, "We've given a lot of coverage to Negro affairs. These people are in our service area, and it's our duty to do so. I think the Kerner Report was unfair in that respect." WXYZ's Bill Fyffe says, "We're making a greater effort to inform the whole community about some of the positive things that are going on," rather than emphasizing crisis coverage and thereby contributing to the inflation of tension.

Police Commissioner Ray Girardin sat in his oversize, wood-paneled office on Detroit's Beaubien Street one day recently and

76   suggested that "Television in its presentation of news is maturing greatly and doing things they never would have done only a few years ago. I can't say enough about how they're handling themselves. They're living up to a heightened awareness of their responsibilities. In this social revolution we're having, they're a vital part of it."

Many knowledgeable Detroiters, even those harshly critical of TV's performance there, admit that television is gradually—though perhaps too gradually—achieving greater sophistication in the handling of minority news. "It seems to me that television news rooms have begun to think through these premises a little better," says Richard Marks. "TV people are awfully bright. It takes a special kind of guy to think in terms of telling a story visually."

But Marks quickly adds that the city's three network-affiliated commercial TV stations have in their news rooms a total of two Negro reporters, and no Negroes at all in significant middle- or upper-layer editorial posts. "It's a scandal, so far as I can see," Marks says. "The medium has never found it possible to hire enough blacks to project news of black people faithfully. The stations don't know how to look for skill nor how to plan for it. If the sensitivity isn't built into those news rooms, how is it to get there? Sometimes Negro reporters bring back Negro news to their news rooms, and it doesn't fit their editors' idea of what's going on, so it isn't used."

Al Dunmore argues earnestly that the problems of America's cities are becoming so complex that big-city news operations now need specially trained reporters in the field of urbanology, "be they white or black." Many TV stations employ experts on science, music and politics, he points out, and the time has come when they need experts in urban affairs. "Not cub reporters with a microphone in their hands," he says, "but specialists, men who really know the inner cities of America. I'm not saying that Negroes are better at this than whites, but often they tend to have a better feel for it."

Detroit's problems in this whole matter are not different from those in scores of American cities having cohesive and unassimilated minorities living at their cores: how to force open the lines of communication and let understanding and cooperation flow through. Detroit, we hasten to point out, has been used in these articles only as a microcosm.

The Kerner Commission's own conclusion, arrived at after broad research in many parts of the U. S., is that: "The failings of the media must be corrected and the improvement must come from within the media." The essence of the Commission's recommendations to the media is in the following paragraph, and is worthy of full quotation:

"News organizations must employ enough Negroes in positions   77
of significant responsibility to establish an effective link to Negro
actions and ideas and to meet legitimate employment expectations.
Tokenism—the hiring of one Negro reporter, or even two or three—
is no longer enough. Negro reporters are essential, but so are Negro
editors, writers and commentators. Newspaper and television policies
are, generally speaking, not set by reporters. Editorial decisions
about which stories to cover and which to use are made by editors.
Yet very few Negroes in this country are involved in making these
decisions, because very few, if any, supervisory editorial jobs are held
by Negroes. We urge the news media to do everything possible to
train and promote their Negro reporters to positions where those who
are qualified can contribute to and have an effect on policy decisions."

Finally, said the Commission, it would be of "inestimable importance to race relations in the United States simply to treat ordinary
news about Negroes as news of other groups is now treated." That's
the heart of it, really; it's the same thing which concerned whites and
blacks have been saying in wordier and less economic fashion for a
long time; it's the almost too-simple "golden rule" which—if tacked
up in all the Nation's TV news rooms—would help bring a new age of
communion and understanding in the city life of America.

To sound reveille at the dawn of this hoped-for age, the Commission suggests formation of a private, non-profit Institute of Urban
Communications which would help train specialists in the reporting
of big-city news and would recruit and place Negro journalists in
jobs where their special viewpoints would do the most good. It would
also review informally the handling of racial news in all its aspects,
and praise excellent performances and condemn shoddy ones.

Whether or not the Commission is right in thinking that one more
institute, bureau or study group is what's needed now is not clear.
But sensitive whites and blacks are tending to agree with them that:
"Along with the country as a whole, the press has too long basked in a
white world, looking out of it, if at all, with white men's eyes and a
white perspective. That is no longer good enough. The painful process of readjustment that is required of the American news media
must begin now."

Political Conventions

According to Professor John Kenneth Galbraith, national political conventions decide nothing and television alone sustains the myth. Other observers maintain that the conventions' major decisions are rarely made in the presence of television; the television viewer is meant only to see the nominating function and the rally to kick off the campaign. Sometimes, as at the 1968 Democratic Convention in Chicago, the viewer sees much more.

That national political conventions are important to television was illustrated early by the increase in set sales accompanying convention coverage in 1952. However, by 1970 the major importance of convention coverage is its influence upon advertising sales and the networks' images. The satisfaction of viewers, critics and sponsors with the coverage of the conventions can pay important dividends to the network for the next four years. In the past, the network winning the greatest ratings during the convention and the campaign has often led the network news field until the next presidential campaign began. And sales people claim that the networks news image definitely affects sales of the entire network schedule.

Thus it is not surprising that broadcasters send more people to each convention than does the party—including delegates and alternates—and that the networks establish elaborate public relations outlets at the convention. And for the same reasons, NBC and CBS have disregarded suggestions made since 1952 to discontinue gavel to gavel coverage. ABC's poor financial position led that network to substitute partial for complete coverage in 1968. Although this "forced experiment" with entertainment programming was successful in attracting audiences during certain hours of the convention, it had doubtful effects on that network's news image.

William S. White (pp. 81-86) maintains that television is an intrinsic, sometimes controlling part of the political convention. He describes several instances where the effect of television was, in his opinion, decisive. The coverage of a single event at the 1948 con-

78

vention helped Harry Truman to gain the Negro vote at the polls.
Television influenced Robert Taft's loss of the Republican nomination in 1952. The presence of television coverage was instrumental
in John Kennedy's choice of Lyndon Johnson as a running mate; and
television worked against Richard Nixon both at the 1960 convention
and in the following campaign.

Television's active role insures that the public is better informed
about the details of the convention, but often only the ostensibly
important and true are shown. According to White, since what occurs
outside camera range at a convention is often more decisive than
activities within camera range, television's ability to expose the true
significance of a political convention is profoundly limited.

The theory that television is far more than an observer and, in
fact, can influence the outcome of a political convention has gained
numerous supporters following television's controversial coverage
of the 1968 Democratic Convention in Chicago. Neil Hickey's four
part article (pp. 87-105) on television and the Chicago Convention
examines the debate regarding the medium's role at and in that event.

Hickey provides background for the controversy in the first
part of his article (pp. 87-93). He discusses the public and official reactions to the coverage and lists the various charges made against the
networks.

The FCC received hundreds of complaints about the coverage
from private citizens and consequently requested explanatory letters
from the networks. Hickey discusses these letters in part two (pp.
93-97), and describes the networks' reactions to the Chicago controversy. He emphasizes the tension that existed between party
and city officials and the press even before the Convention began and
quotes newsmen who suggest that charges of bias and distortion
were inevitable.

In part three (pp. 97-101), Hickey evaluates the objectivity of the
television coverage in Chicago. According to Hickey, to summarize
the nature of the coverage is very difficult; reporters reacted to a complex series of events in various ways. Hickey goes on to quote the
reactions of several academicians to television's presence and importance in Chicago.

In the final part of his article (pp. 101-105), Hickey considers
whether or not events at the 1968 Convention will affect the freedom
of television news and the viewers' trust in its honesty. He concludes
that the controversy over the coverage of the convention has helped
television take a stride toward maturity.

Reuven Frank (pp. 106-115), president of NBC News, defends his

80 network's news coverage of the Chicago Convention and answers in detail some of the criticisms which were levelled at television coverage: that the networks devoted undue time in showing the demonstrations, that television did not show the provocations which led to police action, that broadcasters deliberately interrupted important parts of the Convention. Frank maintains that, in the case of the Chicago Convention, television coverage is being blamed for the event. Frank discusses the anxieties reflected in the letters received by the networks. He points out that many are advocating a form of censorship, and he presents his concept of the purpose of free journalism in a free society. Frank argues that control, even for the public good, is dangerous in the long run.

Television's Role in Politics
By William S. White

JULY 11, 1964

The two great political parties are about to assemble in convention in the old, recurrent drama of American President-making. And television—"the magic lantern," as some of the pros call it with wry, love-hate feelings—is about to offer its quadrennial mixed fare of sound information, stirring entertainment, solid enlightenment, and hokey bravura, first from the Republican gathering in San Francisco, then from the Democrats rallying in Atlantic City.

It will be "coverage" in the most massive and tireless form, if also in a somewhat surface form. The red eye of TV is poked into many corners of those proceedings, even though it still does not reach that famous "smoke-filled hotel room" in which legend says—and sometimes correctly—that the real and final convention decisions are made.

But to say that television only "covers" these conventions is to speak genial nonsense. TV long since has passed from its early status as a mere onlooker. This omnipresent mechanism does far more than merely record the proceedings. It has become not merely an observer but always a vital and sometimes actually a controlling part of the whole show.

No national political convention is planned any more without giving top priority to the magic lantern. Every phrase of the agenda— from the deliberations of the platform committees through the keynote speeches and, finally, to the immense and fateful showdown which is the roll call for nominations for President and Vice President—is arranged with a far more acute and concerned eye on the potential looking audience out in the country than on the people actually in the convention hall. Timing—including the most urgent efforts to have the big thing happen during the prime viewing time— is everything.

The press, of which I have been for some 30 years a part, used to be the elite force, cajoled and pampered only next to the voting delegates themselves. But the press comes in a very poor second now.

81

82 The convention masters do what they can—within reason, of course—
to accommodate us. But their pleading and sustained courtship goes to
that other "medium" from whose gaunt towers the country is drenched
with the image of a convention of hard-working—and hard-playing—
politicians gathered for the solemn purpose of recommending a man
for the Presidency to the people of the United States.

To say that the country is far better informed on the running
details of the convention than it was before TV came to full bloom is
to speak the obvious truth. To say that the advent of TV as a major
convention force has both tidied up and speeded the proceedings,
perforce casting them into some manageable mold for public consumption, is also to say the truth.

But there is another side to this business, and I myself believe
that the powerful and all but pre-emptive influence now exercised
by television is not an unmixed blessing. If the country is indeed told
much more, by way of visual sense, than it used to be told, it is also
told more that is not necessarily so and sometimes shown more of
what is only ostensibly important at the expense of much that is
truly important.

The visual spectacle of the convention, TV handles with incom-
parable skill. Who could describe the dizzy parades, the shouts and
cries from the convention floor in the nighttime, the hurried huddles
and counter huddles, half so well as that camera lens which roves
so all-seeingly, so remorselessly, over the scene?

But a good deal of what is seen on the home screen is "true"
only in a limited and literal sense. When, say, the delegation from
New York is shown at the end of its caucus, the view is precisely a
factual one. Perhaps it tells—and shows—the onlooker that New York
has decided to cast so many of its delegate votes for this candidate
and so many for that candidate. But what it cannot relate is the hard,
inside bargaining, the bruising private thrusts and parries, which have
led to this decision and which may in the end lead to other actions
quite overshadowing this initial action.

TV can tell what and, with great luck, sometimes how. But it
cannot tell why. It cannot expose the true significance of a political
convention, simply because, with rare exceptions, what happens outside camera range is far more decisive than what happens within
camera range.

TV is, therefore, a force both of unrivaled disclosure and of
profound limitations upon disclosure. Its power, at any rate, is quite
beyond question. In 1948 a chaotic Democratic National Convention
in Philadelphia nominated Harry S. Truman for a full Presidential

term in his own right in circumstances that could hardly have offered
gloomier omens for his cause. The Democratic left wing was in angry
rebellion; it was going off in support of the third-party candidacy of
Henry A. Wallace. The Democratic right wing was in sullen revolt;
it was going off with the Dixiecrat candidate, Strom Thurmond, now
a senator from South Carolina. Mr. Truman, it appeared, had the good
wishes of the center of his party—and not much else. Moreover,
he was confronting a supposedly unbeatable Republican adversary
in Thomas E. Dewey of New York.

In that campaign year, I was out in the country trying to determine whether the polls were right in giving the victory to Mr. Dewey
with no shilly-shallying whatever. Here and there I met up with local
Democratic leaders who shifted uncomfortably at the question,
"How's it going?" Like all the rest of us, they had been deeply influenced by the pollsters and pundits. All the same, in instance after
instance, these local politicians had a hunch—they were afraid to
call it more than that—that Mr. Truman was going to get the biggest
Negro vote in history, not excluding that of Franklin D. Roosevelt
at the height of his power.

One local Democratic boss showed me a pile of pencil-written
letters from Negro men and women in his ward. Over and over in
them this phrase, or a phrase meaning the same thing, recurred like
a litany: "Mr. Truman sure stuck his neck out for us at that Philadelphia convention." At Philadelphia, TV—with all its matchless
capacity for flat, surface disclosure and never mind its disabilities as
to interpretative disclosure—had unforgetably shown one climatic
moment in that fateful convention. It had shown that hard-core deep
Southerners waving the Stars and Bars and marching angrily from the
convention hall and out into the night, crying their hostility to Truman
because of the civil-rights plank he had adopted.

The Negroes in the Eastern part of the country had seen that
picture of marching and angry men. It was a stark, simple tableau.
Mr. Truman had, indeed, "stuck out his neck" for them and this they
knew in a deeper sense than any number of printed words could have
conveyed. He did get a historic Negro vote. And he was elected,
polls or no polls, pundits or no pundits. It is possible to make a case
that the medium of TV literally saved his candidacy. I, for one, have
always believed this to be the plain truth of it.

Again, in the 1952 convention at Chicago, in which the forces
of General Dwight D. Eisenhower and the late Senator Robert A.
Taft of Ohio were locked in savage battle for the nomination, what
really broke the Taft candidacy was the charge of the Eisenhower

84   people that the Tafties had "stolen" delegates in Texas. Accusations of "political immorality" of this kind are not treated too seriously by the professionals, for one man's steal is merely another man's legitimate coup in delegate snatching. And parenthetically, for my own part I did not really see that the Taft people had broke a single one of the Ten Commandments.[8]

All the same, a decisive issue was made of the matter before the Credential Committee, which had the job of determining what delegates had been legally sent to the convention and what delegates had come with a cloud over them. That committee decided—most unwisely, given the highly emotional climate of Chicago—to hold its critical session behind closed doors. The silent spectacle of TV cameras trained upon those closed doors struck a blow to the Taft backers from which they never recovered. The country got excited. The delegates heard from the country. And Dwight D. Eisenhower was nominated for President of the United States.

I have always been convinced—and I am quite sure that this was no idle, purely personal notion that the decision of John F. Kennedy in 1960 to ask Lyndon B. Johnson to be his Vice-Presidential running mate on the Democratic ticket was closely related to the power of TV. The late-night session in Los Angeles that nominated Kennedy showed a succession of urban Democratic bosses—of the Catholic faith, as was Mr. Kennedy himself—at the head of the powerful blocs that put him over. Overnight, there was concern in the Kennedy camp that the country would see this as a heavy-handed urban-boss bulldozer movement flinging all resistance out of its way.

This being the realistic estimate of the "image" that had been left with the voters of the country, the problem was to find a responsible means to soften that impression. Lyndon Johnson, a Texan, a Protestant, a man with long and firm ties to rural and small-town America, was the answer. It is in any case all but certain in retrospect that Kennedy could never have won the election without Johnson.

Again, there is no question among old political observers that TV unconsciously worked against Richard Nixon in 1960, both at the convention and, more visibly, in the campaign itself. Nixon not only tends to photograph badly on TV; he also is rarely at home in the medium.[9]

At heart a deeply intense and buttoned-up sort of man, he often seemed on TV to be overly earnest—and overly worried. A sunny confidence, or at all events at least a *seemingly* sunny confidence, is a vast, immeasurable asset to a politician. Nixon's "image" did not suggest such a confidence, whether or not he actually felt it.

The point raised by all this is an important one; and it is this: In any political convention—as, indeed, later in any national campaign —TV has two profoundly seeing capacities which, like the rain, fall alike on the unjust and the just. It can show, with a pitiless, non-committal and purely objective eye, the quality of phoniness in a man or a situation. This might be called the vision of truth. But, equally, it can—without any such purpose and with total innocence of motive —also show unpleasant qualities which are not there. It can enor-mously handicap those unfortunates who are simply not photogenic. This might be called the unintended vision of unconscious falsehood.

Thus it is that television has become not merely a giant-eyed and all pervasive spectator and not merely an indispensable and endlessly involved major part of convention proceedings. It has also become, to a quite important degree, an embodied power of veto over the ultimate decision as to which man should actually be nomi-nated for President. It is an undoubted fact that no major American party these days would willingly nominate the most superb possible candidate, measured in terms of his essential political ability, if he had no capacity to master the great medium of TV—if, that is, he per-sistently "came over poorly" on it.

One of those high-ranking politicians who has always been aware of this is the present [former] President of the United States, Lyndon Johnson. For years—as Majority Leader of the Seanate and to a con-siderable degree even while he was Vice President—Mr. Johnson felt alien to the medium. This was not because he disliked it in any way but simply because there was between his highly individualistic private personality and the great, glowing and highly impersonal personality of TV no real oneness.

In that clamorous 1960 Democratic Convention in Los Angeles Mr. Johnson undeniably "came over" far poorer than did Mr. Kennedy. This was not the least of his many handicaps then in the contest with JFK.

It was only after he became President, in the tragic days of November 1963, that LBJ came to terms with TV. He had never really believed that he could top or even equal the gleaming TV personality that had so well served his predecessor. He came into his own here simply because at last he came to recognize that his problem was not the insoluble one of not being photogenic but simply that on the magic lantern he had been pressing too hard.

Now he simply became himself, became Lyndon B. Johnson. Instantly, the old lack of oneness between Johnson and the medium became instead a new oneness between Johnson and the medium. The cheerful self-confidence that had marked all other aspects of

86   his public career now became manifest in his association with TV; he quit fighting it, and let nature take its course.

. . . .

So it is that the "good" and the "bad" in television—never so deeply, so achingly exhibited as at the great congresses of political parties which are called national conventions—to the detached observer endlessly tip the scales of judgment, first one way and then the other way.

If it classically increases the sense of drama and of audience participation in our politics, it [television] also sometimes dulls the keenest edges of our suspense. That matchless technical skill which combines the lens and the computer produces the final answers for us—tells us who has in fact won and who has in fact lost—long before the climax really should have been reached and exposed.

The drama is foreshortened: and, humanly, we sometimes are not ready for it. It is just as the great jet airliners carrying us to England arrive a bit too soon and so leave the mind—and the stomach—still operating on Eastern Standard Time when we are in fact plunged half a day ahead of ourselves and our emotions, into British Summer Time.

Television in Turmoil

By Neil Hickey

FEBRUARY 8, 15 AND 22, MARCH 1, 1969

Unlike the "old soldiers" of the Army ballad who "never die; they just fade away," the controversy over what happened in Chicago during last summer's Democratic National Convention appears destined neither to die nor fade away, but to linger in some morose corner of the public mind for generations to come.

Almost 90 percent of American households tuned their television sets to the events of August 26-29, 1968; satellites carried live coverage to Europe, Japan and Australia, newsfilm was rushed to scores of foreign networks and stations representing 92 percent of all television homes in the free world.

The 20-year romance which television has enjoyed with American families was seriously shaken amid the charges and countercharges over whether or not TV news fulfilled its responsibility of reporting news objectively to the public. Tens of thousands of letters flooded the three major networks and the Federal Communications Commission complaining that:

Network coverage of the convention was biased against the Johnson-Humphrey Administration and Mayor Richard Daley of Chicago.

TV newsmen in the streets consistently filmed scenes of police violence and clubing of dissenters, but never the provocation which led up to it.

Floor reporters for the networks spent a disproportionate amount of time interviewing anti-Administration delegates and those favorable to the candidacy of Senator Eugene McCarthy; floor men were accused of generating and perpetuating rumors having little basis in fact (principally, the reports of an incipient boom for the nomination of Senator Edward Kennedy).

TV reporters and anchor men engaged in too much editorializing (at the expense of straight news) without labeling it as such.

Networks too often cut away from the podium to show film of riots and interviews with delegates hostile to the majority view.

87

88   TV newsmen were too generous and affectionate in their coverage of the hippies, Yippies and radical leftists who had come to Chicago with the announced purpose of disrupting the convention and creating havoc in the streets.

The networks were bent upon "revenge" for prior restrictions placed by Chicago officials upon their capability for live, remote coverage and their access to the convention floor; and also for the Democrats' refusal to meet in Miami Beach (as had the Republicans) instead of Chicago, a decision which cost the networks millions.

But even such serious charges as those might reasonably fade into distant memory and be blurred by time—except that a series of high-level official investigations promise to keep them in the public eye well into 1969, with effects that will surely impinge upon all future television handling of national political conventions, as well as opening to debate for the first time on a broad scale the very nature and influence of television's involvement in the American political process.

The Senate Commerce Committee and the House Interstate and Foreign Commerce Committee (which have jurisdiction over broadcasting), as well as the House Committee on Un-American Activities, are studying TV's performance in Chicago. So is the U.S. Department of Justice and a Chicago Federal Grand Jury. The National Commission on the Causes and Prevention of Violence, whose full report is due later this year, released an interim study (attorney Daniel Walker's report)[10] which—while sternly accusing the Chicago police of wanton pummeling of dissenters and newsmen— noted that television created the stage upon which the young radicals dramatized their anger and that television thus substantially influenced the behavior of both demonstrators and police.

"There is no question that the protestors in Chicago . . . 'played to the cameras' or that they often did it very effectively . . . ," the Walker Report says. "What the 'whole world was watching,' after all, was not a confrontation but the picture of a confrontation, to some extent directed by a generation that had grown up with television and learned to use it."

The news media, including television, had been reporting for weeks that from 100,000 to one million protestors would converge on Chicago during convention week. But the best estimates now indicate that the demonstrators' recruitment was an almost total flop, and that no more than 5000 of them came to the city from points outside Illinois.

Nonetheless, the advance publicity about their supposed invasion

"played a part in conditioning authorities and demostrators alike as   89
to what to expect . . . ," the Walker Report pointed out, and caused
the mobilization of 25,000 police and National Guardsmen and Regular Army troops to deal with a major insurrection which simply never
materialized but the mere threat of which made law enforcers edgy
and nervous before the convention ever got started.

Another agency which set about scrutinizing TV's role in Chicago
was the FCC, which produced over a thousand letters of complaint
alleging, in general, that "the television coverage did not fairly
present the issues on a number of grounds . . ." and asking the networks to submit justification of their Chicago coverage. While bridling
at this intrusion into their news bailiwick, which they deemed improper under the First Amendment, the networks dutifully composed
and forwarded to the FCC elaborate apologias of their efforts.[11]

By that time, Congress was already back in session and noisily
masticating the whole subject in what *Broadcasting* magazine called
"a climate of almost unanimous Congressional disapproval of the
Chicago coverage compounded with the politically potent reaction
against televised violence that has swelled since the assassination
of Senator Kennedy."

Senator Russell B. Long (D., La.) claimed: "Unfortunately, the
City of Chicago was convicted by the television media without its
side ever being seen or heard." Senator John O. Pastore (D., R.I.),
chairman of the Senate Communications Subcommittee, asked the
TV networks to consider seriously giving Mayor Daley an hour of
free time, as he had requested, to tell his side of the story. (All three
refused, eventually.) "What happened in Chicago has rocked this
Nation," Pastore said on the Senate floor. "Right, wrong or indifferent,
it has rocked the Nation, and so much so that the American public is
confused as to exactly what did happen. How much took place that
did not show on television and how much might have been the result
of provocation are questions needing to be answered. . . ." Mayor
Daley put together an hour show anyway and this rebuttal was aired
on about 150 stations around the country in September.

In a House speech on September 4, 1968, Representative Roman
Pucinski (D., Ill.) told his colleagues: "I believe the television networks did Chicago and its people a disastrous disservice last week . . .
and it is my hope that those responsible will take every step possible
to redress this outrageous and unfair television coverage. . . . I submit to the Members that some of those reporting what happened
. . . reached the zenith of irresponsibility in American journalism. . . ."

Those strong sentiments were seconded by Representative

90 Ed Edmondson (D., Okla.), who rose to say: "Network media personnel such as Cronkite, and Huntley and Brinkley have done violence to the truth by their unfair coverage at Chicago and the public deserves better at the hands of this great industry."

Other congressmen joined the debate in fervent agreement, and finally Pucinski suggested that TV news departments were now afflicted with a "credibility gap" and had better "set their house in order" before loss of confidence in television began to affect the whole national economy. Television, explained Pucinski, has an important role in moving products from factories into American homes, and he worried that if people lose faith in TV news, "how long will it be before they lose confidence in television advertising?"

The attacks persisted from every quarter. Columnist Jenkin Lloyd Jones wrote: "It should now be obvious that television, as it is now used, is the enemy, not the servant, of the political convention. It has become so, not out of malice, but because TV is a medium that prefers drama to uplift, and where both are present it will go for drama every time. . . . It is as though every reporter in town were covering the bawdy houses or interviewing the residents of the drunk tank."

CBS reported to TV GUIDE that of 9000 letters received after the convention, the ratio of critical letters to favorable ones was 11 to 1. NBC got 8542 letters condemning its efforts and 1092 praising them. (ABC did not air full coverage of the convention.) Mayor Daley claims to have received 135,000 letters supporting him, 5000 against.

The trade newsletter *Television Digest* noted the mood of Washington in early September: "We've been covering Washington for many years and never have we observed such a mass of Congressional vehemence against broadcasting." A month later, it quoted a veteran Senate employee as saying: "It doesn't make any difference who wins the Presidency; television is in for one hell of a rough time when Congress comes back in January. Your industry just couldn't be in worse shape, despite the fact there'll be many new faces in Congress."

The Chicago convention is being called the great Rorschach event of recent American history: observers of every bias are interpreting it according to their own needs and fantasies. Similarly, an impressive body of psychological literature attests to the existence of a remarkable phenomenon called perceptual selection, which means that witnesses to an event perceive it—and quite sincerely so—the way they want to perceive it, and reject coldly what their prejudices and presumptions find uncongenial.

For that good reason alone, the Chicago coverage will be a gold

mine for psychologists and sociologists for many years to come. Some 91
TV watchers saw unjustifiable brutality in the streets and repressive
parliamentary rule in convention hall; others saw intolerable provocation by dangerous radicals and an undemocratic refusal by some
delegates to accept the majority's will.

Thus, the vision of Chicago, August 26-29, 1968, which erupted
through millions of television sets in the U.S. and the world, will
have its wise and reasoned partisans for what may be an endless
debate. [The late] Senator Everett Dirksen (R., Ill.), for example,
called TV's handling of both political conventions "an outrage against
the democratic process" and described one particular reportage
from the convention floor in Chicago as "a clear and outrageous
attempt at editorializing and bias."

Ben Kubasik, director of the National Citizens Committee for
Broadcasting, on the other hand, sees TV news' Chicago coverage
as a "whiff of fresh air" and warns that "manipulators" must not be
allowed to intimidate broadcasters from handling the news as their
editorial judgment dictates. The charges against TV, says Kubasik,
"are not so much to deny what took place as to put a muzzle on the
future."

Among the angriest of TV's tormentors have been columnists
Drew Pearson and Jack Anderson, who, in a series of syndicated reports, claimed inside knowledge of a House Commerce Committee
study purportedly confirming that "some of the networks deliberately
went out to slant the news"; that TV directors purposefully photo-
graphed Vice President Humphrey and Mayor Daley in unflattering
poses, even resorting to distorting the TV color; that speeches favorable to the Johnson regime were forsaken repeatedly by the cameras
to focus on some dissident eager for publicity; that the networks
wanted revenge on the Democrats for costing them $3 million by
their insistence on holding the conclave in Chicago instead of in
Miami Beach.

The networks "got their revenge," wrote Pearson and Anderson,
by playing up the violence in Chicago which they had overlooked
in Miami Beach—where six men were killed in street riots during
the Republican Convention. Did TV create news for its own purposes,
the columnists asked? "There is evidence that the TV networks, perhaps in their eagerness to generate high ratings for TV sponsors,
encouraged dissidents to make inflammatory statements and helped
to stir up controversies."

TV news executives scoff at such blanket indictments. The *New
York Post*, which carried the Pearson-Anderson columns, felt moved

92   to publish disclaimers in its editorial columns, regreting that journalists of national reputation should be spokesmen for "men who are really in anguish because the coverage of Chicago did not suppress or minimize unpleasant news." The *Post* added: "The violence in Chicago was not TV's responsibility; any Congressional investigator who claims that it was is guilty of defamation and distortion. The notion that the labors of conscientious TV men under fire were exploited in a network plot to discredit the Democrats is absurd."

It is a fact, however, that the TV networks did exert enormous pressure on the Democrats to keep the convention in Miami Beach, and, as Norman Mailer wrote in his punchy and poetic account ("Miami" and "The Siege of Chicago") of the summer's events: "It is to the Mayor's curious credit that he was strong enough to withstand them. . . . One did not make an enemy of a television network for nothing; they could repay injury with no more than a chronic slur in the announcer's voice every time your deadly name was mentioned over the next 12 months or next 12 years . . . (But) no interlopers for any network were going to dominate the streets of his parochial city, nor none of their crypto-accomplices with long hair, sexual liberty, drug license and unbridled mouths. . . . So Daley was ready to take on the electronic wrath of the semiconductors of the world, his voter-nourished blood full of beef and curses against the transistorized communicatory cabals of the media."

By August 26, when the Democratic Convention was gaveled to order, Chicago was a stage crowded with actors—politicians, protesters, press—eager to perform; a script crammed with conflict and tension had been memorized by all the participants, and each knew his role well; and then the curtain rose on four days of intense drama which is still being reviewed and analyzed in remorseless detail.

In the Presidential campaign which followed, Hubert Humphrey's popularity with the American people fell too low to be retrieved by Election Day; picketers, most of whom had been nowhere near the August convention but had witnessed it on television, dogged his footsteps with cries of "Chi-ca-go! Chi-ca-go!" and thus recalled to still other TV audiences those shocking midsummer events. Many experts felt that—as much as any other single factor—the televised conflict along Michigan Avenue and in the International Amphitheatre had made Richard M. Nixon President of the United States.

Oddly, there seemed even more profound effects than the election of a President; namely, a kind of "social dynamite" (in columnist Max Lerner's words) in the spreading suspicion among both liberals and conservatives that the wells of communication in the U.S. are poisoned. Broadcast news, especially, stood in severe crisis at year's end, fearful of an erosion of confidence among its heretofore loyal viewers (who for long had depended on TV for most of their news); fearful also that its prized journalistic freedoms were about to suffer the most vigorous assaults in television's 20-year life.

Even before the first delegate arrived at the Chicago Convention, antagonisms between press and Democratic establishment were hardening, as each set about ensuring its own vital interests for the days ahead: TV newsmen wanted full access to the sources of news; officialdom of Chicago and Washington were eager to minimize the appearance of dissent both inside convention hall and in the streets. Those goals were in sudden conflict, and the angry debate was staged in full view of 115 million American TV watchers.

So normally dispassionate an observer as CBS's Eric Sevareid felt obliged to say, three days before the convention: "This city of Chicago runs the city of Prague a close second right now as the world's least attractive tourist attraction." David Brinkley grimly suggested that "the Democratic leadership does not want reported what is happening."

TV men contended that a series of events during the convention period added up to firm restraint upon the networks' capability of focusing live coverage on anything but the podium and its parade of speechifiers. For example: a strike of communications workers against the Illinois Bell Telephone Company prevented live coverage of events outside the International Amphitheatre; and a drastic cutback in the number of floor passes given the networks threatened to impede the traditional ferreting out of news by TV floormen.

There were others. Security men forbade the placement of cameras in windows and on rooftops in downtown Chicago, as well as the use of cherry pickers (the large camera cranes) and helicopters. Permission to park mobile vans on any street was denied; no camera locations on any city streets nor in any public parks were permitted, except outside the Conrad Hilton headquarters hotel. Not surprisingly, the networks concluded that party officials did not want live pictures of disruptive violence broadcast to the world and did not want TV reporters fraternizing freely with delegates—especially dissident ones—and airing contentious interviews instead of podium business.

Once the opening gavel fell, more difficulties arose: David Brinkley discerned "faceless, unidentified men" clogging the convention

94   floor with no apparent mission other than "following our reporters wherever they go, listening to every word they say." CBS's Dan Rather was punched to the floor by security men while trying to interview a delegate. Mike Wallace, another CBS floorman, also was manhandled and forcibly removed from the hall. (Of 300 newsmen assigned to cover the streets and parks, 63 of them—according to the Walker Report—were physically attacked by police, and 13 had their recording and photographic equipment damaged intentionally.)

The angriest response to all this came from CBS's president, Frank Stanton, who, in a telegram to chairman of the Democratic National Committee John M. Bailey, called treatment of newsmen "disgraceful," demanded an end to such "shameful practices" and insisted that "strong-arm tactics totally alien to American tradition and law have been used repeatedly to prevent reporters from doing their jobs."

Besides the alleged indignities to themselves, most TV newsmen—who tend to be politically liberal in their personal orientation—were privately convinced that delegates favorable to Senator Eugene McCarthy were receiving less than fair treatment as against those committed to Vice President Humphrey. Thus, rightly or wrongly, an opinion pervaded the press section in convention hall and the TV anchor booths that the Democratic Party wanted no bad tidings of disorder and disunity to leave Chicago, nor any conspicuous repudiation of the policies of President Johnson to be shown.

All of these quarrelsome and unhappy matters, taken together, created a contest of wills between party and press. Normally dispassionate TV newsmen lost hold on their objectivity in the heat of partisanship and in the face of irreconcilable and antithetic interests over such a broad range of issues. (Walter Cronkite, in a moment of rare intemperance, used the word "thugs" to describe some of the convention security guards—a lapse for which he later confessed to being "ashamed.")

Complicating this confrontation was its coexistence with unsettled conditions in the Democratic Party itself, over such matters as the language of a platform plank on Vietnam, argument of the unit rule and the seating of contested delegations, the delicate Paris peace talks, the crisis in Czechoslovakia, and the candidacies of Senators McCarthy and McGovern.

Those factors, combined with a generally turbulent political climate around the country, "made it likely, if not inevitable," as one NBC executive put it, "that charges of bias and distortion would be raised against news media in general and against television in

particular because of television's greater impact." That is precisely   95
what happened.

. . . .

The most detailed response to criticism of TV's performance in
Chicago is in the form of letters from ABC, CBS and NBC to the FCC,
composed at the Commission's request after that agency received
hundreds of complaints from private citizens about TV's handling of
the convention.

An examination of these letters is highly instructive. ABC, for
example (which, unlike CBS and NBC, did not offer full coverage but
rather a nightly 90-minute wrap-up), informed the Commission that,
out of 19 hours and 37 minutes of its preconvention and convention
coverage, only 13 minutes and 49 seconds—or 1.1 percent—were
devoted to film or tape coverage of the disorders between police
and demonstrators. NBC said that it aired more than 35 hours of
convention coverage in the August 26-29 period, of which 36 minutes
were devoted to the demonstrators while the convention was actually
in session, plus an additional 28 minutes during times when no
convention business was going on. (CBS gave no tally in its FCC letter, but CBS president Frank Stanton said in a speech that of 38 hours
and 3 minutes of his network's coverage, only 32 minutes and 20
seconds—1.4 percent of the total—showed protest action.)

These figures were offered as an antidote to the widespread impression that TV news had devoted a disproportionate amount of time
to showing violence at the expense of convention proceedings, and
in support of the belief that viewers simply tend to recall the super-
charged drama of street battles because of their vastly greater impact
on the home screen.

ABC denied favoring the young dissenters at the expense of
Chicago police and noted that its hired conservative voice, columnist William F. Buckley (who shared a platform with liberal author
Gore Vidal), had had plenty to say on the air both in defense of Mayor
Daley and in condemnation of the provocateurs; similarly, ABC
anchor-man Howard K. Smith frequently made statements "supporting many of the actions of Mayor Daley and the Chicago police."

Their operations in Chicago were "so limited," ABC complained,
"that we had only one exterior remote video camera" set up in front
of the Conrad Hilton Hotel, as well as one mobile unit which could
respond only to events already taking place. (All three networks, of
course, were able to use hand-held cameras anywhere.) "The limitations imposed by the city of Chicago as to where we could set up our
(video) cameras, combined with our inability to transmit a live signal

96 from any remote location as a result of the communications workers' strike, necessarily precluded our coverage of events leading up to any disturbance." ABC also denied telling protesters where their cameras would be so that disorders could be staged in front of them.

CBS, for its part, catalogued the factors which complicated the task of reportage: "irreconcilable opposition" both in convention hall and in the streets to an "unpopular war"; well-organized attempts by radicals to exploit antiwar sentiment to disrupt the convention; resort by hundreds of dissidents to "the tactic of goading the police into overreaction"; the resulting loss of restraint by policemen, which caused injury to hundreds of dissenters, newsmen and bystanders; rancor among various factions on the convention floor. Those conditions "contributed to a week which tested to the utmost the ability of television and other news media to do a fair and objective job of reporting," wrote CBS, and added that their efforts "took place under restraints upon the freedom of movement and technical resources of television . . . which have never before been imposed on the medium."

NBC, in its letter to the FCC, said that a reading of viewer complaints suggested strongly that many watchers of the convention coverage simply had "forgotten instances of reporting which contradict their conclusions, while recalling only selectively or inaccurately to suit an argument." In spite of the obstacles, NBC wrote, a review of all their riot film proved that the network had indeed shown the taunts and provocations of protesters, including the throwing of missiles and the tearing down of an American flag.

Was NBC biased against the Administration's Vietnam policies in its selection of delegates to be interviewed and in the comments of its reporters? It was not, said the network. Vietnam was the major issue dividing the convention, and "roughly 40 percent of the delegates voted for the minority plank." Even so, "NBC provided for full expression of support for the majority position."

Did NBC give a distorted account of the convention proceedings, stimulate rumors, create controversy, and cut away from the podium too often? It did not, said the network. Floor interviews on the so-called "boomlet" for Senator Edward Kennedy "reflected activity and interest within the Democratic Party" about the chances of such a move on the senator's part. Nonetheless, the "number of interviewees who expressed skepticism about this possibility outnumbered those who thought the draft movement was still alive." And reports that many delegates were unhappy about the conduct of the convention and the actions of police simply "were a reflection of the fact that there was such dissatisfaction."

Finally, said NBC, it had dutifully shown "substantially all" of the debates on the Vietnam plank, and all nominating speeches. In addition, it had exercised its unquestioned right to present "supplementary coverage from the floor of the convention and outside the auditorium, in an effort to inform its audience more fully" on such matters as the credentials fight, the unit rule, loyalty oaths for Southern delegates, convention security and the events in downtown Chicago. Without such reporting, said NBC, a television news organization "would be serving merely as a passive conduit for approved information. This is not the function of the broadcast or any other journalistic medium. . . ."

Perhaps the simplest summation of network opinion of the Chicago controversy is in the closing words of ABC's reply to the FCC. The events of last August were so "inherently inflammatory," said the network, "and people identified so passionately with one side or the other, that no matter how these events were treated by the news media, there would inevitably have been criticism of the news coverage."

That may well be so, but so far the statement has satisfied no private citizen nor public official who was convinced that television behaved with partisan bad manners in Chicago last August and ought to be restrained from ever doing so again.

A piece of "conventional wisdom" about the Democratic Party's meeting in Chicago last August has it that the press, especially television, portrayed the events as a straight-out contest of good versus evil: the good dissenters (both inside and outside the hall) versus the bad Establishment.

But in fact, many TV newsmen were careful to attempt setting a journalistic balance, even in the heat and confusion of those explosive events. CBS's Roger Mudd, for example, complained during the Wednesday night session, which saw Vice President Humphrey nominated, that the dissenting minority of delegates in the hall were not behaving with suitable good grace. "When you lose a case in politics, you usually accept the vote and go on and try to win it another time," said Mudd.

"It occurs to me that we're suffering at this convention from a massive case of political bad manners," he added, "and the special goat became Mayor Daley." He wondered if the dissidents thought that "this convention could get along without security. They vented their spleen on Mayor Daley and anything he controls. And over the course of the past two or three days I observed what I concluded to be deliberate attempts by the anti-Humphrey people to provoke

98   incidents that would perhaps succeed in disrupting the convention."

He disagreed with Georgia delegate Julian Bond's charge that such important issues as war, poverty and racism had not gotten sufficient hearing at the convention; and he questioned the recurrent notion among some observers that the police and National Guard were totally at fault for the riots in Grant Park and Michigan Avenue. "I talked to reporters last night who were there who said that the police were right," Mudd insisted. "I don't know that we're absolutely correct in calling it unprovoked."

ABC's anchor man Howard K. Smith, the day before the conclave began, defended Mayor Daley's stringent security measures, while calling one of the principal protest organizers (David Dellinger) "Intolerant and bellicose." The Amphitheatre was being cordoned off, said Smith, "from a small fraction of people who, under protection of a very elaborate system of rights, have developed a skill at disruption. . . . Mayor Daley may have overdone it, but if you or I had the responsibility, you or I, too, might say, 'I won't let it happen here next week.'"

On the meeting's final night. Smith summed up by saying that if the convention had been run with a rough hand, "so are all conventions, and they must be. They're big, amorphous blobs of determined men always on the verge of chaos, and without strong handling a convention would last for weeks without any commensurate achievement." He said that the dissident delegates had had the "fullest scope to speak and to act" on every matter of substance.

NBC's Chet Huntley, during an informal on-the-air seminar with his fellows, suggested that many of the young demonstrators were "obnoxious" and were being quite purposeful in their baiting of the police. CBS's Eric Sevareid wondered if the rumors of a Senator Edward Kennedy candidacy were not, at least in part, the creation of TV reporters looking for an intriguing story. In a postconvention speech at Columbia University, Sevareid admitted that "now and then in Chicago, under the exhausting pressures and complexities of those violent events, some of us lost our cool. But not very often, nor did it stay lost very long. We are, after all, human beings. . . . I cannot join with some of my colleagues who make a blanket defense of our work there: but I think the emergence of the full truth will reveal that our efforts were more respectable than a good many critics now seem to think."

All such utterances—and there have been others—by network newsmen suggest that the TV coverage was not quite the simplistic Passion Play nor the blatant partisan exercise which many viewers seem to recall, but a complex, evolving story told in varied fashion by scores of reporters responding to it in diverse ways.

We asked several academicians for their thoughts on the meaning of Chicago *vis-à-vis* television's presence and importance: Professor William Wood of the Columbia University Graduate School of Journalism suggested that events of such high emotional content accentuate people's response to how journalists fulfill their responsibility. "We obviously are not getting a cool, reasoned critique of television's job in Chicago."

The "high-handed" behavior of Chicago officials agitated many TV newsmen into losing their objective sense, Wood says. "We occasionally did perceive reporters' private feelings through their tone of voice, and these are men who are, of course, supposed to be absolutely impervious" to any such lapses. "The network newsmen were required to make many quick decisions based on their news judgments," Wood says, "and here I think the more sensational story prevailed when it sometimes shouldn't have. . . . In a convention, as in other events, you don't constantly have the breaking story at a high pitch. But the networks are eager to hold their audiences, and they must fill time interestingly. So they sometimes latch onto stories which are lacking in substance, and say to themselves, consciously or unconsciously, 'Let's keep this thing going.' "

The events of Chicago have brought some "quiet self-examination" to the networks, according to Wood. "This wave of criticism isn't all bad. The whole world of journalism is thin-skinned. We're liable to yell First Amendment every time we need to. We're not particularly graceful under criticism. But when the FCC demands explanations of network news decisions, then this is a very serious business. I would line up with the networks in insisting that the FCC exercise caution in these matters; otherwise it might lead to some kind of restriction, and that is not the answer."

Penn Kimball, the consulting editor to the Lou Harris survey and also a professor at the Columbia Graduate School of Journalism, believes that the violence at Columbia University during last year's student uprisings exceeded that at Chicago. "Much more brutality was visited upon the Columbia students than on the Chicago dissenters. But in Chicago you had the stereotype of the machine boss in Mayor Daley, whereas in New York you had the picture of a progressive mayor in John Lindsay." Lindsay managed to get through the Columbia revolt without anybody blaming him, Kimball says, but Daley was a "natural villain in terms of broad stereotypes. He is one of the clichés of our time: an old machine politician. The media con-

100 tribute to these stereotypes: they tend to glorify the hero and vilify the villain. As it happens, both Daley and Lindsay are pretty good mayors, each in his own way."

The Chicago riots illustrated a peculiar problem faced by TV news, in Kimball's view. Some of the pain might have been avoided, he feels, if reporters had been assigned to follow the street violence without cameras or microphones, doing an old fashioned news-gathering job on foot, and feeding the facts to their anchor men. "Television tends to limit itself to that aspect of news which they can get a picture of," he says, "and that is a fragment of the total story."

Kimball believes that the Senator Kennedy boomlet began with "a little piece of validity," and then it became advantageous for some delegates—the ones who were fighting for a strong antiwar platform plank—to nurture it. "What is a reporter to make of it when responsible people are telling him Kennedy may be a candidate? There was indeed something to the story, but the boom was never real, and TV—and everybody else—inflated it."

TV newsmen are in "the biggest goldfish bowl in journalism," according to Kimball; they're aware of the inherent pitfalls of their trade and are doing the best they can as honestly as they can to avoid them. He suggests they not be concerned by irate letter writers—even the tens of thousands who expressed themselves after the convention.

Kurt Lang, a professor of sociology at the State University of New York at Stony Brook and co-author (with his wife) of the book *Politics and Television*,[12] feels that networks are indeed dedicated to the "principle" of objectivity in their reporting, and when they make mistakes it's because the story is fast-moving, and because reporters, human and fallible, must view events from some perspective. When TV coverage dramatizes something which transgresses our prejudices, we automatically look for bias in the reporting, Lang says. "The network newsmen surely were guilty of unwitting bias. It was literally impossible to describe that convention the way it happened; it had to be reported from some point of view."

But newsmen, whether TV or print, "must make judgments" about events their professional lives touch, he claims, and that is not easy in the case of events so dependent on television as is a political convention. The reporters are well aware of how much is being staged for their benefit by the convention organizers and so they're fond of taking the viewer backstage and showing him the inner workings. "To keep the political establishment honest is a useful function of television news," Lang adds. "That's the point of journalism and part of the gratification of the profession. The kind of stories a good journalist takes pride in are the ones in which he can point out what the facts are as against what they seem to be."

TV journalists must take some of the responsibility for what happened in Chicago, Lang says. "They inadvertently contributed to the uproar in their search for interesting interludes. But that to me is not the same as slanting the news." In spite of what many people think, according to Lang, the disturbances outside the hall received not too much coverage, but not enough—certainly not enough of the right kind of useful journalistic exploration. TV's cameras and reporters dutifully reported the presence of thousands of young people and their subsequent angry collisions with the police and National Guard.

"But here was a marvelous opportunity before a mass audience to conduct an investigation in depth about what these demonstrations and these young people really meant," says Lang. "Who were they? Where did they all come from? Why, in fact, did they come to Chicago at all? What does it say about our institutions? Why should young Americans walk around waving a Vietcong flag? What moves them to shout, 'I want to destroy the whole Establishment and see it come tumbling down'?"

"Nobody I know in TV has attempted seriously to answer these questions. The networks were covering the violence, all right, but not what it means to all of us for now and in the future." And that, many observers insist, is the better story.

Almost unanimously, the top executives of television's network news departments insist—publicly, at least—that if last August's Democratic National Convention were to happen again, they'd cover it exactly as they did the first time. Many of the reporters seem to feel the same; David Brinkley has said: "If we had to go back to Chicago, I wouldn't change one thing we did, not one shot, not one word."

This posture will strike some TV watchers as gratuitously brazen, especially since television's performance in Chicago triggered the largest outpouring of viewer dismay in the industry's history. But it hints at the chasm which divides TV's defenders from its critics in this bothersome and prolonged debate.

On the one hand, professional TV observers such as Robert Lewis Shayon (in the *Saturday Review*) are saying that the two networks providing gavel-to-gavel coverage "did outstanding jobs reflecting accurately the drama and the truth of the most ghastly week in the history of American politics." The contraposing view is expressed by

102 Representative John Dingell, Democrat of Michigan, who says: "The most charitable thing I can say about the convention coverage is that it was handled very poorly. Either it was biased, or it was handled with such extraordinary incompetence [as] to give that impression."

Such differences, it is now clear, will never be resolved, no matter how many official inquiries are mounted—and they have been numerous—nor how fervent their conclusions in support of one view or the other. The most we can hope for is that the contentiousness will illuminate and redefine certain aspects of television news practices, as well as the country's response to them.

In spite of the networks' public exclamations of retrospective satisfaction with their performance at Chicago, a good deal of private soul-searching has gone on among the high-ranking TV executives, with results that will surely be apparent in subtle ways at future national conventions. TV journalists are determined to improve their hold upon First Amendment guarantees of press freedom; but their superiors in exalted places at ABC, CBS and NBC are understandably chary about ever again alienating such large and vocal segments of their audiences from what is essentially an entertainment and advertising—not a journalist—medium.

That anomaly plagues TV news and leaves it susceptible—rightly or wrongly—to charges of applying some entertainment standards to the handling of news events. As Penn Kimball suggested recently in Columbia University Forum, as long as political conventions are being aired in prime time, they had better "measure up to the entertainment standards" of commercial broadcasting. The goal of commercial TV is maximum audience, Kimball points out, "lured by the high drama of a fight to the finish between the rival gladiators, no holds barred, the loser to the lions. Exciting television, however, can be ruinous politics."

A fair amount of show-biz-style press agentry goes on at political conventions; the networks transport wholesale to the convention sites platoons of staff publicists whose task it is to disseminate to the Nation's newspaper TV editors the good tidings that their network successfully "beat" the opposition to certain news stories and triumphed in the ratings.

This drumbeating is the despair of the best TV newsmen, but it goes on anyway. It telegraphs a habit of mind among television's management people that live coverage of important events ought to be judged by some of the same standards as *The Ed Sullivan Show*. It is unlikely that the Nation's best newspaper will ever bombard TV networks with press releases soliciting acknowledgment of their expertise.

Convention organizers go to great lengths to stage-manage a decent show for the TV cameras, but long stretches of dullness at the podium are unavoidable. So television does its best to keep the show moving, frequently in ways which irritate the participants. It is as though (the politicians feel) they have laboriously prepared a kingly feast of victuals to set before the press; then television arrives like a rich relative, complains that the bill of fare is too low in protein and too high in calories, and proceeds to cook its own TV dinner and masticate it loudly, to the chagrin of the other guests.

Nonetheless, commercial television continues to be a welcome guest at political conventions and probably always will, in spite of such exotic proposals as that of Senator Russell Long, Democrat of Louisiana, who suggests it be barred altogether from reporting them. In the future, he feels the Democratic Party "should arrange to have the convention televised under its own direction and control. Let the party present its case rather than have the commentator present what he, rather than the party holding the convention, would like to have the public see."

The public saw very little, actually, of the convention-related violence, despite the torrent of complaints that the networks had given it disproportionate attention. The riots, to state it simply, were covered badly, not well—more skimpily than their importance dictated—principally because TV could not function with total efficiency under the restrictions imposed by Chicago authorities. The Walker Report noted, for example, that "the Old Town area near Lincoln Park was a scene of police ferocity exceeding that shown on television Wednesday night."

Observers who spent hours at the vortex of the Chicago riots, as did TV GUIDE's reporters, know that the persistent accusation of network failure to show demonstrators' provocation is the weakest charge in the lengthy indictment against TV's handling of the story.

Film cameramen afoot amid police and rioters were obliged to muscle their way from one wharf of violence to the next, racing and stumbling to get their pictures, being buffeted by both sides, and succumbing reluctantly to shouted police orders to turn out the portable TV lights lest they attract brickbats from the rear ranks of protesters. In spite of such obstacles, a retrospective study of network coverage indicates that much provocation was indeed filmed and broadcast; most of the riot film used by Mayor Daley on his hour-long televised defense of his administration's actions was borrowed from the networks and had been aired during the convention period.

But these and other complaints are more significant for what they leave unsaid: namely, that many Americans are weary of bad news,

104 frustrated that the Nation's ills will not surrender to the traditional solutions, confused by the anger and disaffection of so many young people, and suspicious of journalists—especially on television— whose often unpleasant task it is to report this turmoil of our lives in the 1960's. Technically, a responsible news organization has the job of holding a mirror to evolving history; its obligation is to assure that the mirror is as distortion-free as possible. It aspires to total objectivity; but, knowing the unattainability of that goal, tries to deliver at least a full measure of fairness on all events it observes.

If we are to believe the indications—and they probably are transitory—some unmeasured erosion of trust in TV news has occurred since Chicago. So far, no polls have confirmed this, but TV news executives operate on the assumption of its truth.[13]

Former FCC Commissioner Lee Loevinger goes so far as to suggest that "some positive step is necessary to restore public confidence in the integrity of broadcast journalism" in the wake of Chicago and to justify TV newsmen's claim to full participation in the guarantees of press freedom under the First Amendment. He suggests the establishment of an American Broadcasting Council on Fairness and Accuracy in Reporting, a nongovernmental "grievance committee" set up by TV men themselves to hear complaints about breaches of fair journalistic practice and to pronounce censure.

"Today broadcasting stands in greater peril of attack and restraint," says Loevinger, "and in greater need of such an institution, than the medium of print journalism. The peril and need of broadcast journalism are also the peril and need of the American people, for the broadcast media perform the journalistic function for a majority of the American people."

Sociologist Kurt Lang thinks there should be "constant criticism" of TV news. "Television should criticize the Establishment and should expect criticism in return, and not be surprised and alarmed when it comes," he says. He's in favor of an occasional conference sponsored by the FCC to evaluate TV news' performance and serve as a funnel for viewer dissatisfaction. "The networks owe this to the public in return for the large profits they make," Lang argues. It's possible to have public scrutiny without violating freedom of expression, he says. "Nothing rivals the oligopoly that the news staffs of the three networks hold collectively. That's a tremendous concentration of power. I'm not saying they're abusing it, But . . . we not only have no effective regulation now, we have no effective criticism."

Despite TV news' loudly expressed fears, it's likely that the furor over Chicago will subside without having engendered any dramatic restraints upon the medium's press freedoms, nor any large-scale defections by viewers, from television to other sources of news, nor any permanent loss of faith in the medium's credibility as a news organ.

A yes-no answer to the question "Did television at Chicago serve the American public well?" is not possible. The closest to a conclusion that the truly disinterested student can come to is: TV performed conscientiously but fallibly in volatile circumstances. The result—for varying reasons—was unsatisfying to a significant number of Americans, and the offense to their sensibilities must be taken seriously.

TV news has been through a crisis, and knows it. Its live coverage of news events—particularly argumentative ones—will never be the same again. One of the sanest summations of the Chicago experience was that of Richard Salant (president of CBS News, interviewed by the Public Broadcast Laboratory): "There are many things . . . by hindsight and the crucible of experience that we would have done somewhat differently. . . . We learn and we'll be better next time."

The events surrounding the Democratic convention were unique, Salant said, and "we simply had not prepared our minds for all of them. But if the set of circumstances that occurred in Chicago ever occur again, I think we'll report it somewhat differently." Just how CBS would "be better next time" and how "differently" it would report, Salant obviously would—or could—not say. Certainly not with half of Washington ready to seize upon any specific confessions of error as more grist for all the investigation mills.

Still, even his hesitant admission that all was not perfect in television's coverage of the Democratic convention is the beginning of wisdom. As a result of the St. Crispin's Day that was Chicago, Americans have learned a good deal about themselves; and television journalism has taken a giant, although painful, step toward the full maturity it covets so devoutly.

Chicago: A Post-Mortem

By Reuven Frank

DECEMBER 14, 1968

A new love-hate relationship has suddenly burst forth between television and its basic audience. Not between television and the intellectuals and upper-middlebrows, the ones who talk about boob tubes and finally break down and buy one for the kids; the ones who up to 1960 bemoaned the passing of conversation in America (as though they ever listened); the ones who at cocktail parties were always importuning you to do subjects no one would watch—including them. But between television and the basic American audience, the most middle-class majority in the history of man.

They don't watch any less, but after several years of telling poll-takers they trust television above other media of news and information, they are now saying that the era of trust is over. Network mail has reached surprising volume, and the letters which approve are treasured. Politicians hint at punitive actions. Appointed officials and big-name Washington newspaper writers participate in a swelling chorus of rejection, conspiracy-hunting and abuse.

The one crystallizing event which brought this about was television's coverage of peace demonstrators meeting Chicago policemen during the Democratic National Convention. The Federal Communications Commission itself has received enough letters on this one event to prompt it to take the ominous step of directing the networks to evaluate FCC mail and, in effect, justify that coverage. The networks are caught between principle—refusing to participate in what seems to be a clear violation of the First Amendment by the FCC—and practicality—the need to get on the record what really happened.

The details of what happened in Chicago are already fading into memory, but the impressions, the memory of the emotions, will remain. What happened in Chicago seems to be this: several thousand people, mostly but not all young, came there to make their antiwar protest heard. The City of Chicago tried in every possible way to assure that they got no attention. They therefore got more attention, in the country and around the world, than they deserved or dared *107* expect.

The reason was television: not what anybody in television did but the fact of television, the existence of television. It demonstrated the shortsightedness of planning any public event these days without taking television truly into account, because it is just plain there, and its absence would be even more obvious than its presence.

Another thing happened in Chicago that almost disappeared from public discussion the day the convention ended. The convention was a disunited one, and its disunity was patent. Controls imposed on delegates and others entitled to be there may or may not have been unusual but they seemed harsh to the delegates themselves and to the people watching at home. At the center of this storm, also, was Mayor Richard J. Daley of Chicago, delaying and then ordering adjournments, cuing and cutting off band music. The fuss over the peace demonstrators and the police has driven the troubles of the convention itself from memory. The letters make almost no mention of what happened inside the convention hall; and the polls, which show 70 or 60 or 50 percent of Americans siding with the Chicago police against the demonstrators, have not even bothered to poll the country about what they thought of the convention.

Immediately following the convention, the criticism seemed to be concentrated on charges that we had spent undue time in showing the demonstrations and the police actions in suppressing them, and that our reporters and commentators had made statements about the police action which directly or indirectly criticized the police. This was easy to answer because it was simply not true.

The time NBC devoted to direct network coverage of the convention totaled more than 35 hours. The time devoted to the pictures of the demonstrations was 65 minutes, less than three percent of the total time. Of these 65 minutes, 30 were in prime time. (The consideration of prime time is important because Mayor Daley raised it when he demanded network time for his "reply.")[14] Also of these 65 minutes, 12 were a resumé of scenes already shown, a late-night summary of events, and clearly labeled as such. The other networks had similar experience.

I have reviewed the NBC transcript of the 65 minutes in question. To me, it is notable among other reasons for its brevity. The transcript is unusually short for 65 minutes of pictures. It showed no statement critical of the police; it showed almost no value judgments at all. It was simple descriptive material accompanying pictures. Most of the time our reporters said nothing at all, merely letting the pictures

108 be shown. The regularly scheduled programs which NBC News produces reused some of these pictures; and the reporters gave their
analyses as they often do with news events whether they have been
covered live or not. Hugh Downs and others carried on a long discussion during the *Today* program.

From implying that we had shown too much, the criticism shifted
in the week after Labor Day to the implication that we had not shown
enough. The new and larger wave of letters, stimulated, at least in
part, by Mayor Daley's public statements, were to the point that we
did not show the provocation of the police which led to the action we
did show; and then, to a lesser degree, that we did not describe adequately the organization and history of the demonstrations as they
were developed over the months preceding the conventions. It was
criticism of too little rather than too much coverage.

We have only the word of Mayor Daley and official Chicago police
spokesmen as to the degree of provocation. No one denies that there
was some. The transcript of our own 65 minutes mentions it prominently. To accept uncritically the evaluations of various Chicago officials about the high degree of provocation is no more justified than
accepting uncritically the statements of various people in relatively
high public position that there was no provocation at all. Blair Clark
and Richard Goodwin, in behalf of Senator McCarthy's campaign
organization, sent telegrams to the networks asking to answer Mr.
Daley if he were given time on television. They detail what they
consider and state was the entirely unprovoked attack by Chicago
policemen on young McCarthy workers after Thursday midnight of
convention week. The point of all this is that the statements by Mayor
Daley and his associates about the extent to which the demonstrators
provoked the police cannot be accepted without much more information and documentation.

Up until the violence, it was our conscious policy to avoid covering too much of the activities of demonstrators lest we fall into the
trap of doing their advertising for them. Months of "underground
newspaper" ads organizing two streams of the demonstrators were
known to everyone in the news field, and little was done about it for
this reason. During the actual convention coverage, little attention
was paid to the demonstrations Monday and Tuesday night for the
same reason. When open clashes occurred within range of our cameras, which were relatively stationary, there was no longer any responsible reason for withholding coverage.

But all this begs much more important questions. The tone of the
criticism is a lack or loss of faith in television reporting itself. There
is implication after implication, in the letters, in certain newspaper

accounts and comments, that all this came about because of intent, because the networks wanted it this way as a sort of revenge. Revenge that the two national conventions were in different cities, revenge that floor credentials were allotted below what we considered minimum needs, revenge against a catalogue of greedy motives and mythic presences. And if the answer is No, why haven't we stopped beating our wives?

What did this? The nature of the coverage was not substantially different from the nature of the coverage in 1964, 1960 and 1956. Nor for that matter from the nature of the coverage of the Republican Convention this year. There was some criticism of what we did that week, but of manageable and expectable volume. It was more than counterbalanced by open expressions of approval and appreciation.

But in Chicago, the event itself was different, and the coverage is blamed for that. There is no logical answer available other than this one.

Since 1956 it has been our pattern to rely on four floor reporters for reporting events inside convention hall. By interviews and by statements they explain proceedings, expected developments and also currents of thought and action which otherwise would not reach the public. It is our position that the official proceedings of a convention are only a part of the journalistic record of that convention, and this has been the best method we could devise of fulfilling journalistic responsibility to find and report the rest of the story. These four floor men are augmented by reporters and mobile electronic equipment at many locations away from the convention hall, at the convention headquarters hotel, at candidates' headquarters, and at other locations.

Our equipment has improved over the years and our men have grown more experienced. But the basic structure has not changed since 1956. A third element in that basic structure, the least-known element, is a body of reporters covering each principal candidate and as many as 40 of the principal delegations.

The degree to which this entire reporting system was called on to present news material other than the official proceedings was not substantially different from 1964, although many of the letters express criticism of it in a tone which implies 1968 was something brand-new. This is just one more instance where the criticism cannot be taken to mean what its words say. There is no doubt the critics are disaffected or hostile. But they give reasons which were just as valid in previous situations which they did not see fit to criticize.

Lately, when I have had to reply to criticism of our covering more than the official proceedings, I have often gone beyond the simple

110 statement that there is more news at a convention than takes place at the podium and that it is our responsibility as journalists to find it and report it. We spend a great deal of time and effort every fourth year reporting that world-shaking event, the choice of the American President by the American electorate. We cover primary campaigns; the important primary elections; the election campaigns; Election Night; all in detail and depth, deploying all our men and expending network time which sheer business considerations would not necessarily justify. The national nominating conventions are not only themselves important events in this process, but they are the locales of many other events bearing upon this process, some important, some minor.

The managers of the convention have not yet learned well enough to realize what it means that television is there. They know it as a fact, but they do not appreciate it. Television is there and will always be there. Individuals working in television organizations do not make the decisive difference; the fact that television is there makes the difference. Television has been invented and developed and it exists. The politician tends to see this as giving him access to the public. Now the public has access to him. It may be, as has been said, that there were conventions in the past which were even more rigidly managed. But not when people could watch it as it happened, feel that it was they being managed.

There have also been many references, in letters and in print, to the fact that the first pictures of the Michigan Avenue demonstrations interrupted Mayor Carl Stokes of Cleveland, who was seconding the Presidential nomination of Vice President Humphrey. Usually there is an implication of some sinister purpose. Again, the explanation is far longer and more complicated than the original charge.

First of all, it is our practice to try to present the entire nominating speech of every serious nominee, unless truly major news events intervene, but to consider seconding speeches subject to much less stringent criteria for interruption. Mayor Stokes, as I say, was seconding Mr. Humphrey's nomination.

Secondly, when it became apparent that events outside the convention hall would not be available for live television broadcast because of the circumstances of the telephone-equipment-installers' strike, I set down the rule that if we could not cover live, we would cover with television tape as soon as it became available; if tape was ruled out, we should do it with film; and if film was out of the question, we might try the sound signal from walkie-talkies, and show still pictures on the television screen. But we would do what we could, as we could, to discharge our responsibility to the television audience *111* to cover the entire story in the manner it had come to expect. That first piece of television tape was rushed by motorcycle courier from Michigan Avenue to the Merchandise Mart; screened there on a spot-check basis for technical reliability; an editor evaluated it and chose less than four minutes, which was all we could handle; and as soon as it became available, we were ready to use it. Since the speech placing Vice President Humphrey's name in nomination was still being made, we deferred the tape until the nominating speech ended, and used it instead of Mayor Stokes' seconding speech. (Later that night a video-tape excerpt from the speech was used.)

I want to return to the point I made earlier, that the coverage is blamed for the event. I have no competence as a social scientist and the explanation I suggest impinges on those disciplines.

Between 1964, the last convention year, and 1968, the average middle-class American has gone through many wrenching experiences. His tranquility has been shattered. He has been exposed to realities of war in a way no previous generation of Americans has had to face its war. He has seen ghetto riots in his living room. He has watched with horror young people of good background expressing contempt for his dearest values in the way they dress and act and what they say. Berkeley and Hough and Hue; Columbia and Newark and Tet; what he has seen on television has shaken him physically and morally, made him fear for his safety, his savings, his children, his status. The world as reported by television threatens him. It is a short and understandable step for him to conclude that television threatens him. Television has become the object of what psychoanalysts call transference.

This, not any event, nor anything any or all of us working in television organizations did, accounts for the extent and depth of feeling which followed the Chicago convention coverage. Nowhere is this clearer than in the case of the demonstrators who clashed with the police. Since, unlike black demonstrators, their protest is not against being excluded from the fruits of current America, they are particularly hated. They are verbal and symbolic. They don't throw rocks at trains; they lie down in front of cars. They don't carry firearms, but Vietcong flags. They know the words that shock and the words that anger and how and when to use them. They know what cleanliness is considered next to, and some of them intentionally remain dirty. (There is no doubt in my mind that a few came to Chicago hoping for the kind of police treatment they got.)

This unease, this frustrated hankering for tranquility, this com-

112 plex of fears and hates greater than any within living memory underlies this political year, the campaigns, the polls, the emphasis on repression. Minorities who are willing to disrupt can be very disruptive. Our society and our law are supposedly dedicated to the protection of minorities, but the price of disruption of the majority seems too high. This frustration keeps bursting forth and will until there is some solution. Repression is in most cases the conditioned answer, but that seems to too many to be going too far, especially if it happens where they can see it.

If such young protesters are as unpopular as I think in the United States today, it seems to me worth suggesting that by showing their confrontation with the police without at the same time denouncing them, we may have appeared, to those who loathed them, to be supporting them. This was made worse by showing them being beaten. The normal reaction of most Americans is sympathy with victims, any victims in any situations. People who hated the victims were revolted by their own sympathetic reactions. This revulsion was transferred to the medium, television. Knowingly or instinctively, Democratic politicians who felt their cause damaged by what happened in Chicago and because it was seen, used this revulsion as justification.

What is even more interesting is that so many of the letters about Chicago went on to all the other underlying concerns of contemporary America. Many, even most, Americans consider themselves individually threatened these days. There are three sources of threat: racial conflict, the Vietnam War, and dirty young people with long hair. (It is very often pointed out that many of this last group are not young. No letter I have read points out that many of them are not dirty, or that many of them have short hair.) All three threats run through the letters, and therefore presumably through public attitudes, as a single refrain. And yet only the last one is relevant to the event itself. All three are relevant to current attitudes, and especially to the real world as seen on the face of a television set.

Television allows no respite, no selectivity. The newspaper-reader's eye can skip what bores him, ignore what disturbs him. If he has had enough of black militants, he need go no farther than the headline. If he has special distaste for stories about child molesters or Biafran starvation, he can turn to the ball scores without forcing the editor to give up what he thinks are his responsibilities. Not on television.

If *Huntley-Brinkley Report* shows the Vietnam War five days one week and the viewer always watches the *Huntley-Brinkley Report*, he will see the Vietnam War five days that week. He can't skip it or ignore it. So why don't you show some good news? Why don't you say some nice things? Why must we always be faced with aggressive minorities, riots, looting, killing? The fact is we do show good news and say nice things, but not enough to erase the afterimage of the inescapable. The only other answer must be a new kind of journalism.

It's the kind of journalism the French have on their television. And when the crowds went into the streets last May, the television reporting was one of the bigger targets. It had betrayed them and fooled them and lied about them, and everybody knew it. Even that might not be so bad. But if you don't believe a medium of journalism, can you believe it when it gives good news?

As for the news we put out, we put it out because we think it ought to be put out. We are the current stage in the centuries of evolution of our kind of free journalism, governed by tastes and ethics passed on through what is essentially oral tradition, reacting to conditioned criteria of importance and public interest, hemmed in by some law but not much, consciously or subconsciously always responding to the need to be current, relevant and involving. Relevant to what? To the public and what it cares about. Entertainment is a part of all journalism in all media at all times of history. Being interesting is very much a part of why journalists do what they do.

But American journalism as an institution is never venal. (Specific exceptions prove nothing.) It never does things purely for its own gains. Although it is always the product of many subjective decisions, these are made according to some image of what the public wants and the conditioned impulses of journalists of how they should act and conduct themselves. They do not act from self-interest.

This, which is true of newspapers in this country, is just as ture of journalism on television. It is in the nature of American network television today that even its most economically successful activity could be easily replaced with something outside journalism which could make more money. And the biggest, most difficult, most controversial activities in news, such as covering national political conventions and space launchings, go on at huge money losses.

This system of journalism being impelled by internal needs and supervised by internal controls is what we call free journalism. It exists in very few countries. It is the system under which the reporter demands access to facts and events for no other reason than that he is who he is, and his argument is always accepted.

114   That is our system. It is so ingrained, nobody thinks about it very much, and it takes more words to describe than merely to sense. We grew up with it and that's the way it is. It moved over to television journalism automatically, without conscious decision or open debate, although it's full of debatable propositions. These are the propositions being debated most these days, although so far the challengers are mostly emotional and the rational shape of useful debate is not yet evident.

In most countries in the world today, in most societies, at most times of history, this journalism without a social purpose is abhorrent. The social purpose varies with the time and place, but none at all seems like one of those vacuums that we are told nature always fills. In Spain journalists are expected to advance established religion and government; in China, to rally the people; in the Soviet Union, to avoid the frivolous and contribute to the progress of socialism. These purposes exist in constitutions and Organic Press Laws promulgated by people who believe them intensely and unselfishly. Our rationalizations about a public entitled to information freely obtained, about a press which checks on government, about the right of journalists to be free even when outrageous, run counter, in those countries, to moral fundamentals.

And here, today, in the United States, facing a frightening jigsaw of crises for which we are unprepared, many people seem to think that American journalism, and above all American television journalism, should be governed by ennobling purposes. We are castigated for not promoting unity, for not opening channels of interracial communication, for not building an edifice of support for our fighting men, for not ignoring dissent, for not showing good news.

Our system does not now provide for working toward social good. Let us even postulate that there is unanimously accepted social good which television journalism should set itself to achieve or promote. And the decision would be made by five Albert Schweitzers sitting around a table. Whoever put them there could, in time—perhaps far, far off in the future—replace the five Albert Schweitzers with five Joseph Goebbelses, or five Joseph Stalins, or five George Lincoln Rockwells. You see, it's not the five Albert Schweitzers who are important, but the table.

I say the table itself is evil. To those who worry about television, or television news, being too powerful, I say there is no doubt that there is great potential power here, but only if used. The only safeguard is free journalism, journalism without directed purpose, because whether that purpose represents good or evil depends on who *115* you are.

Television is an institution, but its functions are performed by people, by individuals, by citizens, by mature men and women, by parents, by householders, by wage-earners, by patriots. Each of these as individuals may support the purposes people urge on us. I think most do. We try to keep them out of our work as well as we can, being only mortal, frail and otherwise human. Because, as a colleague puts it, the choice is between the truth imperfectly perceived and the social good dogmatically formulated.

If you tell a medium of journalism what to put in and what to leave out, even if you know in your own heart you are promoting the public welfare, even if most people agree with you, then you are changing journalism as it exists in America. Whatever you call it, censorship is censorship, and all censorship is aimed not at the transmitter but at the receiver.

Notes to Chapter 1

1. This figure is from the Roper Research Associates 1967 Report, *Emerging Profiles of Television and Other Mass Media: Public Attitudes 1959-1967*, the fifth in a series of studies of public attitudes toward television commissioned by the Television Information Office. Since multiple answers were accepted, the figure of 64 percent is somewhat misleading. Newspapers, for example, were listed as being the primary source of news for 55 percent in the same study. In the latest Roper study, taken November 14-23, 1968, with 1995 adult respondents, the television figure dropped to 59 percent but the figure for newspapers dropped to 49 percent. Among respondents who named only a single source of most news, television led newspapers, 29 percent to 19 percent.

2. William A. Wood, *Electronic Journalism*, New York: Columbia University Press, 1967.

3. James Reston, *The Artillery of the Press*, New York: Harper & Row, 1966.

4. In September 1969 NBC notified its owned and operated stations that henceforth they would be allowed to editorialize. CBS and ABC owned and operated stations were already editorializing by that time.

5. In the 1968 Roper survey, 63 percent of the respondents felt that stations should editorialize and only 26 percent were opposed to such a practice. But with respect to endorsing political candidates, only 14 percent approved without reservation, 31 percent approved if equal time were given to opposing candidates and the rest either disapproved or were not sure or did not answer.

6. Mr. Hickey feels that since their article was written there has been a real effort at all three networks to confine all but the most urgent bulletins to commercial breaks, station breaks or during credits at the end of a show.

7. Chapter 15 of the *Report of the National Advisory Commission on Civil Disorders* is entitled "The News Media and the Disorders" and is the source for the reference made by Mr. Hickey in this article.

116   8. The bulk of the Texas vote eventually went to General Eisenhower.

9. Richard Nixon was able to effectively use television in his 1968 campaign. For a candid discussion of how this was done, see Joe McGinniss, *The Selling of the President*, New York: Trident Press, 1969.

10. Mr. Walker, Vice President and General Counsel of Montgomery-Ward and Company, Chicago, was charged by the Violence Commission to prepare a "current and comprehensive" report of the chronology of the Chicago disorders. In his report, later published as *Rights in Conflict* (New York: Dutton & Co., 1968) there was a special chapter entitled "Police and the Press."

11. On February 28, 1969, the FCC wrote the three networks informing them of the results of the Commission's investigations into complaints concerning network coverage of the Chicago Convention. The Commission indicated that they were concerned with two major questions: Was reasonable opportunity for contrasting viewpoints afforded with respect to the controversial issues related to events of the period in question? Was there any real evidence to substantiate allegations of staging or distorting the issues? The Commission said their answer to the first question was yes, while their answer to the second question was no.

12. Kurt Lang and Gladys Engel Lang, *Television and Politics,* Chicago: Quadrangle, 1968.

13. The November 1968 Roper survey did not validate this assumption. On the contrary, television gained 3 percent since 1967 as the most believable news source. Respondents were asked: "If you got conflicting or different reports of the same news story from radio, television, the magazines and the newspapers, which of the four versions would you be most inclined to believe?" With no multiple responses permitted, 44 percent answered television, 21 percent newspapers, 11 percent magazines, 8 percent radio and 16 percent did not know or did not answer. The corresponding figures for the 1967 Roper study were 41 percent television, 24 percent newspapers, 8 percent magazines, 7 percent radio and 20 percent did not know or did not answer.

14. All three networks refused Daley's request for free network time. Both NBC and ABC made counter-offers, suggesting that Daley appear on a special one-hour panel program—*Meet the Press* on NBC or *Face the Nation* on ABC. Daley refused the networks' offers, but received an offer from Channel 5 in New York for air time. By September 16 and 17, one-hundred-fifty television stations had aired a one-hour filmed program and several hundred radio stations a half-hour taped program giving Chicago's viewpoint of the disorders. Chicago's Channel 9 and New York's Channel 5 aired the program on Sunday, September 16, opposite a Barbara Streisand special on CBS, *Bonanza* on NBC and the ABC *Sunday Night Movie.* The program obtained a 38.8 share of the audience in Chicago, but only a 14 share in New York.

PROGRAMMING
Chapter 2

Getting
on the Air

Network programming for each year costs the three major television networks more than a billion dollars. Even before the season begins in September, the networks spend over twenty million dollars in the process of deciding which shows will be scheduled for the new season. After the scheduling is finished, the networks devote six to eight million dollars to promoting their forthcoming program fare to the viewers. The loss of commercial revenue caused by using air time for promotion is yet another cost to the network.

The process by which most submitted programming ideas materialize into network programs traditionally has taken close to two years. A small proportion of the estimated thousands of program ideas received by the networks are classified as tentative program projects. By July of the year preceding the season, the networks' list of perhaps two hundred tentative projects is cut at least in half. Most of the remaining projects become pilots by December of the same year; half-hour pilots usually cost anywhere from 100,000 to 300,000 dollars each. The cost of a pilot, of course, depends upon a variety of factors, including length, salaries, shooting locale and so forth.

The selling season begins in January, after the networks have made some preliminary decisions regarding which pilots would be the best potential sellers, should receive the highest price tags, would best fit in the desired program schedule and, therefore, should be given the "hard sell." Of the perhaps sixty to one hundred pilots, approximately twenty to thirty-five go on the air in September, depending largely upon the success in the ratings of existing shows and whether or not sponsors can be acquired for the new ones. Twenty-four new series appeared during the network prime time in 1969-70, including two shows which changed networks.

Because of the spiraling costs of pilots, the networks have been reducing the number of pilots made each year. CBS, for example,

120   made only thirty-five pilots for the 1968-69 season, whereas five or
six years earlier they made an average of one-hundred-fifty. In order
to avoid producing costly pilots, which may not ever be aired, the
networks are increasingly making prior commitments to shows. Advance commitments are most usually made for series which have
stars with proven track records (Doris Day, Jim Nabors, Debbie
Reynolds) or for producers who, being under exclusive contract to a
given network, have, in effect, already been partially paid for producing the program. Such was the case with NBC and David Dortort,
producer of *Bonanza* and, later, *The High Chapparel.*

Quite obviously, the networks need to sell their high-cost programs to sponsors at an even higher cost if they wish to stay in business and make large profits. In 1969-70, the estimate is that one
billion, fifty million dollars will be spent by advertisers in prime-time
network television alone. Sixty seconds of time during *Laugh-In,
Mission Impossible* and *Mayberry RFD* were priced at $65,000 before
the season began, while a minute in the *Doris Day Show, Dean
Martin Show, FBI* or *Bewitched* was priced at $63,000. In all, eighteen
shows had a price tag of at least $60,000 per minute of advertising
time. The lowest asking price for a sixty-second spot in a network
prime-time entertainment series during 1969-70 was $33,000 for
Let's Make a Deal. Even *CBS News Hour/ 60 Minutes*, the cheapest
prime-time network series, was priced at $30,000 per minute.

Given the costs of producing and sponsoring programs, it is not
surprising that television success is determined by survival of the
fittest, the fittest usually being those shows which achieve the highest
audience ratings. Richard Doan (pp. 122-126) explains that while the
demographics of the viewer (age, sex, income and so forth) which a
particular show attracts are becoming of greater consequence to sponsors and programmers, most shows are still renewed or not renewed
on the basis of sheer numbers. Doan discusses the exceptions to this
general rule, shows which may be aired that do not have large ratings.
These can include inexpensive shows, a show the network needs or
thinks it needs to fulfill its commitment to public service, or a series
which a special sponsor wishes to use a prestige builder. But Doan
concludes that, unlike radio, prime-time commercial television is not
the place for minority tastes.

How some of the general principles regarding programming outlined by Doan were applied by CBS in finalizing their 1969-70 prime-
time schedule is illustrated in the account by Richard Warren Lewis
(pp. 127-134) of the February 19, 1969, CBS program conference

with the big five of corporate management. Lewis provides the reader with a unique glimpse of what happened behind the scenes before CBS, the traditional leader in network ratings, released the list of its prime-time programming for the current season.

New shows appear on the networks' schedules each year, and Robert Leonard (pp. 135-137) cites five major questions which the advertising agent generally asks himself before deciding which new show to advise his clients to buy. 1 Is it similar to a proven show? 2 What are the track records of the key people involved in the show? 3 Does the show seem to fit the sponsor's product or the image he wishes to create for the product? 4 Can the series be obtained for a discount price? 5 Can the show offer the sponsor a good CPM, that is, a low cost-per-thousand viewers?

The sponsor's ultimate decision whether to buy a new program is affected by a number of variables, some of which are unpredictable. Neil Hickey and Joseph Finnigan (pp. 138-146) illustrate several of these in their article relating twelve episodes that have occurred in past selling seasons. A salesman's ingenuity or his lack of judgment, an advertiser's immediate positive or negative reaction to a given pilot, an advertiser's negative reaction to even one incident in a pilot, and differences in the tastes of prospective sponsors are among the factors affecting the sale of a program.

Doan and Finnigan (pp. 147-152) discuss the inglorious history of *Turn-On*, a comedy series that lasted one evening and has been labelled a million-dollar disaster. The history of *Turn-On* illustrates many of the significant factors which may influence the process of television programming. *Turn-On* came into being because of the sponsor's desire to copy a successful show with proven producers and, consequently, its failure demonstrated that one cannot always copy success, even when practically the same people are trying to copy their own original. The importance of the sponsor's tastes as opposed to those of the network or its affiliate, the importance of possible rating success as opposed to the individual taste of the station manager, the importance of which pilot is shown to the client and which is aired as the premier show, the importance of the time slot—especially for a mid-season replacement, the potential power of the affiliates to cancel the networks, and the ultimate supremacy of the viewer—even a minority viewer—when and if he makes his views known are all suggested in this article.

Why Shows Are Canceled
By Richard K. Doan

JUNE 15, 1968

Every year it's the same: Two to three dozen weekly network entertainments are summarily done in, rendering millions of TV fans bitterly unhappy. Many of the fans are ready to believe the network decision-makers must be off their rockers. Some viewers vow they've had it—they'll never watch TV again. Some scream bloody murder. "How could you?" they wail. "Those were my favorite shows! All my friends were crazy about them, too. Who do you think you are? Why don't you ask people what they like? You don't seem to know a good show when you see one!"

In extreme cases, the programmers are denounced as creeps who probably don't have enough sense to come in out of the rain. And if they had the temerity to dump a teen-agers' love like *The Monkees*, they're invited to "die, die, die!"

It is a fact, of course, that every TV series—good, bad or downright awful—has a few million friends.

It's also a fact, apparently never quite accepted or understood out there in videoland, that a few million isn't enough. To survive, a show has to have lots of millions of friends, like, say 20 million.

And it's a fact, further, that the people who put programs on and take them off have to rely a great deal on their instincts and experience in putting them on, but they have something more tangible to go by in knocking them off. The word for it is ratings (see pp. 385-408).

Now it's true the networks don't go around asking viewers which shows they like best. The A. C. Nielsen Co. of Chicago does it for them. That is, Mr. Nielsen records what 1200-odd "sample" families actually watch, assuming they watch what they like. And what Mr. Nielsen's folks like, Mr. John Q. Public gets. It's as simple as that. If a viewer's preferences chance not to coincide with those of the Nielsen panel, too bad.

But don't the networks sometimes cross off shows that really are pretty popular? Not if they can help it! You don't see *Gomer Pyle* and *Lucy* and *Bonanza* and *Red Skelton* being scratched, do you?

In fact, you don't see programs rating in the Top 10, or 20, or 30, vanishing at season's end unless the star has elected to quit while he's ahead as Dick Van Dyke did and as Andy Griffith is doing this year; or unless there is some other circumstance beyond network control, such as a sponsor pulling the rug, as Chrysler did last year with Bob Hope's *Theater* series on NBC. No sir, hit shows—Nielsen winners—are too hard to come by to be unloaded willy-nilly.

There's really no great mystery about it: TV programming is governed by the law of survival of the fittest. The fittest being the shows best liked by certain people. Certain people being those the advertiser wants most to reach. The people he wants most to reach being, as a rule, the great, well-washed, middle class, 18-to-49-year-old group. Young adults, they're called in the trade. Kids and older folks the sponsor can ordinarily do without—unless he's selling cereal or Geritol.

The cancellation of shows is merely a weeding out of the weakest by these standards. Mr. Nielsen, it probably needs to be noted, not only counts how many are looking, but describes them by age, income, education, and so forth.

One way to look at it, suggests NBC's astute Paul Klein (vice president, believe it or not, in charge of audience measurement), is to think of TV as a colossal theater seating about 23 million people. Now, everything is relative, Klein points out. For example, the number of people it would take to fill a Broadway theater to overflowing would look like a mere handful in Yankee Stadium. So, in TV's theater, 10 million doesn't look like very much. Fifteen, 16 million isn't enough! Twenty million? Well, that'll do.

What makes anywhere from 20 to 23 million an acceptable "house"? Just that this happens to be about the number of viewers a show gets in average prime time when it pulls roughly 30 percent of the tuned-in audience. There being three networks, most of the TV audience watches one or another of these. In the ratings books, a so-called 30 share (that is, 30 percent, or nearly one-third of the audience) means that a show is making a minimal competitive showing. If it grabs a 40 to 45 share, it's a hit. If it attracts something less than a 30 share, it's in potential, if not actual, trouble. "That means we're in economic jeopardy," Klein says.

Klein is a big demographics man and he also sometimes thinks of the TV audience as a huge "people pie." He explains: "Nielsen ratings are homes ratings. That's the wrong kind of pie. The right kind is people pie. For instance, we're dropping *Tarzan*, which has been getting an acceptable homes rating but hasn't been delivering

124 the right kind of people. Too many kids and old ladies. *Tarzan* people
are worth less to the advertiser than, say, *Star Trek* people. We're
renewing *Star Trek* partly because we got 115,000 letters asking us to,
but also because it delivers a quality, salable audience. It has as many
upper-income, better-educated males watching as CBS has watching
NFL football, which sells for about $65,000 a minute, while *Star
Trek* costs the advertiser only about $40,000 a minute."

Klein's arguments notwithstanding, it's still a show's per-home
popularity that usually spells life or death. Take the 28 weekly series
in last September's network lineups which will not be around next
fall: With the exception of Andy Griffith's show, which will be without
him next fall, at mid-winter renewal time only two of these 27 shows,
Tarzan and *He & She,* ranked anywhere above 50th in the ratings, and
only *Tarzan* had a share-of-audience above 30. Many of the doomed
shows crowded the lower brackets of Nielsen's boxscore, and not
one was the audience's first choice in its time period; most indeed
were third choice. *Tarzan,* as Klein pointed out, was getting enough
homes watching, but not the "right" viewers. *He & She,* a CBS situation comedy introduced last fall, was, it seems, a small *cause celebre.*

"We very much wanted it to succeed," CBS program chief Mike
Dann laments. "We have it gravy time, Wednesdays following *Green
Acres.* It was the darling of the program department. It was the darling
of the 'in' crowd; people like Mike Nichols loved it and bought trade
ads urging us not to drop it. We got more letters favoring it, I think,
than anything we've ever put on. The loyalty was fantastic. Canceling
it was the hardest program decision I've ever had to make. But we
just didn't feel it had quite made it. It averaged only a 28 share and
was usually third in its time period. With a sitcom, you've just got to
get circulation." (Circulation is the currently preferred euphemism for
ratings.) Anyway, CBS had Doris Day, one of the biggest movie box-
office stars, signed for a new comedy series for next fall, and in the
shuffle *He & She* had to go.

Once in a while a series is so clearly a dud that no rating is needed
to spell its doom. Such a one was *Dundee and The Culhane,* an offbeat
Western unveiled last fall. "It was canceled quicker than any program
in CBS history," Dann reports. "In fact, even before it went on the
air! The pilot was great, but I saw seven episodes and read five additional scripts, and I was convinced it was going to be an absolute
failure. We decided in September to replace it in December with
Jonathan Winters."

After a show gets on the air, there is one major factor other than
its inherent appeal which influences its fate. The program's night of
week and hour, and the competition it faces in that time period, help

make or break it. *The Big Valley* and *The Man from U.N.C.L.E.* are **125**
cited as examples in recent times of series that didn't win passing
ratings until moved to more favorable time slots.[1]

Sometimes series survive not only because they are passably
popular and salable to advertisers, but because they also are inexpensive to produce. Cheapies such as ABC's *Dating Game* and
Newlywed Game come under this heading [$20,000 per nightime
program].

Very often, new series doomed to extinction are marked almost
from the opening night. ABC's *Good Company* last fall was such a
one; it couldn't get out of Nielsen's subcellar. If a show debuts to low
ratings but gets favorable reviews, an effort may be made to salvage
it with advertising and promotion, maybe even a time change. If it
bows to high ratings, what the critics say about it doesn't really matter.
But if it comes on to the drumbeat of low ratings and poor notices—
good-by!

Sometimes series will pull respectable ratings for several seasons,
then just "run out of steam," as the programmers put it. That was what
happened this season with *Lost in Space, I Spy* and *Run for Your Life.*

In painfully few instances a series survives despite low ratings.
CBS's Tuesday night news hour is a case in point—actually the only
one remaining in prime time. It exists simply because the network
regards it as a necessary public service. Attracting audience, or at
least maximum audience, is not one of its objectives. Indeed, the very
fact that this CBS documentary series typically interests but a small
percentage of the TV crowd assures ABC and NBC entertainments
at the same hour of claiming higher ratings than they might otherwise
achieve.

Why is there all this premium on high ratings? Because advertisers want, seek and pay for circulation—in newspapers and magazines as well as on TV and radio—and the more viewers a time period
has, the more money a network can charge a sponsor for it. The network and sponsor do not wait to find out how much audience a show
gets before agreeing on the rate; it is negotiated beforehand, based
on estimates derived from prior experience. A network's profits—or
losses—rise and fall, by millions of dollars, with its ability to schedule
programs of utmost numerical appeal. The TV programmer is simply
looking out for his stockholders when he buys or drops a show.

The networks do indeed, from time to time, book specials of
obviously limited appeal—such as CBS's *Sol Hurok Presents,* an
undeniable dose of culture, this season (1968-69)—and sometimes
they are able to sell these programs—for instance, the Dreyfus
Corporation sponsored the Hurok show.

126   In these cases, circulation is not the objective, either of the network or the sponsor. The network books the special out of conscience, as a public service for which the network can get Brownie points from the FCC, Congress and the critics, professional and otherwise. The advertiser buys into such programs for one reason, or a combination of reasons: Association with culture and/or public service will enhance his community image; the program can be expected to grab a class of viewer the advertiser particularly wants his message to reach; the network many times, in order to recoup some of its expenditure, peddles the special for a bargain price. For example, 3M got a four-hour ride in ABC's $2-million "Africa" evening for about $650,000 when the network was unable to scare up any other sponsorship.

It must be said in the networkers' behalf nowadays that when they are asked why shows have been canceled, they seldom resort to the hoary myth that "ratings are just one of many factors we take into consideration." Neither do they profess to see any evil in playing their programming by the numbers. It's just good business, as they see it.

Prime-time commercial TV, in short, is no place for minority tastes, and nobody's making any bones about it any more.

The Man on the 34th Floor
By Richard Warren Lewis

JULY 19, 1969

The thermostat in suite 3435, a windowless conference room in CBS headquarters in Manhattan, reads 78 degrees—just warm enough to discourage total comfort. It is a Wednesday afternoon three days before Washington's Birthday, the date on which the network traditionally makes official its fall program schedule.

Around a bare circular table of polished walnut, plush designer chairs swivel with the Big Five of corporate management: William S. Paley, chairman of the board since 1946; Dr. Frank Stanton, the sandy-haired Ph.D. who is president of CBS Inc.; cigar-smoking John A. Schneider, the "boy wonder" executive vice president and Paley's heir apparent; Richard W. Jencks, red-cheeked president of CBS Broadcasting Group; and Robert D. Wood, recently installed CBS-TV president.

Situated among them are research director Jay Eliasberg, armed with a folder of statistical rating charts for every region of the Nation, and Mike Dann, mercurial senior vice president in charge of programming, the only participant wearing shirt-sleeves.

The imminent four-hour showdown is the culmination of dozens of smaller groupthinks, many of them as passionately animated as a psychological encounter group. No wonder. Some $150-million in annual program revenues rides on this decision-making process.

"These meetings have the internal dynamics of a crucible," explains Marc Golden, former CIA agent and current director of program development. "The whole ball game is played in the winter. But you don't know the score until many months later in the fall."

The pressure has been mounting since the first of January. Everyone in the room, along with some 15 junior staffers, has spent the previous seven weeks analyzing weaknesses in the CBS lineup. Under the most rigid conditions, they have scrutinized those pilot films available for the 1969-70 season, usually at either 11 A.M. or 4 P.M., hours when the flow of creative juices was thought to be at its maximum. No more than one show has been seen at a single sitting.

127

128 If two or more executives watched a pilot simultaneously, they did so in stony silence, observing the front-office rule against any conversation while film was running. Secretaries stood guard at screening-room doors to prevent interruptions.

Additionally, all those assembled have digested projected story outlines and read the composite reports of the Program Analyzer, an audience-testing device created by Dr. Stanton.

Now all eyes are focused on Dann, who stands before two outsized rectangular planning boards he designed. The seven prime-time half-hours between 7:30 and 11 P.M. are printed across the top of the larger Scheduling Board, while the days of the week are listed down its left-hand border. Reading from left to right, each network's current programs are listed in red, blue and tan magnetized cards that cling to its face.

Immediately to the right, one can scan the 14 magnetized cards on the Development Board, representing 14 new hour and half-hour shows—a CBS investment of $5 million. Among the hour possibilities is *Cutter's Trail,* a bloodless Western similar to *Gunsmoke,* with emphasis on a family group headed by actor John Gavin. *The Protectors* is a drama describing the relationships among a mayor, police chief, district attorney and coroner in an American megalopolis.

Lost Flight concerns the passengers on an airliner that crash lands on a remote Pacific island and the way, like more sophisticated Gilligans, the survivors exist. *U.M.C.* (University Medical Center) could stimulate a new wave of doctor stories. Another card reads *Jim Nabors,* indicating a variety hour that CBS is committed to drop into the new schedule. After five seasons Nabors has decided to abandon *Gomer Pyle* for this more imaginative format. The network has already allocated a $200,000 weekly budget for the program.

Smaller cards adjacent to the hour entries designate the latest half-hour contenders in an area that has always been a CBS forte— situation comedy. None of these $250,000 investments shows much originality. They all resemble entertainment that has previously appeared on stage, screen or television.

Houseboat, a series adapted from the Cary Grant-Sophia Loren movie, deals with a widower with four children who hires a maid to care for them. Instead of Grant and Loren, unfortunately, CBS has cast the unheralded Arthur Hill and Danielle deMetz.

Me and Benjy is the latest "heart comedy" by the producers of *Leave it to Beaver,* the basic difference between the shows being the involvement of two families, one of them black. Then there is *Barefoot in the Park,* a "sitcom" featuring a young married couple, based on the hit Broadway play. Ironically, it stars Skye Aubrey, daughter of the deposed CBS president Jim Aubrey, a controversial figure who was fired [in 1965] in apparent disgrace. *Barefoot*'s chances are as likely as those of Aubrey's being invited to lunch in the executive dining room. "The first show has to do with the couple buying a bed and the difficulties in getting it into their apartment and the bed being too small for both of them to fit into," Dann explains. "It's much too risque—especially for a 7:30 show. And that's our greatest need."

Other remote possibilities are a rural comedy starring Minnie Pearl (CBS is already oversaturated with this commodity) and the venerable *Vernon's Volunteers,* a slapstick story about a fire department, previously rejected as a midseason replacement last January.

A more likely prospect for a late-evening comedy spot, should one develop, is *The Governor and J.J.*—Dan Dailey and Julie Sommars bridging the generation gap between a politican and his daughter. Equally promising is *To Rome with Love,* about a teacher (John Forsythe) who moves to Rome with his three daughters. "It's a *My Three Sons* kind of show which reflects the problems of a father with children," Dann reminds the gathering. The producer of *To Rome with Love,* coincidentally, also produces *My Three Sons.*

Pacing the synthetic white carpeting, Dann directs his attention to the larger, multicolored Scheduling Board as he explains his department's recommendations for change.

On Sunday night, *Gentle Ben* has suffered a noticeable decline in the ratings. Dann is unimpressed by a modest letter-writing campaign in which thousands of viewers have pleaded to "Save *Gentle Ben.*" "There are only so many bear stories you can do," he says gruffly. "With *Land of the Giants* and *Walt Disney,* two children's shows opposite it, why don't we try an adult form to give the audience a chance for more selective viewing?" With that, he removes the *Gentle Ben* card from the board, tossing it on the floor.

The remainder of Sunday night seems viable. "*Ed Sullivan, Smothers Brothers* and *Mission: Impossible* are all working fine for us. We don't change."

Monday night seems just as stable. *Gunsmoke, Lucy, Mayberry R.F.D., Family Affair* and *Carol Burnett* all rank high in the Nielsen ratings, just as *Lancer, Red Skelton* and *Doris Day* do on Tuesday night. The *CBS News Hour* lags way behind the opposition, but management policy makes its appearance on the schedule obligatory.

A twinkle comes to Dann's eye when he reaches the *Glen Campbell* card opposite Wednesday at 7:30. In a bold move the previous

130   December, he had decided to cancel *Daktari* weeks before the customary "second season" and replace it with the singer from Arkansas in a musical variety show. This strategem exemplified the highly specialized science of counterprogramming. Dann pitted Campbell against two Westerns, shows that attract older audiences, in an effort to charm the viewer who was not being satisfied in that time period.

Between the time of that move and now, the third week in February, weekly overnight Arbitron ratings ordered by Dann certified that Campbell's hit status was not ephemeral. "Glenn Campbell turned around the whole season," Dann exults, ever mindful of the ratings race with NBC. Furthermore, the show has delivered a substantial carry-over audience to *The Good Guys, Beverly Hillbillies* and *Green Acres*, well-established programs following in its wake.

The 10 P.M. Wednesday period had also benefited from Dann's legerdemain. *Hawaii Five-O* seemed moribund on Thursday night at 8 late last year, winning only a 22-percent share of the audience and position number 80 on the Nielsen list. When Dann moved *Hawaii* to its current hour, it vaulted into the Top 20 the first week and has remained there ever since.

Thursdays from 7:30 to 9 had long been a major disaster area. Both *Blondie,* which opened last season, and *The Queen and I,* its woeful midseason replacement, had been written off as "creative failures" before they reached the air. *The Queen and I* card that Dann takes off the big board is joined by one for *Jonathan Winters,* who failed to attract significant audiences at 8 P.M. Only the *Thursday Night Movies* will be retained.

The Wild Wild West, Friday at 7:30 deserved a better fate. "Maybe it's not a big hit," Dann had earlier explained, "but it's a functional show. It gets a good circulation and it's profitable." The CBS hierarchy, however, recently had become alarmed over the widespread criticism of violence on television and the increasing clamor for Federal regulation. *The Wild Wild West* thus became expendable. Its card is unceremoniously removed.

"On Saturday, Gleason's fine," says Dann, resuming his analysis. *"My Three Sons, Hogan's, Petticoat* and *Mannix* are also solid."

That leaves three and a half hours of programming to replace: two blocks from 7:30 to 9 on Thursday and Friday, and Sunday night at 7:30 to 8. Dann confronts the toughest problem first. "We have tried for three years to do something about Thursday and we have failed. We just can't lick 7:30 to 8."

That very dilemma was preying on his mind earlier in the day when he raised a pair of binoculars to his eyes and gazed at the Henry

Moore sculptures in the Museum of Modern Art's garden 34 stories *131*
below. It was only then that he was able to conceive the solution—
moving *Family Affair* from 9:30 on Monday to 7:30 on Thursday.
The idea appears to have considerable merit. CBS has received
several hundred thousand letters from parents and school groups
requesting that the program appear at an hour more accessible to
younger viewers.

"How does it do in the Rocky Mountain time zone, where it is
played at 7:30?" Schneider asks. Charts supplied by Eliasberg confirm that *Family Affair* is a bigger hit at 7:30 in Salt Lake City than it is
elsewhere at 9:30 and that it attracts an extraordinary number of
under-12 viewers. The switch is quickly approved, even though it
violates an unwritten rule: Never Tamper with a Hit.

The strategy, of course, is to eliminate the rating advantage of
the established 7:30 leader, NBC's *Daniel Boone.* "We really want to
take *Boone,*" Dann declares, ready to administer the *coup degrace.*
He grabs the *Jim Nabors* card and places it on the schedule immediately following *Family Affair.* "In the weakest part of our whole
schedule," he says, "we now have two of the biggest draws that exist
on our network!"

Schneider then addresses himself to the resultant gap on Monday
at 9:30. He complains that *The Doris Day Show* has not realized its
potential, despite a healthy rating. He wants future scripts to take
Doris off the farm, glamorize her and involve her in more contemporary situations. "Not only should the show be redone, but let's
give her a new time period," he suggests. "I think she'd be very compatible just before Carol Burnett on Mondays." The change is made.

To fill the *Doris Day* vacancy on Tuesday at 9:30, Dann nominates
his prime candidate for a late-evening family comedy, *The Governor
and J.J.* By putting it there, he demonstrates his policy of protecting
a newcomer with an established lead-in show, in this case *Red
Skelton.*

To Rome with Love next falls into place as the substitute for
Gentle Ben, gaining majority support for its potential appeal to the
Sunday night family audience, where its opposition primarily appeals
to children.

"I'm worried about *The Name of the Game,*" Board Chairman
Paley interjects, looking back on the loss of *Pyle* on Friday night.
"Your vital point is 8:30 Friday night. If you can stop *Name of the
Game* [a 90-minute drama on NBC] in the first half-hour, you'll retain
the 8:30 audience when your movie starts at 9. If you lose 8:30, they'll
stay with *Name of the Game* until 10."

Dann reduces this worry by shifting *Hogan's Heroes* from Satur-

132 day at 9 into the former *Pyle* position. "Same kind of show as *Gomer*,"
he declares. "Not as big a rating, but it was against NBC's *Saturday
Night at the Movies* and *Lawrence Welk*, which takes all the oldsters.
Hogan's can win, just like *Gomer*."

Noting the remaining hour's gap on Friday night, Frank Stanton
then asks: "What's the one new show that you have faith in more
than any other?" Unanimously, it is *U.M.C.* Conveniently devoid of
sex and violence, *U.M.C.* can be expected to gain support among
both young and old viewers.

"The public appetite has always been around for this," Dann
comments, tentatively placing the card at 7:30 Friday. Whether
accidents and operations are so appropriate so close to the dinner
hour becomes the subject of a vigorous debate. Its outcome: another
place will have to be found.

The easiest spot on the board is Wednesday night at 9. Currently
occupied by the hugely successful CBS comedy block, *Beverly Hillbillies* and *Green Acres*. Their competition is the weakly-rated ABC
movies and NBC's *Music Hall*, whose sponsor is not overly concerned
with big ratings.

"A new story form is always a big gamble," says Dann. "They're
the least likely to succeed. But by putting *U.M.C.* at 9 o'clock and
shoving back *Beverly Hillbillies* half an hour, we would be creating
a hammock between two successful shows—the other one being
Hawaii Five-O at 10 o'clock. That would really not be too much of a
gamble."

Dann also knows that *Hillbillies* producer Paul Henning will not
object to being evicted since he will be following *Glen Campbell*, a
hit show with a similar audience. And *Hillbillies*, which Dann calls
"the biggest hit in the history of broadcasting," had prospered in that
identical position one year earlier.

Next, the dislodged *Green Acres* is assigned the spot vacated by
Hogan's Heroes, Saturday at 9—an ideal sandwich between *My Three
Sons* and *Petticoat Junction*. With the switch of *Hillbillies*, a place
has to be found for *Good Guys*. Friday at 8 looms as a possibility, if
only something substantial can precede it. Nothing left on the Development Board arouses enthusiasm. *Me and Benjy* is not funny
enough. *Vernon's Volunteers* is thought to be poorly executed. *Barefoot in the Park* belongs later in the evening.

"We're dead," Dann sighs. "The entire schedule will not work
unless we have a strong 7:30 comedy." Reluctantly, it is decided to
insert the hour-long *Lost Flight* at 7:30 and move *Good Guys* to
Sunday night, in place of *To Rome with Love*.

"*Lost Flight* can be a functional 7:30 form," Dann remarks, as the   *133*
meeting concludes on a gloomy note shortly before 4 P.M. "It's not
based on violence and it's all right for the kids." But everyone understands that his statements lacks conviction.

Several minutes after an anxiety-ridden return to his office, he
gets a call from Ted Ashley. "I think *Get Smart* is available," Ashley
reports. A slippage in ratings has prompted NBC to cancel the four-
seasons-old escapist comedy.

Dann has always admired *Get Smart*. He feels its comedy-
jeopardy format is reminiscent of the best Bob Hope and Marx
Brothers movies. There is also a precedent for his considering the
acquisition of a faltering series from a rival network—he had salvaged
My Three Sons from ABC and turned it into a durable Top 10 show.

"That's the key to a perfect schedule," Dann thinks to himself,
in growing excitement. "That's the lock. That's my 7:30 show."

He immediately contacts network president Robert Wood and
explains Ashley's offer. "Bob," he says, "I want to go after *Get Smart*."
"Do you think it's strong enough?" Wood asks. "It tied *My Three
Sons* when it was against it," Dann replies, drawing on his memory.
"It's doing very well now. Not great. But Friday night at 7:30 we have
43 percent more children looking in. It's an ideal children's show."
"Go after it if you can get it," Woods instructs.

By the end of the day, Dann has closed the deal for *Get Smart*
and transferred *Good Guys* back to Friday night at 8. He has welded
together a potent, 90-minute block of the same variety of wild, farcical
comedy, an inspired departure for Friday night that involves $35
million in prospective revenues. Several years before, a similar
comedy block concept on Saturday night had ended the dominance of
the NBC movies.

Dann goes to bed thinking that the schedule has been locked. At
1:30 in the morning, he receives another phone call from Ashley,
informing him that it seems doubtful that series star Don Adams
wishes to continue with *Get Smart*. When NBC had learned only
hours before that the show had been purchased by CBS, two NBC
executives descended on Adams' Beverly Hills home, offering him
six specials for the fall season plus his own variety show. Adams indicated that he favored NBC's lucrative proposal.

At 2 A.M., wearing a pair of pajamas, Dann pads barefoot into the
kitchen of his rambling, suburban New York home and places a call
to Adams. For the next three hours, he tries to persuade Adams to
continue with the series. "My goodness," Dann argues, "If you're
against *High Chaparral*, which has an older audience appeal, and

134   *Let's Make a Deal* on ABC, we fully expect you to be a substantial success. It's an unopposed comedy area, the only game in town." He also recites the increased numbers of younger viewers on Friday night and the financial advantages that could accrue to Adams, who owns 35 percent of the show.

"In this business, you should never give up a hit," he advises Adams, speaking in hushed tones so he will not disturb his sleeping family. "Gleason was the only man I know who walked away from a successful show—*The Honeymooners*—and was able to survive in a different format. You are not a man of [that great] stature in the industry, no matter what your capabilities are. You can't assume that by going on an hour variety show you will be just as successful." Dann's impassioned philippics end at 4:55 in the morning.

"OK," Adams says. "Let me talk to my people and I'll get back to you." Dann knows that Adams has scheduled another meeting with NBC at 10 A.M. "With a performer," he says later, "you must really get him to make up his mind at that moment. If you let him get away, he's subject to formidable pressures."

"Don, it's five of 5 in the morning," Dann retorts. "We want you. But at 5 o'clock we'll go another way. There's nothing more I can say that will influence you. You have to tell me right now. We have to announce our schedule today. I have to know one way or the other. I have no choice." There is a pause. "OK," Adams sighs. "I'll stay with *Get Smart*."

In his exhilaration over consummating the $3.5-million deal, Dann cannot return to sleep. He takes a hot shower, shaves, and catches the commuter train to Manhattan for the 8:30 A.M. signing with Adams' agents.

"Right now, we figure we've got the dream schedule," Dann bullishly observes. "We go in confident that we will win the ratings as we have for 14 years. We have no real weak spots."

By Monday afternoon, the first day they go on the market, *Get Smart, Hogan's Heroes* and *Good Guys* are sold out to advertisers. The CBS vice president in charge of sales, on that same day, executes firm contracts for $125 million-worth of business.

"Fifty percent of the reason for a program's success is where it's scheduled," Dann later explains. "To the professionals, we've got a hot schedule. We're practically sold out for the fourth quarter of 1969, the greatest quarter in the history of the company. We're hot on the street."

How Did THAT Show Ever Get a Sponsor?

By Robert Leonard

OCTOBER 16, 1965

"How did that show ever get a sponsor?" "I could have picked a better program blindfolded!" Do you think nasty thoughts like these as you dial across the crazy quilt of new programs blanketing television at this time of year?

Maybe you'd like to know how programs are picked for sponsors. And by whom. I'll be glad to let you in on the ritual. For 10 years it was my job as Vice President in charge of Television at one of Madison Avenue's biggest ad agencies. The sponsors I sold shows to are the blue bloods of American business and the new programs I latched on to were legion.

The television chieftain of the advertising agency, backed by other agency bigwigs, entices the advertiser to gamble on a new show. The price tag is anywhere from two to six million dollars. And there are four things to look for when you're evaluating that new property.

1. *"Likewise, I'm Sure."* This is the safest kind of programming because it carbon-copies some other well-rated program as closely as the laws of infringement permit. As these laws are quite vague, you needn't worry about purchasing a show starring an outspoken housemaid. Of course it shouldn't be called *Hazel.* You might call yours *Ethel,* and of course you can't use Shirley Booth. But she isn't available anyway. Aside from these details, look for similarities of plot, sets and subordinate cast. "Likewise, I'm Sure" programming is a perfect reply to a sponsor who says, "Why don't you ever offer me anything like *Bonanza?* Now there's a wing ding of a show!" You might come right back at him with a drama called *Briganza* that takes place on a big Oregon ranch called the Sequoia, which is owned by Bill Wheelwright who has *four* sons.

2. *Credit Rating.* Here's a surefire sponsor-pleaser. This kind of programming relies on the "track record" of the people who developed the show. The producing company (tell your prospective

135

136 advertiser) is the exciting new Hollywood outfit, Gee-Whizz Films. The principals of Gee-Whizz are Marty McFlaberhoff, who used to be Mr. Big at the old How Come Studios. Marty's the money man; he gives the outfit stability; and for artistic depth he's got Ernie Levenberry, who wrote short subjects for Acme and that famous educational-television documentary series called *Whither Timber,* which dealt with our dwindling woodland resources. Who's going to direct the series? A good question! He's none other than Al Flog, well-known to TV fans for his work in *World-Wide Circus Time,* which was No. 37 in the Nielsen ratings several seasons back. So on down the line, through scriptwriters, film editor and wardrobe mistress.

While you're weighing in the whodunit of a new show, don't forget the cast credits. Usually you're stuck with a star of the luster of say, Maximilian Kolodney, who was last seen opposite Helen Twelvetrees, or maybe Beverly Phlank, who played Tinker Bell in an off-Broadway "Peter Pan". This may discourage you and cause you to insist on some "offbeat names" who can be warped into "a fresh format." I mean something like combining Willie Mays and Chet Huntley in a psychological Western, or Lawrence Spivak playing the role of a kindly football coach.

3. *Integrated Programming.* Now here's an approach to the medium that sponsors really go ape about because their commercials are *integrated!* This means that commercials flow smoothly out of the story—rather than coming as interruptions to it.

Want an example of integrated programming? The sponsor is in the detergent field and the show is called D.S.C. Note how it fits right in with knights or doves and tornadoes because it features the men of the Department of Street Cleaning! If D.S.C. has too much of a military ring to it, we could call our series *Men in Off-White;* exciting episode after episode takes us into the everyday lives of the men who preserve our sanitation; their hopes and fears, their home life; the things they have inside their homes that they've collected in line of duty.

4. *Distressed Merchandise.* Just between us, baby, this is the safest kind of programming to recommend. It doesn't aim very high, so it can't fall very far. You can buy it late in September just before its first telecast. Or better yet, after a few weeks have gone past without a sponsor. The network is desperate. The packager is frantic. The price is slashed! And the concessions you get! Quick-escape clauses! Extra commercial positions!

Why hasn't this show sold before? Maybe it's a real stinker. Maybe everyone who saw the pilot threw up. Don't be discouraged; it

still could be a good show but *offbeat*. No one dared to take a chance.   *137*
Maybe it was put together by the news department in order to win
points from the Federal Communications Commission and they made
it good by mistake. It's got some other handicaps too, like being
spotted right opposite the No. 1 rated program in all television and
as its feed-in—the show immediately before it—it has the lowest
rated show in all prime time.

Well, that's how to pick television shows. There's only one other
thing you should know. How to play the numbers racket. This, pal,
is basic. Businessmen insist on this when slumming over in show biz.

You've got to come up with a rating prediction and express it in
the most sacred of TV numbers—CPM—cost-per-thousand homes of
commercial. How do you come by this figure? You take the weekly
average audience ratings of the time slot during last season's peak-
viewing months (October through April). Then you add 25 percent
to prove you have confidence in the new vehicle you picked. Then
you divide this number into the sponsor's cost per episode of the show
(times as well as talent) and you divide once again by the number of
commercial minutes the sponsor gets per episode. That's the magic
formula, kids!

A friendly tip, however! Don't dare put the CPM in writing.
Because when your television turkey is staggering around next
spring just asking to be slaughtered, the CPM can get your neck, too.[2]

How TV Shows Are Sold

By Neil Hickey and Joseph Finnigan

AUGUST 21, AND 28, 1965

It happens every year, January through April. TV people call it the Selling Season, those few heartbreaking, hilarious, hectic months during which the major networks lock up their prime-time schedules for the following September.

It's a time of triumph and a time of anguish—joy for the winners, desolation for the losers—as inestimable millions of dollars are flung down and snatched up in the great floating dice game which rages over the U.S. in planes and trains, in elevators, on golf courses, and in the plush restaurants of New York and Hollywood, as producers, packagers, advertisers, and network programming bigwigs close the deals which decide the TV fare you'll be fed in the fall.

It's a sometimes grim, often screamingly funny business. We recently quizzed a number of the persons in this impressive drama, in order to bring you a glimpse of the pageantry that accompanies the buying and selling of TV shows.

Our first stop was in the office of John H. Mitchell, vice president in charge of sales at Screen Gems, Inc., one of the largest purveyors of TV pilot films. Mitchell recalled his fervent attempts in 1962 to sell ABC on the *Our Man Higgins* series, which starred Stanley Holloway. Oliver Treyz, then president of ABC-TV, had a stiff and seemingly impenetrable resistance to the *Higgins* idea. He had seen the pilot, and was not quite enthusiastic enough about it to put it in his schedule. But Mitchell continued to press his case.

One day the Screen Gems executive was in New York and telephoned Treyz to deliver one of his many pep talks about *Higgins*. Treyz interrupted impatiently, "Look, John, we've been through all this. I don't have time to discuss it further. I'm in a hurry to catch a train to Washington." That ended the conversation. Mitchell put down the phone and yelled to his secretary: "Find out when the next train to Washington leaves!" Moments later he was out in the street and boarding a taxi for the ride to Penn Station. At the station he bought a ticket to Washington, found the train, and got on board.

As the train pulled out, Mitchell began walking through the train *139* looking for his prey. Finally, in a parlor car he spotted not only Treyz but also Leonard Goldenson, president of ABC, and Thomas Moore, then programming vice president of ABC-TV.

He crept up behind them, then snapped to attention and clicked his heels. The trio of ABC bosses turned to study him. Mitchell saluted briskly, and said: "Higgins reporting, sir!" The ABC men broke into laughter. Mitchell said to them: "You're not going to get away, you know." When the laughing died down, Treyz said: "Anybody who goes to such incredible lengths deserves to be listened to." The four of them discussed *Our Man Higgins,* and closed the deal on the spot. When the train stopped at the North Philadelphia Station, Mitchell got off—the agreement in his pocket—and took the next train back to New York [*Our Man Higgins* lasted one season].

In 1964, ABC was showing the pilot film of *12 O'clock High* to a group of executives from the Doyle, Dane, Bernbach advertising agency, and their very important client, Volkswagen. The group sat in a screening room engrossed, as Robert Lansing and his legions got on with the business of winning the war in Europe. Halfway through the film, an Air Force bomber group dropped an enormous load of bombs on a German city, and it went up in flames and smoke. A heavily accented German voice in the screening room was heard to say: "There goes our factory."

Volkswagen did not buy *12 O'clock High* [the show lasted two seasons].

In the Selling Season of 1964, one of the networks decided to be extremely stingy about whom they showed pilots to. "Sometimes, if you show a pilot to 15 or 20 prospective advertisers, without making the sale," an adverse chain reaction sets in. They 'badmouth' the show around, and pretty soon it's dead as a doornail."

The network decided to pick only the very best prospects, and then show each pilot to only one potential buyer at a time. At all other times, they would not let the prints of the pilots out of their sight.

This was probably sound Selling Season psychology, but it was a move which seriously aggrieved and aggravated the network's team of salesman, whose commissions customarily derive from the sale of these expensive properties. So the salesmen concocted a plan to defend their incomes: They would simply hijack pilot prints, smuggle them out of the network offices, then show them secretly in the homes of likely clients in the rich suburbs of New York City.

140   And that's what they did. In order to facilitate the heist, the salesmen transferred the pilots to cans bearing the names of innocuous
daytime shows—titles not calculated to arouse the curiosity of roving
network executives.

    Finally, on a Sunday morning, a network salesman—using one of
his bootleg prints—sold a very expensive show to a client at the
latter's home in New Canaan, Connecticut. Barely able to contain
his elation, he hurriedly telephoned his superior at the network,
and declared loudly: "I've just sold the _____ show," he said, naming
the proposed series. "A $300,000 order! The client says he thinks the
pilot is great!" The salesman's boss was nonplused. "How in Hades
can he think it's so great if he's never even seen it?" he demanded of
the salesman. Suddenly, the salesman realized he was trapped; he
sputtered, back-tracked, and finally blurted: "He took our word
for it!"

    Some shows—even ones which turn out in the end to be vastly
successful—go to 30, 40 or even 50 possible buyers before finding a
home, and are agonized over at each stop by top-ranking executives
and all their relatives. Others are sold with bewildering ease. Such
was the case with this year's *O.K. Crackerby!*

    ABC invited two men to their New York studios to see the pilot:
Bud Barry, an executive vice president at the Young & Rubicam advertising agency, and a leading executive of the Bristol-Meyers company, who ABC hoped would sponsor the show. They settled into
their chairs in the screening room, and the film came on. Ten minutes
later Barry took out a slip of paper, wrote on it, and handed it to the
Bristol-Meyers man. The note said: "Buy it." He did. The Burl Ives
starrer goes on in the fall [it was canceled the following January].

    Every important network programmer and ad agency vice pres-
ident has a list of vastly successful television series—which he turned
down flatly when they were offered to him. Even the most astute
judges of TV horse-flesh guess wrong some of the time—and live to
regret it.

    In the early 1950's a representative of one of the independent
production companies called on a leading ad-agency vice president
with a pilot which CBS was interested in, but was holding on the shelf
pending buyer interest. The ad man's reputation as a shrewd judge of
entertainment attraction was formidable.

    As the salesman was showing the pilot film, he noticed that his
audience of one was viewing it—a comedy—in stony silence. He
obviously was not amused. At the end, the ad man stood up, glared at

the salesman, and said: "You're kidding, right? It's a joke. This is a put-on." The salesman, aghast, assured him he was serious in offering the pilot. "Well, it's *terrible!*" said the executive. "I've never seen anything so ludicrous. No advertiser in his right mind is going to spend a cent on a clunker like that. Do you think a family in Dubuque is going to watch the misadventures of a washed-up ex-model and illiterate Mexican husband?"

The ad man was not quite perceptive enough to know that Desi Arnaz was a Cuban, not a Mexican, and that *I Love Lucy* would become the most popular comedy series in TV history.[3]

The reasons why pilots sometimes are not bought are as varied as the reasons why they are. The make of a brand of dog food once was invited by a network representative to see a pilot, in the expectation that he might want to sponsor the show.

The prospective buyer sat through the film and was obviously enjoying himself until there appeared on the screen an enormous German shepherd watchdog that was called upon to attack an intruder and wrestle him to earth.

The dog-food man darkened, his brows furrowed. When the film was over, he turned to the network representative and said: "I like the story, but tell me, does that watchdog have to be quite so ferocious?" The network man was puzzled. "Well, of course, He's a watchdog, isn't he?" The other man shook his head. "Bad for the product," he said. "No good for dog food." Thus, a sale was lost for want of a friendly watchdog.

When Bud Austin, now executive vice president at Filmways (producers of *The Beverly Hillbillies* and *Petticoat Junction*) was employed at Goodson-Todman, he was handed a new Western series to try to sell. One of his first stops was at the office of a network programming vice president, to whom he showed the pilot. When it was over, the network man turned to Austin, grimaced, and said:

"That is without a doubt the most miserable, amateurish, nonsensical, badly produced, foolishly written inept and inane hogwash I've ever had to sit through." "You're trying to tell me you don't like it," Austin said. "Right!" said the network man.

Chastened, but not discouraged, Austin next set up a screening for an important executive of the Young & Rubicam advertising agency. The man liked the pilot. In addition, he believed that an important Y & R client, who had headquarters in Chicago, might want to sponsor the series.

Austin and the ad man flew to Chicago the next day, showed the

142 pilot to the client, and—to the jubilation of both of them—he was highly enthusiastic about it. "There's only one thing," said the client. "We've already bought time on . . ."—he mentioned the network which had turned down the series so peremptorily only days earlier—". . . for next season. So naturally, they'll have to approve any series we want to do. But if this one suits them, we'll buy it."

Elated, Austin hurried back to New York, and to the office of the network programming vice president who had been so eloquent in his dismissal of the pilot. Austin confronted the man, and said: "Now about that Western series we were discussing, I want to tell you that. . . ."

The network man broke in and said: "I thought I told you what I think of that monstrosity. It's the most banal, dimwitted, numb-skulled pot-boiler I've seen in years, and I wouldn't touch it with. . . ." Austin broke in, saying: "Wait a minute! Wait a minute. I've found a buyer for it!" The network executive paused and observed Austin silently for a moment. He placed his palms down on the desk, smiled benignly, and leaned forward.

"Bud," he said. "That show is one of the finest, truest, most heart-warming and ennobling Western series I've seen in a long . . . long . . . time."

An ABC executive recalls, when his network was trying to find a sponsor for the *Ben Casey* series in 1961. The Selling Season was running out, and ABC was eager to sell the show and thus lock up its fall schedule.

They telephoned the office of an important potential sponsor. He was not in, but they finally located him at home. "We have a great new show for you," they told him. "Just the thing to move your product off those shelves. Come on over and see it." The client demurred. "I'm about to leave on a two-week fishing trip with my 12-year-old son," he said. "I can't possibly make it today." ABC's men were insistent. "It will take only an hour," they assured him. "This series is bound to be a winner. Bring your son with you, then you can go straight from here to your fishing trip."

The client relented. A short time later he and his son—both dressed for the trout streams—arrived at ABC's studios. They settled into their chairs as the lights went down, and the pilot film started. In a scene halfway through the pilot, Ben Casey was called upon to administer a hypodermic needle directly to the back of a young girl patient. A close-up showed the needle actually entering the girl's flesh. At that instant, a low moan was heard in the screening room, followed by a thump. The client's son had fainted dead away. The film was stopped, the lights came up, and a great deal of fanning, patting, and exhortation was required to revive the youngster. ABC's men were deeply apologetic.

The prospective buyer looked around at them, and said: "If this is what your series can do to a young boy, then I don't want any part of it." He gathered up his rather bleached-out son and went on to his fishing trip. Needless to add, he didn't buy *Casey.*

A week later, however, another sponsor did—the manufacturer of a product competitive with the fisherman's. *Ben Casey,* as is now history, went on to become an enormous success [it ran on ABC for five seasons]. The first potential buyer, who rejected *Casey,* told an ABC man later: "Every time I look at that kid and realize what he made me lose, I could rap him over the head with my fishing pole."

Many would-be television entrepreneurs are not above applying the techniques of the con game to the peddling of TV series. One such aspiring producer even managed to create a series out of thin air by carefully manipulating interest in a property that didn't exist.

The enterprising con man—let us call him Taylor—was employed as a underling at one of the major networks. He evolved an idea for a television series, then set about writing a lengthy treatment of it. When he had the presentation completed, he simply sat back and waited.

A few weeks later, the programming vice president of his network left for a two-week vacation. It was the signal for Taylor to put his plan into operation. He retrieved his presentation from his desk drawer, dated it, attached a memo, and had it delivered to the programming VP's desk bright and early on the first Monday morning of the executive's vacation. That meant it would be on ice for two weeks.

Taylor then began telephoning his many personal and professional friends in the newspaper and magazine business, tipping them off to this "hot new prospect"—the series he had outlined—which he claimed his network had under consideration for its forthcoming schedule. Items began to appear, describing the series and hinting at client interest. Important actors were named as being enthusiastic about starring in the series. Leading TV writers, said the columnists, had been approached about contributing scripts.

All this comprised Step One in the con man's game. As the second step, Taylor then enlisted the aid of other friends in some of New York's leading advertising agencies. He had them telephone the programming VP's office and request copies of a printed prospectus on this series they'd been hearing so much about.

144   The network executive's secretary had to tell them that no such prospectus existed, but that her boss would surely be in touch with them when he returned from vacation. The VP returned to his desk at the end of two weeks to find Taylor's presentation, a raft of newspaper clippings on the proposed series, and what appeared to be impressive sponsor interest from a dozen advertising agencies.

Hurriedly he called in Taylor, registered the idea as being in development, and set about fabricating a prospectus. Taylor then was paid the usual holding fee of $1200 as the originator of the series idea and was made executive producer in charge of developing a pilot film.

It had all gone like clockwork. The con man eventually shot a pilot which was, in fact, good enough to attract sponsorship, and the series went on the air the following autumn.

More than one television series has been created out of thin air, some more legitimately than others. The TV Establishment contains a few dozen men with sufficient horsepower to do so in an aboveboard manner. In 1960, Warner Brothers ABC series *SurfSide* 6 had just such a birth, and the manner of conception illuminates some of the complex scheming which characterizes the Selling Season.

Dick Pinkham, a vice president of Ted Bates advertising agency, had in hand a number of Bates clients who were eager to sponsor a show. None wanted the great financial responsibility of a whole show, but each was willing to pick up part of the tab for a series. Pinkham had the idea he might lump them all together—one of the early ventures in "participating" sponsorship which now is commonplace.

But Pinkham had no show for them. Thus it was necessary to create one—a commercially ironic application of Voltaire's axiom: "If God did not exist, it would be necessary to invent him." Pinkham telephoned William T. Orr, who heads Warner Brothers' TV department in California, and explained the problem.

He told Orr that ABC, which at that time was fighting for sales, would accept any reasonable vehicle in order to get business from his clients. So Pinkham and Orr stayed on the telephone Coast to Coast— for well over an hour—and composed a vehicle. The conversation went something like this:

"Give me a category in which practically every TV watcher is interested," Orr said. "Glamor," Pinkham replied. "Right," said Orr. "And young people." "Glamorous young people," Pinkham contributed. "And glamorous places," said Orr. "Acapulco, New York, Miami Beach."

"Adventure and intrigue," Pinkham said. "And sunshine."   *145*

Orr told Pinkham about a number of young players Warner's had under contract: Troy Donahue, Diane McBain, Lee Patterson, Van Williams. They settled on Miami Beach and an adventure-detective format. They evolved a houseboat to take advantage of Miami's aquatic aspects. All the important details of what eventually became *SurfSide* 6 were decided by the end of the phone conversation. All that remained was for Orr to hand the framework to scriptwriters and have them commence the job of cranking out stories.

Pinkham, for his part, bought time on ABC and began describing to his eagerly awaiting clients this fascinating new series he had "found" for them. It enjoyed a two-year run.

There was once a series called . . . well, never mind, let it rest in peace. The pilot film of this particular Western epic was so bad that even the producer knew it was rotten. "The lead actor mumbled so that scarcely a word could be understood," he told TV GUIDE, in a moment of retrospective candor. "The story was incredible. It made no sense at all. The scenery was palpably fake. The whole thing looked like a nickelodeon movie. The leading lady had one drooping eyelid. The horses were superannuated and swaybacked. It was B-A-D bad."

The pilot had been shown to scores of potential buyers and spurned at every turn. Finally, the producer decided on a bargain-basement technique to unload this horror: With every additional screening to a prospective buyer, he removed a thousand dollars from the asking price. The pilot rapidly was reaching the financial point of no return.

The weary producer arrived at the umpteenth screening, turned on the projector, and slumped down in a seat in the darkness, a dozen feet from two client representatives who had come to see his handiwork. The producer's embarrassment was acute, and he closed his eyes and tried to make the time go faster.

Then he heard the voices of the clients. One was saying: "This is great stuff." "Very exciting," said the other. "I love it." "Terrific story."

The producer perked his ears, scarcely able to believe what he was hearing. But the two clients continued to extol the film. They appeared even to understand what the leading actor was saying.

The producer sat up and began to keep score on his fingers. With every admiring remark from the pair of potential buyers, he restored another thousand dollars to the pilot's selling price. By the

146   time the pilot was over, its price was as high as it had ever been. The two clients stood up, smiled, asked how much, and said: "We'll buy it."

All of which proves that in television, just as in everything else, there's no accounting for taste.

The Show That Died After One Night

By Richard K. Doan and Joseph Finnigan

MAY 17, 1969

It's just possible there's a case for the social scientists in what happened the night of February 5, 1969. That was the night, you may recall, that 16 or 17 million Americans looked in on the premiere of an ABC "second season" series named *Turn-On* and were so violently turned off by what they saw that the network had to call off the series the next day.

That alone made *Turn-On* one for the books. Not many series have played one-night stands. What made it all the more remarkable was that *Turn-On* had been concocted by the very people who cook up the fabulously popular *Laugh-In* every week. How could they have laid such an egg? Worse yet, how could watching it be such a revolting experience to so many people that, perhaps for the first time in TV history, half the stations in a network line-up overnight refused to air any more of the series?

Was *Turn-On* all that "dirty"? "Vulgar"? "Irreverent"? All these words cropped up in the morning-after uproar. Yet a lot of viewers professed not to find the program particularly offensive.

So what was it? Was *Turn-On* so far-out that it disturbed viewers' sense of propriety? Was it something they didn't like to see, so they hated it and were enraged by it, somewhat in the way millions of people reacted to the rioting caught by the cameras in Chicago's downtown last August?

In short, was February 5 a turning point in television history— a moment when the viewers, including critics and not a few local broadcasters, served notice that they felt that TV should not dabble in wildly offbeat, distasteful entertainment?

If an impartial answer is possible, it may be that countless viewers were instinctively repelled by *Turn-On* because they expected it to be another *Laugh-In* and found it instead a strange, frenetic, pointless string of blackouts that added up to a crude fraud. It had no

147

148 emcee, no narration, no apparent theme. It was a collection of unfunny gags and skits bridged by electronic music. For some reason, many viewers were so repelled or confused or antagonized by it, they came away with no real recollections of *what* it was all about!

"All I can remember," one shocked woman viewer told TV GUIDE, "is the word 'sex,' in huge letters, pounding across the screen." It was *Turn-On*'s most sustained sequence, running several minutes. "Sex," its letters changing colors and emphasis—"Sex!", "Sex?", and so forth—flashed in center screen while the faces of guest-star Tim Conway and actress Bonnie Boland flitted in and out of the picture, mugging suggestively at each other, to the tune of throbbing electronic sounds building in intensity.

Conway turned up in many skits, among them a series of police-station booking scenes in which he was the culprit. After being told each time that he was charged with assorted crimes "and first-degree murder," he would demand to use the phone. Thereupon he would, say, order a ham sandwich. It was that funny.

Periodically throughout the half-hour, production credits would turn up. Periodically, flashing lights on a control board would suggest that the whole affair was computerized. To one perceptive viewer, it seemed to represent somebody's notion of how to prove Marshall McLuhan's proposition that "the medium is the message." And it overstrained.

As a spin-off of a currently hot show, it added up to a kind of simple-minded distillation of the dregs of *Laugh-In,* deprived of *Laugh-In*'s fun and stars but gutted by *Laugh-In*'s dirtier intents. It lacked impact. And it wasn't really so obscene as it was just off-color and unsophisticated.

Or so some professional TV watchers argue. Out along the network line, the feeling was that *Turn-On* had plainly gone too far. Don Perris, general manager of WEWS, Cleveland, wired ABC-TV president Elton Rule: "If your naughty little boys have to write dirty words on the walls, please don't use our walls." WEWS, Perris promised, would carry no more of *Turn-On*.

WEWS had a lot of company. "The real reason the show was canceled," one insider confided afterward, "was that there wasn't any network left. It was a case—maybe the first one in history—of the stations canceling out a network." Two days after the ill-fated premiere, it appears, no less than 75 stations, representing about half the ABC line-up for the show, had served notice *Turn-On* was anathema to them.

In city after city, station people reported that their viewers cast the deciding vote. "We just couldn't handle all the calls," says Gene McCurdy of Philadelphia's WFIL-TV. "There were no pros—only antis. We canceled the show right away." In Baltimore, reactions ran "three to one against the show," says Paul Coss of WJZ-TV. "I think we'd have dropped the show even if ABC hadn't." New Haven's WNHC-TV got "an instantaneous and heavy 'no' reaction," according to Howard Maschmeier—even after the station had aired announcements cautioning that *Turn-On* was "for mature viewers." All of the stations had prescreened the show and, as Maschmeier put it, "had misgivings, but felt that the program should have its day in court."

Leonard Goldberg, 35, who at the time was vice president of ABC-TV programming (he resigned that post in early April to become a Hollywood producer), calmly admits there was no alternative to cancellation: "The critics blasted the show. And we heard from the stations *loud* and *clear*. They felt it was not the kind of show we should have on our network. But most importantly, we heard from the viewers. The response was overwhelmingly negative. There really wasn't any decision for us to make—the feeling was so unanimous."

Precisely how many viewers sounded their nays, ABC officials characteristically declined to reveal. There can be little doubt the number was substantial. One source described it as "a tidal wave."

Robert Doubleday, who runs KATV, Little Rock, Arkansas, and is chairman of ABC affiliates board representing the stations airing ABC's shows, says he can remember no previous instance when dislike of a new series was so immediate, violent and widespread. He got letters "from all over the United States"—about 200 of them, he guessed—"saying 'we want to thank you and congratulate you' for canceling the show." The viewers had got his name, Doubleday explained, from news stories reporting his stand against carrying *Turn-On* further.

The Little Rock broadcaster confesses he previewed the show two days before air date, decided it was "in poor taste" and so advised ABC, but he let it go on his channel because he did not like setting himself up "as judge and jury." His viewers didn't hesitate to. They found it not only "dirty" and "irreverent" but "tasteless," he reported.

Doubleday isn't sure, though, the fiasco won't "have a good effect in the long run." He thinks it might have told the Hollywood producers and New York decision makers that most people still have standards of taste and morality. "It would be a good idea," he suggests, "to load these people who do those TV series into Greyhound buses and take them on a trip across the country to show them how the rest of the people live."

150   Who were "those people" who thought the country was ready for *Turn-On?* One was Marvin Koslow, advertising boss of Bristol-Myers, the big pharmaceutical concern. Last spring he approached Ed Friendly and George Schlatter, *Laugh-In's* packagers (who recently won the Producers Guild of America award as "best TV producers of 1968") and asked them to try to come up with a new half-hour TV series. He wanted "something unusual and provocative," says Digby Wolfe, a Friendly-Schlatter executive.

Turn-On had been kicking around as a concept predating *Laugh-In,* according to Wolfe. "Actually, it was closer to the original *Laugh-In.*" Wolfe got the job of producing *Turn-On* and a pilot was taped.

If it was supposed to be a variation on *Laugh-In,* Len Goldberg didn't see it what way. "The name *Laugh-In* never came up in our discussions of the show," the former ABC executive claims. "We were striving for something different. We were seeking a completely new form for TV."

ABC, however, had not come into the picture until after the pilot was made and Koslow and his advertising agency, Young & Rubicam, were shopping the networks for a time slot. CBS and NBC programmers looked at the pilot and turned the show down. "It was not any good," an NBC official indicated. "It wasn't funny, to begin with. And in many areas it was in bad taste." A CBS executive reported, "We said no, thank you. Not so much because the show was dirty but because there was not a joke in it. Also, it was so fast with the cuts and chops that some of our people actually got physically disturbed by it!"

A second pilot was put together—but neither was aired as the premiere. "I don't know why," the NBC man observed, "because the pilot we saw was an Academy Award winner alongside the thing ABC put on the air."

John Naylor, an N.W. Ayer ad-agency vice president who bought a spot in *Turn-On* for the American Telephone and Telegraph Company (Bristol-Myers had decided to share the sponsorship with others), says he saw a pilot but wasn't shown the air show before it was telecast. "We weren't thrilled by the pilot," he recalls, "and the network wasn't either, but they promised to make improvements in it."

Goldberg admits that the show wasn't all the network would have liked it to be. "We recognized that it was going to take a while to refine the idea," he explains. "But we felt we were dealing with very creative people in Friendly and Schlatter and Wolfe, and I still think what we were trying to do was right—we were breaking new ground. . . . Look, we were not trying for another *Family Affair.* This was an effort to come up with a new form."

Was he prepared for the wave of revulsion? "I was surprised, yes," he said. "But then, these are volatile times. You can never be sure *how* people are going to react. The people in this case spoke. *Everybody* spoke! One thing you can say for sure: that audience out there isn't passive."

He felt no need for abject apologies. "I hope," he concluded, "we're big enough to admit we just made a mistake." The mistake cost something over a million dollars—Friendly and Schlatter had scripted nine shows and shot seven of them—but Goldberg at that moment could not say whose loss it would be. A "settlement" was being worked out among everybody involved, he said.

Of one thing there could be little doubt: most, if not all, of the people who had a hand in bringing *Turn-On* to the air had misguessed its fate. Testifying before a Senate hearing on television sex and violence a couple of weeks after the *Turn-On* debacle, ABC-TV president Elton Rule confessed sadly that the network had felt the new series would be "an immense success or an immense bomb—and it turned out to be the latter." He lamely argued that "the form, not the content" had been at fault.

"It was a little bit on the risque side, wasn't it?" asked Senator John O. Pastore (D.,R.I.), one of Capitol Hill's sharpest TV critics (see pp. 340-344). Rule confessed it was. But he also claimed that "we did nothing [in the show] that is not seen on TV every week."

Digby Wolfe remembers: "The first showing was at Technicolor [studios in Hollywood], when ABC, the sponsors and agency saw it two and a half weeks before air. The praise, I think, was unqualified. Marv Koslow said he was delighted. We had implemented all the changes he wanted and delivered him a better show that expected. Len Goldberg added his agreement to these sentiments and said he felt we had a hit."

Producers Friendly and Schlatter still aren't willing to admit they manufactured a bomb. "I'll grant it wasn't something for the *Peyton Place* types," Schlatter snaps. (*Turn-On* had replaced *Peyton Place II.*) "It was designed to get more than passive reaction from the audience. It was really not a show; it was an experience, a happening. It was meant to be disturbing. It was provocative, adult, sophisticated. It was environmental comedy. At no time did we set out to offend. We set out to reflect our times. If we offended, we're sorry. But the fact that it was taken off doesn't mean it was unsuccessful. It only means it's going to take a little time before we can do it again.

"The crime is that this show took a year to produce; it involved 14 brand-new, shiny, young writers, average age under 30, and seven brand-new, young editors, and a lot of other shiny new talent—

all of it snuffed out now because the responsibility for American tastes was put in the stations' hands. It's a shame."

Friendly is equally vociferous. "Television has for so long, as everybody knows, been aimed at the 12-year-old mentality. The audience is used to being spoonfed. What we did was experimental television in prime time. I think you'll see a show in this form in a year or two or three. . . . If *Turn-On* failed, it failed by being ahead of itself. The most unfortunate part of this whole affair is that democracy didn't rule. The vast majority of people never got a chance to look at *Turn-On* and vote how they felt about it." Friendly praised Koslow, the sponsor's ad man, as "one of the real brave guys of this business" for being willing to put up money for *Turn-On*.

But one participant in *l'affaire Turn-On* who can't afford to be identified commented: "There were 300 jokes in that show, enough to offend everybody, regardless of race, religion or national origin. We just went totally wrong in our judgment. I think we just got used to looking at the show and seeing it improve. . . . There were two things basically wrong with it: there wasn't any sort of identification with the audience—just a bunch of strangers up there insulting everything you believe in. And secondly, it wasn't funny enough."

Koslow was the only key figure involved who declined to talk about the show at all with TV GUIDE.

A Friendly-Schlatter secretary was one of the few who had sensed impending disaster. At a party following a press screening of the show, she confided to a reporter: "We're going to get a lot of hate mail." Something over a million dollars' worth, as it turned out.

Daytime Programming

The daytime television audience and the evening prime-time audience differ in two very significant aspects—size and composition. The daytime audience is much more constant. For example, while the average percentage of total television homes viewing television between 7 and 11 P.M. varied between 44.4 percent in July, 1969, and 61.4 percent in November, 1969, the corresponding seasonal variations in daytime viewing (9 A.M.-4 P.M.) were only 24.24 percent and 23.78 percent. Moreover, two-thirds of the daytime audience are women and thus it is much more homogeneous than the nighttime television audience.

Consequently, the daytime audience attracts a more limited and homogeneous group of advertisers than does the evening audience. Over 90 percent of daytime net billings are for toilet requisites, proprietary medicines, soaps and cleansers, and food products. This limited group of advertisers has in turn meant little experimentation in programming.

Soap opera is the main staple of daytime television, just as it was for daytime radio. Nine of the ten top-rated shows in 1968-69 were of this genre; and the soap operas are followed regularly by eighteen million viewers, 70 percent of whom are adult women.

Herta Herzog, in a classic study on the radio soap operas which was first published in 1943, suggested that daytime radio serials had three major attractions: they were a means of emotional release (catharsis); they provided opportunities for wishful thinking (projection); and the advice obtained from the characters helped the listener to deal more effectively with life and its problems. While no major study has been undertaken of the reasons people watch daytime television serials, it is likely the findings would closely correspond with those of Miss Herzog.

During the last few years, soap operas have been becoming progressively more contemporary. This development is part of the general trend in all feminine-oriented media toward more con-

153

154   temporary themes. Also, producers of television soaps are attempting to attract the younger housewives; traditionally, the soap operas have received higher ratings from homes in which the lady of the house is 50 or older, while the housewives in the age bracket from 35 to 49 have not been avid soap opera fans.

The recent changes in the development of the soaps are discussed by Edith Efron and Marya Mannes. Miss Efron (pp. 156-162) considers the major change to be the transition from the fundamental theme of the housewife struggling against overwhelming adversity to that of the male-female relationship. In contemporary soaps, the central source of drama and conflict is mating, marriage and reproduction of the species, and it is from this cycle that the basic value system emerges. The good and the bad people are defined by their approach to sex, their view of marriage and their attitudes toward children. But the sex that the soaps are peddling is, according to Miss Efron, soggy and dreary. The producers contend that their themes are identifiable and realistic to the public; Miss Efron feels that contemporary soaps portray a sick aspect of society and they exploit women by extolling childishness and dependency. The contemporary soaps are, in fact, anti-feminine.

Although daytime serials are finally recognizing some current social manifestations, Miss Mannes (pp. 163-168) feels they still basically portray a world with values and attitudes which are neither relevant to the present nor useful preparation for the future. Miss Mannes compares a real middle-class suburban housewife with her serial counterpart and shows how a number of existing realities are not reflected in the soaps. Suspension of reality is deliberately perpetuated because of the widespread belief on the part of television programmers that a mood of escape is essential to attract the daytime audience and to sell the sponsor's product. This attitude is particularly disturbing to the author who sees the serial drama as an ideal framework to gain new and exciting insights into the human condition.

The quiz shows have, since the Quiz Scandals of the late 1950's, become almost the exclusive province of daytime television and now rank second to the soaps as a daytime staple. Most of these shows are aimed at the younger housewives. Like the soap operas, the quiz shows have been modernized, with a change of emphasis in the latter from financial rewards to entertainment and personalities. The networks, however, still consider the game to be of primary importance, believing that viewers desire a form of escape which occurs when watching ordinary people win big prizes.

Edith Efron (pp. 169-173) disagrees with the networks. She main- *155*
tains that the public is not particularly interested in the monetary
rewards and points out that viewers often cannot even remember what
prizes were awarded on the shows. Miss Efron cites several prominent
psychologists and quiz show producers in support of her contention
that quiz watchers do not crave escape, but rather desire to test their
mental skills and abilities. The networks insist that the great majority
of the daytime audiences are women who are too busy with household chores to have the time or inclination for exhaustive intellectual
experiences. This assumption is based on the failure of several daytime news and talk shows. According to Miss Efron, the networks
confuse public-affairs stuffiness with intellectual programming.

The absence of any research on the IQ distribution in the daytime
(or nighttime) audience leaves the debate unresolved and it is unlikely that more mentally demanding shows will be offered to the
daytime viewer in the near future.

The Soaps—Anything But 99-44/100 Percent Pure

By Edith Efron

MARCH 13, 1965

Some months ago, the sleepy, Victorian world of daytime drama made news. The news was that it had ceased to be sleepy and Victorian. In fact, said the reports, the soap operas were doing something no one could quite believe: "peddling sex."

Announced one astounded critic: "Folks squawking about cheap nighttime sex should harken to the sickly sexuality of daytime soap opera. *Love of Life* details frank affairs between married women and men; *Search for Tomorrow* has a single girl in an affair with a married man, result: pregnancy; *The Secret Storm* has another single girl expecting a married man's child."

And, under the headlines "Era of Souped-Up Soapers" and "Torrid Days on TV Serial Front," *Variety,* the weekly newspaper of the entertainment industry, reported that there was a daytime "race to dredge up the most lurid incidents in sex-based human wretchedness," and cited "a torrid couch scene involving a housewife with gown cleaved to the navel who was sloshed to the gills on martinis, working her wiles on a husband (not hers). The fade to detergent blurb left little doubt as to the ensuing action."

Even a superficial investigation of events in the soap-opera world confirms that these reports are true.

To understand this phenomenon, one must enter the total universe of the soap operas. And if one does, one soon discovers that the central source of drama is not what it used to be in the old days, when the brave housewife, with husband in wheel chair, struggled helplessly against adversity. The soaps have shifted drastically on their axes; the fundamental theme today is, as Roy Winsor, producer of *Secret Storm*, puts it: "the male-female relationship."

More specifically, the theme of nine of the 10 daytime shows on the air when this study was launched[4] is the mating-martial-reproductive cycle set against a domestic background. The outer world is certainly present—one catches glimpses of hospitals, offices, court-rooms, business establishments—but the external events tend to be a foil for the more fundamental drama, which is rooted in the biological life cycle. Almost all dramatic tension and moral conflict emerge from three basic sources: mating, marriage and babies.

The mating process is the cornerstone of this trivalue system. The act of searching for a partner goes on constantly in the world of soap opera. Vacuous teen-age girls have no thought whatever in their heads except hunting for a man. Older women wander about, projecting their intense longing to link themselves to unattached males. Heavily made-up villainous "career women" prowl, relentlessly seeking and nabbing their prey: the married man. Sad, lonely divorcées hunt for new mates.

This all-consuming, single-minded search for a mate is an absolute good in the soap-opera syndrome. Morality—and dramatic conflict—emerge from how the search is conducted. Accordingly, there is sex as approached by "good" people, and sex as it is approached by villains.

"Good" people's sex is a somewhat extraordinary phenomenon, which can best be described as "icky." In *The Doctors*, Dr. Maggie confides, coyly, to her sister: "He kissed me." Her sister asks, even more coyly: "Did you want him to kiss you?" Maggie wriggles, and says: "He says I did." Then archly adds: "You know? I did." Maggie has already been married; her sister has had at least one lover. Coyness, not chastity, is the sign of their virtue.

"Good" people's sex is also passive, diffident and apologetic. In *The Doctors*, Sam, after an unendurably long buildup, finally takes Dr. Althea, a troubled divorcée, in his arms, and kisses her once, gently, on the lips. He then looks rueful, says, "I'm sorry," and moves to look mournfully out the window. "I'm not," murmurs Althea softly, and floats out of the room.

The "good" people act like saddened goldfish; the villains, on the other hand, are merely grotesque. One gets the impression that villains, both male and female, have read a lot of Ian Fleming, through several layers of cheesecloth.

To wit: a dinner between villainess Valerie Shaw and Dr. Matt in *The Doctors* in which Valerie leers, ogles and hints ("A smart woman judges a man by his mouth. . . . Yours is strong and sensual. I'm glad I came to dinner"), announces she will be his "playmate" and boasts throatily, "I play hard and seriously—but not necessarily for keeps."

And in *Love of Life* a sinister chap named Ace drinks in a bar with

158 a teen-age girl who used to be his mistress. "We used to ignite," he breathes insinuatingly. They exchange a kiss—presumably so inflammable that the camera nervously cuts the picture off beneath their chins. "Not bad, baby," he gasps heavily.

This endless mating game, of course, has a purpose: It leads to marriage, the second arch-value in the soap-opera universe. And the dominant view of marriage in the soaps is also worthy of mention. According to the "good" women, it consists of two ingredients: "love" and homemaking.

"Love," in the soaps, tends to be a kind of hospitalization insurance, usually provided by females to male emotional cripples. In these plays, a woman rarely pledges herself to "honor and obey" her husband. She pledges to cure him of his alcoholism, to forgive his criminal record, paranoia, pathological lying, premarital affairs—and, generally, to give him a shoulder to cry on.

An expression of love, or a marriage proposal, in the daytime shows, often sounds like a sobbing confession to a psychiatrist. In *Search for Tomorrow* Patti's father, a reformed drinker, took time out from brooding over his daughter's illegitimate pregnancy to express his "love" for his wife. It consisted of a thorough—and convincing—rehash of his general worthlessness and former drinking habits. "I need you," he moaned. "That's all I want," she said.

In *General Hospital* Connie's neurotic helplessness proved irresistible some weeks ago; Dr. Doug declared his love. They engaged in a weird verbal competition as to who was more helpless than whom, who was more scared than whom, who "needed" whom more than whom. Doug won. Connie would be his pillar of strength.

Homemaking, the second ingredient of a "good" woman's marriage, is actually a symbolic expression of "love." There is a fantastic amount of discussion of food on these shows, and it is all strangely full of marital meaning. On *The Guiding Light* the audience sat through a detailed preview of the plans for roasting a turkey (the stuffing has raisins in it), which somehow would help get separated Julie and Michael together again. On *The Doctors* one ham was cooked, eaten and remorselessly discussed for three days; it played a critical role in the romance of Sam and Dr. Althea.

If domesticity is a marital "good," aversion to it is a serious evil. On *Secret Storm* a husband's arrival from work was greeted by a violent outburst by his wife, who handed him a list of jobs he had not done around the house. His neglect of the curtain rod was a sure sign that he was in love with a temptress who works in his office. Conversely, if a wife neglects her house, the marriage is rocky.

After mating and marriage, the third crucial value in the soap-opera universe is reproduction. The perpetuation of the species is the ultimate goal toward which almost all "good" people strive. And "The Baby" is the household god.

"Good" people discuss pregnancy endlessly. Young wives are either longing to be pregnant, worried because they are not pregnant, getting pregnant or fighting heroically "not to lose the baby." And at whatever stage of this process they happen to be, it justifies their being inept, irritable, hysterical and irrational.

"Good" men, needless to say, are unfailingly sympathetic to the reproductive process and are apparently fascinated by every detail of it. In *The Doctors* you knew one chap was a "good" husband because he referred to himself as "an expectant father" and earnestly discussed his wife's "whoopsing" with his friends.

The superlative value of "The Baby" is best revealed when he makes his appearance without benefit of a marriage license. He is usually brought into the world by a blank-faced little girl who has been taught to believe that the only valid goal in life is to mate, marry and reproduce, and who has jumped the gun. The social problem caused by this error in timing is solved in different ways. The girl has an abortion (Patricia, *Another World*); she loses the baby in an accident (Patti, *Search for Tomorrow*); she gives the baby up for adoption (Ellen, *As the World Turns*); she has the baby and marries its father (Julie, *Guiding Light*); she has the baby and marries someone else (Amy, *Secret Storm*).

The attitude of the baby-worshipping "good" people to this ominpresent social catastrophe is strangely mixed. The girl is viewed as a helpless victim of male villainy: "She loved the fellow too much," said Angie's father sadly in *General Hospital*. Of course, she has acquired the baby "the wrong way" and must—and does—suffer endlessly because of it. Nonetheless, she is having "The Baby." Thus she receives an enormous amount of sympathy, guidance and help from "good" people.

It seems almost unnecessary to say that only "bad" people in soap operas are anti-baby. The fastest bit of characterization ever accomplished in the history of drama was achieved on *Secret Storm,* when Kip's father recently arrived on the scene. He said: "I can't stand all this talk about babies." This instantly established him as a black-hearted villain.

The worst people of all, in the soaps, however, are the "career women," unnatural creatures who actually enjoy some activity other than reproducing the species. With the single exception of *The*

160   *Doctors,* which features two "good" career women, Drs. Maggie and Althea, even the feeblest flicker of a desire for a career is a symptom of villainy in a women who has a man to support her. Some weeks ago, we could predict that Ann Reynolds, in *The Young Marrieds,* was heading for dire trouble. She was miserable over her lost career, she had no babies, and she said those most evil of words: "I want a purpose in life."

It is hardly surprising to discover that even when the female characters achieve their stated ideal, they are almost invariably miserable. A man to support them, an empty house to sit in, no mentally demanding work to do and an endless vista of future pregnancies do not seem to satisy the younger soap-opera ladies. They are chronically bored and hysterical.

They also live in dread of the ever-present threat of adultery, because their husbands go outside every day and meet wicked career women." They also agonize frequently over the clash between their "needs as a woman" and their "needs as a mother."

The male denizens of this universe are equally miserable for parallel reasons. They suffer quite a bit from unrequited love. They are often sick with jealousy, tortured by their wives' jealousy of their careers and outer-world existance. They, too, have a remarkable amount of trouble reconciling their "needs as men" with their "needs as fathers."

So we find, amid all the gloom in Sudsville, a lot of drinking, epidemic infidelity, and countless cases of acute neurosis, criminality, psychotic breakdowns and postmaternal psychosis.

And this, dear reader, is the "sex" that the soap operas are "peddling" these days. It is a soggy, dreary spectacle of human misery, and is unworthy of all those "torrid" headlines. In fact, if one wants to be soured forever on the male-female relationship, the fastest way to achieve this state is to watch daytime drama.

The real question is not "where did all the sex come from?" but where did this depressing view of the male-female relationship come from? Hardened observers of TV's manners and mores have claimed that sex is being stressed in the soaps because it "sells." But the producers of soaps retort hotly that this has nothing to do with it. Their story lines, they insist, simply reflect social reality.

Says Frank Dodge, producer of *Search for Tomorrow:* "We always try to do shows that are identiflable to the public. These shows are a recognition of existing emotions and problems. It's not collusion, but a logical coincidence that adultery, illegitimate children and abortions are appearing on many shows. If you read the papers about what's going on in the suburbs—well, it's more startling than what's shown on the air."

"The moral fiber has been shattered in this Nation, and nothing has replaced it," says Roy Winsor, producer of *Secret Storm*. "There's a clammy cynicism about life in general. It deeply infects the young. It leads to a generation that sits, passively, and watches the world go by. The major interest is the male-female relationship. That's the direction the daytime shows are going in. Some of the contemporary sickness has rubbed off onto TV."

A consultation with some authorities on feminine and family psychology seems to support these gentlemen's contentions about the soap operas. "They're realistic," says Dr. Harold Greenwald, training analyst of the National Psychological Association for Psychoanalysis and supervising psychologist of the Community Guidance Service in New York. "I think they're more realistic than many of the evening shows. They're reflecting the changes taking place in our society. There are fewer taboos. The age of sexual activity in the middle classes had dropped and it has increased in frequency. There is more infidelity. These plays reflect these problems."

Dr. William Menaker, professor of clinical psychology at New York University, says: "The theater, the novel, and the film have always reflected people's concern with the sexual life; and in this sense, what's on the air reflects these realities of life. Increasing frankness in dealing with these problems isn't a symptom of moral decay but rather reflects the confused values of a transitional period of socio-sexual change.

"Unfortunately, the vision of sex that seems to emerge on these shows is mechanical and adolescent, immature. The 'love' seems equally childish; it is interacting dependency, rather than a mutual relating between two autonomous adults. As for anti-intellectualism of these shows, it is actually antifeminine. It shows the resistance of both writers and audience to the development of the total feminine personality. There is no doubt that these shows are a partial reflection of some existing trends in our society; it is not a healthy picture."

Finally, Betty Friedan, author of *The Feminine Mystique*,[5] says: "The image of woman that emerges in these soap operas is precisely what I've called 'The Feminine Mystique.' The women are childish and dependent; the men are degraded because they relate to women who are childish and dependent; and the view of sex that emerges is sick. These plays reflect an image built up out of the sickest, most dependent, most immature women in our society. They do not reflect all women. In reality there are many who are independent,

162   mature, and who posses identity. The soaps are reflecting the sickest aspect of women."

On the basis of these comments, one can certainly conclude that all this "sex-based human wretchedness" is on the air because it exists in society. And the producers' claims that this is dramatic "realism" appear to have some validity.

But does the fact that a phenomenon exists justify its incessant exploration by the daytime dramas? Two of the three experts consulted actively refrain from making moral judgments. Betty Friedan, however, does not hesitate to condemn the soap operas. "The fact that immature, sick, dependent women exist in our society is no justification for these plays," she says. "The soap operas are playing to this sickness. They are feeding it. They are helping to keep women in this helpless, dependent state."

Everything's Up-to-Date in Soap Operas

By Marya Mannes

MARCH 15, 1969

The other afternoon I turned on *The Edge of Night* by accident (I confess to being accident prone) and couldn't believe my eyes. Cookie Thomas was wearing a pantsuit! Was it possible that the makers of soap operas really knew what was going on in the world?

This question is asked by one fairly regular observer of three serials in particular—*Search for Tomorrow, The Secret Storm* and *The Edge of Night* (with an occasional peep at *The Guiding Light*), who cannot therefore claim knowledge of the whole spectrum and of any revolutionary developments introduced into the other nine network soap operas. Certainly, the daytime serial as a whole has finally been reconizing such current social manifestations as drug addiction, youth alienation and revolt, blacks (in small parts), poverty, loan-sharking, mental illness and sex.

And I remember with happy disbelief a very brief scene in which a girl and a boy were having an argument on a park bench about commitment and involvement, about changing society. The girl was all for it, the boy said "Naah," or words to that effect. But at least it was the kind of talk two contemporary kids might have almost anywhere.

As for sex, the pleasures of adultery are now clearly conveyed, if roundly condemned, and marital ties now permit the kind of kissing formerly reserved for illicit couples or moving pictures. For a number of years, moreover, unmarried pregnancies have been an essential staple. Since the decent ladies in the soap have nothing to do in life but give birth, in or out of wedlock, drink coffee, prepare meals, and worry about other people, waiting for Baby is second only to crime and illness in the emotional graph of these small-screen fables.

But in all other ways, soap opera still concerns itself basically with one kind of America: the comfortable suburban life of white, middle-class Protestants, the homes always impeccably neat and

163

164 ultraconservative, the men either lawyers, doctors, small-business-men or newspaper types, the women always perfectly coiffed and smartly attired, the forces of good and the forces of evil neatly opposed, love finally triumphant over obstacles that would have mired Eros himself.

In short they recognize a world that simply does not exist, which is doubtless why the serials fascinate millions of women and sell millions of dollars worth of detergents, cake mixes, deodorants, tooth pastes, polishes and illusions. The major illusion—of reality—is sustained by domestic situations familiar to most people and dialogue so simple and explicit that a dropout would understand it. It is also sustained by men and women who might be the people next door, only better-looking. I refer now to the good people. The bad people—criminals, lechers, career women and divorcées—usually live farther away.

Perhaps the unreality of soap opera can be best conveyed by suggesting certain basic realities that it consistently fails to reflect. Some of these may seem trivial, some are serious. Among the former, let's compare a real woman in her home—middle-class and suburban, if you will—with her serial counterpart.

In the daytime real women do not do their housework in per-fectly pressed little luncheon dresses, with street shoes and coiffures fresh from the dryer. In the absence of their husbands and in the interest of their labors, real wives are often in housedresses or slacks and flat slippers. Their hair is, at the least, inclined to casualness, with detached or errant strands, when it is not—at the worst—in curlers.

Real women have food and condiments on their kitchen counters, books in their bookshelves, and magazines or papers on their living-room tables. Soap-wives never have. Soap-wives never read, do exercises, play musical instruments, have hobbies, take home-courses, serve as substitute teachers, watch the UN on TV, think. Most inde-fensible of all in a program designed for women is this total limitation of their horizons. They are given no independence of mind, spirit or action, as individual human beings; the role assigned them as wife and mother is assumed to permit no extensions and no additions.

It also appears singularly free of the usual human indulgences and small pleasures. When real women have cozy chats in the late afternoon with other women, they often offer them drinks. Soap operas maintain that quaint assumption that good women refuse them even when proffered by a man. Only single or career women lap them up, but that's because they're unstable anyway.

Now for the "parties" in videoland. These little get-togethers 165
of close friends and families are social disasters. If the talk is not
merely a recap of the plot line, it is of an awkwardness that defies
description. It alternates embarrassing revelations with strained
silences which neither the housewife-hostess nor her spouse seems
able to avoid or repair. I doubt if even the dullest suburban group is
as inept in human intercourse or simple manners as these serial
disasters which even liquor cannot ameliorate.

It appears doubtful, in fact, that soap-opera writers have had
any direct contact with really interesting human beings, possessed
of wit or intellect. The only character I can think of in serials who
has a genuine spark of sophistication and humor is Frank Carver of
The Secret Storm, and I don't blame Susan for being hooked on him.
Yet judging from the types presented as writers, or journalists, or
painters, acquaintance with the creative process seems minimal in
soap-opera terms.

The young "writer" (lately invisible) in *The Edge of Night* was
a prime example. Afflicted with a girl-wife of unparalleled stupidity,
he nevertheless told her the "plots" of his hitherto unwritten works,
tapped them out in their small apartment (he refused to live on her
rich father's money) while she hovered anxiously over him, and
betrayed by no word or act that he was capable of coherent thought,
let alone professional routine.

A more intelligent fellow, Nick in *The Secret Storm,* is a newspaper columnist who writes apparently splendid short stories in his
spare time at night in the apartment he shared (until recently) with
his virago spouse. He manages to accomplish this feat while she,
too, not only hovers but reviles him for wasting his time when he
should be getting rich.

Now reporters can write in a newspaper city room surrounded by
a hundred other clattering people, but I know of no free-lance "creative" writer who can get anything done with anyone else in the room,
including his wife.

That goes for artists too, of course, I remember a few years back
a young woman painter married to a young Ames (*The Secret Storm*
again) who daubed away happily in her smock while friend and foe
tramped through her studio, making comments. Since she has long
been absent from the screen, she must have come to no good end
while I wasn't looking.

Again, these palpable unrealities may seem unimportant and
even trivial in themselves. But they add up in the end to television's
prevailing sins: the perpetuation of attitudes which are neither

166 relevant to the changes and needs of present life nor a preparation for a perilous future. And more, that this perpetuation is not the result of ignorance but of deliberate policy. Like most of television entertainment the daytime serials are devised to keep as many people as possible at home in a suspension of reality and a mood to buy. Like "enriched" bread, which is divested of its original nutrient, the soap opera contains just enough additives to make viewers feel it is keeping up with the times. But the injection of real truth, the real society, the real world would, it is argued, provoke an audience resistance, shatter that mood of escape so essential to product-acceptance.

And since the viewer of afternoon soap opera is largely the woman at home, it is equally essential that the image of the full-time housewife be enthroned as the single highest good—and the greatest consumer of our society. She does the buying, and the more she stays home the more she has to buy—or thinks she must.

That is why, although there are 30-odd million American women in the labor market who work either to help support their family or because they want to—and they range from young wives to middle-age wives and widows, the only women on television who have jobs are unmarried girls waiting for a husband or immoral women waiting to pinch someone else's, or just unhappy women who never got their man. Sometimes a married woman with grown children takes a job in a hospital or a library, but the wails of a neglected husband (who is at the office all day) bring her smartly back home where she belongs.

In any case, I can think of only two women—the psychiatrist in *The Edge of Night* and the research doctor in *The Guiding Light*—who apparently were dedicated to their professions (granting always that this dedication was a substitute for The Right Man).

Ponder also that, although the population explosion is second only to the atomic one in its danger to the world, and that millions of American women use contraceptives, the word "pill" is never uttered by any soap-opera female of my acquaintance.

And although, once again, the illegitimate pregnancy is an afternoon TV formula, the only time I heard the hint of abortion raised (if not so called), the word "Murder!" immediately followed it. At a recent international conference in Virginia on abortion, the experts attending it—doctors, psychiatrists, lawyers and churchmen, including some Catholics—came to the almost unanimous consensus that the right of childbirth was up to each woman on the advice of her doctor and that all existing abortion laws should be repealed. In the light of such widespread opinion and the fact that several states are already revising their abortion legislation, some recognition of this vital change, as a human issue worthy of inclusion by television serials, might be expected. It is certainly one agonizingly close to the young as well as to their families.

And here we come again to a major default of commercial programming. Except in news and public affairs and a very occasional drama like *CBS Playhouse*'s "The People Next Door," by J.P. Miller, the sweeping revolt of the young is treated only in the most trivial or stereotyped terms. Teenagers might recognize themselves (although I would doubt it) in *The Monkees,* or in those rock-and-go-go sessions so dear to the record companies, but I wager they would stare with hooting disbelief at what passes for their kind on daytime serials. To be sure, the girls wear long hair and the boys longer hair than they used to and, as I said, the plot line sooner or later includes some alienated youngster with a problem. But what of the new young breed of social and political activists, what of the young idealists and draft protesters who court contempt and prison for their passionate beliefs? Even though they may be a minority, they have affected this Nation deeply and crucially. And I doubt whether any middle-class family in this country is not aware of them or in some direct or indirect contact with them. But not the folks in TV's Oakdale or Monticello. No siree. That wouldn't sell goods in Ohio or Georgia or Texas, to name a few.

And what of the millions of city families living, or trying to live, through strike after strike, through noise and pollution and crowds and the daily brutalities of life? Why can't we be made to feel with them and for them? What conceivable relation to this common reality do these neat serial shadows have?

Soap opera shows us day after day gleaming hospitals copiously staffed with impeccable doctors and charming nurses, but have they any relation to the critical shortages in our national health care, and to the crushing financial burden sickness places on the American citizen? Who do they think they are kidding—or conning?

Think what a chance is wasted by a great medium capable of enlightening while it involves, capable of reflecting the truth of ourselves to ourselves! And what an ideal framework for this is serial drama. The human need for storytelling is as old as man, and the continuing narrative form still holds a deep fascination, in spite of repeated announcements in intellectual circles of the death of the novel.

An immense amount of care and talent and inventiveness goes

168 into the production of soap operas, the acting is often of a high order, and genuine emotions are sometimes evoked by believable scenes. Standards of goodness and decency are made to prevail against the quite grotesque machinations of the bad soap characters, and married love conquers all in the endless serial span, year after year, hospital after hospital, courtroom after courtroom, coffee after coffee.

It may be wondered why an unlimited succession of human woes, sins and follies should constitute what is known as entertainment. But if that is indeed what a great many women want to see, then at least these should be placed within the context of living realities instead of manufactured crises.

No more important challenge could face a writer than a serial in which real people pursued real lives and spoke of real things; in which, indeed, they were being themselves, good and bad; and by which the viewer would gain new and exciting insights into the human condition—free from the soap that leaves a blurring and distorting film.

What a challenge to a writer; and to a network brave enough to let him tell it as it is. Who knows—it might even pay off.

America's Great Spectator Sport

By Edith Efron

AUGUST 13, 1966

Always a staple of network TV, game shows account, this season, for an impressive portion of daytime programming. Out of some 110 hours of weekday network television—otherwise largely devoted to reruns and soap operas—some 32 hours are turned over to games. Indeed, with a brief break for lunch, it is possible to watch 13 game shows in a row from 10 A.M. to 4:30 P.M.—two on CBS, three on ABC, and eight on NBC.

Although it might be described as a minority phenomenon—soaps being far and away the most popular daytime fare—this run of games is particularly startling when one considers that between 10 and 4:30, the Nation's youngsters and adolescents, who form such a huge part of the nighttime audience, are locked away in schools. These shows were unmistakably planned for adults and are unmistakably being watched by adults—about 45,000,000 weekly, 35,000,000 women, 10,000,000 men.

What does this adult craving for games actually mean? If one settles down in front of the set and watches the full sequence of game shows, one will rapidly discover that the games themselves are not stupid. In almost every case, they require some sort of specialized knowledge and highly developed mental skill. Even the much-lamented *Supermarket Sweep*,[6] which has been written off by casual observers as a graceless plundering of supermarket shelves, actually requires detailed knowledge of market prices plus the ability to make arithmetical calculations, involving fractions, at high speed. Most of the game shows, in fact, are actually a series of highspeed, specialized tests of wits. One might almost describe them as little "IQ tests."

The men who create and preside over these shows confirm the fact that the basic appeal of the games is intellectual: "To watch a TV game," says Bob Stewart, one of the creators of *Password* and *To Tell the Truth*, "is to watch the mental agility of other people. You can

169

170   match your own skills with the players. People like to use their own intelligence and to see others use theirs." "The only game shows which succeed are those which stimulate the viewer intellectually," says Ed Vane, director of daytime programming at ABC. "TV games are popular because they test people's ability to think under stress. This has always interested people. Human beings have a survival need to keep their wits strong and alert," says Gene Rayburn, emcee of *The Match Game.*

. . . .

Larry White, vice president in charge of daytime programming at NBC, thus sums it up: "TV games give people a chance to test themselves on general knowledge, specialized information, observation, recall, judgment, deductive abilities. They are popular because they test intellectual qualities. Mental tests, tests of wits, are always very absorbing to people."

Outside of the TV world, various authorities also support this interpretation. Detroit psychologist Roger Callahan, ex-president of the Michigan Society of School Psychologists, declares, "The appeal of the game shows is the same as the appeal of all quizzes and parlor games—they give people an opportunity to exercise their minds." Professor Herbert Hyman, head of Columbia University's graduate department of sociology, declares that several elements probably make game shows popular, suggesting the "traditional American pleasure in a contest" and the "intellectual pleasure of play," among them. Boston psychologist Barbara Klein similarly says: "The appeal of the game shows is obviously intellectual. Very often the excitement lies in high-speed deduction."

It is worth noting that the charge of "greed" for prizes—an interpretation of game-show popularity which has often been leveled against the public—is rejected by almost all these people. Only sociologist Hyman suggests that there may be some viewer "delight in ill-gotten gains." The others write off the public's interest in the monetary rewards as insignificant. "Greed is one of those hokey, worn-out clichés about game shows," says Mark Goodson, producer of many of the games on the air. "Ask people what the prizes are on most of these shows—they can't even remember." Psychologists Klein and Callahan support this, respectively calling the hypothesis of collective vicarious greed "absurd," and "rationally unfounded."

If, as is suggested, an important reason for the popularity of the game shows lies in their intellectual appeal, it seems clear that many million adult viewers of daytime TV are being seriously under-

estimated. This is definitely the view of the game-show men who *171*
work closely with the public.

"I've learned from my experience with the game shows, that there
are millions and millions of mature, alert intelligences in this country," says Allen Ludden. "The game shows," says Bill Malone, "reveal that native intelligence—not necessarily educated intelligence,
but native intelligence—in the viewer is far higher than it is said to
be." "If there's a receptive audience for any intelligent, challenging,
thought-provoking game," says Stewart, "then one has every right to
assume that it is intelligent—that there is popular intelligence out
there."

Over and over, the game-show specialists insist that the daytime
audience needs and would appreciate more intellectually demanding
shows. "They're hungry for the sight of brightness on the air," says
Stewart. "They're starving for intelligent programming," says Ludden. It is the conviction of these men that an adult audience which
genuinely craves mental stimulation can be provided with more
substantial fare by the networks.

When this conviction is presented to the network executives,
however, it meets with a sharp and instantaneous rebuttal. No, say
the network programmers, more mentally demanding shows cannot
be offered to the daytime audience: Says Larry White of NBC, the
network responsible for the majority of game shows on the air, "Most
of the daytime viewers are women. They're working during these
hours—washing dishes, making the beds, answering the doorbell,
taking care of the babies. They don't have the time or inclination to
watch more demanding shows." ABC's Ed Vane makes identically
the same point.

And both executives hasten to add that the rare experiments in
"intellectual" programming in the daytime hours have not been successful. "If you put an intellectual show on the air," says Larry White,
"you know what kind of ratings you'll get." And says Ed Vane,
"People are not looking to television for an expansion of their intellectual range. They are not looking for an exhaustive intellectual
experience."

What is the evidence for this view which contradicts the earlier
observation? It lies in the relative non-success of such news-and-
talk shows as *Calendar* with Harry Reasoner, the Mike Wallace news
show, and more recently, Phyllis Kirk's *The Young Set*—all of which
appeared on TV with a great hullabaloo about up-grading daytime
programming and were calmly ignored by most of the daytime audi-

172   ence. "It's hard enough to get an audience for intellectual shows at night," says Larry White. "Look at *CBS Reports*, look at *East Side/ West Side*. If you put an intellectual show on in the daytime, you'd get zero ratings." "It's hopeless," says Ed Vane. "If it's intellectual, they just won't watch."

The game-show men, however, repudiate this reasoning. Says Ludden: "The networks simply don't understand the difference between native intelligence and public-affairs stuffiness. The viewers are not academic squares, but that doesn't mean they have 12-year-old minds." Malone demands: "Who's deciding what's intellectual anyway? It sounds to me like demagoguery, as if a small group of people have set themselves up to decide what is and what isn't a proof of intelligence." Stewart, too, declares that TV is abnormally polarized between public-affairs shows and inane fiction: "There's very little on the air today that an intelligent but not highly educated mind can find satisfying."

Both psychologists interviewed also reject out of hand the network executives' notion of "intellectuality." Psychologist Callahan declares, "Too often, what passes for intellectual programming on the networks isn't intellectual at all. Too often, it consists of dull, unresolved drama; dull, unresolved discussions; and dull, unresolved public-affairs shows, to which the only appropriate response is—so what? Such shows are mentally frustrating. Most viewers reject them day and night—and rightly so. To judge people as intellectually deficient because they repudiate such shows is absurd."

Psychologist Klein criticizes as "nonsense" the network view that intellectual capacity is determined by a response to any specific category of subject matter or program—and adds: "All that exists in the way of a mental classification of our populace is a bell-shaped curve, representing the full sweep of human intelligence. The networks could reflect three-quarters of this curve, from modest normal up to genius, if they chose to do so. Unfortunately, they don't so choose."

And here the debate ends, as such debates always end—in the full bloom of nonresolution. A pitched battle over the intellectual level of viewers is not a new phenomenon. There is hardly a recorded discussion of any TV programming problem, day or night, which does not dip into the complex question of audience intelligence.

This particular debate, however, is unique in that the advocates of more intelligent programming are not basing their argument on the minority success of prestige nighttime public-affairs shows— but on the minority success of humble daytime game shows. They are not speaking in the name of the formally educated—but in the name of the natively intelligent.

It is a curious fact that native intelligence in the mass audience is rarely mentioned in all the brouhaha about TV programming. Indeed, the issue has been totally neglected in all the broadcasters' earnest studies of the public. According to ABC's Ed Vane, the mass audience, both day and night, has been weighed and measured in almost every material respect; amount of income, number of years of formal schooling, number of children, number of cars, number of washing machines, to mention a few. But no one has yet produced a study for broadcasters on the number of brains—the number of just plain bright people in both the day and the nighttime audiences.

It should be done. Perhaps it can be established that there are many millions of modestly schooled adults in this country who have good minds, and who would actively welcome more intelligent programming. If this is so—and the bell-shaped IQ curve suggests that it is—the networks should make it their business to acknowledge the phenomenon of popular intelligence and program for it accordingly. Indeed, the formal recognition at broadcast headquarters of the existence of multimillions of intelligent "common" men and women could have a profoundly salutary effect on U.S. television.

Drama

In August, 1955, TV GUIDE ran an article entitled, "They Never Had It So Good: TV Becomes the Patron Saint for Nation's Promising Writers." The article's first sentence read: "Thanks to television—that electronic patron of the arts—many a former struggling young writer has been wafted all the way from garret to suburbs."

This article was written at the zenith of the era which is now referred to as "The Golden Age of Television," when writers like Paddy Chayefsky, Gore Vidal, Rod Serling, Reginald Rose, Horton Foote, N. Richard Nash, Robert Alan Aurthur, Tad Mosel and David Shaw were writing dramas for such shows as *Studio One, Philco-Goodyear Playhouse, Lux Video Theatre* and *Kraft Television Theatre.*

The state of original drama for television is now quite different and its decline is considered nearly complete. The compounding of restrictions on television drama from all sides has led to mass desertion by the writers of the Golden Age. Marya Mannes has referred to the great irony that "in a medium that could not exist without the word, the writer has least control over the word, and that in the most powerful means of communication yet devised, the writer is least free to communicate."

Many broadcast historians argue, with much justification, that the total television fare available to the American viewer in 1970 is far superior in quantity, quality and variety than was the case fifteen years ago. Even with respect to drama, it cannot be denied that the great majority of the 343 hour-long dramas that appeared on the eight one-hour dramatic series during 1954-55 were hardly memorable; many were, in fact, poor productions. However, some of television's finest dramatic moments occurred in these shows.

Both Edith Efron and Dick Hobson are concerned with the reasons for the decline of original television drama and the exodus of the television dramatist. Miss Efron (pp. 176-182) discusses the pressures on the writers that are imposed by the NAB Code, the network continuity acceptance departments, the activities of pressure groups,

174

relevant Congressional hearings, the ratings and, finally, self-censorship. The censorship exercised by these forces has "eviscerated"
television plays. Miss Efron feels that unless these forces are controlled, TV drama will completely die.

Hobson (pp. 183-187), writing three years later, documents the
continuing brain drain of television dramatists. In fact, several of the
writers quoted in 1965 by Miss Efron had, by 1968, also left the
medium. Hobson suggests that network programming departments
and business-oriented studios are yet another item which should
be added to Miss Efron's impressive list of restrictive pressures on
the television writer. The executive-level group often assumes its
concept of audience tastes and desires is correct and impresses the
writer with the necessity of catering to the mass audience. Dramatists are warned that only the audience matters and TV is not a medium designed for self-expression. As Hobson explains, dramatists
realize that under the present system this is true and they are going
elsewhere.

Although the lack of good writers is a major factor in the decline
of original television drama, there are other elements as well. Richard
Doan points out (pp. 188-191) that the increasing number of movies on
television has lowered the demand for original television plays. He
believes that the public no longer distinguishes between the various
forms of drama that appear on the home screen.

The high cost of television drama is also a serious drawback,
and according to Doan, an important reason why the critically successful *CBS Playhouse* will be unlikely to herald a revival of the "Golden
Age."

Can TV Drama Survive?

By Edith Efron

According to many diagnosticians of television's ills, drama in the medium is afflicted with a strange and disturbing disease. The disease appeared after a brief "Golden Age" of literary experiment and artistic dedication, and, in the opinion of qualified observers, it has grown steadily worse each season. Its principal symptom is "emptiness"—a mental vacancy, an emotional vacuum, a moral void—as though the plays had been hollowed out by an unseen hand which allows nothing to remain but the bromidic, the passionless, the inane.

A few years ago, a phrase derived from a poem by T. S. Eliot was used to describe the ailing state of television: "a vast wasteland."[7] A line from another Eliot poem may be even more appropriate today: "This is the way the world ends/Not with a bang, but a whimper."

The world of TV drama is whimpering and dying today, and everyone, in and out of the television industry, knows it. In Hollywood recently, six of TV's finest dramatic writers, several of whom have earned Writers Guild best-script awards, were interviewed on this subject. They were: Christopher Knopf, president of the Writers Guild of America, West; Gene Roddenberry, creator-producer of *The Lieutenant;* Bruce Geller, producer of *Rawhide;* Stirling Silliphant, co-creator of *Route 66;* E. Jack Neuman, co-creator and executive producer of *Mr. Novak,* creator-producer of *A Man Called Shenandoah;* Richard Alan Simmons, the executive producer of *Trials of O'Brien.*

Two others were also interviewed: a programming executive from CBS who wishes to remain anonymous, and Thomas McDermott, head of Four Star Television.

Each of these men was asked one basic question: "What forces have eviscerated TV plays?" It took them from a half hour to four hours to answer; the average interview lasted two hours.

In the following excerpts, we give you the highlights of the diagnosis that emerged. It is a strange diagnosis, in that no single

176

element of it will come as a surprise to a well-informed reader; but the impact of the total sum of the elements may shock that same reader; it shocked many of the men as they were making their analyses. "It's like knowing that a man is sick," said one. "Over a period of years, you notice one symptom, then another, then another. And one day, you put them all together . . . and you realize he's got cancer."

The disease that is destroying the dramatic art form on TV is equivalent to cancer in the realm of artistic communication. It is a fatal disease, if unchecked. Its name is "virulent censorship." Here, according to these men, are its major manifestations:

The NAB Code. In 1956, after the Kefauver hearings in Congress, at which representatives of various pressure groups attacked TV drama, television film producers adopted the Code of the National Association of Broadcasters. This Code had been devised to screen out material that might offend public "taste." Among other things, it sets rules for the portrayal of such situations as adultery, suicide, physical violence; it forbids the offending of recognizable social groups; it demands that conventional virtue triumph, that conventional vice be punished. The NAB Code, say the the men interviewed, automatically empties TV plays of almost all meaningful content.

Roddenberry: The horror of the NAB Code is that it exists at all. It reflects the attitudes of the Bible Belt, of the religious orthodoxies, the business community, the Madison Avenue people who, historically, have never been people with fresh, brave opinions. The Code permits only the safest kind of opinion on the air.

Geller: The ethical standards of the Code are those of the most rigid, anti-intellectual and vociferous groups in this country. It is stifling to writers.

Simmons: It enthrones common-denominator attitudes. The writer must avoid attacking the primacy of the state, religious values, sexual values, sensitive social areas. No politics left of Democratic values is tolerated. The cultivated person is made into a buffoon, and the salt-of-the-earth low-brow emerges triumphant.

Silliphant: It is sometimes said that broadcasters ignore the Code. That's absurd. The Code is TV. It's part of their blood stream. They wouldn't know how to disobey the Code. The NAB Code is the intellectual dictatorship under which we all live. It's the barbed wire, the prison guards and the machine guns. It's the lowest-common-denominator bromides of the culture.

Network Censorship. Euphemistically called "continuity acceptance" experts, network censors are hired, say the interviewees, to enforce this tyranny of mediocrity. They screen every word and

178 gesture that goes on the air,[8] with their eyes firmly fixed on mass prejudice.

CBS Programming Executive: To get on the air, a script must win the approval of the largest possible number of people. One therefore avoids what is unpopular. You won't deal, for example, with an ethical issue which might offend Catholics or Jews; it would alienate too large a sector of the audience. You go down a whole list of people representing large blocs of religious, political or social opinion in this country, and you make a list of what they'd be offended by, and you censor it out. Whatever is left is allowed on the air.

Geller: Network censorship has degenerated to the incredible level where the continuity department counts the number of such verbs as "grabs," "strikes," or adjectives such as "roughly," "violently" in estimating whether a script is "suitable."

Silliphant: Sponsor interference is negligible as compared to the NAB Code, and the whole Philistine network with its infantile censorship.

Knopf: Network censors? We talk about them the way they talk about cultural commissars in a police state!

Pressure Groups. The evisceration of content is further reinforced by a continuing barrage by organized minority groups which see the air waves as their "property." Pressuring the broadcasters directly or indirectly through the FCC, these groups, say the men interviewed, are invariably determined to rid the air waves of any concept which does not flatter their collective image, or which conflicts with their official versions of the good and the true.

Roddenberry: The FCC serves as the channel for the pressure groups, for the Catholic Church, the Jewish groups, the nationality and racial groups. The FCC was theoretically set up to see that the rights of the public to their air waves were protected. I number among these rights the right to an interchange of the diverse attitudes and ideas which make up our Nation. Instead of doing this, the FCC is cooperating with these pressure groups in limiting these ideas to a sterile, middle spectrum (see pp. 303-321).

Knopf: There's constant pressure on the networks from professional, as well as from religious and racial, groups. Take the Bar Association. It's very important that their members be shown as noble, virile Siegfrieds going forth to fight the flaming dragon with a lance. A show goes on the air, or they get word of a script—and the screaming starts. Groups request to see the film; they report their findings to committees and to various Bar Associations. Important lawyers then put pressure on studios and networks. A show can be knocked off the

air, knocked out of syndication, or it is rewritten. The compromise is
enormous. Now . . . multiply this by every single profession portrayed on the air to get a sense of the magnitude of the censorship
involved.

Neuman: Poor Mr. Novak sat down and had a snort with a guy—
a drink and a smoke. I averaged 100 letters a day from people who
were horrified to see a schoolteacher drink. A powerful professor in
some Texas university organized a whole protest campaign. NBC
called me up and said, do we have to have Novak drink? I resented it
like hell.

Geller: *Prima facie,* we must treat every member of a minority
group as a saint. There's no way to portray one as a villain. I once
wrote a play with a Negro villain. The kid said, "But I thought you
told me they were good," and the father answered, "I said no such
thing; I told you they were the same as anybody else." It was changed
to an Argentinean. I guess there's no Argentine pressure group.

Silliphant: If I wanted to do a scathing attack on a plumber, I
couldn't do it. A man representing millions of plumbers would put
and end to it. You think that didn't happen? It did. These pressure
groups control the industry.

Congressional Hearings. Because TV is "publicly owned," it
has lost First Amendment protection to a significant degree. TV drama
is the only art form in America which is subject to investigation and
the threat of legislation by Congress. Committee reports on Congressional investigations of sex and violence in television programs
have profoundly affected dramatic content.

Neuman: These dictums to eliminate sex and violence from
drama are destroying drama. There's absolutely no serious work of
literature that does not have violence and sex. And it's up to a writer
to make the judgment as to how it is to be used—not a congressman!
What are we trying to protect human beings from, anyway? Themselves? Sex is the driving force of every man and woman in this
country. As for violence, anyone who tells me to take violence out of
drama—I say, go to hell!

Silliphant: I reacted with horror and nausea to the Dodd hearings.[9] I felt like leading an armed insurrection against the Government, or leaving the country. Because of this Government-regulation
situation, the whole industry was being hauled before a judge, jury
and executioner who had no constitutional right to play these roles
in the domain of art. The First Amendment is like a crucifix. If we'd
held it up before that committee they would have melted away like
vampires in medieval tales. But everyone was frightened. The indus-

180 try buckled under it. The result was an intensification of censorship.

Roddenberry: Senator Dodd has simply imposed additional censorships onto the already dangerous multiple censorships which proliferate in TV. The networks clamped down on violence after the Dodd hearings, and turned to a vacuous comedy which is more repellent than the prior violence. There was a good reason for the violence on the air. Plays must have conflict; conflict is the source of drama. If writers aren't allowed to do shows about ideological conflict, they'll do shows about physical conflict. If you can't show moral struggles over controversial issues, you'll show life-and-death struggles over noncontroversial issues. The excessive reliance on physical violence was caused by censorship. Further censorship is not the solution. All that has happened is that now there's almost no dramatic or climactic material on the air at all.

The "Tyranny of Ratings." In all other media of communication, art is placed directly on the market and survives commercially with the support of mere thousands. On TV, which is organized as a merchandising medium, drama is thrown in as a free giveaway from a manufacturer, in hope of attracting an audience of multimillions. The result is the insanely inflated circulation problem known as the "tyranny of ratings." Translated, say these men, it means a reinforcement of the same mass prejudices imposed on the air waves by censoring groups.

Knopf: A novelist gets on the bestseller list with 50,000 sales. A Broadway play is a smash hit with a thousand people a night. A movie is a success with a million. Only on TV does an artist have to win the acceptance of an audience of 20,000,000—not to mention their pressure groups.

Geller: The ratings problem has often been described as the problem of writing for the common man. This isn't true. It's perfectly possible to write beautiful plays for a mass audience. The Greek plays, Shakespeare, Restoration comedy, all were written for the common man. But that doesn't mean one can write a beautiful play that will be simultaneously appreciated by 50,000,000 common men! It's the size of the audience, a size determined by the sponsor's interests, that forces the art down to the lowest-common-denominator level.

Silliphant: Products are legitimately noncontroversial. Art is not. Products can logically command an audience of multimillions. Art cannot. Good creative writing, with a viewpoint, must necessarily be disturbing, probably offensive, to part of those millions. The statistics determining the survival of TV plays are relevant to advertising, not to art. The very economic structure of the medium is

antidrama. All a writer can hope to do is to rig up pseudo-problems in *181*
bromidic situations, and solve them with cultural clichés, in order to
cater to the lowest common denominator of this impossible audience.

Self-Censoring Writers. The vast majority of writers capitulate to
this diseased alliance of multiple censorships and advertising goals.
The habit of conforming to common-denominator values becomes in-
ternalized, say these men, and the writer learns to think within the
mental strait jacket. Thus the fountainhead of dramatic ideas dries up.

McDermott: People who have worked in this business for any
time develop a built-in standard of selection, a kind of automatic self-
censorship. Ideas that are politically or morally controversial simply
don't come to them. They don't even allow themselves to think of
subjects to which investigating committees might object, to which the
FCC people, the Dodd Committee, the Catholics, the Jews, the
Protestants, the blacks and the whites might object.

Knopf: The censorship of the pressure groups, of cliché values,
becomes a conditioning. The writer actually conditions himself to
censorship. He approaches his work knowing in advance what he cannot do. It's a self-willed slavery to the establishment.

Silliphant: The writer's problem is identical, psychologically, to
the problem of the producers, the networks—it's an acceptance of the
value system of "others," a refusal to battle to assert his own. The
censorships are built-in psychologically. Every writer knows the
restrictions in his bones and in his blood. He knows them without
reading the Code, or the mail from the pressure groups, or the edicts
of the FCC, or the reports of Congressional hearings. It's in the air,
it's on the air, it's at every meeting. . . .

Prognosis: Death. The evisceration of content, initiated by
Government in league with pressure groups—reinforced by advertiser needs—and accepted by broadcaster, producer and writer, is
killing drama on TV. With few brilliant exceptions, the brief history
of televised drama is a disaster. Offered as "free" on the "publicly
owned" air waves, drama is perishing of unfreedom and of social
persecution. And, say these men, the situation is growing steadily
worse.

Geller: The situation gets worse all the time. There's absolutely
no hope of its getting better. I'd like to advocate complete freedom of
expression, but it seems hopeless.

Simmons: The early experiment is finished. The area of struggle
and striving is just about bloody-well zero. It's becoming deader
every season. We're reaching the point of ultimate calcification.

Knopf: The genuine spark of the individual creation is gone.

182   They've traded it for polished mediocrity. This is the only artistic area in America where there's no room for real ability, no place for giants. The best people are getting out. It's intellectual and moral insanity.

Roddenberry: I see no evidence that the tremendous dangers of the multiple censorships of TV plays are understood. If the networks feel they can counter this with their news and public affairs programs, they are sadly mistaken. People are not affected by expository writing, as they are by drama. All over the world we see monuments erected to artists and poets and dramatists. I have yet to see one erected to a crier of news. Drama is more real than reality. It's a distilled vision of the essence of reality. The prime hours of comedy and drama are deeply affecting the Nation and its attitudes today. And the monstrous danger of this heavily censored drama is that it is injecting a false vision of reality into the Nation. It is teaching the American people one lesson over and over again—that life is emptiness, that there is nothing to be concerned with in this world but trivia. What has happened to TV drama is a cultural disaster.

TV's Disastrous Brain Drain

By Dick Hobson

JUNE 15, 1968

What ever happened to Rod Serling—late of *Twilight Zone*— whose name was once synonymous with "TV Writer?" A video dropout. "I'm not a practitioner any more. I couldn't stand the guff. I was ready for the Laughing Academy."

What became of writer Stirling Silliphant, whose *Naked City*s and *Route 66*s were once a repertory theater of contemporary life and times? Another dropout. "Those of us who learned our craft in television are, without exception, abandoning it. We're like Rhett Butler when he told Scarlett as he went out the door, 'My dear, I no longer give a damn!'"

TV's Brain Drain is no mere trickle. A whole generation of Serlings and Silliphants is stampeding out of the medium. They're badgering their agents: "Get me a movie! Get me out of this!" And they're going away "mad." Scrappy Harlan Ellison says: "It's not me deserting a sinking ship. It's the sinking ship deserting me!"

The writers are angry because "nit-pickers," "memo writers" and "company finks" from network programming departments are exerting ever more capricious "creative control" over their scripts. Ellison, who won the Writers Guild award for an *Outer Limits* script, recounts an exchange of dialog during a story conference with the producer of a current adventure show, his four assistants and a certain network executive, a former ad man:

Network Man: When you have the female spy about to open the hatch to flood the sub, I want you to have one of the crew jump her, grab at her face, rip off this rubber mask she's wearing—and she's not beautiful, but really ugly!

Ellison: But why?

Network Man: Because I liked it in *From Russia With Love*.

Ellison: No thanks. It's gratuitous, silly and stolen from someone else's work. I won't use it.

Network Man: You'll do what you're told or you'll never work again in this town!

183

What's going on in the writer's mind at this point? "It's the culmination of hours of demeaning acquiescence on my part, of arrogant
stupidity on his part, of a systematic bastardization of anything meri-
torious and original in my creation."

Did Ellison knuckle under? "On that script I did 17 rewrites, and
after I was off the script, there were eight more. When I saw a rough
cut, I invoked the clause in the Writers Guild contract to have a
pseudonym put on the segment."

There's one detail missing from the above account. In the heat of
the argument, Ellison lost his cool. "I went berserk. I ran amuck. I
hauled back and drove one right into the center of his imbecilic face."
When the shook-up network man got back to the office, he killed
$12,000 worth of Ellison's script assignments for that network.

Writers are angry because their scripts are continually rewritten
and rewritten by "creative typists" to the point of nonrecognition.
Paul Schneider says: "It is painful to watch my stuff on TV. About the
only thing I recognize is my name. On one of my *Bonanza*s the producers claimed they were compelled to rewrite it because the network
ordered them to." Husband-wife writing team Phyllis and Robert
White say: "We know writers who simply refuse to watch their stuff
on TV. We don't have the guts not to turn on the set, if only to marvel
at what they've done to our baby."

The writers are angry even the networks' censorship fails to keep
up with changing mores. Sam Rolfe had a big fight with the censors
over the tame phrase "sex appeal" in an *U.N.C.L.E.* script and they
finally compromised on the more leering expression: "S.A." "At the
end I felt debilitated and drained. Yet you've got to fight each and
every 'sex appeal' battle in order to hold some ground for the bigger
and more important battle of, say, the next script about abortion. If
cowardice became a habit, you'd run away from a more important
fight."

The writers are angry because business-oriented studio heads
are forever intruding into the writers' act, trying to hype up their
stories with phony gimmicks. Even Silliphant, surely one of the most
exceptional talents ever spawned by the medium (he won an Oscar
for writing the screenplay for *In the Heat of the Night*), is not exempt.
In his first two-hour movie-for-TV, *Wings of Fire,* the studio's TV
production chief objected to a love scene, said it was too long, needed
action and instructed Silliphant, "You've got to put a bear on the
beach." Was there any point in explaining to the mogul that there
aren't any bears in the Caribbean, where the story takes place? Silliphant said: "I put a bear on the beach, but it was my last assignment
at that studio. I broke my contract after that."

The writers are fed up with executive-level groupthink where everybody tries to second-guess what will titillate the viewers next. "Have we done Lucy on a trampoline?" "Let's do James Bond in the West." "How about a *High Noon* with women?" Writer Sam Rolfe, co-creator of *Have Gun, Will Travel* and developer of *The Man from U.N.C.L.E.*, was called in to write a pilot, and groupthink handed him the format on a platter. "They said, 'Hey, there aren't many Westerns this year; let's do a Western. Hey, *Perry Mason* is going off; let's put a lawyer in the West.' This pastiche became *Dundee and the Culhane.* I felt jaded before I started."

Series like *Dr. Kildare* and *Naked City* once constituted a kind of literature of contemporary American life; and when *The Defenders* was finally axed, the writers really lost hope. There was nothing left. "TV today in no way grapples with the problems of life," flatly states writer Gene Roddenberry, creator of *Star Trek* and its executive producer. "Our show can get away with statements about the computerization of life or the horror of bacteriological warfare, but only because *Star Trek* is set in the future. On the contemporary level, TV is guilty of the terrible sin of omission."

"Why can't I write a story about Vietnam?" Silliphant wants to know. "Why should entertainment programs be less reflective of life than news programs? The networks say, 'No, the sponsors don't want it.'" But on that score, writer-producer Bill Froug disagrees: "Sponsor pressure is a myth. It is always the network program department that says that the sales department says that the sponsor says that they will withdraw their support of any segment containing such-and-such a theme. But sponsors are never consulted. Sponsors simply stand in line like everybody else."

Among the "sins of omission" cited by Roddenberry, up until *I Spy* broke the ice with Bill Cosby, was the entire Negro race. "When the Writers Guild struck in 1960 on the issue of money, the strike should have been on the issue of *River Boat,* a series supposedly set on the Mississippi. The producers warned us, 'No Negroes.'"

First on Roddenberry's list of TV's all-time "sins of omission" is *I Led Three Lives,* a fictional series although based on activities of an actual FBI agent who infiltrated the U.S. Communist Party. "It was fiction. I hate myself for having written two episodes. It was entirely trumped up."

The writers are angry because, they say, the networks are deliberately debasing the level of TV to the lowest common denominator. The series are becoming more like comic strips—the good guys whiter, the bad guys blacker, the stock situations ever further removed from life.

A current example of the erosion of depth, complexity and the "roundedness" of honest human drama is what happened to *Cimarron Strip* over the course of its first and only season. At the beginning, scriptwriters were advised that "Marshal Jim Crown," the character played by Stuart Whitman, "has true compassion for human failing. He realizes that most men fighting here (homesteaders, cattlemen, cowboys, farmers, Indians, cavalrymen, railroad men) are fighting for something they believe to be their rightful due."

By the end of this season the writers were getting quite a different prescription: "We should avoid stories where Crown has a sympathetic attitude toward the heavies . . . The villains, to be effective, must clearly appear as evil incarnate—no shades of gray; but, rather, totally black . . . We should avoid stories which reflect social problems of the Cimarron period as well as ones of today."

What happened between September and June? The network programming department by edict "simplified" the format to comic-strip dimensions, forcing yet another writer, the show's developer and "supervising producer," Christopher Knopf, to join the mass exodus of writers from television.

The experience taught Knopf, former president of the Writers Guild of America West, something new. "It was the biggest shock in my 18 years as a professional writer. I found that the network knew more about the mass audience than I." His rude shock came with the airing of an early episode of *Cimarron* which the network programming chief had predicted would be "a rating disaster" but which Knopf considered "the best film I'd ever seen on television." The episode—with the marshal as his first-draft "compassionate" self—opened with a 26 rating. At each successive quarter hour the rating kept dropping, for a total of four points, meaning that 6,000,000 viewers had dialed it off. "I knew then that the ultimate I am striving for is not what the audience wants," Knopf concludes from the experience. "It had been my conceit that I could lick the system through good writing. I no longer believe it."

The network was proved to be "right"; the writer admitted he was "wrong." The network was right, assuming that TV's responsibility is to acquiesce in the "dictatorship of the proletariat." But many writers won't make that assumption. Everett Freeman thinks that what is needed is a reversal of the credo that says you have to give the public what it wants!" he says. "The public doesn't know what it wants until it is shown."

Paul Monash, executive producer of both *Peyton Place* and *Judd for the Defense,* and himself a writer (he wrote one of the better

Judds of the season), talks more like his producer self. "TV is not a   *187* means for self-expression. Why aren't those writers in some other medium? This is a medium designed to bring entertainment to an audience. We should ask not whether the writers are satisfied; ask if the audience is satisfied."

In terms of the system today, Monash is "right," and he makes $500,000 a year from the system to prove it. His angrier colleagues go along with him part way. They agree that the audience may not be dissatisfied because what they see is simply what they've been conditioned to expect. They've become addicts of mediocrity. Still they remain unsatisfied because their appetite for the enrichment of their lives, an appetite theoretically inexhaustible, is not being catered to. According to the angry writers: The way the system works today, the people who have been made addicts of mediocrity are the same people whose program preferences are polled so the system can then "give the people what they want."

The writers, what's left of them, are at war with whole echelons of executives—network programming, network sales, rating specialists—who are trying to second-guess what the people out there think they want. The echelons have become known as "they." According to Silliphant: "We used to be able to go in and fight for our scripts. But no producer today speaks for himself. He speaks for 'them.' He'll say, 'They say this story is not in the national interest,' Well, who are they? The producer himself doesn't know."

"They like the most obvious, least demanding material that won't unnerve anyone," says Ellison. "They think there is less risk in imitative programming. Their criterion is fear. They're frightened of getting canned out of their jobs," says Lester Colodny. "They're motivated by only one drive—survival," agrees Froug.

The survival of "they," or "them," depends entirely on their performance in the Ratings Game. "Our real target," says Knopf, "is an incredible complex of graphs and content analyses—the golden rule by which network executives run their operation and dictate what may appear."

"The greatest single feature depressing quality in TV," says Roddenberry, "is how many viewers per dollar will determine what stays on the air. We are all prisoners of our commerce-dominated system. Television is getting worse and worse and worse, and I think it's got to get even worse before it gets better."

Meanwhile, where are the writers? They went thataway.

Is Drama the Thing?

By Richard K. Doan

MAY 11, 1968

CBS Playhouse, it's plain to see, hasn't exactly revived the "Golden Age" of television. Indeed, the infrequent, taped, original dramas presented under this umbrella title so reminiscent of the immortal Playhouse 90 (and obviously intended so by CBS) have made only a slight dent in the drift of TV fare. The networks are more committed than ever to the filmed fodder that guarantees ratings, and the prospect is that next season will see only a token upturn in "meaningful" drama.

The irony of it is that the CBS project has been a notable success. Its first three offerings—"The Final War of Olly Winter," "Do Not Go Gentle Into That Good Night" and "Dear Friends"—were declared hits. The most recent one, "My Father and My Mother," while less ecstatically received by the critics, was no dud.

Over-all, the ratings have been respectable if not sensational.[10] Critically, all four productions to date probably would stand comparison with memorable Golden-era dramas of the late-1950's. The four plays have been expensively mounted, skillfully executed, provocatively themed (the Negro at war, old age, marital strains, the mentally retarded). The airings have triggerd mountains of "Bravo!" mail. The sole sponsor of this season's offerings, General Telephone & Electronics Corporation, has been hailed as wonderfully enlightened for letting the dramas run uninterrupted by commercials. GT&E officials, for their part, have been elated, too.

In short, CBS Playhouse has batted impressively—granted, of course, it hasn't gone to bat any too often.

This impressive record would seem to prove the efficacy of high-class, high-minded drama, thus persuading TV programmers, a notoriously imitative group, to rush out with copies of CBS Playhouse. This seems the least they could do considering their frequent assertions that they are bored with today's prime-time grind and long for TV's Good Old Days.

But no. There will be another clutch of *CBS Playhouse* one-nighters next season—four at least, maybe five or six. *Hallmark Hall of Fame* on NBC, mostly devoted to warmed-over classics, might risk one original. NBC has managed to induce Prudential Insurance to underwrite five dramatic specials, three of them an hour in length, the other two 90 minutes long. They will be based on original scripts with contemporary themes; only time will tell whether they have more serious theatrical intent than, say *Fame Is the Name of the Game.* And that, as of the moment, is about the extent of it.

Why? For heaven's sake, why? Well, naturally there isn't a pat, simple answer. The consensus is that no great, compelling demand exists for original TV drama any more. Hundreds of *CBS Playhouse* viewers have cried "More! More!" But they are not an overpowering voice. (Far greater numbers, for example, cried "More!" for *Star Trek.)*

A reason often advanced for the absence of demand for original TV plays is that the public's appetite for such fare is being satisfied these days by TV's rash of movies, which, after all, are "original drama" of a sort!

Indeed, there is a kind of blurring of public distinctions between the forms of televised drama. Many people thought CBS's studio-taped *Death of a Salesman* was a movie. David Susskind's remakes of film and stage classics this season (*Dial 'M' for Murder,* and so forth) ran on ABC's "movie nights" and often passed as movies. NBC's *World Premiere* features have been accepted as movies, although they really are two-hour filmed TV plays. It makes little difference to the viewer, of course, what trade label a drama carries so long as he is getting name stars in good productions with strong plots. Hence, *CBS Playhouse* productions have blended into the whole of TV drama, simply becoming something to be compared with last night's movie.

Another explanation for the failure of the CBS project to ingite TV's latent dramatic talents is that quality scripts are so hard to come by today. Most people involved with *CBS Playhouse* feel it does well to come up with three or four top-notch scripts each year. Senior CBS programmer Mike Dann, whose personal pride in *Playhouse* knows few bounds, insists he had two advertisers interested recently in emulating GT&E's sponsorship of occasional dramas but couldn't find scripts to offer them.

Not everybody buys this view. Among the dissenters are such Golden-Age TV playwrights as Reginald Rose, Ernest Kinoy and Paddy Chayefsky, who argue that if the medium provided again the

190   kind of wide-open market it once did for teleplays, the writers would produce them.

"Not a single good American play has come to Broadway this season," Dann retorts. "The one and only important movie has been *The Graduate.* We consider ourselves lucky to have had three *CBS Playhouse* hits." Dann confesses, however, he was "completely wrong" back in June 1966, when the series was announced, in believing it would generate new writing talents. "On the other hand," he crows, "we never dreamed we could entice back the great writers who had left TV—the Reg Roses, the Gore Vidals, the Tad Mosels. And here we are with all of them back!"

Dann, it seemed, was slightly premature in his claim. Cheyefsky, author of the memorable *Marty,* was irritated that CBS had trumpeted his return. He insisted he had no commitment to CBS, "not even an idea" for a script. He groused that CBS was "missing the boat" because the series was not presenting "anything controversial," in his view. To this, Barbara Schultz, Dann's petite but powerful overseer of *Playhouse,* responded, "Heaven knows we'd like to do something controversial, *if* it's a play."

Still another reason *CBS Playhouse* isn't being widely imitated, it appears, is the acknowledged fact that it is a loss leader. CBS's net deficit on it is perhaps close to $1 million a year, much of this for script development. About four scripts, costing up to $25,000 each, are commissioned for each one produced. GT&E paid $525,000 for the two-hour "Dear Friends," and $450,000 of this went for production costs leaving a pinch for the air time, normally worth $160,000 per hour.

Of the plunge GT&E took in sponsoring *Playhouse,* advertising boss George Norton recalls, "We were buying a pig in a poke. We went around all last summer without any stomachs." But after the rave notices and fan mail flooded in, he joyfully reported his satisfaction.

Was he unhappy with any aspect of the venture? Yes, he admitted —he'd like to see a few "lighter-side" dramas. "So would we!" Dann reacted. "If we could get a Neil Simon or Buck Henry or Mike Nichols to do a comedy for *CBS Playhouse,* we'd love it! But 95 percent of the writers are people who feel they have to say something serious."

Gutsy or not, incidentally, there won't be any reruns of the *Playhouse* dramas, Dann is sorry to say, because rights and union costs are too high in the case of these taped productions. . . .

Will CBS continue *Playhouse* even if it doesn't ignite a new Golden Age? The question strikes Mike Dann as superfluous. "Of

course!" he snaps. Still, it's lucky for Dann and for *CBS Playhouse*'s   *191*
"Bravo!" crowd that GT&E showed up with another bag of money.
These are no days in TV for shows that don't pay their way.

Comedy

In *The Public Arts*, Gilbert Seldes, a great pioneer of mass media criticism, stated that "comedy is the axis on which broadcasting revolves" because sponsors support and even insist upon a form of entertainment which attracts audiences and leaves them in "a most favorable state for persuasion." Audiences unquestionably are attracted to comedy. Eight of the top fifteen rated series of the 1968-69 season were situation comedies, despite the appearance of new television formats, such as longer shows and the influx of motion pictures and movies made for television.

The television comedy of 1968-69 was not the same comedy which first appeared with the advent of the medium. Comedians reminisce about the old days in much the same way as do other performers with respect to the so-called Golden Age of drama. Sid Caesar, for example, talks of the time that he, Carl Reiner and Howie Morris deviated for almost five minutes from a *Your Show of Shows* script, trying to make Nanette Fabray "break-up."

There is, of course, argument and debate on the advantages and disadvantages of such artistic freedom and on whether or not the quality of comedy was any better fifteen years ago than now. Today, however, the scripts which are placed on cue cards before the show begins are closely followed, and deviations are rare and momentary. The same concerns regarding ratings, sponsor reactions and letters from special interest groups which have plagued television drama have become nearly as prevalent in television comedy; and the comedian has, with few exceptions, been taken away from the audience.

The method by which the laughter has remained in television comedy while live audiences generally have not is explained by Dick Hobson (pp. 194-200) in his discussion of canned laughter. Hobson describes how the Laff Box operates and how the "Laff Boys" manufacture the appropriate "tickle, sharpie and howl." He suggests the attitude of the industry toward canned laughter and its effect upon comedy writers, directors and performers.

Goodman Ace, one of television's best known and most highly *193* paid comedy writers, has referred to writers of television comedies as "the invisible men of TV" and the "ghost writers in the sky." Ace maintains that comedy writers are usually treated by the comedians as the enemy and are rarely given proper recognition, either on the studio set or in publicity regarding the show. With the passing of the impromptu sketch, however, the comedy script has become more significant and, although they are still the invisible men of TV, comedy writers are considered an increasingly necessary evil. Bill O'Hallaren (pp. 201-203) recounts how some writers are exposed to the new comedies that soon will be appearing on the television screen and asked to submit scripts for future shows.

The challenges as well as the restrictions and taboos that face O'Hallaren and his colleagues are outlined by Sheldon Leonard (pp. 204-207) whose successful productions included several long-running situation comedies—*The Danny Thomas Show, Gomer Pyle, USMC* and *The Andy Griffith Show*. Leonard discusses the difficulty of analyzing what makes people laugh, the censorship caused by the tender sensibilities of various interest groups, the lack of a proper training ground for the aspiring comic, and the need for exploring new areas of satire.

The Hollywood Sphinx and His Laff Box

By Dick Hobson

JULY 2 AND 9, 1966

Charley Douglas, King of the Laugh Tracks, isn't talking.

He won't tell who buys his canned laughs, though his clients are estimated to embrace well over a third of the 95 prime-time shows now on the air, including even programs like *The Dick Van Dyke Show* and *The Hollywood Palace* which have their own live audiences ostensibly capable of laughing it up for real.

He won't tell where he begged or borrowed all those prerecorded giggles and guffaws emanating from his mystery machine, known as the "Laff (sic) Box."

He won't discuss the circumstances under which he quit the Electronic Laughter Department at CBS some 10 or 12 years ago and set up shop on his own.

"I won't even talk about why I won't talk," says Charley.

Getting to the nub of the Charley Douglas story is like trying to unlock the Coca-Cola formula. Nevertheless, gang, here's the story:

The Yock Czar of TV is known to employ three of his own boffola technicians, referred to in the industry as the "Laff (sic) Boys" and differentiated only as "John," "Carroll" and "Tex"—all of whom work under a tight security lid. They're not talking either.

Picture if you will Lon Chaney Sr. in *Phantom of the Opera* flailing at the pipe organ in the darkened cathedral crypt and you have some notion of the Laff Boy at work. Hunched over the keyboard of Charley's box on the darkened dubbing stage, his fingers punching at the keys, his feet manipulating the pedals, he wrings forth his fugues and caprices. He's a veritable virtuoso of titters and snorts.

The Laff Boys operate out of Charley's padlocked garage in the village of Northridge in San Fernando Valley. It requires three or four hours to "lay in" the laugh track on *Gilligan's Island*, say, or *Please Don't Eat the Daisies*. There are thought to be five Laff Boxes

195

in Charley's garage, four covered with black, beat-up leatherette, one with brown. A Laff Boy signs out a Laff Box and transports it in his own car to the dubbing stage. There he wheels in the box—about the size of a typewriter stand—on small casters and plugs it into the wall socket. There are two brass padlocks on the lid and no one but Charley, John, Carroll or Tex has ever looked inside.

In the 10 years of Charley's laughtrack monopoly the Laff Boys with their clattering padlocks have become a familiar sight to the producers, associate producers, sound recorders and mixers, film editors, sound-effects cutters and music editors regularly present. If the Laff Box should start acting strangely, the Laff Boys wheel it into the men's room, locking the door behind so that no one can peek. Once smoke began pouring ominously from a crack in the box and the Laff Boy panicked and undid the padlocks right there in front of everybody. Luckily for the Yock Czar of TV, it was too smokey for anyone to see much.

With all his mysterioso hocus-pocus about the padlocks, Charley has stimulated more discussion than if he'd left the lid wide open. Everybody and his brother has a theory about what's inside. But mention of the name "Charley Douglas" and it's like "Cosa Nostra"— everybody starts whispering. It's the most taboo topic in TV.

. . . .

Inside the Laff Box is an amplifier and, some say, a million laughs. Actually, 320 laughs on 32 loops, 10 to a loop. Consequently the various combinations can run into vast numbers. Each "loop" is a length of quarter-inch magnetic tape consisting of 10 individual audience laughs spliced end to end. Each single laugh has a normal beginning, middle and end; so clearly Charley's process is never a matter of merely increasing or decreasing the volume. The Laff Boy can, however, dial down the mixer pot and smother off the end of a laugh if it threatens to cackle on embarrassingly long.

All 32 loops are whirling around simultaneously, ready to be keyed in by the 32 keys, operable singly or in combination. The various keys represent, among other distinctions, short laughs, medium-length laughs and long laughs for use depending on the duration of the "hole" of silence in the sound track to be "filled." There are keys covering the dimension of intensity: loud, medium, mild. And there are separate keys representing the number of laughers, ranging from a few random gigglers up to a coliseumful.

One key called the "presence" activates a loop without audible laughter but with just the sound of breathing, rustling of clothing,

196   shifting in seats. The "presence" is normally used "to fill a hole" of dead silence, though some producers like to have the "presence" around at all times.

There's a "titter key" and a similar "chuckles reel" that's a big favorite with some producers who use it almost exclusively. There's an "anticipation reel" where everybody in the audience says "oh-oh," for insertion when they are supposed to anticipate what's going to happen next. There's a (breath) "intake" reel for surprise reaction, with everybody gasping, and one reel called, recognizably, "oo's and ah's." There are separate keys for cheering, applause, men laughers only and women laughers only. One key activates "sharpies" —those snorts one often hears prior to the main audience roar. There's a "funny-laugh" key for a single idiosyncratic kook laugh—an indication that even maverick individualism can be canned.

Since there are up to 10 laughs on each reel, the Laff Boy customarily has to key-in whichever of the 10 laughs happens to come along next. Yet it is possible for him to pre-set certain laughs. For example, on the "screamer reel," also known as the "mad howl," a producer might specifically request Mad Howl No. 3, in which case the Laff Boy would stop the mad-howl loop and pre-set it to start with the desired howl. In this way, highly specific chortles or sharpies or belly laughs can be requisitioned at will.

A half-hour filmed show like *Bewitched* comes to the dubbing stage in three reels of eight or nine minutes each and the reels are dubbed one at a time, for the purpose of rerecording onto one composite sound track the various individual tracks: music, sound effects and dialog—and in the process to add the laughs. In the first step, the "rehearsal," the film is projected on the screen, below which is ticking away the illuminated footage indicator. Those present try not to talk and concentrate instead on note-taking. The producer might scribble down things like: "Big boffola at 389." The Laff Boy "plays" his box, reacting instinctively, this being the first time he's ever seen the film. The producer and the Laff Boy then discuss the laughs, sometimes with a little argument over whether something is funny. The producer always wins the argument.

The next step is a "take." The Laff Boy pre-sets to the start mark any specific reactions he needs, such as Mad Howl No. 3, limbers up his fingers, wriggles his toes in his stocking feet, and tenses up for the take. He might start by activating keys 13, 24, 52 and 81, then letting up on 52, depressing the foot pedal a smidgen of a push, meanwhile turning the mix dial down, and so on. When the lights come up, the Laff Boy is frequently drenched in sweat.

The trick of the Laff Boy's trade is timing. He can't "jump a gag" *197*
by punching in the laugh too early. There's a difference of opinion
in the laugh game as to how long the pause should be. George Burns,
a pioneer of the "laugh spotting" art, contends it should be eight
frames or one-fifth of a foot of film, which on the screen is a third of a
second.

To manufacture a natural-sounding laugh, the Laff Boy must let
a few "people" in his box anticipate a joke. This is called "giving it a
little tickle." Then he might punch in a "sharpie" just before the main
laugh. The climax of the laugh is equally intricate. He has to punch
his keys so as to "tail out" with a little chuckle and "slide under"
the incoming line.

He must take care not to "laugh" a straight line, not to "cover"
a line of dialog, and never to "bury" a gag line. Gags frequently
build, each capping the last, so the Laff Boy must likewise build and
hold his biggest laugh for the pay-off. But his biggest problem is with
filmed shows made without the benefit of a live audience and therefore without enough space alloted to insert any decent amount of
canned yocks.

They say that some of Charley's Laff Boys have a lighter touch
than others. Only one is universally considered a hopeless square
with no sense of humor whatever, and that is old Charley himself.
Producers wince when they see that it's Charley trundling in the box.
Some have put in standing requests for John only, Carroll only, or
Tex only. Yet everyone likes Charley personally, despite his de-
ficiency in the humor department, and everybody adores the Laff
Boys.

There's a danger in too many rehearsals. They say you've got to
get the Laff Boys in the morning because by afternoon they're all
laughed out and nothing is funny to them any more. They say that
the Laff Boys, being inured to laughs, tend to lay in too many. They
say that the Laff Boys are getting stale over the years.

. . . .

There's something else. Caustic TV critic Hal Humphrey once
wrote: "I'm of the opinion that laugh styles change over the years,
and that a big belly laugh lifted from an old *Martin & Lewis* show
has a spurious tone when one hears it used today in, say, an episode
of *My Mother, the Car.*

To get around those spurious tones of Charley's box, CBS sound
engineers at Television City knocked together a fancier contraption
they call "The MacKenzie Machine" (named for an engineer who
developed the mechanism) which "augments" *The Red Skelton Hour*

198 with prerecorded titters taped right in Skelton's studio, No. 33, and which "sweetens" *The Danny Kaye Show* with canned cackles recorded in Kaye's studio, No. 31. No outdated Martin & Lewis yocks for Red or Danny! Just the freshly canned kind.

All this in an effort to manufacture laughs that sound real and natural and true. Audiences composed of living, breathing, sentient beings, it seems, don't sound too good. "The fact is," says Arthur Julian, a writer on *F Troop*, "real audiences sound phonier than the laugh track. Sometimes they freeze up and act unnatural." Producer Don McGuire, creator of the late *Mona McCluskey*, and author of the forthcoming Doubleday novel *The Day Television Died*, concurs: "Live audiences in from the street are tense and nervous and you don't get their true reactions." Adds *Addams Family* associate producer Herbert W. Browar: "At times, the live audiences yock it up 'too' much. Maybe someone off camera is waving his hands wildly for audience reaction." Sighs Bob Banner, whose company produces *Candid Camera*: "Audiences just never laugh or respond on cue. They do the strangest things."

Live audiences aren't all they're cracked up to be because they can hardly see the performers through the swarm of cameras, announcers, lights, sound men, props, musicians, microphone booms, dancers, cameramen, stagehands, and assorted production assistants. The have to crane their necks up to the monitors overhead to catch what's going on. At that, they can't hear much. The studio public-address system has been cranked way down to prevent sound from leaking back into the mikes and producing that screeching howl called "feedback." Audiences who can't see or hear can't be counted on to laugh at jokes.

The industry's solution—TV's best-known and least-talked-about secret—the Laff Box—is by now endemic, ubiquitous, and here to stay. Pronounces NBC's vice president in charge of TV programs, Grant Tinker: "It's something that's with us every day and night. It's largely a necessary thing."

It wasn't always so. Back in the earlier days of radio there were programs like *Stoopnagle & Budd, Amos 'n' Andy* and *Easy Aces* that tootled along without any hoots and hollers at all. Then it all broke loose. As the late Fred Allen put it: "The worst thing that ever happened to radio was the studio audience. Somebody like Eddie Cantor brought these hordes of cackling geese in because he couldn't work without imbeciles laughing at his jokes."

Enter video, and one of the pioneers of filmed TV comedy, Harry Ackerman, developer of the original *I Love Lucy*, recalls:

"I learned that Lucy was 'dead' on a bare soundstage, so I insisted that we film in front of an audience. It was for the performers' benefit at first, though of course we recorded the audience reaction and learned to 'sweeten' it when necessary." *The Lucy Show* as well as *Hey, Landlord!*, an upcoming series this fall [1966], are the last survivors utilizing the three-camera technique of filming before a live audience.[11] "Why, we have to 'take out' more laughs that we put in!" exclaims *Landlord*'s production executive Lee Rich. ("Desweetening," it's called in the laugh game.) "But it got to be a bore having the audience around," Artie Julian continues. "Even on live or taped shows like *The Hollywood Palace* the engineers started dialing the audience out and using canned reaction."

Certainly no comedy producer is about to show up in a Madison Avenue projection room with his can of pilot film minus built-in laughs. The prospective buyer might not know it's funny; he might not buy. For according to Jay Sommers, creator-producer of *Green Acres*, "People are so conditioned to the laugh track that if they don't hear it they don't know it's a comedy show."

There have been exceedingly few instances of comedy shows sans laughs and those instances aren't likely to fire up a spirit of reform.[12] For its first and second seasons, *Hennesey* had a "titter track." Its third season, the titters were dropped. At the end of the third season *Hennesey* was dropped. A series called *Harrigan & Son* starring Pat O'Brien survived just one season without a laugh track. And season before last, producer Buzz Kulik publicly proclaimed that *Kentucky Jones* would have 'em rolling in the aisles with no laughs, canned or live. Five yockless episodes later, after a grim look at the Nielsens, NBC put through an urgent call to Charley Douglas's garage in Northridge: Send over the box.

Stung to action by the quiz scandals of 1959, CBS president Dr. Frank Stanton hired a sort-of house detective known around town as "Mister Clean," whose job it was to tack title cards like "audience reaction technically augmented" onto the tail end of shows with laugh tracks. That reform lasted half a season or so. Today, you can't glimpse a fast-crawl end-credit for Charley Douglas on any of the dozens of shows yocked up by his outfit, Northridge Electronics.

"We put in sound effects, too, but nobody complains about that," says a puzzled Herb Browar. "Sure, what about creaking doors or spooky music?" asks Artie Julian. "There's no guilt about that, yet everybody has this great guilt about putting in laughs." Sheldon Leonard, whose company makes *The Andy Griffith Show* and *Gomer Pyle, U.S.M.C.*, among others, concedes: "There's an air of shame and

200 self-consciousness about laugh tracks that's not necessary." Then how did these guilts get going? Don McGuire's theory is this: "There are some producers, including myself, who feel guilty about using laugh tracks because it demonstrates a lack of talent. It's an admission on our part that we don't know how to make our shows funny enough."

Funny or not, comedy shows will never lack laughs as long as writers write, directors direct, actors act, and editors edit—all with the Laff Box to fall back on. "Writers are continually aware of the box," Rod Amateau says. "After every gag line the next one has to be neutral so the laugh can cover it." "Directors leave pauses for audience reaction, space for laughs to be laid in," says Artie Julian. "Actors who have worked before live audiences always allow room for laughs," says *Get Smart*'s executive producer Leonard Stern. One has only to recall Jack Benny's hurt stare, George Burns' gaze at the tip of his cigar, or Bob Hope's pretense of sailing right into the next sentence. And "film editors" splice in extra footage after every gag so the Laff Boy will have room for his product.

If some shows seem to yock it up more than others, there's a high-falutin' theory to account for that too: "It is an axiom of the TV-comedy business," Steve Allen explains in his book *The Funny Men*,[13] "that the less realistic you are, the bigger your jokes have to be. If you're not being at least a little true to life, your script has to blast a laugh out of the audience every few seconds because their emotions are not much involved."

The way Sheldon Leonard explains it: "A show with a high degree of reality, as *The Andy Griffith Show*, requires a modified laugh track, whereas *The Beverly Hillbillies* track can be more intrusive."

So why are laugh tracks so all-fired necessary? Theories are multitudinous. "To get the guy in slippers and robe with the can of beer to look up from his newspaper to see what's going on," says producer George Schlatter. "To assuage your embarrassment at laughing at such corny items as Granny's hawg jowls," says producer Rod Amateau. And that's just for starters.

Yet perhaps it's child-star-turned-TV-tycoon Jackie Cooper who gets to the real nitty-gritty of the laugh-track question when he says: "We're manufacturing a reaction to our own creation, yet we'll never know if the people out there are really laughing. It's the put-on of all time."

When Comedy Writers Hunt Jobs, It's Not Very Funny

By Bill O'Hallaren

JULY 29, 1967

Spring and summer may bring to most of the world dreams of frolicking in the woods, loaves of bread and jugs of good stuff; but for the average struggling Hollywood television writer, it's the season for a far different type of fantasy. Because these are the days he dreams of invitations to Advance Showings, those hush-hush screenings of the new shows on next fall's schedule. Whether he gets to go to those screenings will pretty much determine whether he has a fat, successful year, or one in which he gets to put in a lot of time on that novel.

The Advance Showings start as soon as the network schedules are firm, and they help explain why the names of the same few writers keep popping up on so many shows. Of course, any show that reaches the pilot stage had to be written by someone, and we might wonder why that someone doesn't go ahead and write it once the show is sold. Sometimes he does, but often pilot writers are so rich and successful they can't do more than a couple of the shows. Or by the time the thing is sold, they aren't speaking to the producer any more. Or maybe somebody in Sponsorville has decided they aren't the type after all.

Any of these events results in the word going out to agents that the pilot will be screened at the studio at such and such a time, and the producer would like to have some writers drop in and see if they have a "feel" for the show. These invitations are golden, because those who attend the Advance Showings obviously have a long head start on all who have to wait until the program is on the air. In fact, those who have to wait that long might as well forget it.

Anyway, with a little luck a journeyman writer can expect a call from his agent with the word that there's a showing of a pilot that very afternoon. Only a few top writers are being invited, the agent advises, but I was able to squeeze you in. Two o'clock at MGM.

201

The writer, dazzled by visions of multiple assignments, presents himself at the studio gates. Before he can mention his secret rendezvous, the guard jerks a thumb toward the projection building. "All you writers go to Theater 5."

It is soon apparent that "a few top writers" includes all the writers he knows or ever heard of, and a few dozen more just in from New York. Any Hollywood hand can tell, just by watching the crowd pouring into Theater 5, that the pilot to be seen is a comedy, because it doesn't take much practice to spot a card-carrying comedy writer. He's the middle-aged fellow in the gray suit with the forlorn face. Put him cheek by jowl with a basset hound and the mutt looks jovial. The writers who do heavy drama wear flame-colored sweaters, drive sports cars, laugh a lot and worse still are usually seen with blondes draped over their arms.

Studio projection rooms are the last best relics of Hollywood's gaudy past. Enter one, and you can see how it was when the real stars and certified titans ruled the studios and mere mortals groveled at their feet. The best of the projection rooms feature at least a few massive leather chairs obviously imported from some London club, and there are phones, desk areas and rows of colored buttons to press. The leather may be a little cracked now, and the buttons no longer summon platoons of flunkies, but the grandeur lingers.

Once the race for the best of these ego massagers is settled, the writers usually have time to exchange some lively banter about their gallstones, who died lately, mix-ups at the Writers Guild over residual checks, and the rate at which the smog is killing them.

Before the film begins, somebody from the producer's office stands up to welcome the visiting craftsmen. On rare occasions it is the producer himself; more often it is an associate producer; and in many cases the welcome is delivered by some unknown who is never seen by anyone again.

Whoever the speaker, he assures them the show really is in the market for scripts. He also warns that since the pilot was filmed, the network and sponsors have ordered a few minor changes. Nothing to worry about, but the locale has been moved from Venus to the home office of a large insurance firm, and the hero is now a window washer working outside that office, instead of the commander of a spaceship. Actually, as you can see, he's still air-borne, so the change shouldn't be too much of a problem.

The film itself is watched in almost complete silence. The protocol for comedy writers viewing a pilot is never to laugh unless there is a scene so bad, so gauche, that it deserves a reprimand, whereupon a short, despairing cackle is permitted. But they aren't completely impassive during the better offerings. A fine, well-turned comedy bit will often draw an admiring "Hmmm." A really sharp, unexpected line may cause three or four writers to burst into an uncontrollable "Uh." Fledgling producers sitting through one of these showings for the first time have been known to crawl out before the final credits, blubbering for their mommies.

Once the film has been run and the lights return, there's usually an informal critique, whose tenor depends on whether the producer or any of his staff are still present. If the producer does remain, the remarks are likely to be along the line "You've done it again, Harry" and "This one's a cinch to go five years." If the producer and his underlings are safely out of earshot, the evaluations run to "What a turkey!" "Screen Gems had a better version 10 years ago and it flopped," and "What a lousy credit this would be! I wouldn't touch it."

Sometimes the showings are followed by inspirational talks from the producer. The Smothers Brothers situation-comedy pilot, not to be confused with their [network] variety program [which ended in 1969] was previewed on a Friday afternoon at a time when the show was undergoing changes, dissension and the panic of a rapidly approaching air date. Fred de Cordova, the new producer, stood up and said, "I know many of you have wives, home, children, mistresses. A weekend is ahead and maybe you have Little League, lawn mowing, assignations planned. Forget them. Go home and think Smothers Brothers, morning, noon and night. Then call me Monday morning with the ideas that will save this show!" No one will ever know whether it was the Little League or assignations, but somehow the Monday-morning calls didn't save the show.

Why Do You Laugh?

By Sheldon Leonard

FEBRUARY 11, 1961

On the stage, the holdup man thrusts a gun into his victim's ribs and snarls, "Your money or your life!" The victim hesitates, then says, "Well . . ."—and the audience howls! What's funny about that? Does it answer the question if I tell you that the victim is Jack Benny?

A man makes an upsweeping gesture with the palm of his hand and snorts, "Eh!" Why does the audience laugh? Because the man is Danny Thomas.

Durante mutters, "I got a million of 'em!" Funneee! But don't ask for a completely logical reason why.

Why is a joke funnier if you tell it in dialect? Why will a story about Brooklyn get a bigger laugh than the same story placed in Albany? Why do people groan at puns? We who are in the business of feeding television's voracious appetite for comedy don't know all of the answers. We just know these things are so.

Comedy does not survive analysis. If you tell your wife a joke and all you get in response is a puzzled look and "What's funny about that?" don't try to explain. Let it go. Change the subject.

Many scholars have tackled the question of "What's funny about that?" Many ponderous tomes have been written on the subject, emphasizing the importance of catharsis, vicarious participation, empathy and countless other elements in comedy. But if there is one thing about which I can be certain in this uncertain business of making people laugh, it is this: Pack all the academic knowledge of comedy contained in all those learned books into one capacious egghead, and put the possessor thereof on stage with any frayed, old-time burlesque comic to trade ad libs, and the old-timer will leave the professor for dead.

It would be nice if there were a way to intellectualize comedy, reduce it to rules and formulas. It would make us feel so much more secure. As it is, the writer, producer, director and performer may think a piece of material is funny, but the only time they'll know for sure is when an audience tells them so with laughter. And when the people laugh—yours not to reason why; yours but to go ahead and give them more of the same.

It comes down to this: Even though you fracture your friends and they tell you that you ought to be on television, wait a while before you quit your job and spend your savings on a TV wardrobe. Having a wonderful sense of humor is far from enough. Maybe your comedy is too special for mass acceptance, or too personal, or too *chi-chi*, or too far out. If it is and you face an audience with it, you will know how a Roman gladiator must have felt when his eyes swept the assembled multitudes and beheld an array of down-turned thumbs.

Comedy is made up of indeterminate parts of aptitude and experience, such as wit, fluency, self-confidence—and the proper combination of physical characteristics—a comedian is still a long way from possessing the attributes of a star until he has accumulated a vast amount of experience in front of audiences.

A few years back, that wasn't too tough to do. The legitimate theater was booming. Vaudeville performers did as many as five shows a day. All the top comedy shows in radio were performed in front of audiences. Every city of any size had its stock company, or was visited by a repertory company, or chautauqua or a tent show. Road companies were crisscrossing the hinterland. In those days a man could learn his trade. Today there is no place to make mistakes. Somebody uncovers a talented young comic, and whap! they shove him on television in front of 40 million people.

It takes time to make a star. Over the years the great comedians developed an invisible umbilical cord connecting them with the audiences they faced so that they could sense, with fantastic accuracy, how they were scoring. Because of this rapport, developed through exposure to thousands of audiences, they knew when to wait and when to accelerate. They could feel their control of the audience. They knew when the laugh was built up—ready to be released. The sum of these experiences is what is called "timing."

But the generation of giants that had the advantage of countless exposures to audiences via vaudeville, burlesque, audience radio, and so forth, is looking forward to reduced theatrical activity and more time spent clipping coupons, and the bright new comics are lucky to get in front of a theater full of people a couple of dozen times a year. They can do a few appearances on variety shows, or they can play limited engagements in the handful of night clubs that still employ comedy acts, and that's just about it. Meanwhile television sits waiting, hungry mouth agape, for new talent.

Another substantial handicap that besets comedy is the formidable array of taboos that have been set up. You mustn't tell dialect jokes. You can't make jokes about plumbers, lawyers, doctors, schoolteachers, mail carriers, and so on. Stay away from politics, current events, controversial subjects. The list is endless. Which brings us face to face with an ominous question: What is the future of comedy on television? It is bleak, friend. Bleak.

But the industry will find a way to meet the challenge. Whenever a public demand exists, someone finds a way to satisfy it, and the demand for comedy entertainment will always exist. It is as old as communication between men. I'm sure that our ante-diluvian, skin-clad ancestors gathered in front of their caves to yak it up while some slope-browed extrovert gave a Mack Sennett version of how he caught a dinosaur.

People need laughter as they need nourishment and shelter. It is our industry's responsibility to discover and cultivate the talents and skills that go into the creation of comedy. The big producing organizations should sponsor stock companies. This would give new talent a chance to try itself in front of audiences.

The industry must resist the censorship imposed by special groups with ready pens and tender sensibilities. The jokes are not meant to offend. It's too bad if we can't make a joke about doctors, for instance, without spokesmen for the profession sounding off as though we were trying to destroy it. What has happened to our sense of humor? Are we so stuffy we can't take a good joke about ourselves?

We must develop more respect for the accomplishments of our medium. I get very tired of the apologists for television. I don't see any articles in the Sunday book-review sections complaining about the over-all mediocrity of literature, in spite of the fact that 90 percent of the stuff that's put between hard covers is not worth reading. Art critics don't make an issue of the fact that the overwhelming majority of paintings that hang in commercial galleries are not worth wall space. In all other creative areas, it is taken for granted that the commonplace will outnumber the exceptional, but television is always being stoned because you can't view a masterpiece every time you twist the dial.

It's time we stopped apologizing for television's shortcomings and started taking pride in its accomplishments. I am angered and disgusted by those in our industry who rationalize their basic disrespect for television, and their unwillingness to really extend themselves, by saying, "What's the use? The masses don't appreciate good stuff." They talk down to their audiences, and (I'm glad to say)

their audiences, being a lot smarter than they are credited with being,
recognize it and don't like it.

Above all, we must be more daring. We must explore new areas of satire, fantasy and imagination, instead of trying always to be safe. Around pilot time, when conferences are occurring at every luncheon table in Sardi's East and Twenty One, you can hear shows described as "like another *Danny Thomas Show*" or "It's got the same value as *The Real McCoys*" or "It's like *Gunsmoke* only the hero's a sea captain." If you say about your project, "It's not like anything that has been on the air before," beads of sweat will pop out on your client's brow.

But to give the much-maligned client his due, if you've earned his respect and confidence by your track record, there's a very good chance you won't have to worry too much about agency interference. Those boys are perfectly willing to keep their hands off a smooth-running operation. If your show gets into trouble—well, that's something else again.

Those who accept unquestioningly the many restrictions and prohibitions that best the mass entertainment media are headed for mediocrity or failure. Anyone who aspires to a high place must believe in himself—in his taste, his judgment. If you try to please everyone you wind up pleasing no one. Ultimately, the only man you must please is the one you look at when you're shaving every morning.

Sports

In the early years of television, both networks and local stations found sports coverage to be an attractive feature, since it was a relatively cheap way of filling up a great deal of air time. As the medium grew and prime-time audiences multiplied, investments were made in other types of programming and televised sports coverage became largely limited to weekends. Many sports promoters encouraged limited coverage because they felt that television had overexposed their events and had hurt their box office receipts.

By the late 1960's, however, sports coverage was once again a major programming feature. This reversal was caused, at least in part, by the desire of sponsors of items such as beers, razor blades, automobiles, tires, airlines, power tools and insurance firms to reach the male viewer. The result was that before the end of the decade the total hours of sports telecast each year by the three major networks exceeded seven hundred and the amount of money spent annually by sponsors of televised sports was well over 200 million dollars. While prime-time network spots normally cost an advertiser from $3 to $4.50 per thousand homes and rarely more than $5 per thousand male viewers, football and golf were costing the advertiser from $6 to $8 per thousand male viewers. The demand still continues and in most cases the number of advertisers exceeds the number of commercial availabilities.

In spite of the increase in both coverage and demand, however, televised sports generally operate on a very small profit margin and, as Stanley Frank (pp. 210-215) illustrates, the networks actually lose millions of dollars in carrying some of the year's most important and most watched sporting events. Frank indicates that sports are the most overpriced shows on the air in relation to size of audiences and that the networks cannot be expected to continue indefinitely to carry sports at a financial loss as a public service or prestige builder. Frank suggests that sports promoters ought to realize that they are pricing themselves out of the television market and that athletes ought to recognize that a reduction in television coverage would threaten their salaries and pensions.

In his second article, Frank (pp. 216-222) maintains that the resurgence of televised sports has destroyed, or at least drastically altered, the basic concepts or conduct, or both, of every sport the medium has touched—except perhaps the Olympics. Frank claims that television has caused a loss of integrity in football, baseball, bowling, golf and hockey. He contends that the owners and administrators have debased their sports by succumbing to the large fees offered by the networks. Sports attractions have been changed, athletic skills perverted and cash customers short-changed. Frank also contends that television has sometimes deterred game attendance.

William Davey (pp. 223-225) answers Frank's charges and states that Frank is using TV as a scapegoat for all changes that have taken place in sports over the last fifteen years. Davey argues that the changes and inconveniences caused by the medium are minor when compared to the benefits of enabling millions of additional spectators to enjoy a variety of spectator sports. He denies that all the changes in sports are necessarily bad or that television has reduced attendance; on the contrary, attendance as well as viewership of all major sports is higher than ever before and sports themselves were never healthier. Davey believes the sports fans will not allow TV to significantly debase any televised spectator sport.

Melvin Durslag (pp. 226-229) is concerned with the corruption of the sportscaster rather than of the sport. Many sportscasters are characterized by provincialism and pussy-footing, and are not truly significant editorial and reportorial forces in sports. Durslag feels this is caused primarily by a system in which the sportscaster is selected by the team, promoter or ad agency rather than by the station. In these circumstances, the independent commentators with daily shows are the main hope for candid sports journalism, but even here a problem may exist if the commentator's station carries a particular team's broadcasts. Thus, according to Durslag, the most interpretative sports reporting is still found in the newspapers.

Greed is the Name of the Game

By Stanley Frank

AUGUST 9, 1969

Item: CBS is asking $70,000 a minute from pro football sponsors during the upcoming season. Network officials admit the price is "negotiable." They will accept substantially less to fill the schedule that is increasingly difficult to sell.

Item: NBC, operating on a new $50-million, three-year baseball contract, anticipates a loss of $2 million on the deal this season. Barely half the commercial spots on the *Game of the Week* had been sold when the season opened.

Item: ABC recently paid $12 million for the rights to the 1972 Summer Olympic Games.[14] Experts estimate the network will wind up with a deficit of at least $4 million on the telecasts.

Item: NBC paid $2.5 million for the Super Bowl in January but was able to sell only $1.7 million of available commercial time. Production costs and commissions to advertising agencies brought the net loss to $1.155 million on the biggest attraction in sports.

Item: The three major networks will all carry pro football for the first time in 1970. In May, ABC was given 13 Monday night games for $8 million, a cut-rate price, after CBS and NBC flatly rejected Commissioner Pete Rozelle's demands for telecasts in prime time. They insist football cannot compete in the ratings against movies and entertainment programs.

These straws in the wind—as big as uprooted California redwoods—should be clear danger signals to sports promoters that they are pricing themselves out of the TV market. Further, sponsors' resistance to the exorbitant prices networks must charge threatens the structure of athletes' cushy salaries and pension funds that are largely supported by TV revenue, yet both groups are blandly ignoring the economics of broadcasting. The situation can be summed up concisely: sports are the most overpriced shows on the air in relation to audiences attracted. The average cost for commercials on a popular

210

weekly show in prime time (7:30 to 11 P.M.) is $46,000 a minute. That show will draw twice as many viewers as a more expensive NFL game on Sunday afternoon. It will out-pull baseball (except the World Series and the All-Star Game) by a 3-to-1 margin. Other sports, particularly golf, have poor ratings that are even more disproportionate to the fees networks and sponsors pay for them.

"In any other business we'd be arrested for throwing money away," Bill MacPhail, vice president of CBS Sports, says morosely. "We're carrying sports purely as a public service, like news, but we can't take a financial beating indefinitely. Things really will be critical if cigarette advertising is banned from the air.

"To give you an idea of the crazy inflation in sports, we paid the Green Bay Packers $35,000 for all TV rights in 1956. Today, each of the 16 teams in the NFL gets a million and a half bucks a year from us. Costs to sponsors have gone up correspondingly, and the blunt truth is they're not getting their money's worth."

The most significant tip-off on prevailing conditions is that Howard Hughes, who paid $16 million for a 90-percent interest in Sports Network Inc. last year, has remained on the sidelines. He bought SNI, an independent outfit that carries golf, hockey, and college and pro basketball that the networks do not have tied up, after he withdrew a $148.5-million tender offer for 43 percent of ABC's common stock. Hughes had 34 percent of the stock when he suddenly called the whole thing off, citing ABC's "inordinate opposition."

Mr. Hughes can be a vindictive man when the spirit moves him, and he has the money to gratify his every whim. It was predicted that through SNI he would get even with the television Establishment by outbidding it for blue-ribbon sports events. Pete Rozelle has been threatening to peddle pro football on an independent network if the Big Three do not meet his demands. Although SNI has the staff and the equipment to handle football, it has not made a pass at Rozelle. Mr. Hughes may be an eccentric billionaire, but he is not so balmy as to get into a crap game with the odds stacked against him. He has seen too many suckers go broke in the six casinos he owns in Las Vegas.

Dick Bailey, who founded SNI and now is operating the renamed Hughes Sports Network, has bad news for hustlers who thought he would sweeten the pot with his fresh capital. "Sponsors are refusing to pay ridiculous prices asked for events that are a drug on the market," he says. "Team owners and athletes are getting all the gravy, and I have no intention of subsidizing them."

For years, people in sports have been exploiting television as

212 though it were the fabled golden goose, an inexhaustible source of riches. TV revenue assures profits to owners of major-league baseball and football franchises before they sell a ticket, and pro athletes, of course, are the new plutocrats of American society.

Big-league baseball players average $28,000 a year. In the National Football League the average is $26,000. Sixteen basketball players in the National Basketball Association are paid upwards of $50,000 a year; five earn more than $100,000. Lew Alcindor, who has yet to play a game in the league, will collect $1.3 million during the next five years. Joe Namath and Donny Anderson, who were given bonuses of $400,000 and $600,000, respectively, just a few years ago, can moan that they were born too soon when they read of the rewards O.J. Simpson is demanding for lugging a football.

Since attendance has increased slightly, if at all, in the last five years, it is obvious that fantastically inflated salaries are coming from teams' TV income—and that's only half the story. TV also is underwriting players' pension funds that were boosted to giddy levels by recent threats of strikes in baseball and football.

A ballplayer with 20 years of service in the big leagues is entitled to $1945 a month, every month, at age 65. If he played 10 years, he will get $1585 a month. Football players may do even better because their fund is invested in blue-chip stocks. In addition to cash payments, both groups enjoy fringe benefits—paid-up life insurance, medical and dental care for their families, maternity and disability allowances—that could cost some $2500 a year if bought individually.

All this is wonderful for the sweaty heroes, but the overworked golden goose finally is screaming for mercy. "It must be evident that sports are in big trouble when we can't sell the World Series, traditionally the Number One attraction," says Carl Lindemann, vice president of NBC Sports. "Everybody in America knew we were offering open spots to political candidates during the Series last year. Yet the baseball people boosted their price 30 percent on the new contract."

Why did NBC pay it? Lindemann shrugs. "We're caught in a vicious circle of network competition and prestige. We've had the Series for 30 years and it's an article of faith that we must keep it. I suppose CBS feels the same way about NFL football and ABC about college football. One of these days, though, a top executive will look at the balance sheet and say the hell with competing for losses. When that happens, you'll see what John Foster Dulles called an agonizing reappraisal of the situation."

It is unlikely that there will be any sharp curtailment of top events in the near future, but fans must be disturbed by continuing "accommodations" for TV that debase performances. The World Series, for example, always started on the first Wednesday in October. This year, it will begin on October 11—the day after the 1968 Series ended. If the exercises go seven games, the decisive contest will be played on the 19th, when the weather in most cities hardly is conducive to championship baseball.

Why the late start? Well, sir, sponsors must buy the entire Series package. Under the old arrangement, they got big audiences only on one weekend; they died on weekdays, when most male viewers were at work. The prospect of four Saturday and Sunday games, plus a third weekend for the pennant play-offs introduced this year, provides a more marketable package—at higher prices.

Now there is talk of playing weekday Series games at night. Bowie Kuhn, the new commissioner, bridled when the subject was broached, "What's wrong with night games?" he demanded. "The TV audience has doubled since the All-Star Game was shifted under the lights." You can safely bet borrowed money that World Series weekday games will be played at night by 1972, at the latest.

All sports seasons run too long. The networks naturally want all the dates they can get, and league officials are happy to oblige them. Basketball and hockey players bump heads for 82 and 76 regular games, respectively, then struggle through three best-of-seven play-offs to determine the champion. It seems evident that by the time the boys get to the showdown, they are too battered and bushed to play at the peak of their ability.

The extension of the baseball season has compounded networks' headaches in lining up football sponsors. "I hate to admit this because we don't have baseball," CBS's MacPhail says, "but all the talk that football has superseded baseball as the national pastime is malarkey. Whenever a crucial baseball game is opposite football, it kills us in the ratings. This year baseball will be on the air three Sundays in October, making it all the tougher to sell our NFL schedule."

Pete Rozelle, whose TV brinksmanship has turned pro football franchises into instant-money machines, makes token sympathetic noises in discussing the networks' problems. "Sure, I recognize that we may be reaching the point of no return for sponsors. I don't dispute the ratings, but we draw a male audience in the upper income brackets that offers a sponsor intangibles the figures do not reflect."

Contracts that are expiring this season bring $25 million a year to the NFL from CBS and $10 million to the AFL from NBC. Rozelle may get a higher price for the package as the negotiator for both

214 leagues, but he was thrown for a severe loss for the first time when CBS and NBC refused to bid on his grand objective—Monday night games in prime time. In the absence of competition, ABC got the 13 games for $8 million, less than half the proportionate rate CBS is paying on Sunday.

"I think it was a good deal for us," Rozelle says bravely. "The two leagues compete against each other on Sundays, with a resultant loss of ratings. Pro football was not getting the maximum utilization of interest it needs for further development."

"I told Rozelle we weren't interested in football at any price on Monday," MacPhail confides. "We'd never set aside three hours for games on one of our best nights. We have Lucy and Carol Burnett, who will draw twice as many viewers as a top game."

"Rozelle was out of his mind if he thought football could displace *Laugh-In* and the Monday night movie," Lindemann snaps. "Football won't pull a bigger audience on Monday night than it does on Sunday afternoon. Wives will holler blue murder if husbands try to tie up the set after monopolizing it on Sunday. Look what happened last year."

On September 16, 1968, a Monday, CBS carried a game between the Rams and the Cardinals, who were pegged as hot contenders for their divisional titles. Opposite it on NBC was *Madame X*, a turkey described by Judith Crist as "hokum and schmaltz and easier to peel than an onion for the same effect." The football game had a 13.6 rating compared to 27.9 for the movie.

"ABC is so far behind CBS and us in entertainment and news that it's smart scheduling to score some Brownie points with football," Lindemann continues. "I guarantee, though, that ABC still will finish a bad third in the ratings."

The reluctance of the Hughes Network to thrust large, coarse sums at Rozelle would seem to have scotched his threat to sell football to an independent network, but MacPhail is not discounting that possibility. "Rozelle can create his own network. I don't think he's prepared to exert the time and effort it needs, but he has a 50-50 chance of bringing it off. I have enormous respect for Pete. Anything he tackles he does well."

So soft sells and tough talk fill the air, and it is remarkable how people pushing up the prices talk at cross-purposes when it suits their private purposes. Bowie Kuhn revealed that Gussie Busch, owner of the Cardinals, assembled his ballplayers before the season opened and warned them that their mounting salary demands could force an increase in ticket prices that would antagonize the fans.

"My mail shows there is strong public reaction against high   *215*
salaries and pensions," Kuhn added. "I hope players are beginning
to realize the dangers of excessive compensation."

When Kuhn's comment was relayed to Marvin Miller, the player's
bargaining agent who made their strike threat stick last February, he
snickered. "For 40 years, starting with Babe Ruth's $80,000, high
salaries have helped baseball's publicity and image. The commissioner's office proudly announced last year that seven players were earning $100,000 or more. Now Kuhn suddenly is bleeding for the fans.

"The players get only one-third of the money the owners receive
from NBC, leaving a lot of room for negotiation. Everyone ignores
local TV, which pays more than the network fee." (Local TV adds up
to about $22 million.) "Total TV revenue is about two and a half
times player payrolls—without counting gate receipts and income
from concessions," Miller continued. "I agree that you cannot logically expect TV fees to rise indefinitely, but if I had to make a long-
range prediction, I'd bet that baseball revenue will be higher in 10
years than it is today."

Does that mean the players will agitate for a bigger cut of the pie
when the present three-year contract expires? Mr. Miller smiled
cryptically.

Weeb Ewbank, coach and general manager of the New York Jets,
cloaks designs on TV loot behind a disarming approach. His modesty
stunned one and all when, reviewing the Jets' 16-7 upset of the
Baltimore Colts in the Super Bowl, he intimated that his team might
have been lucky. "It's only fair to have a two-out-of-three series in
football," he said. "The Super Bowl is too important to be decided
in one afternoon. One game doesn't prove anything."

Not as long as a sponsor with a fat bankroll draws breath.

What TV Has Done to Sports
By Stanley Frank

FEBRUARY 4, 1967

Ninety seconds remained in the Game of the Decade—hmm . . . perhaps the Game of the Year . . . the day?—when Bud Wilkinson, the TV football analyst, inadvertently gave the show away. Unbeaten Notre Dame and Michigan State were locked in a 10-10 tie and, although the Irish had the ball back on their 30-yard line with the clock running faster than a thief, Wilkinson observed that there still was time for last-ditch heroics that could settle the issue. "Both teams are permitted four time-outs in each half," he explained, "and neither side has taken one yet."

That revelation must have baffled 33 million viewers, for there had been 13 interruptions in the game—12 for sponsors' commercials and an ABC "promo" plugging future events. Four commercials had come after each team's touchdown and field goal. Who called the nine other time-outs? The referee. Why? Strictly for the convenience of TV hucksters.

Critics who blast TV's mounting intrusion in sports point to contrived time-outs as examples of its detrimental influence, but there are far worse abuses. Concessions to TV have destroyed the basic concept of the World Series. Money-grabbing promoters are collaborating with TV in debasing college and pro football, basketball, bowling and hockey. The major networks have been guilty of phony buildups in boxing and golf to pull bigger audiences. With the sole exception of the Olympic Games, conducted by an international organization beyond its control, TV has corrupted every sport it has touched.

Apologists for TV argue that some concessions must be made to sponsors who are spending more than $200,000,000 annually on sports. They contend it's not unreasonable to ask the fans, who never had it so good, to hold still for an occasional sales pitch in return for getting all the blue-ribbon events, except championship fights, on the cuff.

The overruling flaw in this argument is that the integrity of sports

216

has been sabotaged by distorting competitive conditions to accommodate television. The culprits are not the sponsors or network executives. Like all competent merchandisers, they are exploiting every
possible angle to push their products. The blame lies squarely on
owners of pro teams and hypocritical college administrators who have
cheapened their attractions, perverted athletic skills and short-
changed their cash customers for TV's fast bucks.

The conniving behind the scenes is so flagrant that Bert Bell, Jr.
recently quit as business manager of the Baltimore Colts in protest
against the "crass commercialism" of the National Football League.
His father, the leagues's commissioner in the 1950's, sternly resisted
the blandishments of TV and imposed local blackouts to protect the
gate, a restriction that was altered last season. It is significant that
young Bell denounced "the supermarket air that has invaded pro
football" and declared that "the new medium in the NFL is the almighty dollar" a few days before the league announced its revamped
setup for 1967.

With a new franchise in New Orleans bringing the total to 16
clubs, everyone assumed the NFL would adopt the normal alignment
of two eight-team divisions. The moguls, however, unveiled a scheme
for added TV revenue, that set a new world record for barefaced
cupidity. They split the league into four sections, thereby concocting
synthetic semifinal play-offs for the Eastern and Western divisional
titles, a dodge that will bring in $1,000,000.

A typical example of the NFL's capitulation to TV was the game
in Minneapolis between the Vikings and the Packers on November 27.
The kick-off was pushed back to 3 P.M., local time, so that CBS could
pipe the game to lucrative Eastern outlets as the second half of a
double-header. The exercises were concluded under the light of a
silvery, frosty moon. Any reputable bookie will lay 6-to-5 that a bloke
rash enough to sit on a stone slab in the cool of the Minneapolis
evening late in November will wind up under it in a cemetery. When
Viking fans bought season tickets, they had every reason to believe
the games would be played under the most favorable conditions
possible, but the moguls callously gave them a fast shuffle to play
ball with CBS.

College officials who profess devotion to lofty ideals of sportsman-
ship and all that jazz are giving the pros a stiff tussle in double-dealing.
Penn State and Syracuse also delayed their game in November to
suit ABC's schedule and finished in near-darkness on a field without
lights, ruining a close 14-12 game for the players and spectators.
Both schools bitterly condemned ABC's action, but Asa Bushnell,

218 executive director of the NCAA TV committee, retorted that they could have turned down the network's request.

"I suppose they were afraid of losing the TV Fee," Bushnell told me laconically. Each team receives $105,000 [$125,000] for a regional telecast. A national hookup is worth $165,000. Principles are thrown into the trash can when that kind of money is floating around.

It is enlightening to note that eminent seats of learning are so suspicious of rivals' ethics that the major conferences pool TV revenue to curb abuses in the recruiting of players—for all the good it does. Last season each member of the Big Ten collected $90,000 and the Southeastern Conference whacked up $1,005,000. That was only part of the loot. Postseason games fetched fancy TV fees as high as $875,000 for the Rose Bowl, plus gate receipts in excess of $600,000.

"I'm sorry I ever had anything to do with the mess TV has made of college football," says Ralph Furey, director of athletics at Columbia University. He was co-chairman of the NCAA's first TV committee in 1951. "I was naive enough to think TV income would be distributed among all schools. When that was proposed in 1953, the big boys screamed 'socialism' and threatened to sell their games independently if a share-the-wealth policy was adopted.

"Since then, the rich have gotten richer and schools that refuse to compromise their standards to proselyte players have been frozen out of the picture. There's no question that TV has compounded the abuses of big-time football, just as the bowl games did. They're a fatal combination to amateur competition."

Once there were only two postseason games—the Rose Bowl and the East-West game for the benefit of the Shriners' fund for crippled children. In the 1930's the Orange, Sugar and Cotton Bowls got into the act. In recent years the proliferation has reached such ridiculous lengths that there were 20 clambakes this season, most of them cooked up to get on the TV gravy train and plug local chamber of commerce promotions.

Perennial powerhouses that monopolize the TV schedule contend they have stimulated interest in the game and cite the steady increase in attendance as proof of it. Their propaganda was refuted by the report of the 1966 NCAA TV Committee. After weighing such factors as population growth, rising enrollments and disposable income, the committee found that attendance lagged 65.7 percent behind the normal economic indexes. "If television's deterrence on game attendance had been completely neutralized," the report concluded, "college crowds now should total approximately 37.8 million a season instead of the current 25.3 million."

The chief victims of TV's inroads on gate receipts are, of course, small colleges which depend on football to support other sports and intramural programs. The NCAA threw a sop to these poor relations by sanctioning telecasts of four regional small-college divisional championships in December. Each participating team received a big, fat $6250 from TV.

In view of the graver damage TV has done in the structure of sports, the furor over football time-outs is small potatoes. In all fairness, it must be reported that interruptions for commercials are made with the least annoyance to the players and spectators. Both the colleges and the pros follow the same procedure. There are 18 spots for sponsors—two before the kickoff, two following the first and third quarters, two during half time, and three in each quarter. The only time-outs that may interfere with the action are the 12 during the quarters, and the networks have devised a satisfactory formula for handling them.

A liaison man on the sidelines keeping track of the commercials signals the referee for a sponsor's time-out, if one is due, during a natural pause in the game. The pros present no problem; they average five touchdowns and four field goal attempts a game. College games produce less scoring, but the liaison man tries to confine his breaks to intervals when the ball changes hands, as after a punt. Since it takes 20 seconds for the incoming offensive and defensive units to square away, only 40 seconds are added for a one-minute commercial.

Coaches have legitimate squawks when a sponsor's time-out disrupts a team's momentum, and in January at a meeting in Houston recommended a rule eliminating commercials at such times. In the Rose Bowl game last year UCLA complained that such an interruption jeopardized its 14-12 upset of Michigan State when it was trying to eat up the clock. The next day Vince Lombardi blew his stack in a similar situation while Green Bay was beating Cleveland for the NFL title. It is true that such incidents pop up infrequently, however.

"Maybe I'm a sucker to give you fuel for your article," Carl Lindemann, vice president of NBC sports, told me, "but it's a cinch TV will be stepping up its demands. Why try to kid anyone? A vicious circle is in operation. The more promoters ask for their attractions, the more commercials we'll need to get off the hook. CBS already is charging NFL sponsors $70,000 a minute. How much higher can the price go? The only answer is more commercials.

"When we had NCAA football, we started with 14 sales pitches a game, then raised them to 16, and then we had to go to 18. That's not an inviolate number. It's bound to increase."

220   Lindemann's prediction drew an emphatic denial from Pete Rozelle, the NFL commissioner. "Eighteen commercials a game is the absolute limit. Actually, we're far below the NAB Code maximum and we intend to stay there." (The Code permits 16 commercial minutes an hour on daytime shows. This means that during a two-and-a-half-hour football game there can be, heaven forfend, 40 commercials.) "We're making no further concessions to TV. We realize they will spoil our product."

Rozelle's statement is reminiscent of the brave talk baseball people spouted 30 years ago when night ball was introduced in the majors. A team never would be permitted to play more than seven games a season under the lights, the owners vowed. You know what happened. Nearly half the games are now played after dark. It's more profitable that way.

Baseball's surrender to TV is the most abject of all, for it has adulterated the fundamental character of the World Series, still the country's Number 1 event. More than any other game, baseball is a test of a team's strength in depth, particularly its pitching staff. Ty Cobb and Walter Johnson did not play on pennant winners for more than 15 years at the peaks of their careers because their supporting casts were inadequate. The same handicap kept Ted Williams and Stan Musial out of the Series after their appearances in 1946.

Pitching is the pay-off, especially in the Series. A team formerly needed four good starting pitchers when the games were played on successive days. There was a break in the schedule only when a shift in sites involved a train ride of more than 12 hours. Today, a plane can span the continent in half that time, but a day is set aside for traveling after the second and fifth games. Three weeks before the 1966 Series opened, Commissioner William Eckert announced there would be open dates even if the contenders were Baltimore and Pittsburgh, 40 minutes apart by air.

Why? To insure a big Sunday audience for sponsors who pay $3,500,000 for the TV rights. The Series traditionally starts on a Wednesday, and if a team wins four straight—as Baltimore did last year—the show ends on Saturday. Juggling the schedule to give sponsors a sure-shot Sunday game has undercut the emphasis on team balance and enables a club to get by with only two top pitchers. In 1965, when the Series went the seven-game limit, the Dodgers' Sandy Koufax and the Twins' Jim Grant and Jim Kaat started three games apiece. The individual performances were fine, but it wasn't baseball for purists.

A similar tampering job has been done on the format of the premier event in bowling, the National All-Star tournament. The championship once was determined by 15 rounds of preliminary play, then *221* a three-game match between the two top scorers, with the title going to the man with the most pins in all 18 games. TV sponsors, afraid a wide margin before the final match would detract from interest in the show, rewrote the script so that the title now hinges on the scores of only the last three games. Consistency is the hallmark of the great bowler. Under the present system, a lucky streak can win.

The National Hockey League, which has trouble finding enough big-league players to stock six teams, recently announced it is expanding to 12 clubs next season in one fell swoop. The big idea, of course, is to open up new TV markets that will attract sponsors on a national network. The decline in the caliber of play is not important when balanced against TV money in the bank.

It is an old story that boxing was killed by overexposure on TV, but the networks do not like to be reminded that they were accessories to the crime. Deep thinkers in the industry decided that the plug-ugly image of the fight racket had to be made more presentable by boosting wholesome types such as Irish Bob Murphy and Chico Vejar, whose manager was a sports announcer. The prize package, though, was Chuck Davey, a clean-cut graduate of Michigan State. He had one slight fault; he wasn't much of a fighter. Davey racked up an impressive string of victories over carefully selected opponents and sold TV sets like crazy until he had the misfortune to encounter Kid Gavilan, the welterweight champion. Midway through the farce Gavilan, a right-hander, switched to Davey's southpaw stance, boxed his ears off and fractured the bubble with a TKO in the 10th round.

On at least two known occasions TV has resorted to "dramatic license," a euphemism for deception, in golf. A few years ago Sam Snead faked, by his own admission, losing a match to Mason Rudolph after he was disqualified on the 12th hole for having too many clubs in his bag. The producer proceeded with the taping of the match and presented it as a tingling contest down to the final green with no mention of the disqualification. Another time a long-range camera went on the blink during a match between Gene Littler and Byron Nelson. When it was shown on film, the approach shots were faked by stand-ins.

Many suggestions have been advanced for curbing TV's influence on sports, but there seems to be only one solution. People running the events on which so much fervent attention is lavished must draw the line to protect the integrity of their games. Expecting the industry to call a halt is as unrealistic as expecting General Motors to curtail production voluntarily to relieve traffic congestion.

The acid test for TV is coming up this spring when CBS goes into

222   soccer, the most popular game in the world. There are no time-outs in soccer even for injuries; a player separated from his senses and maybe a leg is lugged off the field on a door and his team carries on without a substitute. The action is continuous for 45 minutes in each half. Soccer nuts in Europe and South America have torn down concrete stadia registering their displeasure with gimmicks that violate the traditions of the game. Bill MacPhail, director of CBS sports, was asked what he proposes to do about commercials.

"It's an awful headache," he answered morosely. "They've tried to cope with the same problem in hockey by running tapes of the game after breaks for commercials. The home audience is only two or three minutes behind the action at the end of each period. That works in Canada, but I don't think American fans will go for it.[15] They immediately suspect something fishy is going on and holler blue murder. They want to see the live action, the instant it happens."

He suddenly smiled. "Just got a great idea for the soccer. We can have a dog on the side lines and let it loose every 15 minutes or so. The fans always get a big belt watching a fat cop chase a mutt, and while everyone is convulsed we can run a commercial."

Mr. MacPhail was kidding, of course. . . . You want to bet? [Shortly after the soccer telecasts began, a referee was quoted as saying that eleven of the twenty-one fouls he called in a televised game on May 24, 1967 had been false, so that CBS could get in its commercial quota. Several players said that the referee had approached them before the game and "told us every nine minutes we must stay down." The episode received headline coverage in sports pages around the world and a member of the House Communications Subcommittee indicated that he planned to introduce a bill to amend the Communications Act to ban the rigging of sports contests. This kind of problem was one of the reasons that soccer is no longer on television.]

TV and Sports: A Rebuttal

By William Davey

APRIL 22, 1967

Those of us who happen to be employed in the television indus-try, and who are also sports fans to any degree, are getting used to seeing television raked over the coals for its coverage of sports—good, bad or indifferent. This is usually handled, naturally enough, by newspaper sports columnists who watch televised sports events all weekend and then complain all week in their columns about what TV is doing to sports. Since television enables them to see more events than they could ever cover before, this should add interest and authority to their columns. Sometimes it does, but too often they use up the space knocking announcers, camera angles and com-mercials.

But for a sports buff who might never in his lifetime have an opportunity to see a World Series game, a Rose Bowl game, a heavy-weight championship fight, an Olympic dash, a Masters Golf Tour-nament, a Wimbledon tennis championship, a Stanley Cup play-off game or a Notre Dame football game, television has opened a won-derful world of pleasure.

Whatever the technical or aesthetic shortcomings of TV, many true fans consider it a privilege to have seen some of the great athletes of our time in action: Roger Bannister's mile, a Stan Musial double, a Willie Mays catch, an Elgin Baylor basket, a Valery Brumel high jump, a Joe Louis or Ray Robinson knockout punch, a Bobby Hull goal . . .

Then there is your "veteran sports expert," Stanley Frank, who says that TV debases, corrupts and exploits sports. If there is any exploiting being done, Mr. Frank is doing it. He's using TV as a scapegoat for every change that has taken place in sports in the last 15 years that he thinks is bad.

Mr. Frank begins by mentioning the bafflement of fans watching the Notre Dame-Michigan State football game when, after 13 inter-ruptions in the action, the announcer mentioned that each team had four time-outs left. He says it baffled 33 million viewers. Thirty-

223

224   three million! Whatever their state of bewilderment—and it wasn't really that baffling—what of it? Was it bad?

There were about 80,000 people in the stands that day. Is it a bad thing that 33 million got to see the game? Maybe Mr. Frank was there—in the stands. I wanted to see the game too, but I couldn't make it. Neither could 33 million others. So we watched on TV and we didn't complain about the 13 interruptions (which, in addition to "contrived" ones, included those of TD's, extra points, injuries, quarters, two-minute warnings and half time). But Stanley Frank complains. Why? Because, he says, it was all done "strictly for the convenience of TV hucksters." Nonsense!

Let me tell you, old veteran sports expert Frank, why it was really done. It was done so that 33 million people could have the privilege of seeing the game instead of 80,000. That's the only way the networks can afford to do it, and if the commercials that pay the freight are too much to bear, there's a button on most TV sets that turns them off.

Football, like baseball and boxing—your prime examples of TV-corrupted, debased and exploited sports—are spectator sports, which means that people are supposed to watch them, the more the better. The inconveniences and changes wrought as a result of TV coverage are minor compared to the benefits. If they weren't, the public would soon let the television industry know about it.

These changes aren't made to suit the TV "hucksters." They're made to suit the public, and the public is well suited. Unfortunately, many sports experts deplore changes because it's tough to keep up with them; they destroy ancient traditions and outdate the clichés which make up 90 percent of sportswriting. But that doesn't make all the changes bad, nor does it debase sports.

Baseball night games are mentioned as "being more profitable" (than day games). Of course they are. More people can see them that way. Isn't that the whole idea? And having a day off in the World Series does not "destroy the basic concept" of that series. Nor is it planned that way "to insure a big Sunday audience for sponsors who pay $3,500,000 for the TV rights." It's done so that 50,000,000 people (many of whom work Saturdays) will get to see at least one game in case of a four-game sweep.

There's another sports myth that bugs us apologists, and that's the favorite daily-sports-page-space-filler of all: TV killed boxing. There's no doubt that TV helped—more power to it. But only one thing killed boxing. Boxing killed boxing. In fact it's still kicking the corpse.

Sure, there was Chico Vejar, Bob Murphy and Chuck Davey— all pretty bad. But there was also Joe Louis, Rocky Marciano, Ray Robinson, Carmen Basilio, Joe Walcott and some others who knew their trade. Television has been pretty much out of it for several years and now what do we have? Would you believe Brian London? Bleeding Henry Cooper? George Chuvalo? Sonny Liston's fights would have killed boxing forever if they had been shown—and TV would have been blamed.

However you weigh population growth, enrollments, income and the other factors Mr. Frank mentions to show that attendance is lagging "behind normal economic indexes," one fact is still true. Attendance is up in all major sports and sports were never healthier!

But the big thing is the one that critics insist on ignoring: Viewership is up! Millions of people are seeing games, contests, matches, bouts, competitions—everything. Some are good, some are bad, but little by little we learn and we become more selective. Soon the good ones come to the top and the bad ones drop out.

Spectator sports are not played for sports purists or sports experts —they are played for sports fans! They encourage youngsters to participate; they excite and entertain those whose participation has ended. If television can show Don Larsen's perfect World Series game to millions when only a few thousand could be in the stadium to see it, then TV has performed a service far beyond its ability to corrupt, debase or exploit the sport of baseball.

Sure, television makes mistakes and will make more; but even if it wanted to, it couldn't corrupt, debase or exploit the sports it covers. Fifty million fans won't let it!

When Will Sportscasters Be Allowed to Speak Up?

By Melvin Durslag

JUNE 24, 1967

For openers, Howard Cosell makes it plain that he is a rare object of art, the kind a collector might spend a lifetime seeking. "There never has been one like me before," he informs you, "and there never will be one like me again."

Some of his colleagues say "Thank heavens," but it is undeniable that Cosell, TV-and-radio sports commentator for ABC, is an unusual species. Since nobody discusses Howard with the verve and the enthusiasm with which he discusses himself, we turn the microphone over to him.

"I am a journalist," he says. "I am no house man, no shill and no pretty boy who is on the air only because his looks are merchandisable. I stand for frank, creative journalism in a business in which too many others are the essence of blandness. They stand for nothing. This doesn't mean we have no respectable people in sports broadcasting besides myself. It only means that too many are on the air who are an affront to listeners beyond the age of 6."

Whether Cosell is the god of oratory who will deliver the sports broadcasting children from their furrow isn't known. But two facts are pretty well established: (a) Howard is a fearless, often good sportscaster, and (b) he is romping about a field in which improvement distinctly is needed.

Considering their size and their influence as media, television and radio haven't, in the estimation of many, matured as reportorial and editorial forces in sports. Progress has been noted in some areas, but provincialism and pussyfootism still abound, and political manipulations behind the scenes pose obstructions to announcers, many of whom would do a better job if they didn't fear the system.

"Fear still dominates the industry," says Cosell. "The fear of offending on TV and radio prevents the kind of bold commentary necessary to any major news medium." Those who cover teams on the

226

MELVIN DURSLAG
WHEN WILL SPORTSCASTERS BE ALLOWED TO SPEAK UP?

227

air locally are generally selected by the club and approved by the station, or vice versa. Often the sponsor's ad agency pokes its nostrils into the selection, making the announcer beholden to many masters.

"Announcers have been the slaves of promoters, teams, agencies and the like for too long," says Don Dunphy, veteran sportscaster whose specialty is boxing. "Many years ago, as broadcaster for the New York Yankees, I mentioned casually one afternoon, "The Yanks look jittery today.' . . . The next day I received a note from the front office. It advised me, 'Don't ever make the Yanks look jittery.' We are frightened and squeamish in this business. I think we are ready for the kind of comment that was made over CBC (Canadian Broadcasting Corporation) by Bob Pennington (of Toronto), the color man with whom I worked the Cassius Clay-Brian London fight from England. Pennington told his audience, 'This fight is a disgrace to Britain. And the British Boxing Board should consider withholding London's purse.'"

At the local level, announcers covering the teams today usually fall into two groups. One—the more objectionable—is known as the "homer," which is to say he identifies personally with the home club, referred to usually as "we" and "us." He does this in most cases because he is encouraged to do so by the club management or the school, which controls his employment and which couldn't care less about quality journalism.

The other type of broadcaster covering the home team is impartial and objective for two reasons. First, he prefers to be. And second, the club or the school allows him to be. "In all the years I did the games for the Boston Red Sox," says Curt Gowdy, "I never insulted the intelligence of our listeners or made a fool of myself by rooting for the home team. Tom Yawkey, the owner, said, 'I listen to your broadcasts, too. Just give me the game as it happens—and leave the rooting to me.'"

The objective reporter is, of course, an improvement over the "homer," but not the last word in TV-and-radio journalism, either. Since he is a captive of the club owner and perhaps the ad agency too, he is restrained from offering in his broadcasts all the information related to his beat.

Say, for instance, sharp words have been exchanged between a football coach and his general manager, and a condition less than harmonious prevails. This is news not likely to be passed along to the listeners. Nor are they likely to question the wisdom of an ownership when a Frank Robinson is traded to another team and in his first year wins just about all the decorations for batting. "There is no

228 doubt but that the announcers on the beats must put the brakes on themselves," says Les Keiter, a seasoned Philadelphia sportscaster. 'The good ones try their best to keep their dignity without committing professional suicide. And the bad ones don't even try to keep their dignity."

At the national level, announcers doing, say, baseball and football, normally are hired by the networks, pending approval of the team, or the league or association whose games are broadcast. And often the ad agency enters the picture, too, as it does at the local level.

. . . .

If, as Les Keiter says, broadcasters who work the beats must apply the brakes, who is permitted to step on the accelerator? For the most part, this luxury belongs to the independent commentators with daily shows. They appear to be the main hope of the TV and radio industries for frank sports journalism.

In some instances, these commentators come through with the real story, but the system is against them. Say, for example, a local station locks up the broadcasts of a baseball or football team. To the station this is a valuable property, promotionally and financially. So the tendency, in most cases, is for the station to play ball with its team, build it up and avoid hard comment on what might displease the club management. The material delivered by the commentators on those stations isn't necessarily distorted; it is just watered. And there also are occasions on which the news is eliminated altogether.

"When you work for a station that carries a team's broadcasts," says Jim Healy, director of sports for KABC-TV in Los Angeles, "you don't get notes ordering you to give the best of it to your station's team. It is just understood that you will. And if you say something that offends the team, the owner won't come to you. He will go directly to.the station management."

A onetime color man on a Los Angeles Rams broadcast, Healy admits he knew his place. "The Rams played a terrible first half in Chicago," he recalls. "They had five passes intercepted. I had a half-time guest—a newspaperman—who, to my horror, began, 'The Rams look like a volleyball team out there today.' I quickly got him off the subject, because I knew it was my job to get him off the subject. Either that, or go sell neckties for a living. . . . Now I do two nightly shows for a station that has no local teams under contract. This means that my commentary is not restricted. I am permitted—in fact, encouraged—to say what I think. And I do."

Van Patrick, director of sports for the Mutual network, and sportscaster for the last 30 years, points to another obstacle to unflinching journalism on the air. "The big ambition of the young announcer," he says, "is to cover a local team or bust out of his town and catch on with one of the networks. Knowing that offended team managements can impede his progress, he is often going to proceed under wraps."

The presence of "under wraps" journalism on TV and radio has resulted in an increased effort on the part of the better newspapers to offer readers information they aren't likely to glean from the other media. Unable to compete with TV and radio on live coverage, the papers have, to a large extent, concentrated on interpretive reporting, on comment and on intimate stories related to the live news.

One listening to the broadcasts of the Los Angeles Dodgers, for instance, never discovered that manager Walter Alston, irritated by players griping about the bus, asked the driver to stop—and invited anyone who wasn't happy to meet him outside. This choice news morsel was carried in the newspapers. Nor did those tuned to New York Yankee games ever hear that a group of players had been fined by the manager for drinking and disorderliness in the Newark airport bar.

"Sportswriters like to pour it on us and call us gutless," says Curt Gowdy, "but there is plenty of politicking and home-town rooting and sins of omission in the sports pages, too." True, a lot of bad journalism abounds in the sports pages of America. But what incisive and unrestricted coverage there is in the daily media, still is dispensed, for the most part, by the newspapers.

Will TV and radio ever remove the wraps altogether? "I doubt it," says Howard Cosell. "The fact I've been permitted to stay around is a miracle."

Gowdy is more optimistic. "TV and radio are growing," he says. "Before long, stations and networks are going to demand complete autonomy in the hiring of sports announcers. Once the announcer needn't worry about agencies and team managements, his work will improve."

Will the teams refuse to go on TV? "For the kind of dough they are getting," says Gowdy, "I think they will go along."

Advertising

Marshall McLuhan has stated that historians will find in advertising "the richest and most faithful daily reflections that any society ever made of its entire range of activities." It has been estimated that the average American adult is exposed to approximately 650 advertising messages a day. The greatest single source of exposure is television. John Kenneth Galbraith argues that "the industrial system is profoundly dependent upon commercial television and could not exist in its present form without it . . ."

More than one-fifth of television air time is devoted to commercials. More than two thousand advertisers spend about two and one-half billion dollars each year for television time, not including the costs of producing commercials. Procter & Gamble alone spends more than 112 million dollars annually for advertising on network television. The production of a one-minute commercial costs the advertiser an average of from $22,000 to $25,000, and, as has been indicated, one minute of network prime time costs up to $65,000.

The television commercial has been referred to as an American art form which is the ultimate in mixed media—sight, sound and sell. The average cost of producing a minute commercial is now about five times that of producing a minute of a prime-time entertainment program. Stanley Kubrick, who reportedly spent 11 million dollars producing the movie, *2001: A Space Odessy*, has estimated that if a movie were made with the same care as a television commercial, the movie would have to cost 50 million dollars to produce.

Because of the continually higher costs of advertising on television, there is some question as to whether or not the proportion of total revenue from television advertising will continue to rise in comparison to that from advertising in other media. However, there is little doubt that advertisers will continue to spend increasing amounts in television advertising. The widely held belief that television is the most effective way of reaching large numbers of potential buyers is supported by the apparently successful use some firms have made

230

of television advertising. Alberto Culver, for example, experienced a   *231*
rise in sales from 1.5 million to 80 million dollars from 1956 to 1964
while almost exclusively using television as a means of advertising;
and largely through television Lestoil managed to thwart the competition of Procter & Gamble, Lever Brothers and Colgate-Palmolive
and to raise its sales figures from $150,000 to 100 million dollars in
just three years.

The playlet commercial has long been a main fixture of television
advertising. Peter Andrews (pp. 233-235) discusses the dramaturgy
rules for this modern-day passion or morality play and draws some
comparisons between the playlet and the Greek drama. Andrews
feels that the playlet is an effective means for selling and he analyzes
some of the techniques for dramatizing the product performance.

To Patrick Walsh (pp. 236-238) the commercial is the avant-garde
of change and both reflects and accelerates the societal trends and
mores far more than does the rest of television programming. This also
applies to production techniques and music; the producers of commercials use and improve upon new techniques of modern film-
making long before these are assimilated into regular programming.

Are we sure television commercials really do sell products? Are
the successes of Alberto Culver and Lestoil really representative of
the impact of television on sales, or, as some of television's competitors argue, are these two special cases, from which no generalizations can be drawn? Martin Mayer in his two-part article (pp. 239-
245) indicates that no one really knows the answers to these questions.
Television advertisers fall back on the "what-else-could-it-be"
rationale whenever their use of television and their increase in sales
are simultaneous. Research does seem to suggest, however, that
attempts to persuade the viewer to make an immediate purchase of
a specific product are more successful than presentation of abstract
ideas. Mayer describes two methods of pretesting commercials but
notes some limitations of each. In the end, it is usually the cost-per-
thousand which determines where and when the advertiser uses
television.

The time of airing is only one of the variables which may determine the success of a commercial. Repetition is another variable and
Richard Doan (pp. 246-248) explains that research findings regarding
its effect are still inconclusive. The sponsor still determines how often
his commercial is repeated and how long it stays on the air on the basis
of his own response to the commercial, how well he thinks it sells,
how much money he is able and wants to spend, and how much the

232 commercial is talked about. Doan enlarges upon the fact that the success of a commercial does not necessarily rest upon its popularity; in fact, quite the opposite may be true.

The effectiveness of the use of color in TV commercials is being tested and the results are positive. Judy Jobin (pp. 249-251) discusses some of these findings: for example, increased involvement with color commercials. Predictions are that by the end of 1970, 47 percent of TV homes will have color and by 1975 this figure will reach 75 percent. In view of the apparent success of color, black-and-white commercials, in all likelihood, will become increasingly rare.

The Commercial's The Thing
By Peter Andrews

MAY 16, 1964

Any television viewer who uses the commercial break as a time to open another can of beer may be missing some of the most gripping drama the small screen has to offer. After all, what are the empty, courtroom histrionics of Perry Mason compared to Calvin saving a marriage with a can of Ajax? What is some routine frontal lobotomy by Ben Casey compared with Katy Winters making sure her girl friend uses new, more effective Ice-Blue Secret so that she won't offend on that special date?

The play has become the thing wherein Madison Avenue shall catch the conscience of the consumer. And the playlet commercial, sometimes called the "situationer" or "instant passion play," is creating its own New Wave on television. In the last five years the playlet commercial, with its real-life dramatizations of man's never-ending struggle against dirty sinks or bad breath, has become a staple commodity in the huckster business. The trick is to write a morality play that runs exactly 58 [or 28] seconds. The script must follow dramaturgy ground rules as rigid as those of the classic Greek drama, never using more than 130 [or 65] words.

"I average a dozen rewrites and five major meetings per script," said one anguished writer. "I suppose you could call them writers' conferences but they're more like semiliterate bull fights. We'll fight for hours between ourselves and the client over the choice of a single word." "The playlet is quite close to ancient Greek drama," an account supervisor added. "The Greeks wrote about the gods and their relationships to man. We show the viewer the relationship of our product to his life."

If you think substituting Mr. Clean for Zeus in 58 seconds is easy, try it. Here is a guided tour through the basic plot of television's latest sub-art. The explanatory remarks are from advertising-agency playletwrights.

The first scene introduces the characters. "You establish your people by location. Put them into an immediately recognizable situation—behind a sink, in an office or at the launderette." In *Oedipus*

234 *Rex,* Sophocles used up about 20 lines before mentioning that the crops were failing and the cattle were dying. The neoclassicists of commercial-land don't have that kind of time. The horror of a dingy kitchen floor or a less than sparkling wash gets thrashed out immediately. "It's like starting a melodrama with the heroine already strapped to the plank and the buzz saw approaching."

Within 10 seconds things really start going downhill. The whole situation is clearly out of control. Those stains will never come out and it is simply impossible to clean those hard-to-get-at places. What's worse, there is often the threat of exposure. The bridge club is coming over and then everyone will know. "Never underestimate the power of guilt."

Suddenly, there comes that magic moment. Josephine pulls out a can of Comet, Calvin sprinkles a bit of Ajax around or Wally Cox starts popping Salvo tablets into the washer. The product, Madison Avenue's answer to the *deus ex machina,* has arrived. In a really fancy commercial the introduction of the product is coupled with a "Rejection Scene" where inefficient Brand X is banished forever. Nowhere in the history of English letters is there a rejection scene to match the contempt, much less the conciseness of, "Get rid of that greasy kid stuff and get with Vitalis."

Now comes the part the sponsor has been waiting for, even if you haven't. It's the "Proof Scene." "This is really the guts of your commercial. It's here that you explain and show whatever is distinctive about your product."

In Shakespeare, there is usually that nice scene near the end when everything has already happened, while you look for your shoes underneath your seat. No playlet commercial misses its own "Reprise Scene" where all are rhapsodic because of their shining floor or because they don't have to brush after every meal any more.

And, finally, as surely as the sun sinks slowly in the West, the playlet ends on a "Package Shot" of the product so everybody can remember who the real star of the show was.

"For products like soaps and cleansers and shampoos, the playlet is ideal," said an account supervisor. "In the first place, you're appealing primarily to women, with whom the playlet format is particularly effective. Secondly, there is little difference in price and, frankly, not very much difference in product performance. But with a playlet you can dramatize what differences do exist. That helps product personification and identification."

Product identification is further helped by having a single character running through all of the commercials. The running

character in each commercial series is chosen, in Madison Avenue
terms, "for personification of the product benefit." Ice-Blue Secret's
Katy Winters is cool, calm and never ruffles under pressure. Ajax's
Calvin is old and reliable, but he keeps up to date. Spic & Span's
Sophie is a cheerful, beefy girl—just the right size for those big
cleaning jobs. And Mr. Clean is exactly the sort of miracle-working
wonder man you'd expect to see walking around New York wearing
one earring.

The only difference between producing a 58-second commercial
and an hour-long spectacular is that the total cash budget for the commercial is higher. While the initial cost of a playlet runs [anywhere
from $200 to $200,000] about $10,000, it is not unusual for a big ad-
vertiser to buy $1,000,000 worth of air time to show each playlet. The
average life span of a playlet is a little more than six months. During
that time more people will see it than have watched every theatrical
production in America for the last 100 years. And that's show business
with a capital "B."

Commercials and Our Changing Times

By Patrick Walsh

MAY 25, 1968

Even as I write this, television is changing faster than at any other period in its history. But it's not really regular programming that is changing so radically: It is in the commercials that the revolutions heralded and protested, ballyhooed and feared in our national periodicals, can be most easily observed. I refer, of course, to the drug prevalence, the sexual revolution, and the massive alterations in the way people look, dress and act—the new freedom (or, if you will, the "new permissiveness").

In a nation taught to have a horror of drugs (but which uses them to an astonishing degree), which has traditionally had a phobia about sex (and a positive fascination with it) and which has emphasized conformity in both dress and hair, commercials are mirroring some strange things indeed.

According to a Bufferin commercial, "It's a turned-on day," and you'd best be turned on with it. Pepsi comes to the rescue because it, according to the commercials, "turns you on." Make no mistake; being turned on means just that, and the traditional route has been something at least as effective as marijuana. If your kid drops acid or blows a little pot to get turned on, it is obviously not a Good Thing. But what about that turned-on world we accept?

And why should a guy get expelled from school, threatened and cajoled by his parents and bugged by half of society because he has long hair, when whole gangs of people are on television peddling everything from Valvoline to bear grease to hold down your Lennonesque locks?

People who make commercials are always aware of changing trends and mores. It is true that various inroads have been made on our national psyche by such recent shows as *The Smothers Brothers Comedy Hour* and *Rowan and Martin's Laugh-In*, but it really is the commercial medium that knows "where it's at"; certainly not the situation comedies or Westerns, or the great majority of variety shows or panel shows, or even most of the talk shows and soap operas (which deal, respectively, mostly with innuendo and *double entendre* and a simplistic morality-play attitude). The common denominator here is a rejection of the tremendous ground swell of change appearing all over the country. Just as Maynard Krebs in *Dobie Gillis* bore no resemblance to a representative of the late-Fifties beat mystique, neither does 90-odd percent of popular programming resemble the hedonism of the Sixties.

As soon as there's something new in the world—the hip world of youth, swinging music and radical fashions—the hipper commercials, the luxury-selling commercials, will latch on to it (home products— detergents, floor waxes, bleaches and that ilk—are not particularly interested in swinging). Commercials for things meant to make one look more attractive (cosmetics and the like), to make one more desirable (deodorants, toothpaste, and so forth) or just feel plain luxurious (cars, travel and such) all display an imagination and/or a hipness and/or an open sexuality which are incongruous in relation to most other television programming, and, indeed, to much of American society.

A ginger-ale ad portrays a very lively yacht party, replete with bikinied young things, which may go on all night. Anybody staying out all night on a situation comedy would be cause for major trauma.

Motorcycles, until recently the *betes noires* of our society, turn up in commercials with startling regularity. Mini-skirts, to many a good minded American the harbingers of doom for all that is proper in our Judeo-Christian culture, abound in commercials, and have from their very inception (they're finally beginning to show up in regular programming now).

Teeny-bopper types have frugged, boogalooed, and slopped their way through commercials for soap, deodorents, soda pops and heaven knows what else—and they are very often accompanied by rock groups, flashing psychedelic lights and other of the various accouterments of the more famous discotheques. Female flesh shows up a lot, with bikinis on beaches for sun-tan-lotion ads, bare backs for shampoos or bath oils, or the aforementioned mini-skirts for just about anything.

Aside from the carnal aspects of many commercials, there are many technically sophisticated things about television's better one-minute spectaculars. Quick cutting, radical lighting, montages, hand-held camera techniques (later picked up for *The Monkees*), dramatic zoom effects, soaring pan shots, and sometimes astonishing color work

238   can be found in commercials but hardly anywhere else on the tube.

Where music is concerned, the hip commercials are, far ahead of most programs. While the situation-comedy people still think that rock is something akin to mid-Forties Woody Herman played loud, the commercial folk know better. "The Plymouth Win-You Over Beat Goes On" is, in reality, an alteration of Sonny Bono's (Sonny & Cher) song "The Beat Goes On," as sung by Petula Clark, another rock singer. A lot of people who think they hate the Beatles have probably been pleased by an attractive theme played behind a Chevy commercial on *Bonanza.* It bears a fascinating resemblance to "Norwegian Wood," which was written by John Lennon and Paul McCartney. Good rock pervades the swinging commercial. (The world of the TV commercial has kept a lot of fine jazz musicians alive, too—Paul Horn, flute; Pepper Adams, baritone; Clark Terry, trumpet; Ed Shaughnessy, drums, are just a few little-known but highly respected men to be heard in commercials.)

"The times they are a-changin'," and the commercial is often in the avant-garde, influencing the masses, propagandizing the future, subtly but inexorably showing tomorrow today. And even some of the more conservative and staid advertisers seem to be thinking new thoughts. "Geritol," traditional sponsor of *The Amateur Hour,* was co-sponsor of an early edition of *Rowan and Martin's Laugh-In,* one of the most youthful and offbeat shows ever to hit the air. Something is happening!

Does TV Advertising Make You Buy?

By Martin Mayer

JANUARY 8 AND 15, 1966

For six hours every day the television set is on in the home of that mythical personage with the enormous buying power, the Average American Householder. At least 65 minutes of that six hours are given over to commercial messages, which means 90 separate messages a day; 630 a week; more than 32,000 a year. For the privilege of putting such messages before the Average American Householder and his Friends, advertisers in 1965 paid about two and a half billion dollars.[16]

Did they get their money's worth? Oddly enough, nobody knows. As Charles K. Raymond, former technical director of the Advertising Research Foundation, wrote in a recent issue of the *Harvard Business Review*,[17] "Virtually no large manufacturer knows how much of his profit was caused by his advertising." From ratings surveys, market research studies, "recall" interviews and the like, the advertiser can say for sure that a lot of horses have been let to the water. And the incessant disappearance of goods from the stores into the homes means that somebody has been lapping it up. But no one can say for sure that these particular horses have been persuaded to drink.

Some commercials, unquestionably, have moved merchandise. The split head for Anacin, the white knight for Ajax, that genial tiger for Esso—all these presented a new view of a product that was itself virtually unchanged, that was still for sale at the same places for the same prices, and suddenly the "tonnage" zoomed. Only the new commercials could explain the change.

In the present state of the art of research, these what-else-could-it-be? measurements are most advertisers' only way of judging the effectiveness of their commercials. Such tactics work fine when the sales increase is a big one, but usually it isn't. Normally, over the life of a single advertising campaign, there isn't anything left over as a sure thing after the computers have calculated the *possible* benefits

239

240 to sales from special store promotions, tax cuts, new packaging, the messy divorce of the competitor's regional sales manager, hot spells and the like. So you can't prove anything. Justifying their advertising expenditures to their stockholders, most managements must fall back on something like the remark once made by advertising researcher Paul Gerhold, "If you think your advertising doesn't pay, just stop it for a while and see what happens."

A lot depends on what you're advertising. Alberto-Culver, which has sales about one-half of 1 percent of the sales of General Motors, spends more on TV commercials than GM does. Wrigley spends on chewing gum seven times as much as Swift spends on meat; and Consolidated Cigar spends more than giant Mobil Oil.

The perfect product for a television commercial is a new beauty aid sold at a rack beside the cash register in the store. The commercial demonstrates the product, suggests you too could look like that by using it, and shows the package—which stays in the mind enough to be remembered when seen while the money is actually in hand. Because nobody who buys beauty aids is really wholly pleased with the way she (or if it's hair tonic, he) looks, there is almost no brand loyalty to fight against. And because hope springs eternal, the new grease has a built-in edge.

The worst product for a television commercial (not counting things like drop-forge machinery which are unlikely to interest the Householder) is probably the one that requires the grasp of an abstract idea followed by a special trip to a place not on your normal daily route. Not many advertisers who have tried television have abandoned it, but the Florists Trans-world Delivery Association is a case in point. Back in 1959, after sponsoring several shows, FTD decided TV couldn't persuade viewers to send flowers by wire, and so bowed out [FTD has since gone into TV spot advertising].

Many television commercials, of course, do not aim to make an immediate sale of a specific product. Even at $35,000 to $55,000 [$65,000] for a single nighttime commercial minute on a network, an advertiser may feel he gets his money's worth just by building his name. Squibb introduced the electric toothbrush; but when General Electric put out a similar item ("Progress Is Our Most Important Product") it took away much of the business. Such image-building can be done in print, too—GE, AT&T, Du Pont and Kodak all spent more in magazines than they did on television in 1964—but the TV commercial intensifies the mood created by print advertising.

Some commercials are aimed as much at the salesman as they are at the consumer. Avon Products, which sells through housewives picking up some commission income in their spare time, advertises in daytime television to give its amateur order-takers a model they can follow when they ring the next doorbell.

Pete Cash, president of the Television Bureau of Advertising (TvB, the industry-wide promotion service), is intrigued by the possibility of using television to promote selling while the car is at the gas pump. For years, by literature, visits from representatives, commission arrangements, manufacturers have been trying to convince servicemen that they can be salesmen, too. Now, Cash says, television has done it: "Through television, Purolator got hold of the eyeball-to-eyeball market, the service station, where you've got the customer locked up for three or four minutes."

Sometimes the purpose can be to make a little company seem more prominent in its field. A Midwest fishing-tackle maker, Shakespeare, bought occasional inexpensive minutes on the *Today* show and was delighted at the improvement of its booth positions at sportsman's shows.

Department stores and discount houses use television just the way they use the big "advertised special" in the newspapers—to pull people into the store, where they will buy more than they planned to buy. "People shop at certain stores by habit, and you want to break that habit pattern," Pete Cash argues. "Well, the newspaper can't say, 'Now, wait a minute!' But a forcing television commercial can, by its intrusiveness."

"That line about 'I know half the money I spend on advertising is wasted, but I can never find out which half,'" said Horace Schwerin, proprietor of the Schwerin Research Corporation. "Whoever said it first—whether it was John Wanamaker here or Lord Leverhulme in England—he was way off. An optimist. The fact is, all but about 10 percent of the money spent on television commercials is wasted. The amazing thing is that television pays out, running at an efficiency of 10 percent."

It will be understood that Schwerin is not merely expressing an opinion. He also has something to sell: a service which "pretests" commercials in a way that allows Schwerin and a number of advertisers to give a direct measurement of selling effectiveness.

The procedure is a very simple one. People whose names have been selected at random from a telephone book are invited to come to a theater to see the screening of a new television show. When they get to the theater, they fill out a questionnaire about themselves. Part of the questionnaire is a list of brands in a product group, and each member of the audience is asked to check the brand he would like

242   to receive if he wins a drawing. To make sure people mark their true preferences, low-priced products are offered to the winner in case lots. The drawing itself follows, and there is a winner (his choice of brands is never announced, to make sure people are not influenced by it).

Then the audience sees the television program, and as the show proceeds, an announcer's voice asks people to check on an answer sheet whether or not they like certain moments. In the program Schwerin has embedded the commercial he is testing. When the show is over, the audience is asked to comment on the commercials, too, and to write down what they recall about the advertising. And then another copy of the brand listing is handed around, each member of the audience checks which brand he would like to win, and there is a second drawing. The second checkoff is the business end of the machine.

Between a third and two-fifths of the commercials Schwerin tests show no results—that is, the number of people in the audience who check the brand after it is advertised is about the same as the number who checked it before it was advertised. All kinds of commercials—rock 'em, sock 'em; honey-chile; mood—work on occasion and fail on occasion. Every so often a commercial shows a *negative* score—it persuades people who thought they liked this brand that they really don't. (The two biggest negative results involved commercials featuring aggressive women—one set in a home with a nagging wife, for an electric razor; the other set at a bowling alley, for a soft drink, with the girls trouncing the boys.) But most show some small positive pull.

On the basis of 20 years' experience, Schwerin has developed "norms" for each kind of product. "There are people who are loyal and people who are not loyal," Schwerin says, "depending on the product group. With beauty products, 35 percent are not loyal; with cigarettes, only 9 percent are not loyal." If a commercial produces more switching than is normal for this product, Schwerin rates it as a strong commercial; if it produces less switching than usual, he recommends that the advertiser and the agency go back to the drawing board.

These Schwerin tests obviously measure something, and among the advertisers who think they measure selling effectiveness are such sophisticated people as Alberto-Culver, Pet Milk, Goodyear, Miles Laboratories, Westinghouse and AT&T. Almost all advertisers and their agencies "pretest" a commercial in some way. Some use their own versions of the Schwerin approach, others show an audience just

the commercials, and then ask what people remember and whether *243*
they liked it.

This "playback" information may or may not be useful to the
advertiser. Occasionally it can reveal individual viewers' hostility
to the brand—"My cat won't eat it," a woman wrote of a pet-food
brand in a Schwerin test, "and most cats I know are the same." Sometimes people's recollections will reveal a disturbing distraction in
the commercial: "Woman almost hit a truck in the commercial and
kept smiling." And every once in a while the comments of these first
test viewers will tell the advertiser about a selling argument he didn't
even know was there—as in the famous Kool spot of television's
early years which opened with a picture of a breaking chain just
to get the people's attention and thereby conveyed a vague feeling
that "Kools help you break the chain-smoking habit." Most "playback" questioning is straightforward, common-sense stuff, which
would make a psychiatrist smile. Some ambitious advertising agencies do hire psychiatrists to perform "depth interviews" and profound explorations of what people *really mean* when they say after
watching a commercial that all laundry soaps are the same.

Many advertisers spend substantially more money in a different
kind of testing, looking for substantially more certainty. They will go
out into the field with a new commercial, buy television minutes in
anywhere from half a dozen to 30 cities, run their new commercial
in half of the cities (the "test markets") and their old commercial in
the other half (the "control markets"). If sales go up in the test
markets, presumably the new commercial is the more effective.[18]

Researchers have to be pretty good to pull this one off, partly
because it's hard to control what advertising the people see and
partly for deeper reasons. In 1964 Jack Gold, then of the Mennen
Company, showed that any three test market areas, averaged together,
were likely to be off from 20 percent to 25 percent in predicting how
sales will move nationally. But if the experiment is carefully designed,
it can give an advertiser an excellent notion of what he is doing. In
1959, for example, economists from the U.S. Department of Agriculture extended to the study of advertising effectiveness the complicated techniques agronomists had developed to test the effectiveness
of different kinds of fertilizer (no offense intended). As a result they
were able to say with a high degree of certainty that farmers wishing
to sell more apples should advertise the numerous ways housewives
can use apples rather than their health-giving qualities.

Testing can be and has been used to decide what sort of television show goes best with the commercial. "I'm sure the news strip

244   is good for drugs," says Robert Foreman, who recently resigned as head of television for Batten, Barton, Durstine & Osborn. "There's a rub-off—believability and timeliness. And I know the news shows are dangerous for airlines, because they have to worry about crashes. But that's pretty specific. Otherwise—and I've spent a lot of my career and a lot of my blood trying to build climate for commercials—it doesn't seem to make any difference. You'd think a period piece would be a bad setting for a modern convenience appliance, but then you look at the way Chevrolet sells on shows full of stagecoaches [e.g., Bonanza]. There are lots of theories. Some say if the show is dull before the commercial, it's better, because then you don't get a 'heightened lull.' But what good is that? You don't get any audience, either."

For most advertisers, indeed, the whole question of the effectiveness of commercials reduces to the simple business of audience size. What television offers first of all is the enormous audience—85 percent of all American homes at one time or another during the course of an average day. The effectiveness of the commercial itself strikes many advertisers (including some of the most experienced and successful) as a number on a roulette wheel: You may hit a winner, but you'd better not count on it. These advertisers measure the effectiveness of their commercials simply in terms of the number of homes they reach divided by the cost of the time—the "CPM," or cost-per-thousand, which is the Rock of Gibraltar of the industry. They make up their budget on the assumption that they want to secure so-and-so many "exposures," assuming a fixed value for each time the commercial actually appears on the home screen.

What *Fortune* magazine once called the Chinese water-torture method of advertising, dripping messages on the viewer's skull day after day, makes people hate commercials. Bob Foreman, while despising the approach, warns against underestimating it: "Familiarity," he says, "is the greatest selling tool there is." Still, when one considers the communication power of television at its most persuasive —its ability to get overnight and almost universal recognition of a new personality, a new product, a new slogan—the use of the medium for endless repetition seems a fearful waste.

According to Professor Gary A. Steiner's CBS-sponsored study for the Bureau of Applied Social Research, Columbia University (see pp. 411-418), three-quarters of the American people will "agree" with a statement that "Commercials are a fair price to pay for the entertainment you receive." But 16 percent think commercials are misleading, 11 percent think they are an insult to intelligence, 17

percent think they are boring, and 8 percent think they are in bad taste. *245*
Probably not much can be done about it: So far as these matters can
be measured, the most unpopular commercials (the patent-medicine,
deodorant, toothpaste jobs) are also the most effective. I believe the
headache-remedy commercial is *supposed* to give you a headache, to
encourage your use of the product. "After all," an agency head once
explained, perhaps seriously, "aspirin gets stale on the shelf, and it's
most effective if you use it up fast."

In one area, however, improvement might be possible. Steiner
found that of all critical statements about commercials, the one that
drew the widest agreement (63 percent) was, "Most commercials are
too long." Schwerin, whose service works for British as well as American advertisers, has found that commercials there score as well as
commercials here—even though all British commercials are only
30 seconds long. "We venture the guess," said a Schwerin newsletter
in 1964, "that if—by some miraculous decree—all U.S. television
commercials were given a maximum duration of 30 seconds, everyone would adjust to the new state of affairs very quickly with no loss
in effectiveness or sales."

Combine a cut to 30 seconds with the development of more informative testing procedures to help advertisers improve the sales
efficiency of commercials, and TV might be able to give an hour a
day back to the public.[19]

"You've just destroyed," said an advertising man rather bitterly,
hearing this suggestion, "the whole foundation of the way this business runs." But what's wrong with that?

A Word About Commercials

By Richard K. Doan

JANUARY 14, 1967

Are you no longer swept off your feet by the white tornado? Is that bad-breath routine about to drive you batty? In short, do you pine for fast, fast relief from those deadly familiar commercials? And does it seem to you that advertisers ought to know it when they're rubbing your fur the wrong way time after time, day after day, night after night, week after week—yes, even year after year?

Relax. They know what they're doing. And they don't mind irritating you. Not, at least, as long as they're getting through to you. Not as long as you remember their brand, and buy it.

You say you wouldn't buy that brand if you were starving to death and it would save your life? It matters not. You must be in a minority. The experts say it doesn't work that way. Most people will buy a highly competitive product if they think it best even if its TV advertising rubs them raw. Take Madison Avenue's word for it. The boys there aren't laboring to make you love them. All they want to do is sell you.

They have no rules about how long a TV commercial or selling theme shall run. Sometimes a spot's longevity is determined simply by how much the sponsor has, or wants, to spend. Sometimes, as with cold remedies, it's a passing event.

More often the determining factor is how well a commercial sells. As one Madison Avenue expert put it: "Especially in the drug field, an advertiser may get what he considers a satisfactory commercial and spend against it almost to the end of time." The Aerowax people, for instance, liked the gimmick of machine-gun bullets spattering off "jet-age plastic" so well that they kept this theme going for four years.

"One reason you'll see a commercial repeated over and over," explained John Bergin of the Batten, Barton, Durstine & Osborn ad agency, who created the successful Dodge Rebellion campaign and who's also involved in selling Pepsi-Cola, "is that the cost of producing commercials has skyrocketed in recent years. It's running up to

246

$50,000 (and sometimes even more) to film a single minute. If Holly- *247* wood spent proportionately as much for movies, every one of them would be a *Cleopatra!*"

But how does an advertiser know when his spot has run its course? Judging by what the agency oracles say, nobody has anything resembling a pat answer. Suggested Paul Gerhold of the J. Walter Thompson Co.: "When people stop talking about your commercial, it's time to pull it off."

Huge sums are regularly spent by the sponsors and their agencies trying to find out whether people are "talking about" their TV spots. This is done by so-called follow-up interviewing of householders, usually by phone or by door-to-door canvassing.

It may come as a shock to many viewers, but these surveys seldom bother to elicit feelings of irritation engendered by a sales pitch. That just isn't considered important. "Some of the most irritating commercials have been the most successful," says Richard A. R. Pinkham, whose Ted Bates agency has been noted for some of the hardest sells in TV (for Anacin, Carter's Pills, among others). He assured an inquirer that if he and this agency had any such selling job to do over again, "we'd do it just the same way."

Frank Kemp at the Compton agency, who oversees campaigns for such products as Tide, Gleem and Ivory soap, sided with Pinkham's viewpoint. "Nearly everybody supposedly hates those commercials," he remarked regarding a well-known headache remedy's spots, "but they sell. The point is, we're not trying to make people love us; we're only trying to sell."

Pinkham, incidentally, claimed it is more often the sponsor himself rather than the TV audience "who gets bored first with a commercial." "We sometimes have a problem keeping him, not the audience, from getting irritated by it," he reported. He declined to identify any of his clients who have begged for relief from their own ads.

Perhaps the most surprising part of all, however, is the fact that the billion-dollar advertising business has no clear picture yet of the impacts of repetitious selling. The Schwerin Research Corporation, an outfit that has spent years probing the subject, confessed recently in a report on "The Economics of Wear-Out": "The life cycle of a television commercial is a difficult phenomenon to chart or even to comprehend."

Studies suggest, the firm said, that "the incessant drip" of repeated commercials "evidently splashes off more than it soaks in," possibly because consumer resistance hardens as the pitch gets more familiar or because the commercial has done all the convincing it's

248 going to. But nobody really knows what massive doses of advertising are doing to TV watchers, according to Schwerin.

"What happens," the researcher wondered, "when the consumer is exposed to a thousand advertising impressions a day—when he may be exposed to the same piece of advertising several times a day—when he is liable to see it again and again for months or even years—and when he is simultaneously exposed to more or less the same competitive claims in the product field?"

Viewers may not have a scientific answer to that one, but they might give Mr. Schwerin some choice opinions.

Why Color Commercials Are Successful

By Judy Jobin

SEPTEMBER 2, 1967

Madison Avenue's manipulators, according to the latest study[20] of color television and its effects, are discovering that color TV's selling powers drastically outstrip those of its monochromatic poor relation.

The point is, everyone knows that roses are red and violets blue. But when you watch black-and-white television, you see dingy gray roses. Consequently, there's a credibility gap. You don't get really *involved*. And that is the key word, says the "Psy-Color-Gy" report. That's the name of this scientific examination of the impact of color television on that most precious of commodities, the psyche—and on its neurological in-laws, the emotions.

"Psy-Color-Gy" represents the combined efforts of Robert M. Hoffman, vice president for marketing and research of a group called Television Advertising Representatives; and Dr. Ernest Dichter, head of the Institute for Motivational Research.

"Color," says the report, "is a state of mind; color is emotion." Which means, that you are highly susceptible to color because you are, face it, largely an emotional creature. Witness the answers given by more than 400 average housewife, mother and grandmother types who participated in the battery of tests and interviews devised by Dichter and Hoffman.

The first of these was a carefully controlled experiment to measure the advantage of color commercials over their black-and-white counterparts. Identical commercials (20 in all), of both the tinted and untinted variety, were screened before six groups totaling 300 women. After each screening the subjects were asked to respond—positively, negatively or neutrally—to eight statements concerning their emotional reactions. There were enough more ayes for color commercials than for black-and-white to give color, right now, a 17 to 34 percent advantage—and a *potential* advantage of better than 50 percent.

However, what's big news for advertisers doesn't necessarily

250   have to be good news for the public. A few hypersensitive persons
have been known to react so violently to certain colors that they fell
into a sort of stupor known as "color shock"; but that's not in the realm
of possibility for most viewers. About the worst an average color-set
owner can realistically expect is an occasional, rather silly lapse from
normal behavior. (And by the way, the longer you own a color set,
say the researchers, the stronger its impact will be. Tests also revealed
that you'll be more sensitive to color if you're under 40.)

The symptoms of this malady, manifested by several participants in the study, may well become the most popular psychological
hang-up of the next decade. They're unsettling at best. Dr. Dichter
describes, for instance, the "Aha! experience," which is more likely
to be induced by color commercials than by black-and-white. The
Aha! experience is that moment of truth when Hannah Housewife,
on seeing a color image of, say, Jawgrab Denture Adhesive in pale
lavender, gasps with insight and cries jubilantly, "I saw that in the
supermarket yesterday and that's just how it looks!"

There's a chance that Hannah, only temporarily unhinged, may
emerge relatively unscarred from that near-epiphany—but only to
another neurosis. Even more rattling, for instance, is color television's
ability to diminish by one-half the viewer's psychological distance
from the goings-on in the mini-screen world. This tends to create a
dangerous sense of intimacy.

An example is the case of a wanton Bronx housewife who relates
"When I watch color I feel like I can reach right out and grab whatever
I am watching, especially that Illya Kuryakin.[21] He's so sexy." Luckily
for Mr. Kuryakin, color can do nothing to reduce *physical* distance
between the desired and the desirous. And unfortunately for our
Bronx housewife, neither Mr. Kuryakin nor a reasonable facsimile
can be purchased at her local A&P.

The Hoffman-Dichter study classifies a variety of polychromatic
viewing experiences, including deep "emotional involvement . . .
security," for instance, which means, in the poignant words of a Baltimore housewife—"With color I feel part of whatever is going on,
even in commercials." And what *that* means, in terms of television's
realities, is that you're going to experience an intimate, albeit foolish,
psychosomatic involvement with the commercial world's distressing
crises: headache, backache, dingy washdays, and the lot.

In fact color brings television much closer to being an element
of "massage" as Marshall McLuhan defines it: "The medium is what
happens to you." And it doesn't happen rationally, so you can't fight
back. Color works subtly—it indicates mood: Blue is peaceful, it

allows you to take mental short cuts; red means stop or it means pain. None of that has to be verbalized. Thus the advertiser, with less explaining and describing to do (he no longer has to say "Look for the red-and-white package"), has more time for his actual sales message.

Dr. Dichter describes exactly how color TV will "happen to" the viewer. The latter may be shocked and bewildered to find himself engaged in an absurd practice called "mental rehearsal" in which he unconsciously rehearses the use of a product in his mind. And from there it is a logical step to the so-called "opening night"; that is, to the actual purchases of the product.

Another effect of color—the clarification of background and detail —can have morbid side effects. Witness this shameless display from an elderly Florida woman. "You get all the details. One night we actually spotted on one of the performers a couple of black hairs on her skin. It was clear and real. You wouldn't have been able to see it on black and white television." The same lady also expressed interest in seeing sunburn commercials in color. "That commercial where the girl is in pain would show up very well in color."

On the other side of the coin, color effected a minor miracle in Phoenix, Arizona, where a hard-of-hearing housewife reported: "Since we got our color television, I don't need to turn the volume up. For some reason, I can hear better when I watch color shows." That happened because color adds a dimension of depth.

"Psy-Color-Gy" reports that, according to results of its word test, people feel "friendly" rather than "reserved" toward color television. Which is really a very nice way to feel toward TV, considering the time devoted to it.

The aesthetic element can't be overlooked either. Several years ago, David Sarnoff, who pioneered for color as far back as 1930, lyricized: "What is a rose in black and white? What is this world without color, without the clouds and skies and the rainbow?" What is it, indeed?

Blacks
on the Screen

By 1968-69, blacks were starred or co-starred in fourteen prime-time network series. Twenty-one of the fifty-six nighttime dramatic shows had at least one regular black performer. An increasing number of blacks were appearing in a wider variety of commercials and were being given primary roles in many of them.

The appearance of blacks on camera is very recent. In 1965, all three networks were monitored for five consecutive hours and during that period just three blacks appeared on screen, two of them for less than one minute. A survey of commercials aired during sports telecasts in 1966 revealed that blacks appeared only five percent of the time, even though Negro atheletes comprised almost half of professional basketball and close to one-third of professional football and baseball. Moreover, those blacks who did appear in the commercials surveyed were usually extras in beer, cigarette, soft drink and automobile advertisements; no blacks were included in commercials for gasoline, food, banks or insurance companies, or clothing. In 1967, only 2.3 percent of all television commercials used blacks.

The reasons commonly given for the large increase in the appearance of blacks on television in 1968-69 were several. These included the pressure of social change which was accelerated by the civil rights movement; the success of Bill Cosby in *I Spy*, the Kerner Commission Report which charged TV with "tending to ignore the fact that an appreciable part of its audience is black" and called for the use of more black actors; the assassination of Martin Luther King; an increasing recognition by advertisers of the buying power of blacks and the ability of television to reach them; and finally, as one reporter put it, "a willingness on the industry's part to further the cause of social justice as long as it is in vogue and doesn't cost money."

Although the number of Negroes appearing on television is growing, there remains a very significant problem: that of making

the increased appearances of blacks truly meaningful by increasing
understanding between the races. When undertaking to resolve this
issue, the television industry will have to deal with many difficulties
which relate to what Robert Lewis Shayon has referred to as "the
dilemma of how a subculture can at the same time preserve its unique-
ness and contribute to the consensus that must cement a variety of
subgroups in a pluralistic society."

Many obstacles will need to be overcome, and the answers will
need to be found for many questions. How can the black performer
keep working and yet avoid a new Uncle-Tomism? How can he avoid
complete accommodation to prevailing white styles of television and
at the same time take advantage of an opportunity to enrich the general culture by his special experience? How and when will television
overcome the present tendency to stereotype the black as a kind of
Super Negro who sounds white and looks black, who, until recently,
never had bad breath or needed cosmetics, who is almost always an
official upholder of the law (that is, a policeman, a military man)
rather than an average citizen or even a lawbreaker? How can the
racial barriers in broadcast unions be broken? How will the industry
overcome the resistance of blacks to enter broadcasting, either because they are suspicious of "tokenism" or totally unprepared psychologically, as Shayon feels might be the case with regard to the less
educated. Finally, there is perhaps the most crucial question of all:
How should television handle the racial issue? Is Godfrey Cambridge
correct when he says that "issues are often best handled by indirec-
tion" and that a direct assault on the racial question will cause "blacks
and whites in perfect harmony to switch over to whatever fantasy is
left"?

Professor Martin Maloney (pp. 255-258) suggests the rather formidable difficulties of characterizing blacks on television. He sketches a
brief historical survey of blacks on the home screen, indicating just
how invisible the blacks have been. Now that the blacks are visible
and will probably be even more so in the future, what are they going
to look like? Maloney points out that at the moment the black people
on television are differentiated by only their color. He presents three
alternatives available to writers and producers; but he feels that the
outcome will most likely be a continuation of the present attempt to
assimilate the blacks into white roles and white stories.

Art Peters (pp. 259-264) contends that the increase in appearances
by blacks on television is laudatory but not sufficient. Blacks need to
be presented as fully-developed living characters, complete with

254   good and bad features, with whom the audience can become truly involved. Peters feels that television could accelerate and even lead social change by increasing awareness and racial understanding. Instead the medium is merely keeping pace with trends and reinforcing existing images of the Negro by mirroring an American society in which blacks play a limited role, usually as auxiliaries to whites.

Black Is the Color of Our New TV

By Martin Maloney

NOVEMBER 16, 1968

Diahann Carroll, in the NBC series *Julia*, is, I believe, the fourth black actress to star in a series on American TV (Ethel Waters, Hattie McDaniel, and Louise Beavers each played the title role in *Beulah*), and Diahann seems to be the third black performer of either sex to have her own network television series. Nat King Cole and Sammy Davis Jr. preceded her, but if *Julia* succeeds, she will be the first and only successful member of this last, lonely trio.

As Arnie Toynbee used to say in Western Civilization 101, History teaches us that a black star in a TV series—any black star, any TV series—will cause militant bigots to besiege their local stations. This time, I doubt that history is right. Not that American audiences don't include a rich and gaudy array of bigots; it's just that they don't seem to have as much clout as they once did. People like Bill Cosby, late of *I Spy*, Nichelle Nichols of *Star Trek* and Greg Morris of *Mission: Impossible* have established themselves firmly as regular and successful television performers; the next step, inevitably had to be a series in which a black actor or actress was the star.

The main problem with TV ventures like *Julia*, as I see it, is answering the question, "But what are TV blacks going to be like?" Some people feel that when, after 20 years of reflecting American culture, TV has gotten around to recognizing the presence of some 22 million blacks in our midst (surely the slowest double-take in history), the images which emerge on the screen should show "typical" people in "true-to-life" situations. This is known technically as the Tell-It-Like-It-Is-Baby syndrome. The Tell-It-Like-It-Is people would presumably come up with a grim and defiant tale in which Miss Carroll would appear as an abandoned wife, trying to raise seven kids in a rat-infested slum on relief.

The producer of *Julia*, Hal Kanter, an expert at contriving TV comedy, has a different set of stereotypes to offer, derived more from

255

256 *Ozzie and Harriet* than from James Baldwin or LeRoi Jones. Julia is a fairly prosperous nurse and a war widow with one child. Kanter says that the series is "a situation comedy with no laugh track."

I hope, as Kanter does, that TV audiences will supply the laughter. It would be pleasant to have Miss C. around for a while—and besides, TV can stand to be much blacker than it ever has been.

There can be no doubt that the blacks are on TV; they've been on the way since 1962, though only a few of the reasons for this sparse showing were made clear last March, when Michael Dann, CBS vice president for programming, testified before a committee. He explained the absence of blacks in television entertainment by pointing out that TV had not been willing to pervert the truth about American life by depicting black governors or business executives, blacks at the 21 Club or in Beverly Hills swimming pools, when in fact there aren't any. CBS writers, he said, try to avoid "artificial situations." This seems a fair and adequate explanation—if you believe that such dramas as *Lost in Space* and *The Beverly Hillbillies* and *The Wild Wild West* derive from the great realistic tradition of Zola, Ibsen and Dreiser.

Behind this sort of instant defensiveness, however, and more or less in private, there have been serious and well-intentioned discussions of the problem by TV executives. The resulting decision seems to have been to admit more blacks to Televisionland, in everything from commercials to Westerns. The remaining question is: what are they going to look like when they get there? It's a hard question to answer, because, until recently, blacks in TV have been only slightly less rare than aardvarks or unicorns.

A quick canter through the history of programming reveals how nearly invisible they really were. Most of their appearances were as "guests"; a TV set-owner might, over the years, have become reasonably familiar with the look and sound of Louis Armstrong, Sammy Davis Jr., Mahalia Jackson and a few others. Harry Belafonte has done an occasional special. Sidney Poitier appeared years ago in a *Philco TV Playhouse* drama, Ossie Davis starred in "The Emperor Jones" for *Kraft Television Theatre*, and *Hallmark Hall of Fame* produced "Green Pastures."

As for series comedy, there was always Eddie Anderson as Jack Benny's valet, Rochester; there was *Beulah* (a maid); and of course, there was the immortal *Amos 'n' Andy*, which gave black performers a little TV work more or less by accident. This enormously popular radio series was written and performed by Freeman Gosden and Charles Correll, both white, who somehow conveyed the impression

that they had learned about blacks mainly by studying Eddie Cantor's **257**
burnt-cork routines. *Amos 'n' Andy* represented its characters as
happy, unreliable buffoons. When it came to TV in 1951, the Gosden
and Correll roles were played by genuine black actors. The series
lasted on CBS and in syndication until 1964, when pressures from
civil-rights groups finally forced its withdrawal. As of that date, *Amos
'n' Andy* was clearly the most vigorous, continuing effort made by
television to show what blacks were "really like."

The principal series which might be though to compete for this
distinction were, in fact, no competition at all. A musician named
Bob Howard once had a successful series called *Sing It Again*, but
this was in the early days of the medium, long before TV became big
business. In 1957, Nat King Cole starred in a network series which
failed because no sponsor would support it. In 1966, Sammy Davis Jr.,
appeared in his own weekly series, an inept offering which faded
quickly.

In short, the black American has been the invisible man—or,
at least, one of the invisible men—on U.S. television. Consider an
episode which happened in Harlem, in 1963. A civil-rights organization offered local children one silver dollar for each black face they
could spot on TV (no baseball players included). Over a period of six
Saturday afternoons, the organization paid out exactly $15.

The uncomfortable truth may just be that, exept for the long
series of marches and demonstrations from Selma and Ol' Miss to
Resurrection City, and especially except for the protests, sit-ins and
riots, TV might be today as lily-white as it was 10 years ago. The civil-
rights and black-power movements provided news of a dramatic
voltage which television simply could not—and did not—ignore.

TV drama didn't become integrated in a major way until 1965,
when Bill Cosby accepted a co-starring role in the NBC series *I Spy.*
Cosby's success—he received three Emmys—created a new figure
in TV drama: what has come to be known as the "black second banana."
In its present usage, the term refers to the part which Gabby Hayes
used to play in Western movies, that is, the pal and/or assistant of the
hero. Cosby didn't look or sound much like Gabby Hayes; but then,
the whole climate of entertainment is much cooler these days. He
was followed by a handful of other blacks in subsidiary roles: Hary
Rhodes in *Daktari*, Don Mitchell in *Ironside*, Greg Morris in *Mission:
Impossible*, Ivan Dixon in *Hogan's Heroes.*

All this clearly constitutes a trend, which is something TV understands. During the present season, black actors are popping up all
over the place. Michael Dann, for instance, seems to have recanted

258   on his earlier stand for uncompromising realism in TV drama. CBS
has introduced a black engineer into the *Family Affair* and a black
marine into *Gomer Pyle, USMC.* NBC has *Julia,* Flip Wilson, and a
black physician in *The Doctors.* ABC has done very well too. Their
fall line-up has included *The Mod Squad,* with Clarence Williams III,
and *The Outcasts,* co-starring Otis Young. *Peyton Place*—ever an
avant-garde effort—will present an actual "friendship" between a
white girl and the son of a newly arrived black family.

Meanwhile, the long, unsettled spring and summer of 1968
produced a plethora of documentaries and specials about and for
blacks: a rerun of NBC's *Same Blood, Same Mud,* the CBS series
Of Black America, ABC's *Time for Americans,* and the NET *Black
Journal* were outstanding examples. Possibly in an effort to ease a
potentially dangerous season, the networks, with some help from
local stations, created an odd programming effect. Almost the only
original, first-run programs last summer were of the "black special"
variety.

In current ghetto slang, the word "gray" refers to a white who is
more or less tolerable to blacks. The above rundown of recent and
current programming might suggest that network TV is going to be
pretty gray this year.

Frankly, I have my doubts. Characterizing TV blacks will not
be easy. The alternatives seem to be three in number: you can resort
to the old, happy-in-blackface stereotypes, and revive *Amos 'n' Andy;*
you can cast blacks in essentially white roles and white stories, playing marginally with the fact that they have problems which are not
shared by most whites; or you can abandon the ready-made characters
and familiar stories, and try to develop quite novel and original ones,
though not necessarily in the Tell-It-Like-It-Is style.

The first alternative is unthinkable in 1968, and probably won't be
adopted except through a colossal blunder. The third calls for a sort
of originality and creativity which is rare in any mass medium, and
which, if found, would probably prove more embarrassing than
valuable to TV programmers. This leaves us with the second alternative—the one toward which TV writers and producers have already
gravitated.

Whether whites or blacks will be prepared to tolerate the Black-
in-whiteface sort of character and story, in a day of White Citizens'
Councils and Black Power militants, is hard to predict. The hypnotic
power of familiar TV images is great. But so is the white-black division
in U.S. audiences.

What the Negro Wants From TV

By Art Peters

JANUARY 20, 1968

There was a time, 15 years ago, even 10 years ago, when Negroes were a rarity in television and the inclusion of a colored actor or actress in drama or situation comedy in anything other than a menial servant's role was guaranteed to produce controversy, raring debate, angry reaction from Southern viewers and possible sponsor withdrawal. Today, in this the enlightened age of civil rights, the barriers of race have been lowered and Negores are gaining acceptance in television.

Unfortunately, they are gaining acceptance as *Negroes,* not as human beings. That is, they are seldom shown as rounded, breathing, living characters with whom the audience can become really involved.

Part of the problem is, of course, that television to a large extent mirrors American society, in which, despite substantial gains, the Negro still plays only a limited role. This raises the key question of whether television should not make an effort to lead rather than just to keep up with the parade.

George Norford, high-ranking Negro executive with the Westinghouse Broadcasting Company, has this perceptive observation: "Television is doing a lot to improve the Negro image, but not nearly enough. When all of television's good deeds for Negroes are lumped together, they are still so infinitesimal they are almost lost in the over-all big picture.

"It's not enough for television merely to reflect the existing Negro subculture in its drama programs. Television can and must use its persuasiveness and power to create a new acceptance among whites of the Negro and a new awareness on the part of the Negro himself of his own ability and potential. Television could be the catalyst, the force that creates and promotes racial understanding. By merely keeping step with current social trends instead of taking the lead in seeking

259

260 new horizons in race relations, television is missing out on a signal opportunity to contribute."

P. Jay Sidney, veteran Negro actor who has appeared in more than 200 television dramas, takes this position: "Negroes rarely get the opportunity to portray human beings on television. They are usually cast in the role of auxiliaries to white people. Their only reason for existence on the screen, their *raison d'être*, is for the benefit of white people in the story."

Bill Cosby, star of the espionage series *I Spy* and television's most celebrated Negro actor, says: "Writers and producers seem to think you need a special reason for a role to be played by a Negro— that he has to pounce on someone or be pounced upon. Because of this, Hollywood has helped to promote a negative image of the black man. When a Negro comes on the screen, the audience immediately tenses up. They know they are about to witness some violence, whether physical, verbal or emotional. If someone were to make a film about a Negro who didn't have any great conflict because of his color, who loved and was loved by a black girl and raised a black family, the audience would come back to see it again, looking for some hidden meaning."

In this way two Negro actors, intimate with television and the movies, sum up not only the plight of Negro actors and actresses, but the problems of their flesh-and-blood counterparts in real life as well. The fact is that many Negroes feel that only grudging desegregations has been achieved and that the real goal of integration remains tortuously beyond reach.

Walter Carroll, sales manager for KDIA, the San Francisco area's largest Negro radio station, maintains: "There have been three civil-rights acts passed in the last 10 years, but it has not made that much difference." What difference there is and there is a difference, comes in the number of roles awarded to Negroes, a growth reflecting the growth in civil rights.

The Negroes are, in fact, seen in a variety of dramatic roles on network programs. However, Norford is right when he says TV's acceptance of Negroes parallels that of society at large but doesn't blaze any new paths. Unless they are cast as servants or entertainers, Negroes are rarely involved in dramatic scenes which show America at play, be they at country club dances or church socials.

Negroes are almost never cast as judges, airline pilots, boat captains, college presidents, cowboys, bank executives, salesmen, editors or engineers. Negroes are generally accepted in television dramas these days as policemen, teachers, FBI agents, soldiers, doctors, espionage agents, radio-and-electronics workers and detectives.

There are notable exeptions, of course, as there are to most rules, but even when a Negro is cast in the role of an executive or professional man, his demeanor by necessity is usually servile or compliant, seldom domineering, harsh or superior. And ironically, the same ground rules which forbid Negroes to be cast as domineering executives usually prevent them from portraying criminals, unless, of course, they are penitent or remorseful.

In discussing these problems, actor Sidney referred to his testimony before a Congressional committee which, five years ago, was investigating charges of discrimination in the TV industry. "It's been five long years," he declares, "but things haven't changed much for the black man in television. Casting directors have now latched onto the idea of placating civil-rights groups by placing a Negro in a key role here and there, perhaps as a policeman or a nurse. Earlier, the Negro was portrayed in films as a maid or a teethchattering, knee-knocking, 'Feet-don't-fail-me-now' flunky. But, even today, the Negro remains a servant, at least psychologically, in the movies and on television. His roles are a little more sophisticated, to be sure, but he is nevertheless a servant, a type of auxiliary to white people."

Sidney cites his own experience last spring when he was hired as a regular in an important supporting role on the popular daytime soap opera *As the World Turns.* "I was supposed to be a research physician in that series," he says, "and yet, emotionally and dramatically, I did not exist as a person. My whole function in those 14 segments was getting a white boy out of jail. I was a nonperson in the plot, a one-dimensional figure with no life of my own. I didn't have any problems. There were no things about which I was personally glad or sad, nothing toward which I personally aspired. I had no past, no future, no family. I existed only for that white boy. I was, in other words, an auxiliary, not a human being." His tone suddenly becomes vehement. "Hell!" he explodes. "Life is not just going to your laboratory every day."

Unlike most of his contemporaries, Sidney has not been content merely to voice his concern about the status quo. During the past five years he has launched a one-man crusade against the industry, picketing television studios which don't hire Negro actors and actresses in representative numbers and buying ads in trade publications excoriating advertising agencies and sponsors for failure to use Negroes in televised commercials. Despite his militancy, Sidney is one of the milder voices in the growing clamor against discrimination in television programming.

Fifty-one-year-old Florence Kennedy, outspoken Negro woman lawyer, who for many years has been active in civil-rights endeavors in New York City, says, "Let's face it, the situation has reached the crisis stage." She believes that millions of black Americans subconsciously regard television in the same manner as the downtrodden peasants in some foreign country might regard a ruthless dictator who flaunts his power and wealth while his subjects grovel in poverty and destitution.

"Television," she declares, "feeds the frustrations and angers of the black masses by showing them a way of life they may never enjoy, a world from which they are forever barred. Although the ambitious Negro through sheer perseverance may rise above his circumstances and attain a position and money, enabling him to buy the luxuries of life—a new car, a boat, a fancy home with swimming pool—he remains an outcast from the mainstream of society, unable, because of his color, to actually belong. Television, by excluding the Negro from most of its programs, helps to reinforce this image of rejection."

Paradoxically, the sound and fury are mounting against television at a time when the industry appears to be doing more than ever before in the Negro interest. Television's highest-ranking executives, convinced that most of the verbal brickbats are being thrown by a few misguided, uninformed and possibly envious persons, speak in wounded, exasperated tones of continuing Negro protests.

"There are five times as many Negroes appearing on television in feature roles today as there were only a few years ago," points out one well-known producer. "Frankly," he declares, "most of this fuss is being kicked up by Black Power groups. I think that the responsible Negro leaders are aware of the tremendous strides that Negroes have made on television."

The "responsible" Negro leaders are indeed aware of some progress, but they are not at all happy about it. Whitney Young, executive director of the National Urban League and a recognized moderate on civil rights, contends: "Perhaps stations would be more aware of their responsibility if they employed more Negroes. Federal law requires that any business holding a government contract must furnish proof of fair employment practices. Yet the Federal Communications Commission regularly grants valuable licenses to television and radio stations without such requirement, even though there are some notorious violations."[22]

George Norford, who, in addition to his position at Westinghouse, coordinates the activities of the Broadcast Skills Bank, an agency developed by the networks in conjunction with the Urban League to recruit, train and employ Negroes for the broadcast industry, contends that progress is being made behind the cameras. He says: "Negroes on TV cannot all be Bill Cosbys or Sammy Davises or Nichelle Nicholses. Some have got to be just plain Joe Smith, technician; Harry Brown, accountant; Bob Jackson, writer. This is where roughly 92 percent of Negroes employed in TV are. Indeed, this is where most people employed in the industry are."

Another hopeful note is sounded by Mike Dann, vice president of programming for CBS-TV. "The Negro has achieved status and he has attained the highest responsible positions in American life," Dann declares, "and if we in television are accurate writers and producers, we will show the Negro in various occupations and endeavors not for the sake of recognition, but for the sake of accuracy."

Although Dann believes that television is slowly but surely getting around to fairly representing Negroes in dramatic roles, he agrees with Sidney that television continually fails to portray the Negro as a flesh-and-blood human being. "I think the real problem is creating dramas which really make you care about the Negro as a person," he says. "We do not have enough dramas in which the Negro portrays the kind of character with whom you can really identify. I think it is because the Negro is cast all too frequently in the role of a helpful person in solving someone else's problem, a type of person whom you don't really care about as a human being and who functions solely in support of the hero in the play."

The subject is obviously a sensitive one at the networks. At NBC, Mort Werner, vice president in charge of programming, declined to discuss it at all, sending word down through an aide, Charles Smith, that the network prefers to stand on its record. Smith, in turn, pointed out that NBC has "pioneered" in developing such Negro television stars as Leslie Uggams, Nichelle Nichols, Bill Cosby and Don Mitchell. Next year [1968], Smith said, Diahann Carroll will be the first Negro woman star of a weekly television drama series.

Significantly, neither Cosby, who already is an NBC star, nor Miss Carroll, who soon will be, is satisfied with television's treatment of the Negro in drama roles. In a recent first-person newspaper article, Cosby declared that Negro children in big-city ghettos have few black

264 heroes to pattern their lives after other than the dope peddlers and pimps who wear diamond rings and drive flashy cars and who are impressive because they have found a way to beat the system. Noting that most Negro doctors, lawyers and other professional men move out of the ghettos once they attain a measure of success, Cosby feels that the image of these hardworking, ambitious, successful black men is lost to Negro children.

"It is the responsibility of TV and films to build a better image for the Negro," Cosby insists. "I see no reason why there can't be films with Negro cowboys who can shoot and ride and do all these things that people respect in a cowboy. Why can't there be black pilots in war stories?" Miss Carroll echoes Cosby's sentiments. "It is important that Negro children have symbols with which they can identify," she declares. "They must be taught to have pride in their blackness, and television can help them establish this identity."

Civil-rights leaders and performers in the industry agree that as long as television continues—by ignoring the credentials of Negroes as human beings—to emulate the white society it serves, the medium will remain a negative force operating against the interests of the black man.

The dilemma is perhaps best summed up in the words of actor P. Jay Sidney: "The image that Negroes have had since they were first dragged off of slave ships has been that they are something less than human. As long as this image persists, it will be impossible for any civil-rights laws that are passed to be enforced. When a Negro applies for a job, he not only has to qualify, he has to get past the image the white interviewer has of him. That image may have been reinforced only last night on TV."

Women
on the Screen

Television, caught as it is between public service and private enterprise, is in the unenviable position of having to reconcile the monetary advantages of popular acceptance and the responsibilities of public welfare. The television industry stands accused of failing to participate constructively in the drive of the blacks to receive their full measure of citizenship. It also stands accused of failing to recognize and support the equality of women.

The criticism that television has reinforced society's notion of the stereotyped Negro is also applied to its role with regard to women. The medium is said to be a primary influence in the perpetuation of traditional attitudes regarding the inferiority of women and television is criticized for being instrumental in the stifling of women's attempts to achieve their identity and make greater contributions to the community.

Betty Freidan (pp. 267-275) maintains in her two-part article that "the feminine mystique" has pervaded television along with the rest of society and the image of women presented on the air in commercials, soap operas and game shows is that of an incredibly stupid, insecure, miserable female. The rest of the medium presents no image at all, even though the face and the body may be there. Miss Freidan argues that the mystique of the mindless, sex hungry female and the passive housewife is creating millions of unnecessarily mindless, martyred housewives and is making our whole society as well as television sick in the process.

Marya Mannes (pp. 276-280) discusses the absence of female television comentators or newscasters. The negative attitudes toward women of authority which are prevalent in society are equally prevalent in broadcasting. Miss Mannes points out that the only recognized female authority on national television is Julia Child, who is

266   permitted to do her thing in woman's so-called natural environs, the kitchen. Although women are necessarily accepted in entertainment, they are not accepted in the public affairs or documentary fields. Miss Mannes hopes that someday broadcasters will be as concerned with public interest as they are with public acceptance and that the many women who have something valid to say and contribute will have equal opportunity to disseminate facts, opinions, ideas and insights.

Television and the Feminine Mystique

By Betty Friedan

FEBRUARY 1 AND 8, 1964

If the image of women on television today reflects—or affects—reality, then American women must be writhing in agonies of self-contempt and unappeasable sexual hunger. For television's image of the American woman is a stupid, unattractive, insecure little household drudge who spends her martyred, mindless, boring days dreaming of love—and plotting nasty revenge against her husband. If that image affects men—or reflects, at least, the men who created it—then American men, in their contempt, loathing and fear of that miserable obsessed woman, must be turning in revulsion against love itself.

This is the rather horrifying feeling I had after sitting for several weeks in front of my television set, trying to reconcile the image of woman projected by television commercials and family situation comedies, by soap operas and game shows, with the strangely missing, virtually nonexistent image of woman in all the rest of television: the major dramatic shows, the witty commentary, serious documentary or ordinary reportage of the issues and news of our world.

In fact, the most puzzling thing about the image of woman on television today is an eerie *Twilight Zone* sense that it is fading before one's eyes. In the bulk of television programs today, and even, increasingly, in commercials, one literally sees no image of woman at all. She isn't there. Even when the face and body of a woman are there, one feels a strange vagueness and emptiness, an absence of human identity, a missing sexual aliveness—is it a woman if it doesn't think or act, or talk, or move or love like a person?

Behind that fading image, the non-woman on the television screen, I found, talking to producers, network decision-makers, agency executives, an even more unpleasant image: their image of those millions of American women "out there" watching that television screen, controlling that dial, determining those ratings—the

267

268   American housewife who, they say, "has taken over television" as she is supposed to have taken over control of her husband, children, home, the U.S. economy and the Nation generally. Put the two images together—the woman on the screen and the one watching it—and you see how television has trapped itself in the feminine mystique.

The feminine mystique is the name I have given to a way of looking at woman that has become epidemic in America during the last 15 years. Based on old prejudices disguised in new pseudo-scientific dogmas, it defines woman solely in sexual terms, as man's wife, mother, love object, dishwasher and general server of physical needs, and never in human terms, as a person herself. It glorifies woman's only purpose as the fulfillment of her "femininity" through sexual passivity, loving service of husband and children, and dependence on man for all decisions in the world outside the home: "man's world."

In my book, *The Feminine Mystique,* I showed how this sophisticated mishmash of obsolete prejudices (woman's place is in the home; woman is inferior, childlike, animal-like, incapable of thought or action or contribution to society) has been built up, since World War II, by psychologists, sociologists, educators, marriage counselors, magazines, advertising, and by a combination of historical coincidences (depression and war, the bomb, the population explosion, the stepped-up speed of change in the world) and misunderstood needs and frustrations of men and women themselves. The result of the feminine mystique, I maintain, is to stunt the growth of women, robbing them of identity and making them virtually displaced persons in our fantastically growing society. Forcing women to live vicariously through love, husband, children, I submit, is not only making women sick for lack of a self but making love and marriage, husbands and children and our whole society sick.

This whole process is projected on television to such an extreme that the question is not only what the feminine mystique and its stunted, dehumanized, sick image of woman is doing to real women and their respect for themselves, or men's love and respect for men—but what it is doing to television.

Consider first that drab, repulsive little housewife one sees on the television screen. She is so stupid that she is barely capable of doing the most menial household tasks. Her biggest problem is to get the kitchen sink or floor really clean, and she can't even do that without a kind, wise man to tell her how. ("To think that just a few months ago I was in college and now I'm a wife and mother," she weeps on the television commercial. "I want to be everything Jim

wants in a wife and mother. But he says I'm inefficient, I can't cook
and clean. I've tried and tried and I just can't get that sink clean.")
Her biggest thrill is when with that old man's magic help (which
comes in a can), she gets that sink clean.

Her other biggest problem is how to keep doing all that cleaning
and still keep her hands "feminine." She is so unattractive and feels
so insecure that she needs all the help and mechanical contrivances
modern science and industry can supply to keep her man from leaving
her. ("How long has it been since your husband took you dancing . . .
brought you flowers . . . really listened to what you said? Could it be
that gray in your hair?" Bad breath? Irregular bowels?)

She isn't even adequate as a mother to her children. ("Even the
most careful mother can't completely protect her family from household germs," the kind, wise man reassures her. "Is there really more
than one vitamin?" she asks him, having never finished fifth grade
herself.) In fact, she is barely capable of feeding the dog. (That wise
old man has to tell her how to get the mutt out of his "mealtime
rut.")

Less than a fifth grader, more like that simple animal in her
capacity to understand or take part in modern human society, this
television-commercial woman has no interest, purpose or goal
beyond cleaning her sink, feeding her kids, and going to bed. The
whole world beyond her home—its politics, art, science, issues,
ideas and problems—is evidently beyond her comprehension. For
not only is there no television image of a woman acting in the world,
but the programming of daytime television and, increasingly, even
prime time, assumes she has no interest in it, or ability to understand
it. She lives only for love.

But beneath the sacred exaltation of marriage, motherhood and
home in the soap operas and the religious tones of the commercials,
there is a crude assumption on the part of television decision-makers
that all those women out there are panting through their boring days
of mindless drudgery in a state of permanent unappeased sexual
hunger. From a little after 8 in the morning until the late, late hours
after midnight, they evidently want from that television screen only
the image of a virile male. At least this is the superficial reason given
for that disappearing, virtually nonexistent image of woman on the
television screen, and the preponderance of male cheesecake ("beefcake" is it called?). "It's women who control the dial, and what a
woman wants to look at is a man—a man with sex appeal, a man who's
available to her," I was told, over and over again, up through the ranks
of television decision-makers.

270   Several years ago, when the networks were under attack from the
Federal Communications Commission, CBS put on a daytime news
program. The producer, new to daytime, suggested a woman commentator. The network brass said he was out of his mind. In simple
four-letter words they explained to him that of all things the dames
didn't want to see at 10 A.M., it was a woman. They wanted a man they
could jump right back into bed with. But CBS did put a news-oriented
show, *Calendar,* into that 10 A.M. time period, and hired actress Mary
Fickett to act as Jill-of-all-trades. She did the household commercials,
acted as pretty little straight man to commentator Harry Reasoner, and
now and then made some forays into the more serious business of
the program on her own. The condescension with which he talked
down to the women out there may have marred his sexual charm.
Calendar died [after almost two years].

On the MGM lot, producer Irving Elman explained to me why
his show *The Eleventh Hour,* and *Dr. Kildare* and *Mr. Novak* at the
same studio, and several other major series, are built around two
men—a young bachelor and a middle-aged widower. The bachelors
such as Dr. Kildare and Ben Casey are available for a fantasy affair
with the younger housewives; the widowers like Dr. Starke in
The Eleventh Hour are available for the older housewives. In *The
Defenders* the older lawyer, Lawrence Preston, is the object of affection for the over-40 crowd; his son, Kenneth Preston, can be embraced
by the young mothers. "There is more sex appeal if he is a widower,"
Elman explained. "It makes him more available. If he were married,
his wife would be in the way. And if he were divorced, the women
wouldn't like it. It would be too threatening. Marriage is sacred."

The double standard involved here almost seems unfair to men.
Madelyn Martin, long-time writer of the *Lucy* shows, explained:
"You can't package a dramatic show around a woman because women
want only to look at a man, and they don't want their husbands to
look at other women." The housewives "out there" are evidently so
insecure that they can't face fantasy competition from a woman on
the screen not only for their own husbands, but for their fantasy extra-
marital amours either. "We have to be very careful to keep Kildare
from getting seriously involved with a woman," MGM executive
producer Norman Felton said. "Women love stories where there's
the suggestion of romantic involvement, but they resent it if he even
kisses the girl on the screen. That kiss jars the viewer's fantasy that
she is the one with whom he's having the love affair." This, of course,
is one of the great advantages of the hospital to television; the romance
never has to be consummated because the woman patient neatly dies.

"One of the high spots was Kildare's romance with that girl who died *271*
of leukemia," Felton reminisced.

If housewives control the dial, why, with no women at all, are
Westerns perennially so popular? "Beefcake" of course. *Bonanza,*
for instance, really gives the panting women a choice of sizes and
ages—four unmarried men: Daddy and his three sons. According to
reports, the producer has been toying with the idea of letting one of
the four get married but, evidently out of consideration for all those
women "out there," hasn't had the nerve to let it happen yet.[23]

If the image-makers are right in theorizing that a woman "never
wants to look at a woman, only men," is sex really the reason? "Love"
is hardly the emotion the television woman seems to feel for that man
she clutches so possessively. In the soap operas it is more like a
martyred suffering, a noble endurance. ("Get married, stay home,
suffer," a high school boy summed up woman's fate, after he had spent
a week at home, sick in bed, watching daytime television.) On *I
Love Lucy, The Danny Thomas Show*, and other family comedies, that
television housewife, far from "loving" or even "liking" her husband,
seems positively obsessed with the need to wipe him under the door
mat, get revenge against him, control him, manipulate him, show him
up for the despicable, miserable worm he really is, and establish once
and for all who's really the boss of the house. As if, over and over, she
must show herself to be somebody by forcing him to his knees—
getting him to admit her unquestioned superiority as the boss of the
family.

That warfare is, of course, limited to the family and the house,
since the woman is always, and only, a housewife. But sometimes,
lately the woman who gets revenge against the huband isn't actually
his wife, but a paid servant or housekeeper like Hazel. (Less competition to those women "out there," since the paid housekeeper
doesn't actually go to bed with the husband? Yet, in the essential
motif of the family comedy—revenge against the male—Hazel, the
housemaid, is indistinguishable from the television wife.)

Since the women in these comedies aren't ever allowed to over-
reach that definitive level of dullness and unattractiveness (otherwise
would they offer too much competition for the supposedly dull, unattractive housewives out there?), the husbands must also be shown
as stupid, unattractive boobs for even a semblance of believable
suspense or conflict. It is perhaps a tribute to real male vanity, or real
male contempt of the female, that television critics often complain
of this silly-boob image of the husband, never noticing that the wife
in these situation comedies is an even more silly boob. Evidently, in

272 order to retain her "femininity" that wife always has to lose the battle in the end—or rather, demonstrate her true superiority by magnanimously letting the poor fool think he won it. (As on *The Danny Thomas Show* when, after he has subverted her complicated plot to make him give her a mink coat for Christmas, she shames him—by bringing him his rubbers and raincoat in the rain and catching near-pneumonia—into tape-recording abjectly that he loves her, in front of the whole Tuesday afternoon bridge club.)

In the daytime soap operas, the martyred superiority of the wives doesn't even have to be demonstrated; it's just mysteriously, axiomatically *there.* Since the housewives in *As the World Turns* and all the rest must conduct their warfare with men day after day, during the day, the major dramatic problem seems to be to get the men home to be manipulated. It is amazing how often those busy lawyers and doctors and businessmen on television soap operas come home for lunch! But the neatest trick—which simultaneously accomplishes revenge and keeps the man home permanently to be controlled, or perhaps just to provide the soap-opera housewife with someone to talk at—is to paralyze the husband and put him in a wheelchair.

However it is accomplished, the real emotion played to by this image of woman who supposedly lives-for-love is hate. As a former network vice president in charge of program development put it: "They [those housewives out there] don't want to look at husbands who are nice or strong. They only want to look at attractive younger men or old codgers out of the battle between the sexes. In the average dame's life the husband is the enemy, the guy you have to manipulate, push around, be happy in spite of. When the daytime serial features a strong husband, and the wife is not the controlling one, the rating is invariably low. The husband becomes acceptable only if he is manipulated by the good, kind, loving, all-wise wife."

But why is there no image of women on television engaged in anything else but that so-called war between the sexes? After all, it is only in the family comedies that men appear as such stupid boobs. The bulk of television features men engaged with more or less valor in action in the world—curing the sick, coping with social problems in *East Side/West Side,* Mr. Novak teaching in the classroom, cowboys in Westerns, supermen zooming into outer space, detectives, and variously engaged individuals in dramas and specials that are concerned with something beyond intramarital warfare, to say nothing of news and documentaries about real issues of the world beyond one woman's house.

Could the very absence of any image of women active or triumphant in the world explain the dream of revenge and domination over the male, the sexual insecurity and self-contempt and even that supposedly unappeasable sexual hunger which television plays to, in its nasty image of the American housewife?

Why is there no image at all on television of the millions and millions of self-respecting American women who are not only capable of cleaning the sink, without help, but of acting to solve more complex problems of their own lives and their society? That moronic house-wife image denies the 24,000,000 women who work today outside the home, in every industry and skilled profession, most of them wives who take care of homes and children too. That image also insults the millions of real American housewives, with more and more education, who shape U.S. culture, politics, art and education, by their actions in PTA, League of Women Voters and local political parties, and who help to build libraries, art galleries and theaters, from Detroit to Seattle, and even strike for peace.

Why for instance, isn't one of the leads in a program like *Mr. Novak* a woman teacher? I asked MGM executive producer Norman Felton. He explained: "If you have a woman lead in a television series, she has to be either married or unmarried. If she's unmarried, what's wrong with her? After all, it's housewives we're appealing to, and marriage is their whole life. If she's married, what's her husband doing in the background? He must not be very effective. He should be making the decisions. For drama, there has to be action, conflict. If the action is led by a woman, she has to be in conflict—with men or women or something. She has to make decisions; she has to triumph over opposition. For a woman to make decisions, to triumph over any-thing, would be unpleasant, dominant, masculine. After all, most women are housewives, at home with children; most women are dominated by men, and they would react against a woman who suc-ceeded at anything."

But that housewife in the family situation comedies in only too unpleasant, dominant and masculine. She is always triumphing, not over forces in the outside world, but in that endless warfare against her own husband or children. "In comedy it's all right," Felton said. "You're not supposed to take her seriously; you laugh at her." Could there be a serious drama about a woman in the home, a housewife? "We couldn't make it dramatic—and honest," he said. "Most of a housewife's life is too humdrum. If you showed it honestly, it would be too dull to watch. Maybe you can get away with it in a hospital. After all, how many dramatic cases does a doctor or lawyer have in a year? But if you tried to do it with a housewife, no one would believe it. Everyone knows how dull the life of a housewife really is."

Thus, if television's only image of women is such a "dull" housewife, there is, in the end, no action or dramatic conflict she can engage in except that warfare with her own husband or children. Unless she gets sick and goes to the hospital, where she can die nobly of a brain tumor. "It makes sense that women are only figures of comedy," said Madelyn Martin, writer of *Lucy*. "When you think of traditional figures of comedy—the short guy, the ugly one, the man with the big nose, the Negro or Jew or member of any minority group—comedy is a way of turning their misfortune into a joke. It's a way of being accepted—'Look at me, I'm funny' and 'Don't anybody laugh at me, I'll laugh first.'"

If women are the one majority in America that resembles an oppressed minority, it's not because of actual deprivation of right, or opportunity, or human dignity, but simply because of that self-ridiculing image—the mystique of the mindless female, the passive housewife, which keeps girls and women from using their rights and opportunities and taking their own lives seriously, in time. In an examination scene in a *Mr. Novak* episode, a high school girl takes the blame for her boy friend's crib sheet to protect his future as a would-be physicist. "It's all right," she says, "let them blame it on me. I'm not going to college or anything. It won't matter to me." Why doesn't it matter to her, her own life and future? Why, in high school, does she already play the martyred, passive wife? No need to work or study in school herself, or plan her own future, the image says. All she has to do is get that boy to marry her—the sooner, the better—and he'll take care of her life.

Do anything you can to hook that man, all those images of women on television say, because you aren't or can't be a person yourself. But without studying, or working, or doing anything yourself, you can be a "housewife" at 18. And get all those expensive things for wedding presents, just like *Queen for a Day*—a lounge chair, a dishwasher, a whole set of china, baby furniture, even a free trip to the beauty parlor every week.

Is it a coincidence that millions of real girls who have grown up watching television—and seeing only that emptily "glamorous" housewife image of women—do not, in high school, have any goal of their own future except being such a passive housewife? Is it partly from lack of any self-respecting image of a woman as a person herself that so many stop their own growth in junior high to start that frantic race to "trap" a man, get pregnant in high school, or quit college to take a "housework" job in industry, to put their husbands through medical or engineering school. By seducing real girls into evading the choices, efforts, goals, which would enable them to grow to maturity and full human identity in our society, television's image of women is *creating* millions of unnecessarily mindless, martyred housewives, for whom there may never be a thrill or challenge greater than the dirty kitchen sink.

These new teen-age housewives—the growth-stunted young mothers who quit school to marry and become mothers before they grow out of bobby socks themselves—are the female Frankenstein monsters television helped create. And they may writhe forever in that tedious limbo between the kitchen sink and the television game show, living out their century-long life ahead, in a complex world which requires human purposes, commitment and efforts they never ever glimpsed. How long can even television channel their pent-up energies into vicarious love affairs with Dr. Kildare, vicarious revenge against that husband who is surely not their real enemy?

How long will boys and men love women, if this nasty, vengeful martyr is their only public image of woman, and becomes an increasingly vengeful private image? The female Frankenstein monsters, after all, are created by the minds of men. Does the new plethora of widowers, bachelor fathers, and unmarried mature men on television, who pay a maid or houseboy, or soon perhaps, a robot to get the household drudgery done, signify unconscious rebellion against that "housewife" altogether? Do they really want her for a wife? One suddenly realizes that there are no real love stories on the television screen—in the sense of the love stories that one can still see in the old movies with Ingrid Bergman, Joan Crawford, Norma Shearer, Claudette Colbert and all the rest. No love stories, no heroines—only those housewife drudges, the comic ogres who man the war between the sexes.

Television badly needs some heroines. It needs more images of real women to help girls and women take themselves seriously and grow and love and be loved by men again. And television decision-makers need to take real women more seriously—not for women's sake but for their own. Must women only be used as diaper-and-pot-holders for the male news commentators? Must they be shown only as paid or underpaid dishwashers for fear of making real housewives uncomfortable?

Should Women Only Be Seen And Not Heard?

By Marya Mannes

NOVEMBER 23, 1968

Walter, Chet, David, Eric, Frank, Ed—wonderful guys, superb professionals, and we know them better than anybody else in the world, except for our husbands. For they come into the room every night and tell us what the score is and where the action is, and we don't care if they're handsome or homely, or 40 or 50 or 60, because they have authority, they have presence, they have experience and reason—and because they are men.

That, in fact, is the clincher. For if there were such a thing as a top women commentator on television with the same attributes, would we feel the same way about her as we do about these men? I suggest that the answer would be No. And I suggest that the reasons for this No lie in attitudes toward women of authority that are shared equally by the broadcasting powers and the public they purport to serve.

These are questions that assail at least one of the very small handful of women—myself—allowed to comment on matters of the life and death on television: specifically through a brief weekly commentary on New York's educational TV station, Channel 13, and occasionally on ABC-TV's news program. While I consider myself fortunate to be one of this tiny band, I cannot help wondering about a representation so token that it is virtually nonexistent in a population of which half are women. Of these women, admittedly, the ones with the requisite wisdom, experience and presence to communicate with a large public are indeed a minority. But still they exist by the hundreds in the arts, the sciences, the political scene, and above all, in literature. Who sees them on television, not as panelists, but in their own right as voices of authority?

The answer is, invariably: Pauline Frederick, reporting to us on NBC from time to time from the United Nations. But her durability could be explained not only by her obvious competence and pleasing presence but by the fact that she is more of a reporter and interpreter of events than—in the sense of being a catalyst of thought—a commentator. The opinions expressed are those of others: almost no personal attitudes toward individuals or events are apparent. You might say that this was also true of Cronkite and Huntley and Brinkley and McGee, if not of Sevareid and Newman. Yet even these masters of fact, of objectivity, manage to convey their own stamp and stance: a way of looking at things which is entirely theirs. This Miss Frederick lacks, thereby remaining totally uncontroversial. Like Marlene Sanders of ABC, for instance, her function is certainly more than that of a newscaster in that she edits the wire-service reports and news releases as they come in and—exerting selection and a sense of priorities—prepares her own newscast. Both supplement their reports with interviews, on-the-spot observation, and extensive background reading.

The newscasters, on the other hand—mostly personable young men throughout the country who appear on your screen and describe the day's events—merely read the scripts handed to them by their newswriters. Yet even in this category of neutral news wholly free of opinion, women are seldom visible, although in many other countries they are familiar presences on the home screen.

Again, why not here? Certainly we allow pretty young women to explain the weather on television or tell us what Mrs. Nixon wore at a rally or what Lynda Bird Robb likes to eat. And the networks often send them "on the road" and even—in the case of Marlene Sanders, and Liz Trotta (NBC)—on a Vietnam tour.

Yet it is a fact that the only national television female of real authority is Julia Child. That is not merely because she is a superb human being but because her opinions are confined to that natural and universal passion, Food. Nobody can knock a woman Doing Her Thing in a kitchen. And nobody cares if she doesn't look like Raquel Welch or have her hair done by Kenneth. In fact, quite properly, they care for her more because she is, simply, herself.

But, put a woman behind one of those desks with buttons and monitors and let her rip? For one thing, she should look young and smooth-faced, and who can be that after 20 or 30 years of training, involvement and experience? And who—as one network executive was heard to say—"wants to look at a middle-aged dame, especially if she's bright?" A vice president suggested that women like that were regrettably apt to remind the men in the audiences of their wives or mothers—or mothers-in-law: always talking or laying down the law, presumably. A man can take it from a man, although he may wince at

278   the debonair sophistication of a Buckley or a Vidal, because after all he knows what he's talking about. Besides, objectivity has long been claimed (with little evidence) as a masculine virtue, and while opinion is therefore a male prerogative, it is a female flaw.

To a lesser degree this is true of print too. Newspapers have some very fine female political correspondents and general columnists who report and comment on major issues, but it is very seldom that they are quoted either by pundits or the public. They are hardly ever on the editorial page of daily or weekly newspapers, for that is the sacred male domain. If a woman of any distinction says anything or does anything of public importance, she lands on the woman's page with the recipes.

And when women move into fields of exposure or reform—to wit, the late Rachel Carson and insecticides in her book *Silent Spring*, or Jessica Mitford and the undertaker business in *The American Way of Death*, or former Senator Maurine Neuberger and cigarette advertising and the tobacco industry—the reactions of outrage from the particular interest exposed invariably include the implication that the attacks were unfounded (the woman didn't know her facts) or hysterical (women are emotional, hence wholly subjective). Women novelists, from Rebecca West down to Jacqueline Susann (yes, the graph is steep) are all right, and women mystery writers are universally embraced. And there is always, of course, Margaret Mead, especially if she sticks to primitive tribes. But at least the male public does not expect such women to be beautiful or sexy: success is enough.

In a recent article in *The New York Times Magazine*, newsman Bob Teague of NBC complained that he was weary of being complimented by whites because he was a Negro rather than because he did a good job. The parallel with women in broadcasting is obvious. Since our representative is even less than token, we are oddities, often praised mainly because we are women.

The fact is that television is primarily a medium of entertainment, and that's presumably where women belong. Public affairs are male affairs, and that's where they don't belong—except in the early-morning hours. In spite of its appalling title and climate of gush, the women on *Girl Talk* occasionally tackle the facts of life between a rash of commercials. And now, on the new WNBC discussion show called (of course—and stupidly) *For Women Only*, Aline Saarinen and her guests really come to grips with major subjects. This the housewives can hear, but not the general public. Women may have borne the sons who go to war, but in prime time when do they speak of

war? They conceive the children, but when—in prime time—do they   279
express their opinions on the Pope's encyclical?

There is still, let's face it, a deep resistance to the career woman
as such, no matter how feminine she may be. And this resistance is
quite understandable in the case of militant females who bulldoze
their opinions with strident voices, contorted faces and guerrilla
tactics. Even worse, perhaps, are those silken-voiced, super-groomed
ladies who use the guise of femininity to conceal a vaulting and
implacable ambition.

But the time will come, hopefully, when it won't matter whether
facts and opinions, ideas and insights are communicated by a man or a
woman, or whether, if a woman, she is young or not young, neither a
fashion model nor a Playboy centerfold.

Heaven forbid that we should ever replace Walter and Chet and
David and Eric and Frank and Ed, whom we love dearly. All we are
asking—and by we, I clearly mean those women who are qualified
by training and experience to communicate, those who are deeply
committed to the society we inhabit—we ask only that our voices be
heard more often and more widely in matters that concern us all—
men and women—equally. Surely it is an abnormal situation when
major discussions and news panels addressed to world events are
composed, almost invariably, only of men. As women we might not
only be able to offer special and different insights, but it might make
for a more peaceful world if we did.

Our job as women, after all, is to create and not destroy. We have
learned through centuries of instinct and experience how to preserve
a family; and that family has now been extended to our town, our
state, our world. We are committed to keeping house; and that
house has now become our city and our Nation. We must clean the
air we breathe, the streets we live in and the land and water that
sustain us.

The machinery of peacekeeping is as much our function as that
of our men. It is our boys who are killed in war; it is unplanned,
unwanted children borne by women who bring the starvation,
poverty, and congestion that lead to war. It is love for the wanted
child that should make our voice in the forming of his future as
essential as that of our men.

On a more immediate level, I believe that women have a special
way of looking at things and feeling about them that men by their
very nature often lack. This can concern matters that might seem
trivial but could be very important. It is a kind of intimacy of vision,
a direct human approach which can often be more revealing of truth

than the "grand design" or portentious abstraction projected on the media by most men. When I see the inevitable row of men questioning a President or a public figure in the news, asking whether he still believes such and such that he said in such and such a speech of October 8, I wish some woman would ask what he does in his spare time, what writer or painter or music he most likes, how he communicates with his son, what he misses most, what he wants most. Just as men should be often assigned to interview women, I wish women were often the probers of men.

If only for variety, the female presence as a commentator of the human as well as of the political scene would be an asset. In the recent manned Apollo launch and orbit, the combination of Rene Carpenter and David Brinkley added a refreshing dimension and new insights.

So—gentlemen of television, leaders of broadcasting—what are you waiting for? Could it be that you are more concerned with public acceptance—than with the public interest? Could it be that because you are men, you see only your own image?

Notes to Chapter 2

1. *Big Valley's* initial opposition included *I Spy. The Man From U.N.C.L.E.* opened against *The Red Skelton Hour* on CBS and *McHale's Navy* on ABC, both top-rated shows.

2. Since the writing of this article in 1965, the practice of a "guaranteed cpm" has become more prevalent. Under this concept, the networks unofficially and often secretly promise the advertiser additional network air time, free of charge, if the show in question does not deliver a predetermined size of audience.

3. *I Love Lucy* premiered on October 15, 1951 and ended on June 24, 1957 when Ball and Arnaz decided to do a monthly show. The *Lucille Ball-Desi Arnaz Show* ran in 1957-58. The *Desilu Playhouse* began in 1958, with "The Ricardos" appearing almost every month. It is interesting to note that despite the immense success of *I Love Lucy*, the show lost its first sponsor, a tobacco company, because the company felt the show was not helping the sale of its product.

4. The nine daytime shows referred to by Miss Efron are *Love of Life*, *Search for Tomorrow*, *Secret Storm*, *The Doctors*, *General Hospital*, *The Guiding Light*, *Another World*, *As the World Turns* and *The Young Marrieds*. All of these shows except *The Young Marrieds* are still on the air. According to Miss Efron, *Edge of Night*, the tenth show is not a "soap opera"; it is a serialized melodrama whose hero is a criminal lawyer, and its events bear little resemblance to those described in this article.

5. Betty Freidan, *The Feminine Mystique*, New York: Norton, 1963. An essay by Miss Freidan regarding television's portrayal of the American female may be found on pp. 267-275.

6. A 1965 game show devised by David Susskind in which husbands raced around a supermarket to see who could grab the most expensive groceries from the shelves within a specified period of time.

7. On May 9, 1961, Newton Minow, a contributor to this collection (see pp. 488- *281*
493), made his first address to the National Association of Broadcasters Annual Convention as Chairman of the Federal Communications Commission. In that address he said: "When television is good, nothing—not the theatre, not the magazines or newspapers— nothing is better. But when television is bad, nothing is worse. I invite you to sit down in front of your television set when your station goes on the air and stay there without a book, magazine, newspaper, profit-and-loss sheet or rating book to distract you—and keep your eyes glued to that set until the station signs off. I can assure you that you will observe a vaste wasteland. . . . Is there one person in this room who claims that broadcasting can't do better?"

8. News and documentary programs are not within the province of the continuity acceptance departments. Actually, since the payola and quiz scandals of the late 1950's, only ABC has officially kept the name "Continuity Acceptance." CBS renamed this function "Program Practices" and NBC calls it "Broadcast Standards." CBS is the only network not to have its own written programming code. Its Program Practices people say they rely on the NAB code and precedent for program guidelines.

9. Senate Hearings on Television and Juvenile Delinquency held in 1961-62. The hearings report in 1964 claimed that television was operating as a "school for violence" (see pp. 511-515).

10. The ratings for the four CBS Playhouse presentations were: *The Final War of Olly Winter* (January 29, 1967)—20.3, that is, 20.3 percent of television homes were watching the program; *Do Not Go Gentle Into That Good Night* (October 17, 1967)— 17.1; *Dear Friends* (December 6, 1967)—22.6; and *My Father and My Mother* (February 13, 1968)—20.1.

11. The only shows in 1969-70 utilizing the three-camera technique of filming before a live audience are: *Here's Lucy, The Governor and J.J.,* and some variety shows.

12. In 1969-70, *Julia* and *Room 222* are two of the few shows without a laugh track. *The Courtship of Eddie's Father* is an example of a show with what the industry defines as a "very light" track.

13. Steve Allen, *The Funny Men,* New York: Simon & Schuster, 1956.

14. Production costs for covering the 1972 Summer Olympic Games are expected to exceed 2 million dollars, making ABC's total rights and production costs over 14 million dollars. The Summer Olympics telecasts illustrate how the costs of acquiring and improving coverage are spiraling. Rights and production costs have risen from $600,000 in 1960 to 1.3 million dollars in 1964 to 7.7 million dollars in 1968 to an estimated over 14 million dollars in 1972.

15. While American fans have not been enthusiastic about the practice of running tapes after commercial breaks, Canadian fans have been upset over other changes in hockey caused by television, such as changing the Center Line into a broken line so that it will show up better on the home screen.

16. This figure included radio time sales. In 1968, television time sales were slightly over 2 billion dollars while radio time sales exceeded 1 billion dollars for the first time.

17. Charles Raymond, "Must Advertising Communicate to Sell?" *Harvard Business Review,* September-October 1965, pp. 148-159.

18. For an interesting account of how Port Jervis, New York, was used as a test market without the town or other competitors knowing it, see "How They Turned a Town into a Test Tube," *TV Guide,* December 10, 1966.

19. Despite the fact that the thirty-second commercial has become the dominant unit of time in television advertising, the amount of time devoted to commercials has not been reduced. On the contrary, the lack of available time slots to run advertisements has resulted in recent pressure to increase commercial minutes per hour during prime time from six minutes to seven minutes.

20. For further information regarding this study, see *Television Age*, May 8, 1967.

21. Illya Kuryakin, played by David McCallum, was one of the two leading characters in *The Man From U.N.C.L.E.*

22. In June 1969, the FCC adopted a series of rules designed to insure that all licensees afford equal opportunity in employment. Broadcasters are now required to file annual statistical reports on minority group job participation and also to adopt and submit detailed equal employment opportunity programs. The Commission will refer complaints of discrimination to appropriate equal opportunity agencies for investigation. In July 1968, the FCC had ruled that a broadcaster who discriminates in employment is not operating in the public interest. But that rule did not require periodic showings of compliance.

23. When Pernell Roberts, who played the oldest son, Adam, left the show, his place was taken by David Canary. Canary, as the friend and ranch foreman named Candy, kept the choice of sizes and ages intact.

CENSORSHIP AND CONTROL
Chapter 3

Censorship
and Control

Television is unquestionably the most controlled and highly censored of all the mass media. Formal and informal external sources of control or censorship or both include the Congress, the Federal Communications Commission, the Federal Trade Commission, the Anti-Trust Division of the Justice Department, the Food and Drug Administration and, ultimately, the courts. As has been indicated throughout Chapters I and II, control of programming and censorship of content can also be exercized by the individual stations and staffs, the Code Authority and the Code of the National Association of Broadcasters, the continuity acceptance departments of the networks, sponsors, advertising agencies and the individual writers or artists. Programming is further influenced at various times and in varying degrees by pressure groups, feedback from audiences, ratings and television critics.

The broadcasters themselves took most of the initiative in persuading the Government to institute external, legal controls over broadcasting. The uncontrolled use of broadcast frequencies in the 1920's caused chaos; and as a result, many broadcasters appealed to the Government to regulate the use of the frequency spectrum. Among the many concepts incorporated into the Radio Act of 1927 and the Communications Act of 1934, two are of particular importance to an understanding of why such direct Federal control is applied to broadcasting.

The first concept is that station ownership should be licensed by the Government because of the limited number of broadcast channels available. At the time broadcasting was being developed there were, for example, many more newspapers than there were available channels for broadcasting, and anyone who was able to do so could establish his own newspaper, magazine or film company. Thus it was felt that broadcasting had to be federally regulated and should not be subject to the First Amendment guarantees that other media enjoyed.

286   Today, this concept still prevails despite the fact that there are presently more radio and television stations than there are daily newspapers, magazines, or motion picture companies producing feature films. One-newspaper cities far outnumber single-station television cities and, in our present economy, to establish a television station is often cheaper than to start a daily newspaper. Through UHF and cable, far more television frequencies are now available. However, in June 1969, the Supreme Court, in unanimously upholding the Fairness Doctrine which will be discussed at some length in this section (pp. 303-321), ruled: "Scarcity is not entirely a thing of the past. . . . While there are substantially more individuals who want to broadcast than there are frequencies to allocate, it is idle to posit an unabridgeable First Amendment right to broadcast comparable to the right of every individual to speak, write or publish."

A second concept and basic rationale for strict legal control of broadcasting is that broadcasters use public property—the air waves—and should be subject to special control by representatives of the public: that is, the Congress and its regulatory agencies. In some imperfectly defined way this differs from, say, the magazines which use the mails and need mailing permits to distribute their products. Thus, while the Government does not license commercial magazines or review their performance at periodic intervals, it not only has the right, but also the duty, to license and regulate broadcasting stations in "the public interest, convenience and necessity." In its June 1969 decision, the Supreme Court held that "A license permits broadcasting, but the licensee has no constitutional right to be the one who holds the license . . ."

The Federal Communications Commission is the government agency most responsible for the orderly use of the frequency spectrum. In the first part of his three-part article (pp. 290-295), Martin Mayer provides a brief historical background of the Commission's establishment in 1934 and its mandate from Congress to regulate broadcasting in "the public interest, convenience and necessity." The Commission's authority is based on its ability to revoke broadcasting licenses. Mayer points out, however, that even though the Commission cannot be ignored by the broadcasters, its actual operation is severely restricted by the law, the Congress, the courts, a small budget and a tremendous workload. Mayer contends that, since the FCC serves the public, as long as the public seems to be generally satisfied with television, the Commission will be very hesitant to use its only real power.

In part two (pp. 295-298), Mayer discusses the FCC's attempts to regulate networks and the attempts by some Commissioners to circumvent Section 326 of the Communications Act which specifically prohibits FCC censorship or interference in free speech. Mayer illustrates the diversity of opinion existing among the Commissioners by presenting two Commissioners' contrasting views. He notes the requirement that the Commission be politically divided: four members from one party and three from the opposition. Of course, this rule often can mean a change in official Commission policies when one Commissioner is replaced.

The final part of Mayer's article (pp. 298-302) is devoted to some of the significant policy issues which the Commission now faces. The FCC was established primarily to handle technical problems and it has exerted its greatest influence in this area. Broadcast technology is now changing, and with cable television and satellites (see Chapter 6), broadcasting may become a common carrier much like the telephone. Mayer points out that the critical decisions of how the use of satellites will be controlled and what restrictions will be placed on cable TV are, at this time, in the jurisdiction of the FCC. He feels that the FCC has the opportunity to stop "spinning its wheels" and play a far more significant role in affecting broadcasting's future.

Edith Efron (pp. 303-309) discusses the FCC's Fairness Doctrine and the problems it has raised. Spokesmen for the political right and left invoke the Fairness Doctrine for their protection and simultaneously blame it for the suppression of their views. Miss Efron feels that the confusion results from the "notable abstractions" in the Doctrine. The problems of defining "fairness" and "objectivity" result in newscasters and documentarians conforming as closely as possible to a safe, middle-of-the-road view. However, the middle-of-the-road is also a position, and millions of American viewers who are to the left and right of the political spectrum feel they are being actively deprived of an equal voice on the air waves. Miss Efron advocates the adoption of a "spectrum theory" as a solution to the broadcasters' inhibitions which are imposed by the Fairness Doctrine. She feels that the proportionate use of newsmen representing the total spectrum of political views would insure the public's receiving a glimpse of U.S. political life as it really is.

Four prominent Americans reply to Miss Efron's comments and her support of the spectrum theory. Dean Barrett (pp. 310-312) maintains that reasonable fairness and balance in the treatment of news and public affairs are attainable. In fact, Barrett feels that coverage is healthier than Miss Efron seems to indicate. In his opinion, the spec-

288   trum theory outlined by Miss Efron would provide "a cure even worse than the ailment" she seeks to rectify. The solution lies, rather, in leaving broadcast news to trained, disciplined reporters, and providing more forums for a broad range of outspoken views.

Senator Pastore (pp. 313-315) defends the Fairness Doctrine. He states that television's middle-of-the-road approach to controversial subjects is caused by the broadcasters' timidity and lack of responsibility. Pastore does feel, however, that broadcasters have reason to feel inhibited, but not from the results of the Fairness Doctrine. He maintains that broadcasters need to be freed of some governmental restrictions and suggests that a good beginning would be an extension of the license renewal period.

William Buckley (pp. 316-318) agrees that the problems cited by Miss Efron are extremely significant, but he suspects that a satisfactory solution may not be possible. Buckley argues that the spectrum theory would suffer from the same problem of practical implementation of theoretical ideals that hinders the effectiveness of the Fairness Doctrine. It would be impossible to rule objectively on whether or not the spectrum was completely covered or responsibly weighed. He proposes that in cities where there are two television stations, there be complete freedom for all broadcasters whose loyalty to the U.S. is unquestioned, and that pay-TV be established in communities whose popluation is over fifty-thousand.

The last commentary (pp. 319-321), by Professor Arthur Schlesinger Jr., emphasizes that the Fairness Doctrine is merely a guideline and not a set law. The Doctrine needs to be applied to each particular case; the significant question is who shall apply the guideline? Schlesinger suggests that an agency of appeal, made up of broadcasters and members of the public, be set up to judge the merits of individual charges or cases. According to Schlesinger, the area of news broadcasting as opposed to documentaries, commentaries or editorials should retain pure objectivity with a predominance of fact over opinion as its guiding principle.

FCC Commissioner Nicholas Johnson (pp. 322-329) agrees with the television industry that censorship has become a very serious problem in this country. However, he emphatically denies any relationship between censorship and the Federal Government. Johnson's premise stated here is that television censorship is the result of fear on the part of broadcasters to incur the displeasure of the private interests from whom the television industry receives its profits: cigarette companies, car manufacturers, soft drink companies and the like. Information vital to the public welfare is being suppressed according to

Johnson, who supports his contention with a number of examples. *289*
Johnson restates the Jeffersonian principle: "The way to prevent
error is to give the people full information . . ." and points out that
the American people in fact are not receiving complete information
about their own affairs.

CBS News president Richard Salant (pp. 330-337) emphatically
denies Johnson's accusations, at least as they relate to CBS News. He
attempts to demonstrate that Johnson is 100 percent wrong on all
counts by taking each of the Commissioner's specific charges of suppression of evidence and avoidance of damaging facts and indicating
how the charges do not apply to CBS's news operation. Salant maintains that during his tenure at CBS no issue, topic or story has been
selected or omitted and no news treatment has been affected because
of pressure or censorship by corporate management, advertisers or
his associates at CBS News.

The FCC

By Martin Mayer

NOVEMBER 19 AND 26, DECEMBER 3, 1966

Of all the alphabet agencies spawned by Franklin Roosevelt's New Deal, the FCC—Federal Communications Commission—is the one most likely to be in the news and in the minds of people who are not lawyers or politicians or part of the business the agency regulates. Family television sets are on for six hours a day, and the FCC is the only official Government body that has anything at all to do with what appears on those screens. The air is public if anything is, and people look to the FCC, often hopefully (because everybody has his own grudge against something in television), to make clear what they expect from the broadcasters.

In fact, however, Government regulation of broadcasting started off less as a help to the consumer than as a service to the industry. What was killing broadcasting (and infuriating listeners) back in the 1920's, when regulation began, was the fact that two signals on the same (or nearly the same) frequency will instantly interfere with each other if they carry into each other's territory. There was no way for the broadcasters themselves to keep intruders out of their frequencies: Only the Government could do it. In 1927 the confusion became desperate, and Congress established a Federal Radio Commission[1] with the power to grant broadcasters exclusive licenses to their frequencies. The Commission was to keep its hands off the question of how the public air was used: The responsibility was strictly to decide who should have the use of it.

The new Commission reported to the then Secretary of Commerce, Herbert Hoover; and among its first employees, in 1928, was a young law student named Rosel H. Hyde, who stayed with the agency after Congress had made it an independent Federal Communications Commission in 1934, and [was until September, 1969] is still there—as Chairman. Considering how close to impossible the FCC in recent years has found the revocation of any broadcasting license it is interesting to note that the Radio Commission in its first two years ordered out of business completely 150 of the 732 stations that were in operation when the agency began work.

290

Though the seven Commissioners don't much like to hear it (and neither does the President, who appoints them subject to confirmation by the Senate), the FCC is fundamentally a branch of Congress. Its reason for being is to write the laws (the official word is "rules") which a fast-moving business like broadcasting provokes in greater numbers than a busy legislature like Congress can provide, in detailed complexity greater than a technically ignorant body like Congress can understand. Thus, the "independent regulatory agencies," of which the FCC is one: Congress delegates certain of its powers to make law, setting down the standards within which the agencies must work.

In the case of the FCC, these standards are, as Judge Henry J. Friendly once put it, "more than usually meaningless." Empowering an administrative agency to decide whether or not railroads should be allowed to shut down a line, Congress had told the Interstate Commerce Commission to consider "public convenience and necessity." Liking the phrase, but feeling it was somehow incomplete, the men who wrote the Communications Act in 1934 told the FCC Commissioners that in awarding broadcast licenses they should be guided by "public interest, convenience and necessity."[2] But it is one thing, not too difficult, to determine whether a given slice of the public needs rail service; something else to decide whether it needs a radio or TV station—and something else again, wildly different, to conclude that one man rather than another should be awarded a broadcasting license because this fellow will use his license (a gift of the Government, which may be worth millions) to serve "the public interest, convenience and necessity."

Nobody "owns" a broadcasting license in the normal sense of the word "own"—every three years a license must be renewed. At that time, the FCC can simply put any broadcaster out of business by taking away his license and giving it to somebody else. Every so often, a new Commissioner threatens to do just that to lots of broadcasters (this direct threat, rather than the publicized phrase about "a vast wasteland," was what the television industry most remembered about Newton Minow's maiden speech as Chairman in 1961). The new Commissioner makes these threats soon after he learns that if he can't revoke licenses he almost can't do anything.

The FCC does have limited authority to impose small fines[3] but as a practical matter its powers are restricted to life and death— keep the license or give it back—as though a judge's only choice in dealing with a burglar were to set him free or order him electrocuted. Moreover, the only grounds on which the Commission can properly

292 deny a renewal is clear proof that the station has failed to serve public interest, convenience and necessity. "The Commission," says an officer of the network, "is trying to enforce something it can't even define. You can't make a crime out of a mystery—that's Kafka." So in the end nothing happens.

Given the existing law, the political context and prevailing judicial attitudes, not much can happen, officially. What most interests everyone except an engineer is the quality of the programs on the air—but the Communications act specifically forbids the Commission to supervise program content. Though many Congressmen cheerfully declare themselves in favor of regulation, a number of them (like the Johnson family) own at least some piece of a television station—and the rest rely on the good will of local broadcasters to carry their reports from Washington free of charge. The vagueness of the standards laid down in the Act makes courts reluctant to support the Commissioners when the losers in an FCC contest take an appeal—in one recent stretch, the Court of Appeals for the District of Columbia overruled the FCC in nine straight cases.[4] Finally, the FCC is still to a degree under the shadow of the bad name it acquired, deservedly, during the years when the Truman and Eisenhower Administrations threw a few bones to political grifters in the form of Commission appointments. One Commissioner from that era died while under criminal indictment, and another resigned while under Congressional fire.

Even if the law were more flexible, the Congress and the courts more sympathetic and the past more reputable, the FCC would be in constant trouble. Budgeted at about $17,000,000 [$20,000,000] a year, with only about 1500 employees[5] around the country, the agency is charged with licensing all broadcasting, including, for example ham operators, police cars and radio-summoned taxicabs; and all interstate or overseas messages on wire, including long-distance telephone calls, telegrams, and so forth.

In addition to routine field checking of whether stations are using more power than authorized, keeping their log books correctly and generally behaving themselves, the agency must handle 3000 formal applications of one sort or another every day. The 300-odd matters on which the Commissioners actually hold a hearing make an argued case-load twice that of the Supreme Court, but account for only one-thirtieth of one percent of the applications that must be processed. The rush, always under outside pressure, means that quite important decisions are often made sloppily: The Commission was saved only by the Korean War from the consequences of a decision

that would have saddled the industry with color television that could
not have been received on a black-and-white set; and nothing saved
television from the FCC's decision to mix VHF and UHF stations
in the same markets, thereby guaranteeing at least the initial failure
of the UHF band.

In a report to John F. Kennedy shortly before he assumed the
Presidency, James M. Landis, once dean of the Harvard Law School
and head of the Civil Aeronautics Board, wrote that the FCC "seems
incapable of policy planning, of disposing within a reasonable period
of time the business before it, of fashioning procedures that are
effective to deal with its problems." A similar investigation today
would yield an only slightly more charitable result—but there is
nobody to blame. It's hard for a man to keep his tie on straight, let
alone sort out an infinitely long list of business and financial affairs
in a neat and orderly manner, if he's forever on the run.

One result is an air of frustration and irritation with one's colleagues that hangs in the halls at the Commission's offices . . . During
the 32 [36] years of its existence the FCC has had 16 [17] Chairmen
(counting Rosel Hyde twice, because he also held his current post for
the first year of the Eisenhower Administration). None of them ever
advanced from this job to a greater public office.

Still, the severity of the punishments the Commission theoretically can impose means that no station owner can risk ignoring it.
"They're worried about their licenses daily, weekly, monthly,"
says a Washington lawyer who earns his living basically by feeding
information out from the FCC to station owners across the country.
"When the inspector walks into their offices, they want to know exactly what he'll be looking for." The Commission has never disciplined any station severely for limiting its service to claptrap, but
it has threatened to do so—and there might always be a first time.

The grounds for such action would be the station's failure to live
up to the promises it made (heavy local coverage, attention to public
affairs, service programs, and so on) while arguing for its original
license or a previous renewal. "In my time there," says the Washington lawyer Paul Porter, who served as Chairman shortly after the war,
"my friend Cliff Durr was playing left end, and when renewals came
up Cliff would make this comparison between promise and performance. If there was a raving disparity, as there often was, Cliff
would say we should have a hearing, and I would go along. It got so
we had half the industry on temporary licenses; we didn't have
enough hearing examiners to handle the business. We discovered
that of 26 clear-channel (radio) stations, only one or two had farm

294 directors; we made a lot of jobs for county agents. Then we issued a blue-book 'Public Service Responsibilities of Broadcasters'[6]—and said, Go and sin no more. It had a short-term salutary effect."

The FCC has recently been moving back toward some measurement of promise versus performance. Broadcasters now make their promises on new and much less detailed application forms, which require them only to pledge that certain rough percentages of broadcast time will be devoted to 1. News, 2. Public Affairs, 3. All other programs, exclusive of entertainment and sports. "It looks much less restrictive than the old form, which had seven specific categories,"[7] says [former] Commissioner Lee Loevinger, "but that makes it more significant." The important category will be the "everything else"; rather than trying to hold the stations to their percentages, the Commission will require a minimum, some of it at hours when people may actually be watching, for local or unusual programming. The requirement will probably be leaked informally to the Washington lawyers rather than issued as a rule, because a rule can be knocked down by Congress or the courts, while "regulation by lifted eyebrow" can make most station owners nervous enough to change their schedules.

Members of the viewing public can sometimes make the eyebrow lift, too. "We get letters from people," says William Ray, director of the Commission's complaint bureau, "simply saying that there's too much crime and violence, or that there shouldn't be wrestling on television. We recommend that they make their views known to the licensee, and we send the station a copy of the letter. Sometimes, when the complaint is specific—on such and such a commercial at such and such an hour the sound was too loud, the advertising agency has been notified that this commercial will not be shown again. All complaints go into the folder to be looked over when renewal application comes in; and we call the attention of the renewal people to what the folder contains." No station wants too many letters in that folder, so viewers (and pressure groups) have a little leverage.

Ultimately, though, neither the angry viewer nor the FCC itself has any great leverage, because the public as a whole is not unhappy with the television service it receives; and the Commission is supposed to serve the public. A few years back, FCC hearings were held in Chicago and Omaha to determine what people thought of their local TV stations; when it was suggested that the next stop might be Iowa, the Iowa legislature formally resolved that the FCC should stay out of its state. Though there is always a danger that such an attitude can slop over into a refusal to regulate at all, Chairman Hyde can argue

convincingly that "stations are under constant community examination every hour that they're operating."

In most cities, anyway, not many people care much one way or
the other about their local station, because they don't watch what the
local station puts out. What they watch, what they love or hate (and
what they want the FCC to do something about) is the programming
that comes from the networks.

When the word "broadcasting," is used, most people mean the
networks and their programs. But the law under which the FCC operates was written on the old Jeffersonian model of a nation of competing small farmers, each with his own little independent broadcasting station, each entitled to absolute free speech. Though NBC
was already in business with two permanent radio hookups when the
first Radio Act was passed in 1927, nothing in that law or the Communications Act mentions networks.[8]

Still, if there is nothing in the law that gives the Commission
power to regulate networks, there is also nothing that keeps the Commissioners from trying. Perhaps the most significant decision the FCC
ever made was one that ordered the National Broadcasting Company
to sell off one of the two radio networks it then controlled (the separated network became ABC).[9] Moreover, because the networks make
most of their money on the five very-high-frequency stations each of
them owns and operates,[10] and the FCC could make a rule forbidding
networks to own stations, any letter from Washington receives a
respectful (not to say excited) reading at the headquarters of every
network. As a senior executive of one of them puts it, "The Commission says it has no authority to regulate networks, but it acts
just as though it does."

When the FCC speaks of programs, however, it stands on much
softer ground. Section 326 of the Communications Act flatly states
that the law shall not "be understood or construed to give the Commission the power of censorship . . . and no regulation or condition
shall be promulgated or fixed . . . which shall interfere with the right
of free speech." Testifying before a Senate committee in 1960, Frederick W. Ford, then Chairman of the Commission, said that "I don't
see how we could possibly go out and say this program is good and
that program is bad. That would be a direct violation of the law."

Other Chairmen, especially the Kennedy appointees, Newton N.
Minow and E. William Henry, have felt that there were (or at least
should be) ways around Section 326. They saw it as their mission to
improve what was broadcast on the public air. And the issue is not

296   completely clear-cut, even to those who feel strongly that the FCC has
no business in this area (a group that includes Chairman Hyde: "The
law forbids me from interfering in programming," Hyde says, "even
if it doesn't forbid some other Commissioners").

The Commission's power over broadcasters comes from the fact
that all licenses must be renewed every three years, and in considering whether or not to renew a license, the Commissioners are
permitted to look into the kind of service the station can be expected
to give. Studying this question in 1960, the Commission listed fourteen areas in which to judge a station's performance. The first two
dealt with opportunities for local self-expression and the development of local talent; then there were demands for religious, educational, children's, public affairs, editorial, agricultural, news and
sports programs; weather and market reports; "Service to Minority
Groups"; and (14th) entertainment.

Such requirements remain unreal, however often they are stated,
and even if met they would not necessarily improve television.
Judge Henry J. Friendly in his Holmes lectures at Harvard asked
leave to doubt "whether the Commission is really wise enough to
determine that live telecasts—of local cooking lessons, for example—
so much stressed in the decisions, are always better than a tape of
Shakespeare's Histories." Sometimes the insistence on local programming can have harmful effects. Because it was understood that
the FCC wanted every station to present at least half an hour of local
programming between 6 and 11 every night, NBC's Chicago station
for more than a year did not carry Huntley-Brinkley: The difference
between Central and Eastern time worked out to mean that there was
no other half-hour every day which could be sacrificed to local talent
without losing important money from sponsors and (perhaps almost
as important) infuriating local viewers who wanted to see a network
entertainment show.

Formal intervention in programming by the FCC (apart from very
occasional rulings that a station must give equal time to someone to
answer a political broadcast) has almost always been an effort to cut
the ties that bind networks and their affiliated stations, or networks
and advertisers, or networks and program suppliers. Following the
quiz-show scandals of the late 1950's, the FCC strengthened an
"office of network study" in the agency. In part on this group's recommendations, the Commission during the last decade has ended the
once-standard practice of "option time" (by which a station in signing
an affiliation agreement pledged itself to carry network shows on
certain hours if the network requested the use of the facility). It also

has outlawed the "must-buy list" (by which the networks could force *297*
advertisers to purchase time on a number of major stations if they
wanted the use of the network at all).

Nothing to date has made much difference in the networks'
domination of the public air, and nothing is likely to do so. In terms
of quality, some of the results of FCC action have probably been unfortunate. With the loss of option rights, networks were compelled to
make even more certain that every program they sent out would be
highly popular, because many stations were cheerfully prepared to
show movies (which would allow them to keep all the mondy advertisers spent for their time, instead of turning over most of it to the networks) whenever a network show couldn't guarantee a big audience.

The FCC may lack the legal power to influence network programming, but its powers in other areas are so extreme that a few words
dropped in the right ears can be remarkably persuasive. Perhaps the
most extraordinary example of informal intervention was the call
from Chairman John C. Doerfer in 1960 which brought down to the
FCC for a little conference the chiefs of all three networks. Doerfer
had no rule to propose; indeed, he had not discussed with his fellow
Commissioners much of what he was about to say. But he was insistent—and he noted that President Eisenhower agreed with him—
that each network must present a public affairs program every week
in evening time at an hour when no two such programs would conflict. The network officials had known that something of this sort was
in the wind ("The FCC is a sieve," one of them says), and they were
prepared. The antitrust laws, they said sympathetically, forbade any
such collusion among them: Indeed, their lawyers were concerned
that they were meeting together to discuss programs at all, even under
such distinguished auspices as those of Chairman Doerfer. At this
point Doerfer reached into his desk and pulled out a letter from the
Attorney General, an official opinion that collaboration among the
networks for this purpose would not violate the antitrust laws. Presently, without any Commission action, the networks were following
Doerfer's suggestions [since 1967 they sometimes haven't].

Again, when Newton Minow became Chairman he told the heads
of the networks that he, Jack Kennedy and Bobby Kennedy were all
distressed by the programs their children watched Saturday morning
and at the cocktail hour on the weekdays; and now that the networks
knew their audience was displeased, they would wish to offer more
serious children's programs. This worked, too, but not for long.

The extreme positions on the Commission have been represented by Kenneth A. Cox from the State of Washington and Lee Loev-

298 inger from Minnesota.[11] Both are liberal Democrats, lean Westerners, intellectual and rather austere. For all these similarities, they agree on virtually nothing.

"I think the Commission was created for the purpose of regulating," Cox says. "Right now, part of the regulating should be to make the networks establish program categories and use them. If we don't have the authority, the courts will tell us; if our policy is wrong, then Congress should change the statute."

"What the regulators are saying," Loevinger replies, "is that we don't want to censor, but people have to be responsible for what goes out. Implicitly, they're saying that the FCC must make the judgment of what is responsible. That's just the kind of censorship that some European governments exercise over broadcasting—and the Congress, the Court and the people have repeatedly said that they do not want the FCC given that authority."

The Commission, which must by law be divided 4-3 between the two political parties, tends also to be divided 4-3 on issues like program regulation. When E. William Henry resigned as Chairman, for example, the trade papers buzzed with speculation as to whether he would be replaced with a "regulator" like himself or a lawyer like Loevinger.[12]

But not everywhere. "This business," says a very senior officer at one of the networks, "is 80 percent to sell goods, and it will keep grinding along as it is. Whoever's on the Commission you're not going to change broadcasting with the devices available to the FCC. The intelligent people in broadcasting, even when there's an action pending that scares them and even when they go along with it, don't really regard the Commission as a big ogre—just as something that's spinning its wheels."

The Federal Communications Commission was established in 1934 primarily to handle technical problems, and even today more than half its staff is engaged in engineering work. Each Commissioner is assigned his own engineer, independent of the agency's engineering offices, to help him know what he agrees with. The Commissioners themselves, like most people who hold such jobs in Washington, are likely to be lawyers; and many of them go on in later years to represent broadcasting stations in matters before the Commission. Many of them hang on their walls a certificate testifying to completion of a course given by the Capitol Radio Engineering Institute.

It is probably fair to say that the bulk of the FCC's decisions over the years have been technical, and the rest have been commercial or political in a rather vulgar sense. (Franklin Roosevelt, annoyed at the overwhelming support given to Wendel Wilkie by the Nation's newspapers, instructed James Lawrence Fly Chairman of the FCC to see to it that the same "bunch of bums" didn't take over broadcasting too; and it took a threat from Congress to amend the law to persuade the Commission that ownership of a newspaper should not be regarded as a negative factor in assessing the qualifications of an applicant for a broadcasting license.)[13]

When television came, the Commission did give a nudge to the educators, reserving for them 242 (now 632) channels on which commercials could not be carried (and giving them a preference on regular channels: One of the first TV stations was established by Iowa State University, as a self-supporting, commercial operation).

But government, like a television network, is designed to give people what they want. Where the majority feels strongly about something, the minority makes do. And governments cannot come roaring into the market place, disturbing all the patterns of going businesses, without the most urgent reasons of public policy. So the FCC, making gestures toward the values of protecting minority interests and guaranteeing diversity of service, has fundamentally gone along with the intensely commercial use of the public air by a restricted number of licensed people who have a virtually unrestricted power to decide what they will and will not broadcast. The public as a whole is not dissatisfied. . . .

There is little sentiment on the Commission, and nearly none in Congress, to rock this particular boat. But "technology," as E. William Henry put it shortly before his resignation as Chairman, "is not standing still; it will not preserve forever—or even until that long tomorrow—the type of broadcast system we have today."

The first premise of American broadcasting is no longer clearly true and will soon be clearly false: There is less need now and will be no need in the future for the broadcasting station that "owns" a slice of the public air and controls in its special interests what will go out on its facilities. The spread of CATV (community antenna) systems (see pp. 581-585), and the near prospect of a communications satellite which can rebroadcast directly to people's homes on dozens of channels at once, suggest that broadcasting in the future can be built on the premise of the common carrier, like the telephone company. Anyone with a program who can pay the (relatively small) time charges for the use of a channel on the satellite would have the right to broadcast, just as anybody with the price of the call can pick up his telephone and dial long distance.

300   This fall, Texaco, which has sponsored the Metropolitan Opera Saturday afternoon radio broadcasts for a quarter of a century, wanted to make a big institutional splash by telecasting the opening night of the Met's new $50,000,000 theater at Lincoln Center. The company was prepared to pay for the privilege—but no network would sell the time, because that Friday night was one when some of the new programs were to be introduced, and the Nielsen rating of a series might suffer if its first show were pre-empted.

Every so often, documentary film makers, reputable people with affiliations as solid as Time-Life, ask to buy time for their product on the networks; and the networks refuse on the grounds that stations are now held responsible to the FCC for their programs, and except where a political party buys the time (which is a separate question in the law) they cannot risk potentially political films they do not control.

In 1966, Fred W. Friendly resigned from CBS because the network had decided not to carry live from Washington the Senate Vietnam hearings. Every year, producers make pilot films for new entertainment series, which are looked at by the networks and rejected—even though, often enough some advertiser is prepared to sponsor them.

All these problems, serious and ridiculous, are caused by the short supply and long expense of transmission facilities, either to the stations or on the air. Even in the current infant state of the art, satellites can greatly increase the number of channels available for transmission to stations and greatly reduce the price (the Ford Foundation has estimated a reduction of more than 75 percent). Eventually, direct satellite transmission to homes could blast open the technical and financial bottleneck of the limited number of stations in each locality. Meanwhile, CATV systems, rapidly expanding across the country, have the technical capacity (if not, at present, the program resources) to add literally dozens of channels to what is available on the home screen. Oddly enough, there is more room for information on a wire than there is in the air.

"There are highly significant policy issues in space," says Chairman Rosel Hyde. "Who will be the authorized user of the satellites? Who will own the earth stations? Will the satellite supply only to networks or to stations—and what about this talk of supplying directly to the home?" The issues have been further confused by the Ford and Comsat proposals to use the profits from communications satellites for the support of educational television—proposals which assume that these satellites will serve no function other than to replace the existing wired and microwave relays that make the broadcasting networks possible.

Inevitably, an agency like the FCC sees these questions mostly *301* from the point of view of the industry it regulates. All regulatory agencies, as Dean James M. Landis pointed out in his report to John F. Kennedy, suffer a "tendency toward industry orientation (which) arises primarily from the fact that of necessity contacts with the industry are frequent and generally productive of intelligent ideas. Contacts with the public, however, are rare and generally unproductive of anything except complaints."

Dealing with the CATV question, the FCC seems to have looked first to the convenience and necessity of the stations. Most of the rules that have been laid down so far aim to keep CATV systems from bringing outside stations into any area where the local service is technically adequate. . . .

Generally speaking, the "liberals" on the Commission (those who believe broadcasters should be held to higher standards of public interest) have demanded narrow restrictions on the CATV systems; the "conservatives" have been for giving the new ventures their head. "We can't permit CATV to distort and frustrate the established pattern," says Commissioner Kenneth Cox, whom the networks regard (respectfully) as one their strongest antagonists at the FCC. What worries Cox and his colleagues is that local coverage and local service will disappear under the impact of big-city stations available everywhere. . . .

On the other hand, Chairman Hyde, whom Jack Gould of *The New York Times* recently described as "the most conservative member of the FCC," feels much more uncomfortable with the new rules against CATV: "It looks," he says, "like we're protecting stations against competition." Hyde is also less concerned about damaging the local part of TV: "Why should we sit here and tell the folks they have to see what's going on in the county when the whole opportunity of broadcasting is the wider experience?" But Hyde, too, is worried about "chaos in the program market" and puzzled by the odd and uncertain legal question of who owns what in a program that is being broadcast.

The big question to come in regulating the use of communications satellites will present these issues in an aggravated form. Unfortunately, the FCC, like all Government regulatory agencies, was established to make small decisions by a Congress which said it reserved the big decisions for itself; and all the Commission's modes of operation are designed to deal with trifles. When the law that created Comsat was passed,[14] nobody had imagined the possibility that satellites might make broadcasting itself a true public utility rather than a mostly private business. So Congress gave the FCC

302 virtually unlimited authority over the companies that run communications satellites: The agency must approve their financing, their purchasing policies, their fees, and their decisions about the customers they will accept. As a result, almost by accident, the FCC has new, drastic and probably unwanted power over the future of television—and will probably keep this power, though Senate hearings indicate that some congressmen and senators now feel the matter is too important to be left in the Commission's hands.

"It seems inevitable," Joseph V. Charyk, president of the Communications Satellite Corporation, told the annual meeting of the National Association of Broadcasters, "that we will continue to move toward the effective establishment in metropolitan centers of what will amount in fact to a communications utility." In the next few years, FCC rulings will hasten this motion or try to stop it. For the station owners and their allies in Congress, and very possibly for the public, the stakes here are very much higher than they have been in the usual rule-making debate about the number or the decibel-count of commericals, the ownership of programs, the right of the networks to option time from affiliates, and so forth.

Control of the satellites gives the agency its first real chance to stop "spinning its wheels" and get the wheels moving somewhere. "The satellites," says Chairman Hyde, looking back on 20 years as a Commissioner and 38 years of involvement with government regulation of broadcasting, and ahead to the years of space hearings, "are where the glamor is going to be."

Is Speech on Television Really Free?

By Edith Efron

APRIL 11, 1964

At a recent Congressional hearing, a Socialist arose and denounced the suppression of left-wing political views on the publicly owned air waves. Pointing out acidly that "Abraham Lincoln, in the campaign of 1860, represented a minority political viewpoint," Aaron Orange, spokesman for the 74-year-old Socialist Labor Party, said: "We agree with Justice Hugo Black who stated, 'There is no progress possible anywhere where the differences of people are stifled, their voices are not able to be heard, and where they all speak as one voice . . .' It is simple logic that creating the opportunity for a wider presentation of one view, while at the same time suppressing . . . the expression of all other divergent views, is the very antithesis of democracy. . ."

At another recent Congressional hearing, a conservative rose and similarly denounced the suppression of right-wing political views on the publicly owned air waves. Congressman Durward Hall (R., Mo.) attacked the "one-sided editorializing" that goes on in all three networks "in the guise of public-affairs shows." He said: "If there were signs of diversity, I would not be so concerned. But one does not hear or see one network show today which seems to be 'liberal-oriented' and one tomorrow which seems to be 'conservative-oriented.' They all fall into the 'liberal' category."

In the last few years, a strange new phenomenon has emerged: the battle by large groups, both right and left of center, for access to the publicly owned air waves. Not only do these groups charge that their views are excluded from the air waves, they also charge that they are frequently subject to ideological attack on the air, without the opportunity to defend themselves.

This cry from far-flung points of the political spectrum that free speech is being inhibited by broadcasters in general—and by the networks in particular—is the latest and most disturbing development

304 in the history of America's only Government-regulated communications medium.

And there can be no question but that a specific Government regulation lies at the root of the trouble. Its name is: the "Fairness Doctrine." It lays down the principles to which broadcasting news and public-affairs departments must conform. And, paradoxically, the spokesmen for the left and the right are simultaneously blaming it for the suppression of their views and invoking it for protection. To understand the paradox, one must understand the Fairness Doctrine.

This doctrine is a modification by the Federal Communications Commission of its own 1941 ruling known as the "Mayflower Decision."[15] This historic decision forbade broadcasters to express their own thoughts on controversial issues, and had the peculiar affect of abolishing almost all controversial thought from television. In 1949, the Fairness Doctrine was developed to rectify this situation. "It granted the broadcaster the right to express his views—provided he also sought out and presented 'all sides of controversial issues.' This presentation of 'all sides' was to be 'fair,' 'non-distorted,' 'nonpartisan,' 'non-one-sided,' 'equal,' 'equally forceful.'"[16]

Officially, the Fairness Doctrine is intended to be the guardian of diversity of thought on the publicly owned air waves; and its various provisions are intended to solve the age-old journalistic problem of "impartiality" versus "slanting"—concealed or "covert" editorializing. Unfortunately, "slanting" is strangely difficult to pin down. Said FCC Chairman E. William Henry: "Overt editorializing presents little problem . . . but editorializing may take other less-identifiable forms . . . It is very, very difficult to draw the line as to what is editorializing." And Congressman Oren Harris (D., Ark.)[17] commented further: "We get into the problem of deciding whether a news analysis is editorializing when it is slanted . . . Who is going to decide? Isn't it largely how we might feel as individuals toward a particular news report?"

With this question, Mr. Harris isolates the central—and unresolved—dilemma of the Fairness Doctrine. In any given news report or documentary on a controversial issue, a treatment that seems eminently "fair," "impartial" or "objective" to one viewer, may seem eminently "unfair," "slanted" and "biased" to another. The truth is that the Fairness Doctrine contains a set of noble abstractions to which most would subscribe in principle—but upon which no two appear to agree in practical application. It is, in consequence, one of the most unintelligible regulations governing the broadcasting industry.[18] At the recent "editorializing" hearings, one broadcaster,

Clarence Jones, president of WQIZ, St. George, South Carolina,
blurted out: "Just what is the standard of fairness? Who knows? I
don't understand it. I don't know what it requires me to do. I wish I
did."

Given the confusion that reigns over the issue of "fairness" or
"objectivity," how do the networks approach the problem? Curi-
ously enough, both CBS and ABC profess to find it marvelously
simple. In a host of policy statements they have blandly laid claim to
total "fairness." They contend that "fairness" or "objectivity" consists of ordering their staffs to report on events in news programs and
interpret events "in depth" in documentaries without any reference
to, or expression of, their own opinions.

James Hagerty of ABC, while still news chief, stated ABC policy
thus: "We're trying to be objective. We present both sides fairly. We
are reporters. We get interpretations from 'other' people and present
them. If anyone on this network is expressing his own opinion—well,
if I catch him, I won't permit it." (Elmer Lower, his successor, confirms this policy and amplifies: "Our aim is to present news accurately, fairly and with balance. As networks, ABC Radio, and ABC
Television do not present opinion' [they do present "commentary"]).

And Richard Salant, while news chief of CBS, said, "We believe
in objective coverage. Our reporters do not cover stories from 'their'
points of view. They are presenting them from 'nobody's' point of
view." [Eric Sevareid "comments," as opposed to "reports" or
"editorializes."]

This is not the position taken by NBC, which lays no claim to
offering the public an opinion-sterile product. "We feel," says NBC
News chief William McAndrew, that news events require interpretation to give them reality. We offer our staff men a wide latitude of
interpretation." There is reason to suppose that on this matter NBC
is closest to accepting reality. The claim that "no-opinion" journalism
can exist is dubious. Indeed, it is branded an outright myth by some
of the most responsible men in the business.

News, they say, is "always" a form of editorializing. Quincy
Howe, a former president of the Association of Radio-Television
News Analysts, says: "All news presented on radio and TV editorializes. The newscaster editorializes in what he emphasizes and what
he plays down, in what he omits and in what he includes." David
Brinkley is in agreement. "News," he says, "is what I say it is. It's
something worth knowing by 'my' standards."

Documentaries, too, say expert communications men, are carriers
of a dominant point of view. A documentary, they point out, is far

306 more than a filmed debate by two teams of men with opposing ideas about a problem. It is the producer's interpretation of that problem "and of the controversy itself:" This interpretation is guided solely by the producer's opinions. And these opinions are controversial—as the storms of protest in the Massachusetts Legislature over CBS's *Biography of a Bookie Joint,* and the anger among conservative congressmen over NBC's *The Battle of Newburgh* amply attest.

The documentary, say its producers, is necessarily a form of editorializing. Says John Secondari of ABC: "It is absolutely impossible to write, broadcast, or put together pictures without having a point of view." Says Gerald Green, who produces documentaries for NBC: "It is impossible not to have a point of view. Once you start selecting facts and choosing what and whom to put on the air, a point of view is implicit." Says Don Hewitt of CBS: "Of course, the 'in-depth' news documentaries do take a point of view . . . It has to be understood that personality has to come through."

This all adds up to the plain fact that the allegedly impartial air waves are awash with unidentified editorial opinion. Yet this situation is not precisely the networks' fault. The truth is that the networks, like all broadcasters, are in the grip of an impossible dilemma: They are bounded on one side by the fact that it is impossible for a human being to combine words or pictures without smuggling in value judgments—and they are bounded on the other by a Fairness Doctrine which demands an indefinable "impartiality" in news and public-affairs programming.

How have they resolved the conflict? Their solution, official statements notwithstanding, is an unhappy one. It consists simply of making sure that newscasters and documentary producers conform as closely as possible to a safe, middle-of-the-road point of view. Dominant network opinion is thus described: "It's conformist," says ABC's Howard K. Smith. "As compared to the other media, TV is by far the most colorless, the most cowardly." "The prevailing opinion of this network, I'd say, is moderate," says NBC News chief Mc-Andrew. "We have the political spectrum interpreted by moderates. Rightists call us liberal, labor people say we're in the middle." "The networks are in the hands of corporations which see the world the same way—as moderate liberals," says CBS's Hewitt. And the FCC's Henry says: "I'd say the prevailing network opinion is middle-of-the-road. Of course this middle position isn't 'no' position. It's 'a' position. Whatever it is, so far as the Fairness Doctrine is concerned, it's well within it."

It seems clear that a definite political point of view prevails on network broadcasting. Whether one calls this view "moderate," "middle-of-the-road" or "moderate liberalism," it is the unidentified political filter through which the viewer is permitted to view the affairs of this Nation. And yet, as Mr. Henry says, the middle position is "a" position, it is not "no" position. What's more, it is not the "only" position in America, and may well not be the majority position. The political middle is just what its name indicates—it is the "middle band" of the U.S. political spectrum, and it does not reflect the views of millions of Americans who represent a vast reservoir of diversified political opinion, both left and right of center, not to be confused with the Communists, racists or religious fanatics at the far fringes of the spectrum.

Spokesmen for these millions have come to feel that they are being actively deprived of an "equal" and "equally forceful" voice on the publicly owned air waves. They do not wish to be examined, interpreted and seen exclusively through "moderate" eyes; they wish to do their own examining, interpreting and seeing on the air. They are protesting vehemently against the token role they are allowed in a medium which has given a monopolistic status to the middle-of-the road mind.

There are those, today, who would revoke the Fairness Doctrine altogether, on the grounds that it is absurd to have a Government regulation for the express purpose of protecting diversity of expression, if its principal effect is to stifle it. At a recent meeting of the Radio-Television News Directors Association, 60 percent of those present voted that the doctrine had impaired their "editorial integrity."[19] And, according to FCC Chairman Henry, "There are a number of congressmen who would like to see the doctrine abandoned."

One of these irate congressmen, Glenn Cunningham (R., Neb.), a member of the House Communications Subcommittee, questions the legal premise behind the Fairness Doctrine—the Mayflower Decision itself. He says: "The problem of political slanting in one direction stems from something deeper than the Fairness Doctrine. It comes from that regulation which deprives broadcasters of freedom of the press. Until regulation is reduced to the function of an electronic traffic cop, and broadcasters have freedom of the press, broadcasting will never have the political diversity that the other media all have."

This view that broadcasters should have freedom of the press has grown in Congress—but it is not yet a majority position. Many still argue that it is not just the ambiguous Fairness Doctrine which causes the slanting-to-the-middle, but the timid interpretation placed upon

308   it by the network. And, despite the seriousness of the intellectual dilemma imposed by the doctrine on the networks, there is a certain justice to this claim. A monopolistic middle-of-the-road viewpoint was not legally imposed on the networks by the FCC. The collective huddling around the political centerline was a voluntary self-constriction on their part. There always was—and still is—an alternative interpretation of the Fairness Doctrine: "proportional representation."

Chairman Henry has this to say: "As far as the Government is concerned we say that the broadcaster should present contrasting viewpoints on issues of public interest. The question of whether an issue is of public interest depends, in part, on the number of people interested in it. Minority views are entitled to proportional representation, so to speak." "Proportional representation," taken literally, can mean nothing more or less than the "spectrum theory" of broadcasting—a well-established method of presenting a broad range of political positions on the air based on the statistical prevalence of such positions in the country. "The spectrum," says Mr. Henry, is "perfectly permissible under the Fairness Doctrine."

Practically speaking, what would the "spectrum theory" mean? "It would mean this: That the men who staff the news and public-affairs departments would represent all the polar political positions in this country. They would cover and interpret news from these identified points of view, like by-line newspaper reporters and columnists. They would produce documentaries on social and political issues from these different identified points of view."

With the "spectrum" method, the network product would become both politically more realistic and livelier. Newscasts, presented by men with frankly contrasting, rather than implicitly identical, viewpoints, would cease to be blindly repetitive; the art of controversial commentary would be revived; and such phenomena as socialist documentaries on capitalism, labor documentaries on business, *laissez-faire* documentaries on the welfare state, and conservative documentaries on U.S. foreign policy could appear. Above all, the "spectrum" method would allow the public to get a glimpse of U.S. political life as it really is, a violently colored dramatic spectrum of conflicting ideas, aspirations and goals—undulled by an artificial middle-of-the-road filter.

The plain fact is that the United States is not ideologically homogenized. And network TV has no business pretending that it is, even in the face of a desperately ambiguous legal situation. If, as we are told, the air waves "belong" to the totality of the American public,

there is little excuse for "not" using the "spectrum theory" of broad- *309*
casting.

The Fairness Doctrine "is" an endless source of torment and
confusion to the broadcasting industry and, as such, it merits the
condemnation it is increasingly getting. But to the degree that the
networks have retreated before the doctrine's ambiguities—to the
degree that they have voluntarily rejected the maximum intellectual
diversity that was legally possible to them—to the degree that they
have placed the crucial realm of political coverage in the hands of an
intellectual monopoly—they are responsible for the bitter struggle
for air time by major groups that we are seeing today.

The "moderate" interpretation of the Fairness Doctrine has
turned the networks into a giant communications system which
trudges down the middle of every road, waving the banner of non-
commitment. It has produced a strange, soggy tyranny of "medium"
opinion on the air waves, prophetically described in the Senate Report on Freedom of Communications: "It is in the quagmire of moderation that intellectual integrity suffers the most."

Is Speech on Television Really Free?

By Dean Barrett and Senator John O.
Pastore

APRIL 18, 1964

Dean Barrett

Miss Edith Efron has honestly summarized various views on the so-called Fairness Doctrine and has written a skillful and intelligent diagnosis. However, it is a diagnosis of a potential ailment more than of present actual conditions. Her prescribed cure, I fear, is wide of the mark and might be far worse than the ailment. My own reactions and appraisal can be summed up in four points:

1. Conditions are much healthier than Miss Efron and others think. It is doubtful that "moderate" interpretation of the Fairness Doctrine has "produced a strange, soggy tyranny of 'medium' opinion on the air waves."

Many of us who are far from television addicts can recall witnessing countless advocates of minority views, even "extremist" views, arguing their cases with vigor on television screens within the last year. We have heard such immoderate segregationists as James Kilpatrick of Richmond and Governor Ross Barnett of Mississippi, such complete integrationists as James Baldwin, and even such a far-out fringe operator as Malcolm X. We have heard Adlai Stevenson glorify the UN, Barry Goldwater alternately condemn and condone it, and more extreme characters sanctify and crucify it.

One of the frequent complaints is that the ultra-views get no hearing on the air waves and that broadcasting is dominated by the "moderate liberals." Yet we find the super-conservatives, in their *National Review*,[20] proclaiming they are shut out of academic forums, major magazines, and the daily press, and "only" broadcasting provides them a regular outlet. In brief, we should recognize that the offbeat holder of minority views gets more of a hearing on the air waves then in any other "mass" medium.

2. Reasonable fairness and balance in the treatment of news and

DEAN BARRETT AND SENATOR JOHN O. PASTORE
IS SPEECH ON TELEVISION REALLY FREE?

311

public affairs are attainable—when the job is entrusted to trained news specialists who are disciplined in placing news integrity above all other considerations. And, though aberrations may occur in occasional stories or broadcasts, an extraordinary degree of long-run balance can be achieved.

We are aware that some articulate Americans dispute this view. Certain labor leaders contend that almost all major media are conservative-controlled. Some ultra-conservatives see all working men as engaged in some sort of liberal conspiracy. And Henry Luce, sincerely advocating that news be filtered through a particular set of value judgments, has steered *Time* toward what he considers "point-of-view reporting" and what detractors call "slanted reporting."

Nonetheless, some years of experience in training and observing professional journalists have convinced this writer that a remarkable degree of fairness can be achieved. We can observe this in most of the output of the Associated Press and the United Press International and in the news columns of our best newspapers. We can observe it, I insist, in the news and public-affairs output of our networks and better independent stations.

The outlets mentioned, moreover, have covered not just the major partisans but the spokesmen of less orthodox and even "extremist" views. To illustrate the point, what reasonably informed American is unfamiliar with at least the broad views of Robert Welch and the John Birch Society, Elijah Muhammad and his Black Muslims, to say nothing of more respectable elements like the Buckleys and Goldwaters or the Reuther brothers.

3. The "spectrum theory" in the form defined by Miss Efron would provide a "cure" even worse than the ailment she sees. Miss Efron suggests that the staff members of news and public-affairs departments should "represent all the polar political positions in this country" and would "cover and interpret news from these identified points of view" and "produce documentaries on social and political issues from these different . . . points of view."

Then Miss Efron compares these opinionated broadcasters with "by-line reporters and columnists." In that one phrase she underscores the flaw in her whole proposal, I think. The "by-line reporter" in respectable American journalism is paid to "report" and to do so with all the responsibility, integrity and balance he can command. If he is good enough to deserve the byline, the reader should not detect any slant, any bias, any point of view. The columnist is an entirely different animal; he is generally paid to express an opinion, just as is an editorial writer, and the reader knows this.

312   Having news output handled by a whole range of outspoken partisans, with their views consciously injected, could well lead to journalistic bedlam. The theory seems to presuppose that the citizen who gets his racial news through a journalistic Ross Barnett and then through a journalistic Martin Luther King would somehow be better informed than one whose news is reported to him through Cronkite and Huntley. It also assumes that a William Buckley or an I. F. Stone would be capable of a reasonable facsimile of factual reporting. This is doubtful, despite the highly articulate character of both men; they have been practicing causists for too long.

The advocate and the reporter are of necessity two different types, and the latter has learned, through tough discipline, to subordinate any personal views to the goal of reportorial honesty. He has also seen enough of the fallibilities of the causists to become suspicious of violent partisanship. Hence it is only natural that the good news reporter and the good news editor should be moderates, both avoiding personal bias.

4. Where, then, does the solution lie? It lies, I think, in leaving the broadcast news reports and documentaries in the hands of those trained in the rigorous discipline of reporting honestly, of giving the same attention to the distasteful as to the palatable. If one of these begins injecting clear bias into his work, for heaven's sake fire him. But don't scrap the whole system and turn the job over to professed causists.

With that settled, let us try providing for the expression of a multiplicity of strong views clearly labeled as such. How? First, by engaging an array of articulate causists to voice their views as strongly as they wish in commentaries clearly announced as opinion; these would correspond roughly to the newspaper columnists. The idea is not entirely new; it was once tried in mild form by ABC, among others. It could be tried more expertly. Second, stage more of the round-table forums embracing partisans of various positions.

In brief, let us solve Miss Efron's problem by providing more formus for a broad spectrum of outspoken views. But leave the news and the documentaries to the professionals who are trained to be ruthless in practicing editorial integrity. In the meantime, let us encourage all the FCC Commissioners, broadcast executives, and members of Congress to continue giving their attention to the whole problem. For it has many facets, none of them subject to easy, pat solutions.

Senator Pastore

I cannot agree with the critics of the Fairness Doctrine who contend that its principal effect is to stifle diversity of expression.

Under the guidance of Government regulation, radio and TV have become integral parts of our society. The public has become dependent upon such media for information, views, and facts. The broadcaster is duty bound to stimulate thought, encourage discussion, and offer programs that will sharpen the public interest in important subject matter whether it be an issue on national, state or local level. The Fairness Doctrine gives him this latitude. It offers the broadcaster and the network full discretion in choosing the method and format in achieving this objective.

To say that the Fairness Doctrine is responsible for leading the broadcaster down the too-moderate middle-of-the-road approach is to me far-fetched in logic and a reflection on the maturity and integrity of the industry. The broad criteria enunciated by the FCC do not, in my judgment, inhibit the broadcaster in the presentation of controversial subject matter. In fact, the very opposite is true. For the keystone of the Fairness Doctrine—and indeed of the public interest —is the right of the public to be informed and to have presented to it the conflicting views on issues of significance.

Therefore, the Fairness Doctrine imposes a firm obligation on a broadcaster to afford opportunity for the discussion of such conflicting views. If the broadcaster takes a middle-of-the-road approach on a controversial subject, I feel it is not because of the requirement of the Fairness Doctrine, but because the broadcaster is not living up to his responsibility.

Furthermore, the record is very clear that a single case does not exist where a licensee has been refused a renewal of his permit only because he violated the Fairness Doctrine. Indeed, the opposite is true. A significant case which proves the liberality of the FCC is the so-called Pacifica case where the Commission said: "We recognize . . . such provocative programming . . . may offend some listeners. But this does not mean that those offended have the right, through the Commission's licensing power, to rule such programming off the air waves . . . No such drastic curtailment can be countenanced under the Constitution, the Communications Act, or the Commission's policy, which has consistently sought to insure 'the maintenance of radio and television as a medium of freedom of speech and freedom of expression for the people of the Nation as a whole'."[21]

I fully realize that in spite of the liberality of the Commission's policy, it does not guarantee a licensee that someone will not file a protest against him, be that person a conservative, a liberal or a middle-of-the-roader. Procedures must always be available to permit the filing of complaints, but this does not mean that a broadcaster must take the safe way out and merely stick to the middle of the road and avoid his responsibility in bringing to the public, information, views, and facts of a significant issue.

I have continually repeated in public and private my firm belief that the broadcaster has the ingenuity, the courage and the imagination to select and present the issues of our times in a constructive and stimulating fashion. That there are exceptions to this must be conceded, but I feel that they fall in the minority.

It would be naive on my part, however, not to realize and admit that some timidity does exist on the part of the broadcaster with a tremendous investment at stake. That fear, imaginary or real, centers about the "heavy hand," so-called, of the FCC as renewal time comes about every three years. But the remedy is not the abandonment of the Fairness Doctrine, which is the only guarantee that a diversified and free society has in such powerful media of information.

I feel, therefore, that the broadcaster requires and deserves a stronger sense of independence than he now enjoys. I suggest a review of the time element of the renewal process to promote both independence and responsiveness on the part of the broadcaster.

As I have indicated, the Commission by its Pacifica decision has stated quite firmly its liberality of interpretation. Interpretation depends on the composition of the Commission at any one time—and the Commission is changeable and does change in complexion from time to time.

Serious consideration should be given to extending the renewal period from three years, let's say, to five years as a step forward in "unshackling" the industry. To be sure, this could be only a beginning—an approach, so to speak—to be considered among other measures and methods which would give the broadcaster a more secure and independent attitude of operation.

In making this suggestion, I am perfectly aware of all the hurdles and restraints involved. Judging from our experience in seeking to amend the Equal Time provision of Section 315 of the Communications Act, these are changes not easily achieved.

However, recalling the Great Debates of 1960 and the industry's performance in that field, we must conclude that the broadcaster has become quite matured and he is entitled to be accepted and trusted.

The unquestioned advantage to all our citizens is now a matter of *315* history. To me, then, it is the area of expanded opportunity and extended time for service that should be explored. Consider it, if you will, an incentive for responsibility to be accepted—and intelligently and honorably discharged.

But let us not denigrate the Fairness Doctrine—or discard it. Indeed, what are the alternatives? What is the logic to the plaint that a Doctrine predicated on fairness must breed unfairness? There is none.

I believe that the Fairness Doctrine affords the broadcaster all the flexibility he needs to move ahead with daring, imagination and integrity in these critical times when the public interest demands all those qualities from mass media. The challenge—and choice—is his.

Is Speech on Television Really Free?

By William F. Buckley, Jr. and
Arthur M. Schlesinger, Jr.

APRIL 25, 1964

William F. Buckley, Jr.

I congratulate Miss Efron for poking her nose into the matter and asking us all to give some thought to the dilemma of the television broadcasters. It "is" a dilemma, for which I do not think there is an absolutely satisfactory solution to be found. For it comes down to this: Television channels, because they are limited in number, are in effect public utilities. This means, theoretically, that those persons or corporations who are licensed to run them may not treat them as private property, to do with as they uniquely see fit. There needs to be a guardian of the public interest, and that guardian, almost necessarily, is the Government of the United States.

At this point the dilemma emerges. Everyone who has observed the history of governments knows, or should know, that in the last analysis they tend to be much more dangerous to the freedom of the citizenry than any private group within a society tends to be, even a monopoly. So that on all those occasions when one turns over to the government fresh supplies of power with which to regulate the public interest, we are handing over to the principal source of potential public harassment, additional power with which to afflict us.

But what are the alternatives? One is, of course, a continuation of the status quo. The trouble with the status quo, says Miss Efron—and her views on this point are widely shared—is that in reaching for a formula by which to guard the public against indoctrination by the broadcasters, the Government has set up criteria which (a) are incorrigibly ambiguous (what indeed is "fair" treatment of a controversial subject?) and which (b) conduce to a dismally dull fare which deprives the listener of the excitement of public controversy and threatens to pickle the whole industry in a Volstead-like blandness, unsuitable to the keener appetites of American life.

That potential blandness is, as I say, something that threatens us, rather than something that has finally crystallized during the past

316

decade of television. There was nothing bland, or even objective, in *317*
such programs as Edward R. Murrow's on Senator Joe McCarthy; or
in Reginald Rose's on the lives of Sacco and Vanzetti; or in Every-
body-and His-Cousin's on the Revival of the American Right Wing.
In all of these there was plainly visible a gut prejudice, on one side of
issues about which, in fact, there are two sides. And I am not aware
that the FCC singled out these programs, or others like them, for
criticism. But the recent memorandum by the FCC, stressing the
necessity to give time to those who hold opposing views, has been
widely interpreted by television and radio broadcasters as a warning
against tendentious broadcasts. Edward R. Murrow did offer Senator McCarthy time for rebuttal on the famous occasion in 1954.
Whether he was impelled to do so out of his own sense of fairness, or
whether the sword of the FCC twitched above his head, one does not
know; but I do agree with those who say that a rigidly enforced rule
requiring the granting of equal time for the expression of contrary
views would effectively put an end, for all practical purposes, to any
venturesome political thought on the air waves.

Miss Efron's proposal is that, in place of the Fairness Doctrine, a
so-called "spectrum theory" be instituted, by which broadcasters
would be encouraged not to mute opinions but to present unmuted
opinions ranging right across the political spectrum. She would look
forward, under the revised situation, to "such phenomena as socialist
documentaries on capitalism, labor documentaries on business,
laissez-faire documentaries on the welfare state, and conservative
documentaries on the welfare state, and conservative documentaries
on U.S. foreign policy."

Her proposal suffers, it seems to me, from precisely the same
order of difficulty she is seeking to avoid. Just as it is almost impossible to specify, in difficult cases, what is a fair, and what an unfair,
presentation of a political event (for example, a sit-in demonstration),
it would be almost impossible for anyone to rule objectively on
whether the spectrum was being comprehensively covered, let alone
responsibly weighed.

Where does the spectrum end, and crackpottery, whether of the
mischievous or of the harmless variety, begin? I ask that quite seriously. There are responsible people in the United States who do not
believe that the John Birch Society is crackpot, even if they agree that
some of the views of its founder are. And there is a distressingly
large number of people in this country who hold that the presentation
of the Communist view of things is clearly a part of the responsibilities of covering the left end of the spectrum. What about the views of

318 George Lincoln Rockwell? Are his proposals for dealing with the Jewish and Negro races going to be enthusiastically aired under the spectrum theory?

My point is that no mathematical construct—such as the spectrum theory—is going to solve essentially philosophical problems. In modern politics, the need is to examine not "all" points of view, but all "respectable points of view"—but there we are right away back with the same problem of definition that the Fairness Doctrine has gagged over.

Suppose one were to modify Miss Efron's proposal to read something like: the spectrum "short" of those extremities which the broadcasters will take the responsibility to ignore. Are we then left without problems? Unfortunately not. Miss Efron talks about "proportional representation." It is easy enough to apportion time to the Republican and Democratic candidates with mathematical accuracy (that is, by giving them each equal time). But what about the socialist? Or the anarchist? Are they to have equal time with Democrats and Republicans? If not, how much less than equal? One-half time? One-fourth time? For every conundrum Miss Efron lances, another one sprouts up: because, I repeat, the problem is not of the kind that can be solved by the imposition of mathematically-formulated thought.

It seems to me that the only thing to do is to take a deep breath and jump in. I would favor the passage of a law giving all broadcasters about whose loyalty to the United States there is no reasonable doubt (that would not be an innovation: Loyalty risks aren't allowed to obtain licenses anyway) the right to broadcast anything they want, in any way they want, but only in those cities which have at least two television stations. I would expect abuses of this privilege to be controlled by community action. And to guard the interest of the minority, I would favor legislation directing the FCC to make available licenses in any community of over 50,000 people, for the construction of pay-TV stations, through which the pressures of the consumer are most keenly exercised, both positively and negatively. The Government's role would then be limited primarily to anti-monopoly action (there is nothing the Government can do about a natural oligopoly). It is, I think, to the credit of the FCC that it has not, in general, abused its great powers; but the rule of law requires that administrative agencies should not have great powers which they are potentially able to abuse. I should think the Commissioners would welcome relief from the responsibility of deciding whether KPPA-TV in Dubuque has been devoting too much time or enthusiasm to the projected fluoridation of the city water.

Arthur M. Schlesinger, Jr.

The air waves are publicly owned. They are not anyone's private property to be used according to passing whim or interest. They are accessible only through public license and can therefore be properly expected to observe public standards and serve public purposes. Since the air waves are an extraordinarily powerful means of communication and influence, the public has a large stake in the way they are used: And since this is a free society, committed by the Bill of Rights to the protection of diversity in opinion and expression, the public interest surely requires that television and radio support the Founding Fathers' vision of a free and diverse republic.

Up to this point, it is all straight-forward enough. If television and radio were to become the instrumentality of a single opinion, this would constitute an obvious misuse of the air waves and defiance of the Constitution. The hard problem now arises: What steps can be taken to insure that the multitudinous opinions of our society find expression over the air waves? This is the problem which the Fairness Doctrine has sought to answer. The Doctrine is valuable as a general recognition of the Government's obligation to do something to stimulate and assure liberty of expression on the air waves. But Miss Efron's article offers a concise account of the difficulties the Doctrine has encountered in practice. The problem is whether anyone can think up anything better.

Critics of the Doctrine say that it holds up an impossible ideal of "impartiality" or "objectivity." As an historian, I can claim a certain acquaintance with this controversy. Of course, no human being can escape his own preconceptions; and, of course, the fact of selection inevitably implies the act of interpretation. I am glad to note that broadcasters are getting interested in these classic issues of epistemology; but I would caution them that acknowledgment of the pervading subjectivity of human knowledge does not mean that all knowledge is equally tainted, or that objectivity does not remain a useful ideal, or that one cannot come closer to this ideal in some fields than in others.

Newspapers contain, in the main, three categories of opinion-bearing materials: news stories; feature stories, comic strips, and so forth; columns and editorials. Television and radio have their three equivalents: news broadcasts; documentaries, satires, and so forth; commentaries and editorials. It is clear that the ideal of objectivity is most likely to be approximated in the news category, where fact, on

320   the whole, predominates over opinion. No matter how impassioned a Yankee fan a news broadcaster might be, it will still be hard for him to distort the baseball scores. I would therefore see no reason why objectivity should be thrown overboard as the guiding principle in the news category. No matter how sympathetic one might be to the "spectrum" approach, I do not think that a television station should feel obliged to ask a member of the John Birch Society to read the news bulletins one night and a Communist the next.

The real problem has to do with the second and third categories: how to protect the interest of diversity in areas where opinion predominates over fact. We must first understand, I believe, that there is no conceivable way to reformulate the Fairness Doctrine to make it work automatically for every situation. It will always be, not a self-executing ordinance, but a guideline to be applied to each particular case. It will always be a matter of judgment.

The question then arises: Who shall apply the guideline? Who shall make the judgment? Here, it seems to me, some new machinery ought to be established which would give those who believe themselves the victims of unfair attack a way of seeking redress. The existing machinery is either excessively informal—complaints to the station or network—or excessively formal—complaints to the FCC. Might it not be possible for the broadcasters themselves to set up an agency of appeal made up of industry and public members? Such an agency could serve as a means of judging the merit of complaints and could help propose ways to encourage the expression of competing opinion. The FCC would remain available as a court of last resort.

Identification of what one group or another might legitimately regard as opinion unfair to itself is only part of the question. The other part is the problem of seeking out and presenting alternative opinion. There are obvious technical difficulties here. One might consider, for example, giving the editors of the *New Republic* and the *National Review* a half hour each on television to do anything they want; but, however skilled Mr. Harrison and Mr. Buckley are at putting out their magazines, there is no reason to suppose they could put on a good television show. Perhaps the idea of the spectrum will have to be pursued within the studio or network. In any case, it is the right idea; and it should be developed with the object of giving all significant elements of opinion opportunity for expression on the air waves.

In short, I see no reason for abandoning the Fairness Doctrine. The idea of extending "freedom of the press" to the air waves makes

no sense, of course, so long as channels and frequencies are limited. *321*
The idea of the freedom of the press is based on the fact of unlimited
legal freedom to start a newspaper; but there is no such unlimited
freedom to open a television station. Maybe UHF will change all this;
but, until it does, "freedom of the press" will have no relevance to
the air waves. Instead, the broadcasters, working with the FCC and
the general public, should confront the problems raised by the
Fairness Doctrine and seek in an orderly manner to construct the
machinery which will provide a fair way to give its injunctions
full effect.

The ideal should always be more debate, more discussion,
more controversy. It surely is not beyond the ingenuity of American
broadcasters to figure out how this can be done.

The Silent Screen

By Nicholas Johnson

JULY 5, 1969

Julian Goodman, president of NBC, believes that television "is now under threat of restriction and control." Frank Stanton, president of CBS, says that "attempts are being made to block us." Elmer Lower, president of ABC News, thinks he may "face the prospect of some form of censorship."

I agree. Censorship is a serious problem in our country. My only dispute with these network officials involves just who is doing the censoring. They apparently believe it's the Government. I disagree.

NBC recently cut Robert Montgomery's statements off the air when, during the *Johnny Carson Show,* he mentioned a CBS station being investigated by the Federal Communications Commission. Folk singer Joan Baez was silenced by CBS when she wished to express her views about the Selective Service System on the *Smothers Brothers Show.* Now, of course, the entire show has been canceled— notwithstanding the high ratings and its writers' recent Emmy. Sure there's censorship. But let's not be fooled into mistaking its source.

For at the same time that network officials are keeping off your television screens anything they find inconsistent with their corporate profits or personal philosophies, the FCC has been repeatedly defending their First Amendment rights against Government censorship. Just recently, for example, the FCC ruled—over strong protests—that the networks' coverage of the Chicago Democratic convention was protected by the Constitution's "freedom of the press" clause. In other decisions, the Commission refused to penalize radio station WBAI in New York for broadcasting an allegedly anti-Semitic poem, or a CBS-owned station for televising a "pot party."

Many broadcasters are fighting, not for free speech, but for profitable speech. In the WBAI case, for example, one of the industry's leading spokesmen, *Broadcasting* magazine, actually urged that WBAI be punished by the FCC—and on the same editorial page professed outrage that stations might not have an unlimited right to broadcast profitable commercials for cigarettes which may result in illness or death.[22]

322

This country is a great experiment. For close to 200 years we have   *323*
been testing whether it is possible for an educated and informed
people to govern themselves. All considered, the experiment has
worked pretty well. We've had our frustrations and disappointments
as a Nation, but no one has been able to come up with a better system,
and most of the newer nations still look to us as a model.

Central to our system, however, is the concept of an educated
and an informed people. As Thomas Jefferson said, "The way to
prevent error is to give the people full information of their affairs."
Our founding fathers were familiar with censorship by the King of
England. They were going to replace a king with a representative
Congress. But they were concerned lest any American institution
become powerful enough to impede the flow of information to the
people. So they provided in the First Amendment that "*Congress
shall make no law . . . abridging the freedom of speech . . .*" Why
"Congress"? I believe they assumed Congress would be the only
body powerful enough to abridge free speech. They were wrong.

A lot has happened to the creation and control of information in
this country since 1789. That was an age of town meetings and hand-
bills. Today most information comes from the three broadcasting
networks, ABC, CBS and NBC, and the two wire services, Associated
Press and United Press International. As Professor John Kenneth
Galbraith has reminded us in *The New Industrial State*,[23] 70 years
ago the large corporation confined itself to mass production in heavy
industry. "Now," he writes, "it also sells groceries, mills grain, pub-
lishes newspapers and provides public entertainment, all activities
that were once the province of the individual proprietor or the
insignificant firm."

It is easy for us to forget how large, profitable and politically
powerful some corporations have become. In 1948 about half of all
manufacturing assets in the United States were controlled by 200
corporations; today a mere 100 corporations hold that power. A single
corporation such as American Telephone & Telegraph (one of the
FCC's many regulated companies) controls the wages and working
conditions of 870,000 employees, purchases each year some $3.5
billion in goods and services, has assets of $37 billion, and has annual
gross revenues in excess of $14 billion. This gross revenue is several
times larger than the combined budgets of all the Federal regulatory
commissions, the Federal court system, and the U.S. Congress; larger
than the budget of each of the 50 states; a larger operation, indeed,
than all but very few foreign governments.

I am not suggesting that large corporations are inherently evil.

324   Not at all. They have created much of our wealth. I am merely urging that we be aware of the fact that large corporations have both the incentive and the power to control the information reaching the citizenry of our free society.

Sometimes corporate pressures to control what you see on television are just plain silly. For example, in his book *TV—The Big Picture*,[24] Stan Opotowsky reports that "Ford deleted a shot of the New York skyline because it showed the Chrysler building. . . . A breakfast-food sponsor deleted the line 'She eats too much' from a play because, as far as the breakfast-food company was concerned, nobody could ever eat too much." Often, however, corporate tampering with the product of honest and capable journalists and creative writers and performers can be quite serious. Sometimes there is a deliberate alteration of content; sometimes needed information is squeezed out by more profitable "entertainment" programming.

On February 10, 1966, the Senate was conducting hearings on the Vietnam war. Fred Friendly, who was president of CBS News at the time, wanted you to be able to watch those hearings. His network management did not permit you to watch. If you were watching CBS that day you saw, instead of George Kennan's views opposing the Vietnam war, the fifth CBS rerun of *I Love Lucy*. Fred Friendly quit CBS because of this decision, and subsequently wrote *Due to Circumstances Beyond Our Control*[25] to tell the story. He began his book with the quotation, "What the American people don't know can kill them." Indeed it can. In Vietnam, about 35,000 so far. We have been shown miles of film from Vietnam, it's true. But how much has television told you about the multibillion-dollar corporate profits from that war?

There are many other situations in which censorship exists side-by-side with large profits—and disease or death. The tobacco industry spends about $250 million a year on radio and television commercials designed to associate cigarette smoking, especially by the young, with fishing, football, the fresh air of the great outdoors, sexual prowess, and all other desirable attributes of a fun-packed adult world. In exchange for this investment, the industry sells on the order of $9 billion worth of cigarettes a year. Would it really surprise you to learn that the broadcasting industry has been less than eager to tell you about the health hazards of cigarette smoking? It shouldn't. Just recently, for example, a United States congressman alleged that the president of the National Association of Broadcasters had suppressed from Congress and the American public revealing information about the "substantial appeal to youth" of radio and television ciga-

rette commercials. The relation of this forgetfulness to profits is clear: *325*
cigarette advertising provides the largest single source of television's
revenue, about 8 percent.

The FCC has ruled that broadcasters can't present one point of
view on a controversial issue and censor all others just to serve their
own beliefs and profits. The "Fairness Doctrine" requires that all
viewpoints be presented. The FCC applied this doctrine to cigarette
commercials. And what was the response of the broadcasting industry? It fought the decision with all the economic and political
strength at its command. It has finally gone all the way to the Supreme
Court to argue that a doctrine which limits its power to keep all information about the health hazards of cigarette smoking from the
American people is a violation of broadcasters' First Amendment
rights!

Or how about the 50,000 people who die each year on our highways? Their deaths are due to many causes, of course, including their
own intoxication and carelessness. But how many television stations
told you—either before or after Ralph Nader came along—that most
auto-safety engineers agree virtually all those lives could be saved if
our cars were designed properly? Nader, in *Unsafe at Any Speed*,[26]
speculates about "the impact which the massive sums spent ($361,-
006,000 in 1964 on auto advertising alone) have on the communications media's attention to vehicle safety design."

Television certainly didn't take the lead in telling us about unfit
meat, fish and poultry. (Chet Huntley was found to have been editorializing against the Wholesale Meat Act at a time when he and his
business partners were heavy investors in the cattle and meat business!) Bryce Rucker, in *The First Freedom*, notes that:

> Networks generally have underplayed or ignored events and state-
> ments unfavorable to food processors and soap manufacturers. Recent ex-
> amples are the short shrift given Senate subcommittee hearings on, and com-
> ments favorable to, the 1966 "truth in packaging" bill and the high cost
> of food processing. Could it be that such behavior reflects concern for the
> best interests of, say, the top-50 grocery-products advertisers, who spent
> $1,314,893,000 in TV in 1965, 52.3 percent of TV's total advertising income?[27]

What could be more essential than information about potentially
harmful food and drugs?

All Americans are concerned about "the crime problem." Have
you ever stopped to wonder why the only crimes most of us hear about
are, in the words of the Presidential Commission on Law Enforcement
and Administration of Justice, "the crimes that are the easiest for the

326 poor and the disadvantaged to commit. . .'"? What we haven't been told is that much of the crime in the United States is "white-collar" crime; that the rich steal as much or more than the poor. As the Crime Commission Report defined it:

> The "white-collar" criminal is the broker who distributes fraudulent securities, the builder who deliberately uses defective material, the corporation executive who conspires to fix prices, the legislator who peddles his influence and vote for private gain, or the banker who misappropriates funds. . . .

Did you ever find out from television, for example, that a single recent price-fixing case involved a "robbery" from the American people of more money than was taken in all the country's robberies, burglaries and larcenies during the years of that criminal price fixing? The Crime Commission declared that "it is essential that the public becomes aware of the seriousness of business crime." Why is it the news media do not tell you about these threats to "law and order"?

One could go on and on. The inherent dangers in cyclamates (the artificial sweetners in soft drinks) have been so widely discussed in Sweden that the government is considering prohibiting their use. The danger is scarcely known to the average American.[28] Most of the Nation's 160,000 coal miners have "black lung" disease (the disintegration of the lung from coal dust) in one form or another. Mine operators may refuse to pay for fresh-air masks—or support workmen's compensation legislation. Some television stations in coal-mining areas have, until recently, refused to televise programs offered them by doctors about this serious health hazard. Reports differ, and no one knows for sure, but one current sampling showed that 20 percent of the color-TV sets studied were emitting excess X-ray radiation. Natural-gas pipelines are exploding as predicted. And did you know that the life expectancy of the average American adult male has been declining in recent years? The list goes on almost without end.

Note what each of these items has in common: human death, disease, dismemberment or degradation, great profit for manufacturers, advertisers and broadcasters, and the deliberate withholding of needed information from the public.

Many pressures produce such censorship. Some are deliberate, some come about through default. But all have come, not from Government, but from private corporations with something to sell. Charles Tower, chairman of the National Association of Broadcasters Television Board, recently wrote a letter to *The New York Times*, criticizing its attack on CBS for "censoring" the social commentary on the *Smothers Brothers Show*. He said,

There is a world of difference between the deletion of program material by Government command and the deletion by a private party (such as a broadcaster). . . . Deletion by Government command is censorship. . . . Deletion of material by private parties . . . is not censorship.

Another *Times* reader wrote in answer to Mr. Tower:

Mr. Tower's distinction . . . is spurious. The essence of censorship is the suppression of a particular point of view . . . over the channels of the mass media, and the question of who does the censoring is one of form only. . . .

He's right. The results are the same. You and I are equally kept in ignorance, ill-prepared to "prevent error," and to engage in the process of self-governing which Thomas Jefferson envisioned—regardless of who does the censoring.

A number of talented people within the broadcasting industry recognize its failings. One of the Nation's leading black announcers told me of his first job as a disc jockey. He was handed a stack of records, but forbidden to read any news over the air. Said his boss: "You're not going to educate the Negroes of this community at my expense." A high ABC network executive was recently quoted in the pages of TV GUIDE as saying, "There are many vital issues that we won't go near. We censor ourselves." Eric Sevareid has said of the pressures involved in putting together a network news show: "The ultimate sensation is that of being bitten to death by ducks."[29] And the executive editor of the *San Francisco Chronicle* has warned: "The press is in danger. Not the exciting kind of Hollywood danger, but of dissolving into a gray mass of nonideas." For it is also a form of censorship to so completely clog the public's air waves with tasteless gruel that there is no time left for quality entertainment and social commentary, no time "to give the people full information of their affairs." Mason Williams, the multitalented one-time writer for the Smothers Brothers, has left television in disgust and written a peom about his experiences with "The Censor," who, he says in conclusion,

Snips out
The rough talk
The unpopular opinion
Or anything with teeth
And renders
A pattern of ideas
Full of holes

328

> A doily
> For your mind

Your mind. My mind. The mind of America. The Rolling Stones said it long ago:

> When I'm drivin' in my car,
> When the man comes on the radio,
> He's tellin' me more and more
> About some useless information . . .
> Supposed to fire my imagination? . . .
> I can't get no satisfaction![30]

Many Americans are trying to say something to each other. But the media haven't been listening. And you haven't been told. So some have turned to violence as a means of being heard. All you've been shown are the dramatic pictures; you know there's something happening." But like the Everyman of Bob Dylan's song, "You don't know what it is, do you, Mr. Jones?" The "Silent Screen" of television has left you in ignorance as to what it's all about.

The time may soon come when the media will have to listen. From many directions come suggestions for change. Law professor Jerome Barron says the courts should recognize a "public right of access to the mass media." Free speech in this age of television, he believes, requires that citizens with something to say be permitted to say it over radio and television. Suppose you approach a television station with a "commercial" you have prepared either supporting or protesting the President's conduct of the Vietnamese war. It may no longer be sufficient for the station to say to you, "Sorry, we don't like your views, so we won't broadcast your announcement"—as a San Francisco station did last year to those trying to express their point of view regarding a *ballot proposition*! As the U.S. Supreme Court said a few days ago in the Red Lion case, upholding the constitutionality of the FCC's Fairness Doctrine:

> There is no sanctuary in the First Amendment for unlimited private censorship operating in a medium not open to all. Freedom of the press from governmental interference under the First Amendment does not sanction repression of that freedom by private interests.[31]

It is too early to know the full, ultimate impact of this decision.

In Holland, any group that can get 15,000 persons to support its list of proposed programs is awarded free time on the Dutch Television Network for a monthly program. There is even an organization for tiny and often eccentric splinter groups without 15,000 supporters. If a similar experiment were conducted in this country, groups in-

terested in electronic music, drag racing, handicrafts, camping, as well 329
as the League of Women Voters, the National Association for the Advancement of Colored People, local school boards, theater and drama associations, the Young Republicans (and, who knows, even the Smothers Brothers), could obtain television time to broadcast programs prepared under their supervision.

Or each network might devote a full one-third of its prime time (6 P.M. to 11 P.M.) programming to something other than entertainment or sports. It could be nonsponsored cultural, educational and public-affairs programming. If the networks were required to stagger such fare, then at any given time during the 6 P.M. to 11 P.M. period of greatest audiences the American viewer would have an alternative, a choice. There would still be at all times two networks with the commercial-laden, lowest-common-denominator mass entertainment of situation comedies. Westerns, quiz shows and old movies. The third, however, would have something else.

It would be wholly inappropriate for me as an FCC Commissioner to insist that broadcasters present only the information, ideas and entertainment that I personally find compatible. The FCC does not have, and would not want, the responsibility for selecting your television programs. But it would be equally irresponsible for me to sit idly by and watch the corporate censors keep from your TV screen the full range of needs, tastes and interests of the American people.

The television-station owner, not the network, has ultimate responsibility for his programming. But somebody has to select his programs, you say; nobody's perfect. You're right. An all I'm urging is that, when in doubt, all of us—audience, networks and Government—ought to listen a little more carefully to the talented voices of those who are crying out to be heard. In short, I would far rather leave the heady responsibility for the inventory in America's "marketplace of ideas" to talented and uncensored individuals—creative writers, performers and journalists from all sections of this great country— than to the committees of frightened financiers in New York City. Wouldn't you? I think so.

I am delighted the networks have raised the issue of censorship in America. I hope they will permit us to discuss it fully.

He Has Exercised His Right to Be Wrong

By Richard Salant

SEPTEMBER 15, 1969

Federal Communications Commissioner Nicholas Johnson's article in TV GUIDE is shocking, if true. It is just as shocking if it is not true. And as it relates to CBS News, it most certainly is not true.

Commissioner Johnson claims that, for economic reasons, broadcasters withhold information and suppress discussion of issues vital to Americans. Therefore, he concludes broadcasters are hypocritically concerned about government censorship since the real evil is self-censorship arising out of broadcaster timidity and economic self-protection.

Much of Commissioner Johnson's article relates to broadcast journalism. To the extent that Commissioner Johnson deals with entertainment, I will leave to those responsible for that programming the task of examining Commissioner Johnson's accuracy, although the inaccuracy of his charges against television journalism necessarily raises serious questions about the rest of his charges.

But I can speak only in respect of broadcast journalism—and only for CBS News. And for CBS News, I state flatly that Commissioner Johnson is totally, completely, 100 percent wrong—on all counts.

Let me start with the most general aspect of Johnson's frightening world of fantasy.

In the 11 years I was a CBS corporate officer and in the six years that I have been president of CBS News, to my knowledge there is no issue, no topic, no story, which CBS News has ever been forbidden, or instructed directly or indirectly, to cover or not to cover, by corporate management. Corporate management at CBS has scrupulously observed that vital doctrine of separation of powers without which honest journalism cannot thrive—the separation between the corporation and an autonomous news organization.

Second, the separation between CBS News and the sales departments of the CBS radio and television networks and their advertisers

330

has been complete. CBS News has no sales department. Its function is to choose the topics and stories and to prepare the broadcasts; the sales departments and the advertisers play no part in that process. No topic has ever been selected or omitted, and no treatment has ever been affected, by the imagined or expressed wishes of an advertiser. Long since, the policy has been established that CBS News makes the broadcasts and the advertiser makes and sells his products, and never the twain shall meet.

Third, there has been no *self*-censorship: I—and to the best of my knowledge, my associates at CBS News—have never avoided a topic or altered treatment to protect, or to avoid displeasing, corporate management or any advertiser. As I have stated, anybody in the organization who avoided a topic or distorted his normal judgments in the treatment of a topic in order to avoid offending the economic interests of any advertisers, or to please CBS management, would thereby betray his professional heritage and would disqualify himself from working with CBS News.

So much for the general principles. As far as I have gone to this point, the issue between Commissioner Johnson and me is, to the outsider, bound to be inconclusive: It is his work against mine, and I would not blame any third party who knows neither of us for giving the nod to the Commissioner, since I have a personal stake in my own reputation and the reputation of my CBS News associates and he at least *appears* to be a responsible, neutral government official with the public interest at heart. So let us turn to each of the specific charges of suppression and avoidance which Commissioner Johnson advances to prove his general thesis. Taking them one at a time, the record shows he is wrong all along the line. His batting average turns out to be .000. At most, he proves himself to be a pitcher with more speed than control, rather than a hitter.

Item: Commissioner Johnson writes that "We have been shown miles of film from Vietnam, it is true. But how much has television told you about the multi-billion dollar corporate profits from that war?"

Plenty. We have included in our broadcasts the stories of Vietnamese corruption, of the operations of American business firms in Vietnam, and of war contractor costs. Example: Congressman Pike's disclosure of the sale to the Defense Department of $210 worth of generator knobs for $33,000. Example: A two-part report in June 1969 on Pentagon waste and overruns.

Item: Commissioner Johnson, stating that cigarette advertising "provides the largest single source of television's revenue" asks,

332 "Would it really surprise you to learn that the broadcasting industry has been less than eager to tell you about the health hazards of cigarette smoking?"

Well, if it did surprise you, it would only be because you have not been watching CBS News. We have dealt continuously and in depth with the health hazards of cigarette smoking, long before the Surgeon General got around to his report and long before Commissioner Johnson publicly decided to become concerned about the problem. We started a long time ago, on September 19, 1962, with the *CBS Reports: The Teenage Smoker*. We broadcast a special on January 11, 1964, *On Smoking and Health*, the day the Surgeon General's Report was issued. On April 15, 1964, we broadcast an hour documentary, *CBS Reports: A Collision of Interests*, a detailed review of the health, economic and public policy issues raised by cigarette smoking. In our national health tests broadcast early in 1966, we again dealt with the hazards of smoking. We did another special hour-long broadcast in the beginning of 1968, *National Smoking Test* (about which *Newsday's* television critic commented: "It took courage on CBS' part to show the way. Especially since as the program mentioned the cigarette manufacturers are TV's largest advertisers. Viewers are in the network's debt"). We came back to the subject in the *21st Century* series, in a broadcast entitled *The Wild Cell* (February 2, 1969). We included stories in many of our other regularly scheduled broadcasts—for example, in *Calendar* on lung cancer and smoking in April 1962—and repeatedly we have covered in our regular news broadcasts all the developments—up to and including an interview on Thursday, July 3, with the current Surgeon General on cigarette advertising and the hazards of smoking. A quick count shows that since June 1963, our regularly scheduled news broadcasts have included 84 special film stories on cigarettes (including the showing of the American Cancer Society's anti-smoking film—in January 1967; and the attack by E. William Henry, then Chairman of the FCC, on television cigarette advertising—in March 1966).

Item: Commissioner Johnson refers to the "50,000 people who die each year on our highways" and then asks ". . . how many television stations told you—either before or after Ralph Nader came along—that most auto-safety engineers agree virtually *all* those lives could be saved if our cars were designed properly?"

I do not have a nose count of the number of stations. But, again, before the issue became very fashionable to discuss, CBS News did a one-hour pre-emptive, prime-time special May 13, 1966, *Crash Project—The Search for a Safer Car*—featuring Ralph Nader. If Com-

missioner Johnson's extremely selective perception has excluded that   *333*
broadcast from his mind, I call to his attention this excerpt from a
review in *Variety*, May 18, 1966:

> Of more significance, however, than the arguments pro and con on car
> design was CBS' lack of inhibition in confronting one of the giants of adver-
> tising and letting the chips fall where they may. Thus a direct comparison of
> two competitive makes was shown with a tester from Consumers Union
> detailing the faults in one car and extolling the virtues of another while iden-
> tifying both by name. This is indeed strong stuff and certainly more than
> most of the newspapers of the country would do under similar circumstances.

And on auto safety, CBS News did not hit and run: We have gone
back to the subject not only in our *National Drivers' Test* broadcasts
but in 44 different reports in the Morning News and the Evening
News since April 1965—dealing with the charges against the automobile industry and with the call-backs, including a demonstration
of exactly what some of the defects leading to the call-backs were.

Item: Commissioner Johnson quotes Bryce Rucker as stating
that "Networks generally have underplayed or ignored events and
statements unfavorable to food processors and soap manufacturers.
Recent examples are the short shrift given Senate subcommittee
hearings on, and comments favorable to, the 1966 'truth in packaging'
bill and the high cost of food processing."

Wrong again—in our news broadcasts, we covered those hearings
and included statements of consumer representatives and witnesses
in support of the bill. We have reported stories relating to alleged
abuses in food processing. Just a few examples: On March 24, 1969,
in the Evening News with Walter Cronkite, we reported the FTC
allegation that the Campbell Soup Company had been putting clear
glass marbles in bowls to make its soup look thicker in television
commercials. And we reported the story of the dangers involved in
pesticides' contaminating cranberry sauce; the story about the dangers of botulism in canned tuna fish and the mass recall of canned
tuna; the unfit meat story as it developed; Ralph Nader's testimony
attacking the standards of intrastate meat packers; and the Government action against the Colgate-Palmolive sandpaper commercial.

Item: Commissioner Johnson asks, "What could be more essential than information about potentially harmful . . . drugs?"

He just asks; he doesn't say that we didn't cover it. He was lucky
because if he had said it, he would have been wrong. Time and time
again, we have reported such stories as the thalidomide story, the
FTC allegations relating to aspirin and bufferin, the Government

334 action against drug price fixing, the hearings on the excessive cost of drugs, including Italian cut-rating and American profiteering in Latin America, the charges relating to dangerous side effects of the birth control pill, the FTC action against Geritol and Tums—both heavy advertisers with CBS. On July 9, 1969 (after Commissioner Johnson's article) we reported briefly on the recent reports of the National Academy of Sciences on the ineffectiveness of drugs and pharmaceuticals; we came back to the subject for a more detailed report on July 11.

Item: Commissioner Johnson states that television fails to report on corporate crimes and he makes specific reference, although not by name, to an important case of price fixing.

If I can guess what price fixing case Commissioner Johnson is talking about, we most certainly reported it.

Item: Commissioner Johnson writes about "the inherent dangers in cyclamates (the artifical sweetners in soft drinks)" and implies that television's failure to cover that story results in the danger's being "scarcely known to the average American."

Wrong again. On the Morning News of April 11, 1969, we did a piece, running 7½ minutes, concerning cyclamates, and we also reported the story in the Evening News.

Item: Commissioner Johnson *seems* to say (sometimes his pen is quicker than the eye) that we ignored the "black lung" disease story— the dangers to miners' lungs resulting from coal dust.

The pattern is familiar: He is wrong; we did not ignore the story. We covered it in reporting the hearings in Washington and in West Virginia on the issue, and in a special broadcast on February 11, 1969, entitled *Danger! Mines.*

Item: Commissioner Johnson refers to the fact that "one current sampling showed that 20 percent of the color-TV sets studied were emitting excess X-ray radiation." Again he doesn't say so but the implication is that we didn't cover it.

Wrong again: We did—as long ago as August 1967 when we reported that the Surgeon General called for action on such radiation.

Item: Commissioner Johnson states broadly that we avoid stories of "human death, disease, dismemberment or degradation."

Let him drop into my office some time and see the viewers' mail that comes across my desk complaining that that is *all* we ever talk about, and criticizing us bitterly for not emphasizing more good news. Was Commissioner Johnson otherwise occupied during our almost nightly Vietnam coverage, or when we broadcast such documentaries as *Harvest of Shame, The Silent Spring of Rachel Carson, The Tene-*

ment, Christmas in El Barrio, The Poisoned Air, Men in Cages, Hunger in America? And our continuing series on one street in a Washington, D.C. ghetto, Columbia Road on the CBS Morning News.

Commissioner Johnson finds it easy to make out a case by simply ignoring what we have done. His implication is that, in deference to advertisers, we stay away from any news unfavorable to consumer products. As we have just seen, he is wrong on every one of his specifics; we have covered each of the cases he mentions. And we have done other consumer stories as well which involved industry and network advertisers: For example, the housewives' boycott of supermarkets protesting high prices; the gas station game and prize practices; the dangers of flammable toys and clothing; toy guns and other war-like toys; the trading stamp story; lumber industry activities in the forests, concerning which we did also broadcast a documentary entitled *Bulldozed America;* the dangers of pesticides (see also the two-part documentary, *What Are We Doing to Our World?*); automobile insurance practices involving racial discrimination and arbitrary cancellation of policies; retail credit abuses (concerning which we also did a one-hour documentary entitled IOU $315,000,000,000); automobile warranty abuses; the dangers of cholesterol as a cause of heart and other diseases, caused by meat fats, butter fat, margarines and other shortenings and vegetable spreads (*CBS Reports: The Fat American*).

And, of course, implicit in Commissioner Johnson's thesis is the charge that about the last thing which we would ever do is report stories unfavorable to CBS or CBS News itself. But again, the facts are to the contrary: For example, we have reported the charges against television for its alleged violence and effect on juvenile delinquency. We reported the charges that CBS "staged" a pot party; we reported former Secretary of Agriculture Freeman's attack on the accuracy of the CBS News documentary *Hunger In America.* And as to Commissioner Johnson's favorite subject, the Smother Brothers, it was CBS News which, last Fall, even before the storm broke, did a segment of *60 Minutes* with the Smothers Brothers expressing their view-points about their role in television and their relationship to CBS; and it was CBS News which, on the day after their contract was canceled, included the only network interview with Tommy Smothers reacting to the CBS action.

As Commissioner Johnson says in his article "one could go on and on." And the *facts*—about which one could go on and on—destroy the fantasy about which Commissioner Johnson goes on and on. Others—perhaps more scholarly and careful than Commissioner

336 Johnson—have examined the question of television news' integrity and independence, and have come to quite different conclusions. Thus, Herbert J. Gans, a sociologist who is making a long-range study of the mass media, stated:

> Despite the old stereotype that media employees report the news as their owners and advertisers see fit, this is not true of national television and magazines, however true it may be of the local press. People who work in the media I have studied so far are surprisingly free from outside interference on the part of non-professionals and business executives, and can decide on their own what to cover and how to cover it.[37]

It may well be that the Commissioner is to busy attending to his official duties, and making speeches, and writing articles, to permit him to know what really goes over the air. But Commissioner Johnson shows signs not only that he has no time to *look*, but he also has no time or inclination to *read*. For one of his lowest—and most mistaken blows—comes in his invocation of Eric Sevareid as a witness to support his thesis. In a paragraph explicitly devoted to management and advertising interference and pressures, Commissioner Johnson states that Eric Sevareid "has said of the pressures involved in putting together a network news show: 'The ultimate sensation is that of being bitten to death by ducks.'"

Never underestimate the carelessness or the disingenuity of Commissioner Johnson. Eric Sevareid indeed said exactly that several years ago. But if Commissioner Johnson could have seen from the Sevareid statement itself, or from checking with Eric directly, that Eric (see his letter to TV GUIDE, July 19) simply was not talking about management or advertising interference or pressures. Eric *was* talking about what plagues us all in television journalism and for which not even Commissioner Johnson can supply a solution: the cumbersome apparatus of television journalism, with all its cameras and lights and technicians and layers of personnel which are inherent in the complex nature of our method of transmission. Eric was contrasting this with the simplicity of a reporter or a writer for print who can sit in a corner by himself, type out his story and send it in. All Commissioner Johnson had to do was to read the Sevareid statement—or if that was too much trouble he could have done what any journalist would do—check it.

The ultimate issues which Commissioner Johnson raises are important indeed. They involve the independence and integrity of broadcast journalism, free of management interference and advertising pressures—and free too from government dictation or coercive suggestion. I happen to think that Commissioner Johnson has some esoteric and erroneous notions about the First Amendment. (Incidentally, the credit he bestows upon himself and his associates as the champion of the First Amendment in the Commission's handling of the complaints concerning our political convention coverage is not quite justified. The Commission's *actions* in that case were rather less noble and rather less sensitive to the First Amendment than its belated words. After all, the Commission transmitted *every* complaint that it received and required us to address ourselves to them—including hundreds that, only months later, it announced were not within its permissible authority.)

I also happen to think that the spirit, if not the letter, of the First Amendment would at the very least, compel a man in his position—a government agent who, through his licensing power, has the power of life and death over broadcasters—to be exceedingly careful and accurate when he undertakes public statements about what broadcast news does and does not do and what it ought and ought not do.

But, as I have stated elsewhere, the First Amendment includes the right to be wrong. Commissioner Johnson has certainly exercised that right.

[The following letter appeared in TV GUIDE, September 27, 1969: "Let anyone who has watched prime time network television decide for himself. As Mr. Salant knows, little of it is 'news.' As for TV news, it's not that it's done nothing; it's just too little too late. Walter Cronkite says we have barely dipped our toe into investigative reporting. Ed Murrow said '(Corporate management) makes the final and crucial decisions having to do with news and public affairs.' Many former TV newsmen agree. (See, e.g., book by Salant's predecessor in office: Fred Friendly, *Due to Circumstances Beyond Our Control.*) Let's hope for equivalent candor from a future, noncorporate Dick Salant."

Nicholas Johnon
Federal Communications Commission]

"Permissiveness"

Along with the limited number of channels available for broadcasting and the principle that the air waves are public property, yet another rationale for extensive external, legal controls of broadcasting has evolved. As Senator Pastore suggests in this section (pp. 341-342), television is considered to have been invented to serve the family in the home and, as is the case with any other electrical appliance, the user is at the mercy of the appliance once he turns it on. The concept that the person in the home must have television and must turn it on has apparently become generally accepted as a truism. The viewer does not have the same choice he may exercise with respect to other media—for example, not going to a movie, not buying a paper, not subscribing to a magazine. Thus the argument is that the Government must insure moral and ethical content of television programming.

In an interview with Richard Doan presented here, Senator Pastore (pp. 340-344), Chairman of the Senate Communications Subcommittee and a recent outspoken critic of sex and violence on television, contends that the public has a right to expect decency from television. He feels that the increasing crudity in television programming must be checked and he suggests the broadcasters adopt "rules of reason." If the propriety of a given show is in doubt, it should be submitted to the NAB Code Authority for prescreening and review. CBS is openly opposed to this suggestion and maintains that the actual licensees, the network affiliates and, perhaps, the television critics are the proper agents for prescreening, if this is necessary. The positions of NBC and ABC are less clear; Pastore claims they both fully endorse his proposal, but spokesmen from the two networks claim the issue has not yet been fully examined. In the meantime, Pastore has been instrumental in instituting a thorough study of the relationship of televised violence to actual violence (Chapter 5, pp. 510-528).

In the wake of Senator Pastore's suggestion to increase the role
of the NAB Code, Richard Doan interviewed Stockton Helffrich, Code
Authority Director. The interview (pp. 345-349) provides insights into
how Helffrich views the Code and the relationship of the Authority
to the NAB and the networks. His comments reflect what determines
priorities for monitoring done by the Authority, the Code Authority's
position on prescreening programs, and the importance of the Code
in the eyes of the industry and the public.

Pastore contends that television "is an entirely different medium"
from the movies and movies can thus contain more material that is
"out of bounds." Peggy Hudson (pp. 350-355) discusses the problem
of showing the new, "out of bounds," movies on the home screen. She
reviews the effects of the latest, most lenient, Hollywood production
code. According to Miss Hudson, the televising of these "gamier"
films will prove difficult for several reasons. They may violate the
NAB Code; they may earn disapproval from the FCC or the advertiser; and the advanced publicity for some films make them attractive
box office fare, but too notorious for television. Miss Hudson suggests
that Hollywood could start making "buttoned-up, toned-down" versions of their films for television. She also reports there is speculation
that the more realistic films now being made for theaters may help
bring about more sophisticated standards for television films.

On November 1, 1968, the Motion Picture Association of America's new rating system went into effect for newly released movies.
The three network chief censors comment on the code (pp. 356-358)
and state that the networks intend to continue to make independent
judgments about which films the television audience should see,
regardless of the given film's MPAA rating. The network censors
acknowledge, however, that they can expect a greater number of
viewer complaints if an X-rated film, even an edited version, is aired.

Senator John O. Pastore's Campaign to "Clean Up" Television

Senator John O. Pastore Interviewed
by Richard K. Doan

MAY 24, 1969

Well, it's an old chestnut, this idea of permissiveness, risque performances, vulgar gestures, jokes that are a little too suggestive, anything that is subtle. After all, I am sophisticated enough to stand it, and most American people are—but day by day it has been getting worse and worse and worse, and a lot of people are very much disturbed about it.

Many of the broadcasters take the position—and the networks particularly—that they don't get all that many letters about it. Well, people don't write to stations and networks like they write to congressmen, you see, and I have heard from many people. I go to church on Sunday and I'm stopped by half a dozen people who make a complaint about it. Or I have people visit with me or I go to a social affair or I go to a civic club, and it's continuous. I've been swamped with complaints.

And yet the industry seems to feel there isn't much to this, and that's the thing that has disturbed me. There's a great deal to it.

Now, I'm not saying that this is so prevalent that all television is bad. No, I'm saying that 90 percent of television is good. But I'm a little confused by the logic being used by the networks on this question of prescreening. This is not an original idea with me. You will recall that about seven years ago that *Bus Stop* show [an ABC series] was very controversial. So much so it was taken off the air. Well, after a speech I made at the National Association of Broadcasters I had a meeting in this office. I had Mr. LeRoy Collins, who at the time was president of NAB, and Robert Sarnoff, who was head of NBC, and Leonard Goldenson of ABC and Frank Stanton of CBS; and they sat in this office, and the man who raised the question of previewing was Mr. Collins, the broadcasters' own representative. He took the posi-

340

tion that the Code [the NAB Code of Good Practice] itself was nothing *341* more than a lot of beautiful words and a facade, in effect, unless it was properly implemented. And his position was that the only way you could implement it was by prescreening; in other words, to give the Code Authority the right, when necessary, to screen some of those programs before they get on the air, not after they've been seen by the public. The old adage is: an ounce of prevention is worth a pound of cure. Now, that's what this is all about.

But frankly, nothing has happened since 1962. The situation has grown worse and worse. Of course, the argument has always been made, how can you say that the violence, the crime and the sex shown on television are related to human behavior? Well, you can get as many people to say yes [it has an effect] as you can get to say no, depending on who commissions the study. But the Surgeon General made a very exhaustive study of cigarette smoking and its relationship to lung cancer, and once he took a very affirmative position that this was so, all these other quick studies began to crumble and collapse. So I feel that if we can get a thorough study by the Surgeon General as to the relationship [of televised and actual violence] it'll be much more convincing, and then I think a great deal more will happen.

In the meantime, I've always felt we have a rule of reason. It's a rule of reason. There isn't a man I've met in the broadcasting industry who doesn't know the difference between right and wrong, who doesn't know when a joke has gone too far, when a dress is cut too low, when the feminine body is too much exposed, when a joke begins to lose its subtlety and becomes a vulgarity—and that has happened!

Now, they're always saying, well, this is a permissive age. Well, maybe things that were once spoken in a whisper are now spoken in a loud voice. Crime has always existed, although we have more of it today. Sex has been with us since Adam and Eve. But the fact remains that television was invented to service the family in the home. It's an entirely different medium than a moving-picture theater. With a moving picture, you can read a review. If you feel it's going to be a picture that's a little out of bounds, you don't buy a ticket and you don't go. But when you turn on that knob, that knob, and you hear from a licensee of the Government, you expect something decent. And you have a right to expect something decent.

Q: Senator, do you personally see a relationship between sex and violence on TV and the violence and permissiveness we're experiencing in this country today?

A: Oh, I think there's a connection. But on the other hand, I

342 could be refuted very easily, because I'm not a psychiatrist. I'm not a psychologist. As a parent, though, I think it makes a lot of difference. After all, if my young daughter is sitting with me and I see something that I don't like, I blush. I'm 62 years old and I blush! But I blush for her. And I certainly don't want her to see it.

Now, I get a lot of letters from mothers who tell me this sort of thing. I received a letter from a woman who told me her 13-year-old daughter and her 8-year-old boy were watching *King Kong* [a movie] on television, out in Kansas City. Well, this boy became so agitated that he went and got his BB gun and shot it right at the set! Now that's how it agitated and excited him. I don't know what *King Kong* was about, but to answer your question, it does affect some people.

You see, if everybody had a high IQ and if everybody were sophisticated and intellectual, you might not have this problem. But we're dealing with society as a whole. Now, I'm not saying that television has to be reduced to a moronic level. I'm not saying that at all But there's a responsibility here that's much greater than it might be in the motion-picture industry or on the Broadway stage or even in newspapers and periodicals. This is a much more sensitive field.

Q: Are you prepared for the possibility that the Surgeon General might report he couldn't prove a causal relationship between televised and real violence?

A: Well, it isn't a matter of being prepared for it. It's a matter of waiting to find out if that is so.

Q: As you know, Senator, Dr. Frank Stanton of CBS and others have contended it hasn't even been possible to devise a methodology for measuring the effects of viewing.

A: Well, of course, they've always taken that position, and that's where the catch comes. I'm trying to find out whether they're right or wrong. I think we ought to cross that bridge when we get to it.

Q: Do you see some parallel between the smoking-cancer investigation and this probe of TV's violent effects in that it might take a period of years—maybe even 10 years—to make a case?

A: Well, we don't have to wait for that time to pass to make certain changes that I think will be in the public interest. And I think we've already started.

Now, there was the president of NBC who came before our committee, a very wonderful man, Julian Goodman, who told me he was blessed to have a 6-year-old son and that he was a little disturbed about some of the Saturday morning children's programs and he had them changed. Now, after all, there was something wrong!

All I'm saying is, look, you're sensible people. You're men of the world. You're fathers of families. You know the difference between

right and wrong. There's so much about this you can do on your own! *343*
Then, when you get to the marginal cases, maybe you need a Surgeon
General's opinion.

Q: One of the things they contend in the industry, Senator, is
that your complaint is a little late. They say they have cleaned up
much of the violence in the last year or so. Have you seen any visible
improvements in programming in this respect?

A: Oh, yes, I certainly have, and I applaud it. And I'll tell you
how it happened: it happened as a result of the Presidential Commission on Violence. I mean, that's the trouble: unless they're prod-
ded they don't do it; and while I applaud them for what they've done,
I say it came about because they were all ushered in before the violence commission—and then the changes began to take place!

Q: I gather, Senator, that it would meet your specifications as
to prescreening if the networks just submitted their programs for
review by the Code Authority when requested to do so.

A: Yes, I would allow them to use discretion. For instance, you
take *The Sound of Music.* Now, you wouldn't want to prescreen that.
Everybody knows that's a good movie.

Take *My Three Sons,* Who has to prescreen *that? The Doris Day
Show, The Jackie Gleason Show . . .* there are so many shows they
know beforehand are all right.

But then you have certain programs where the habit has been to
indulge in a little bit more freedom. Now, I'm not saying these should
be eliminated. But these are the ones that should be looked at. Then
you wouldn't have a proposition like *Turn-On*—and I don't always
want to be picking on the same show—where they had to pull it off
the air because it went too far.

You remember the questioning by our committee about this
show. I mean, there was a reluctance to say exactly why it was taken
off the air and finally I butted in and asked, "Wasn't it taken off because it was too risque?" and the fellow [Elton Rule, president of
ABC-TV] said, "Yes."

Now, that's it! That's it!

Q: But you are willing for the networks to be the final arbiter,
irrespective of the Code Authority's judgments?

A: Well, I don't think you could deny that. They would be put
on their full responsibility. I would hope, you see, that this would
have a very salutary effect not only on the networks and affiliates, but
on the producers themselves. After a while, they would understand
better, all around, the guidelines within which they must work. And
we'd remove much of the doubt.

Q: Do you have any legislation in mind?

344   *A:* No, no. For the time being, of course not. I'm not suggesting Government regulation. I'm opposed to Government regulation, because I think they can do this job on their own. Not only that, I tell you very frankly, we don't want to do anything here that will impinge on the basic constitutional rights of freedom of speech. I'm very strong on that.

       Q: Do you have a feeling you are carrying this ball all alone?

       A: No, I am not. As a matter of fact, I went into the Senate restaurant the other day—my son was in; he's a doctor at the Yale New Haven hospital and he was down visiting me—and at the next table was a senator and his wife. I had never met his wife, but as he was going out, he introduced her to me and said, "By the way, as you were walking in, I pointed you out to my wife and she told me she had seen you on television, and she agrees 100 percent with what you've been saying." So, maybe some senators aren't with me—but I have an idea their wives are!

       More than senators' wives are with Pastore. Shortly after this interview, President Nixon wrote the Senator, backing his request for a Surgeon General's probe. "I share your deep concern and strongly applaud your vigorous criticism of what you regard as a misuse of this great medium," the President said.

A Conversation With Television's Chief Censor

Stockton Helffrich Interviewed
by Richard K. Doan

AUGUST 23, 1969

Q: In your opinion have the TV networks been living up to the NAB Code?

A: I would say yes. In the area of violence, they have cut 'way, 'way back. We are finding less and less to challenge on this score.

In the matter of sex, I think there's greater candor in some of the network programming, a more matter-of-fact approach to the boy-girl relationships of life, but I feel the networks have been astute in responding to a greater openess on the part of the audience, while not pressing it too far.

In *Laugh-In,* for instance, they're obviously trying to accept and go along with current attitudes, but not to a point where a thing is spelled out too explicitly. If something is of a nature that it goes over the heads of the younger set—and of us older squares, too, for that matter!—then it isn't going to injure anybody. The rest of the audience—the in-betweens, the new generation and others—are able to bring to their viewing whatever backgrounds they need in order to infer whatever they want to from it.

Q: Are you saying that *double-entendres* are all right?

A: With qualifications. I think I'm saying that. *Laugh-In,* as the case in point, is an approach to topical humor, including sexual humor, which to me rather consistently and effectively stops short of going too far. The show has an ability to make an allusion and if you understand it, all right, but it pursues a policy of evil being in the eyes of the beholder. If you read more into it than they say, OK; that's because you're sophisticated. Now that's like something for everybody! It's hard to get into trouble if you do it that way.

Q: How did you feel about ABC's ill-fated *Turn-On?*

A: It happened we inadvertently missed that show. We normally monitor every premiere. I asked for a rescreening of it because I received one or two station comments on it. Personally, I felt it was heavy-handed and did not, in some sequences, stop while it was

345

346 winning. It might have succeeded, I think, if they had approached it just a little more gingerly.

Q: If the networks have cut 'way back on violence, as you say, doesn't it suggest there formerly was too much?

A: There may have been. We don't know. For all the research done on the subject, we aren't certain what the effect is of a given piece of violence or depictions of conflict generally. But we do know there is public concern about violence and a fear that the broadcast media might have been contributing to it, so we've inhibited ourselves out of a preoccupation with that concern.

Q: Have you looked into the Saturday morning children's cartoon programming? Have you felt it was too violent?

A: We monitor TV programs on a priority basis, our first priority being the action-adventure category—adventure, Western, suspense, detective, that sort of thing. Our second priority is children's weekend fare. We've seen marked changes there, too. Basically, I find it slapstick. It is not overboard, in my judgment.

Q: Was your office a factor in getting the networks to cut back on violence?

A: I think we were a factor, but I believe the networks would have done it anyway, of their own volition.

Q: How much monitoring do you do?

A: Our surveillance of network programming has more than doubled, almost tripled, since last fall.

Q: Why was it stepped up?

A: We got a specific mandate from our TV board [of the NAB]. They asked us to do "intensified" monitoring, as they put it, after the assassinations of Martin Luther King Jr. and Senator Robert Kennedy. These assassinations, of course, had a very strong impact on our whole society. That naturally includes the broadcasters, who felt a deep concern. They wished public good will, and a number of them made deeply moving statements on this. So they said, well, we have a self-regulatory arm of NAB that's set up to deal with things in the public interest, so let's concentrate on this area. And we have been doing so.

Q: Senator Pastore praised your Code of good practice as "reading like the Ten Commandments." Do you agree it's that good?

A: In its over-all credo I think it's a desirable document. There is no question, though, that its interpretation requires more and more flexibility, and this stretching can reach a point where we must question the applicability of some of the proscriptions of the Code to the times in which we live.

Q: You're saying the Code may need updating?

A: I feel there are areas in which it is not adequate to the situa-

tion. The world is changing, and I think that where the Code flatly *347*
proscribes things without allowance for exceptions under certain
circumstances, the text should be revised. It's hard to pinpoint specifics without a script in front of you.

Q: You'd make the Code more lenient, you mean?

A: Leniency may not be the right word, but yes, I think so.
Society is tolerating greater candor, and the Code endeavors to respond to the sentiments of broadcasters and viewers alike.

Certainly there is no wish by broadcasters to offend anybody or
to go in for clearly salacious material. But I think that broadcasters
in the last year or two have been increasingly aware that big changes
are occurring in our society. This is, after all, the era of the Pill and
the Bomb, and such things affect our attitudes. This doesn't mean we
adopt a no-holds-barred attitude, but we do try to react to what the
public feels is quote right unquote.

Young people today, for instance, are more honest and candid in
their approach to sex. And I think we might bear in mind that there is
a rather well-known psychiatric principle, developed by a man named
Legman (or at least he helped develop it), that to the degree you
censor out simple human expressions of sex, sexuality, and such, you
create a vacuum that violence tends to fill.

Q: Does it work in reverse? Does sex fill a violence vacuum?

A: I don't know. Love does. Or mutual involvement does. Sex,
however, really is a complex area of concern to us. Basically we try
to take a reasoned approach to it. We try not to corrupt the innocent
and not to frustrate the intelligent.

Q: Was your office involved in any way in the CBS cancellation
of the Smothers Brothers?

A: No, that was an internal matter with CBS and did not involve
us at all.

Q: What is the NAB's position on Senator Pastore's proposal
that the networks ought to submit their programs to the Code Authority for prescreening?

A. Our position, I'd say, parallels that of many broadcasters,
including the networks: a concern that this could lead to prior censorship. Actually the networks and Code Authority have been practicing
to some extent, except in CBS's case, substantially what the Senator
proposes. ABC has already shown us nine of the pilots for its new fall
series and we expect to preview the other one shortly. NBC has
shown us four of theirs. It's a consult-and-advise arrangement. If
we question somthing, it's up to the network to decide what to do
about it. If we disagree after-the-fact, either of us can urge a review by
the Code [Review] Board.[32]

Q. What exactly do you feel Senator Pastore was trying to achieve with his proposal?

A. He was trying, I feel, to make broadcasters very conscious of their responsibilities. I think he made very clear statements that he wished to avoid censorship *per se.*

Q. How do you view the U.S. Surgeon General's inquiry, which Senator Pastore instigated, into the effects of TV violence on children?

A. Difficult though it may be to do, bona-fide behavioral research would be desirable. I think Senator Pastore has urged something the broadcasters welcome. We'll just have to see what the findings are.

Q. Why does your practice of monitoring on-air programs and asking a network to change or delete something before a program's second showing amount to less censorship than asking the same thing before the program is broadcast the first time? Wouldn't less harm be done if something objectionable were never broadcast at all?

A. Well, doing something prior to broadcast literally would give a group like ourselves tremendous power. Even if I were the most benign and intelligent and wise sort you could find anywhere, I think that under the First Amendment many Americans would question what the situation might be if somebody else, of a different character—a blue nose—were in my job.

Now, I might have some kind of personal objection about something in a show, but at least when a program has already been broadcast, other people's judgments can be weighed against mine. Is there audience reaction supporting my view? Do the stations agree with it? The value of hindsight is not to be underestimated.

Q. Can you think of an instance of how the Code has been applied lately?

A. Well, in the last year we added a provision to the Code stating that unsafe practices should not be apparent in either commercials or in programs unless consistent with plot or characterizations. We raised this point when we saw a screening of NBC's new fall series . . . *Then Came Bronson,* filmed prior to our adoption of this standard. It stars a James Dean-type who rides a motorcycle and he was shown not wearing a helmet while riding it. But it turned out NBC already was alert to this and had taken steps to put him in a helmet.

Q. Do movies present many Code problems?

A. Not really. The networks do an expert job of editing movies to delete objectionable scenes. For instance, *The Apartment* is a good movie but tends to dot every "i" and cross every "t"; it overdoes some of the points relating to the use of Jack Lemmon's apartment.

The network edited out 20 minutes of this and what was left was, *349* believe me, a much tighter, tauter, better script. It was not emasculated.

Q: Do many viewers seem to know of your TV Code and how it works?

A. Well, I think we could stand a good deal more public awareness. Our Code Seal is recognized, we know that. But I don't think it results in much audience action. I wish frankly there were more. I'd like to hear from more of the public, or at least see them let their local stations know what they think. But, you know, it's a lot like politics and other matters: people deplore and cluck and tsk, tsk, but they don't do much about it.

And if you don't hear from people, you just have to assume you are doing pretty much what they want and expect.

How Will TV Handle Sexy Movies?

By Peggy Hudson

JULY 22, 1967

Hollywood's new production code was the opening gun in a "Battle of the Boudoir" which is helping shape the future of living-room television. Now that the new code has freed Hollywood from many old taboos, U.S. producers are making movies sexy enough to cause even foreign filmmakers to sit up and take notice. And, needless to say, these sexier films have caused quite a stir right at home among movie addicts and TV moguls.

The addict wonders when some of these gamier movies might appear on his home TV screen. The moguls are wondering what to do about this alarming trend. Both have just cause to wonder. One movie alone—John Huston's yet-to-be-released *Reflections in a Golden Eye*—deals with such Freudian themes as homosexuality, voyeurism, sadism and self-mutilation.

The movie buff's reasoning runs thus: Television is using movies of more recent vintage. As TV's stockpile of "first-run" films is exhausted, the time lag between wide-screen and home-screen showings is being narrowed. Ergo: Soon the television industry will be forced to show the current bumper crop of sexy feature movies.

Things are not as simple as that. Soon we'll see why—and also get an idea of why the TV moguls are worried. First of all, Hollywood's straying from the primrose path is not a mere whim of the industry. It was necessitated by hard economic facts. The new code came as a much-needed shot in the arm to Hollywood producers who had sought in vain to compete with ever more sexy foreign imports.

For more than three decades Hollywood's hands had been tied by the old production code's taboos against scenes portraying "lustful embraces" or the explicit treatment of "illicit sex." Finally, such a daring foreign film as the Swedish *Dear John*, a drama which succeeded in remaining romantic despite its sexually graphic episodes, reportedly has already grossed over $3 million for its United States distributor alone. And it may eventually earn as much as $4 million.

350

It's easy to see, then, why the new, more permissive code brought a great deal of movie industry jubilation. Even Jack Valenti, president of the Motion Picture Association of America, seemed hardly able to suppress enthusiasm when he was asked if the new code, in easing the ancient taboo against nudism, would allow movies in some instances to picture bare female breasts. "Yes," Valenti replied— and quickly proved a prophet. Almost immediately after Valenti gave this historic green light, the film treatment of James A. Michener's novel *Hawaii* was released showing scenes of native girls whose breasts were covered with nothing more visible than the new MPAA code.

Even more daring movies were soon to follow. One of these was *The Tiger Makes Out,* starring Eli Wallach and Anne Jackson, who head the company producing this sexy farce. The old Hollywood code specifically barred seduction or rape as a target of comedy. Certainly rape was hardly a thing to smile at. But *Tiger's* hero is a Greenwich Village mailman who plans to rape the first pretty girl he sees. His plan is foiled by a bored Long Island housewife who somehow succeeds in turning his attention from thoughts of rape to reflections upon Rembrandt and other cultural pursuits. Wallach is one of the few movie producers to be found these days who shows a sublime indifference toward codes—whether for movies or television. "I'm still going to try to rape the woman and amuse the American public," he swears.

Another film joining the move toward sexploitation is Otto Preminger's *Hurry Sundown.* It deals with a husband whose hold on his wife is frankly sexual. The movie's climactic scene comes when he unbuttons her blouse and arouses her in one of the most graphic expositions of the "art" of love-making yet to be offered wide-screen audiences.

Getting any of the above-mentioned movies on the home TV screen would be no mean feat. This doesn't suggest that some of them might not end up playing to living-room audiences in one form or another. But the problems posed could be enormous.

Television's own Code, put out by the National Association of Broadcasters (NAB), is written in general terms and appears at first blush to be almost as liberal as Hollywood's new code. In fact, NBC's director of Broadcast Standards, Carl Watson, insists: "There's practically no play or story that cannot be done with artistic restraint in a way that's acceptable to the mass audience." But as Howard Bell, [former] director of the NAB Code Authority, points out: "TV standards will always have to be somewhat tighter than those for the

352 theater. There has to be more control for those exhibiting films in the living room, where control of who sees what is more difficult."

The television industry also has at least two Big Brothers constantly watching it. One is the advertiser. Few ad men are eager to associate their products with a movie that is controversial. The other "brother" is the Federal Communications Commission, which keeps a critical eye on what one of its former Chairman termed TV's "vast wasteland."

Apparently oblivious to these facts of life in the television industry, many of Hollywood's newer movies continue to exercise their new-found sexual freedom. Yet their producers may find themselves unable to sell even heavily censored versions of their newest products to the television market. As one high-placed but anonymous TV executive puts it: "Film-makers have got to accept the burden of how they merchandise their movies. They have to live with the image they create. If it hadn't been for its advertising, *La Dolce Vita* would have been on television three or four years ago. But now it's a 'red flag.' They sold the movie as an orgy. They made their money by exploiting it as a sensational motion picture. We know it's not sensational but the public doesn't."

Psycho is another example of how easily spooked TV executives can be. CBS reportedly paid $400,000 for this Alfred Hitchcock thriller—and quickly showed an advanced stage of jitters. The movie's original air date was postponed as a matter of good taste because of the Valerie Percy murder. Both the suspense film and the Percy case revolved around the brutal slaying of a beautiful young woman. But the postponement of *Psycho* only served to draw more attention to the controversial nature of the movie. Protests were registered by a few individuals and stations and *Psycho* was [temporarily] shelved as a network show.

Unlike *La Dolce Vita*, *Psycho*—at least in its trimmed state— is relatively free of amorous activities. But television-wise it shared one flaw: It had become too notorious. If television programmers are still afraid of "notorious" movies, what is the fate of more quiet but even more "mature" films? They may still end up on home screens— if the fanfare accompanying them doesn't frighten away prospective TV buyers. One television executive whose job it is to study such things told us how the blouse-unbuttoning scene in *Hurry Sundown* could be handled, for example: "I'd show the scene up to where he begins to unbutton her blouse. Then I'd take the frame and blow it up and crop it at the shoulder line. The adults would know what is happening. The scene could easily be salvaged for TV." Technology

could blend with the aesthetic in making this movie acceptable to   *353*
home audiences. But other movies present larger problems which
may be insurmountable for TV buyers. *Reflections* may be one to
find it hard to pass through the golden eye of this needle.

Despite the exceptions—Wallach, who doesn't seem to care, and
Huston, who may also defy a code or two as the mood moves him—
most of today's moviemakers are forced to recognize the shotgun
marriage that has wedded Hollywood to the television industry. As
an indication of the "dowry" involved in this industrial wedding,
CBS and ABC recently agreed to pay $92.3 million for films to be
shown on TV. ABC agreed to pay 20th Century-Fox $5 million for
a mere two showings of *Cleopatra*, the first scheduled for 1970. NBC
is paying United Artists $115 million for the right to telecast 94
films over a nine-year period.

The answer to the problem of sexier movies versus TV could lie
in the perfection of any one of several techniques. Hollywood producers, for example, finally have admitted that they have been
"doctoring" their export movies for years. They have shipped some
countries extra film footage featuring nude and much more sexy
scenes.

Eli Wallach, who appeared in *Genghis Khan*, says two versions
were shot. "In both, the Mongols arrived and were bathed by slave
girls," he explained. "In the American version, the slave girls were
wearing little. In the European version, they wore nothing." With
such precedent, it would seem relatively easy—at least to the unini-
tiated—for Hollywood producers to put a third version of their products on the drawing board—a buttoned-up toned-down TV model.

But finding a topflight producer to agree to such an undertaking
isn't always so easy. Sidney Lumet—who not only admits his TV origins but who sees no big problem in turning out good films designed
expressly for the TV audience—recoils at the idea of producing a
Jekyll-Hyde movie, one version for the neighborhoods and the other
for the living room.

Lumet, whose long string of movies includes *The Group, The
Hill, Fail-Safe* and *The Deadly Affair,* defends Hollywood's newly
relaxed standards. His movie *The Pawnbroker* first was given a condemned rating by the Legion of Decency (now the National Catholic
Office for Motion Pictures), but was later changed to "morally un-
objectionable for adults" when Lumet maintained *The Pawnbroker's*
controversial nude scene was intrinsic to the film's artistic merit.
Lumet says he knows of several producers who have been asked to
turn out TV versions of their movies, but vows he won't make movies

354   two ways. "If you're able to make movies two ways, you should shoot the less sensational way and forget the other. The more sensational way would be just for the sake of sensationalism."

Marvin Schwartz, producer of *The War Wagon,* seems to agree with Lumet: "Making a picture two ways means making two different pictures," Schwartz maintains. "You can't take the same theme and bastardize it for TV. If you reshoot scenes, that changes the story. You might as well do a completely different one."

Though Schwartz is a comparatively new name on the marquee of Hollywood credits, he reflects the old Hollywood school of thinking. He insists Movies can get along without TV. "We are making films for the theater, not for TV," he says. "If TV wants the movies—good, that's gravy. But if a movie is good, it will make money without TV."

Some of the more established names in Hollywood, however—those such as Otto Preminger—seem more in the mood to reach a rapprochement with TV. Preminger not so long ago lost a court suit to prevent what he insisted was an excessive number of commercial interruptions in the televised showing of his movie *Anatomy of a Murder.* Now he not only admits he was pleased by CBS's slightly trimmed showing of *Advise and Consent,* he also says he could easily abide by TV's Code and make movies for the networks.

Preminger confesses that he was "surprised" that the homosexual theme of *Advise and Consent* was left intact in the telecast of the movie. But he maintains that if he were to make a movie for TV, he could reach an "understanding" with a network to avoid any taboos, as long as he knew of the restrictions in advance. "If the network would say, 'Look, we don't want homosexuality,' or 'we don't want'—lets say—'an automobile accident because our sponsors won't like it,' or 'we don't want you to say anything bad about smoking,' I could easily avoid it. That wouldn't kill me. I can't discuss the whole world in one film. . . . I only wouldn't like it if I had done a show or done a film, and it was cut later because of such taboos. I think that is ridiculous."

. . . .

Some of the more optimistic producers feel that the television audience will remain content neither with standards nor strictures based on old-movie concepts. But Lumet and Schwartz, for example, predict that television will follow Hollywood's new lead toward liberalization—if not license—in "adult" subject matter.

"Movies made under the new code are doing big business not because they say 'damn' and 'hell' but because they are more adult in concept," says Schwartz. "People are seeing these movies—and then going home to watch TV the next night. They are having to pay to 'grow up' now. Eventually they'll be able to do the same thing in front of their TV sets.

"The new code is taking a leaf from foreign films. For years American films depicted boy-meets-girl. But most of them still take an hour and a half to get the couple in bed. In foreign films, the boy and girl start in bed—then the film takes them out to tell their story. I think the new code means we're becoming more realistic about people—and TV will benefit."

Lumet contends that as movies become more "realistic," so will television. "The gulf between TV and movies narrows if the picture has been successful," he says. *The Bridge on the River Kwai* had no censorship problems—but if it had, they would have gotten by. There are slight double standards. As the interdependence between TV and the movies becomes greater—and it is becoming greater— TV will move more and more toward the movie level."

The New Movie Code

DECEMBER 7, 1968

Hollywood's new movie-classification system won't really affect what we'll be seeing on our home screens. TV intends to go right on playing to the 8-to-80 audience, even if that means skipping some of those "adults only" pictures or whacking out their flagrantly sexy, violent or profane scenes.

The Motion Picture Association of America's rating system in effect for movies released since November 1, 1968, stamps them either G for "general audiences," M [GP] for "adults and mature young people," R: persons under 16 [17] may be admitted when accompanied by a parent or adult guardian, or X when no one under 16 [17] should be admitted. Enforcement is voluntary and left to the exhibitors. MPAA is concerned entirely with theater showings and makes no pretense of suggesting what is acceptable movie fare for TV.

Unanimously, the network censors say they'll take note of the MPAA ratings but expect to go on, as in the past, making their own independent judgments about what TV audiences should see. All this doesn't really help TV people pick which pictures shall be seen in prime time. Indeed, it probably just adds a new headache.

A networker who is most passionate on the subject is NBC's chief censor, Ernest Lee Jahncke, a 31-year radio-TV veteran. In Jahncke's view, MPAA president Jack Valenti's scheme for "rating" pictures to protect the young from too-adult stuff is "a cop-out that permits the movie industry to go its lewd ways without cleaning up its product at the source. A lot of people producing movies," he snaps, "seem to confuse the shock values of eroticism with adult significance. It's possible you know, to address yourself to adult topics without using barracks-room language."

Still, the NBC official and his CBS counterpart, William Tankersley, both commend Valenti for trying to give parents a movie guideline. "It's a timid step that can't hurt," Jahncke says. "A good step toward protecting children," Tankersley says.

ABC's Grace Johnsen, who has been passing on shows at her network since 1947, is less enthusiastic. "I've always been opposed to putting a stamp on anything," she explains. "You only invite certain people to look at it."

Miss Johnsen, Jahncke and Tankersley—a trio with more than 90 years' broadcasting experience among them—concur that what can pass on TV in the matter of sex, violence, crime and profanity is a question for seasoned judgment which can't be spelled out *per se* in specific guidelines.

"We feel, in putting any picture on the network," says Tankersley, "that no one's morals should be lowered by viewing it. Certain films, of course, are generally known to be more 'adult' than others, but most people are aware of such pictures. Even so, we edit all movies so no child would be hurt by them." He suggested CBS's cutting of *Night of the Iguana* was a case in point: "Nobody was offended by it."

If anything, the new ratings will just tend to add to a present problem, Tankersley noted: "When we book a movie that has been widely advertised as 'for adults,' even though we've deleted its objectionable elements, we get letters objecting to our running it. Now, I suppose, we'll get more such mail, because people will be aware of these ratings." He conceded the public has no way of knowing the network has excised raw and rough parts. "It would be a cop-out," Tankersley says flatly, "for us to throw up a flag (an on-screen warning) saying a film was 'for adults only'."

The CBS official admits that some thought is given to how many teenagers are apt to be around at the time a movie is shown. "There are more kids watching Friday nights than on school nights," he points out, "so we may run a picture on Thursday night that we'd be less inclined to run Friday night."

Lee Jahncke defended his decision to run *Never on Sunday*, a movie about a happy prostitute. Jahncke confesses NBC got "quite a bit" of flak from its viewers. "But I don't think we corrupted any morals," he insists. "Basically it was a comedy." He pondered a moment. "Maybe we were wrong. Look, we're not infallible. We put on 52 movies a year. Judge us by the 52, not just by one!"

Viewer mail these days, all three of the censors say, complains at times about the editing of movies in the belief that something has been deleted as objectionable, whereas it has been cut to shorten a film to TV's time limitations.

People today are generally more sophisticated in their TV tastes than they used to be, the ABC standards director notes. "In the early days we got complaints that ballet dancing was obscene," she smiles. "That never happens any more."

The three networkers are divided on the trend, if any, in pictures. Miss Johnsen feels that the pendulum is swinging back toward lighter,

358   more wholesome things. We're going to have cleaner films." Tankersley doubts it, saying, "This year's pictures are rougher than last
year's, and I don't see any evidence of a swing."

Jahncke is sure Hollywood is on a premeditated sex kick, as yet
unslackening. He remembers a lunch conversation five or six years
ago with Geoffrey Shurlock, MPAA production-code head who now
bosses the new ratings system. Shurlock told him in essence, the NBC
man recalls, You people in TV have taken the play away from us
[the moviemakers] in violence and we can't compete with you there.
So we'll divide it up—you can have the violence, we'll take the sex."
And Hollywood has done so with a vengeance, Jahncke believes.

Violence

Concern has been manifested about the speculated effects of televised violence on various segments of our society, particularly children and young people, since television's inception. Monitoring studies which enumerated the number of killings and displays of violence aired over a given time period were already prevalent by the early 1950's and these were often cited when other nations were preparing to establish their own regulations of television programming. By 1954 the Senate had held an inquiry into the effects of the mass media, particularly television, upon juvenile delinquency.

The possible relationship between television and juvenile delinquency continued to be of public concern in 1961. Because the number of programs stressing violence was increasing and because the NAB seemed not to be fulfilling its promise, made in 1954, to adequately police the industry, the committee headed by Senator Thomas Dodd of Connecticut held another inquiry. This committee concluded its three-year investigation in 1964; it stated, "on the basis of expert testimony and impressive research evidence . . . a relationship has been conclusively established between televised crime and violence and anti-social attitudes and behavior among juvenile viewers." Although Senator Dodd's committee acknowledged that its interpretation of the research was supported more enthusiastically by the professionals dealing with delinquents than by researchers, it maintained that television seemed clearly to be functioning as "a school for violence."

The committee made four major recommendations: The networks should work together to plan improvements in children's programs. The NAB Code should be revised to provide more effective sanctions. A system should be developed to enable viewers to express their views. A "co-ordinated large scale research attack" should be launched to gather more precise information concerning the impact of television on juvenile behavior (the Dodd Committee is discussed in the section about children's use of television, Chapter 5, pp. 511-516).

After the assassinations of Dr. Martin Luther King and Senator

359

360   Robert Kennedy in 1968, President Johnson appointed a National Commission on the Causes and Prevention of Violence. In September 1969, the Commission released its Report on violence in television entertainment programs.

The Commission stated that it was "deeply troubled" by television's "constant portrayal of violence" not in any genuine attempt to focus artistic expression on the human condition but rather in "pandering to a public preoccupation with violence that television itself has helped to generate." Although television entertainment based on violence might be effective merchandising, the Commission felt this to be an appalling way to serve a civilization—"an appalling way to fulfill the requirements of the law that broadcasting serve the public interest, convenience and necessity."

The Commission reinforced the concept that television's impact upon children is significant. Moreover, according to the Commission, television projects an image of the adult world which is "by and large an unwholesome one" and teaches the child "moral and social values about violence which are inconsistent with the standards of a civilized society." The Commission stated, "it is reasonable to conclude that a constant diet of violent behavior on television has an adverse effect on human character and attitudes . . . " and, "We do not suggest that television is a principal cause of violence in society. We do suggest that it is a contributing factor." Although the Commission acknowledged that much remains to be learned about the effects of media violence, "enough is known to require that constructive action be taken at once to reduce the amount and alter the kind of violent programs which have pervaded television."

Just prior to releasing the report, during its final drafting, the Commission decided to add several qualifying remarks. The Report points out that the Commission's findings were based on content analyses of 1967 and 1968 programs and that a great deal of violence had already been eradicated. Since about 18 months are required for programming decisions to be reflected in network schedules "the test of network intentions to reduce violence on television, as these were expressed in the spring and summer of 1968, can properly begin with this year's television season." The Commission warned against making television a scapegoat for the increased violence in our society and declared: "We urge that those who read our statement do so carefully, without exaggeration of its findings, remembering that America also experienced high levels of crime and violence in periods before the advent of television."

The Commission did indicate, however, that the industry was still not doing enough to meet the issues in question. For example, the NAB Code has no meaningful standards which could be applied to reduce the number of programs which, because of basic formats, require violence as the principal means of resolving conflict. Also, the networks have failed to conduct their own research on the effects of televised violence. Nevertheless, the Commission directed its recommendations to the industry, advocating internal change rather than governmental intervention. In fact, according to its Chairman Dr. Milton Eisenhower, the Commission "put absolutely aside the thought of censorship."

The Commission put forward four recommendations to the broadcasting industry. The airing of cartoons containing serious non-comic violence should be abandoned. The industry should reduce the number of crime, Western and action-adventure programs and limit the airing of these types of programs to the later hours, after 9 P.M., when children presumably are no longer watching. Programs in which violence is a routine and acceptable way of solving problems should be avoided; resorts to violence should have unusual and undesirable outcomes. More research about televised violence must be conducted and the industry should devise policies, standards and practices concerning televised violence, which are "more responsive to the best evidence provided by social scientists, psychologists and communications researchers." The Commission also emphasized the importance of parental supervision of children's viewing habits; parents should express disapproval of objectionable programs and approval of good programs to the networks and stations. The Commission thought most families would prefer not being exposed to large doses of televised violence.

The Report was immediately attacked on the grounds that the charges were based on analyses of programs of past seasons. Industry officials claimed that many of the Commission's recommendations had been effected by the time the report was released. At CBS, for example, president Dr. Frank Stanton said, "few will now find the content of Saturday morning children's programs objectionable" and vice president for programming Mike Dann was quoted in the *Wall Street Journal* as saying, "You'd need a microscope to find any violence in our schedule now." NBC president Julian Goodman took issue with the Commission's definition of violence as "the overt expression of force intended to hurt or kill." Goodman argued that under this definition a single minor incident would classify an entire program as "violent," regardless of its quality and value or the dramatic circumstances in which the incident occurred.

In addition to the report of the Violence Commission, yet another investigation of televised violence is being undertaken. At the request

362   of Senator Pastore the Surgeon General's office has agreed to conduct a one-year study in which it will attempt to prove that televised violence does in fact cause anti-social behavior. This study, already in progress, will cost the Government up to one million dollars. Pastore's hope is that the Surgeon General's twelve-man Scientific Advisory Committee on Television and Social Behavior will obtain the same kind of positive evidence regarding the effects of televised violence as was gathered by the Surgeon General with respect to the ill-effects of cigarette smoking. A discussion of some of the problems that will be faced by the Surgeon General's task force and the general difficulties in trying to obtain scientific proof of the relationship between televised violence and anti-social behavior is found in the section on children's use of television in Chapter 5 (pp. 510-528).

In 1952, Professor Charles Siepmann, in *Television and Education in the United States,* stated that no solid evidence existed regarding any psychological effect of television on children or adults and "if one is looking for scientific proof on this matter, one will not find it. It is a matter of judgment and opinion." However, Siepmann also said that "the absence, whether now or in the future, of scientific corroboration provides no alibi for lack of serious thought and discussion of the problem and for lack of responsible action stemming from reasoned and reasonable judgment of the possibilities in the situation."

Seventeen years later, Professor Percy Tannenbaum told the National Commission on the Causes and Prevention of Violence that with respect to obtaining proof of a causal relationship between televised and actual violence, "The verdict you seek is not proven and will not be in my lifetime or in the lifetime of this commission." He went on to emphasize that the question of violence in society is so urgent, "we should move directly to measures of regulation and control instead of merely waiting for confirmed evidence about media effects."

The Violence Commission requested Dean George Gerbner of the Annenberg School of Communications at the University of Pennsylvania to obtain more detailed information concerning the amount and form of televised violence. A summary (pp. 364-370) of the fifty-page report, *Dimensions of Violence in Television Drama,* submitted by Dr. Gerbner and his associates to the Commission reviews findings related to nine questions: How much violence occurs in network televised drama? In what sorts of shows does most violence occur? Was there less violence in the fall of 1968 than there was in the fall of 1967? What was the nature of the violence which occurred? How much killing is there in televised drama? Who are the violent people in these shows? Where does the violence take place? How is violence dealt with and what does it all add up to?

Gerbner's answers to these questions formed the basis for many of the Commission's criticisms and conclusions. While there is general agreement that some of the answers are now dated, there is considerable debate over just which answers are dated and to what degree.

Senator Pell, like his fellow Senator from Rhode Island, Senator Pastore, has been an outspoken critic of violence on television. The Senator (pp. 371-375) contends that although freedom of speech should not be limited, television has no more right to breed violence than does the meat industry to sell tainted meat. The industry's argument that there is no scientific proof to support the idea that television breeds violence is accepted by the Senator. He points out, however, that television's financial existence is based upon the premise that the medium does influence the minds and actions of people. This being so, he finds the premise that programming does not affect people to be untenable. The industry also maintains that it should not be singled out from other means of communication. Pell considers television to be quantitatively and qualitatively different from other media. He feels research must be encouraged and compares the situation regarding televised violence in America with that in England. His hope is that the industry in this country will regulate itself.

Professor Martin Maloney (pp. 376-380) argues that the current crusade against violence on television is frequently hypocritical, generally ridiculous, totally pointless and genuinely dangerous. He submits that these crusades against television violence are in fact damaging because they camouflage the real issue: increased violence in society. Television's immense popularity makes it a popular subject for investigation and controversy. However, according to Maloney, television is the poorest of all the media for conveying any real impression of violence in its entertainment programming. The small screen, unreal color and assembly-line products for mass consumption are detriments to realistic portrayal.

How Much Violence Is There on Television?

JULY 12, 1969

In network television drama:

Eight out of every 10 plays contain some violence.
It occurs at the rate of 7 times per hour.
There are 600 separate acts of televised violence per week.
Half of the leading characters act violently.
One out of every 10 kills somebody.

These are a few of the findings in a remarkable report recently turned over to the National Commission on the Causes and Prevention of Violence. When it began its work last year, in the aftermath of two shocking assassinations, the commission knew that the concern about violence in America was accompanied by widespread suspicion that television has been a significant factor contributing to that violence.

But, though everybody talks about TV violence, nobody knows very much about it. How much of it is there? What forms does it take? There were no reliable answers. The Commission decided to get some. It asked Professor George Gerbner, dean of the Annenberg School of Communications at the University of Pennsylvania, to head a team of investigators at this graduate research institute to study and report on "the extent and nature of violent presentations" in television drama. Collaborating with Dean Gerbner in the study were Professors Martin Brouwer, Cedric C. Clark and Klaus H. Krippendorff, staff associate Michael F. Eleey, and scores of graduate student monitors.

Now that report is in the hands of the Commission, in the form of a 50-page mimeographed volume entitled *Dimensions of Violence in Television Drama*. Because of time limitations—the researchers were given only two months to come up with the answers—it is described as a "bare bones" report, with every little interpretation of the raw quantitative data. Still, it is a unique document: the only body of evidence nailing down precisely what television violence amounts to.

364

That evidence is summarized in the following pages. Before *365* getting to it, it is necessary to insert a few words about how the research was conducted and what it covered. Those readers who would prefer digging right into the meat of the report may skip the two explanatory sections that follow this one. Dean Gerbner has announced plans to repeat the study each year as part of a general project providing systematic information about trends in the representation of social issues in the mass media.

How was the study conducted? First, you have to understand that the report does not necessarily tell you how violent television is now. And it certainly doesn't tell you how bloody it's going to be next season, when, according to current indications, the networks will attempt to lower the level of violence in their shows. It does cover one week of programs telecast during October 1968 and another week of programs from the same period of 1967.

The week of October 1 through 7 was chosen as a typical week of American television, and all dramatic programs shown during the peak family-viewing hours of those weeks—during prime evening time and Saturday morning, to be precise—were monitored or screened.

The study was limited to network shows and to dramatic shows. Dramatic was interpreted to include any fictional story—cartoons, situation comedies, melodramas, movies—everything from *Magilla Gorilla* to *The Night of the Iguana* (both of which actually were part of the survey). Dramatic programs accounted for 60 percent of all network offerings. The other 40 percent—off limits to the researchers —comprised variety shows, game shows, and news or documentary presentations (some of which, presumably, contained scenes of actual violence).

How is "violence" defined? For the purposes of the study, it is defined as "the overt expression of force intended to hurt or kill." Within this over-all definition, specific guidelines were set forth for the searchers.

How much violence did they find? We had better start with the fundamental—and staggering—statistic that opened this article: 8 out of every 10 plays contained some violence. The violence varied, obviously, in degree, in frequency, in quantity, in content; but there it was, in 80 percent of all plays, whether they were come-

366 dies or tragedies or cartoons. (The word "play," as used throughout the report, refers to any self-contained fictional presentation of any length, from a five-minute *Banana Splits* cartoon—of which there can be several within one *Banana Splits* hour—to a three-hour movie epic.)

How frequently were acts of violence (harmful actions directed by one character against another)shown? Seven times an hour, on the average, ranging from 5 per comedy hour to 24 per cartoon hour).

A total of 1215 separate acts of violence were counted during the two October weeks surveyed. Exactly 183 plays were studied; 149 of them contained violent episodes—adding up, altogether to 872 violent episodes (a violent episode being "a scene of whatever duration which concerns the same agent [of violence] and the same receiver"—anything from a fist fight to a battle scene; a violent episode can contain several specific acts of violence).

Every major character in a TV play had more than an even chance of inflicting violence on someone. There were 455 major characters ("principal" roles "essential" to the story) altogether: 241 of them committed violence.

In what sorts of shows does most of the violence occur? No surprises here. Almost all action programs (crime, Western, adventure, and so forth) and cartoons contained some violence—97 percent of the action shows, 95 percent of the cartoons—while the incidence of violence in comedy shows was considerably lower, though not insignificant (67 percent).

There was considerable pressure at the beginning of this season to decrease the amount of on-the-air violence. Did the networks have less of it in the fall of 1968 than in 1967? No, say the report, "If anything, there was a slight (4 percent) increase in the proportion of hours devoted to programs containing violence."

Yet within this apparently more violent framework there does appear to have been a slight decrease in the rate of violent episodes and acts per program. The acts figure was 11.1 per violent play in 1967 and 10.5 in 1968.

Now we know how much violence there is—or has been—but what is the nature of televised violence? This much can be said about the violent acts shown on television: They were usually performed at close range—in 7 out of 10 conflicts the parties were "within easy talking distance." There was usually a weapon involved

—6 times out of 10. Half the time the victim was a stranger to his attacker.

Most of the time the violence was unreciprocated—"6 out of 10 violent acts evoked no response from their victims; they could not or did not resist."

Violent encounters were usually between males—more than 8 times out of 10. Only 7 percent of all violent acts were committed by women, and they were the victims of only 6 percent of all the acts of violence.

If there were witnesses to violent scenes, they were usually passive spectators—half the time there were no witnesses at all, one-third of the time witnesses were present but showed no re-actions, in 9 percent of the cases witnesses "assisted or encouraged violence" and in 8 percent of the episodes they tried to prevent it. "On the whole," the report states, "it is safe to conclude that violence is rarely shown as unacceptable."

Physical pain was not a visible result of most violent acts—at least three-fourths of all violent acts left the participants looking good as new. When you consider violent episodes, however (remember, they may be the sum total of a number of violent acts), the toll mounts. Half of the episodes produced physical injury or death. Two casual-ties per episode was the average. In 14 percent of all dramatic programs—whether violent or nonviolent—some "gory details of physical injury (blood and wounds)" were shown.

Most violent encounters were between clearly identified "good guys" and "bad guys"—8 out of 10. Half of the time the goodies initiated the violence; half the time the baddies started the rumble. But the goodies took it on the chin more often, even though they could be expected to come out ahead by the time the last commercial rolled.

How much killing is there in television drama? The figures speak eloquently for themselves: One out of every 10 leading charac-ters killed another person. One out of every 20 was killed. One out of every 10 televised acts of violence resulted in death. One out of 5 people who committed violence killed somebody.

Who are these violent people? They are usually male, in the prime of life and unmarried. Good guys or bad guys? You can toss a coin.

To delve into this more deeply, lets start with sex—which is seldom where things start on TV because there aren't enough women

368 to go around. In the make-believe world of television drama males outnumber females by 4 to 1. Among those characters who commit violence, males lead 6 to 1. There are 8 times as many male killers as females and 7 times as many male corpses.

Every age group had a piece of the violent action, but young-adult and middle-aged characters bit off more than their share. They accounted for 9 out of every 10 killers and 8 out of 10 fatal victims. Young adults were most likely to kill; middle-aged folks were most likely to get killed.

Marriage is a reliable hedge against trouble on TV. Most of the people who inflicted or suffered violence were unmarried.

Lawmen and lawbreakers figured prominently in the survey. They made up one-fourth of the entire dramatic population of television, and they comprised one-third of all violent characters and one-half of all killers. More violence was committed by criminals than by lawmen; but when the agents of law and order became violent, they were just as likely to kill somebody as were the nogoodniks. Seven out of 10 lawmen committed acts of violence, with 2 out of 10 becoming killers. Private eyes were just an eyelash less violent (67 percent), but they rarely injured anyone fatally.

Classifying television's violent people by racial or ethnic characteristics provides some illuminating information about the way drama represents contrasting segments of our population. In the world of TV fiction, foreigners and nonwhites were more likely to indulge in violence than were white Americans: "Major characters playing violent roles included half of all white Americans, 6 out of every 10 white non-Americans and nearly 7 out of every 10 non-whites."

White foreigners were the most likely to be killers; nonwhites were the least likely. And, comparing all whites and all nonwhites, 28 percent of the violent white characters became killers, while only 10 percent of the nonwhites did. On the receiving end, foreigners and nonwhites died more often (proportionately) than did white people.

Where does the violence take place? Far away, generally. As the statistics on violent foreigners and nonwhites imply, the settings for the violence are likely to be outside the normal experience of the majority of viewers—old or futuristic or foreign. If you see a man on horseback, a train speeding through the Balkans or a space ship in flight, you can be almost 100-percent sure that violence has come along for the ride.

As the report puts it: "Whenever the place of action was not

limited to the U.S. along or not localized to a city, town or village, or
whenever foreign themes or people other than majority-type Americans were significant elements in the story, violence prevailed in 9
out of every 10 plays." In contrast, contemporary urban or rural settings "dominated the locales of the great majority of nonviolent
plays."

*From the point of view of law and justice, how is violence dealt
with?* Most of the violence, obviously, was illegal, though much of it
was provoked by acts which were themselves flagrantly violent and
illegal. But the question of legality or illegality seldom arose. In only
2 out of every 10 violent plays was due process of law—arrest or trial—
shown or implied as a consequence of major acts of violence.

When official agents of the law became embroiled in violent
episodes, they themselves contributed to the violence two-thirds of
the time. In 4 of 10 episodes they initiated it; in 3 of 10 they responded
violently to violent provocation; in 2 of 10 they suffered violence and
were unable to respond; and in 1 of 10 instances they responded to
violence in a nonviolent manner. The report's conclusion: "Police
restraint in the face of violence was rare."

What, then, does it all add up to? It seems to add up to the fact
that for the period of this survey, at least, violence had become a conventional, accepted part of almost all of television's dramatic presentations. Again, this was a quantitative study, and the effect of all this
television violence on viewers cannot easily be separated from the
effect of violence in other media—newspapers, magazines, books,
movies, and so forth—upon those same viewers.

On television, violence is, on the whole, presented as a customary
method for dealing with a problem.

How this is affecting viewers of all ages who are exposed to it—
that's a question this study did not seek to answer and does not attempt to answer. Presumably the Commission on Violence will come
to grips with this frightfully complex issue, now that it has a clearer
picture of the violent content of television.

Testifying before the commission last fall, Dean George Gerbner
said: "The study of this content is like the study of the climate or of
the tides in the ocean. It will not tell you what you and I will do or
where you and I will go, but it will tell you which way the cultural
wind blows or the cultural tide flows. It will tell you what all of us
are exposed to and, therefore, what enters in one way or another into
all that we do."

370   We have not yet learned how to control our weather, but we can do something about those cultural winds and cultural tides. We can change their course if we, as a Nation, choose to do so.

Television Violence is Harmful

By Senator Claiborne Pell

FEBRUARY 1, 1969

A few months ago *Rowan and Martin's Laugh-In* awarded its 1968 Emmy Award to a distinguished series, "Finger Painting and How I Licked It." This might be read as a commentary on the current efforts of a number of people, myself included, to find an effective and fair means of assessing and reducing the incidence of violence in television.

The controversy is one in which there has been generated, deliberately one would even guess, too much heat and too little light. The broadcasting industry, well financed, is able to leap into the fray, waving the banners of Constitutional freedoms. In the absence of rational discussion these banners play upon our legitimate concern that our government shall not become the arbiter of taste or content in any of the communications media. Here let me make it clear that my position in this article is concerned only with the quality of day-to-day "entertainment" programming on TV, and not in any way with legitimate news coverage.

As a member of the Drafting Committee of the Democratic Platform Committee in Chicago, I introduced, and the Committee adopted, a statement condemning violence in television. It called on the FCC to exercise its licensing powers as a means of controlling such content if the industry failed to do so. Needless to say, the broadcasting industry sped into action, and the proposed plank was considerably diluted en route to the floor of the convention. I am pleased, however, that the platform did at least express mild concern and I am confident that the small flurries of activity in this area will soon grow into a careful and reasonable balancing of private freedoms and the public interest.

Whether or not the FCC is entitled or should be entitled, to review program content, the fact remains that the air waves are public property and should be viewed as a public trust. I would prefer that the industry itself undertake to serve as fiduciaries of that trust, and

371

372 perhaps the mere threat of government action will push it in that direction.

I do not favor any limitation of our Constitutional rights to freedom of speech; neither do I favor the right of any industry to sell tainted food or dangerous drugs free of regulation, nor the right of the television industry to breed violence in our society if indeed it does.

The basic question of course is just that: what is the effect of violence in the mass media . . . and why should we concern ourselves with television particularly when our daily papers, not to mention comic books, and even fairy tales, are full of all kinds of mayhem? If violence in television is a factor in breeding violence in our society, what is the responsibility of the industry in exercising the vast power of that medium? And what is the responsibility of the government to protect its citizenry from the industry's pursuit of profit by frequent appeals to the lowest spectrum of public taste?

It is my understanding that the principal argument of the television industry against regulation, or at least its publicly stated argument, is that there is no proven connection between violence in television and violence in our society. In terms of scientific proof that is true. But we are not dealing with chemical equations or physical properties; we are dealing with the minds of people, particularly of the young, something that we know relatively little about.

I believe we can say that there are always a certain number of psychotic or potentially psychotic persons in our society, who may well be influenced by constant exposure to violence which has the kind of immediacy of impact that violence in television has and which newspaper articles or other media do not.

More important, it seems to me that the television industry has itself answered the question affirmatively. Its financial foundation rests entirely upon the principle that television does influence the minds and actions of people. Fortunes have been spent to prove the proposition that advertising campaigns can induce people to buy products. And are these products sold by a straight message that says buy this? Certainly not. Cigarettes are sold because a virile young man is cruising on a yacht with a beautiful girl . . . The examples are endless.

If this is meaningless, if television advertising does not induce people to do things, then should we not happily dispense with advertising, end the shrill demands upon our attention and presumably reduce the cost of the products it sells? Unthinkable? Perhaps. But, if unthinkable, the industry is then left with the untenable position that its advertising time can motivate people but its programming times does not.

A second argument of the industry is that television should not be singled out as distinct from films or books or newspapers or other forms of communications. One answer, in my opinion, is that television is both quantitatively and qualitatively different. As to quantity, it is an appalling statistic that, if we project the present rate of school attendance and television watching, we find that by the time a child of 2 is 18, he will have watched more than 17,000 hours of television, or better than 60 percent more time than he has spent in the classroom.

Several months ago, after the death of Senator Robert Kennedy, the *Christian Science Monitor* undertook a survey of television programming. *The New York Times* report of that survey was headed, "84 Killings Shown in 85½ TV hours on the 3 Networks." The survey recorded no fewer than 372 acts of violence or threats of violence, including 162 on Saturday morning, when the audience included a great many children. The early-evening survey showed a murder or a killing every 31 minutes. TV presents not only the fact of violence in our society (and violence is a fact which I do not expect television to ignore in favor of finger painting) but an endless, repetitive quantity of fictional violence.

And what do the largely white-oriented programs, the depiction of violence in a white society, do to the children in the black ghettos? What do they see but a world of the white man in which these things are acceptable, and even desirable?

These are great and troublesome questions in a troublesome time. They are not questions to be facilely answered or submitted to the final judgment of the balance sheets. I suggest that neither we the audience nor the executives of the television industry have faced up to the fact that the power of television is such that it cannot evade greater responsibilities, nor hide behind the pressures of advertisers. We no longer apply the doctrine of *caveat emptor*—let the buyer beware—to the hapless purchaser of what may turn out to be tainted goods. Should television be permitted to slough off its responsibilities by saying in effect, *caveat spectator*—let the watcher beware?

Qualitatively, too, the impact of television is different. It is more immediate, more real, than the written word. If a picture is worth a thousand words, how much more is that picture worth when it is live and constant?

In short, logic suggests that there must be some connection between violence in television and violence in society. We can and

374 should encourage greater research efforts to define that connection more exactly. Such research is now being financed by the British Independent Television Authority through a university-based research center. And in Great Britain, as elsewhere in Western Europe, the problem has been thought sufficiently serious to impose standards governing scenes of violence and the use of dangerous weapons.

Even if the effects of violence in television are not precisely measurable, what price are we to pay in the senseless assassination of great leaders by faceless men; what price are we to pay in the annual slaughter of people in this country by guns on a scale unknown anywhere in the civilized world? Certainly, television is not the only villain, and its regulation not the only cure. But anyone who suggests that the greatest medium of human communication now in our possession has no power to influence the minds and actions of people is either dangerously obtuse or deliberately evasive.

Pending more extensive research, what can reasonably be done without invoking the specter of censorship and government control? It seems to me that all of our experience with government regulation of industry would suggest that there is a reasonable distinction between regulation and control, just as there is a reasonable distinction between liberty and license.

A first reasonable step would be a proper overhaul and enforcement of the present Code of the National Association of Broadcasters. The Code deals with the depiction of violence, and all the major networks subscribe to it. But the Code's enforcement machinery operates only after the fact—after a program has been aired and a complaint received.

One official of the Code-enforcement office, when asked, could recall no specific instance in which sanctions were applied. This is not surprising, since it is commonly known that the present Code is more honored in the breach than in the observance, at least as far as violence is concerned. The self-regulation of the industry in the realm of "blue" material is more extensive—which only proves it can be done.

In Great Britain the television industry undertakes, itself, to scrutinize all programs at all stages of production before air time in accordance with a set of very specific standards of acceptability. And there the rate of homicide per 100,000 of population is .7 percent compared to our rate of 6.1 percent—more than eight times as great.

The British Independent Television Authority, in its broadcast standards, states that "great care should always be taken in the presentation of scenes . . . in which easily acquired and dangerous weap-

ons are used. It is a simple fact that guns and swords are not easily   375
come by, while knives, bottles, bars and bricks are. It is not good that
children with a tendency to violence see them in frequent use."

Unfortunately, in our country guns are also easily come by and
should not be seen in frequent use.

And in Sweden, which is famous for its graphic portrayal of sex
scenes in films, all films and all television programs are subject to
review and approval of any scenes containing violence. In this country
we seem a good deal more worried about our children's exposure to
sex than we are about the possibility that they might shoot someone
or be shot.

I would be the first to concede that when we venture into the
realm of ideas we are on more dangerous grounds than in the regulation of the securities industry, for example, or of food and drug content. To suggest that the quality or content of any communication
should be judged by the safe and cautious standard of bureaucrats is
not a solution which should appeal to any serious person—even
though it is arguable that the level of taste determined by the advertisers is lower still.

It is not, however, necessary to confuse unwanted and undesirable censorship of program content with establishment or reasonable
standards of acceptability which should govern the use of a public
trust, the air waves. I see no reason why adequately precise, determin-
able and fair standards cannot be worked out within the industry,
with a nudge from the public and the government, or why those standards, if they are thereafter abused by any licensee, should not carry
with them a penalty adequate to ensure that they will, in fact, be
observed.

The TV industry might well heed the history of government
regulation of abuses, which indicates that the one sure way to bring
about regulation is for the industry to take no reasonable measures
when they are needed. And one sure way to prevent such reasonable
measures is for the television industry to let loose a thundering herd
of irrelevant sacred cows in defense of its territory and at the expense
of the public, whose heritage it is.

Television Violence Is Not Harmful

By Martin Maloney

JANUARY 25, 1969

Some months ago, while drifting and dreaming through the evening hours with Johnny Carson, I collided squashily with what I can only describe as the New American Morality. The Carson show that evening was the standard product and included the customary mildly vulgar jokes, interspersed with jocular references to Miss Priscilla Goodbody, a mythical NBC censor. Then Peter Lawford sidled into view, and within seconds Miss Goodbody had ceased to be a figure of fun and was suddenly transformed into a real and hostile deity, something on the order of Moloch or Baal of the Phoenicians. The reason was simple. Miss Goodbody, formerly in charge of Sex and Scatology, had now apparently become responsible for the elimination of violence on NBC.

Mr. Lawford, it appeared, had a movie to plug—a comic opus called *Salt and Papper.* And yes, he did just happen to have some films clips along with him. At this moment, and quite unexpectedly, came—as they say in the trade—the weenie.

Carson's mobile face abruptly took on a look of preternatural solemnity, causing him to look rather like Sergeant Joe Friday confronting a child molester. Was it true, he asked Lawford, that NBC had refused to show two of the clips because they were deemed excessively violent? Mr. Lawford nodded humbly and allowed that NBC had; fortunately, however, one scene from the film had been certified as chemically pure and was even now in the projector.

So, having paid appropriate tribute to the New Morality and at the same time provided the film with an invaluable plug ("At Your Local Theater! The Movie NBC Didn't DARE to Show!!"), they rolled the clip.

I had two reactions to this episode. First, that Miss Goodbody has not yet really learned her trade. The film clip showed two (newly) obscene objects, a p-st-l and a d-gg-r, the latter of which was used in

376

an unsuccessful effort to stab a British cop. Second, that I really don't like Miss Goodbody in her new role any better than I liked her earlier manifestation, when she was professionally dirty-minded.

In a general way, I find myself more and more exasperated at the current great crusade against violence, much of which seems to be directed against television. I feel this way because the crusade, as it bears on television, seems to me (a) frequently hypocritical, (b) generally ridiculous and (c) almost totally pointless.

The tragic deaths of Dr. Martin Luther King and Senator Robert Kennedy were, of course, elaborately covered by the press, television and radio. When the verbiage which resulted produced, *inter alia,* a hypothesis that the United States is a sick society, the commentators at once accepted their own hypothesis, without much evidence, as incontrovertible fact, and began to set an example of preliminary penitential breast-beating. Historically, American middle-class audiences have always reveled in such charges leveled against them and their country, and have usually enriched and made heroes of their authors, from Charles Dickens through Philip Wylie to Paul Goodman. The new indictment was thus assured of success.

President Johnson, employing a standard politician's stratagem designed to simulate vigorous action without actually disturbing anything, appointed a commission to study the nature and causes of violence in American life, the agenda of which were to include an assessment of violence in the mass media. Possibly the President was not aware that violence as a psychological, social and historical phenomenon had already been exhaustively investigated, and that the distilled results of this effort were on tap at the Library of Congress. He must have been told, however, that the Report of the Kerner Commission on urban problems, then recently issued and largely ignored by officialdom, had had a good deal to say on the subject. In spite of these considerations, the new commission was appointed and no doubt, within a year or so, will tell us how violent we are, and why. I can hardly wait.

Early in July a group of some 50 congressmen penetrated, with their usual acuteness, to the heart of the matter and asked the Federal Communications Commission to conduct a 30-month study of the social impact of TV violence. Chairman Rosel Hyde replied that if Congress would furnish the funds, the FCC would do the study.

Meanwhile, the broadcasters responded to the crisis promptly and confusingly. Following the appointment of the Presidential commission, TV executives appeared in smartly tailored sackcloth to confess and repent, belled by Dr. Frank Stanton of CBS. Dr. Stan-

378 ton's statement, though pious, was a little ambivalent; he said that while CBS would of course do nothing to compromise the artistic integrity of its producers and writers, the network would take immediate steps to eliminate the gratuitous violence which presumably had heretofore adorned its offerings. CBS was followed in this announced policy by NBC and ABC.

Soon the reports from the dream factory, West Coast branch, began to flow in. Haggard and ulcer-ridden producers, writers and directors, particularly of Westerns and cop-and-robbers yarns, were reported as striving manfully to suggest that the battery, mayhem and slaughter so essential to melodrama were indeed taking place—but just off camera. Whether they considered employing messengers and a chorus of elders to describe all this bloodshed, in the manner of ancient Greek tragedy, the reports do not specify. The reform wave swept farther, picking up some curious flotsam along the way. At NBC, the *Get Smart* series was to be purged of its notorious excesses. ABC reported the elimination of one episode of *The Flying Nun* and— weirdest of all—the cancellation of an episode of *The Dating Game* because one of the participants had once been Mrs. Jacqueline Kennedy's [Onassis] cook.

Some penitents within the TV ranks were probably sincere enough, though one might question their judgment a little. William Bell, author of the soapy *Days of Our Lives,* took a page in *Variety* to explain that drama without violence is "invariably finer drama."[33] (Shakespeare, Marlowe and Euripides would have been astonished at this statement; but then, they didn't know about soap opera, which is the only known dramatic form in which characters talk each other to death.)

. . . .

What fascinates me in all this tohubohu about violence is the easy economy with which the crusade has moved from the "sick society" motif to a concentration on the mass media (the bacteria in the national system) and then on to television as the chief germ. John Wayne and his Green Berets are happily clobbering the Viet Cong in movie houses across the Nation. No newspaper publishers, no matter how assiduously his sheet may dish up and serve murder, rape and mayhem, has yet bared his breast and cried, *"Mea culpa!"* (One publisher did announce that he was discontinuing "Dick Tracy" and "Little Orphan Annie" because of the bloodshed they featured.) Indeed, to my knowledge, only one impresario of popular culture has come near equaling the TV people in nervousness: the proprietor of the Royal London Wax Museum, in Chicago, delayed the unveiling of some new images of Bonnie and Clyde until a gun could be removed from Clyde's waxen hand.

Why this obsessive notion that TV, of all possible institutions, must be the villain of the piece? The main reason, I suppose, is that television is enormously popular, and we retain enough of the old Puritan mentality to be deeply suspicious of anything so many people enjoy. If the hula hoop had somehow achieved the popular status of TV, and the average American in 1969 spent say, 11 hours weekly rotating a plastic ring around his middle, the phenomenon would undoubtedly attract hordes of psychiatrists, journalists and politicians in search of a cause.

To be sure, there is violence in television, as there is in newspapers, books, the theater or any other medium dealing largely in melodrama and farce. But for the purpose of conveying any real impression of violence, television is surely the poorest of all the media. The miniature pictures, gray on gray, are capable of transmitting only a highly abstract image of reality; and the color—when there is color—is bright and artificial and unreal, charming enough but suggesting a fantasy world in which nothing very serious could happen. And above all, television—the most "mass" of the mass media—is largely an assembly-line product, like canned tomatoes or processed cheese, and the assembly-line motto for an age of consumption is "milder, much milder." If television were highly flavored, to create powerful and memorable experiences, we wouldn't be able to watch so much of it. So it isn't.

I am worried about violence—the real violence in which blood flows and lives are destroyed. I am concerned when police officers club demonstrators, when armed soldiers actually fight snipers from building to building in American cities, when I get the daily body count from Vietnam. If anything is poisoning our lives and weakening our society, it is this reality—and not the fabrications of television writers and producers. I have been sickened by some few episodes on TV in recent years: by the sight of Jack Ruby pistoling Lee Harvey Oswald before the very faces of his gaping guards; by the spectacle of a South Vietnamese police official casually murdering a prisoner; by the stunned shock of the faces of Robert Kennedy's supporters as they realized the import of that off-stage gunfire; by the savage and horrifying spectacles provided by TV news during last summer's Democratic convention. As for the antics of Maxwell Smart and the Flying Nun, I can only say that if they imperil the Republic, then the Republic is past saving.

In the long run, I think that the crusade against violence on

380 television is not only ridiculous and pointless, it is also genuinely dangerous. It is a distraction. It is a crusade without risk, pain or hard decision; and if we join it, we may very well never find out where the social action really is.

Just for openers, I can tell you one place where the action is not. It's not on the Johnny Carson show.

Notes to Chapter 3

1. Section 3 of the Radio Act of 1927, Public Law 632, 69th Congress, February 23, 1927.

2. Section 307 of the Communications Act of 1934, Public Law 416, 73rd Congress, June 19, 1934 (Amended in December 1964). The Act, as well as most of the documents cited in the notes to this Chapter may be found in Frank J. Kahn, ed., *Documents of American Broadcasting*, New York: Appleton-Century-Crofts, 1968.

3. Fines are now limited to a maximum of $10,000. The FCC is presently attempting to substantially raise that maximum.

4. As indicated in the introduction to this Chapter, the courts have increasingly been supporting FCC actions and rulings and, in fact, have recently criticized the Commission for not being strict enough.

5. Only about 250 of these 1500 employees are in the Commission's Broadcast Bureau which oversees the broadcast industry.

6. Commonly referred to as the Blue Book, this policy statement was issued by the Commission on March 7, 1946. It has been largely superceded by the 1960 Programming Policy Statement, issued by the FCC on July 29, 1960.

7. The seven categories were (1) Entertainment, (2) Religion, (3) Agriculture, (4) Education, (5) News, (6) Discussion and (7) Talks. The form did, however, include blank spaces preceded by the numbers (8) and (9) and category (10) was Miscellaneous.

8. Section 303(i) of the Communications Act does, however, give the Commission authority to make special regulations to stations engaged in "chain broadcasting."

9. The order was the result of the promulgation by the Commission on May 2, 1941 of its Chain Broadcasting Regulations. These regulations, amended on October 11, 1941, were upheld by the Supreme Court in 1943 in the case of The National Broadcasting Co., Inc., et. al. *v.* United States et. al., 319 US 190.

10. In recent years, ABC Television network operations have lost millions of dollars. The losses, however, were more than offset by the large profits of ABC-owned and operated stations.

11. Loevinger, a contributor to this anthology (pp. 453-457), is no longer a Commissioner.

12. President Johnson restored "conservative" Hyde as Chairman, but appointed "regulator" Nicholas Johnson as the seventh Commissioner. An article by Commissioner Johnson appears in this section (pp. 322-329).

13. Recent efforts of the Anti-Trust Division of the Justice Department to restrict cross-media ownership have resulted in the FCC's beginning to consider ownership of a newspaper as a negative factor in assessing the qualifications of applicants for new licenses or renewals.

14. The Communications Satellite Act of 1962, Public Law 624, 87th Congress, 2nd Session, was passed on August 31, 1962. The creation of Comsat was authorized in Title III of the Act.

15. In the Matter of the Mayflower Broadcasting Corporation and The Yankee Network, Inc. (WAAB) 8 FCC 333,338, February 16, 1941.

16. This equality is not the same as equal time. Strict equal time applies only to *381* free broadcast time given to political candidates during a campaign (see pp. 488-497). The Fairness Doctrine calls for giving "reasonable opportunity" for opposing positions on controversial issues of public importance. It is under the Fairness Doctrine that the FCC has ruled that anti-cigarette commercials must be aired and that persons or groups attacked on the air must be notified and allowed free time to reply.

17. Congressman Harris was the Chairman of the Communications Subcommittee of the House Commerce Committee, which is charged with the task of overseeing FCC action and formulating broadcasting legislation.

18. The regulation is sufficiently confusing for the NAB to periodically send its members some questions and answers illustrating the latest FCC rulings on the Fairness Doctrine. These questions and answers are a separate part of the Political Catechism discussed in note 13 on p. 558.

19. The RTNDA was largely responsible for taking the question of the constitutionality of the Doctrine to the Supreme Court. See Nicholas Johnson's article on pp. 322-329.

20. *National Review*, November 5, 1963.

21. In re Pacifica Foundation, 36 FCC 147, January 22, 1964.

22. *Broadcasting*, February 10, 1969.

23. John Kenneth Galbraith, *The New Industrial State*, Boston: Houghton Mifflin, 1967.

24. Stan Opotowsky, *TV-The Big Picture*, New York: Dutton & Co., 1961.

25. Fred Friendly, *Due To Circumstances Beyond Our Control*, New York: Random House, 1967.

26. Ralph Nader, *Unsafe at Any Speed: The Designed In Dangers of the American Automobile*, New York: Grossman, 1965.

27. Bryce Rucker, *The First Freedom*, Carbondale: Southern Illinois University Press, 1968. p. 106.

28. In October 1969, three months after this article was published, the Federal Food and Drug Administration banned the selling of products containing cyclamates.

29. In a letter to the editor published in TV GUIDE, July 19, 1969, Mr. Sevareid wrote: "In his July 5 article, 'The Silent Screen,' FCC Commissioner Nicholas Johnson writes: 'Eric Sevareid has said of the pressures involved in putting together a network news show, "The Ultimate sensation is that of being bitten to death by ducks."' He has not only taken this out of context but has placed it in a context of his own imagining. The line related to the endless little practical problems, such as timing, lights, makeup, prompters, cues, etc. It had nothing to do with any form of censorship—self-censorship, company censorship or sponsor censorship. For nearly six years I have been doing almost nightly broadcasts which involve opinion on the CBS Evening News. Not once have I been even faintly aware of any censorious pressures from any sponsor. Only once has a TV script of mine been kept off the air by reason of its contents; that was done several years ago and by an executive no longer with CBS News."

30. Copyright Immediate Music Inc. 1965. Written by Mick Jagger and Keith Richards. Used by permission. All rights reserved International Copyright.

31. Red Lion Broadcasting Co., Inc., et. al. v. Federal Communications Commission, et. al. United States, et. al. v. Radio Television News Directors Assn., et. al. United States Supreme Court, June 9, 1969, Nos. 2 and 717, October Term, 1968.

32. The Code Review Board, consisting of nine code subscribers (including the networks) appointed by the President of the NAB, considers appeals of the Code Authority Director and may prefer formal charges leading to suspension or revocation of a code member's seal. If the Review Board decides to prefer charges, a hearing is held before the NAB's Television Board of Directors, a fifteen-man body which includes representatives of each of the three networks. Since subscribing to the code is voluntary and more than one-third of the nation's stations are not subscribers, it is rare for a station to have its code seal suspended or revoked.

33. There is considerable disagreement among writers and producers as to the merits of the latest crusade against violence on television. Some, like producer-writer Christopher Knopf, one-time President of the Writers Guild, support Bell's stand and the present efforts to eliminate most of the violence from television. Others, like producer-writer Roy Huggins (*Run For Your Life, The Name of the Game*) are concerned about the networks' timidity in the face of sponsor and Congressional pressures and their decision to avoid certain important subjects and artistic or socially relevant treatments because of the anti-violence crusade.

AUDIENCE

Chapter 4

Ratings

The networks' great concern with ratings, which was discussed earlier (see, for example, Richard Doan, pp. 122-126), was illustrated at the end of the 1968-69 season. In May 1969, CBS and NBC issued conflicting opinions on the results of that season's prime-time "ratings war." NBC claimed a tie; CBS claimed that NBC improperly counted premier week in September while both ABC and CBS were still airing re-runs. So, CBS argued, it won the war with a ratings average of 20.3 to NBC's 20.0. *Mission Impossible* provides an example of the importance of ratings to a program; the asking price for a minute of advertising time on that program (before two of its stars left the show) jumped from $45,000 in 1968-69 to $65,000 in 1969-70, primarily because of the high ratings the show had received.

The nature, methodology, accuracy, and weaknesses of broadcast ratings as well as their use and misuse were of very little concern until 1963. Before that time, almost blind reliance was placed on ratings even though many were improperly conducted and were providing misleading and sometimes totally false information. The abuses in ratings were not publicized and were generally ignored when known because everyone connected with the ratings system seemed content. The networks were making large profits and the advertisers usually enjoyed increased sales. Although there was no substantial evidence that increased sales were the result of television advertising (see Martin Mayer, pp. 239-245), advertisers were quite willing to assume that TV was worth the expense and that ratings were providing sufficient information on which to base accurate decisions for purchasing programs. Agencies were satisfied with the ratings so long as the sponsors were happy.

A series of Congressional hearings, culminating in the Harris Committee Hearings of 1963 publicized the deficiencies of broadcast ratings for the first time. Testimony revealed that all sorts of abuses were prevalent and they affected all of the major radio and television ratings services. Methodologies—such as, meter, diary, personal interview, telephone coincidental, and telephone recall, mailed

386   questionnaire—were inefficiently and improperly implemented. There were mistakes and cheating on the part of field personnel; "fixing" of results to benefit and, hopefully, satisfy subscribers to the ratings service; faulty sampling procedures and calculation of results; inaccurate or incomplete information concerning (a) how the sample was drawn, (b) how closely the final sample compared with the original statistically ideal designed sample, (c) the degree of cooperation from the respondents in the final sample, (d) the length of time the sample was used before it was changed, and (e) the statistical limitations of the data, including sampling error. The Hearings revealed a tremendous variety of additional "oversights" and "slipups" by the ratings services, many of which partially or completely invalidated their survey results.

Although the methodologies used by the ratings services are by their very nature somewhat imperfect, the ratings have been improved considerably since 1963. Recognizing that a lack of confidence in ratings could lead to chaotic conditions within the industry and invite more extensive government investigations and, perhaps, greater governmental supervision and control, the major trade associations within the industry formed the Broadcast Rating Council. The Council has developed minimum standards of performance for ratings organizations, and gives its seal of approval for adherence to these standards. Ratings reports now include information regarding sample design and composition, sampling error and methodology used in obtaining results. In addition, television advertisers and their agencies have become more demanding and sophisticated in their use of ratings because of increased competition from other media and the spiraling costs of television.

However, confusion and major deficiencies still exist, and, as Richard Doan suggests in the following article, may never be completely eliminated. Competition between ratings services still results in conflicting claims by the competitors. Charges and countercharges regarding which service and which methodology provides the most accurate information tend to make all rating data suspect. The emphasis is still on quantitative rather than qualitative data. The compiling of immediate viewing information rather than the investigation of long-range viewing trends still receives the almost exclusive attention of the services and their customers. The basic question of what exactly is being measured remains unanswered. Finally, as Doan and A. J. Nielsen indicate here, the ratings services themselves acknowledge areas of improvement and maintain that more accurate and useful information could be obtained if the necessary funds were forthcoming.

In the first part of his article (pp. 388-393), Doan suggests the difficulties of obtaining accurate ratings. He summarizes the advantages and some of the major criticisms of the Nielsen meter method and, at the same time describes weaknesses in other ratings methodologies. Doan points out that there are a number of different types of statistics provided; an example is the "share-of-audience," that is, the show's attractiveness as a percentage of television homes watching television at a given time. This figure is becoming increasingly more important than the traditional ratings figure. Doan emphasizes the importance of scheduling to the success of a show and the size of its ratings.

Doan devotes the second part of his article (pp. 393-397) to a discussion of the more sophisticated methods of audience measurement which may someday become the primary concern of broadcasters. "People data," that is information regarding who watches which programs and the viewer's reactions, can result in better balanced programming and more efficiency for sponsors who will be able to aim for a special audience. However, there are some obstacles to the compilation of people data which will be difficult, if not impossible, to overcome. In the meantime, many of the conclusions regarding the audience's identity, behavior, and trends are based on educated guesswork.

A. C. Nielsen, Jr. (pp. 398-402) defends broadcast ratings, more particularly the Nielsen ratings. Ratings are the scapegoat of television according to Nielsen. He contends that ratings are objective, impartial estimates of which programs are viewed; they are not intended to be a critical measure of a program's intrinsic merit. He describes the Nielsen methodology and comments on the degree of accuracy the Nielsen ratings achieve, which, he feels, is sufficient for the customer's purpose and his willingness to pay. Nielsen reiterates Frank Stanton's statement that rating television programs is the democratic way of counting votes and giving the public what it wants.

Dick Hobson (pp. 403-408) indicates the increasing importance of demographics to sponsors wishing to reach a particular segment of the total audience. Hobson lists the top ten viewing preferences for a six-week period in 1967 by geographical region, income, educational level, occupation, age, and sex. He points out that the term "Top 10" can have several different meanings and includes some examples of how the different breakdowns provide useful information about the audience for specific programs and program types.

The Ratings, How Can They Be True?

By Richard K. Doan

MARCH 11 AND 18, 1967

One thing everybody—even A. C. Nielsen, the supreme TV-audience estimator—will admit: Ratings aren't exactly accurate. At best they're only somewhere near the truth. The eternal, never totally answered question is, how near?

Apart from that, ratings also are not what most people presume them to be—a measure of the intrinsic popularity of programs. Ratings are basically a reflection of audience preference for one telecast over others on the air at the same time. Hit shows are a product in part of advantageous scheduling, and flops of improper timing. Thus the well-advertised Top 10 is inherently a fallacious compilation!

The oversimplified definition of a rating is that it is a nose count, a 20 rating for a show in Nielsen's book is supposed to indicate that 20 percent of the TV homes tuned it in. Right there is the first "yes, but." Nielsen reports only homes tuned—not even homes watching—because his "audimeters" attached to sets record only that the set is on or off, and which channel it is tuned to. Nothing about who, if indeed anybody, is watching.

The next source of flaw is that, of necessity, neither Nielsen's nor anybody else's survey polls the whole audience. It isn't possible. The compromise is sampling—in Nielsen's case about 1200 homes whose TV preferences are supposed to be typical of about 55 [59] million others.

That's the part that galls many people outside TV, and even a few inside. How, they demand, can one family correctly represent what some 50,000 look at? The answer is that expert statisticians agree that a 1200 sample is enough if—and it's a whopping if—the sample is a correctly drawn scale model of the population. In fact, three experts evaluating TV ratings for Congress [Harris Committee Hearings] several years ago were willing to defend an ideally selected sample of only 400 homes as the basis for a national poll!

Nielsen officials feel the sampling theory is gaining general *389* acceptance. They say they get little mail these days quibbling over it. To those who still harbor reservations, A. C. Nielsen Jr., president of the firm founded by his father, is inclined to quip: "If you don't believe in sampling, be sure—the next time you have a blood test— to get yourself pumped dry . . . make them take it all!"

Next question: So sampling's all right, but how good a cross section is Nielsen getting? His statisticians insist they are pretty happy with the quality of it. So do network researchers, although they'll privately concede Nielsen didn't keep his panel in tune with U.S. Census trends until they insisted upon his overhauling it drastically a couple of years ago.[1]

The Broadcast Rating Council, an industry group set up at the behest of Congress to "accredit" and police TV-and-radio ratings services, also seems generally satisfied with Nielsen's current sample. As proof that they must be doing something right, the Nielsen people love to point out that 28 in every 100 car owners drive Chevrolets and two percent drive Cadillacs—exactly, as it happens, the proportions found among today's Nielsen families.

Nobody reasonably denies that TV needs some measure of the audience it reaches. As an advertising vehicle if nothing else, it must try to tell sponsors how much exposure their advertising messages are getting. Ratings correspond to print media's circulation figures. The similarity ends there. Ratings, in case it needs saying—and apparently it does, repeatedly—are not to be confused with opinion polls. Nielsen "counts the house," not how "good" or how "bad" a show is.

People are often surprised that ratings of competing services disagree. If they differ, it's because they have measured different people at different times under differing circumstances with differing methods of interrogation. All that competing surveys can be expected to do is show some logical correlation. These are the basics of ratings life.

Horrendous stories have been told of ratings being influenced by homes leaving a set on for 24 hours at a stretch with nobody watching, or turned on to "amuse" a pet dog, or to keep the family cat warm. These tales, true or not, are inconsequential. As Nielsen correctly points out, Rex Sparger, a one-time Congressional investigator who tried to rig the ratings of several network shows early in 1966 to get material for a book, would have somehow had to discover the identities of scores of families from Coast to Coast and have induced them to watch or not watch certain programs in order to seriously deflect the ratings of individual shows, even on a one-time basis. "The case

390 proved," said a relieved Nielsen official, "That nobody can conspire in any meaningful way to rig the ratings."[2]

On the other hand, in settling for Nielsen's mechanical devices as a preferred method because they eliminated human guesswork about set usage, the industry settled for half a loaf. The other half is knowing whether anybody really is watching, and how closely.

Nielsen has tried to bridge this gap by resorting to one of his chief competitor's [American Research Bureau or ARB] tools, the viewer diary, to find out the "composition of the audience" (that is, the number, age, sex, education, income, and so forth, of those watching). Nielsen's demographics have a technical weakness: In order not to overbother his metered families he gets a separate set of homes to keep diaries, then assumes that the same composition of audience exists in the metered homes.

Nielsenites point to "amazingly consistent" corroboration by the diaries of prime-time viewing patterns recorded by the meters. In the next breath the Nielsen people will attack the diary as an inefficient device. It "understates" the daytime audience, they claim, because housewives don't want to put down how much daytime watching they're addicted to, and at night the Old Man fails to write down how late he really stayed up. "We'll never know the whole truth," Gail Metzger, Nielsen's glib young director of statistical research, supposes, "until the day comes when we can strap an Audimeter on people's eyeballs. Until then we've just to thank God we've at least got those meters on sets."

Nielsen's industry defenders are full of theories, which they'll expound at the drop of a doubt, about why all systems of audience sampling other than meters find less viewing than Nielsen's machines report. They argue that the diary and the "coincidental" phone call ("Are you watching TV right now?"), [used by Trendex and Hooper] . . . fail to discover all the viewing really being done, especially on second and third sets outside the living room. Door-to-door interviewing [used by Pulse] is similarly faulted on grounds that many people at home and watching TV won't answer the door, especially at night, and thus are counted as not at home and not watching. The door-knockers, it's true, typically get no response at a third of the homes, while phone callers get no answers to nearly 20 percent of their calls.

Suppose it's right that ARB and Trendex and other surveys are to some extent shortchanging the TV audience count—is it possible Nielsen is "overstating" it?

Jay Eliasberg, CBS research boss and hottest denouncer of of Nielsen skeptics, concedes there is approximately 3 percent "overstatement" in Nielsen's evening ratings "because of cooperation bias." He regards this as insignificant. Some researchers less devout about Nielsen think the bias has to be much greater.[3] They snort derisively at a Nielsen claim that field workers are getting the meters into 75 to 80 percent of the homes they select. "Nobody ever gets better than 50 percent cooperation," the head of a big research firm insisted, "and I'd doubt Nielsen gets more than 10 percent of the homes he goes after." Some other researchers echo this sentiment.

Dr. Peter Langhoff, president of ARB, refused to be drawn into public criticism of Nielsen's survey except to say that "any technique is imperfect. . . . If there are imperfections," he added, "the great fault is the failure of the public to cooperate properly." He thought people should "consider it an obligation like jury duty" to respond conscientiously to polls.

The awesome complexities of efficient sampling were illustrated in the findings of an industry-financed study[4] (cost: $100,000) of the differences in viewing habits of people who participate in surveys and those who decline to take part. Cooperators were found to watch "significantly more" than non-cooperators, even 20 percent more in the case of certain programs, suggesting that all surveys are inevitably somewhat inflated.

It is in the use of ratings that the tricks of the ratings game reach a fine art little appreciated by the general public. To begin with, there are specially compiled ratings to meet specific competitive needs. Such a one is Nielsen's 30-market weekly report. Since it polls only major cities where the three networks all have outlets, ABC is inclined to tout these ratings in preference to Nielsen's national figures, in which CBS and NBC are strongest because they have more stations than ABC in small cities and rural areas. A case in point: In the national Nielsens late last winter CBS's *Andy Griffith Show* led ABC's competing *Felony Squad*, 26.0 to 18.8. But in the 30-city survey, *Felony Squad* outrated Andy, 21.2 to 20.2.

A gauge used by the networks almost more than ratings is share-of-audience, the percentage a show pulls of the audience watching at the time it is on. A weekly program is expected to muster a 30-share for a passing grade. If its share falls below 25, the series is in danger. In short, if a program can't lure about a third of the available watchers, it is apt to be tabbed as unequal to network competition. Public affairs programs, like CBS's Tuesday night news hour, are not subject to this rule of thumb. It is recognized that such programs cannot be expected to attract as great numbers as entertainment shows.

Scheduling is at least half the battle in the ratings war. Michael

392   Dann, CBS senior vice president of programming, has said, "Hits are
not the function of programming." He was oversimplifying. What he
meant was that a program's time slot can be as great a success factor
as its inherent appeal. It is common talk that ABC's *The Fugitive*
owed its long-running success in part to the fact that it faced weak
competition from the CBS news hour. *Bonanza, The Dick Van Dyke
Show,* and *The Man from U.N.C.L.E.* are among notable cases of series
which did not soar to ratings glory until they were shifted from their
original time slots.[5]

Jim Aubrey, the CBS czar who drove that network's ratings to
dizzy heights before he fell from grace, attributed his feat in great
part to his knack for scheduling. He was a whiz at calculating "audience flow" and "cradling" new entries between established hits.

The deceptiveness of ratings as a true barometer of program value
was perhaps never more dramatically illustrated than on the night
when CBS ran a Grade-B, a-go-go beach-party movie called *Gidget
Goes Hawaiian.* It captured the biggest rating any prime-time feature
had ever achieved with the exception of *The Wizard of Oz* (*Bridge
on the River Kwai* [and *The Birds*] subsequently topped it).[6] Many
people were at first puzzled, but the reason for the phenomenon soon
became evident: The alternatives were a nondescript ABC semi-
documentary and an NBC special on the British elections. Most
viewers, habitually seeking escape fare, chose *Gidget*, puerile as it
might be.

Ratings are shaded by still other facts, such as how many stations
"clear" a network program at its scheduled time. Local outlets often
blackout network shows, or delay them until off hours (afternoon or
late-night), in order to run locally originated movies or syndicated
series. Mort Werner, NBC program boss, recently contended that
The Monkees would be a Top 10 hit if more NBC affiliates carried it.

The networks analyze ratings information 60 ways, constantly.
There is a method in this confusing madness. It supplies them with
contrived alibis for programming defeats as well as contrived grounds
for claims of superiority.

Thus, this season NBC has been able repeatedly to preen itself
as "No. 1 network" on a basis of average evening ratings, while CBS
has been able to point with pride to domination of the Top 10—below
Bonanza, that is. It is common competitive practice to tote up "half-
hour wins" and who's ahead on a per-night basis as added fodder for
the claims mill. Let no one imagine that ratings are not the spice of
network life. One cynic in the research business went so far the
other day as to describe the pursuit of ratings as TV's "search for the
holy grail."

Another highly sophisticated researcher confided, "The way to 393 win any game, you know, is to make your own rules. The networks, in setting up business with Nielsen, made up rules TV could win by." He added that he would have his hearer's hide if this observation were ever attributed to him. There are forces at work, though, that could change the rules. Some of Nielsen's best friends at the networks are privately predicting that his "homes ratings" will be a thing of the past in less than five years.

Broadcasters have to concede that their Prime Source does not have all the answers. Even assuming Nielsen's simple count of Homes Using TV is accurate enough "for the purposes for which intended," as TV researchers so often put it, it leaves a lot to be told. Exactly who is "using" the TV in these homes? And what do they think of what they see?

Nielsen explores the "who" part periodically by getting a separate batch of homes to keep viewing logs (diaries) showing which members of the family looked at what. Socioeconomic data (income, education, and so forth) also are extracted. The statisticians call this "people" data—in contrast, in the case of Nielsen ratings, to homes data. There is a growing conviction in TV and Madison Avenue circles that the medium must have, and indeed is destined soon to get, a new set of audience measurements "rating" programming in such definitive terms.

Those who dream of a better numbers game than the one they now live by are convinced it is the means to more diversity and quality in TV. "People ratings," they believe, would define the audience appeal of each show and describe the kind and number of viewers grabbed by it. Since everybody must be susceptible to some kind of TV, they argue, and since there are sponsors eager to reach every kind of audience, such a better-refined ratings system would salvage TV from subservience to the lowest common denominator and usher in a dreamed-of-millennium of truly well-balanced programming.

That happy day, it's admitted, will not arrive without a struggle. Extracting detailed vital statistics from vast numbers of people on a week-in, week-out basis is terribly expensive. Inducing people honestly to describe themselves (how much money they make, and so forth) and to report what programs they not only like but will look at (versus what they think they should say they like) is difficult.

And selling programs to sponsors on the basis of appeal to only part of the audience—even if the part is the money-spending adults— would be a new way of life for everybody concerned. It has been far easier for TV to woo advertisers with big "boxcar" homes ratings. The

394 sponsors and their agencies have accepted the total-homes figure
because it made them feel good. It made the audience look so big.

What has been undermining this blissful state is a growing, gnaw-
ing feeling in advertiser and agency circles that there just could be
something to the loose talk all around about defections in the audience. The feeling is sensed that TV, for all its razzle-dazzle, is something of a [$2]-billion pig in a poke, glamorous as an advertising
vehicle, of undoubted potency, yet terribly expensive and surprisingly little defined as to its exact reach and effectiveness, considering
the vast fortunes pumped into it to sell goods. Off the record, the
worry in some quarters is that audience demographics could turn up
now-hidden realities that business would not care to live with. Like
too many kids watching.

Answers differing from Nielsen's are readily to be found in the
statistics of TvQ, a national opinion poll conducted by the Home
Testing Institute of Manhasset, N. Y. HTI asks people to rank programs according to what they like.[7] Lately, for example, *Bonanza* has
been the No. 1 choice in TvQ, as it is in Nielsen's Top 10; but there
the agreement between the surveys tends to end. In December, *I
Spy* ranked fifth with TvQ, 40th in Nielsen; *Mission: Impossible* was
seventh on the TvQ chart, 63rd on Nielsen's, and so on.

TvQ finds age-group preferences in TV fare widely disparate.
Last December, *Bewitched* and *I Dream of Jeannie* led the Top 10 of
kiddies 6 to 11; *The Monkees* and *I Spy* were the favorites of teen-
agers, while young adults most preferred the Saturday and Thursday
night movies, and adults over 50 went most for *Lawrence Welk* and
Bonanza—in that order!

Perhaps no more striking illustration could be found of how much
better public-affairs programming can do on a demographics basis
than TvQ's finding last winter that the *CBS News Hour* ranked as the
fourth most-favored series among adults! In Nielsen's homes ratings,
this series typically lands near the foot of the list. (Nielsen believers
will contend that this only proves again that people claim they "like"
certain programming, then don't watch it.)

ABC was able last fall, however, to call on Nielsen's own com-
position-of-audience breakdowns to show that *Stage 67*, which had
tough sledding in the homes ratings, was TV's top-ranked evening
attraction in terms of the proportions of its audience in professional
and white-collar homes and homes where the head of the family was
college-educated.

This is the sort of point the advocates of "people ratings" are
prone to make in arguing their virtues. Norton Garfinkle, whose New
York-based Brand Rating Index tells blue-chip advertisers and their

agencies what products the TV audience is buying, pushes specific buying habits of the audience as the answer to TV prayers for better programming.

"The whole public-interest debate," he says, "has been concerned with whether we should keep programs of a cultural nature on the air even though they don't produce big homes ratings. Now we seem to have a way out of this log jam because we can establish the fact that programs with cultural values also can have certain marketing values."

Some top-rank network ratings experts—ABC's Paul Donkin and NBC's Paul Klein, among them—agree with Garfinkle that "people ratings" will supplant the Nielsen homes numbers, maybe in less than five years.

Arthur C. Nielsen Sr., the 69-year-old founder and board chairman of the firm bearing his name, confesses that the word "ratings" probably was an "unfortunate choice" of name for the figures he compiles. It somehow connotes a stamp of quality, saying a show is good or bad, whereas all the rating is supposed to represent is an estimate of the number of homes tuned in. But Nielsen and his son, A. C. Jr., president of the company, presumably are assured that in any event theirs will go on being the name of the ratings game. They are now trying to sell their clients (the networks, sponsors, and agencies) on an "instantaneous" homes ratings service. The 1200 or-so homes with Nielsen "Audimeters" recording their viewing on film, which the house holders mail into Chicago every two weeks, would be wired directly into a central monitoring board to provide a daily record of the homes' TV watching.[8] Much as people in TV, being hooked on the ratings habit, would like Nielsen "dailies" over breakfast, there is some belief that this offer of overnight homes figures is too late to stem the tide of demographic desires.

As matters now stand, TV's statisticians, starved for data, subsist in part on sheer speculation. To countless questions about audience identity, behavior and trends, they can only hazard guesses. They call it "hypothesizing." It has to substitute for fact.

One of the networks' best hypothesizers, NBC research vice president Paul Klein, has some engaging theories. He is firmly convinced, for instance, that TV watching in upper-class homes rose last summer in part because of air-conditioning. "The poorer people have to get outdoors for a breath of air in hot weather, while the better-heeled ones can just sit there in their refrigerated digs, watching TV," he reasons. "I've told our people here that if they want the biggest audiences for quality programming, put it on in the summer!"

Klein believes also—and some others in TV share this view—

396   that the avowedly disenchanted TV viewer really is looking, but he is watching only movies, sports, Johnny Carson and other noncontinued types of fare, rather than weekly series, in the belief that he thereby isn't "getting hooked" on the medium. "It salves his guilt feelings," Klein suspects. "Probably if you offered him something called *The Upper-Class Beverly Hillbillies,* he'd condescend to watch it. Then he wouldn't feel so guilty."

Nielsen's meters lately have recorded a slight rise in total TV viewing—not in prime time, peculiarly enough, but in "fringe" periods such as weekends and late evenings. Neither Klein nor Nielsen nor anybody else knows precisely why. They think color TV is a growing lure and the presence of more second and third sets in homes is prompting added viewing. Sports, they guess, could be accounting for more weekend watching. Otherwise they're mystified.

Aside from the plague of such uncertainties where millions of dollars are involved, there is the deeply imbedded awareness, in high industry quarters, that the tyrannous Nielsen Numbers are virtually synonymous with corporate profits. TV is indisputably profit-oriented, "people's air" or not. The network able to claim No. 1 rank by virtue of even fractional domination of the savage evening-averages race cashes in, as NBC did this season, because Madison Avenue rides the ratings bandwagon.

In consequence the programmers are forever under pressure to deliver maximum ratings. The logical ultimate is to drive all programming toward types found to deliver the biggest numbers. It is not ludicrous to suggest that all of prime time would be a succession of *Bonanzas* if the public would sit still for it.

One of the effects of this frenzy is the frequent cancellation of shows that have millions of viewers rooting for them. The cheering is in vain except in rare instances, because a series, though highly popular with a vast minority audience, is a dud to the network if it is in the lower-rated brackets. This is one of the realities of TV life least understood outside.

There are conscientious people in TV's executive suites who are not enamored with this ruthless way of competitive life, who would welcome any devices they could live with that would enable them to shoot more often for programming quality without getting clobbered in the numbers race. Industry leaders like [former] ABC-TV president Thomas W. Moore have yearned publicly for some form of extra ratings points for TV culture or for exclusion of do-good programs from the numbers count. Unfortunately, nobody has come up with a workable panacea.

The Nielsenites say they're prepared to probe deeper into the
TV audience, but they have lost $17 million to date in this field (actu-
ally a minor part of the Nielsen market-research operation) and they
are not about to lose more. If TV wants more refined numbers, it's got
to pay for them. Privately, the Nielsen people suggest that the broadcasters have been pretty miserly in their research spending, considering TV's prosperity.

A troubling question is whether it is even possible to get totally
reliable audience data. Writer Martin Mayer, in an industry-financed
primer titled *The Intelligent Man's Guide to Broadcast Ratings*,
concluded that the "almost ideal" ratings service would be one employing "about 2000 well-trained, reasonably intelligent, highly
responsible ghosts." Ghosts, he suggested, are only beings who could
get into TV homes unnoticed and find out all about their inhabitants
and what they watch and like without arousing biases and influencing
their behavior. Anything short of this, Mayer thought, has got to be
a compromise.

And compromises produce doubts. Earlier this season Richard
Bluel, producer of *The Green Hornet*, told a Hollywood reporter he
had concocted a *Hornet* plot in which the hero kidnaped those 1200
Nielsen families, held them on a mountaintop, and finally ransomed
them off to the networks for $10 million. Bluel was burned up over
the *Hornet's* low ratings, and admitted: "I probably wouldn't be saying this if my show were doing better."

Until the day comes when those absolutely honest and omnipresent ghosts take over the ratings business and nobody ever again
can question the veracity of a TV rating, plots like Bluel's will strike
the fancies of countless people in and out of TV ranks. What can't be
proved is bound to be debated, especially by those who don't like
what is claimed.

Nielsen Defends His Rating Service

By Arthur C. Nielsen, Jr., with Theodore Berland

NOVEMBER 7, 1964

Did you ever watch someone start on a bowl of soup? He stirs the liquid, lifts the spoon to his lips, and sips. He has just tasted a sample and rated it; whether he adds salt or not depends on that random spoonful. You'll notice that he never denounces the spoon when there is too little salt. Not so in TV ratings—despite the fact that rating techniques employ some of the most advanced statistical methods known, and some of the most sophisticated electronics.

Ratings are today's TV scapegoat: Shows with low ratings blame the raters; those who think television quality can and should be elevated blame the raters; and some owners of magazines and newspapers which lose advertising revenue to television attack the raters. As the Nation's most listened-to rating, the Nielsen Television Index (NTI) often is the target of these attacks. After years of patience, I'd like to rise to its defense.

First, be sure you clearly separate "ratings" from "programming." While one may affect the other, they are not the same. Ratings are television's batting averages—they indicate how many people programs are hitting. They are not critical measures of any program's intrinsic merit. They observe, with objectivity and impartiality, the relative appeal of an given program by measuring how many households are tuned to it. Blaming the ratings when you don't like a popular program is like blaming the soup spoon.

Those who would castigate commercial television, incidentally, should remember that it is wholly supported by advertising revenues. Advertising can be effective only if it reaches people. That is why sponsors want programs that attract the largest audiences containing the kinds of people who might buy their products. Whether we like it or not, weighty cultural, educational or artistic shows seldom attract large audiences.

A show's rating is an estimate of how many families watch it.

398

Nielsen ratings estimate how many households have their TV sets   *399*
tuned to which network shows. We keep tab by connecting automatic
recorders (Audimeters) to a cross section of the Nation's TV sets.
These Audimeters are placed out of sight—in closets, basements,
and so forth—and by electronic "photographs" on film, record min-
ute-by-minute whether the sets are on or off, and to what channel they
are tuned. This record is kept 24 hours a day, week in and week out,
and the film records are mailed back to our production center twice
a month, when the sample home receives a fresh film magazine.

In Chicago, the film records are run through large data-processing
departments, where information is inspected for errors that could
mean broken equipment or power failures. Typically, information
from approximately 90 percent of the sample homes is included in
each report.[9] (The rest may be eliminated because of home power
failures, late mail-ins, and so forth.) Then the information is transferred to punched cards and matched against TV program schedules.
Finally, the information is fed into computers.

If there were Audimeters in every American home wired to a
giant central computer, we could know instantly how many American
households were tuned to what at any moment. Unfortunately, there
is no computer large enough to do this job—and even if there were,
it would cost too much to get the ratings by this method. More practical and far less expensive is the method we use which gathers information from a scientifically selected "sample" of homes.

How a sample of homes (we use about 1100 [1200]) can properly
reflect the actions and tastes of 52,600,000 [59,000,000] homes is
completely mysterious to many people. I know because this was a
topic we went into thoroughly with a Congressional committee in
1963. Yet sampling is a basic part of our lives. There's the man sipping
soup; the doctor diagnosing your illness after laboratory examination
of a few drops of blood; your gas-station attendant judging crankcase
dirt by the bit of oil on the dipstick.

. . . . .

Perhaps the best-known evidence that sampling is practical is
found in political polling, where a sample of voters is questioned.
Polls, however, face a much more difficult task because they are
measuring "opinions" and "future action," rather than precise matters such as whether a TV set is on or off, or how many packages of a
given brand have been sold in a particular store. Despite these difficulties, predictions of nationally known political poll-takers, in
recent years, always have been within a few percent of the actual
Presidential vote.

Unfortunately, there are no such figures as final election results

400 with which to check the accuracy of television ratings. But our television rating sample is selected by the same general principles as are
the retail store samples we use in the Nielsen Retail Index, by far the
largest division of our company. We very accurately measure the sales
of thousands of such products as soap, beverages, foods and drugs so
it is reasonable to assume that the TV ratings are similarly accurate.

We're all used to seeing such vital statistics as the U.S. cost-of-
living index or total unemployed. These statistics were all obtained
from samples. Like TV ratings they are estimates—and are not "precisely" accurate. It is impossible to know exactly what the "true"
cost of living is or the "exact" number of people who are unemployed.
Yet these Government estimates based upon samples are very useful
and are accurate enough for the intended use.

How accurate are the Nielsen television ratings? Let's take a
program with a rating of 30—perhaps one of your favorites, like *The
Beverly Hillbillies.* When our report says that the show has a rating
of 30 we mean that our best estimate is that 30 percent of all homes
with TV sets are tuned to the show. Now that's an estimate based on
our sample, of course. The truth could be higher or lower. Statistical
mathematics tell us that 19 times out of 20 such a rating obtained from
a perfect probability sample will be off by less than 3 points—here
between 27 and 33 percent.

The ratings could, of course, be made even more accurate by
using a larger sample. But to cut the error in half—say, from 3 points
on a 30 points to 1½ points—would mean not just doubling the sample size, but increasing it "fourfold." This in turn would make the
ratings cost nearly four times as much. While we would have no objection to increasing our prices 300 percent, we strongly doubt that
our customers would approve!

"Sampling errors" are inherent in ratings, cost-of-living figures
and other statistical estimates. There are also other types of errors.
But they are small and in all probability wouldn't change the rating
user's decision about a particular program.

For example, some people say that just because a TV set is on
does not mean anyone is watching it. This is true. All of us may leave
our sets on now and again when we aren't viewing. But we have made
thousands of phone calls to homes to find out how often this happens.
On the average only about one set in a hundred is on with no one
viewing it.[10] This can't affect significantly the accuracy of our rating.

Another criticism our ratings sometimes get from nonstatisticians
is that each Audimeter home represents approximately 50,000 homes.
Repeated often is the story of an Arkansas woman who disliked Jack

Paar's remarks about a situation in Mississippi and turned him off every time his face appeared. Because her set was metered, the story goes, she felt she had special power in getting him off the air.

First, such criticism ignores the fact that many other viewers may also have been offended by Paar. Second, while this woman statistically did stand for many other viewers, she did not specifically represent them. She was just one individual viewer in a sample of households containing over 3500 viewers. Since her action represented only one individual out of 3500 she could have very little effect on the rating, because the rating was based upon what the 3500 people did—not just one, or even a handful.

Separately, she represented no one. To understand this point, consider the picture on your TV screen. Look closely and you will see it is a series of lines—actually 525 in number. Looked at together, these lines form an image of what the camera sees; but any one line is by itself meaningless.

Unlike the line you might pick out on your TV screen, homes that have Audimeters are not selected haphazardly. They are part of the sample of the population systematically selected according to methods devised by top statisticians, both in and out of the Nielsen company, using data from the U.S. Housing Census.

Every housing unit in the country is assigned to a small census area, technically known as an enumeration district. A computer picks the houses to be used in our sample from these districts in such a way that every house in the country has an equal chance of being selected. The computer selects say, every 10th house on a street but does not supply the addresses. Hence, a special force of Nielsen men must go out and get the addresses of every house chosen. This is how the Nielsen "Master Sample" is developed—at a cost of more than $250,-000.

But, the job still is not complete. Our regular field men then travel to these computer-selected homes and ask to install our Audimeter. The families are paid for this cooperation.[11] Most households accept; alternates are selected for those who don't.

Thus the sample, in many ways, reflects the actions of the millions of viewers. One check, for instance, showed that 26 percent of the sample families own Chevrolets and 2 percent own Cadillacs. National license registrations show that 25 percent of American families own Chevrolets, and 2 percent own Cadillacs.

In other words, our TV ratings are reasonable estimates of the public's viewing habits. They are not represented to be the "exact" numbers of homes tuning in a given program. They are, however, very

402   useful in indicating to broadcasters how certain shows are doing—in relation to other shows and over certain periods of time to show trends in viewing. Our customers tell us that the accuracy is about right for their puposes.

We can never know "exactly" how many eyes are on *Huntley-Brinkley* or "exactly" how many sets are tuned to *Captain Kangaroo* at any minute. But ratings such as NTI give the best approximations there are.

TV ratings are a tool designed for a specific job. With their limitations kept firmly in mind, their users get from them valuable and highly useful information otherwise unavailable. Just as you do when you sample a bowl of soup. So, if a sponsor decides that his offering needs more salt, don't blame the spoon! And most important to the viewing audience, ratings are the democratic way of counting the vote in terms of number of homes watching. It's the broadcaster's way of "giving the lady what she wants."

Who Watches What?

By Dick Hobson

JULY 27, 1968

Southerners watch Westerns.
Eggheads dig Gleason.
Literates prefer Don Adams.
Less-literates go for Jim Nabors.
Blue collar workers choose countrified situation comedies.
Affluents prefer movies to anything else.
Lawrence Welk is boss with the Geritol Tribe.
Sophisticates pick specials.
Everybody likes Tennessee Ernie Ford.

If it sounds like plain common sense, it is that and more. It all derives from highly sophisticated demographic surveys designed to show just who watches what. Gone are the days when it's enough to say that a program rates in the Top 10 or 20 or Top 40. Today's sponsors want to know the "demographics."

These elaborate sampling surveys would never have been undertaken were it not for the insistent demands of TV merchandising. Yet the facts themselves remain uncontaminated by commercialism. The findings are sound sociology. We can forget consumer products for the moment and focus on the Sociology of Viewing Preferences—who watches what.

The following "demographics," determined by the A. C. Nielsen Co. and excluding specials, reflect the tastes of America over a six-week period from October 23 to December 3, 1967.

First, consider the U.S. as a whole:

U.S. TOP 10

1. Lucy Show
2. Andy Griffith
3. Bonanza
4. Red Skelton
5. Gunsmoke

6. Family Affair
7. Jackie Gleason
8. Gomer Pyle
9. Saturday Movies
10. { Beverly Hillbillies
     { Friday Movies

Here we see that there are three "countrified" comedies (*Griffith*, *Pyle* and *Hillbillies*), two Westerns (*Bonanza* and *Gunsmoke*), two variety shows (one "countrified"—*Skelton;* one "citified"—*Gleason*), two family comedies (*Lucy* and *Family Affair*), and two movie nights. This is just a start. Industry wants to know the viewer's age, sex, geographical location, income, education, occupation and a lot more.

Nielsen begins by breaking down viewing preferences by geographical region. For contrast, consider the Top 10 ranking shows for the South and the Northeast:

TOP 10 IN SOUTH	TOP 10 IN NORTHEAST
1. Gunsmoke	1. Jackie Gleason
2. Bonanza	2. Smothers Bros.
3. Andy Griffith	3. Dean Martin
4. Lucy Show	4. Ed Sullivan
5. Gomer Pyle	5. Friday Movies
6. Red Skelton	6. Saturday Movies
7. Family Affair	7. Lucy Show
8. Virginian	8. Thursday Movies
9. Daniel Boone	9. Tuesday Movies
10. Beverly Hillbillies	10. My Three Sons

The South's Top 10 is similar to the U.S. as a whole, with eight shows in common. Conspicuously absent are movies, orginally made for a more sophisticated theater audience. Also missing is *Gleason,* an urban taste. In their place are two more Westerns.

The Top 10 in the Northeast has only four shows in common with the U.S. nationally. Out are all the countrified situation comedies and Westerns. In are the citified variety shows which occupy the top four places. *Gleason* leads the pack. The Northeast has two more movie nights.

Comparing Northeast and South, the two regions have only one

show in common: *Lucy.* For the rest, their tastes are dissimilar. In   *405*
movies, it's 4 to 0. In variety shows it's 4 to 1.

So much for geography. Breakdowns by income give us a new
look:

TOP 10 FOR INCOMES UNDER $5000	TOP 10 FOR INCOMES $10,000 & OVER
1. Lucy Show	1. Saturday Movies
2. Gunsmoke	2. Dean Martin
3. Andy Griffith	3. Friday Movies
4. Red Skelton	4. Andy Griffith
5. Lawrence Welk	5. Thursday Movies
6. Bonanza	6. Smothers Bros.
7. Gomer Pyle	7. Family Affair
8. Family Affair	8. Jackie Gleason
9. {Ed Sullivan / Virginian	9. Tuesday Movies
	10. FBI

Tastes of the lower income group are similar to the U.S. as a
whole except that movies are out, *Gleason* is out, and *Welk* and
Sullivan are in.

The most conspicuous feature of the upper income group is the
prominence of movies—four of the Top 10, including the No. 1 show.
The upper income groups have three citified variety shows and the
first dramatic show to appear in these ratings, *The F.B.I.*

In comparing the two income groups, the uppers prefer movies
and drama, the lowers prefer Westerns and situation comedies.
In the variety field, the uppers prefer *Gleason, Martin* and *Smothers,*
the lowers prefer *Skelton, Welk* and *Sullivan.* Education changes
the picture again:

TOP 10: GRADE SCHOOL EDUCATION	TOP 10: 1 + YEARS OF COLLEGE
1. Lucy Show	1. Saturday Movies
2. Andy Griffith	2. Mission: Impossible
3. Gunsmoke	3. Smothers Bros.
4. Red Skelton	4. Dean Martin
5. Bonanza	5. Jackie Gleason
6. Gomer Pyle	6. Tuesday Movies
7. Family Affair	7. Bewitched

8. Lawrence Welk	8. NFL Football
9. Virginian	9. Thursday Movies
10. Jackie Gleason	10. Get Smart

The Top 10 for the grade school educated mostly follows the national rankings except for the exclusion of movies and the addition of *Lawrence Welk* and a Western.

The Top 10 for the college educated, however, is dissimilar. *Gleason* and movies are all they have in common with the U.S. as a whole. Next to *Saturday Movies*, the highest rated show is a drama, *Mission: Impossible*. Their two situation comedies, *Bewitched* and *Get Smart*, are considered more sophisticated than *Lucy* or *Pyle*.

Classifying TV households by education of the head of the household, the Nielsen Company estimates there are 15.3 million homes in the grade school category and 12.7 million in the one-plus years of college. Grade school types prefer Andy Griffith and Jim Nabors; college types prefer Elizabeth Montgomery and Don Adams. The grade school educated go for *Skelton* and *Welk*; collegers like the *Smothers Brothers* and *Dean Martin*.

The blue collar Top 10 generally goes along with the U.S. as a whole, but the white collar Top 10 has more movies, citified variety shows, and a drama, *Mission: Impossible*. Blue collars comprise 48 percent of all TV households; white collars 36 percent.

TOP 10: BLUE COLLAR	TOP 10: WHITE COLLAR
1. Andy Griffith	1. Saturday Movies
2. Lucy Show	2. Dean Martin
3. Bonanza	3. Andy Griffith
4. Red Skelton	4. Smothers Bros.
5. Beverly Hillbillies	5. Mission: Impossible
6. Gunsmoke	6. Jackie Gleason
7. Gomer Pyle	7. Tuesday Movies
8. Bewitched	8. Family Affair
9. Green Acres	9. Thursday Movies
10. {Family Affair / Saturday Movies	10. {Friday Movies / Lucy Show

The blues have two Westerns in their Top 10 to the whites' none, four country comedies to the whites' one. Both like *Lucy* and *Andy Griffith*.

There is strikingly little overlap between the Top 10's of the South and of the Northeast (one show) between those of the Under

$5000 and the Over $10,000 (two shows), between the Grade School
Only and the One-Plus Years of College (one show), and between the
Blue Collar and the White Collar (four shows). The next time one
hears the phrase "Top 10," it is fair to ask which Top 10.

On the other hand, there is a great deal of overlap in the Top
10's of the South, the Under-$5000 income group, the Grade School
educated, and the Blue Collar workers, which we shall consider
together under the heading "Just Plain Folks." Almost as much overlap is found among the Northeast, Over-$10,000 income group,
One-Plus Years of College, and White Collar workers, an aggregation
which some advertisers call "Sophisticates."

A goodly number of "specials" were aired during the six-week
period under study. They were excluded. Were these taken into account, the Top 10's of the Sophisticates would include between
five and eight specials; the Top 10's of Just Plain Folks would include
only one or two. The Tennessee Ernie Ford special is the only one
that consistently scored as well with both.

Further demographic breakdowns are regularly conducted by the
Home Testing Institute of Manhasset, Long Island, and expressed
as numerical "TvQ" scores. Whereas the *Nielsen* ratings are based
on a sample of [1200] homes and show merely whether the household
TV set is switched on and, if so, which channel the set is tuned
to, TvQ scores are based on a survey of 2000 individuals in 750
families and go further to measure attentiveness and degree of enthusiasm for programs.[12]

The shows in TvQ's Top 10's are generally more sophisticated
than those in Nielsen's because they are programs the viewers are
interested in rather than possibly just the best of a bad lot—the least
bad at the time period. Significantly, Nielsen's two big rating leaders,
Andy Griffith and *Lucy,* are entirely absent from TvQ's Top 10's.
In fact, *The Lucy Show* fails to appear on a single TvQ Top 20 breakdown.

The following demographics, supplied by HTI, reflect the tastes
of selected age and sex categories in November 1967, during the
period under discussion:

TOP 10 AMONG CHILDREN 6-11	TOP 10 AMONG TEENAGERS 12-17
1. Flying Nun	1. Guns of Will Sonnett
2. Second Hundred Years	2. Second Hundred Years
3. Family Affair	3. Monkees
4. Monkees	4. Star Trek

408

5. Gomer Pyle
6. Bewitched
7. Beverly Hillbillies
8. Gentle Ben
9. Off to See the Wizard
10. Walt Disney

5. Smothers Brothers
6. Flying Nun
7. Saturday Movies
8. I Spy
9. Dragnet
10. Family Affair

TOP 10 FOR
ADULTS 18-34

1. Saturday Movies
2. Friday Movies
3. Thursday Movies
4. Wed. Movies
5. Mission: Impossible
6. Tuesday Movies
7. Dean Martin
8. I Spy
9. Sunday Movies
10. High Chapparral

TOP 10 FOR
ADULTS OVER 50

1. Lawrence Welk
2. CBS News
3. Bonanza
4. Walt Disney
5. Virginian
6. Family Affair
7. Gunsmoke
8. Dean Martin
9. Gomer Pyle
10. Daniel Boone

From these Top 10's as well as from other HTI Top 10's that fill out the total age and sex picture, some new sociological perspectives emerge:

Family Affair appeals to children, teen-agers, women, and middle-aged and old people—everybody, in fact, but young adults.

Westerns are most liked by men of all ages and old people. There are no Westerns in the Top 10's of children or women [except for women over 50].[13]

Movies are the Top 10 choice of young adults but not of children (it's bedtime) or the elderly.

The Flying Nun is No. 1 with children and No. 6 with teen-agers, and appears on no Top 10 for older folks.

It should be no surprise that the No. 1 show for the age group 50 and older is *Lawrence Welk.* Other shows in the Top 10 of the Over 50's—and for no younger age group—are *The Virginian, Gunsmoke* and *Daniel Boone.*

Shows that are Top 10 choices of husbands but not of housewives are Westerns and action-adventure series. Housewives prefer movies.

Gentle Ben, of course, is strictly a kiddy passion, and *The Smothers Brothers* a prime teen taste, but *Gomer Pyle* is something of an anomaly, appearing only on the two Top 10's at either end of the age spectrum: children and adults over 50. Certainly something to ponder.

Other Audience Feedback

Even with all their weaknesses, ratings are the most relied upon means of obtaining information about the television audience. However, there are other ways in which the broadcasters have received information about viewers' reactions to specific programs and the medium in general.

In 1955, CBS president Dr. Frank Stanton, himself a pioneer in communication research, proposed "a comprehensive, impartial nationwide study of what the public wants from television and what it means to the public." Five years later, CBS gave a grant to the Bureau of Applied Social Research to undertake the study, because, according to Stanton, "we owe it to our audience as well as ourselves to establish some systematic method of inviting the public to participate in shaping what we do.

The findings of that research study, published in 1963 in *The People Look at Television,* are discussed in the following interview (pp. 411-418) with the late Dr. Gary Steiner who directed the study. Professor Steiner's research is still the most comprehensive attempt to record viewer reactions toward television. In his interview, Dr. Steiner states some of his more significant conclusions: Different population segments have different evaluations and attitudes toward television. The prevailing opinion among viewers is that there is a division of labor among the mass media. There are widespread feelings of guilt regarding the amount of time spent in front of the set. The intellectual is enthusiastic about the programs he himself watches, and neither the intellectual nor the average viewer have specific suggestions for new programs or types of programs. Attitudes and actual behavior differ: the request is for more informational programs, yet entertainment formats—even the programs most frequently criticized—are actually being selected.

410   Edith Efron (pp. 419-423) discusses the importance of mail received by the networks. She describes the systems by which the stars, producers, sponsors and networks deal with letters, and she also outlines the networks' processes of analyzing the mail. The mail, even when not answered, is taken seriously according to Miss Efron. Viewer mail has caused performers to be hired or fired; it has been influential in shows being put on the air and returned to the air; it has changed programming content, production details, program scheduling and even the personality habits of on-screen performers. Miss Efron points out that although viewer mail is obviously not the dominant factor in television decision-making, it does have an effect on the medium.

Richard Ahles (pp. 424-426) reviews telephone audience feedback received by a Hartford, Connecticut, station during 1968. The calls this station received were nearly always complaints—usually made angrily. The complaints normally followed the interruption of regular programming for live coverage of extremely important news events. However, Ahles does feel that telephone calls to the individual station can provide useful information, and he relates one incident in which the station reinstated a program because of viewer response over the telephone.

There have been several efforts to organize citizens for the purpose of influencing television programming. Richard Doan (pp. 427-431) discusses these efforts and summarizes previous attempts by the older, established viewing organizations—the American Council for Better Broadcasters, the National Association for Better Broadcasting and the National Audience Board—to prod the medium's decision makers into reform. The networks have not responded and so these attempts have, except in minor cases, failed. Doan suggests that the newest viewing organization, the National Citizen's Committee for Broadcasting may have a better chance of making itself heard because of its financial backing and influential members.

The Steiner Report:
The People Look at Television

Dr. Gary Steiner Interviewed
by Roger Youman

FEBRUARY 23, AND MARCH 2, 1963

Q: Dr. Steiner, what was the purpose of the study?

A: Its purpose was to develop a comprehensive base line of factual information regarding the way the American viewer actually feels about television and about the uses he makes of it. We are certain that it is the most comprehensive study of this type that has ever been done.

Q: What are your findings based on? Opinion, fact or what? Where does the information come from?

A: In the spring of 1960 we conducted lengthy personal interviews with 2500 adults across the Nation, using a questionnaire that incorporated a variety of specialized techniques designed to measure attitudes and feelings somewhat beneath the surface, as well as more straightforward questions. Our respondents were selected by standard statistical means to assure a representative sample of the adult population. The interviewing was carried out independently by two separate survey organizations: Elmo Roper and Associates, and National Opinion Research Center at the University of Chicago. This allowed us to compare the results of the two surveys—which, incidentally, were virtually identical on all major issues.

In order to get some indication of how expressed attitudes correspond to actual viewing behavior, we also interviewed a sample of viewers whose actual TV habits we already knew. They had participated, three to six months earlier, in a rating survey conducted by the American Research Bureau, and ARB supplied us with diaries containing the names of the shows these viewers had watched.

Q: That was 1960. How can you be sure that your findings are still valid?

A: We recently completed a follow-up survey. We established that responses to the major questions are unchanged since 1960.

Q: Let's find out about those responses. How does the general public actually feel about television and the job the industry is doing?

A: The average viewer finds television an important and positive contribution to everyday life—in fact, he names it as "the single devel-

412   opment of the past 25 years that has done the most to make life more enjoyable, pleasant or interesting." In the average home the set is in use five to six hours a day. The typical viewer is likely to spend some time relaxing with television almost every evening and to find that the most enjoyable part of the ordinary day. So when the set breaks down, this is among the most serious of everyday crises. As a result, one quarter have the set repaired within half a day; half of them have it fixed by the end of the day; and more than 80 percent take care of it before a week has gone by.

But importance—even routine usage—doesn't necessarily mean great satisfaction. And on the matter of satisfaction with "television in general" we find that there is no such thing as a "general public." Evaluations of television and attitudes toward it differ tremendously among different population segments, and especially so according to education. The bulk of the viewing public—those viewers with no more than a high school education—ordinarily discuss television in glowing terms. It is not terribly "originial" or "imaginative," but it is "relaxing," "interesting," "informative" and "exciting." With increasing education, reactions become less positive. The college-educated viewer is not nearly so unqualified in his praise, and the 5 percent of the viewing public with education above the college level becomes critical of "television in general."

But "television in general" isn't too meaningful a concept. We really should get more specific.

Q: Fine. Let's talk about viewing. Why do people watch television? What are they looking for? What do they get out of it?

A: We have a very clear indication of a division of labor among the mass media of communication. As compared with radio, magazines and newspapers, television is far and away the entertainment medium. And this is true all the way across the educational ladder. All viewers—highbrows included—agree that television is the most entertaining of the four.

The average man is also likely to find television his best source of information, as, for example, in providing "understanding of the candidates and issues in national elections." But the better educated are likely to turn to print—especially to magazines—for their intellectual insights.

Radio is generally recognized by all as bringing "the latest news most quickly," while all groups agree that newspapers "provide the most thorough news coverage."

In line with the fact that people watch television principally for entertainment is the fact that they normally describe viewing as a very relaxing activity. Everyone—the highly educated included—agrees that television provides many enjoyable, relaxing hours. But the better educated are less willing to settle for that—or at least to say they do.

Among viewers in general, and especially among the better educated, there is an undercurrent of shame—a word—about the sheer time consumed in front of the set—the many "nonproductive" hours. For example, we showed our interviewees a series of cartoons depicting people watching TV or reading or attending a movie or playing golf—a variety of leisure activities—and asked them to match the cartoons with a series of thoughts such as "Am I lazy!" or "This is really interesting" or "Another evening shot." On the one hand, people matched the thought "Am I lazy!" with the television scene more frequently than they associated it with any of the other leisure pursuits. Forty-nine percent associated it with TV, as compared with 12 percent with reading, 3 percent with movies and 2 percent with golf, to give you a few of the figures. But, by the same token, 42 percent described televiewing as "the perfect way to relax," again more related with that thought than with any of the other leisure activities.

The contrast with reading is especially revealing. Reading is considered relaxing and worthwhile; television is relaxing but "I really should be doing something else." Listen to this viewer: "I sure enjoy television, but so often I worry because it makes me fall behind on my reading." No one says, "I sure enjoy reading, but so often it makes me fall behind on my television."

Q: How does this affect parents' attitudes toward their children's viewing?

A: The same kind of conflict is apparent. TV keeps the kids out of trouble and out of the parents' hair; but it also keeps them out of their homework and out of bed.

Perhaps as a partial justification for the fact that they allow so much viewing by their children, parents attribute widespread educational benefits to the medium. And, incidentally, those people who admit they use television for baby-sitting are far more likely to mention these "educational" benefits. Sometimes they seem to reach pretty far—one parent said: "I don't mind what they look at because even in those Westerns with all of the shooting and killing they show people how to protect themselves. You notice how a man will push a door open carefully before he goes in if he thinks someone may be behind it?"

Perhaps related to this basic conflict is the fact that many viewers ask for more informative programming for themselves—for some

414 constructive by-product that might make those leisure hours more worthwhile as well as relaxing.

Q: That brings us to the question of programming. How do people feel about what they are being offered?

A: As was the case when we asked viewers their opinion of television as a whole, we found out that the general public feels generally good about programs in general. But again there are important differences hiding behind that term "general." Praise of most programs, for example, decreases sharply with increasing education. But here we find an interesting departure from the generally more critical pattern of the well-educated viewers. They are far more critical of programs in general than is the average viewer, but they are far more complimentary about the programs they themselves watch. And they are especially apt to praise the informational value of their shows.

In short: Most people like most shows; intellectuals less so. Everybody likes his shows; intellectuals more so.

Q: What kinds of programs do viewers say they like most?

A: The programs they mention as current favorites come principally from the light-entertainment categories—specifically action, comedy, variety, light drama—and so do the greatest moments from television's past, the personalities and shows the viewers would like to bring back. And that holds for viewers of all educational levels.

Within the light-entertainment category we find that there are about as many fans of each specific type of show—Western, situation comedy, and so on—as there are people who mention these as least-liked shows. For every enthusiastic fan of a program type, there is likely to be a satiated or disinterested viewer. So the survey results do not point to a simple change in program composition that on balance would satisfy more people than it would dissatisfy.

Q: These favorites come from present and past offerings. But what would people like to see that isn't on at all now? What changes or improvements in programming do they suggest?

A: Viewers have little to suggest in the way of specific new television programs or types that are not currently available. But there is a very general request: Viewers say there should be more informational programming on the air—that there is not enough "education," "information," "food for thought." And while this is true across the educational spectrum, it is the better-educated segment of the audience that is most consistent and insistent in this demand.

Q: Is that because they now watch more informational programs than their less-educated neighbors, and would like to have still more available? Or could they simply be trying to impress the interviewer?

A: To get some clues, let's take a look at what television diets our various educational groups actually select. As you recall, we analyzed some viewing diaries kept by respondents who had previously participated in a rating survey conducted by the American Research Bureau.

First of all everyone—highbrows included—watches mostly light entertainment. Roughly two-thirds of the average television week is devoted to easy relaxation such as action, comedy, variety, light drama, and sports programs. In addition all segments select a healthy slice of newscasts, which account for 25 to 40 percent of the programs they watch.

When it comes to heavier fare—serious drama, classical music, heavy information such as public affairs presentations—we find that this constitutes a very small part of the viewer's week. Such programs come to less than 10 percent of the average diet; and even people with education beyond college devote only 15 percent of their viewing to them.

Q: But isn't that because they have mostly light entertainment to choose from? After all, if two-thirds of the programs on the air are light entertainment, then most of the time there is nothing else available.

A: We examined that possibility by looking at what people selected during those hours when they had a choice between light and heavy fare.

With respect to public affairs, we found that the better educated are slightly more apt to choose such presentations, but they too turn overwhelmingly to light entertainment. To be exact, during time periods when there is an informational, public affairs broadcast on the air, the college-educated viewer will turn on the competing light entertainment four out of five times.

By the same token, when we compared viewers who in our survey specifically asked for more information with those who said there was already enough of it on the air, we found that both groups consistently selected in favor of light entertainment when they had the chance to watch public affairs telecasts.

So there is little evidence in support of the argument that viewers watch so much trivia because trivia is all they are offered—that they would watch informational programming if it were more often available in convenient, prime-time hours.

Q: But public affairs is only one category of serious programming. How about more substantial entertainment, such as serious drama or classical music?

A: Here the story is quite different. The college educated will

416 turn from light to heavy entertainment when it is available. The average viewer will not. And those who ask for more serious television programming back up this response with a much higher selection rate for serious drama.

The situation becomes clear when we look at hours when viewers have a choice between all three: light entertainment, heavy entertainment and public affairs. In such time periods we find the general public favoring light fare; and the more sophisticated, better-educated viewers giving up "escape" in favor of substantial entertainment. But among all groups, the public affairs presentations run a very poor third—less than 10 percent of the selections.

In short, people do select; but except for their regular newscasts, they select what they consider the most entertaining, not the most informative, television diet.

Q: Then how do you interpret the fact that viewers—and especially the better educated—ask for more information so frequently?

A: That's hard to say. I can only speculate. One interpretation, of course, is that they don't really mean it—that they are only saying what they think is expected of a well-educated respondent. But there is another possibility: Perhaps they mean it quite sincerely, but not for their own consumption. Maybe they consider it in the same light as, say, speed limits or integration—they recognize the need for information as a need for the country in general. They themselves don't need television for information—after all, they have their serious magazines and books—but they think the average man needs to be enlightened in this day and age.

Q: Isn't there another possibility? Maybe they think the present information programs just aren't good enough. Could it be that what they want is not more of the same but better information shows?

A: That, of course, is a possibility. But remember, it is the present —not better—light entertainment that usually attracts these viewers away from the heavy shows; and they cite the present information shows as the kind of television they would like to see more of. They are not electing to watch nothing, but rather to watch those programs they most frequently criticize. That is the point.

Q: Let's turn to another subject. We hear a lot of talk about TV violence. What did you find out about viewers reactions to this type of TV fare?

A: Most people, and especially parents feel that there is far too much violence for children to see—not only in adult programming but also in shows designed specifically for youngsters.

Their concern is not chiefly on moral or psychological grounds but on physical grounds. Children can imitate so many dangerous *417* things they see. Accordingly the violence that gets the most criticism is that which is imitable; not the fantastic violence depicted in cartoons, or even on crime shows. It is the eye-gouging, slapping, hitting over the head—not mowing down with machine guns—that causes the greatest concern.

Q: What about commercials? What do viewers think of them?

A: Commercials are clearly the audience's No. 1 object of annoyance. Annoyance doesn't often reach the point of exasperation, but it is consistent and it is widespread. Most viewers, interestingly, would not "prefer television without commercials," but most of them do agree that commercials are too long and, especially, interrupt too frequently. This last, by the way, is the major complaint. It is not that commercials are misleading or dull or in poor taste or seductive. All these come in for their share of criticism, but the key frustration is the fact that they intrude so often and in such crucial places. The viewer feels that the networks and stations really ought to do something about this.[14]

Q: Are there particular types of commercials that they like or dislike more than others?

A: Yes. There is very close agreement about which product categories most often offend and which do the best job of entertaining and informing. (That, of course, may have nothing to do with how good a job they do of selling the product, which perhaps is at the root of the problem.) Commercials for beer, food and automobiles seem to be the favorites. Those for bathroom products are most often criticized, followed by ads for cigarettes and undergarments.

Q: Dr. Steiner, what does it all come to? What advice would the viewer give the men who are responsible for television programming if he had the chance?

A: We have seen that people differ on many of the most important issues. But to oversimplify, for the sake of summarizing, the "composite viewer" would probably make the following suggestions:

"First and most important, give me more programs that are fun and worthwhile—programs that I find relaxing and entertaining but, at the same time, are in some way informative, uplifting, useful."

Next, he would say: "You really should be able to figure out how to produce programs that are safe for the children and that attract and hold their attention. If you must have violence, please make it unrealistic, not easily imitable."

Third: "Bear in mind that with me and with my children television is a daily routine, not a highly selective, once-in-a-while ac-

418   tivity. So the average level of programming is much more important to me than programming at its best. Personally I would rather have you raise the quality of all programs by 10 percent than put on a few outstanding shows during the year. In short, I would rather be sure of healthy food daily than have gourmet dishes once in a while at the risk of food poisoning the rest of the time.

"About those commercials: I realize that they pay for the programs and sponsors have a right to have their say, but why do they have to interrupt in the middle of the show to do it? Also so many of them are silly or insulting to the intelligence or in poor taste, especially the ones for bathroom products. But I know you broadcasters aren't responsible for that. However, I do hold you responsible for the placement of commercials.

"I realize that many of my problems with television stem only in part from programming. What often bothers me most is my own use (or misuse) of the set. I would like to be more disciplined about my own viewing and that of my children, but it's an awfully hard thing to control. That's why I'd appreciate some help from you in making those hours a little more worthwhile.

"Television could certainly stand improvement. But, all things considered, you're doing a good job."

What They Do With Your Letters

By Edith Efron

DECEMBER 31, 1966

Barbara Walters, *Today* reporter, sits and giggles over a letter. It says: "How dare you show that painting of a naked woman on the air?" Burton Benjamin, executive producer of *The 21st Century*, sighs over a letter. It says: "Can you supply me with a bibliography on learning theory?" Don Adams, star of *Get Smart*, chuckles over a letter. It says: "I've just written a song called 'Get Smart.'" Mark Goodson, game-and-panel-show producer, grins over a letter. It says: "What does Orson Bean 'mean' when he says, 'I went to Philadelphia and it was closed'?" Allen Funt, producer and host of *Candid Camera*, groans over a whole pile of letters. One says: "Your suits are too tight." Another says: "Your suits are too loose." A third says: "Your tie sticks out from under your vest." A fourth says: "You slump." Chet Huntley, NBC newsman scowls darkly over a letter. It says: "I love you, I love you."

The day has begun in the television world. The mail has arrived. It falls upon the TV folk like a terrifying white deluge. No one knows the exact count—but it's at least a million, every year; and it comes from every city, every town, every hamlet in the United States.

The letters applaud: "Enjoyable, please continue . . . pleasing and informative . . . exciting and excellent reporting . . . funny show, very relaxing . . . clever . . . wholesome and patriotic . . . true family entertainment with nice clean fun. . . . "

And they hiss: "Horrid . . . people are not morons or idiots . . . trite . . . abominable programming . . . social outrage . . . inconvenient hour . . . ridicule of a fine American tradition . . . an insult to adult intelligence . . . full of temptation and trash. . . . "

What happens to the applause and hisses? Do the TV people really pay attention to them? The answer is: You bet your life they do. Series stars, who get the most mail, the great bulk of which is picture requests, have systems set up for handling it. Don Adams, for instance, gets between two and three thousand letters a week. His

419

420   mail is screened by two people. He pores over 100 or 150 a week himself.

Independent producers like Mark Goodson and Allen Funt have secretaries to screen their mail for them. "Knotty or critical mail is given to me. I'm curious to see it," says Goodson. "I get the critical mail, special mail from universities, and VIP mail. I read it avidly," says Funt.

Sponsors too, or rather their top advertising executives, read their mail avidly. At Burlington Industries, sponsor of *The Ed Sullivan Show* and *ABC Stage 67,* advertising director Jack Hanson gets all viewer mail. "I read every word of it personally." At American Telephone & Telegraph, which sponsors the *Bell Telephone Hour,* advertising manager Jack Howland gets all the letters. "We read them, every one."

As for the masses of letters addressed directly to the networks—including tens of thousands a year forwarded by TV GUIDE's Viewer Service—they are processed with dispatch. People specially hired to read and answer "standard" viewer mail (that is, generalized "I like," "I don't like" letters) cull out all specialized questions, gripes and VIP letters for assorted on-screen luminaries, producers and executives to answer.

What proportion of viewer letters is actually answered is impossible to say. NBC has files indicating that more than 177,000 viewer "communications" to the network itself were answered last year. The individuals interviewed, with only one exception, say they answer all mail. The exception was Allen Funt. "We started to acknowledge all letters," he explains, "but we don't do it any more. It's too time-consuming and too expensive. Now we only single out unusual letters." It is probable that Mr. Funt is by no means unique in this matter.

Those who don't get answers, to tell the truth, aren't missing much, except the thrill of seeing an envelope with a famous name in the upper left-hand corner. The vast majority of answers are courtesy formulas, mass-produced by secretaries.

Whether answered or not, however, the mail is taken seriously. At CBS, a breakdown of the contents of the letters is made and circulated among executives. At ABC, Ellen McKinnon, head of the viewer mail office, keeps executives and producers informed of "trends" in the mail. "Right now," she says, "I am keeping Leonard Goldberg (vice president in charge of programming) informed of responses to the shows." And at NBC, the study of the mail almost constitutes a small industry. At this network the viewer mail office, run by Kathryn Cole with a staff of seven, prepares detailed analytical charts of mail responses—approval, criticism and inquiry. These charts are broken down into a series of classifications, subclassifications, and sub-subclassifications. "At the end of every month," says Mrs. Cole, "a detailed report on this total breakdown goes to the chairman of the board, to the vice presidents, and to all producers who request it. It reflects the audience reaction for the month."

Does anything come of all this letter-reading and letter-analysis? Yes—a lot comes of it: "People are hired because of the mail." An ABC vice president says: "The mail of disappointment was tremendous when Robert Lansing was dropped from *12 O'clock High.* It was certainly a factor in casting him as a lead in *The Man Who Never Was.*" Mark Goodson says: "If we get an absolute deluge of positive mail on a performer, we'll call him again. The same is true for a replacement emcee."

"People are fired because of the mail." This is difficult to prove because no TV executive would publicly admit it. But a well-established NBC star says, off the record, "I know positively of one case of a female celebrity on a show who was fired because the mail was so negative. The people simply couldn't stand her."

"On-screen personalities change their personal habits because of the mail." Allen Funt says: "They're mindful of my clothing. I'll always hear it if they don't approve of my suits. And God help me if there's a wrinkle." He tries hard to look elegant. Barbara Walters reports: "I got three hundred letters in one week about my long hair. People didn't like it. They said I looked phony and glamorous. It wasn't a morning image. I cut my hair really because of the letters."

"Dramatic content is changed because of the mail." Although taped series, made long in advance, are unresponsive to immediate mail, the daytime dramas, which are live, quiver sensitively to immediate viewer response. Says NBC's Kathryn Cole: "The producers of daytime drama are very anxious about the mail. *The Doctors,* for example—if they're going to make a drastic change, or inject something unexpected, or introduce a controversial subject, they're eager to know audience reactions. They act on the mail. They take suggestions."

"Production details can be changed because of the mail." Says Allen Funt: "Occasionally a letter gives me insight into what we're doing that's wrong. One viewer pointed out that all the time we were describing the spots we were all alone on stage, without props, and that it wasn't interesting. I realized he was right. The next day, I started using props." He adds: "I'm very responsive to the mail. If

422 the cleaning lady criticized the show two minutes before we went on the air, I'd be tempted to change it. It's my 'mishugass'" ["craziness"].

And the ABC vice president says: "We got a lot of letters complaining about the loudness of the music of *Peyton Place*. We've lowered the volume."

"Shows can be put on the air because of the mail." *Sing Along with Mitch* was originally planned as a one-shot program. It got so much favorable mail, says NBC's Kathryn Cole, that "the sales promotion people were thrilled," and a series was produced.

"Shows may return to the air because of the mail." "There's been a lot of spontaneous mail on *The Avengers*. About a thousand letters, and not one unfavorable one," says ABC's Ellen McKinnon. "We're putting it back on the air because of that."[15]

"Program timetables may be changed because of the mail." The ABC vice president, again, says: "If enough people say, 'We want our children to see a certain show; put it on earlier,' we listen. It's happened. We've changed schedules for that reason."

"Summer reruns are scheduled by the mail." "When they're rescheduling movies," says Kathryn Cole, "they'll call me to find out what the mail was like, the first time around. They'll shy away from movies getting a little more criticism. Also, in rescheduling a series, they'll be guided by past mail responses."

"And sponsors make pro and con decisions because of the mail." "The letters are a sales tool," says one advertising man. "If a batch of good letters comes in, they're in the hands of the sales-promotion boys the next morning. And within a few hours they're waving them under a sponsor's nose." Speaking for one sponsor, Jack Howland of AT&T says: "Mail is one of our research tools. It does guide our judgments. Years of mail, along with other factors, for instance, gave us a feeling the old format of *Bell Telephone Hour* had run its course."

The mail is obviously not the only, or even the dominant, factor in television decisions. As Mark Goodson says, "The mail is just a minuscule sampling. In the last analysis the real voice of the people is ratings." But, as an ABC vice president also says: "It definitely affects us. If people from different parts of the country say something, if there's a trend—and I don't mean thousands, I mean 10, 20, 30— we do pay attention."

Viewer letters—more than a million of them a year—are having their effect on the medium. And it's not surprising at that. The potentates of this industry are entertaining and informing an invisible audience—with only a string of Nielsen figures to guide them . . . and their own canned laugh tracks to listen to.

   And that is why, if you walk into any television office early in the   *423*
morning, you will see them all—from the chairmen of the board and
the presidents down to lowliest girl Friday—sitting and poring over
letters, chortling over them, scowling over them, stewing over them,
losing sleep over them. In the last analysis, however, the silent ratings, not the mail, are the decisive factor in TV decisions. But this is
show business. And, ratings or no ratings, the show folk are starving
for real live applause and hisses.

A Station Just Can't Win

By Richard F. Ahles

APRIL 26, 1969

If WTIC-TV had paid strict attention to the complaints of some of its viewers during 1968, the Hartford, Connecticut, station wouldn't have bothered to carry:

1. The President's State of the Union Message.
2. The UN hearings on the Pueblo.
3. Secretary of State Rusk's testimony before the Senate Foreign Relations Committee on the war in Vietnam.
4. President Johnson's announcement that he wouldn't run again.
5. Coverage of the assassination and funeral of Martin Luther King.
6. Coverage of the assassination and funeral of Robert Kennedy.
7. The national conventions.
8. Apollo 8's flight to the moon.

These televised events led all others in the number of telephoned complaints they inspired from the station's viewers. Apollo 8, occurring as it did during the football season, caused many complaints not only in Hartford but all over the Nation. In his column in the January 4, 1969, issue of TV GUIDE, Richard Doan took astounded note of the "disinterested viewers" who called television stations to complain when a National Football League game was interrupted for the first transmission of TV pictures from Apollo 8.[16]

The stations weren't astounded. They're accustomed to complaints whenever regular programming is interrupted for anything—anything from a special to extraordinary news.

At WTIC-TV, where they keep a daily record of telephone calls from viewers, 103 people were angry enough to complain about missing a few minutes of football for the Apollo pictures, but nobody called to say that showing the Apollo pictures was a good idea. This is the usual pattern. In the fall of 1963, when Yale professor Frederick Barghoorn returned to the United States after being imprisoned in the Soviet Union, WTIC-TV pre-empted the first 16 minutes of the Sunday night *Judy Garland Show* to present the professor's homecoming news conference. Seventy-six viewers telephoned the station in those 16 minutes and 75 of them complained. This in an area where Walter Cronkite's evening newscast gets higher ratings than a lot of entertainment programs.

The 103 complaints WTIC-TV received about the Apollo pictures were the biggest batch since August, when the Democratic and Republican conventions kept the switchboard humming with calls from people who preferred summertime reruns to living history. The relatively calm Republican convention inspired more complaints than the raucous Democratic convention in Chicago. During the GOP gathering, 159 people called to complain that the sessions were too long and not nearly as entertaining as the programs they usually see. Later in the month, only 74 were similarly unhappy with the Democrats. The network's controversial coverage of the clash between demonstrators and police didn't get much of a rise out of WTIC-TV's audience in southern New England. The station's record of phone calls for August 28, 1968, shows that three people called to protest the "brutality" of the police; three said Walter Cronkite wasn't doing a good job; and two just wanted to say how happy they were to see the hippies getting what they deserved.

WTIC-TV—and a lot of other stations—keep telephone records because calls are one means of determining the interests and desires of the television audience. There are many reasons why a television station should try to determine these interests and desires. To cite only one, the Federal Communications Commission requires it.

But there are also many reasons why a station should consider the interests and desires expressed on the telephone as something less than the voice of all the people. The voice heard on the telephone is often angry, sometimes profane and almost always opposed to the finer things television has to offer.

On April 9 last year, 67 viewers called WTIC-TV to complain about missing the regular daytime programs for the King funeral, and one viewer called to thank the station for carrying the funeral. The score on the [Robert] Kennedy funeral was 32 to nothing in favor of complaints.

Having discovered the term "bad taste" somewhere, many callers attack pre-emptions on the grounds that the station is guilty of "bad taste" when it deviates from normal programming and presumably confuses the viewer. On March 16 a caller objected to a Saturday morning news conference, saying "it's in bad taste to have news Saturday mornings when the children are home watching cartoons."

Not all the calls are complaints about regular programming being

426   pre-empted, of course, and many do provide valuable information for
WTIC-TV. "A couple of seasons ago," says Kendall Smith, the station manager, "we concluded the nighttime version of *Password* had
run its course and we dropped it. Hundreds called—and wrote—to
protest our decision, and as a result, we put it back on the schedule."

During the furor over violence on television following the assassinations of Dr. King and Senator Kennedy, 71 viewers called to protest violence on television—but one called to say: "I enjoy violence
on TV and want to see more, not less. None of this kindergarten stuff."

Who Speaks for the Viewer?

By Richard K. Doan

JUNE 7, 1969

The voice of the TV viewer is heard in the land, but, collectively speaking, it's far more of a spontaneous chorus, rising and falling in elation or despair, than it is an organized response to watching television. As for efforts to rally TV consumers *en masse* to exercise some degree of united influence over what goes out over the air, the history of such movements is one of conspicuous futility. In two decades of surveillance of the medium by self-appointed tastemakers, not one discernible result of their dictates is to be found, at least at the national level.

Of course, there's always a first time—and it could be near at hand. A National Citizens Committee for Broadcasting has come on the scene with unusual backing and star-studded cast, and is determinedly making waves.[17] It may make them in vain and ultimately go away. Then again it may not.

Up to now TV largely has gone its way, reacting substantially to just one form of viewer response—the ratings—the while suffering nothing more acute than a passing case of nerves from occasional epidemics of vieweritis in the form of massive mail or phone calls.

Through it all the question of who speaks for the TV audience has remained conveniently moot. Legally, the Federal Communications Commission is presumed to be the public's watchdog, but the FCC over the years has been charged with being as much a guardian of the radio-TV *status quo* as it is a defender of the "people's air waves."

The networks, not exactly noted for gossiping about matters distasteful to them, including gratuitous criticism, claim they have virtually no truck with the country's three long-established major viewer organizations—the Madison (Wisconsin)-based American Council for Better Broadcasts (ACBB), the Los Angeles-based National Association for Better Broadcasting (NABB), and the New York-based National Audience Board (NAB). Network spokesmen, careful not to offend, state that pronouncements and surveys issued by these

427

428 groups are always "studied." But when pressed, the network officials find it impossible to recall any instance when a viewer organization singularly influenced a network decision.

It falls, then, on the tube-watcher societies to document any sway they've exerted over TV's programmers. Such evidence is all but nonexistent. "'Claiming' is not our long suit," ACBB's grandmotherly executive director, Dr. Leslie Spence, avers. "We were part of the efforts of many groups to save *Captain Kangaroo*" (the CBS children's show once threatened with cancellation). "And some years ago the Three Stooges were routed from three stations."

Dr. Spence, a retired university professor, confesses that ACBB's membership (about 7,000, not counting "cooperating parent and women's groups) is "pitifully small in comparison with the population," and she plaintively adds, "It's surprising how many people say they are concerned about the quality of broadcasts and yet do nothing, isn't it?"

Before undergoing a name change a few years ago, NABB was known as NAFBRAT (National Association for Better Radio and Television). The target of this organization is TV violence. "They're body counters," a TV industry spokesman scoffed. "They're always adding up the killings." Last summer, in a typical blast at TV, Frank Orme, NABB's full-time factotum, accused the networks of having "fostered the manufacture and engineered the world-wide distribution of an immeasurable mass of graphically illustrated torture, murder, sadism, horror and callous brutality."

In times past NABB has corralled some well-known names. The late Lee De Forest, "father of radio," at one point was an NABB vice president. Newton Minow still is listed as a director. The current NABB president is James V. Bennett, retired chief of the U.S. Bureau of Prisons.

"NABB's main problem always has been money," says one of its directors, Robert Lewis Shayon, the *Saturday Review* TV critic, "They've never had more than pennies." He feels that NABB has had no visible impact nationally, although he believes it got a Los Angeles station once to cut back on violence in children's viewing hours.

NABB does break into print occasionally. Columnist Drew Pearson likes to quote NABB surveys to show how calloused TV is. Last December Representative Hall Boggs (D., La.), a member of the President's commission on violence, waved an NABB report at CBS president Frank Stanton, a witness before the commission, and demanded to know "how long" the public would have to wait for TV to get off the violence kick. The papers picked it up.

NAB, unlike NABB, is a genteel critic. Not to be confused with *429*
the National Association of Broadcasters, the TV industry's main trade
group, the National Audience Board is the personal do-good project
of a well-to-do, 57-year-old New Yorker named Peter Goelet. Purely
from a sense of need for it, he reputedly has poured something over
$250,000 into the undertaking since 1954. He has claimed an NAB
membership of "3000 civic leaders identified with 58 major organizations" such as women's clubs and civic and religious groups.

Goelet's chief vehicle in his personal crusade is a periodic
bulletin called the *Viewer.* It often features interviews with industry
and government officials. "The Board was never conceived of as a
critical sounding board," says Peter Rankin, Goelet's dedicated
second-in-command. "Its aim primarily is to serve as a bridge between public and industry . . . to exchange viewpoints." Goelet
doesn't believe in "stirring things up and getting people mad at you—
there's no point in that," Rankin argues. (He reported that Goelet
was under doctor's orders not to give any interviews.)

Has NAB changed anything in TV? Rankin claims NBC toned
down its loud commercials after NAB came up with "some technical
how-to's and rationales." Last June, *Business Week* magazine reported that "after criticism from the National Audience Board, both
CBS and NBC scrubbed some mayhem-filled cartoons from their fall
Saturday morning schedules." An NBC spokesman called both of
the NAB claims "presumptuous." A CBS official also denied that
NAB triggered a cartoon cleanup.

If the prodding of TV by ACBB, NABB and NAB has been something less than impressive, then what chance does the new National
Citizens Committee for Broadcasting stand of making its views felt?
The answer: maybe not a good chance, but a better one. NCCB has
far the most impressive backing and makeup of any viewer movement
yet launched. Never before have major foundations kicked in funds
for such an effort; never before have the cudgels been taken up by
such an aggregation of public figures.

Like him or not (and he leaves little choice), NCCB's chief
agitator, Thomas P. F. Hoving, the director of New York's Metro-
politan Museum, knows how to attract attention and doesn't mind
doing so. Backing him as NCCB trustees are the likes of Harry
Belafonte, Robert Montgomery, John Kenneth Galbraith and Marya
Mannes, and tagging along as troops are such prominent folks as
Leonard Bernstein, Paddy Chayefsky, Bill Cosby, Henry Morgan,
Mike Nichols and Leslie Uggams, plus such movers-and-shakers as
R. Buckminster Fuller, E. William Henry, A. Philip Randolph and

430   Whitney Young, Jr. Helping Hoving ride herd on this blue-ribbon panel is a full-time lieutenant, Ben Kubasik, a former TV critic and one-time press officer for CBS News.

For openers, NCCB got grants totaling $255,000 from the Carnegie, Ford, Alfred P. Sloan, W. K. Kellogg, 20th Century and Danforth foundations. Since then, the William Benton Foundation has kicked in $200,000—an 11th-hour contribution which saved NCCB from collapsing completely when it ran out of money a couple of months ago.[18] Consumers Union has added a token $5000, and Hoving himself has donated $18,000, received from McGraw-Hill as advance royalty on a book he is writing about what's wrong with TV.

Kubaskik, who carries the NCBB ball most of the time, blusters, "Nobody thinks anything can be done about TV. We happen to think it can be changed. What we desperately need, though, is hundreds of thousands of people saying, 'No! This isn't what we want in TV!'" Then change can come through existing laws and the FCC, Kubasik holds. And if the FCC won't do the job, NCCB will go into the courts for relief, he warns.

"Petitions, letters to the sponsors, and that sort of stuff does no good," Kubasik argues. "That's the kind of thing the industry holds in contempt."

NCCB's ploy is direct pressure. In March 1969, for instance, Hoving and a dozen of his committeemen got five of the FCC Commissioners to sit down with them over lunch to swap views. Kubasik insists the FCC is "receptive" to NCCB's goals.

The recent furor over TV sex and violence, however, doesn't strike NCCB as a Great Cause. "Sure there is too much violence on TV," Kubasik says, "and we think it does have an influence on young people. But sex and violence are phony issues. The real issue is the trash on TV. We're always told how much violence there is in the Bible and Shakespeare, you know, but how much of the Bible and Shakespeare do you see on TV? No, we say if we had quality programming on TV, we wouldn't be bothered with complaints about sex and violence."

What is NCCB shooting for? For one thing, more prime-time attention to minority tastes in programming. "We want balance in that schedule," says Kubasik. "The broadcasters have got to serve all audience tastes, not just the great mass taste."

NCCB also is pumping for local public hearings on TV-station license renewals, is seeking informal meetings with network brass to exchange views, is looking for opportunities to speak up on such issues as public TV (the committee recently issued a study proposing a 4-percent tax on commercial TV revenues to support public TV) and is taking pot shots at anything that seems to be fair game (example: the networks' prediliction for all-out coverage of assassinations, funerals and Apollo missions prompts Kubasik to carp: "there's nothing left in TV public affairs but death and space!").

So far NCCB has been "an egghead platoon" with no provision for admitting interested viewers. But a mailing has just gone out to 26,000 "key" citizens, seeking grass-roots sentiments toward NCCB's objectives.[19] "We'll encourage formation of local citizens committees," Kubasik reports, "but we want them only loosely amalgamated with us." Right now NCCB has only about 180 hand-picked members.

A qualification for identifying with NCCB obviously is lack of hesitation about assailing the TV establishment. Kubasik, an enthusiastic heckle-raiser, tosses off such barbs as, "We just can't have so much power (over TV) residing in so few hands," and, "All we're trying to do is bend the quality of TV programming upward."

The question is: how many want to march to this drum?

Should the Audience Reign Supreme?

Frank Stanton has stated that the essence of democracy is to give the people what they want. The public should set the standards of television programming by either accepting or rejecting what is offered. Stanton believes that the basic elements for implementing cultural democracy are ratings as well as other types of feedback which have just been discussed.

This position assumes access to accurate information about public reaction to television. Even if more accurate feedback could be obtained through improved broadcast ratings, more representative and numerous phone calls and letters, and more effective audience groups, two important questions regarding Stanton's position would remain. First, does the public know what it wants? After deciding in 1934 to carry New York Philharmonic programs on Sunday afternoons, William Paley was told that there was no audience for classical music. He reportedly replied that CBS would create one, which it did. Audiences have been created for other types of programming as well, quiz shows for example. Second, even if the public knew what it wanted and made its wishes known, should these be the sole criteria for television programming? In other words, is cultural democracy desirable?

Professor Harry Skornia (pp. 434-436) critically examines the assumption that television should consist of what the public wants. He argues that this philosophy implies that the public knows what it wants, the public is an "it" rather than a "they," and the public's wishes can be accurately gauged. Skornia questions all of these assumptions and bases his arguments on the problem of defining "the

432

people"; people behave differently as Market or Audience or Public.
He does not accept the concept that the ratings accurately transmit
what the public wants. Skornia submits that wants are not a sound
standard for determining values; the standards for our laws and democratic government were established by needs, not wants.

One criticism of the position illustrated by Stanton, that the public
should receive what it wants, is that the consequence is frivolous and
wasteful television. Professor Arnold Toynbee (pp. 437-441) blames
this waste on both the viewers and the "commercial purveyors." He
feels that the viewer's childish, abysmally low standards result from
the change in the character of work brought about by the Industrial
Revolution. Factory labor creates boredom and the laborer desires
undemanding recreation. The more educated office worker is a victim
of escapism. Toynbee indicates that historically, undirected leisure
was misspent and today's increased leisure, because it has no direction, will tend to lead to social, cultural and moral regression if
unchecked. The television networks, or commercial purveyors, are
reluctant to raise their standards for fear that people would stop
watching, but Toynbee feels it is important to make the public raise
its sights. He suggests that a spiritual revolution may well be the
necessary solution.

Gilbert Seldes (pp. 442-445) lists seven important mistakes made
by the "highbrow," "egghead," "ultra-intellectual" critic of television.
These are important, he feels, because the statements made by the
intellectuals soon appear in the newspapers and eventually become
the fashion. Furthermore, this type of intellectual criticism is perpetuating the gap between the well educated and the average citizen,
a gap which is not desirable in a democracy. He urges intellectuals to
attempt to acquire understanding as a first step toward closing the gap,
and suggests that much improvement in the medium could be brought
about by well-intentioned, well educated, intelligent critics.

Don't Give Viewers What They Want

By Harry J. Skornia

SEPTEMBER 18, 1965

Do you go to a lecture to hear what a man wants to say about a subject? Or do you go to have him tell you what you want to hear?

Does an atomic scientist change his subject from fission to his latest trip through the Alps because it would be more entertaining and he has excellent slides available?

Ratings are based on the assumption that stations should broadcast What the Public Wants. This premise should be examined.

A few years ago journalists were criticized for providing too little news about nuclear fallout. Editors explained that before press coverage of this problem could be increased, the public must demand it. The chicken-and-the-egg relationship in such a statement is obvious. From what, if not from news, is the public to know that such information is available? Or how is the public to know that fallout is or was reaching dangerous levels, and therefore should be considered news?

The market for news items—like that for products—can be either created or not created. Years ago speakers, artists, and writers had things to say. The available media—print, podium, and radio—dictated only the subject's form. Now the communicator asks the public: What do you want said? The dangers of carrying the What-the-Public-Wants practice to an extreme are obvious.

But this is only a small part of the problem.[20] The slogan "Give the public what it wants" implies, first, that the public "knows" what it wants. Second, it implies that the public is an "it" instead of a "they." Third, it implies that there is a clear and accurate way for wants to be transmitted to the decision makers.

Alan Thomas has said[21] that people play three roles in relation to TV—as Audience, as Market, and as Public.

As Audience, people are a series of unconnected homes or individuals. Because they are so unconnected and isolated from each other, they cannot set standards—which is what Frank Stanton and others say they do. The Audience exists only from moment to moment. The Audience's vote is expressed by ratings. And the ratings count "sets" rather than "people" or likes and dislikes in general.

As *Market,* the people become buying units—economic rather than human entities. Market success is measured by sales and profits; that is, dollars. Market, too, is temporary. It is created by advertising.

As *Public,* public exist in their capacity as "citizens." People who may vote "for" a program as Audience (through ratings) may, as Public (citizens), vote "against" the same program if they find the sponsor dishonest. As a part of the Public, a man may even support stricter government regulation to correct indecencies, dishonesty, rigging, deceit, excessive violence, or any other objectionable content in the very programs he voted "for" as Audience (by tuning in) and may even have voted for as Market (by buying the product).

The role of Public makes the citizen ask himself what is the "responsible" thing to do, rather than merely what is it he likes or wants. This role is the only continuing and rational one of the three. Only in the role of Public do the people operate as a nation. Only in this role have they an accurate mechanism for voting—the ballot box. The Public has voted for the creation of regulatory agencies by voting for congressmen who wrote legislation to create these agencies. As Audience or Market, people may want lewd programs, or dope; as Public, or citizens, however, they will ask for limitations on both.

So the behavior of citizens as Audience is likely to be quite different from their behavior as citizens, when they are asked for a considered and responsible decision for the good of their country, their children, and the general welfare.

The Public regulates. The Audience watches programs and laughs at regulation violations. And the Market buys. Only in their role as the Public do the people recognize their "duties" and "needs" as well as their "wants" in the perspective which democracy requires.

To quote ratings, then is not to quote the Public—it is only to quote the Audience—it means 1. quoting appetite instead of hunger, 2. want instead of need, 3. irresponsibility instead of responsibility, 4. short-term instead of long-term, 5. irrationality instead of rationality. Yet Audience (ratings) is the constituency which the broadcast industry so often quotes in support of its programming.

Newton Minow in 1961 told the industry[22] that his personal random survey of children showed that most of them preferred candy to spinach, movies to Sunday School, and soap operas and game shows to school. There is nothing wrong, he said, with giving children

436   some of the things they want—but we pass laws requiring attendance at school—which is clearly in violation of children's freedom. The fact that democracy is based on laws indicates that you simply cannot let children or anybody else do whatever they want.

Even for adults, "want" is not a sound standard for determining value. "Hunger" and "appetite" are not the same. Traffic laws and the controls placed on certain drugs are examples of the rules needed in all areas of life.

The give-the-public-what-it-wants philosophy fails to take into account that the satisfaction of "needs" is more likely to insure survival of individuals as well as of democracy than the satisfaction of "wants." People do not necessarily "want" what they "need." Needs are objective, and they represent requirements; they are relatively lasting. Wants, on the other hand, are subjective. They are irrational and can be created by all kinds of irresponsible temptation and lures. Something a man "needs" is something it is harmful for him not to have. What he "wants" may actually be harmful.

Television: The Lion That Squeaks

By *Arnold J. Toynbee*

DECEMBER 4, 1965

Television is not the only one of our marvelous modern means of communication that is being largely wasted on frivolities. The same sad tale is told by the headlines and advertisements in the evening newspapers—and not only in the evening one—all over the world.

There is a contrast here, and a misfit, that is striking and painful: On the one hand a technology that is a *chef-d'oeuvre* of intellectual creative power and ingenuity; on the other hand a prostitution of this product of mature human genius to serve childish tastes. A pessimist, looking into the future, might predict that this really shocking combination of incongruous means and ends will condition mankind into becoming a race of technician-morons—creatures that will be lower than our prehuman ancestors in terms of truly human values.

What causes this disconcerting trend? Can it be arrested, reversed? One thing, for certain, is "not" the cause. It is not the inventors' fault that their inventions are being so deplorably misused. The apparatus with which our inventive geniuses have endowed us is neutral. It could be used, just as easily and effectively, for the highest purposes as it is being used for the lowest purposes today. It is, in fact, happily, being used already, though, so far, only on a relatively small scale, in education. If this potent new instrument is being so largely misused at present, the fault lies not with the human inventors of these mechanical genies; it lies with their human users.

Which set of users is chiefly to blame? The viewers of television or the commercial purveyors of it, who stand between the viewers and the inventors? They share the blame, I should say. If the viewers were to stop viewing such inferior stuff, then sheer commercial self-interest would push the purveyors into giving their customers something better. Conversely, if the purveyors did give the customers something better, they would be educating the public to raise the standard of its demand.

437

438   Insofar as the viewers' present abysmally low standard is low by the viewers' own choice, and not because this standard has been imposed on them by the purveyors, what is it that accounts for the viewers' childishness? I think there are several causes on which one can put one's finger.

One cause of present-day childishness in grown-up people is the change in the character of the work by which an ever-increasing proportion of the world's population has come to be earning its living since the beginning of the Industrial Revolution. The mechanization of the world's work has been lightening mankind's physical labor, but this at the price of imposing on the factory worker a psychological curse from which the preindustrial farmer was free. This curse is the curse of boredom.

The farmer's work on an unmechanized farm of the traditional kind is laborious. He must work from dawn to dark, year in and year out; his cows, sheep, and fowls require as constant attention as human infants. But, by the same token, a farmer's life is never dull. A human mother does not easily get bored with her gruelling job of bringing up her children, and the farmer does not get bored—in the sense of time on his hands—with his livestock and crops.

On the other hand, how can the factory worker's life "not" be dull? The "means of production" that he is tending are machines processing "raw materials"—a poor exchange, in psychological terms, for his farmer-grandfather's fields and pastures and crops and cows. The factory worker's relation to the machinery is impersonal. If the wheels are to be made to pay, they must be kept turning 24 hours in the day, so the machine-tender works on a shift; the machine is not his own, in the sense in which the farmer's cow and crop are his.

The factory is not only kept in operation all round the clock, it is insulated from the elements. A thermostat automatically keeps it at whatever temperature the technician chooses; and rain and hail can batter on the factory roof without any effect on the work that is going on under the roof's shelter. The control of the environment inside the factory walls makes the output regular and predictable, but it consequently makes the job of producing the output dull.

The factory worker will be able to hand over to the next shift, and to leave the building, the moment his stint of work is completed. He may come out physically fresh; but he is likely to find himself psychologically jaded. What he craves for, in his off-time, is recreation; and, of course, he is tempted to choose the kind of recreation that makes the lowest spiritual demand on him.

The middle-class office worker is also making the same choice, without having the same excuse. In his case, perhaps, the cause is not so much boredom as it is anxiety. His higher education has made him more acutely aware of problems—political, social, moral, and spiritual —that are baffling him. His flight from these cares to soap-box opera is a case of escapism.

Moreover, the incentives to seek frivolous distractions are growing in strength. The problems that create anxiety become more menacing, and daily work becomes more boring as automation's pace accelerates. Working hours are continually becoming shorter and leisure hours correspondingly longer; and here we have a second cause of the public's present choice of forms of recreation that are frivolous and childish.

For the mass of mankind—for everyone except a tiny privileged minority—leisure was, till within living memory, a blessing, or curse, of which they had had hardly any experience. Abundant leisure has now suddenly descended on them while they are still psychologically unprepared for coping with it.

This social revolution (it amounts to that) has been sudden because the pace of technological advance has become so fast. People are still unprepared for it because the pace of psychological change has always been slower than the pace of technological change—and the pace of psychological change cannot be speeded up, to match, by any ingenious mechanical inventions. In the fable, the tortoise won its race against the hare—but turn the live hare into an electric hare, and what chance is left to the tortoise for keeping pace with that?

When human beings are given leisure, they misuse it unless and until they have educated themselves to do better than that. I have mentioned the tiny privileged minority that enjoyed a monopoly of leisure in the premechanical age. By the 18th century, this minority had already had about five thousand years for learning how to use its leisure for social, cultural and spiritual purposes.

But what is that privileged 18th-century minority's record? It flattered itself that it was an élite. Yet, for one Voltaire, Franklin, Rousseau, Jefferson, or Wesley, there were thousands who misspent their leisure on hunting, gambling and philandering.

The frivolities on which the majority is now largely wasting its recently acquired leisure have, on the whole, less vice in them than the leisured 18th-century minority's frivolous pursuits had. That, however, is a small mercy to be thankful for. The misspending of leisure, even on comparatively innocent frivolities, will lead to social, cultural and moral regression if it continues unchecked.

In our attitudes towards this evil, we cannot afford to be indulgent

440 or complacent. We have to get the viewer of television to raise his sights. How far does this depend on him, and how far does it depend on the policy of the commercial organization that purveys to him those silly programs to which the viewer is now giving an appallingly high proportion of his viewing time?

Here, I am afraid, we are caught in a vicious circle. The purveyor of television, like other tradesmen, is primarily concerned to sell his wares as profitably for himself as he can; and this consideration governs his policy. Shall he try to raise his viewers' standards by giving them programs that will be rather higher than the level of their average present demand as estimated by the purveying firm's customer-research department?

The purveyor shrinks from venturing on this public-spirited experiment. He shrinks because he fears that, if he did raise the standard even one inch above the average level of demand, there might be a mass flight from television. The purveyor therefore allows himself a margin of safety. He sets the level of his wares below the average level of demand, not above it, and this poor-spirited policy gives him greater freedom of play; for his researchers tell him that he can depress the level of his wares at least 12 inches below the average level of demand before his low-brow customers will give up television in disgust because they are finding it too banal to please even them.

Can this vicious circle be broken? No doubt there is some hope to be found in the spread of higher education. In this sphere, television is already beginning to be used for constructive purposes. But it is only in our time that higher education has become accessible to the majority, and the first generation of children who receive it have to come to it without the help of any cultural background in their homes. It is only in the second or third generation that the effects of higher education in school and college begin to become cumulative by creating a fund of culture in the home to give the high school and university student's education an initial boost and a perpetual encouragement.

Will this hoped-for effect of the spread of higher education be enough to produce an improvement in the quality of the average demand of television viewers? We are relying here on education in the formal sense, and this may be capable of producing a change for the better in taste.

But will just educating the head be enough? The head cannot run far in advance of the heart; and, for bringing about a change of heart, something more than an improvement in formal education is required.

A spiritual revolution is needed; and, here, I think, we are touching   *441*
the heart of the matter. We are putting our finger on what is wrong,
not just with present-day television, but with present-day Western
life. In present-day Ethiopia there is no commercial television yet,
but for centuries there have been viewers there. What they come to
view—sometimes walking many miles over the mountains—is the
pictures of the Bible story on the walls of their churches.

Our own medieval ancestors, too, were viewers of that kind. In
our time, we have lost the lofty vision and the serious purpose with
which our forefathers used to be inspired by their ancestral religions.
This inspiration has now been lost by many people who still attend
church and temple and mosque. How is this vital inspiration to be
regained? The future of television, and of everything else, will depend on our answer.

The Petulant Highbrow and TV

By Gilbert Seldes

JANUARY 2, 1960

Over 20 years ago I invented egghead criticism of television. I am not boasting and not confessing—I am presenting my credentials for discussing the subject. In May 1937—10 years before Tuesday night became the property of Uncle Miltie—I wrote a piece for the *Atlantic Monthly* called "Errors of Television." I committed the crime of which all intellectuals are accused: I wrote about TV without seeing it. My only excuse was, there was none to see. I was predicting. Nevertheless, when, today, I hear Dr. Frank Stanton, the president of CBS, denounce "intellectuals who delight in blanket charges about television without showing any evidence of ever looking at it," I know that I started it all.

Since that time I have been connected with about 2000 hours of television—as producer, director, writer, emcee or panelist—but I remain an intellectual critic of the medium. I haven't made all the mistakes of the highbrow critics—because three months after that magazine article appeared, CBS invited me to take charge of making TV errors for them.[23] But I am sympathetic to the angry critic—and I think I know why he carries on the way he does.

As I see it, the basic approach of the ultraintellectual is this:

1. He takes for granted that the worst example of any type of program—the silliest domestic comedy or the most brutal crime picture—is average or typical.

2. He assumes that the "quality" program is excessively rare and has no considerable audience.

3. He doesn't compare TV with the actuality of other forms of entertainment. He tends to talk about "the art of fiction" or "the dramatic art" as if 90 percent of the books and plays offered to us each year weren't unmitigated trash. And he tends to compare *Father Knows Best* with *Oedipus Rex*.

4. He blames on television whatever he doesn't like in America

442

or in modern life generally. This ranges from juvenile delinquency 443 to the cold war and, if the critic is good, can project into the future.

5. He believes that television is what it is because it sells soup and soap. No matter what proof that state-operated, noncommercial TV develops the same characteristics, the sponsor remains the villain.

6. He can be totally unaware of change—if the change is upward. He knows that *Studio One* disappeared and *Desilu Playhouse* is on—he never seems to hear about *Playhouse 90* or *Sunday Showcase*.

7. He wants more programs suitable to refined taste and isn't really interested in raising the total level of entertainment. Actually— by percentages—the amount of highbrow stuff on the air is enormously disproportionate to the tiny number of intellectuals in the country. Statistically they would be entitled to as much time per day as it takes for three station identifications and one time signal.

If they're as wrongheaded as all that, why pay attention to the intellectuals? The millions of people who tune in and enjoy almost everything and buy all the products advertised have never even heard the names of these critics. If they could translate the language in which the criticism is expressed, they'd probably say these highbrows are sourpusses and shrug them off. Yet in 1959 the TV industry collected a thumping lot of money and set up the [Television Information Office] to publicize TV and specifically to combat its "bad press," its unfavorable criticism—just as the movies about 10 years ago set out to prove that "the movies are better than ever." Why?

In the first place, what the eggheads say today, the average newspaper critic will be saying tomorrow. Which means, in the second place, that there is a partial truth in what these critics say, even if it's only the truth that TV is made by fallible human beings and, therefore, it isn't perfect and it's a good thing to haul people over the coals and make them do their best. Parallel to Point One, there is a danger zone in all popular entertainment when people can turn against it, and if it's the smart thing to sneer at TV, this can penetrate down to the average person and have a bad effect. TV is always under the guns in Congress, for instance, and if a strong tide is running against it, any kind of laws might be passed.

There is another reason for attacking bad-tempered and uninformed criticism by intellectuals. It is that well-informed, intelligent criticism could do the industry a lot of good. I do not mean only what highbrows write or say on lecture tours. I mean the day-to-day comment that intelligent people make to one another.

444   In relation to TV today, the hostile one-sided critic is making the same mistake he made in the 1920's about the movies and about jazz. Nowadays the State Department sends jazz bands around the world as ambassadors of good will. Thirty years ago if you said a kind word for jazz, the music lovers denounced you as if you had violated the sanctuary and thrown bricks at city hall into the bargain.

As for the movies, there is a mild expression, peculiarly apt today. It comes from a scholar who (as it happens) struck it rich, James Truslow Adams: "It is not a cheering thought to figure the number of people who are thrilled nightly by a closeup kiss on 10,000 screens compared to the number that see a play of O'Neill's."

Well, today, or a week from tomorrow night, or sometime soon, there will be a play by O'Neill on not 10,000 but 40,000,000 screens, and the fact that the owners of some of them will prefer to see a close-up of a kiss, or a farce, or a Western is the price we pay for free selection. The Adamses who disliked the movies transferred their dislike to radio, and their descendants dislike television. They perpetuate the gap between the educated intellectual and the average man and woman—and in a democracy like ours, this isn't a good thing. In my opinion, the intellectual loses more than the average man by this separation, but our society suffers most.

I said I thought I knew why the intellectual behaves as he does. Let me say first, in his favor, that he pays the ultimate tribute to radio and the movies and television when he calls down the wrath of heaven against the producers. He says, in effect, "These things—which you conceive of merely as trifling entertainments—are terribly important. These aren't fun, they are lessons, teaching people what is admirable in the world. They are creating new ideals for the future. Our children will grow up believing there's no better world than that of *Dragnet* and quiz shows—and how are they going to cope with the tough world that's being created for the children behind the Iron Curtain?"

This is the critic's strength. On the other hand, the extravagance of the criticism renders it null. It leads nowhere. And the reason is that the highbrow critic isn't really attacking what television does—he is defending his own interest which, by and large, is the empire of the printed page. That is why I say that the highbrow critic, although he looks at the TV screen far more often than Dr. Stanton imagines, doesn't see what's going on there. His training and his tradition and his prejudices prevent him from observing the actuality. He sees what he expects to see and what he expects to see is popular perversion of

the whole culture that has come down to us through centuries of the   *445*
printed word.

What's happening to all of us is that we're going through a revolution. The prime communicator before the invention of printing was the preacherorator; after that, print—the newspaper and the book and the magazine—took over. Now the power of print is being challenged. Power is shifting to the electronic medium, to the speaking image on the screen. Naturally, everyone who has spent years in the study of books, everyone who has written for print, everyone who has learned to respect whatever is between covers, feels resentful at the instrusion of the new force. I add myself to them and say, "We have a vested interest in print and you, the managers of the electronic mass media, are lowering the value of our investment."

But as a citizen, I say that we who have had the great advantage of a book education owe it to the community to make terms with the new medium. If we are better educated than the average, we ought to be better able to use the mass media for the general good. I believe that we have in these media, pre-eminently in television, precisely the instrument we need for narrowing the gap between high- and lowbrow. I think also that in the quarrel between the two, the highbrow has been the petulant one and it is up to him to stop nagging his adversary and stop sneering at what other people seem to enjoy—and to make the first step toward reconciliation, which is, of course, to acquire understanding.

Notes to Chapter 4

1. The Harris Congressional Hearings of 1963 revealed that some of the Nielsen homes had been in the sample since the 1930's, when Nielsen first started measuring radio audiences. Nielsen maintained that the advantages of a more permanent sample, including economy, detection of trends, ability to conduct specialized kinds of research, and so forth, outweighed the dangers of the sample's becoming less representative. But pressures from a variety of forces resulted in Nielsen's having what he claimed to be an entirely new sample by 1965, and since that time a sample turnover of 20 percent is reportedly made each year.

2. Nielsen and Sparger settled a suit out of court, with Sparger's agreeing not to publish a recounting of his attempts to rig the ratings.

3. C. E. Hooper, Inc. claims the bias of both the meter and diary method averages about 14 percent, running from a low of 2.5 percent inflation between 9 A.M. and noon on weekday mornings to a 14 percent inflation on weekday afternoons. Hooper is considering becoming a full-scale competitor to ARB and Nielsen in local television ratings.

4. The study was financed by the Committee on National Television Audience Measurements and conducted by Eric Marger Associates. It is described in the booklet,

446 *How Good Are Television Ratings?*, by Martin Mayer, released in February, 1966.

5. *Bonanza* originally came on the air in September 1959 on Saturday evenings opposite *Perry Mason*. *The Man From U.N.C.L.E.* premiered in 1964 in competition with *The Red Skelton Hour* and *McHale's Navy*, both rating hits. *The Dick Van Dyke Show*'s initial opposition in 1961 was the second half of *Laramie* and *Bachelor Father*.

6. In January, 1968, *The Birds* attracted the largest audience ever for a movie shown on television. It achieved a 38.9 Nielsen rating.

7. TvQ ratings are obtained by a mail questionnaire sent to over two thousand families a month. Viewers are asked to rank programs as follows: (1) One of My Favorites, (2) Very Good, (3) Good, (4) Fair, (5) Poor, (6) Never Have Seen.

8. Nielsen is having difficulty in obtaining sufficient support from his subscribers for such a service. He does, however, plan to have an "experimental" instantaneous service in Los Angeles by the fall of 1970.

9. Critics of Nielsen question his assumption that the information from the other 10 percent of sample homes would not affect the ratings results.

10. Nielsen critics claim the figure is 5 to 10 percent higher. Part of the discrepancy relates to the criteria used in defining what constitutes viewing the set.

11. Traditionally, families accepting meters have been paid fifty cents every two weeks plus one-half of all their television repair bills. The use of trading stamps to reward rating cooperators has become more prevalent among the other rating services.

12. See note 7.

13. If women are separated into age groups, it becomes apparent that Westerns are big favorites of women over 50. *Bonanza, Gunsmoke* and *The Virginian* have long been very highly rated by older women.

14. Effective September, 1968, the NAB code was altered to limit the number of interruptions within a program to two interruptions for a thirty-minute show and four for a sixty-minute program. Prior to this time, the code limited the total number of commercial minutes and the number of announcements that could be aired consecutively, but there were no definite limitations placed on the number of interruptions that could occur during a program.

15. More recent examples of letters keeping shows on the air include *Star Trek*. See Stephen E. Whitfield and Gene Roddenberry, *The Making of Star Trek*, New York: Ballantine Books, 1968, pp. 393-399.

16. On December 22, 1968, CBS interrupted the NFL Western Playoff Game between the Baltimore Colts and the Minnesota Vikings for an Apollo 8 report. The report lasted seventeen minutes, twenty-six seconds and cut into a little more than the last two minutes of the first half and most of the halftime activities of the game. A video tape replay of the action missed by the viewer was run when CBS returned to the game.

This episode was just over one month after the NBC *Heidi* incident. On November 11, viewers of the AFL regular season game between the Oakland Raiders and the New York Jets missed the last minute of the final quarter because NBC decided to begin the children's special *Heidi* on time. Unfortunately for NBC, the Raiders scored twice during a nine-second interval in the final minute of play to beat the Jets 43-32, and the fans who had sat through the entire game missed both touchdowns. The switchboard at WNBC in New York reportedly broke down, due to a tremendous number of calls from irate football fans.

17. The National Citizens Committee for Broadcasting was originally established in May 1967 as the National Citizens Committee for Public Broadcasting. In October 1968, following the resignation of Newton Minow from the Committee board as a result of Board Chairman Hoving's charges that there was collusion between commercial TV networks and AT&T to keep the public from being informed, the Committee announced a change of its name, an expansion of its board of trustees and an increased concern with all broadcasting, including commercial TV networks.

18. In January 1969, Board Chairman Hoving announced the launching of a five-   *447*
year $5 million funding campaign and indicated that although foundations would be ap-
proached, the Committee expected to obtain most of its support through private individuals and businesses. In February, executive director Kubasik notified trustees that
several staff members had already been released and that lack of funds might force the
organization to disband "toward the end of March."

19. In October 1970, the NCCB will host a National Strategy Conference on Citizens Rights in Broadcasting. From 1500 to 2000 persons are expected to attend.

20. An elaboration of the following comments by Professor Skornia may be found
in *Television and Society*, New York: McGraw-Hill, 1965, pp. 121-123 ff.

21. Alan Thomas, *Audience, Market, Public: An Evaluation of Canadian Broadcasting*, Occasional Paper No. 7, University of British Columbia, Department of University Extension, April 1960.

22. A portion of his "vast wasteland" speech of May 9, 1961. See *Equal Time*,
p. 54.

23. Between 1937 and 1945, Mr. Seldes was the first Director of Television
Programs for CBS.

EFFECTS

Chapter 5

Television's Role

Dr. George Gerbner, dean of the Annenberg School of Communications at the University of Pennsylvania, gave the following general appraisal of the role and effects of television upon society when he testified before the National Commission on the Causes and Prevention of Violence.

In only two decades of massive national experience television has transformed the political life of the nation, has changed the daily habits of our people, has molded the style of the generation, made overnight global phenomena out of local happenings, re-directed the flow of information and values from traditional channels into centralized networks reaching into every home. In other words, it has profoundly affected what we call the process of socialization, the process by which members of our species become human.

From its very beginning, television's actual and potential functions have been the subject of continuing debate. Lee Loevinger, former Federal Communications Commissioner (pp. 453-457), feels that it is necessary to separate television's present role from its potential role and examine each separately. He reviews five theories of broadcasting which attempt to explain its use and suggest its major function. He considers all five inadequate, primarily because none is consistent with all the present established facts about mass media. Loevinger then presents his own "reflective-projective theory." He refers to television as an electronic mirror which reflects blurred images into which the viewer projects his own vision of society and himself. Loevinger contends that this theory provides a better understanding of television, bringing the "is" and "should be" of the medium closer together by accounting for observable facts and suggesting television's natural function. According to Loevinger, this function is to strengthen our common culture and sense of national unity and purpose by permitting us to share daily in a common reflection of society.

451

452   Loevinger's observation that television is a shared experience strengthening our common culture is reflected in the other articles presented here. Dr. Karl and Jean Menninger (pp. 458-460) maintain that television, although a means of communication, is basically a form of communion. They suggest that television is a presence; it has become a modern equivalent of the old family hearth, with the family sitting around the fire or doing their chores in front of it. Yet television also can bring to us common experiences with millions of others when important events occur.

Russell Lynes (pp. 461-464) states that television has five functions: to inform, instruct, enlighten, entertain, and transport. He briefly evaluates television's performance of each of the first four functions, then discusses at some length its ability to transport. This ability to convey images of places, events, even styles, has added a significant dimension to man's experience. Lynes also emphasizes television's role in breaking down regional differences and standardizing taste and expectations. He argues that television, by exhibiting middle-class standards to the underprivileged, has contributed to the recent urban upheavals.

Lynes talks about television's role in eliminating pockets of isolation. There are still millions of Americans who are not able to receive a single television signal where they live. These people do not participate in the common culture and share the common experiences nor are they transported by television in the manner described by Loevinger, Menninger or Lynes. Professor Edward Morris (pp. 465-468) discusses the impact television has had on an Appalachian community in eastern Kentucky. He emphasizes the great educational values of television for culturally and socially backward people, something which, as Morris points out, educated urban critics fail to keep in mind.

Television, according to the late Eleanor Roosevelt (pp. 469-471) is "one of the blessings of our period of history" for older citizens. It distracts them from the boredom and loneliness of age; it provides them with contact with the rest of the world and it gives them the opportunity to share in events and ideas with younger people. Most elderly people withdraw because they feel unable to share a useful life, but television can and does alleviate this tendency. Of course, television could play an even more significant and constructive role in increasing the happiness and usefulness of the elderly. So too, the older citizen, according to Mrs. Roosevelt, could play a valuable role in helping to improve television.

There Need Be No Apology, No Lament

By Lee Loevinger

Maybe television really isn't very important—it doesn't necessarily influence people just because they watch it for hours on end. That is about the most charitable opinion expressed by six eminent intellectuals writing in TV GUIDE in 1966.[1] Similar derogatory views appear almost daily in newspapers and magazines. Meanwhile millions of people, a large part of the population, spend every evening watching the tube. A recent survey disclosed that only 14 percent of slum homes in one large Eastern city took newspapers, but 100 percent had television sets.

What's going on, and is it good or bad? A rational approach recognizes two separate questions here. The first: What is television actually doing? The second: What should it be doing? In the voluminous writing on the subject, there has been little effort to separate these questions. Most critics are so anxious to tell us what they think television should be that they neglect to examine what it actually is.

A fairly comprehensive review of what has been written shows five general theories of broadcasting: First was the hobby theory. When we were winding wire coils on old cereal boxes, making condensers (capacitors) out of tinfoil and waxed paper, using "crystals" and "cat whiskers," and listening on earphones, the real joy of radio was getting the most distant stations. A boy in St. Paul, Minnesota, thrilled to hear KDKA simply because it was in Pittsburgh. After World War II, much of the interest in television was the novelty of getting a picture in your own home. In those days people enjoyed manipulation of the device as much as programs, and broadcasting was more a hobby than a means of mass communication. Radio is still a hobby for more than a quarter-million licensed amateurs; but most of us have long since become more interested in programs.

When broadcasting declined as a hobby, it grew as a news medium. In the early 1930's newspaper publishers tried to prevent

453

454 broadcasting of news. A separate radio news service was established, but finally publishers conceded the rights of broadcasters, and news wire services were offered to radio stations. Public reliance on broadcasting has grown since then until now a Roper survey indicates more people look to television as a primary news source than to newspapers. This has led numerous observers to the view that the journalistic function is the principal and proper role of broadcasting.

Others see the journalistic theory as emphasizing mere news reporting too much, while neglecting social influence. They point to the vast audience of broadcasting, larger than any other medium in history both in numbers and percentage of population, and claim this offers a chance for great social influence. Since social problems are now so urgent, this leads to the conclusion that broadcasting is, or should be, an instrument of social reform. This view sees television as a means of doing quickly and easily what home, school, church and state have been struggling to do slowly and painfully for years. A similar view is official in some countries, especially Communist ones, which subject broadcasting to strict government control because of its supposed social and political influence.

Recently some philosophers and scientists have rejected the journalistic and social-reform theories in an effort to discover what broadcasting actually is, rather than starting with their own ideas of what it ought to be. The best-known of these is Marshall McLuhan, a Canadian professor now at Fordham, who has become the Billy Rose, or perhaps the P. T. Barnum, of the academic world.[2]

McLuhan's thesis and slogan is, "The medium is the message." This means that each medium changes the environment or creates a new environment, and consequences of this change are more significant than the messages carried. McLuhan regards all media as extensions of human senses, and points to effects of such sense-extensions through printing, radio and television. McLuhan says mass media created "the public," and argues that this fact is more important than any particular message.

Most recently William Stephenson, a social scientist at the University of Missouri, has suggested "the play theory of mass communications,"[3] based on novel, technical and ingenious methods of investigating and measuring attitudes. Stephenson says play is activity that is self-sufficient and pursued for the pleasure in it, while work involves effort undertaken for some ulterior purpose, such as production of goods, ideas or profit.

Mass communication is engaged in for pleasure, not for information or improvement. For example, people look first in the newspaper to read about events they have been involved in and already know about, as a football game they have seen. This shows they read newspapers not for information but as play. The "fill," the ordinary content, of mass communications is neither debasing nor escapism, but a buffer against anxieties and tensions of modern conditions. Culture and national character are formed by songs, gossip, sports, dances, competition and other forms of communications pleasure. The role of mass communications is to maximize communications pleasure and individual freedom in a world of increasing social controls.

Each of these theories has some useful and accurate observations, but none is wholly adequate to explain obvious facts about television and radio. These are:

First, that broadcasting, especially television, is the most popular communications medium in history. It is the first truly mass medium reaching all classes and groups in society.

Second, American-type broadcasting has universal appeal. Even such typically American programs as Westerns are popular throughout the world, as is American popular music. Public demand has forced even government-operated broadcasting systems to present such programming.

Third, broadcasting is increasingly performing the journalistic function of news reporting for a growing segment of the public, while literacy and prosperity are increasing.

Fourth, television arouses strong emotional reactions in both critics and public. Strangely, those who say they dislike television seem to be as regular in their watching and passionate in their views as those who like it.

Fifth, television is largely disdained by intellectuals, both genuine and would-be. Some publications do not consider it respectable to write about television without disparaging it.

Sixth, broadcasting has become more a part of ordinary life than any other means of communication, except possibly talking. It is clearly a component of our common culture.

Testing the five theories we have described against these facts requires a more detailed analysis than is possible here, but such analysis shows that each is consistent with some, but not all of the facts. The difficulty is that each theory has focused on one or a few aspects rather than the whole complex picture. We can better understand broadcasting in modern society if we regard it as an electronic mirror that reflects a vague or ambiguous image.[4] As society is complex and many-faceted, broadcasting reflects a variety of images. These are never precisely focused and completely clear.

456   Society is reflected in the media mainly as an organized group or groups. But the audience watches as individuals. Looking at a blurred or vague image, different individuals see different things. This is because everyone engages in some projection, a common psychological process which consists of attributing our own attitudes, ideas or feelings to perceptions we get from the environment.

Psychologists use projection in the Rorschach "ink-blot" test by showing a series of ink blots to different persons and asking each to say what they mean. The different things people "see" in ink blots indicate ideas, attitudes and feelings of the observers.

All of us interpret observations according to our attitudes. To a child, *Alice in Wonderland* and *Gulliver's Travels* are stories of adventure; to an adult they are charming and fanciful allegories. Similarly, television programs mean different things to different people, and mean different things to one person at different times, depending upon attitude and mood.

Regarding television as an ambiguous mirror reflecting a slightly blurred image of society in which each viewer sees, by projection, his own vision of society and self, explains the observable facts. Television is popular because, as a reflection of society, it is responsive and adapted to mass attitudes and tastes. It increasingly performs the journalistic function because it is immediate, personal and comprehensive. Television is often better than personal observation as it can go further, faster and see more, yet conveys a sense of personal presence and participation.

There is emotional reaction to television because by projection each person sees some of his ego in his perception, so he reacts as though statements about television were about hinself—which they are so far as they involve his impression of television.

A simple test shows how projection involves ego and emotion. Hide and watch people passing a mirror. Almost no one can resist looking at his own image, and few fail to show some reaction. Or try taking pictures and showing them to the subject. People love to see pictures of themselves but never say they are flattered.

The intellectuals are alienated by television because they want to see images of themselves, as they think they are, and instead they see images of the common man and the mass of society. But television is an element of our culture because it shows things of common and universal interest. National culture is not found in museums or formed by graduate schools or universities. It is composed of common habits and patterns of living of people in daily activities, and of the common interest in entertainment, sports, news, and even advertising. The "fill" or ordinary run of material in everyday broadcasting is a more important part of common culture than the occasional artistic triumph or esthetic masterpiece. Whether or not anyone thinks this is the way things should be, observation shows that this is the way things are. The "reflective-projective theory" which regards television as an ambiguous mirror in which each viewer sees an image of both society and self is simply descriptive of known facts.

This view does suggest the role television is best adapted to serve. One of our most pressing needs today is to strengthen our common culture and sense of national unity and purpose. The only media that reach enough people or touch people intimately enough to achieve this are radio and television. Whether television lifts us to esthetic or intellectual heights or elevates our artistic standards is less important than whether it helps us achieve a common culture and sense of national unity and purpose.

It is more likely to do this by responding day after day to the wants and tastes of the million-strong masses than by straining for approval of scornful intellectuals. There need be no apology and should be no lament for a broadcasting industry which provides the mass of people with programs they watch and enjoy daily. Disdainful talk about television seeking "the lowest common denominator" misses the important point. Culture is not arithmetic, and the cultural denominator of popular programs may be the highest, not the lowest, that is truly common. The important point is television does achieve a common denominator in society.

If there were less programming it might be of better quality. But the character of life depends upon everyday experience more than upon great infrequent ceremonial occasions. Amiability at the breakfast table is more important to a happy marriage than design of the wedding gown.

As television lets us share daily a common reflection of society and helps us see a similar vision of our relationship to society, it builds a common culture to unite our country. This now appears to be its natural function and highest ideal. It is enough.

Television—The Comforting Presence

By Dr. Karl Menninger
with Jean Menninger

MAY 18, 1968

Two pieces of information which came to me recently started a train of thought about television. The first was a news item. A man was quoted as saying that, although he detested air conditioning, he had just installed a cooling unit in his office because it helped to drown out the noises of the city. The other bit came from a college girl who had been presented with a turtle-shaped electric appliance which had no other function than to make a whirring sound, halfway between the sound of an electric razor and an electric fan. The sound, described as extremely soothing and reassuring, was said to be a great aid to studying in a college dormitory.

These items suggest that silence is not only unattainable but not necessarily desired. Sounds—and lots of them—are an inescapable part of life in the city. Peace (for people) seems to lie not in escaping from sound but in making it acceptable, comfortable, reassuring, even noncommunicative. The sound must not have a pronounced, foot-tapping rhythm nor an arresting loudness, but should produce a feeling of intimacy and companionship. No rhythm, no melody, no racket—just a presence.

Until this was explained to me by my college friend, I had not reflected upon this function of television for perhaps thousands of persons, although I have sometimes entered homes where the television was turned on while every member of the family was engaged in some activity—playing cards, reading, sewing, studying, writing, cooking or even using the vacuum cleaner.

"It helps me concentrate," says the student. "It gives me a feeling of life around me." says the housewife, "something going on—friends at hand." "It's sort of scary without it," said one schoolchild.

I thought of the traditional picture of young Abraham Lincoln reading by the light of an open fire in a log cabin and wondered if

one might not say that the television receiver has become the modern   *459*
equivalent of the family hearth. In a semidarkened room the family
encircles it. It moves and flashes and crackles. Pictures leap up
before the eyes; corn is popped and meals are eaten around it. Now
and then it needs attention and adjustment, somewhat akin to making
up a bed of coals. Older people doze off comfortably beside it. The
convalescent child and the visiting friend are often included in the
circle.

While I was considering this picture, remembering many Sunday
evenings when I had glimpsed, over my small daughter's head, Lassie
trotting on innumerable errands of mercy, I came upon some corroboration of my ideas in an article by Richard Schickel in the June 1967
issue of *The Urban Review.*

"Television," he said, "is less a means of communication ('the
imparting or interchange of thoughts, opinions, and information by
speech, writing or signs') than it is a form of communion ('act of
sharing, or holding in common; participation, association; fellow-
ship')."

Schickel had noted, as I had, that television is often an accom-
paniment to the routine activities of the household. Statistics indicate
that the television set in the average American home is turned on
about five and a half hours per day, but much of the time it is accompanied by a background of housework or homework or relaxation—
talking, eating, phoning, resting.

Then, suddenly, some great occasion or natural drama breaks in
on the routine and we are all transfixed by the extraordinary fact of
witnessing history as it occurs—the space flights, the death of a
President, the Middle East crisis. These are the hours when the
television set becomes a tie that unites us with people all over the
Nation, even the world. For a time we are experiencing the same
scenes and sounds as thousands or millions of other concerned
persons.

There is comfort and growth in such experiences. Our sympathies
are engaged, our thoughts are excited and our horizons are expanded
through sharing sorrow and tension and acts of courage. There is a
deep craving in all of us to feel part of a cosmic experience which
involves us and others. We need to know how other people live and
strive, succeed and fail, meet disaster and tragedy and success.

Here, too, there is a reflection of high moments around the family
hearth, when the hunter, the soldier or the sailor recounted his adventures or the peddler or the political candidate or the circuit rider
brought romance and news of the world into the family circle. I

460   remember that one President [Roosevelt], using television's electronic predecessor, called his radio reports to the Nation "fireside chats."

The visions that we see in the flames as we sit by the fire are our visions. Let us work to make them better, not in fantasies and illusions, but in the perception of truth, remembering that we are in the company of millions of others who participate with us in the experience of viewing our world.

TV can be a gentle soporific—a "relaxant"—to many; but its great future lies in waking us up.

It already serves to re-create or extend the universe for many people of restricted lives: For so many of the lonely it glorifies existence; for the inhibited it can enrich the imagination. Part of the changes for the better that should take place in the world depend on information—and television often conveys that information: It shows us just how bad some things are in some places, and we can never be the same after having seen them. This throws a heavy burden on the fidelity and integrity of television.

May it live up to the task!

The Electronic Express

By Russell Lynes

FEBRUARY 24, 1968

It seems to me that television has five functions to perform or, if you prefer, purposes to serve. The first of these is to inform. The others are to instruct, to enlighten, to entertain and to transport.

The informational techniques of television are remarkable indeed. They have been highly developed by the news departments of the networks and by local stations, and if I have any quarrel with them, it is that they are not used and exploited enough. I am one of those viewers who looks at television only occasionally when it is not being a reportorial medium. It reports ably after the fact, but it is when it is being a substitute for one's own eyes, watching action as it happens, that it is at its most miraculous. Who will ever forget the sun reflected in the eyes of Robert Frost so that he could not read his poem at President Kennedy's inauguration? Who will forget the McCarthy hearings, the moment when Ruby shot Oswald, the smoke billowing from burning Detroit last summer? Television is the most remarkable transmitter of news ever devised, because it is the first to be instantaneous. It could, to be sure, use its potentialities better than it does, and in time it will.

I am not sure how competent a medium it is for the second of its purposes—for instruction. But that is my fault, not its. I have not subjected myself to educational television of the sort that teaches one how to use information, and heaven forbid that I should get up in time for *Sunrise Semester* or any of its kin. There are as many opinions about the purposes of educational television as there are television critics (and who today isn't a television critic?); my own opinion is that, like all other television, it ranges from excellent to abominable, but is best when it is least pretentious, least arty, least self-consciously high-brow. Indeed it is best when it is reporting and casting light on what it reports and when it explores subjects which admittedly are of no interest to many people but are passionately (or potentially) interesting to a limited audience. I find myself interested in looking at a one-act play by Turgenev, for example, even when I find it

461

462   nonsense; I am grateful for having been given the opportunity to decide. I have been enlightened (my third purpose of television) even if I have not been entertained—my fourth purpose.

I decline to comment on television as an entertainment medium, other than to say that it is a perfectly reasonable medium for entertainment and, like the theater, radio, the movies, night clubs, tent shows, vaudeville, burlesque and circuses—all of which it tries to be—it is only as good as the minds behind it and the performers in front of it. I cannot see that TV has added to entertainment's stature of diminished it. How could it? It is only a medium, not a mind or a talent.

But it has added a dimension to man's experience by its remarkable ability to transport. When people talk about transportation they usually mean physical conveyances—trains, planes, cars, ships—and not those things that transport ideas, and not only ideas, but environments—places, situations, manners, fashions, enthusiasms. As a medium of transportation television has moved people further and faster (indeed with the speed of light) than anything ever has before. This new conveyance undoubtedly will become far more comfortable and refined with time, but it is not likely to become any faster than however many hundreds of thousands of miles a second it is that light travels. Books, by comparison, are cumbersome, newspapers confusing, magazines fragmented, though let no one say a word against the printed page in my presence. Without pausing to argue with the currently celebrated Professor ("The Medium Is the Massage") McLuhan, I would like to contend that those traditional ox-cart and tricycle methods of transportation of the mind, written and printed words, are not likely to be replaced by electronic images, though I admit that McLuhan's prose style is a strong argument for abandoning them.

Let's look at a few of the remarkable effects of this medium of transportation on our lives. Obviously it takes us not only to the far corners of the globe but into space as well; it lets us see our planet as no one has seen it before except in science fiction. It lets us, for example, participate (by communications satellite) in an art auction that is taking place simultaneously in New York and London, allowing us to be on two continents at the same time, watching men's minds work as though they sat across the table from us. They know no more what will happen the next moment than we do, a kind of transportation no book or newspaper or magazine could conceivably duplicate. In a sense television has made isolation, unless it is self-imposed, all but impossible in our country, where the ratio of sets is approximately 1 to every 2.6 people.

The elimination of pockets of isolation has effects on the conduct *463* of society, on attitudes, on manners, on language, on fashions of dress and thought and enjoyment and recreation. If you take a group of young people, for example, who live in the Ozarks and subject them to the rock 'n' roll dance parties of their contemporaries in Chicago, something inevitably happens to the folkways of teen-agers in the Ozarks. Their clothes are going to take on many of the same character-istics as the clothes of the youngsters in the Middle West; so are their gestures, the ways they wear their hair, the length of their skirts, even the slope of their shoulders, the pitch of their pelvises and the fashion-ably vacant and faraway look in the eyes. A century ago it used to take a change in women's fashions, for example, a full decade to get from the Eastern Seaboard to the banks of the Mississippi. The impetus for change in fashion now arrives with the speed of a television signal and becomes reality as fast as manufacturers can get the goods into local stores. Changes in hair-dos don't have to wait for manufacturers.

The effect, of course, is to weaken the traditional regional dif-ferences which have been characteristic of our country (as they are of most countries) and eventually, along with other mass media, TV will go far to hasten their elimination. Trains, trucks and refrigeration have already made the national diet pretty much the same every-where; they have put what were rare delicacies, available only in cer-tain places, on tables everywhere; indeed they have in many respects taken away some of what we used to consider seasonal delights. TV will carry this reduction of regionalisms still further.

As Leo Rosten pointed out in this magazine several years ago,[5] TV will inevitably tend to make all parts of the country abandon re-gional accents for a common speech. It used to be that people con-sulted books of etiquette to find out what custom dictated as the proper way to do things. Now, no matter where one lives, television brings into living rooms a continual flow of examples of currently acceptable modes and manners. It is not my impression that television sets out to be an arbiter of manners, but it is one all the same, and it inevitably reflects middle-class standards of acceptability.

I do not think that this is the place to debate the virtues of middle-class standards (though it is a delightful subject to debate), but I do think that it is worth pointing out that the display of these values by television to people who cannot afford to achieve them has unques-tionably been a contributing factor in the urban upheavals of the last few summers. Television has been one of the most potent ways of keeping the standards of an affluent society constantly before the eyes of tremendous numbers of people who have not the means to enjoy its benefits and very little hope under present circumstances of

464   attaining such means. It would be easy to say that this flaunting of wealth has been a flag waved before the eyes of a bull until it finally in fury charged, with revenge and devastation its single goal. But looked at it in another way, it can be argued with sound reason that this flag has revealed to people demands which they have every right to make. It has shown them what they are missing that others take for granted. It has raised their sights. It has, in fact, raised hell by transporting people out of their slums to the threshold of another world of which the door has not been opened to them . . . except electronically.

Any means of communication is considered dangerous by a great many people who believe that the transmission of any ideas but their own is dangerous. To these timid people television must be the most frightening medium of all. To some of the rest of us it is the most promising. At its best it informs, instructs, enlightens, entertains and, above all, transports. It moves people, it moves places and ideas, and in a democratic and intensely mobile society like ours, what better service could it conceivably perform, and what medium could conceivably perform it better?

Pippa Passes, Ky., Joins The Nation

By Edward Morris

JUNE 18, 1966

In Pippa Passes, Kentucky, Jed Clampett is considered an out-right hick. For all his millions and Los Angeles at his disposal, Jed remains farther behind the times than the Eastern Kentucky mountaineer who is still making payments on a second-hand television set and who has seldom traveled beyond the county seat.

Knott County—where Pippa Passes is located and where I teach—is one of the most isolated and culturally deprived areas in America. It has no locally published newspaper, no radio station, no bookstore, no indoor theater, no tavern, not even a bowling alley. Some of its narrow valleys are so rugged that mail has to be taken in on muleback.

But Knott County has television via a community antenna system, and TV is doing more to educate the people about the realities of modern life than all the teachers have ever done.

Only a few years ago, there was no significant contact between Eastern Kentucky and the "outside world." The scattered area newspapers and radio stations devoted themselves almost exclusively to local matters. Salaries were so low that teachers from other parts of the country generally were unwilling to come here. Those who did were often faced with such suspicion and resistance that they left or adopted the local attitudes.

But television had an easier time of it. Sets became relatively cheap to purchase. (Even today refrigerators and stoves are the only appliances out-selling them.) Distant stations beamed in network programs and quickly lured the mountaineers away from single-minded attachment to local radio. More important, television, unlike the typical outsider, did not criticize, did not demand, did not so obviously condescend. Seeing no overt threat to their old ways of life, the people succumbed to this pleasant intruder. And the first thing one knew, square dancing was out and frugging was in.

465

466   This switch to the new ways became vividly apparent to me when I attended my first college dance here. No more than 10 of the 300 students are from outside this region, so I expected to see gingham and hear the Virginia reel. But what I saw and heard was a bucolic *Hullabaloo*.[6] Aside from the barnlike structure which grumbled to the vibrations, everything was disappointingly normal. Knowing that Arthur Murray had established no outposts here, I asked some students where they had learned their orgiastic pacings. Punctuated by snapping fingers came the consistent answer: "Television, man."

The most noticeable change television brought about, and probably the most valuable one, was to show the people the identity between themselves and other Americans. They have learned through newscasts and "specials" that poverty is no more exclusive to them than it is to the Harlem slum-dweller, that their sub-standard educational system has its counterparts in other states, and that their ballads are at once the prized obsession of the scraggly folksinger and the urbane musicologist.

"You don't know how good it made me feel," one mountaineer confessed with wry satisfaction, "to see Lester Flatt and Earl Scruggs on *The Beverly Hillbillies*. I've liked their music for 15 years, but I didn't think the whole damn country would go for it." Tennessee Ernie Ford and Eddy Arnold were also part of the mountain tradition long before television made them everybody's darlings.

As the identity increases, it becomes easier for outsiders to be accepted into this formerly closed society. Pippa Passes and the surrounding communities swarm with the "war-on-poverty" workers, many of whom have become not only trusted advisors to the people but also their close friends.

Television is influential at every age level. One grade-school teacher, working in a section even more remote than Pippa Passes, said he found a direct correlation between the interests and achievements of his students and their degree of exposure to television. "They pick up things from television adults never think about," a second teacher explained. "They see 'mesa' in their geography books, and it's just another dull word to learn. But when Fury is on that mesa, it means something to them. And how do you tell them what an ocean is like when they've never seen anything bigger than a creek they can jump across? *Sea Hunt* shows them."

But this incidental learning from television doesn't end with grade school. My wife, while sitting in on a class last semester, noticed a freshman girl riffling idly through a book of art prints. Suddenly the girl did a quick double take and held up a reproduction of Grant Wood's "American Gothic." "Look! New Country Corn Flakes!"

She was not being cute—she simply had never seen the painting   *467*
before. One would be hard-pressed to imagine a more delightful, if
elementary, introduction to art.

In my English classes the effects of television are ubiquitous.
Take, for instance, the intrepid and irritatingly quotable Maxwell
Smart. His "Would you believe . . . ?" and "Sorry about that" came so
trippingly off the tongues of my students that I was impelled to lecture
on comic emphasis, clichés, and inappropriate and limited diction.
Since these often dreary subjects needed to be taught, it was comforting to have a relevant example for a change.

On the positive side, I may now refer to Hitler with reasonable
assurance that students can identify him by decade and nationality.
Even when they watch the most saccharine of programs, such as
The Donna Reed Show, they are being exposed to better grammar and
vocabulary than is commonly used in their homes and public schools.
The more they watch, the more rubs off on them. And because there
are so few other diversions here, students are abnormally avid fans.

Were they to watch less avidly, they still could not avoid the
growing preoccupation with Vietnam. Yet, unlike their fathers who
left the mountains for the first time to fight in World War II, the youth
have not looked to the Vietnam war as an escape exit or as the unquestionably honorable thing to be engaged in. Next to campus intrigues
and basketball, nothing is talked about so much here as Vietnam. But
I know of no student who has found college so oppressive and the war
so attractive that he has dropped one to participate in the other.
Students do not, obviously, know all the ramifications of the war,
but they are fairly objective about it. World War II was distant, and the
sounds of it that filtered through these mountains were mainly the
sounds of gallantry. Television has added sight to sound, and the sight
is sufficiently grim to arrest purely emotional responses.

The older generation, given the harsh leisure of unemployment,
learns from television, too. Not long ago, as I sat on a rickety store
porch so authentic it looked phony, I was accosted by an old-timer of
6o or so who inquired if I thought our space program was tampering
with "the will of the Almighty." It seemed he was a member of a
fundamentalist sect which considers that man's God-given domain is
the earth—and no more. Before I could protest my ignorance of
theological niceties, he rambled into such a minutely detailed account
of our most recent space shot and its consequent evils that he sounded
for the world like Jules Bergman with a drawl. I later learned, although I could not have guessed it, that the man was barely able to
sign his own name.

For the mountain housewife, television has been helpful in a way

468 no other medium could ever have been. Besides giving her a substitute for education and travel, it has acquainted her with labor-saving products to the point of revolutionizing (and that *is* the right word) her household routine.

A friend told of visiting a local home in anticipation of eating a fabled "country" meal. What he ate was instant mashed potatoes, a "packaged" dinner, "brown-and-serve" rolls, and instant coffee. "It used to take me half a day to get a meal like this," he reported the wife as saying proudly.

The gourmet's taste buds may writhe at such short cuts, but to the housewife they are sheer deliverance. She has, because television has shown her a way out, more time to think and more to think about. A suburban wife can dispense with television and still learn about new products on her many visits to the supermarket; but the country wife, who may go to the store only once or twice a month, has to know of them in advance. A grocery-store owner at the county seat said he is so besieged for new products his far-flung customers see on television that he could easily double his range of offerings.

Certainly, one cannot justify the relatively low intellectual demands of television on the single ground that it is educating backward mountain dwellers. But backwardness is not peculiar to this region. Television's critics have failed to take into account the many places like Pippa Passes, where *most* viewers do not belong to book clubs, have never had the chance to visit museums or art galleries, are not totally convinced of the efficacy of regular tooth-brushing and are not aware that uncritical enjoyment is a cultural sin. In short, the frame of reference from which the critics operate does not exist for most viewers.

But because television has been so attentively watched here in the Appalachians, it is inevitable that its shortcomings will increasingly be noticed. Hopefully, as the level of appreciation rises, so will the quality of programming.

Recently, at the home of a mountaineer friend, I heard one of his children implore the other to wait until a certain popular program was over before they adjourned to play outside. "Let's go," the second one snapped impatiently. "You know it's going to be the same old stuff." And so, in naive Pippa Passes, another television critic was born.

Television's Contribution to the Senior Citizen

By Eleanor Roosevelt

OCTOBER 17, 1959

I do not happen to be one of the people who are fortunate enough to have a great deal of time to watch and analyze what television is now presenting to the public, but I find that many of my contemporaries get a great part of their information from television programs and that many of their interests stem from what they have seen and heard on television.

I have, as you know, reached 75 and know many of the limitations that come with age. TV can supply many pleasant hours as well as much information. No matter what one's age, one can develop new interests and TV will help older people to develop these interests.

As our senior citizens find themselves growing older, they realize that because of their physical difficulties they are no longer able to have the personal contacts with others and they cannot have the experiences which give validity to their taking part in home life and social contacts generally. Through TV they can often see something which the rest of their family perhaps has gone out of the home to come into personal contact with—a ball game, an inauguration, a convention, the arrival of an important foreign visitor, a thousand and one happenings that other members of the family may not even have an opportunity to see at all, or may only see for one passing moment. In watching TV the senior member of the family is probably seeing everything there is to see. So when the family comes home and discusses a topic, the elderly member does not need to feel left out of the discussion because TV provided full participation in the actual situation. I think this is one of the significant contributions which keep older people from feeling cut off and diffident about the validity of what they may think or feel in discussions with younger people.

Many older people are alone a great deal. In their late years they may choose to live alone rather than to find themselves in the environ-

469

470   ment of a young family where they feel they may be a burden or where they find themselves exhausted by the life that of necessity must stir around them. Even if they live with younger people they may find themselves often left out of the young activities. So they live alone and they are lonely, for the best that can happen to older people is that they will have family and friends who will come in to see them occasionally. They must learn to live with themselves. Physical handicaps may keep them from doing many things which before occupied much of their time; but if a sense of loneliness comes over them they can turn on television, see people and hear them talk, listen to beautiful music, often watch a show as well as if they went to a movie or theater far away.

The old, like the very young, crave identification and remembrance. A child will often demand attention just for the sake of feeling that he is an individual and that you know him as an individual. Old people do the same thing just out of a sense of wanting so desperately to be recognized as people and not to be shoved aside without much thought and treated as though they were pieces of furniture. If they have something interesting to talk about, something that perhaps gives them a little closer touch with the experiences of younger people, they cannot be ignored. So we must think of all these things which bring life and interest to our older citizens, things which keep them cheerful and undemanding.

People who are lonely are apt to make family and friends feel guilty that they cannot be with them more often. Yet the life that younger people lead today makes it difficult for them to find time to drop in on an older person who is no longer active in the same fields. TV, I think has made it possible for older people to learn to live alone happily, and that is one of the greatest contributions that can be made to people who have lost their life's partners and must live for a considerable number of years perhaps with serious handicaps and restrictions. If they have been intellectuals all their lives, as long as their eyes hold out they can read and that will help wipe out loneliness. But eyes suffer too with age, and television is probably a good change when one finds the need to give one's eyes some kind of variety.

Just because TV has such possibilities for reaching the lives of older people and, of course, of the younger people too, particularly of children, it seems to me that the responsibility of those who work out programs is very great. They should have in mind their most constant audiences—children and older citizens and housewives. The older citizens are the ones who are most apt to reflect at length on what they have seen or heard and to use it for good or ill in their *471* contacts, whatever they are, with other people. If they find that they know what the younger people are talking about and that they have a contribution to make, it will immeasurably add to their happiness. They will sift programs they see through their own experience and this may be a valuable help, for the stations can use the reflections and reactions of the older people to the programs they devise and produce. It will give the older citizens an added interest, for they will feel they are taking part in improving or increasing the value to others through sending in their thoughts on certain TV programs.

TV can be used also to give older people an opportunity to help in different projects for different organizations if the organizations advertise on TV when they can use senior citizens in one capacity or another. This would bring happiness to the older people, for it would make them feel that they could be useful. They could even be told of situations in which their influence in the community could be used to advantage, and this would give them great satisfaction.

Whether programs are good or bad or offer opportunities for work or service, just as they are now there is no question in my mind but that to our older citizens television is one of the blessings of our period of history.

Politics

Robert McNeil, in his book, *The People Machine,* attributes to television the most radical change in political communication in the history of this country. He states: "No other medium has brought the ideal of an informed electorate so close to reality, yet poses so serious a threat of reducing out politics to triviality." Harvey Wheeler, writing in the *Saturday Review,* has said that television has created a new system of personality politics and, with the aid of "flying cadres of media experts," is destroying the two-party system. Michael Arlen has suggested in the *New Yorker* that we know next to nothing about the candidates except what we are told on television through political ads or short film clips and simplistic passages of speeches. *The New York Times,* on the eve of the 1966 election, said in an editorial that "television has created a new reality, or at least a new way of looking at reality for millions of viewers. . . ." According to *The New York Times,* "How a man looks and projects himself is more persuasive than the facts about his experience, competence or depth of understanding." And Joe McGinniss claims, in *The Selling of the President 1968,* that "the response is to the image, not to the man" was the credo of the 1968 Nixon campaign, and a combination of salesmen, cameramen and speechwriters was hired to adjust Nixon's image through skillful use and manipulation of television.

Television's importance to the politician has grown to the extent that, by 1968, Theodore White, author of the series of books, *The Making of the President,* was quoted in TV GUIDE: "Our thinking is so strongly shaped by television it terrifies me." Television exposure has become an absolute necessity for most major office seekers. More and more candidates are spending the great bulk of their campaign funds for television appearances, which are timed, whenever possible, to obtain maximum exposure on the evening newscasts. Television gives the politician a huge audience: for example, in 1968 twice as many people were able to see a single Richard Nixon political advertisement on television than had seen him in person in 1960 when he visited all fifty states.

472

This situation poses serious problems for politicians and is of **473** great concern to political observers. One area of debate is the charge, re-inforced by McGinniss in his study of the 1968 Nixon campaign, that television manufactures candidates, or images of candidates, and that the viewers see only what the candidate and his advisors want them to see. The defense is that the television camera actually penetrates the candidate and reveals his true character and beliefs, giving a true impression of his capabilities for the office.

Gene Wyckoff suggests, in *The Image Candidates,* that the candidate's character is universally perceived on television regardless of political predispositions because the viewer has media predispositions to see candidates in terms of television stereotyped desirable and undesirable characters. Charles Thomson wrote in the Brookings Institute study of *Television and Presidential Politics* that "television can unmask a charlatan, if those responsible for the use of camera and microphones want to do so." But he also indicated that those in control and responsible for directing the candidate's appearance could make him acceptable as well. Joseph Napolitan, consultant to the Democratic National Committee, has gone so far as to say: "If you had unlimited funds you could elect a nonentity to office." However, Frank Stanton claims that television cannot create synthetic personalities, it can only unmask them. Senator Jacob Javits agrees, saying television transmits a searching, accurate image of the candidate.

Another cause of considerable concern is referred to by *The New York Times* as "this intrusion of television and show-business values into serious politics." Jack Gould states: "For better or for worse, the present day politician is a performer and showmanship is now a factor in his and his country's life." Leonard Hall, long time Republican Party leader maintained that by 1955 candidates were being chosen who could "sell themselves" because of the importance of television coverage. Gilbert Seldes is concerned because he feels that the wrong commodities are being sold. He suggests that television has put value on speed versus contemplation and quickness versus quality of wit.

Most of the selling comes in packaged, one-minute political advertisements. This too has caused concern and debate. Some recent research indicates that the continual repetition of an advertisement can almost unconsciously affect buying habits of the public. This would indicate that people may be quite susceptible to political advertisements, particularly those for a candidate running for a minor office.

474   Many political observers are irritated by the influx of ad men who engineer the television campaigns of the candidates. Neil Compton, in *Commentary,* has referred to them as the "political mercenaries" who are ready to help sell anyone's candidacy subject to the usual commission on gross billings. Critics were particularly upset when one of the ad men responsible for the very successful but controversial 1966 "faceless" campaign spots for Governor Rockefeller publicly analyzed how "We looked at the Governor in the only way we knew to look at him . . . as a consumer product." Television political advertising is further criticized for its superficiality, slickness and "jinglism"; the ad men defend themselves by citing some of America's pre-television political slogans, such as "Tippecanoe and Tyler Too."

Perhaps the greatest and most dangerous problem related to the political use of television is the cost. Air time and commissions are so expensive that a politician of average financial means may not be able to afford sufficient television exposure. Theodore White was quoted in TV GUIDE as saying "the corruption of politics by the need for money for television time is almost as great as it became under the old-time party bosses who needed money to buy votes at the saloon." Presidents Kennedy and Johnson both supported the concept by which the Federal Government would pay the major costs of campaigning for both parties. In September 1969, the Twentieth Century Fund's Commission on Campaign Costs in the Electronic Era, headed by former FCC Chairman Newton Minow, proposed a plan by which broadcasters would be required to provide a series of half-hours in prime time for use by presidential and vice-presidential candidates at half price. These programs, which would be aired simultaneously over every broadcast station and CATV system in the country, with allowances only for time zones, would be paid by the Federal Government. In October 1969, hearings began on a Senate bill to require broadcasters to provide specified periods of time at reduced commercial rates to all legally qualified Senate and House candidates.

Arthur Schlesinger, Jr. (pp. 477-482) assesses the impact of television on American politics in 1966, stating that the evidence is inadequate, contradictory and inconclusive. Schlesinger first discusses the four types of coverage through which television affects the political process: news, pseudo-news, interpretation and party programs. Actual news coverage is the most significant because the reality of the events themselves still exert the greatest influence in shaping political judgment. Although television serves to bring the candidate closer to the voters, Schlesinger feels that the trend to substitute one-minute political commercials for full-length, or even fifteen-minute, speeches is damaging both to the candidate and the public. Television has significantly affected nominating conventions, but its influence on the rest of politics is marginal. The republic will adapt to television and, according to Schlesinger, television, used as a supplement to other means of information, could do much to enrich our politics.

By 1969, Professor Schlesinger (p. 483) had re-evaluated his assessment. He feels he underestimated the impact of television and the electronic revolution on politics. The traditional political structure has been undermined by television's closing of the gap between the individual voter and the government. The result is that the voter has a sense of individual powerlessness. Schlesinger suggests that the public is becoming frustrated and irritable.

Neil Hickey (pp. 484-487) discusses the dramatic increase in the costs of campaigning via television and he summarizes the various proposals to lower the costs of television time. The problem is compounded now that spot announcements are considered more desirable than program time. According to Hickey, neither of two of the most commonly proposed solutions, modification of the equal-time provision in the Communications Act or a form of Federal subsidy for office-seekers, is likely to be effected in the near future.

Former FCC Chairman Newton Minow and *Washington Post* television critic Lawrence Laurent (pp. 488-493) advocate the repeal of Section 315, which contains the equal-time provision, in the Communications Act. The authors contend that, even after being amended in 1959, the provision, originally incorporated in the Radio Act of 1927, is hopelessly out of date. They support their argument with descriptions of some of the problems of interpreting both the original provision and its amendment. For example, is the television appearance by an incumbent President a bona fide news event or a political program? The authors propose that Section 315 be replaced with the requirement that broadcasters make available four hours of free prime time to each of the two major parties during the month before the election. This time would not be for the candidates but for the parties, to be used as they see fit. Minority parties would receive lesser amounts of time proportionate to the votes they had previously received or the petitions they could obtain. Minow and Laurent mention an incidental advantage to their proposal, shortening the Presidential campaigns.

Nine broadcasting and political leaders were asked to reply to the Minow-Laurent proposal (pp. 494-497). Included are replies from two

476 network heads, two station managers, the President of the NAB, the campaign manager of a minority party and three members of Congress. Predictably, all those representing broadcasting advocated the repeal of Section 315, but only one felt the Minow-Laurent proposal was acceptable. Also predictably, the other respondents disagreed with the plan, although both Senators did support either partial suspension or modification of Section 315.

Politics and Television

By Arthur Schlesinger, Jr.

OCTOBER 22, 1966

The time has come for a preliminary assessment of the impact of television on our politics. More and more Americans, it appears, are forming their impression of the world on the basis of the things they see on the tiny screen. Recent surveys report television as the main source of news for more than 50 percent of our voters, and *Broadcasting* magazine could plausibly argue in 1964 that television had become the "Nation's primary news medium." This widening influence of television over American life raises the question how TV is affecting the basic character of our political system and whether it is strengthening or weakening the workings of our democracy.

Some observers, for example, claim that television is producing a more alert and better-informed electorate; others that it is reducing our politics to a mixture of high-pressure salesmanship and beauty contests. The assessment is bound to be preliminary because the evidence is inadequate, contradictory and inconclusive. But TV GUIDE is to be commended for posing the question; and I am glad to offer an historian's tentative thoughts on a complex problem.

Television touches politics in a number of ways. For purposes of convenience, one may perhaps distinguish four types of coverage: 1. news programs, 2. pseudo-news programs, 3. interpretation and 4. party programs. It may be well to discuss each category and then attempt a general appraisal.

News. Probably the greatest influence in shaping political judgment is still the reality of events themselves. A depression, a war, a debate over national policy, constitutional rights protected or denied, economic securities enlarged or imperiled, bills passed or defeated: Such facts remain the great determinants of political opinion. And it is in communicating these facts that television has had its most impressive success.

A notable recent example was the coverage of the hearings on Vietnam before the Senate Foreign Relations Committee. I have no doubt that future historians will conclude that these hearings opened

477

478 a new phase in the Vietnam debate. Before the hearings, most people had suppressed any disquietude they may have felt over the deepening national involvement in Vietnam on the assumption that the President had more information and no doubt knew best. But the hearings had the clear effect, for better or worse, of legitimatizing dissent. If eminent generals, diplomats and senators were unhappy about our actions in Vietnam, then the ordinary citizen felt free to indulge in his own doubts. And the hearings not only opened up debate over Vietnam; they also ended the taboo which had so long prevented discussion of American relations with Communist China. Would these hearings have had the same effect had they not been on television? I think plainly not—and all the more credit therefore to the NBC network which carried them in full.

Television, through the vivid reporting of actual events, can thus incite new thoughts and emotions in the electorate. It also has the effect in many cases of heightening the sense of popular participation in public matters: Thus the McCarthy-Army hearings undoubtedly made many viewers feel, as they had not before, that the Wisconsin Senator was a threat not just to other people but to themselves. When sustained over a long time, this increased sense of popular participation can alter somewhat the workings of political institutions. It seems already, for example, to have reshaped so basic a device in our politics as the Presidential nominating convention (see pp. 80-117).

For most of our history, the convention was a relatively closed powwow for professional politicians, who get chummily together, discussed their candidates, made their deals and presented the results to a passive public. People might have exclaimed, "Who is James K. Polk?" when they heard (via telegraph) the outcome of the Democratic Convention of 1884; but they did not feel indignant over the fact that the name of the nominee meant so little to them.

Television has changed all that. The dark-horse candidate, emerging unknown out of smoke-filled rooms for nomination on the 46th ballot, is probably a thing of the past. The tiny screen has made the public an active partner. The feedback is too quick and intense to encourage any convention to risk ditching the favorite of the national audience in favor of a crony of the party professionals. In addition, television has had the happy effect of making conventions shorter. It is safe to assume that the Nation will never again have to endure 103 ballots, as it did during the Democratic Convention of 1924.

Conventions, of course, with their inherent drama and suspense, are particularly well adapted to the inquisitive camera. But even television's day-by-day reporting of politics has undoubtedly given the

electorate a larger knowledge of public personalities and a greater   *479*
acquaintance with public issues. News coverage, I think, represents
television's best contribution to democratic responsibility.

Pseudo-News. By "pseudo-news"—a subclassification of Daniel
Boorstin's general category of "pseudo-event"[7]—I mean the creation
of news on the initiative of the medium. Perhaps the term is unnecessarily invidious; for often the news thus elicited is entirely legitimate. Lawrence Spivak's *Meet the Press* and its various imitators, for
example, have greatly advanced public enlightenment through the
years by their interrogations of national figures.

On the other hand, some pseudo-news is mischievous and irresponsible. When President Johnson issued his challenge to the intellectual community some months ago, a news television crew descended on my office in the evident hope that I could be stimulated
to denounce the President. This seems a factitious attempt to manufacture conflict (though, in justice to the program, when I said that
I considered the President's remarks appropriate, they filmed the
interview anyway and put it on the air).

My feeling is that organized shows in a press-conference format
serve a useful purpose but that television interviews designed to
lure or trap people into sensational statements they would not otherwise make can be dispensed with. It is necessary to add, though, that
television did not invent this technique; it is another bad habit it
picked up from the press.

Interpretation. Editorialization on television has taken the form
of thoughtful personal comment (Howard K. Smith, Eric Sevareid)
or, with the recent encouragement of the FCC, of editorials by local
stations. Neither form has thus far had very striking results. I do
not know whether television has an inhibiting effect on comment;
but certainly no television commentator has spoken with the pun-
gency or authority of Elmer Davis on radio, and men like Smith and
Sevareid often look more constrained on the screen than they used to
sound over the loud-speaker.

In the past, networks have attempted panel discussions, like the
NBC series *The Big Issue* a few years back. This is still done a good
deal locally and on educational television. Unquestionably these
programs have improved the level of political discussion, in part
because they permit the suggestion of subtleties and complexities in
public problems. But, possibly for this reason, such programs do not
seem to have been pursued very diligently by the networks.

What television has done most successfully in the field of interpretation is the analytical documentary—the kind of thing that

480 Murrow and Friendly used to do for CBS, the *NBC White Papers,* the Bell & Howell shows. At their best, such programs have dealt with problems at a reasonable level of complexity and have been a highly effective form of public education.

Party Programs. By this I mean time purchased by political parties and leaders, or otherwise made available to them. This, I would say, has been the area of television's most conspicuous failure; and the trouble here begins with the nature of the medium itself. For the effect of television has been to cheapen political discourse, steadily reducing its length, its substance and its rationality.

Sixty years ago an audience which traveled many miles to hear William Jennings Bryan or Robert M. La Follette hold forth on railroad regulation or tariff would have felt cheated if the oration lasted less than a couple of hours. The coming of radio set in motion the shrinkage of the political speech, first to 45 minutes, then to half an hour. Then came television. I can recall the insistence of the TV men in Adlai Stevenson's headquarters in 1956 that half an hour was far too long; unless it were a national crisis, 15 minutes, they said, represented the outer limit of the attention span of an American audience.

Now the 15-minute speech is itself almost a thing of the past. The most sinister statistic in political telecasting is the one which records the ominous rise of the spot announcement. Hyman H. Goldin, a former FCC aide, has estimated that 60 percent of the money spent by candidates on television in recent general elections has gone for spots; the proportion of funds invested in program time has been steadily declining.

This development can only have the worst possible effect in degrading the level and character of our political discourse. If it continues, the result will be the vulgarization of issues, the exaltation of the immediately ingratiating personality and, in general, an orgy of electronic demagoguery. You cannot merchandise political candidates like soap and hope to preserve a rational democracy.

While this drift to spot announcements is in great part the preference of the candidates themselves, the industry cannot be held wholly guiltless, for it would much rather sell spots than program time. Both the candidates and the industry, however, prefer to blame the condition on the audience, which, both claim, will simply not sit still for thoughtful disquisitions on public policy. No doubt a large part of the mass audience could not care less about an intelligent discussion of issues. But there remain a substantial number of viewers, even if less than a majority, who do care. Does not television have an obligation to this important minority, too, as well as to *481* the service of democracy in general?

The ultimate answer to this question lies in the movement which must some day come toward the diversification of the viewing public; UHF and pay-TV will no doubt make it easier for the medium to reach specialized audiences. In the meantime, one wonders whether more free time should not be made available to candidates, especially in Presidential elections. If democracy depends on rational communication, if television is now the dominant communications medium and if television licenses are granted, according to the Communications Act, with a view to the "public interest, convenience and necessity," then it would seem that one of the richest industries in the country might make systematic provision for free time for public debate, at least during Presidential elections.

I recognize that informally the industry has done a considerable amount of this. But I wonder whether it is doing enough to discharge the obligations which come with its highly profitable licenses. Is it not really pretty important to give the electorate a chance to hear a man who wants to be President, even if this outrages people who would prefer to see *The Beverly Hillbillies*?[8] In addition to lowering the level of the party debate, television may give an initial advantage to the poised, photogenic, otherdirected, manipulable candidate.

The rush of professional actors into politics is an obvious consequence of the television age. One shudders a little to think what would have happened, for example, to the Adamses or Jackson or Lincoln if television had existed in the early years of the republic. On the other hand, television is a relatively unsparing medium; it consumes material voraciously, in politics as well as in comedy and drama; and while it may lend itself to slick first impressions, it probably is not hospitable to sustained phoniness and fakery. In the long run, I think, genuine qualities—intelligence, integrity, humor, firmness of purpose—will win out over calculated effects. The Kennedy-Nixon debates of 1960 was a case in point.

The Balance Sheet. Where do we end up? I do not think that television has wrought a revolution in our political system. American democracy will adapt itself to the tiny box as it has to a series of technological changes from the start of the republic. The effects of television—apart from the nominating convention—have been mostly marginal. It would seem that, through news programs and, to some extent, through pseudo-news programs, television has somewhat widened public acquaintance with issues and personalities; but that, aside from documentaries, its efforts at interpreting the significance

482 of news tend to be superficial; and that its party political programs have encouraged the oversimplification of issues and favored the smooth and bland over the rough-hewn candidate. If voters had to depend on television alone for the information on which they base political judgments, the results would undoubtedly be poor for American democracy.

Yet, so long as television is considered a supplement to newspapers, magazines, political meetings and solitary midnight brooding by individual citizens, and not a substitute for them, it has in certain respects enriched our politics. And it could do so much more. Its power to convey the quality of political leadership is vast; the agony of grief which ran around the world when John F. Kennedy died after a short thousand days as President was obviously in part a result of the way television had made him a cherished figure in remote lands. If television would recognize an affirmative obligation to elevate the level of our politics, and applied as much thought and talent to this as it does to selling detergents, it might play a great role in helping make our democracy more rational and responsible.

Addendum

Arthur Schlesinger, Jr.

JANUARY 21, 1969

I now feel that I underrated the impact of television and of the electronic revolution in general on politics. It seems clear that recent changes in the means of communication—above all, the rise of television and of public opinion polls—have hastened the decay of the traditional political structure. For a century, a series of institutions— the political machine, the trade union, the farm organization, the ethnic federation—have mediated between the politician and the voter, passing back and forth between them and representing each to the other. But, with the advent of television, the voter increasingly bases his judgment not on what his party boss or labor or farm or ethnic leader tells him but on what Walter Cronkite or David Brinkley shows him.

One result has been to sap the strength of the traditional mediating institutions and to begin the liquidation of the traditional brokers of American politics. Another has been to increase the sense of individual powerlessness, since the broker can no longer serve as the voter's channel to government. The citizen can't argue with the image on the tiny screen, and all he has is the vague hope that he might some week be selected to register his views with George Gallup or Louis Harris. The rise of television will soon leave politicans to stand face to face with a diffused, frustrated and irritable public opinion. This is bound to have significant consequences for the political process.

Beyond all this, I have no doubt that Mr. McLuhan is right in contending that the electronic revolution will affect our modes of perceiving experience in ways and with consequences that we can at this time only dimly foresee.

How TV Has Raised Campaign Costs

By Neil Hickey

APRIL 20, 1968

In November 1968, we witnessed the 46th episode in the series of American Presidential-year campaigns; to say that vote-stumping habits have changed drastically in that time is to commit serious understatement. The hundred years between Lincoln and Kennedy help make the point: In 1860, Abraham Lincoln never left Springfield, Illinois, nor made a single speech, and his whole national campaign cost $100,000. John F. Kennedy in 1960 traveled 44,000 miles in 43 states, made 360 speeches, spent $11 million of his party's money and an undetermined amount of his own.

Television, in its own gilt-ridden way, has been the biggest single influence upon recent alterations in the art and science of political campaigning—and not the smallest of its effects has been the rampaging cost of public office for parties and individuals. Between [1960] and [1964], political broadcast expenditures increased by [70] percent, and between [1964] and [1968] they increased by [another 70] percent to a total figure of [$58,900,000]. The overall costs for all political activities at all levels of government in [1968] ran close to [$300,000,000] thus broadcast expenditures constituted [about 20] percent of all political spending, making it perhaps the largest single drain on the coffers of office-seekers.[9]

About a half-million offices in this country are filled by the election process—sheriffs, aldermen, clerks and treasurers, as well as Presidents and senators. By far the greatest share of those aspirants never get near a television camera nor spend a cent for the purchase of TV time. But the ones who find television exposure the *sine qua non* of their ambitions for public life are immediately caught up in a round of competitive time buying which can double or triple their already oppressive outlays.

That's fine if your name is Rockefeller or Kennedy or you have the good fortune to be an incumbent President with the tentacles of power

which that condition supposes; otherwise you're in a bit of a pickle   *485*
and had better start ingratiating yourself with potential rich contributors, who will then have a vested interest in your future and your
voting habits.

The problem has no dearth of solutions—most of them requiring
action by the Federal Government—and no chance that either of two
proposed solutions will be effected in the foreseeable future.[10]
One solution is a Federal subsidy for the ragged pocketbooks of the
office-seekers. The other is modification of the Federal Communications Commission's so-called "equal-time" provision (Section 315a
of the 1934 Communications Act) which would allow networks and
stations to give free time to major-party candidates without having
to offer the same to minor-party candidates, crackpots and publicity-
seekers. (Except for bona fide newscasts, news interview shows and
news documentaries and on-the-spot coverage of bona fide news
events, which don't count, broadcasters must "afford equal opportunities to all other such candidates" for an office any time they let
one candidate go on the air free.)

Even so, legislation proposed on this subject in the past has
never quite satisfied all the people involved. "All the suggested
remedies are difficult," TV GUIDE was told by Dr. Herbert E.
Alexander, director of the Citizens Research Foundation of Princeton,
N. J., and the acknowledged leading expert on the whole subject of
campaign spending. "Some of these bills are ridiculous," he says.
"They require broadcasters to give free time to candidates for the
Presidency, the Senate and the House. But what happens in areas
where a single station is received by eight or 10 or 15 Congressional
districts?" It then becomes a problem of how the station could
equitably allocate to scores of candidates the opportunity for a fair
share of the available time.

Another difficulty, as Dr. Alexander sees it, is the rather more
mechanical problem of overlapping jurisdictions. New Jersey, for
example, has no VHF station, so that a candidate who wants to reach
potential voters in a Congressional district of that state must acquire
time on New York or Philadelphia stations. If he buys it, he's wasting
perhaps 70 or 80 percent of every dollar he spends on viewers in
New York, Connecticut and Pennsylvania who can't vote for him; and
if he wants to claim free time (assuming some modification of Section
315), would stations across the border in New York and Philadelphia
really have to give it to him? (There are 40 or more Congressional
districts within listening range of many metropolitan New York
stations.)[11]

486   One of the genuine peculiarities of the whole dilemma is that program time as such—free or otherwise—simply is not as highly valued now as it once was. Spot announcements of one minute or less are favored. In 1960, according to an FCC survey, the Presidential candidates bought 9000 television spots, and in 1964 that figure leaped to 29,300. For campaigns at all levels in 1964, 73 percent of TV stations' charges were for spot announcements.[12] The reasons are obvious; campaigners have deduced a low tolerance among TV viewers for bald and prolonged political exhortation. A spot announcement, like a commercial, is on and off before the viewer can leap up and flick to another channel.

So he's been exposed to the candidate's face and slogan before he can help himself; if that happens often enough, the viewer in the end may be "sold" the candidate, much as he is sold a bar of soap. He still knows nothing about the issues nor has he any insights into the candidate's character, but he's been conditioned by the sloganeering and may develop the knee-jerk response.

This avidity by campaigners for spots bothers such observers as Dr. Alexander, who feel that the only reason at all for broadcasters to give away time is to advance the public's knowledge of important issues and incidentally, absolve part of their legal responsibility to operate their stations in the public interest. Spot announcements simply don't accomplish that.

Theodore C. Sorensen, an advisor to two Presidents, devoted himself recently to methods of "reversing the scandalous rise in campaign expenditures." He has proposed lofting a trial balloon during this election year—for the Presidential and Vice-Presidential offices only—and then observing how its lessons might be applied across the board in subsequent campaigns.

Sorensen wants to suspend the equal-time requirements of Section 315 and then ask the networks to "pledge the donation, free of charge, . . . of one hour of prime time, scheduled at the same hour on each network, during each of the eight weeks immediately preceding the November 5th election." Four of those broadcasts would be used for joint appearances or debates between the two Presidential candidates, and the other hour would be divided into half-hour segments for each candidate to use as he wished.

Also in Sorensen's "package" is the suggestion that Congress "prohibit . . . the purchase of network time segments greater than five minutes in length" to put an artificial ceiling on the parties' broadcast spending; he hopes that the campaigners would then make corresponding reductions in their broadcast budgets.

Sorensen's solution corresponds with that of the television in- *487* dustry itself, to the extent that he'd suspend 315 and let another provision of the Communications Act—the so-called Fairness Doctrine—protect the rights of minor-party candidates. But other experts have always been suspicious of tampering with Section 315. Dr. Alexander, for example, says, "I don't think the Fairness Doctrine is an adequate substitute for Section 315, and for that reason I've been very wary of the industry's position. I don't quite trust them to administer such a thing."

It's likely that someday a workable formula to solve the dilemma will be arrived at—a system of "differential equality of access," perhaps, in which the major parties will get their television time free, and minor-party candidates will be offered free time in accordance with their registration or the size of their vote in a previous election.

In Great Britain, it's all handled more simply: the BBC and the ITA (the commercial system) tell the several political parties how much time they're ready to hand over free, and then the party leaders get together and work out a formula—based on relative strengths in previous elections and seats in Parliament—for the way the time is to be divided up.

Dr. Alexander sees the over-all picture in the U.S. this way: "The political parties have defaulted by failing to develop broad-based and steady sources of political funds. The Government has defaulted by failure to provide meaningful legislation to assist candidates and parties to reach the electorate. And the broadcasters have defaulted by failing to meet their obligations to politics. . . ."

A Proposal for Unshackling Television

By Newton N. Minow and Lawrence Laurent

JANUARY 30, 1965

To those who study communications the most amazing thing about the 1964 political campaign is that voters, politicians and broadcasters survived it with senses still in good working order.

It was a campaign in which the Federal Communications Commission ruled: A United Fund appeal by President Johnson might require all stations to give "equal time" to all political candidates for President. A news conference by President Johnson—attended by reporters from all networks and from periodicals all over the world— did not qualify as exempt from the "equal-time" laws. Among other things, the FCC ruled, it was not a "bona fide news event." A 17- minute speech by the President, however, on American reaction to a change in Soviet Union leadership, a Chinese Communist nuclear explosion and the results of the British elections was exempt from "equal-time" requirements.

Does this sound like the logic of the Red Queen ("It takes all the running you can do, to keep in the same place. If you want to get somewhere else, you must run at least twice as fast as that!") in *Alice Through the Looking-Glass*? Indeed it does. Yet, in fairness to the seven members of the Communications Commission, they—like the politicians, the broadcasters and the public—are victims of antiquated legislation, muddled legal precedents and a wavering, quavering public policy.[13]

What is needed is a complete overhaul of the law and some common sense about modern political campaigning. I have a suggestion for overhaul of the so-called "equal-time" law, Section 315 of the Communications Act—which I will go into in a moment—and I believe this recommendation could go a long way toward solving,

if not solve entirely, the heretofore vexing equal-time problems of **489**
past campaigns.

The Law—Section 315 of the act and the 1959 amendments—
is hopelessly out of date. It says, in essence, to the Federally licensed
broadcaster: If you give or sell broadcasting time to one candidate
for a political office, each of his rivals must be given or sold "equal
time." (The rules also require that the same rates, same discounts,
and other terms apply to all.)

This law made good sense when it was written into the Radio
Act of 1927.[14] There were only a few hundred radio stations, and congressmen were concerned that time would not be made available to
all persons who sought an office. The same language was carried over
into the Communications Act of 1934 and, with minor refurbishing,
it stands in a time when the United States has [more than] 6000 radio
stations and [690] television stations.

Still, the law might be simple to administer if there were actually only two parties in our much-praised (by both parties) "Two-
Party System." But there are more than two political parties, and the
smaller parties want equal time too.

Broadcasters usually had a simple way to avoid a Niagara of free
political time. Since the splinter parties are usually poorly financed,
they are unable to buy expensive broadcast time. Therefore, the
broadcasters willingly sell time to the two major parties and avoid
the whole question. This means that the cost to the two major parties
keeps going up. No one even argues any more that television is the
single most expensive item of the national campaign.

Those 1959 amendments, mentioned earlier, made certain kinds
of news programs exempt from the equal political time rules. Congress was jarred into enacting this legislation when the FCC applied
the law, literally, to a mayoralty election in Chicago. Here's what
happened:

In Chicago, there is a frequent candidate for almost any office,
named (legally, he says) Lar (America First) Daly. At last count, he
had run for various offices more than 20 times and had yet to win an
election. In 1959, Mr. Daly was a legally qualified, write-in candidate
for Mayor and he wanted "equal time" after Chicago television
stations broadcast filmed news coverage of incumbent Mayor Richard
Daley greeting the President of Argentina.

Lar (America First) Daly appealed to the FCC, and the Commission ruled that Daly, indeed, was entitled to just as much television time as Mayor Daley had received.

This led a Congress that was not amused to exempt certain kinds

490 of programs from the equal-time requirements. The exempt programs are:[15]

1. Bona fide newscast.
2. Bona fide news interview.
3. Bona fide news documentary (if the appearance of the candidate is incidental to the presentation of the subject or subjects covered by the news documentary).
4. On-the-spot coverage of bona fide news events (including, but not limited to, political conventions and activities incidental thereto).

This leaves, of course, the need for a definition of "bona fide." In legislative hearing, Congress decided the test would be whether the program is under the control of the broadcaster. If control rests with the politician—if he can control content or the questions to be asked in an interview—then the program is not bona fide and is subject to the equal-time law. A second test is whether the program is one that is regularly scheduled. This gets away from the special documentary, produced and broadcast solely in connection with an election.

Along the way, the FCC has ruled that an appearance by a television station's weather reporter, who was running for the Texas House of Delegates, was not subject to equal time. An Indiana municipal judge appeared regularly on a *Traffic Court* telecast. He became a candidate for mayor and his rival appealed to the FCC. The program was ruled exempt. A Texas congressman filmed a "report" each week and sent it to a station in his home district. It was telecast as a segment of a regularly scheduled news program. Upon appeal, the FCC ruled that such a program wasn't exempt from the equal-time law, because the content was controlled by the congressman.

Such minor cases provided the background for the weird (but completely legal) activities that took place in the 1964 campaign. In September, President Johnson was scheduled to make a formal, televised appeal to citizens for support of the United Fund. Station owners asked the FCC if this would be subject to the equal-time law. The answer: Each station must decide for itself whether the President's appearance would be a bona fide news event. The chairman of the Republican National Committee advised networks that he would not ask for equal time, but the networks avoided the program.

On September 30, in response to a letter from the Columbia Broadcasting System, the FCC ruled that President Johnson's news conferences would not be exempt from the equal-time law. The FCC said these were not regularly scheduled, and, furthermore, the FCC indicated, were not subject to the control of the broadcaster. This reasoning drew an angry dissenting opinion from Commissioner Lee *491* Loevinger. He noted that one publication had referred to FCC equal-time rulings as an "inventory of idiocies" and, added Loevinger: "I . . . protest the addition of another item to this inventory."

Loevinger also noted that the FCC had ruled a "Governor's Radio Press Conference," broadcast weekly, was exempt. Loevinger wrote: "The only relevant point of difference between the Governor's press conference . . . and a Presidential press conference is that the Governor's press conference was held weekly whereas the Presidential press conference is held only when the President believes there is news."

But if things were difficult after this ruling, they became worse after President Johnson's October 18 report on international developments. Dean Burch, Chairman of the Republican National Committee [now FCC Chairman], called the speech "political" and demanded that the three television networks and four radio networks give equal time to the Republican Presidential nominee, Senator Barry Goldwater of Arizona.

The networks, citing a 1956 decision, said the program was exempt from equal-time requirements. The National Broadcasting Company made one exception: It was willing to give Burch 15 minutes to state the Republican position on the three items dealt with by the President. Burch took the 15 minutes. He dismissed the three developments discussed by President Johnson, and devoted most of his television time to discussing current morality and appealing for funds with which to buy TV time for Senator Goldwater. He said he needed "about $500,000" to match the grant the networks had made to President Johnson.

Burch didn't stop there. An appeal to the FCC was rejected. The Court of Appeals heard arguments and voted 3-3. This, in effect, upheld the FCC and cleared the way for the case to go to the Supreme Court. By a 6-2 vote, the Supreme Court declined to hear the case, but Associate Justice Arthur Goldberg had a biting dissent. He cited a number of FCC rulings which he said "have not been wholly consistent" and he added: "These varied holdings of the Commission and the express language of the Act confirm my view of . . . the need for full immediate argument and speedy decision of this case.

"The importance of the question is, I believe, plainly apparent. . . . The statute reflects a deep congressional conviction that in our free democratic system all qualified candidates should be given equally free access to broadcasting facilities regardless of office and regardless of financial means if any candidate is granted free time."

492   Mr. Justice Goldberg added that nothing in the statues made a
President who is also a candidate exempt from the law. (Meanwhile,
CBS said it received and refused equal-time requests from Eric Hass,
Socialist Labor Party; Clifton DeBerry, Socialist Workers Party;
Louis E. Jaeckel, the American Party; and Yetta Bronstein, the Best
Party.)

The Republicans tried once more. The fourth appeal was made to
the FCC under the 15-year-old "Fairness Doctrine" that compels a
station to give all sides a hearing on controversial subjects. The FCC
decided, 5-1, that Burch had no case.

And this was only one of the most striking examples of the great
confusion that surrounds all the laws of political broadcasting. There
were complaints from Texas (Senator Yarborough vs. Republican
George Bush) to the Virgin Islands (concerning a disc-jockey candidate) to California (where the Socialist Labor Party demanded time
equal to the debate between Democrat Pierre Salinger and Republican George Murphy).

Is there no way out of this madness? There is a simple, direct way
out. I hope it will appeal to the public and also to the problem-
ridden men who must deal with the enchanted quagmire of political
broadcasting rules. The solution involves two compromises.

First, the politician must decide to trust the broadcaster. He must
decide that his safety lies in the number and variety of stations and
that the best interests of the people will be safeguarded by this diversity. This faith calls for complete repeal of *Section* 315 *of the Communications Act,* abolishing every segment of the "equal-time"
law. This leaves political broadcasting to the broadcaster, although he
must still answer to the FCC on questions of balance, fairness and
public interest when his three-year license comes up for renewal.

The first step, then, is to give the broadcaster the same kind of
political freedom that the press enjoys. We would say to him, "We
believe that your own civic interests and the desire to appear fair
to your listeners will make you work for the public interest."

A companion measure, however, goes with this and it may be
the lowest price any group ever paid for freedom. The second step
is to make available, during the month preceding Election Day,
four hours of "prime" free time to each of the two major political
parties.

This would tend to limit political campaigning. Radio and TV,
along with the jet airplane, have made the July to November campaign
a tedious bore, a burden of massive proportion to the campaigners,
and a needless anachronism. The time would be assigned to the party,

not the candidate, and it would be the job of the chairman of the National Committee to decide how this time would be used. The four hours could not be in those favorite hours for public service broadcasting, between Midnight and 7 A.M. It would have to be in prime evening time, when most citizens find it convenient to look at television.

Lesser amounts of free time would be assigned to minority parties, on the basis of the number of votes, or the percentage of votes that a minority party received in the preceding election, or petitions it could muster in this current election.

The campaigns, most of us agree, are much too long. For this reason, the offer must be limited to the last month of the campaign. The guarantee of four free hours, of course, does not prevent either major party from buying as much time as it can find or the broadcasters wish to sell.

For the broadcaster, loss of revenue in eight hours—every fourth year—would be a small price to pay for political broadcast freedom. From all accounts, broadcasters are already spending a comparable amount of money every election year on headache pills. An example has already been set by one broadcaster, Thad Sandstrom of WIBW, Topeka, Kansas. He sold no political time in 1964. He gave time to all candidates and reported his happiest election year in history. There were, for once, no complaints.

The furor and arguments of recent years have been created by over-concern for the broadcaster and the politician. Actually, broadcasting laws are not intended to give solace and contentment to station owners; nor are they written for the convenience or advantage of politicians. The laws are supposed to be for the benefit of the citizen who needs the greatest possible information about candidates and issues before making a choice in the privacy of the voting booth.

To make the complexities of political broadcasting disappear, all Congress has to do is to put the voter first.

Political Leaders, Broadcasters Debate the Minow Plan

MARCH 24, 1965

'*But their suggestion . . . seems unrealistic*' Frank Stanton, CBS President.

The Minow-Laurent article puts the case for the repeal of the abortive equal-time law concisely and persuasively. It is a most valuable contribution, with both deep insight and the orderly presentation of little-understood facts, to a discussion that is frequently bogged down in distortions and irrelevancies.

But their suggestion that broadcasters be required to put free time at the disposal of the national chairmen of the two major political parties seems to me unrealistic. Such time might well not be used in the interests of the voter, for face-to-face discussions like the Presidential debates of 1960, but for carefully planned set pieces and campaign advertising, solely in the interests of the party.

Providing lesser amounts of time to minority parties according to their votes in previous elections serves no significant purpose. Whenever a minority party has been a meaningful factor in an election, it has usually arisen out of conditions in the election year and the party did not even exist during previous elections. What constitutes adequate time for a minority party depends upon immediate circumstances.

Messrs. Minow and Laurent soundly remind us that the best assurance of the broadcaster's acting responsibly and fairly in presenting issues and candidates is his obligation to operate his station in the public interest. Rigid legal requirements can only impede his usefulness.

'. . . *the wrong way of doing the right thing*' Robert W. Sarnoff, NBC Chairman of the Board

Mr. Minow makes a most articulate and persuasive case for repeal of the "equal-time" provision of the Communications Act. Many

494

broadcasters, including myself, have long advocated this move. We still do, and Mr. Minow's support in this effort to gain for the broadcaster a journalistic freedom equal to the print media's is indeed welcome.

We do not, however, accept the premise that we must trade for this freedom, and, consequently, we disagree with his "compromise" proposal of requiring broadcasters to allot specified amounts of free time to major and minor candidates.[16]

Mr. Minow characterizes this proposal as possibly "the lowest price any group ever paid for freedom." The response to that, it seems to me, is that no other individual or industry is required to pay for a Constitutional guarantee. If the principle of freedom of the press is valid at all—and what American believes it is not?—broadcasters should not be singled out as the group obligated to pay for that freedom.

In short, Mr. Minow's proposal is the wrong way of doing the right thing. It is discriminatory and confiscatory. If increased exposure of candidates and issues is its aim, why not also require railroads and airlines to furnish so many miles of free transportation to the candidates and their entourages or hotels to extend complimentary food and lodging?

What Mr. Minow proposes is to compel broadcasters to do what they have been, and are, effectively prevented by law from doing on their own. It would subvert the broadcaster's ability to apply journalistic judgment in presenting vital information to the public.

' . . . *there is a middle course* . . . ' Senator Warren G. Magnuson (D., Wash.)

As you know, this provision has been the subject of extensive hearings by my committee over the years. . . .

In 1960 I co-sponsored S. 3171, a bill which made it mandatory for a broadcaster to make a certain amount of time available for the Presidential and Vice Presidential candidates. Following hearings, Section 315 was suspended for the 1960 campaign, permitting the broadcaster to make the time available for the Presidential and Vice Presidential candidates.

My committee reported a similar suspension for the 1964 campaign but, unfortunately, it was not enacted. I voted in favor of this bill in the committee and on the floor. I have an open mind but there are a number of questions that have to be considered before an across-the-board repeal can be accomplished. I believe there is a middle course, at least in the initial instance.

496   ' ... *further relaxation of Section 315*' Senator John O. Pastore (D., R.I.)

I am a firm believer that there should be further relaxation of Section 315. On a number of occasions I have introduced legislation that would suspend Section 315 to include Congressional and Gubernatorial as well as Presidential and Vice Presidential candidates. This would permit the broadcaster to demonstrate by action his ability to deliver on the promises he is now making.

It is my judgment that the broadcaster has reached a point of maturity and if the shackles are removed, he will be able to make more effective use of this powerful medium in enlightening the public during a political campaign. As to those who may have doubts, . . . I should point out that the Fairness Doctrine would apply and Congress can always reinstate the provision of Section 315 if there is abuse.

' . . . *no one has found a better . . . program . . .* ', Representative J. Arthur Younger (R., Cal.)

A broadcaster, licensed and supervised by the Government, cannot possibly enjoy the same individual enterprise freedoms enjoyed by the press, which is not licensed, supervised nor regulated by the Government and where the individual functions in a field where any person is privileged to start a newspaper or magazine so long as he has financial backing to do so. On the other hand, no one, regardless of his wealth, can establish a radio or TV station without being licensed by the Government and being subject to Government regulation and supervision.

I have come to the conclusion that no one has yet found a better or more workable program than now enjoyed by the broadcaster under Section 315.

' . . . *in complete agreement . . . on repeal . . .* ' Mike Shapiro, General Manager, WFAA, Dallas

I'm in complete agreement with Newton Minow on the repeal of Section 315 of the Communications Act and his reasons for same. Speaking personally, and not as a director of NAB, I think the four hours of prime free time for the two major political parties has a great deal of merit. I would suggest no more than one hour per week, per party, be allocated in the month prior to election. Otherwise, if both parties decided to utilize this time in the last week the public—again —would suffer with political time taking over their choice of programs.

' . . . *we cannot agree with the proposal . . .* ' Vincent T. Wasilewski, President, National Association of Broadcasters.

The NAB also advocates the repeal of Section 315, but we cannot
agree with the proposal to require broadcasters to give free broadcasting time to each major political party. As former NAB President
LeRoy Collins wrote in January 1962: "To require the radio and television industries to provide their facilities free of charge to certain
Presidential candidates, without imposing similar requirements on
other types of communications, is a public policy I am confident you
would not support. We see no valid reason for requiring the broadcasting industry to bear the full brunt of this expense, while exempt-
ing entirely other media of mass communications such as newspapers
and magazines."

' . . . *repeal the equal-time requirement*' C. Wrede Petersmeyer,
President, Corinthian Broadcasting Corporation
His solution is a trade. Broadcasters should be required to give
four hours of free time to each of the two major parties (with lesser
amounts to the minor parties) each Presidential election year. In
exchange they would get relief from Section 315. For this broadcaster, at least, it's "no sale." . . .
What's the solution? It's easy. Congress should repeal the equal-
time requirement. Once done, there will be a much more meaningful
coverage of campaigns and political candidates by radio and TV
stations. Broadcasters will at least be free to exercise some journalistic ingenuity in portraying candidates and probing issues.

' . . . *minority parties . . . first to suffer* . . . ' Nathan Karp, National Campaign Manager, Socialist Labor Party
Aside from the statutory obligation to make the minimum periods
of free time available to each of the two major parties, the broadcasters, who are dominated by selfish corporate material interests,
would be free to determine who and what shall be heard over the
publicly owned air waves. The fact that minority political parties and
their candidates would be the first to suffer by no means guarantees
that they would be the only ones . . . Nine companies own three-
quarters of the stations reaching 40 percent of America's TV homes.
(As) FCC Chairman Henry observed: "Repeal Section 315, let
these nine agree to support one Presidential candidate, and that
candidate is halfway home."
In these crucial times . . . it is of the utmost importance that the
modern media of mass communication—radio and TV—be kept open
for the widest possible discussion of the problems facing us and
their possible solutions.

Children

The following section consists of six of a series of eight articles that appeared in TV GUIDE in the Fall of 1969. It would be most appropriate to introduce the series by repinting the editorial which appeared with the first of the series on October 11 of that year.

No aspect of television is discussed more—or understood less—than its possible effect on children.

Whether the forum be the Senate of the United States, a PTA meeting, a cocktail party or a women's-magazine piece, opinions on what viewing may do to—or for—youngsters are expressed freely and vehemently. With facts hard to come by, "psychologists and child experts say" or "plain common sense" are the criteria most often cited. Exactly which psychologists and child experts and exactly what they say are rarely specified. And "plain common sense" is hardly conclusive proof of anything.

Now that our government is investigating television for the third time in 20 years, we are again being inundated with frightening assertions and baffling contradictions about what it does to youngsters. The Senate's Communications Subcommittee holds well-publicized hearings. The National Commission on Violence issues statistics on the amount of mayhem children see on their screens. The Surgeon General uses a $1,000,000 Government grant to study television's effects. All of which provides fuel for those who advocate censorship.

Meanwhile broadcasters and advertisers seize on national concern as further reason to indulge their natural predilection for bland programming.

It is time that someone—and we believe it is TV GUIDE's responsibility —set down exactly what is known and what is not known about how television affects children.

This was the assignment given seven months ago to staff writers Edith Efron and Neil Hickey. They were assisted in their research by Judith Jobin and Susan Ludel of our New York office. The completed articles, and the stacks of research material, were reviewed for scientific accuracy by a research consultant in psychology.

These articles are not easy reading. The subject matter is too important to sugar-coat and the issues we are concerned with do not always lend themselves to journalistic simplification. We are dealing with scientific studies, and it would be unfair to the experts who conducted them, and to readers, if we glossed over difficult concepts.

This is a rather unusual caveat to introduce a series of magazine articles, but then this is the first time a publication has offered a full statement re-

498

viewing the scientific studies of television's effect on children. Much in the
series is surprising and dramatic, and may shock those who think that un-
specified "psychologists and child experts" or "plain common sense" provide
all they need to know on the subject.

THE EDITORS

In part one (pp. 501-505), Miss Efron reviews research findings
regarding the significance of television as an instructional force
and a source of knowledge. She explains that there is general agreement that for pre-school children TV is an educational bonanza which
exposes the child to things he otherwise would not see. The findings
concerning television's significance to the intellectual development of
children over six, however, are contradictory. Miss Efron indicates
that there are three schools of thought on the matter: those saying
that television is a positive intellectual influence, those saying it is
a negative intellectual influence, and those who feel it is of no influence at all. Most experts agree that the brighter the child, the
sooner he disappears from the ranks of heavy viewers. This suggests
that the general intellectual and informational level of television
programming for children is unnecessarily, even harmfully low.

There has long been considerable debate over whether or not TV
is teaching the wrong values to our children. In part two (pp. 505-510),
Miss Efron emphasizes the subjective nature of this debate: that is,
the value systems of those engaged in the debate determine their
impressions of and attitudes toward the values being disseminated
by television. While all agree that television is planting values in
children's minds, disagreement is rife regarding what television
should be, and is, teaching our children about good and evil, truth and
beauty, images of man and life, personal relationships, morality, and
socio-political problems.

In part three (pp. 510-516), Miss Efron suggests some of the problems that will plague the Surgeon General's office in its current attempts to ascertain the relationships between scenes of sex and violence on television and anti-social behavior among young people. She
reviews the still unresolved debate, between the chain-of-ideas
theorists and the perceptual-stimuli theorists as to how children comprehend TV plots, that pervaded the Dodd Senate hearings in 1961-62.
Those hearings ended with much controversy over a laboratory experiment by perceptual-stimulus psychologist Albert Bandura and
the author notes that this experiment has generated a whole school of
similar experiments since 1962. According to Miss Efron, these experiments have been important in generating a belief that the Surgeon

500   General's current study will result in more definite findings and conclusions than did the Dodd hearings of almost a decade ago.

The Bandura "school" has attracted much attention because its findings seem on the surface to imply that television violence triggers normal people (as opposed to psychopathic personalities) to commit violent acts and thus tends to influence children toward aggressive behavior. In part four (pp. 516-522), Miss Efron shows the inaccuracy of this implication, demonstrating that Bandura and those who have simulated his techniques disavow some of the several interpretations of their research. She discusses the experimental methods pioneered by Bandura and summarize criticisms of these methods raised by other psychologists and academics. After interviewing Bandura and several of his colleagues and supporters, Miss Efron is doubtful that a careful study and evaluation of the "new" violence experiments by the Surgeon General's twelve-member advisory committee will result in any startling conclusions regarding a causal relationship between televised violence and anti-social behavior.

In part five (pp. 522-528), Miss Efron reviews and elaborates upon the controversy over the experiments by the Bandura "school." She concludes that the seemingly frightening results of these experiments are somewhat illusory when the difference between play aggression and social aggression is taken into account. Turning from experimental research on the effects of televised violence to other types of research on the effects of television on behavior, Miss Efron emphasizes that the latter is equally dependent upon learning theory. Yet, the science of learning theory is a new one with few firm principles and little agreement regarding the methods of determining the sources of human behavior.

In the final part of the series (pp. 528-535), Neil Hickey contends that although television's effects upon children cannot yet be adequately evaluated, some knowledge has been accumulated which could assist perceptive and concerned parents to reach some conclusions about the best use of television for children in the home. This knowledge could also assist television programmers who should, for example, be concerned about the early mass exodus of brighter children from the medium. Hickey offers some opinions given by experts regarding what television for children should be. Mere reduction of the amount of violence and sex is not sufficient. Television's main task is to create a cafeteria of program types to give children a wide option of things to view. The ideal should be to capture the child's imagination by exposing him to the real world and its people.

What is TV Doing to Them?

By Edith Efron and Neil Hickey

OCTOBER 25, NOVEMBER 1, 8, 15, 22, 29, 1969

In a recent article on the controversies over TV's alleged effects on children, a national magazine cheerily wrote as follows: "On one point most educators agree: Video Boy is becoming a sort of peewee pundit. He knows, for example, the finer points of docking in space, can distinguish Bach from Bartok, and is a storehouse of such miscellany as the fact that whales' backs get sunburned and peel."

Is TV really a significant instructive force on the national scene?

The answer—if academic standards are used—does not add up to the above cheery estimate. Whatever TV may be doing, it is not producing a nation of peewee pundits. Here is what is known, today, about TV's effects on the child's scholastic development:

If there is any type of child in America who profits wholeheartedly from the home screen, it's the toddler—that wide-eyed little illiterate who is overwhelmingly curious about the world. He usually starts exploring the screen at age 2, at first captivated, according to Dr. Louise Ames of the Gesell Institute, by "the light and bright and motion."

By age 3 he understands a good deal of what he is looking at and has distinct preferences. Says Dr. Ames: "From 3 on, they're exposed to all kinds of things they wouldn't have seen a generation ago. Their knowledge is tremendously wide."

Preschoolers are difficult to test, and the only studies that have actually been made of their TV intake are in the realm of vocabulary. First graders who've done a stint before the set have vocabularies that are as much as a year or more ahead of those of nonviewing tykes.

The brighter the preschooler, the more he sops up from the screen. But the duller children derive special profit too. And according to Dr. Phillp Roos, executive director of the National Association for Retarded Children, "TV has proven to be quite a successful teaching tool with educable retarded children."

All in all, for *babies*—whatever their brain power—TV is an educational bonanza.

502   By the time the child is in elementary school, however, the TV-learning picture gets exceedingly diffuse. By 6, a child is absorbing information from dozens of sources—family, friends, neighbors, school, magazines, radio, movies, books and even occasional glances at the newspapers. No one can untangle, with any precision, what he's picking up from TV, as distinguished from these other feed lines. Consequently, there is a lot of speculation going on.

Pro-TV opinion has it that entertainment programming—which is just about all the small fry watch—continues to have considerable academic merit long after babyhood has passed. Observers in this camp claim that while the child is absorbed in the adventures of comedy families and Western heroes, "incidental learning" is sneaking in. "I believe this incidental learning is considerable," says sociologist Charles Winick of City College of New York. His view is shared by virtually all researchers.

Some of this incidental learning is solid grounding in the three Rs and vocabulary enrichment. Jess Stein, editor-in-chief of "The Random House Dictionary of the English Language," says: "To a small child, especially a child growing up in a deprived environment, the exposure to several hundred words clearly spoken and logically used is of enormous educational value."

Parental lore, of course, is full of hilarious—and nonacademic—illustrations of incidental learning. Professor Issac Asimov, biochemist and science-fiction writer, relates that one day after he received a large silver object as a present, his 9-year-old asked, "Hey, what are you doing with that champagne bucket?"

"Where did you hear about champagne buckets?" demanded the astonished professor. "Oh, I see them all the time on *The Three Stooges*," replied his worldly offspring.

And one magazine-writer mother reports gleefully that she was serving tea to three ladies from the PTA one day when her 5-year-old wandered in to inquire: "Mummy, what's a premarital relationship?"

But instructors report that knowledge of a more seemly type is being steadily absorbed by the youngsters. Said a rural teacher in Kentucky: "They see 'mesa' in their geography books and it's just another dull word to learn. But when Fury is riding that mesa it means something to them!" (see pp. 465-468).

Librarians, too, report that TV is educative and say that there have been rushes on local libraries across the country as small-fry viewers discover, first on television and then in their original book form, such exciting works as *Robinson Crusoe, Robin Hood, Treasure Island, The Legend of Sleepy Hollow, Heidi* and *Little Women*. Says Mrs.

Helen Prange, director of Children's Services in a Stamford, Conn., *503*
public library: "TV stimulates children's curiosity. They ask for a
lot of books, especially in science. When characters like Daniel Boone
and Davy Crockett are on the air, there's a lot of reading on frontier
life."

Finally, there are those who say that TV viewing goes hand in
hand with high scholastic achievement. Wilbur Schramm, who has
done the largest TV study in America, involving 6000 children, has
positively established the fact that the brightest children in the
country with the highest marks are very heavy TV viewers.

Says Schramm: "Typically, the bright children are early starters.
They usually begin earlier to watch TV. In the early school years
they're more likely than the others to be heavy viewers of television."
There is, in sum, a solid argument that TV is a healthy educational
force.

But don't rejoice too soon.

This optimistic picture is severely undercut by a contradictory
set of claims—and they emanate from equally reputable academic
sources. Many scholars believe just as strongly that TV is a hindrance
to a younster's intellectual development. And there are studies in
several countries to support this idea.

In the 1950s U.S. researcher Lloyd Scott did a small study in the
University of California and reported: "Children who view more
TV achieve less proficiency in arithmetic and reading, and are signifi-
cantly inferior in total achievement to those children who view less."

In England in 1958, researchers Himmelweit, Oppenheim and
Vince found that TV did not increase the older child's knowledge;
that a net gain was found only for "the very young and the dull";
and that bright children who watched TV tended to fall behind children who didn't.

In Japan in 1962 Takeo Furu did a study and found that seventh-
grade boys who watched TV were not progressing in reading ability
as fast as seventh-grade boys who didn't watch TV.

This gloomy school of thought also suspects that TV isn't stimulating book reading at all but may be reducing it. Dr. Eleanor Maccoby
says today, "I think there is an undesirable effect on reading ability,
but no studies exist to prove what I belive. I suspect, although I can't
prove it, that there may be a shift away from print to visual and
auditory learning. This may be slowing up the learning process. You
can't view as fast as you can read."

Finally, researchers universally reported that the worst students
in U.S. classrooms are almost invariably heavy TV viewers. On the

504 basis of this last fact alone, many TV "pessimists" consider television to be a negative intellectual influence.

As if this contradictory testimony were not sufficiently bewildering, there is a third group of researchers whom we shall call the "neutralist." They have studied by far the largest number of children —a confirmed total of about 10,000—and they report, with massive statistics to back them up, the strange conclusion that after a few years in public school a viewing child ends up with no increase *or* loss of knowledge that can be traced to TV.

Like everyone else studying the TV-learning problem, the "neutralists" have compared viewing patterns with classroom marks. And over and over again, in studies that cover a span of 17 years in three countries—the U.S., England and Japan—they are flatly unable to find any "significant" connection at all. Reports Dr. Eleanor Maccoby, "If you take the simple bare facts of classroom marks, you get *nothing.*"

Why the total failure to uncover any results? Because enormous amounts of TV are gulped down by child geniuses *and* child morons, by the most brilliant students *and* the worst failures. As CCNY sociologist Charles Winick states the scientific dilemma: "If the two groups you could most heavily count on to demonstrate a difference *don't* demonstrate a difference—you're nowhere."

General-knowledge tests and creative extracurricular activities fare no better than school marks, according to the "neutralist." On both sides of the Atlantic, the two biggest studies—Himmelweit and Schramm—tell us that TV isn't causing a ripple of "significant" change in these realms.

Finally, as for TV's effect on book reading, the "neutralists" offer no conclusive answer. On the whole, they say, bright children still tend to read books, and dull children still tend not to, but how TV has affected the reading picture no one is certain.

What does this stream of "insignificant" or uncertain information mean? Is it possible that hours and years of TV watching are actually giving children no information of cultural value? All observers deny this. Both Schramm and Himmelweit suggest that TV *is* teaching, but is not saying much that the children are not hearing elsewhere. The result: you can't measure it by an academic yardstick.

And that's roughly where we stand, today.

There, however, is one genuinely objective index of TV potential for intellectual instruction. It's a startling one, and it is almost inexplicable that the entire country doesn't know it already, because it has been on record for eight years. It lies in one small but highly

significant statistic that emerged in the Schramm study—the age at
which a bright child begins to yawn in the face of the set:

That age is: 10.

Schramm reports, after studying 6000 children: "Sometime
between the 10th and 13th year (fifth and eighth grades), a striking
change occurs. The more intelligent children tend to disappear from
the ranks of the heavy viewers. . . . The difference is quite dramatic.
. . . The higher the child's intelligence, the less his viewing."

The bright children obviously reach what Schramm calls "satura-
tion point" the soonest, and the middle and lower intelligence groups
follow suit shortly after. The average "yawning age" is 12.

This conclusion is not Schramm's alone. The identical "yawning
age" was discovered in England by Himmelweit. "I believe everyone
would agree that 12 is the average age at which healthy children grow
bored with the set," says Dr. Winick.

The reasons for the early exodus from the set of the bright children are numerous—but one of the most crucial is a desire for mental
stimulus. Explains Schramm: "TV ceases to challenge them as it
once did. Many of them are seeking greater challenges and rewards
in print media . . ."

If one can conclude anything from this bright 10-year-old exodus
—and virtually every student of the medium concludes it—it is that
the general intellectual and informational level of the entertainment
programming is unrealistically, even harmfully, low. In England,
psychologist Hilde Himmelweit let out the following blast:

"It seems to me a devastating indictment that, while 10-year-olds
still pick up some knowledge from television, by the time they reach
13 only the dull ones do so, and that the more intelligent the child,
the less the TV hold becomes. Is it perhaps that much of the evening
entertainment is at the level of a 10-to-11-year-old?"

Schramm and most TV researchers in America are saying exactly
the same thing—without the polite British question mark at the
end.

"Everyone knows what values are! Everyone knows what's
right and what's wrong!"

This earnest cry by a U.S. senator, uttered in the course of an
impassioned harangue against certain developments in TV programming, is not unique. Indeed, it's a sentiment shared by millions
of Amercians who also feel that *their* values—namely, *their* view of
the Good, the True and the Beautiful—are self-evident, and that if
"the other guy" disagrees, he is viciously wrong-headed.

506   This widespread view is the essence of the worst battle raging over TV today—the Battle of *Values*. The battle cry, stated simply, is this: "TV is teaching the 'wrong' values to our children."

Because the various legions besieging TV are using the same battle cry, it is frequently assumed that they mean exactly the same thing by it. They don't. They disagree gravely and irreconcilably in their value judgments of Man, of Life, and of Good and Evil.

The differences begin at the base—with the very building blocks of TV programming, the specific shows that are on the air. Even on this primary level, critics dedicated to child welfare are in belligerent disaccord about whether or not any given show is Ethical, True or Beautiful.

The quarrels range through every kind of programming that children see—everything except late-night fare. Here are some typical value clashes:

The National Association for Better Broadcasting, formerly the National Association for Better Radio and Television (which describes itself as a nonprofit corporation dedicated to the advancement of the public's interests in the broadcasting industry), describes *The Heckle and Jeckle Show* as a cartoon series of excellent quality, simultaneously, the PTA magazine called it "just a heap of rubbish."

NABB said of the *Mighty Mouse Playhouse:* 'The little super-mouse is a delightful fantasy," while the PTA snapped: "Recommended for mice."

In the area of programming for older children, NABB declared of *American Bandstand:* "The whole atmosphere lacks grace and gaiety"; while the PTA declared it had "gentle manners, good taste and gaiety."

And NABB declared of *Whirlybirds:* "The element of crime makes it unsuitable for children." PTA said it was "straight, clean, absorbing adventure."

The same type of absolute artistic-moral disagreement has occurred over the prime-time series which are the children's major entertainment fare. The American Council for Better Broadcasts set up an advisory chain of critic-correspondents with the following typical results: Of *Gunsmoke* the critics said: "Too gory and violent" and "suitable for family viewing." Of *Lost in Space* critics said: "marked by violence, greed, selfishness, trickery and disregard for accepted values"; and "imaginative, with good moral concepts."

Since devoted "right-thinkers" have never been able to arrive at identical judgments about TV specifics, it should surprise no one to learn that they are clashing just as violently on TV generalizations.

Here are some of the major value questions being debated today:

What picture of Man is TV "teaching our children"? Some people, including many of the Nation's top TV critics, have de- nounced the idealized TV hero as "artificial" and "unreal." They have declared that this view of incorruptible Man is "escapist" and psy- chologically damaging to children.

Others, like Drs. George E. Gardner and Elizabeth Makkay, Harvard Medical School psychiatry professors, applaud the ideal- ized hero as healthy, and a psychological necessity for children. "Children crave such people," says Dr. Gardner. "They have a need to identify themselves with heroes."

Yet others, like Stanford's Wilbur Schramm, author of *Television in the Lives of Our Children*, criticize the idealized heroes because the ideal is rendered irrelevant to contemporary productive goals. The heroes, says Schramm, are "generally depicted as figures out of history, dressed in period costumes . . . (or) fantastic figures who drive space ships."

And finally, there are those like Eric Sevareid, who denounce the "cult of the antihero"—the newfangled "hero" who's weak, neurotic and often corrupt. He maintains that this trend is being carried "to a point where heroes and heroines are made of burglars and brutes," and suggests that this perverse idealization of ignoble people is debauching the young.

What picture of Man is TV "teaching our children"? *Take your choice.*

What picture of personal relationships is TV "teaching our children"? Some critics denounce the view of human relations on the air as mediocre and vapid. They label the roseate family comedies, with their marital twin beds, their minute hassles and homilies pure "Bible Belt," or "middle-class mythology." They declare them socially unrealistic and childishly evasive about the psychological and sexual facts of life. As TV producer-writer E. Jack Neuman (*Mr. Novak*) has put it: "Sex is the driving force of every man and woman in this country. What are we trying to protect human beings from, anyway? Themselves?"

Others insist that TV is quite realistic, within the limits of half- hour playlets and the proprieties; that the situation comedies portray the wholesome essense of life as it is lived by the middle-class majority. The correspondents of the American Council for Better Broadcasts repeatedly discribed such family shows as "realistic," and as "showing the real problems of parents and children." The people in them, they assert, are "just like the people next door."

508   And then there are those who denounce TV for avidly rooting around in pathology. Schramm criticizes the prevalence of "inadequate fathers"; a national magazine declares that "adults are often depicted as bickering, tension-ridden morons." Others charge TV with besieging the young with visions of tasteless heterosexuality and even more tasteless intimations of sexual perversion. Psychiatrist Lawrence S. Kubie goes so far as to charge TV with portraying "diseased and uncontrolled sexual behavior."

What picture of personal relationships is TV "teaching our children"? *Take your choice.*

What picture of moral conflicts is TV "teaching our children"? Some denounce TV's Good vs. Evil shows for a virtually unceasing flow of intense physical conflict. Cartoon shows, declares Ivan Tors, creator of *Flipper*, are "full of violence, mayhem, sadism, cruelty and everything a child should not see." As for the prime-time Sheriff-Cop-FBI-Army-Navy-Space-Police versus Badmen programs, many, like Dr. Kubie, charge these shows with being vehicles of "bodily mutilation, torture, hate and destruction."

The authors of the report of the National Commission on the Causes and Prevention of Violence claim that this violent contest between good and evil "fosters moral and social values in daily life which are unacceptable in a civilized society."

Many others, however, deny that the Good vs. Evil shows are corrupt. They maintain that the stylized violence is understood as symbolic, and they defend the entire category as morality plays. Scientist-fiction-writer Isaac Asimov, along with other unaroused intellectuals, cheerfully describes the symbolic Good Creature vs. Bad Creature cartoons: "They deal with heart-stopping, mind-numbing adventures. . . . Will the Fantastic Four or the Herculoids or Spider-Man or . . . Space Ghost defeat the forces of evil? Rejoice . . . for they will, they will!"—and he quotes a child authority to allay adult panic: "The good guys *gotta* win."

What picture of moral conflicts is TV "teaching our children"? *Take your choice.*

What picture of sociopolitical problems is TV "teaching our children"?

Again, the divisions of opinion are similar. There are those who claim that most prime-time entertainment evades the very existence of serious sociopolitical problems, that almost none of America's current agonies penetrates the thick screen of fantasy. Others declare that they do penetrate—but in a "whitewashed" and falsely "embellished" form—a la *Julia,* the family comedy starring a beautiful

Negro widow who is largely indistinguishable from a beautiful white widow, save for her color. Academy Award-writer Stirling Silliphant (*In the Heat of the Night*) charges there is a new trend toward "stereotyping" a glamorized Negro.

Then there are those who feel, like a Methodist director of Christian Education, that TV is offering children a realistic and conscience-provoking education in social problems: "TV is opening windows, airing some of the sickness in our modern life—poverty, illegitimacy, discrimination."

And, finally, there are those who charge that significant social groups are being antiglamorized—that they are being converted into ugly grotesques. Journalist Nicholas Hoffman blasts the caricaturing of political dissenters of the right and left in prime-time shows. "The programs denude controversial figures of sanity—conservatives, hippies, black activists, whoever is 'dangerous.' They are allowed to keep their . . . distinguishing lingo . . . but the believable context disappears, so they look like dangerous nuts . . . maniacs. The impression is left that the only tenable approach to reality is a vapid consensus held together by the Boy Scout oath."

What picture of sociopolitical problems is TV "teaching our children"? *Take your choice.*

Finally, what picture of American Society is TV "teaching our children"?

Again, the same polar positions prevail. Princeton historian Eric F. Goldman accuses TV of being actively reactionary—of being "a blockage to a fresher, fuller, brighter way of life . . . it is a counter-revolutionary force."

Some, like sociologists Paul Lazarsfeld, Robert Merton and Wilbur Schramm, see TV as a vehicle that perpetuates current middle-class values. Schramm says: "The media dare not do anything that might alienate large segments of their audience. Thus, they dare small changes, but not fundamental ones; and their whole impact is to retain the status quo."

Some, like President Nixon, Senator John O. Pastore, a host of Congressmen, and millions of disgruntled middle-class citizens, declare that TV *should* reflect the status quo, and respect the values of the middle-class majority; and they charge TV with being too often intent on desecrating them.

Some, like the authors of the Violence Commission's report, say TV values generate "a distorted and pathological view of society" among the poor.

Finally, some, like editor Russell Lynes, declare that TV, just

510   *because* it projects middle-class values, is operating as a revolutionary force. "The display of these values by television to people who cannot afford to achieve them has unconsciously been a contributing factor in the urban upheavals."

What picture of American Society is TV "teaching our children"? *Take your choice.*

If you survey these various charges and countercharges, you are virtually forced to certain conclusions:

That the deepest issue at stake in the Great Value Battle is the stuff of which all holy wars are made—*morality*, both personal and social.

That the battle is recognizably similar in pattern to the ethical-political battles raging nationally off-screen.

That much of the shouting supposedly on behalf of children is going on because the *other* guy's "self-evident truths" are on the air.

And that, in the last analysis, the values that TV is dispensing vary according to the eye of the beholder.

A great many people understand the subjective aspects of this national uproar over TV, and a great many don't. But whatever they understand, they are united in the awareness that the Tube is unquestionably planting values into children's minds, and that they personally dislike a good many of them.

Many, including irate legislators, are seeking the connection between TV's "wrong" values with the disturbing social upheavals of the day. They are putting pressure on the sociologists and psychologists to come up with a set of answers to the question: "What are 'TV values' doing to our children?" They want these answers scientific. They want them simple. And, unfortunately they want them yesterday.

———————

For several years the U.S. press has been filled with reports of the sexual and political rebellion of "youth"—and the consternation of their "elders." Some months ago, imbedded in these reports was the following UPI item:

President Nixon yesterday endorsed a one-year study to gauge the impact of the televised sex and violence on the Nation's youth.

In a letter to Chairman John O. Pastore (D., R.I.) of the Senate Communications Subcommittee, Mr. Nixon said, "I want you to know that I join you in supporting the proposed one-year study of the possible relationship between scenes of sex and violence on television and antisocial behavior among young people."

Pastore proposed the study by the Surgeon General's office   *511*
during recent Senate hearings on television violence.

With this word of Presidential approval, the third major governmental investigation in two decades moved into action to examine the "sex and violence" being beamed by the TV networks at American children.

It is obvious, of course, that as it is generally used, the phrase "sex and violence" has to be short for *"the wrong kind of sex and violence"*—since the "elders" are not objecting to marriage, to police forces and to armies.

It is also a fact that the Surgeon General's task in seeking to ascertain the "impact" of TV plays on the human mind and conduct is scarcely simple.

The reason: every major ingredient of the problem—art, morality and human learning—is still scientifically classified as unconquered or subjective terrain.

As we reported last week, a TV play that is "true," "good" and "beautiful" to one American can be "false" and "vile" to another; and what is "right" behavior to one American is "wrong" to another.

As for learning, social scientist Eleanor Maccoby says, "We are nowhere near figuring out how to *explore* these learning issues yet. We hardly even know what *questions* to ask."

In sum, the object of the Surgeon General's "one-year study"— the relationship of a series of unknowns—is a great frontier mystery so far as science is concerned.

The two previous full-scale Senatorial investigations—the Kefauver hearings in 1951 and the Dodd hearings in 1961-2, have already faced this dismal truth in spades. After summoning legions of moralists, sociologists and psychologists to discourse on the implications for children in the values of TV plays, both hearings ended under an avalanche of contradictions.

And both concluded with a helpless cry for more basic research in the realm of human consciousness.

There is every reason to suppose that the upcoming study by the Surgeon General's office will culminate in the same helpless cry.

There are several ways for the concerned citizen who lacks an elaborate scientific education to get a clear idea of what the Surgeon General is up against. The first is to understand the shoals on which the preceding Government investigations were wrecked—shoals which still exist today.

The Dodd hearings—to discuss only the most recent inquiry— were virtually a test-tube rehearsal for the current scene. They

512 started in 1961, accompanied by strong warnings by the Senator, who declared: "The outlook is grim. Something must be done. Sociologists, psychologists and other scientists have pointed out . . . that television programs saturated with crime, violence and brutality are dangerous to our children and youth . . ."

Strangely enough, when the principal sociologists and psychologists themselves testified, the "outlook" did not seem quite so "grim." In fact, it was not even clear if there was an "outlook" at all:

Dr. Ralph Garry, Boston University psychologist and consultant to the Dodd committee, and sociologist Peter Lejins, then member of the White House Juvenile Delinquency Commission, declared candidly that there was no evidence linking TV to juvenile violence. "It is impossible to the satisfaction of the true scientific method to prove a connection." said Lejins.

The collective ignorance of the social scientists on the subject at hand was summed up by sociologist Carl Perian, the Senator's administrative assistant, in this way: "*All fields of study involving human behavior are equally in the dark concerning the motives and drives that make men behave the way they do.*"

You might think, under these circumstances, that they all went home promptly, and saved the taxpayer some money. But they didn't. They settled down for several seasons of arguing—almost entirely about "violence," "sex" apparently proving too precarious a subject even to fight about.

And as the arguments unrolled about art, morality and learning—about one million words of them—they finally jelled into one discernibly basic debate. It was a highly academic debate—about the nature of plays and how the human mind grasps them—and, since this is the core debate of the current period, here is the net of it:

There were two schools of thought. One declared that plays must be analyzed in terms of an *interlocking series of ideas or concepts.* The other said plays must be analysed in terms of a *separate series of "stimuli" or perceptions.*

What does this argument actually mean? Simply this:

Either: A play is what the *chain-of-ideas* people say it is—namely, a story about, let's say, a noble-hearted man who loves a virtuous girl whose puny inheritance is stolen by an evil old rancher. Thereupon, the hero gallops after the evil old rancher and gives him the clobbering of his life, returns the heritage to his girl and lives with her happily ever after.

Or: A play is what *the perceptual-stimuli people* say it is—namely, a sequence of separate sensory experiences, of which the critical one is the big clobbering scene, which consists of wham! and pow! and the sight of a fist on a jaw, and a body flying through the air, and a crunch and BLAM!

Why does this argument matter enough to fight about it, off and on, for two years at a Senatorial hearing?

Because, depending on these interpretations, both schools of thought draw different conclusions about the effects of plays on children. To wit:

—The chain-of-ideas people insist that children understand TV plots and can thereby learn the valuable old moral lesson: crime does not pay.

—The perceptual-stimuli people insist that such scenes of clobbering serve as stimuli which may "trigger" the children to clobber others.

Needless to say, when the two schools confront each other, communication is less than ideal. At the Dodd hearings, perceptual-stimulus advocates served as witnesses and consultants to the Senatorial investigating committee, and challenged the chain-of-ideas men—writers and executives in the TV industry—to a series of battles, all revolving around this issue.

Thus, at the hearings, such testimony as the following was given by Mrs. Clara Logan, president of the National Association for Better Radio and Television, who had counted patches of "violent stimuli" for a single week in November 1960:

We witnessed the following: 144 murders, 143 attempted murders, 52 justified killings, 14 cases of drugging, 12 jail breaks, 36 robberies, 6 thefts, 13 kidnapings, 6 burglaries, 7 cases of torture, 6 extortion cases, 5 blackmails, 11 planned murders, 4 attempted lynchings, 1 massacre scene with hundreds killed.

The chain-of-ideas men, denying the validity of this approach to plays, fought back with irony—hurling even more horrible "violence" statistics at the committee, taken from great literature, such as Shakepeare's plays.

Again, perceptual-stimuli advocates backed chain-of-ideas men into a corner, and tried to make them account for every bit of "violence" in specific TV plays. Thus sociologist Carl Perian "debated" the recalcitrant Grace Johnsen, ABC-TV's continuity acceptance director, as follows:

PERIAN: Mrs. Johnsen, I am referring now to the actual sound effects of the crunch, when the fellow stepped on his hand in the immediate scene that followed with his heel.

MRS. JOHNSEN: Crunch?

514   PERIAN: Yes . . .

MRS. JOHNSEN: I'm afraid I missed that, Mr.Perian. I don't think there was a crunch. . . . There was the commotion of what was going on in the room.

PERIAN: I think there was a rather loud sound effect.

MRS. JOHNSEN: Well, the acoustics are't too good here. I may have missed this point.

PERIAN: We have seen the film several times, and I think there was a rather loud sound, and if you did not hear it, naturally, you cannot comment on it. Now you did hear the retching of the villain at the point where he had consumed too much water, did you not?

MRS. JOHNSEN: I don't think he was retching.

PERIAN: I see. Thank you.

Then the futile clashes transferred themselves to the direct arena of children's consciousness.

The perceptual-stimulus advocates claimed that many children up to the age of 13, and many adults as well, were completely incapable of following the television storylines. Thus Dr. Ralph Garry quizzed producer Richard Lewis of Revue Studios as to whether he thought adults grasped the connection between the "middle" of a Western and the "end." Mr. Lewis, a chain-of-ideas man, said he thought normal adults, and 13-year-olds as well, did understand the connection between the beginning, middle and end of a play. The argument deadlocked.

Again, Dr. Garry informed William T. Orr, vice president of Warners, that 8-year-olds could not understand the plots of Cheyenne, or their moral ideas. Mr. Orr challenged this:

MR. ORR: Do they understand good from bad or right from wrong?

DR. GARRY: They are still in the process of learning it.

MR. ORR: The reason I ask the question is that the Western is a simple form. The white is usually pretty white and the black is pretty black. . . . I believe children, even children under 6, can understand a simple story of who is right and who is wrong . . .

Indeed, the entire Dodd hearings were nothing but one vast deadlock over this central issue of children's comprehension, which was chewed over and over again in a variety of forms.

The hearings ended on a controversial high point. They presented a report on a laboratory experiment by a perceptual-stimulus psychologist, Dr. Albert Bandura. Dr. Bandura had exposed children to an unbroken patch of "aggression"—an analogy to "TV vio-

lence"—and his report caused astonishment in the chain-of-ideas
ranks.

Specifically, Dr. Bandura had filmed a lady who took a mallet and, for eight minutes, pounded a huge rubber "Bobo" doll—the kind that bounces back when you smack it—shouting such things as "Pow!" and "Sockeroo!"

He showed the film to a group of 3- to 5-year-olds. The children were then given a small selection of toys, including a mallet and a huge "Bobo" doll. Most of the children imitatively pounded the "Bobo" doll with the mallet, and shouted "Pow!" and "Sockeroo!"— but also played with the other toys.

A control group of children who had not seen that film were given the same choice. They played with the other toys more, pounded "Bobo" less, and did not shout "Pow!" or "Sockeroo!"

Dr. Bandura claimed his experiment showed that the perception of "aggression" caused children to "learn aggressive behavior."

Many sympathizers with the perceptual-stimulus school agreed with Dr. Bandura's conclusions; Senator Dodd found his experiment "impressive," But advocates of the chain-of-ideas school were unimpressed. A snappish exchange took place between the Senator and ABC's then vice president in charge of programming, Oliver Treyz, who declared that his network would not air "a lady pummeling a 5-foot doll for 10 consecutive minutes" and denied that this was "analogous to what is shown on TV."

Even some prominent social scientists were unimpressed. Sociologist Wilbur Schramm said he did not believe that the vast majority of normal children could be "triggered" to aggression in this manner.

"Television by itself cannot make a normal, well-adjusted child into a delinquent. This is almost the unanimous conclusion of research and clinical investigation," he said, and he concluded that only an already "psycopathic" child could be so "triggered" to violence.

And thus Senator Dodd closed his hearings on an anitclimactic note. On March 19, 1962, he wrote a letter to the Secretary of Health, Education and Welfare suggesting that HEW write to universities across the country requesting suggestions for research in the vacuum areas of human learning: perception, concept formation, comprehension, value formation, and the cumulative effect of television viewing.

And that was the inconclusive end of the Dodd hearings—very much like the end of the Kefauver hearings a decade before.

516   So now, here we are, only seven years later. The functions of the human mind are still a major mystery to science. Art and moral values are still areas of violent subjective controversy. And yet a new study has been launched.

Why does the Surgeon General think there is anything to be gained from another go round on the subject?

Many reasons. But one stands out strikingly: in the last few years, Dr. Albert Bandura's "Bobo" doll experiment has generated a whole little "school" of such experiments, and the scientists involved all claim that they have proved Dr. Bandura's thesis—that the perception of "violent" stimuli causes "aggression" in viewers.

These developments have been publicized in the scientific press and are the premise of the brief report of the National Commission on Violence. They are the subject of intense controversy today—a complicated replica of the controversies described in this article.

These new experiments are expected to be an important element in the Surgeon General's considerations.

1961: *"All fields of study involving human behavior are equally in the dark concerning the motives and drives that make men behave the way they do."*

—Sociologist Carl Perian,
at the Dodd hearings on TV violence.

1968: *"It has been shown that if people are exposed to televised agression, they . . . learn aggressive patterns of behavior. . . . There is no longer any need to equivocate . . ."*

—Psychologist Albert Bandura,
professor at Stanford University

On the face of it, these two quotations appear to suggest that since Senator Thomas Dodd's initial inquiry into the effects of TV "violence," there has been an astonishing breakthrough in the sciences of Man—a breakthrough that allows psychologists to measure the impact of TV on the human mind and human behavior.

And yet, as we have previously reported in this series, no such breakthrough has occurred. Indeed, in this year of dubious grace 1969, sociologist Wilbur Schramm of Stanford University says of all research in this area: "We must not expect too much. Experiments on such a subject as this are extremely hard to design and conduct, not only because of the difficulty of unraveling the skein of a life to find the sources of complex behavior, but also because of the moral

impossibility of experimenting on a child as one could upon an in- *517*
animate object or a laboratory animal."

Nonetheless, for a second time within a decade, a little hurricane
has blown up over TV "violence" in the broadcasting-government
world. And within the eye of this cultural-political hurricane stands
one particular psychologist: Dr. Albert Bandura of Stanford.

As we reported last week, Dr. Bandura was the star witness at
the Dodd hearings seven years ago—with the first recorded laboratory
experiment on the "effects of TV 'violence'" on human behavior.
The Senator found the Bandura "Bobo doll" experiment "impressive" and expressed a determination to set the whole problem before
the Surgeon General.

A few months ago, at the hearings of the National Commission
on the Causes and Prevention of Violence, Dr. Bandura—now
reinforced by the supportive experiments of a half-dozen or so
colleagues—found another powerful ally: FCC Commissioner Nicholas Johnson. Mr. Johnson traced the "causes of violence in our land"
in significant part to TV "violence," and quoted the lines by Dr.
Bandura which stand at the head of this article.

One of those who listened attentively to the testimony was Senator John O. Pastore, member of the Senate committee that super-
vises broadcasting. So struck was he with waht he was hearing that
he, too, recommended that the Surgeon General study the "scientific
findings" in this field. A year-long study has begun to determine
the "anti-social" implications of TV "violence."

Dr. Bandura and his colleagues have clearly impressed a few
men who have great power over American broadcasting. Why?
Because, as psychologist Richard Walters has put it: "A series of
laboratory studies by Bandura and his co-workers . . . present the
strongest evidence . . . that children should not be exposed to aggressive models if the goal of our society is to reduce violence."

But there is still another reason. The Bandura "school" represents a surprising development in the social sciences. To date, studies
have indicated almost universally that a *psychopathic* personality
could be "triggered" to violence by a fictional scene of conflict.
The Bandura school, however, appears to be suggesting that *normal*
people might also be "triggered." And they are suggesting it by means
of laboratory experiments.

As Dr. Bandura puts it: These experiments show that "if people
are exposed to television aggression . . . they learn aggressive patterns of behavior." Other members of this "school,"[17] too, report
that their experiments show that exposure to "filmed aggression"

518 produces "aggressive behavior." Dr. Leonard Berkowitz, one such experimenter, has published an article in the *Scientific American*, the headline of which reads: "Experiments Suggest That Aggression Depicted on TV . . . Can Arouse Certain Members of the Audience to Violent Action." And the National Commission on Violence states that "available research evidence strongly suggests . . . that violence in TV programs can and does have adverse effects on individuals."

From all this you might conclude that the proof is in—that the worst fears of many have been justified: namely, that to *perceive* violence is to *act* violently—an alarming electronic form of "monkey see, monkey do."

Oddly enough, Dr. Schramm, an enthusiastic advocate of these experiments, says: "There is little in the research to justify pushing the panic button."

Why shouldn't we "push the panic button" if, in fact, TV "violence" is hurling normal people, normal children into violent attacks on people?

The straight answer is that, despite all the disturbing statements quoted, nobody has as yet produced a basis for this charge. If you will reread the statement by the National Commission on Violence and that disturbing headline in the *Scientific American*, you'll discover the significant word "suggest." These experiments *suggest* that there may be "adverse effects," and they *suggest* that certain people may be triggered into violence by TV—they do not *prove* it.

Indeed, a good many scientists flatly dismiss the idea that these experiments even "suggest" any such thing. And to know why, you have to know something about the experiments. We found the facts a touch academic but well worth pursuing:

The first thing to know is that these experiments were generally designed in a certain way:

1) The experimenters showed a little film strip to one group of youngsters, but not to another.

2) This film strip, or "pictorial stimulus," was intended to represent TV "aggression."

3) They then placed each child in a room where he was allowed to be "aggressive."

4) They finally compared the "aggression" of both groups to see if the filmed "aggression" had made any difference.

But what did this term "aggression" mean, as used by these experimenters? What, for example, did they mean by "filmed aggression"?

They meant actions like this: two cartoon creatures bopping each other around[18] . . . a lady pummeling a big plastic Bobo doll[19] . . . a cartoon weed trying to "choke" a flower[20] . . . an adult pretending to be a child spanking another grown-up "child."[21] . . .

And what did the experimenters mean by child "aggression"? In one case "aggression" was the desire to see the experimenter "pop" a balloon, in answer to the question: "Do you think it would be fun to see me pop this balloon?"[22] . . . In another case, "aggression" was the number of times a child socked a Bobo doll[23] . . . In another case it was playing rowdily with dolls[24] . . . In another case, it was the preference to play with a little mechanical 6-inch doll which struck another doll, rather than to play with a ball in a cage[25] . . .

What kind of results did these experimenters get? The children who saw the "filmed stimulus" all marched into the playroom and played in a manner that indicated they'd been influenced by the film-and-game situation. They bopped the Bobo doll more if they'd seen the lady bopping the doll. They played with the doll-hit-doll toy more if they'd seen the cartoon creatures biffing each other around. They wanted to see the balloon "popped" more, etc.

This is what the Bandura-"school" experimenters mean when they say they have shown that TV "violence" causes "aggressive behavior." It is not what most people—or most politicians—think screen "violence" or human "aggression" mean. The National Commission on Violence, in fact, defines "violence" as "the overt expression of force intended to hurt and kill."

Dr. Schramm says of these, and of other like experiments[26] involving adolescents: "The numerous laboratory studies in which aggression has been increased and aggressive behavior encouraged by viewing aggressive film . . . are clearly of concern to us." Obviously, if the tube were "triggering" normal children or adults into "hurting and killing," it would be of overwhelming concern to us.

But is it? Did these experiments in a play situation prove that the tube has that effect? Is the "aggression" of a child popping a balloon to be equated with the "aggression" of an adolescent hoodlum mugging someone in a park, or with that of a Sirhan Sirhan assassinating a Robert Kennedy? As Milton Dickens, a mass-communication research expert, says: the problem in trying to "apply" these results is that the "aggressive behavior in these experiments involved *not other adults or children* but *toys and dolls*."

There are sterner criticisms on record. Psychologist Ruth Hartley, member of the American Board of Examiners in Professional Psychology and a recent director of research projects for the National

520 Institute of Mental Health, has done, for CBS, a book-length demolition job on these experiments. Says she: "These people are playing games with semantics. They're using the word 'aggression' in a sense that is totally different from the popular or dictionary meaning of the word. These experiments are utterly irrelevant to 'violence' in life."

What do these play-tests actually prove? The experimenters themselves are not sure; their conclusions contain logical implications which they disavow.

For example, Dr. Bandura states: "It has been shown that if people are exposed to televised aggression, they . . . learn aggressive patterns of behavior."

When we asked Dr. Bandura if this means "TV teaches people to *behave* aggressively," he said no.

"Some people have misunderstood the purpose of my Bobo-doll experiments," he says. "They were designed only to determine to what extent a child *learns* about behavior from television."

Thus, Dr. Bandura is saying that all he has shown is that if a child watches a fight on TV, he *learns* about fights. This, he adds, has nothing to do with hostility or an impulse to attack people: "*Most aggressive patterns of behavior are learned without any intent to harm.*" And finally, he says: "One would use quite a different experimental procedure if one were testing for aggressive or punitive behavior *to other people.*"

In short, according to Dr. Bandura, he has *not* been testing for antisocial behavior at all.

This is different from what his experimental language implies— and from what some have assumed Dr. Bandura has been saying.

Similarly, Drs. Mussen and Rutherford wipe out the frightening implications of their experiments. They say: "There is no evidence in this data to suggest that . . . those who increase in the measure of aggression shown here, become more hostile toward the other children." Again, in basic English, they, too, are saying that their laboratory definition of "aggression" is not the same as real-life "aggression"—i.e., physically attacking others.

Similarly, Dr. Berkowitz dissolves the antisocial implications of all these experiments in an acid bath of such strong qualifications as these:

—He claims TV can cause "normal" people to become "aggressive"—but adds the "important qualification": "such actions by normal people will occur only under appropriate conditions."

—He denies the "monkey see, monkey do" theory: "The linkage

between what the person sees and what he will do afterwards is
not necessarily close."

—He dismisses the worst social implications of these experiments
by saying that they "have not shown that youngsters who watch
film aggression often, will develop persistent antisocial patterns
of behavior."

—He also says that exciting "violent" TV films, in fact, can *soothe*
people: they *"provide relaxation and enjoyment,"* and can make
angry people feel *"calm."*

—And he finally points out that the number of "aggressive
incidents" traceable to the tube is "quite low."

To cap the climax, psychologist Richard Walters, member-in-
good-standing of this same school, says that "value judgments" are
implicit in the word "aggression": "The concept of aggression . . .
thus has limited usefulness in guiding social-psychological research."

In other words, then: what's "aggression" to you isn't "aggression" to me—and these "objective" experiments are therefore expressions of the private value judgments of the experimenters.

In similar fashion, all the members of this school end up by
undercutting or repudiating the terrifying implication that TV programs can hurl normal people into assaults on other human beings.
Yet these are the very implications that have won them stage center
in Washington. In his most recent major study, Dr. Schramm, who, we
repeat, is a friend of this school, sums up the only conclusion justified
by all available research, including that of the Bandura group. His
words reveal the extreme mildness and vagueness of the actual
"scientific" findings: "We can assume a high probability that under
some circumstances, *some* films produce undesirable effects in *some*
children." And he suggests that social scientists address themselves
to finding out *"what* films, *what* circumstances, and *what* children."

He suggests it because they do not *know.* And, as of this moment,
they are not near knowing. Most important of all, if you read the fine
lines of their studies, they do not *claim* to know. The much publicized
report of the National Commission on Violence contains an avowal
that was not publicized: "It is difficult to design studies linking human
behavior and personality formation to media content in view of the
vast array of other variables in the social environment that converge to shape a person's conduct and values."

By the time one finishes hearing what the Bandura school and
their supporters have to say about these new "violence" experiments,
one ceases to understand why they have been hustled into the Surgeon Genral's office as if Rome were burning and Dr. Bandura

522   were a fire extinguisher.

A clue to this mystery may be found in a comment by Dr. Joseph Klapper, director of CBS research, when he testified before the Violence Commission: "These studies are apparently much more widely discussed than they are read. . . . It is a great misfortune."

In 1951—one year after Senator Estes Kefauver's hearings on the psychological effects of TV "violence"—one of the greatest psychologists of this Nation rose at a professional meeting and delivered an obituary on a laboratory orangutan, who had spent weeks trying to fit a square peg into a round hole.

He said: "It died working on more complex problems than are investigated by most present-day learning theorists."

He went on to say that the science of psychology, which for experimental subjects mainly uses rats, had been degenerating for 15 years, and he climaxed his speech thus: "If we face our problems honestly . . . the theoretical psychology of the future will catch up with, and eventually even surpass, common sense."

The psychologist was Dr. Harry F. Harlow. His audience was the Division of Experimental Psychology of the American Psychological Association. And the speech was his presidential address.

In 1967—five years after Senator Dodd's hearings on the psychological effects of TV "violence"—another prominent psychologist, Dr. Ludwig von Bertalanffy, blasted: "Let us face the fact: a large part of modern psychology is sterile and . . . doesn't see the obvious. . . . It is the expressed or implicit contention that there is no essential difference between rat and man which makes American psychology so profoundly disturbing."

In 1969—just a few weeks after Senator Pastore recommended that a new study of the psychological effects of TV "violence" be undertaken by the Surgeon General—Dr. Robert Lockard, in an article in *American Psychologist*, blasted current psychological theories of man, many of which emerge from rat experiments, as invalid.

One of the ironies of broadcasting is that broadcast regulators are increasingly turning for guidance to a profession which has a penetrating understanding of rats but which knows its understanding of people to be precarious.

In a quarter of a century the social sciences have produced some 150 studies that consist mainly of clashing theoretical interpretations of psychological phenomena that no one yet understands.

Here's a quick run-down on about 25 years of research—on

"violence" and on "everything else," which is mostly learning 523
theory.

First—"violence" research.

Between the mid-1940's and the early 1960's no firm principles were established by any of the research. Investigations generally consisted of surveys of large groups of children and individual studies of very disturbed or delinquent children—and neither type of research proved that TV was "triggering" hostile or "violent" behavior.

This absence of findings isn't because psychologists weren't hunting for TV-caused evils. They were.

In fact, the "triggering" or "conditioning" or "brainwashing" hypothesis had come from psychology itself—right out of Pavlov's conditioned-dog experiments via the modern rat labs, and had already saturated the culture.

Arthur Koestler, prominent scientific writer as well as novelist, says: "In the imagination of the masses, the dog on the laboratory table, predictably salivating at the sound of a gong, has become a paradigm of existence . . . and the word 'conditioning' . . . has become a key formula for explaining why we are what we are. . . ."

The strange fact is that in the court of popular opinion the "brainwashing" findings were in before anyone had ever found them.

Of TV researchers in particular, sociologist Charles Winick of the City College of New York says: "The few people who work in this field all feel they know in advance what results they're going to get."

Unfortunately for such advance "knowledge," the findings have never turned out to conform to expectation.

In 1962, sociologist Wilbur Schramm, testifying at the Dodd hearings, summed up all studies up to that time. He reported them innocuous; declared, in defiance of "conditioning" dictum, that children manipulated the tube, the tube did not manipulate children; and concluded that only a child "psychopath" could be "triggered" to a "violent" act by the sight of conflict in drama.

The outbreak of political violence last year brought the "conditioning" issue to the fore once again. At the recent Violence Commission hearings, Government officials learned that there was new research material, this time suggesting that *normal* people could be "triggered" to violence, or "brainwashed" into violence over a long period of time. This is more sedately referred to as "the cumulative effect of TV violence."

But the truth is: nothing in fact was really new—and nothing had been proved about TV's capacity to "condition" normal or any other

524 people. The *methods* of "violence" research seemed to have changed; they were now laboratory experiments in how learning takes place. But the *results* still added up to zero.

Last week we told one-half of the story about these new experiments. Now we will tell the other. To do so we must recap a few facts.

The group of learning experiments that caused the major excitement were conducted on adults and children by psychologists Bandura, Walters, Lovaas, Mussen, Rutherford and Berkowitz. These were pure "conditioning" experiments: they set up a restricted "stimulus" and studied the "response."

They were, in fact, conducted like modern rat experiments—some by Walters and Lovaas being duplicates of specific rat experiments done years before. Most often these learning experiments excluded ideas and reasoning—both from the film and from the reports on the subjects' reactions.

This small group of experiments arrived at virtually identical findings: they seemed to have shown that if the "input" is "filmed aggression"—the "output" by the human being is "aggressive behavior." On the face of it, short-range "conditioning" seemed to be validated—and the implications of long-range "cumulative effects" were staring everyone in the face.

Oddly enough, these frightening results turned out to be illusory after the experimenters explained what they meant by "aggression." The experimental children had engaged only in *"play aggression"*—namely, they had batted dolls and toys around. The filmed "aggression" had *not* precipitated them into *social* aggression —i.e., acts of physical violence against human beings or property.

The experimenters themselves were cautious about claiming they had proved direct TV "conditioning" leading to social violence, and most of them actively withdrew such implications from their studies.

That is where we ended last week.

In addition to these experiments, there was conducted another batch of similar learning experiments, also based on the principles of the rat lab, and most of them also eliminating ideas and reasoning from the film and from the experiment.

These experiments had received far less publicity. Indeed, their existence was not even hinted at by the National Commission on Violence in its headline-making report. They were done by psychologists Albert, Emery, Maccoby, Wilson, Siegel, Feshbach, Rosenbaum, De Charms, Thibauf and Coules, as well as Lovaas. And they had very different results.

Some flashed "violent stimuli" at children and adults, and the subjects showed *no* alteration of conduct; some resulted in *less* of the laboratory-defined "aggression." Some got *inconsistent* results. And some got inconclusive results. Somehow in *this* set of experiments the "input" did not result in the same "output" and the human subjects, old and young, did *not* behave like laboratory rats.

In sum, this *total* body of findings is contradictory—which means only one thing: *no proof.*

But even this does not end the story. The nagging fact remained that one small group of psychologists did appear to be duplicating *something* in those tests, although there was no agreement among scientists as to what it was. This fact was built up by some psychologists in their writings and downgraded by others until, inevitably, two clashing conclusions have emerged:

One, that psychology was on the verge of proving that TV "violence" could "condition" normal people to "violence"; or two, that experimenters had wittingly or unwittingly influenced subjects and results to conform to "rat-conditioning" theory.

One statement by Dr. Walters virtually conceded the terrain to those who suspected manipulation: "The subjects . . ." he cautioned, "were tested *in situations in which aggressive behavior was permitted, instigated or even demanded . . .*"

The resultant controversy seemed rife with slander. Dr. Bandura, in particular, was the object of the charge that his experimental methods were dubious. It was so widespread that it ended up in a casual handout from the Television Information Office (a subsidiary of the National Association of Broadcasters), which informed people by mimeograph that: "Other social scientists were critical of the way the experiment was designed, and they questioned the value of Bandura's conclusions."

But Dr. Bandura was scarcely the only one suspected of methodological misdemeanors. Virtually all of his colleagues were, as well. The best-known attacker is Dr. Ruth Hartley, member of the American Board of Examiners in professional psychology and a recent director of research projects for the National Institute of Mental Health. She was hired by CBS to analyze this body of research, and she did so in a full-length technical volume. She charged: 1. semantic confusion, 2. verbal obscurantism, 3. experimental slovenliness, 4. challengeable premises, 5. debatable interpretations, 6. equivocation, 7. illogic, 8. experimental manipulation, 9. unjustifiable extrapolation, 10. evasion of internal contradictions, 11. evasion of external contradictions, 12. slanted reporting . . . and other offenses against reason. Her overall conclusion, with a slight note of respect for certain aspects of Dr. Walters' work: bad work—and no proof.

Psychologist Hartley was widely murmured about in certain

526   professional circles as having "sold out" to CBS. She says: "You can't *imagine* the attacks on me. It happens to everyone who doesn't say TV is hurting children. Well, never mind. The experiments still don't prove a thing."

Needless to say, these experiments have strong friends as well as foes. One friend is sociologist Wilbur Schramm, who was hired by the movie industry to analyze this psychological research. Unlike Dr. Hartley, Dr. Schramm does not analyze scientific methodology in his report, and he makes no technical evaluation of the experiments. He does little more than sum them up. He accepts the experimenters' definition of "aggression," and he personally suspects that doll play can be applied to life. He considers the research important.

However, Dr. Schramm, too, reports that these findings are contradictory and that the meaning is not "entirely clear." His over-all conclusion: significant work—and no proof.

Dr. Schramm has not been attacked as having "sold out." But his own competence as a judge of "basic research" has been challenged by Dr. Fredric Wertham, who, for that matter, also attacks the experimenters' research methods: "Artificially set-up experiments to measure aggression are not adequate, because children are not rats."

In turn, Dr. Wertham, who indicts TV "violence" from his base of the "anecdotal" clinical method, has been subject to charges of less-than-ideal scientific lucidity. Prof. James Halloran of Leicester University says: "I don't feel that Wertham supports his case with valid or objectively measurable evidence."

What is the resolution of this row?

There is none.

This is where the issue stands.

The only unity in the entire situation is that experimenters as well as friends and foes agree completely on one thing: *This learning research does not scientifically prove that the sight of TV "violence" conditions the viewer, child or adult, to violent behavior—whether short-range or "cumulative."*

Or, to put it a bit differently: There is no proof that the human child or adult sitting in a living room looking at TV is psychologically similar to a rat sitting in a cage staring at a blinking light.

And so much for TV "violence" research.

Now . . . what-about the "rest" of TV research? The "rest" is also "learning theory"—without the focus on violence." It consists largely of attempts to discover how children acquire ideas of different kinds from plays. *These attempts have resulted in no firm principles to date.*

Such general studies on how children learn do not get the attention in the press and government that "violence" research gets. They should. Because without "learning theory," nobody will ever understand children's behavior at all—"violent" or otherwise: *How* a child learns from the tube, and how be *evaluates* that information, will determine what ideas and values he accepts, which in turn will influence how he behaves.

How *do* children learn from the tube?

Do they think conceptually?

Do they perceive clusters of images?

Do they grasp ideas?

Do they make moral judgments?

What determines which ideas they select and reject?

Do they distinguish between fantasy and reality?

There are no definite answers today any more than there were when these very issues were fought over at the Dodd hearings.

"Learning theory," in fact, is in a seriously primitive state. We have already noted Eleanor Maccoby's statement: "We are nowhere near figuring out how to explore these learning issues yet. We hardly even know what questions to ask. I'm not sure," she had continued, "we would even have the technical means to answer the right questions, once we figure out what they are."

And Dr. Ernest R. Hilgard says: "There are no laws of learning which can be taught with confidence."

We can report with certainty that no one is about to arrive at any such laws in the near future.

Why?

Because behind the chaos in "learning theory" lies a disastrously unresolved controversy at the heart of psychology itself. It is almost never discussed in the popular press.

It is symbolized by Dr. Wertham's statement: "A child is not a rat."

Built into these simple words is a battle that has burned its way through psychology like a forest fire—leaving chaos in its wake: Does man have a *mind*—or doesn't he? Or is he an oversized rodent?

For many decades between World War I and II a school domiated academic psychology that formally claimed *man had no mind*. This was the school that first equated rat and man. And although few psychologists still discuss the issue today, the no-mind doctrine has left a destructive legacy. Says psychologist and statistical expert Dr. George Weinberg, author of "The Action Approach":

528   "Nearly all psychological experimentation still assumes *implicitly* that human beings are mindless creatures capable of being explained by an 'input'-'output' system.

"Nearly all experimenters have a vested interest in this view since they don't know how to set up or conduct experiments allowing that people can *think* about the 'input' and make their own decisions about it.

"Statistical statements about multitudes do not compensate for this. So, the chaos continues. Little has been done so far to give us principles that we can use to predict human behavior."

Translating Dr. Weinberg's statement into TV terms, you get the paradox of: rat experiments reproduced using people . . . "learning" experiments which rule out thinking and ideas . . . charges of "rigging" to shelter vested theoretical interests . . . mutual denunciations for illogic and unscientific procedure . . . clashing conclusions . . . chaotic non-results . . . the contents of this article.

This chaos caused by the no-mind, rat-man tradition has paralyzed psychology—hence TV research.

For the third time this theoretical chaos and attendant controversy has been deposited in the lap of the state for inspection—this time in the person of the Surgeon General. The resultant study promises to be cautious. The Surgeon General has resolved not to formulate policy on the basis of it.

We will learn its contents about a year from now.

———————

"For some children under some conditions, some television is harmful. For other children under the same conditions, or for the same children under other conditions, it may be beneficial. For most children, under most conditions, most television is probably neither particularly harmful nor particularly beneficial."

That famous quotation from the 1961 study by Schramm, Lyle and Parker (*Television in the Lives of Our Children*) encapsulates all that we know—some say all that we will ever know—about the effects of television upon children.

And what, indeed, does it tell us?

Very little, obviously. Human beings, including children, are simply too complex, and the influences upon them too diverse, to allow any more precise conclusions about how a single factor in our lives—in this case television—alters our thinking and our behavior.

All of which is not to say that we know *nothing* about television in relation to children. A tiny residue of certain knowledge settles at the bottom of the great murky vat which contains all the studies, experiments, polls, graphs, essays and sudden hunches about children vis-a-vis the little box called television. For example:

• The most potent single influence upon what a child watches on television is what his parents watch.

• In homes where parents take the trouble to offer attractive alternatives to TV, the children watch less TV.

• A child who watches "too much" television usually is suffering some emotional distress which is causing him to retreat into TV watching. It's not that he's fascinated with the programs. He's unhappy—consciously or not—with his home life, his school life, or his relations with his friends.

• Bright children discover television early, use it heavily, then drift away to other pursuits around age 12; less intelligent children remain enthusiastic viewers for longer.

• The quality of most network TV designed specifically for children is limited by the networks' competitive desire to attract maximum audiences for advertisers—usually the makers of toys and breakfast foods.

Such truths, scarce though they may be, can lead perceptive and concerned parents to some conclusions of their own about how television can best relate to their family life. For example, many child experts have pointed out that parents who tune in spontaneously to TV's discussion programs, concerts, documentaries and drama specials invariably induce similar tastes and appetites in their children—especially when the program becomes a jumping-off point for a simple discussion at home of what it all meant.

For example, a family watching a TV version of "Death of a Salesman" might be led to ask their children how they felt about Willie Loman's kind of traveling life, whether they thought the two sons acted properly toward their parents, and if the mother reminded them of their own.

In such ways, tiny ideational seeds are planted in the child's mind that will grow blossoms later on. At certain ages, children benefit from such small probes and questions which pique them. Answers will come aplenty in time. The prior problem, however, is: What are the right questions?

Dr. Leon Eisenberg, chief of psychiatry at Massachusetts General Hospital, told TV GUIDE: "There is some good material on television right now—*Captain Kangaroo* and *Misterogers*, for example. The value of such programs can be increased if parents join the children in watching, and ask questions, and carry over some of

530 the activities into the rest of the day. Too many parents use television as a cheap baby sitter, and that's bad in two ways: first, the child may be exposed to material which is confusing and harmful to him, and second, it may cut him off from his peers, reading and other activities."

"There's a socialization process that goes on," says Dr. Edward L. Palmer, research director of the Children's Television Workshop. "Children come to like what their parents impart value to. In subtle ways, parents wield great influence on what their children watch."

Example is by far the best persuader. It is hard, claims Schramm, to make a river rise above its source. If public affairs, ethics, science, nature and other such topics are not discussed in the home, "is the child easily convinced that they are important enough to view on television?"

This crucial influence of parents and their life styles upon offspring's habits—including TV-usage patterns—can scarcely be overestimated. That opinion was unanimous among all the experts TV GUIDE interviewed.

In homes where a parent reads to the child and is reasonably attentive to his natural curiosity and desire for actual experience rather than vicarious experience, the child automatically watches television less.

Of course, it's just as possible that insensitive parents, rather than attracting their children into real-life pursuits, can drive them into TV-watching as a refuge. Dr. Lawrence Zelic Freedman, of the Center for Advanced Study in the Behavioral Sciences, has written: "When televiewing is, in fact, excessive . . . it is reasonable to assume that the behavior is symptomatic of intolerable stress in [the child's] environment—whether conflicts in the home, frustrations at school, or among his peers—or of brewing anxiety or emotional instability within him."

Schramm puts it a slightly different way: no child is likely to be harmed very much by television if he has warm and secure social relationships and has no serious psychological troubles. Dr. Eisenberg says: "Prolonged and exclusive watching of television is most sharply seen as an indication of something wrong with the child's social adjustment. A child who is a poor reader or whose parents are not available to him may fall into this. *If TV were filled with the most wonderful content, it would still be detrimental if it kept the child from playing with other children, from studying and so forth.*"

Most children in their early years benefit intellectually from television—in vocabulary-building, in absorbing a general set of cultural

values, in stocking their minds with concepts and facts which otherwise they wouldn't have learned that early. "I suspect that TV informs and instructs in its own way as much as colleges do," says
Dr. Palmer. "TV has a greater educational influence than all the formal establishments devoted to education. *So for a parent to say,
'I don't let my child watch television' is to relegate him to cultural
deprivation.*"

Palmer surmises that TV "just must have a lot to do" with a child's
acquisition of simple, basic knowledge about his country and his
world; the fact that there are such things as Presidents and policemen and soldiers and that they perform certain functions. As children
approach adolescence, however, the brighter ones decide spontaneously that TV has taught them all it can, and turn to books, magazines, records, movies and social activities. The less bright children
tend to remain heavy users of TV.

Part of this decline in usage by brighter children seems attribut-
able to the high content of fantasy—instead of reality—in children's
TV. The more imaginative child, as he grows older, is hungrier for
information than for pure entertainment. Child psychologists have
suggested that a medium so potent in the transmission of information
—about nature, science, ethics—is derelict when it opts instead for
the wispy, fragile world of fantasy, whether live or animated.

Schramm says this: "Do we consider our children so slight a resource that we can afford to bring them up on an intellectual diet
of such a kind? Do we really believe that this is the way to make
leaders and thinkers?"

In addition, it is a fact that most adults—including television
programmers—chronically underestimate how much a child can absorb and understand. One psychologist told us that he believed *any*
principle could be taught to *any* child, as long as it was translated
into terms familiar to the child.

Says Dr. Eisenberg: "Children often are simply not treated
seriously enough. I don't mean that first-graders should be reading
War and Peace. But some of the truths about life contained in *War
and Peace* certainly *can* be taught to children."

Children's programs are afraid to talk about death, says Eisenberg, but many children already have been privy to the deaths of
relatives and friends. "They'll have confused ideas [about it] unless
we bring some clarity to the subject," he says.

But all such altruistic concerns are simply not the principal
preoccupation—nor can they be—of TV programmers in the American
system of commercial television: the networking structure which

532 places the advertiser's interests first and the audience's second. "What has held back children's television . . . for 20 years is the commercial interests of the broadcasters," says Dr. Gerald Lesser, Bigelow professor of education and developmental psychology at Harvard University's Graduate School of Education.

"I have faith in kids. I'm not saying that the programs produced for children have terrible, harmful consequences. But it's meaningless junk that can be put on for little expense and makes a lot of money. The quality of most of it is abysmally bad. Not enough thought has gone into it. Commercial exploitation has produced an endless, grubby bag of cartoons."

Lesser and a number of other psychologists we talked to, lament this fixation by children's programmers with "winning the ratings battle." As long ago as 1961, Schramm and his colleagues were concerned about it, and all the same factors are still operative today:

"We sympathize with television broadcasters for the competitive pressure of the sponsor system. . . .Because of this competition, the networks also are forced to be tough-minded about program ratings—for example, even to discard some lower-rating and higher-quality programs because they influence the rating of programs next to them. It is necessary to maximize the drawing power of the schedule at the cost of experimentation with 'quality.' This undoubtedly represents a severe problem to commercial broadcasters. We consider that it also represented a shortsighted attitude which may produce immediate profits, but will ultimately result in harm to both sponsor and broadcaster."

Occasional specials sprinkled into the children's TV schedule mitigate this condition somewhat, but not sufficiently to satisfy most child experts, who feel that the networks produce quality specials almost against their better judgment and only to keep the critics at bay.

"Children's television gets by on good intentions," Lesser says. "They'll frequently take a classic children's book and destroy it. But those programs are rarely subjected to critical analysis in the press, and the networks automatically get a high mark just for effort. But if we ever get beyond this stage of applauding them for merely being well-intentioned, then we can make progress."

He thinks that television has never truly captured the imaginations of children, nor moved them, as much as a handful of authors—Lewis Carroll, E. B. White and illustrator Maurice Sendak, among others—whose special genius has been in touching the minds of children. And that's due partly to the fact that writing TV programs for children has never been the highly prestigious undertaking that 533 would attract the best creative minds.

But what *should* children's television be? That is the pertinent question since 1. children watch so much television (an average of 50 hours a week), and 2. about two-thirds of intellectual development occurs before a child even starts his formal education (according to University of Chicago psychologist Benjamin Bloom).

What kinds of programs *would* satisfy the social scientists and psychologists and educators who are unhappy about the current state of "kidvid" in the United States? We asked that question of a dozen or more specialists while researching this series of articles, and discovered a surprising consistency in their recommendations.

Principally, they favor "reality" as opposed to "fantasy"—stories and essays and mini-documentaries about the real world, meticulously produced with young people in mind. Eisenberg, for example, would like to see programs with "role models" for children to pattern themselves after. "Let them see what doctors do, and what astronauts, writers and poets do. That way they can form career ambitions."

Nobody says that slapstick should be eliminated from children's TV schedules. In small doses, it's a pleasing and helpful satire of all the silliness that goes on in the adult world, and children understand it as such. Similarly, children are quick to perceive the essential foolishness of an adult who is "talking down" to them in patronizing fashion.

But television's chief task ought to be to create a variety of options, a "cafeteria" (in the words of one psychologist) of program types so that children would have at least the *chance* of browsing among reasonable alternatives and picking the best. "Right now, we have no decent range of options," says Dr. Lesser. "There are a few good programs like *Misterogers* and *Captain Kangaroo,* and after that it's mostly cartoons and things like *Romper Room* and *Bozo the Clown,* which are purely exploitive."

Dr. Sheldon White, professor of psychology at Harvard's Graduate School of Education, says it would be most beneficial to "put before children organized essays on the life around them," with special attention to the needs of children who prefer more serious TV fare. Networks should give at least as much thought, he believes, to what will be good for the children as to what will be good for the ratings. "They have found out that fast slapstick will draw the maximum audiences. Maybe all attempts to break that mold will meet with defeat."

The value of the medium to children is to show them places and

534 events they otherwise wouldn't see, since children, obviously, don't have the chance to get around very much. *The ultimate accomplishment—according to TV GUIDE's sampling of experts—is to catch the child's imagination by showing him the world, what its possibilities are, how people get along in it, how they interract with each other, and what his place in it might be.* This can be done either through fiction or fact.

TV can also provide the child with information on "folk heroes" —such as Thomas Jefferson, Charles Lindbergh, Daniel Webster, Jonas Salk, Mark Twain, the astronauts, among thousands of others— whose achievements might spur the child to study these lives further, and perhaps even say to himself, "Maybe *I* could do something like that." At the moment such a question forms itself in the mind of a child, television has performed a true and lasting service to the Nation's health and future.

Such goals require a cadre of creative people in the ranks of TV programmers—writers, producers and directors, as well as sociologists and psychologists—which has not materialized thus far in the 25-year life of television in America: creators in sufficient numbers and of sufficient dedication to employ the medium of television to its highest potential in speaking to children.

The National Commission on the Causes and Prevention of Violence stated in part in its report released September 23: "Although all of the networks say that they are keeping abreast of current research on the effects of violence on viewers, until recently . . . each has taken the position that the research . . . is *wholly inconclusive. . . .* We believe that the television networks, network affiliates, independent stations, and other members of the broadcasting industry should recognize the strong probability that a high incidence of violence in entertainment programs is contributing to undesirable attitudes and even to violence in American society. It is time for them *to stop asserting* 'not proved' to charges of adverse effects from pervasive violence in television programming . . . when they should instead be accepting the burden of proof that such programs are not harmful to the public interest. Much remains to be learned about media violence and its effects, but enough is known to require that constructive action be taken at once to reduce the amount and alter the kind of violent programs which have pervaded television."

The networks were quick to reply that they had already eliminated the largest bulk of "violence" from their new programs during the many months in which the Commission was preparing its study. Chairman Milton S. Eisenhower acknowledged this but pointed out

that the old, violent network programming was now being syndicated   *535*
as reruns and that it would probably take a decade for the stations to
work these shows out of their programming. That put the case up to
the individual stations' managements.

It is patently inadequate, however, for TV programmers merely
to create shows which do *not* display violence and which do *not* flaunt
sex. What is required is the more positive action of fashioning shows
which utilize, to best advantage, television's vast potential for reaching the minds of children—of touching them and moving them and
enlarging them.

The constant questioning about the effects of sex and violence on
children—questions which, to date, are unanswerable—has left many
with the illusion that this is the only aspect of TV to be concerned
with. This is not true. What is required quite as urgently is for broadcasters—both commercial and noncommercial—to marshal the effort
and the money and the will to create children's programs which have
point and pith and imagination.

When that happens, we will know that American television is
taking its responsibilities to children seriously.

Other
Effects

Television's immense popularity assures that its reflections of all aspects of culture and society are subjects of observation and comment. Jess Stein, editor of *Random House Dictionary* (pp. 538-540), states that there has been an explosion in the English language and that television is a major causal influence. Television is performing much the same function as did the Elizabethan dramatists nearly 400 years ago, when the only other English-language explosion took place. Although Stein agrees that television has a limited vocabulary, it disseminates new words and expressions with incredible speed. Stein feels this is particularly true of newscasts. Television also provides good models of properly spoken English and helps to unite the different regional dialects without destroying their accents. Television, via satellites, will broaden the reach of English, according to Stein, and more and more people throughout the world will gain at least a rudimentary knowledge of English.

Louis Nizer (pp. 541-544) applaudes the fact that many of the old stereotypes and inaccuracies relating to lawyers and courtroom proceedings have disappeared from television. This is partly the result of the American Bar Association's provision of several lawyers to "offer guidance" to motion picture and television producers. It is unfortunate that time limitations of television dictate the use of false devices to condense a trial which would, in reality, last days or weeks, into thirty- or sixty-minute segments. Nizer feels that these devices are technically inaccurate, emotionally inauthentic and give the public a false impression of the thoroughness of the judicial system. He concludes that fictional trials on television are a mixed blessing; but suggests their potential negative effects would be considerably reduced if a warning announcement that the tiral is partly symbolic, not a faithful representation, were shown at some point in the program.

Martin Mayer (pp. 545-549) discusses the impact of television in the media market place on the older forms of organized mass entertainment and information. Mayer claims that television has virtually

536

destroyed the bottom layer of American popular culture: comics,
pulp magazines, radio serials, grade-B movies. Television's effect
was first and most keenly felt by the radio and movies, but they were
able to adapt. According to Mayer, television's longest and bloodiest
war is with the magazines which had earlier performed the same advertising function that television now fulfills. Television may ultimately kill magazines because of more lenient rules and under-the-
table competition. Mayer suggests that the Government and the FCC
could probably prevent the death of magazines by requiring that
network transactions be placed on public record.

Professor Louis Kronenberger (pp. 550-553) contends that, without belittling its virtues, television's effect on American life is uncivilizing and at times anticivilizing. Although television is the
supreme cultural opportunity, it is rife with brutality, crudities,
timidities and imbecilities—this does not refer only to the programming. Kronenberger characterizes television's off-screen atmosphere
as being "as civilized as gluttony."

A defense of television is conducted by Professor Martin Maloney
(pp. 554-557). He maintains that the business of figuring out the
horrid effects of television is a small American industry; condemning
television is a sort of addiction among intellectuals. According to
Maloney, whatever the industry says or does is considered wrong and
usually harmful. He suggests that the ills of society have always been
attributed to the dominant means of public communication and cites
charges made regarding the social effects of movies and radio. Research on the effects of the medium are inconclusive, but Maloney
feels that it is ridiculous to blame all of contemporary society's problems on television.

Is Television Killing the English Language?

By Jess Stein

DECEMBER 24, 1966

It has been suggested that television is going to be the ruin of the English language: that the medium has the paralyzing power to homogenize thought and speech; that it deliberately avoids the exercise of variety in its vocabulary and repeats the same words over and over again; that, for fear of losing a viewer, it panders to the uneducated; that it is bringing about destructive changes in the structure of our speech which will eventually make it an inadequate, muddy, unattractive, and ineffective form of communication.

I heartily disagree. For the past seven years we at Random House have been in an exhaustive survey of the English language. We spent some $3,000,000. We engaged the services of more than 350 lexicographers, technicians, editors and consultants in 158 different fields of knowledge. We found that the language was now changing so fast we had to turn to computers and data processing equipment in order to give our staff enough speed to keep up with it. We analyzed every form in which the language exists, both written and spoken, from newspapers down to the labels on medicine bottles, and right through to tape recordings of radio and television programs.

We knew that the English language was going through a veritable explosion. In those seven years of research it became apparent that one of the major factors in the phenomenal explosion of the English language was the American television industry.

What is happening to our language today has happened only once before in its history. The one comparable language explosion took place nearly 400 years ago, during the Elizabethan Age, and it was influenced strongly by the appearance of the Elizabethan theater— the theater of Shakespeare, Marlowe and Johnson. In terms of language development, the television industry is performing the same function as was performed by those geniuses of long ago.

"How can that be?" people will ask. "The works of Shakespeare alone contain some 24,000 different words. Television seems rarely

538

moved to use more than those 850 words that make up Basic English. **539**
Television commercials assault the sensibilities with hysterically
overinflated adjectives, like 'whiter than white,' which can only serve
to deflate the effectiveness of the words. Prime time is filled with
the studied ineloquence of shows like *Combat!* and *The Beverly
Hillbillies.* Where is the genius of Shakespeare in all of this mediocrity?"

At first sight this is a difficult question. It's obvious that television's Shakespeare hasn't appeared—yet. But the answer is simply
that the question is irrelevant. Because of the industry's vast resources
and the magnitude of its range, it doesn't need to be inspired by
genius in order to be effective. Shakespeare didn't cause the social,
technological, scientific, political and cultural revolutions of his age.
He simply recorded them. He held "the mirror up to nature." The
television industry can reflect the full range of human experience and
human achievement by assigning a hundred men to each of the tasks
that Shakespeare had to tackle alone.

If it is true that the American people are repeatedly exposed to
the verbal mediocrities of soap operas and hillbillies, it must be remembered that they are also galvanized by television coverage of
space shots, marches on Washington, documentaries and *Huntley-
Brinkley Reports*—all of which disseminate new words and new
expressions with incredible speed.

Two years ago the word "Gemini" was used by most people only
to refer to a sign of the zodiac. Today it has a totally new and different
meaning. Words like *telemetry, gantry, retrofire* and *Birchite* are
all vividly understood by nearly everyone in the country. If those
words had been dependent solely on the print media for dissemination and explanation, I wouldn't have been able to use them as
examples in this article today. Too many readers wouldn't have understood them, yet. Television commentators are able to establish new
words with unparralleled speed and accuracy.

Of even more importance is the role that television fills in providing good models of effective spoken English. Residents of different
parts of the country, who speak in differing dialects, are universally
exposed to an education by the most articulate and well-spoken
people of our time. Announcers, actors, newscasters, even politicians, have become scrupulously aware of the necessity to make
their speech clearly intelligible to all people in all parts of the country.
As a result of the medium's broad reach, those in even the most
backward and culturally deprived communities, such as Harlem or
Appalachia, have a window to the world of clear language.

540   Television is a great leveler, but so far it has not caused the Southerner to lose his drawl nor the New Englander to forsake his twang. It has, however, insured that neither of these speech characteristics will grow so far apart that they could become entirely separate languages. It provides a basic melodic line, so to speak, on which different people in different localities may improvise, with the assurance that their neighbors, near and far, will be able to understand them.

The dearth of variety in television's vocabulary does seem regrettable when one considers that in a whole week of broadcasts the average soap opera makes use of only a few hundred different words, but it is hardly destructive. I found that soap operas and situation comedies make use of the same words that I would choose in those situations. In fact, to a small child, especially a child growing up in a deprived or difficult environment, the exposure to several hundred words, clearly spoken and logically used, is of enormous educational value.

Television broadens our language horizons. It makes us aware of what effective English is—as well as what it isn't. As the television industry broadens its reach, via satellites, across the world, the future of the English language will grow even brighter. It has been estimated that one out of four people in the world speak some English. In confirmation of that estimate, it's interesting to note that Russia has been beaming part of her radio propaganda broadcasts to non-English-speaking countries in English! Within half a century, fully half of the world's population may be speaking our tongue at some level of proficiency.

Does Television Tip the Scales of Justice?

By Louis Nizer

JUNE 22, 1963

A few years ago the American Bar Association designated several attorneys to offer guidance to motion-picture and television producers who wished to present court proceedings with reasonable accuracy.[27] This aided the process of ridding the entertainment media of the stereotypes which had previously filled the screen.

Some writers who had never been inside a courtroom, but who followed the hackneyed concepts of predecessors, stopped depicting the lawyer as a shouting idiot, sneering at the witness while waving a forefinger menacingly under his nose. They gave up the tired and false plot in which the lawyer was a servile mouthpiece for the gang leader, taking orders with the same acquiescence as the ugly gunmen who surrounded him. Judges were no longer shown as either knaves or pompous fools who dozed during crucial testimony, or ogled the blonde gang moll on the stand. The motion-picture and particularly the television screen began to approach authenticity, and in so doing achieved superior dramatic impact.

The judicial system, being a human one, has many imperfections, but it is perhaps man's noblest institution. The law is not a science; it is an art. It is, therefore, not, as some people imagine, a precise set of unyielding rules. It is more like a living organism, to be molded in accordance with social and philosophical standards of the community and imbued with the sanctity of reason.

Recently television has abounded in court dramas. This is understandable, since trials have always been the sure climax of literature. To what extent do these fictional court dramas on television reflect the essence of the real judicial system? We may be obliged to them, for recently they have depicted the lawyer, judge and procedure with sufficient veracity to obliterate once and for all the distorted stereotypes of yesteryear. This may be a negative virtue, but it is high time the false image of the lawyer in our society was corrected, because the

541

542   injury was not only to him, but to our whole judicial system. The enemies of democracy must have gotten comfort from our self-imposed contempt for our system of justice. Programs like *The Defenders* and *Perry Mason* reveal the lawyer as an honorable fighter for his client's cause, dedicating his zeal and devotion to serving justice. This is in the great and true tradition.

The difficulty arises chiefly from the elliptical manner in which television trials must be conducted in order to accord with time and production necessities. Within a half hour or an hour the drama must be wound and released. All the care of the judicial system to sift and test testimony must be sacrificed. Since the fictional trial cannot last days or weeks as in real life, the scriptwriter often resorts to false devices. Recently, when only two minutes remained (including commercials), the lawyer addressed the witness, explaining his theory of how the crime had been committed. The lawyer, of course, had not been sworn. He was not subject to cross-examination. Any objection by his adversary would have halted the lawyer's speech in its inception. Yet, in the guise of "suggesting" to the witness, he made an exposition not founded on the evidence. Then to my surprise he wheeled, pointed to someone conveniently seated in the courtroom and triumphantly announced that he was the culprit who had committed the deed. That poor wretch didn't even have time to come to the front of the camera. Right where he sat, he screamed, "I did it! I did it!"

In another episode, Perry Mason's adversary makes an objection to clearly inadmissible evidence. Mr. Mason replies, "I thought, your Honor, we were here to hear the entire truth." The judge looks reprovingly at the objector, who shamefacedly withdraws his objection and sits down. One would think that the rules of evidence designed to exclude irrelevancy, which might distort the truth, were its enemy.

Another frequent denouement of the fictional court scene is the collapse of the witness when entrapped by a contradiction. He resorts to instant confession or is so shattered emotionally that his attorney looks to the judge for a merciful dismissal of his own case. The same error occurs in fictional motion-picture trials. In *Judgment at Nuremberg* a German professor testifies for the prosecution but is destroyed by the admission extracted from him that at one time he signed an oath of fealty to Hitler. This revelation, which would barely have made a dent in him in a real trial, causes him to totter from the stand a broken man. Similar illustrations abound of how the fictional trial scene adjusts itself to its own requirements distorting the truth. My quarrel with them is not that they are technically inaccurate. One

may grant an author considerable license. They are emotionally un-
authentic and give a false impression to the public of the thoroughness of the judicial system, "the jewel in the crown of democracy."

The necessities of television have mothered another invention—
the slugging lawyer who depends on his fists more than on his wits
to topple the evildoers. Television has created other hybrids: Mr.
District Attorney, who is a roving sleuth of heroic proportions (real
district attorneys, living sedentary lives at their desks, must remove
their silver rimmed eyeglasses in amazement at this depiction);
and now lawyers like Sam Benedict, who are combinations of a tough
Marine, a rollicking Mickey Spillane and a righteous FBI man. The
producer's need for an extensive cast is reduced, and the dramatic
action simplified by resorting to a character who combines a rough
tongue and a good heart, or to one who has the dramatic flair of
Sherlock Holmes combined with the scholarliness of Oliver Wendell
Holmes, or to one who combines the uncanny eye of Charlie Chan
with the forensic skill of Daniel Webster. Television has even trans-
planted the old, reliable soap opera into the courtroom as a domestic-
relations drama. Instead of organ music, there is a chorus of "I object,"
"Overruled" and the oath being administered by the bailiff.

The fact is that the flamboyant type of lawyer like Bill Fallon
(who once drank poison in the presence of the jury to demonstrate
it was harmless—and then had his stomach pumped in the anteroom)
is obsolete. There were few of this genre anyhow. Today juries are
sophisticated, and a case can be won only by the presentation of hard
facts. Only if a lawyer can stand on such a structure of truth can he take
off in emotional flight with any effectiveness.

Television trials are very often exciting or they wouldn't pervade
the air. It is not as entertainment that they fail but as true evaluations
of the real judicial process. They present a mixed blessing. On the one
hand they give to the public a heroic view of the trial advocate fighting to protect his client's rights. On the other hand their picture of the
judicial arena is so distorted by abbreviation and artifice that the public may be misled concerning the true majesty of the judicial process.
District attorneys have complained that jurors criticize them for not
producing certain evidence or eliciting facts on cross-examination
which the jurors—judging by what they've seen on TV—think he
should have done, though legally improper in an actual trial. So
fiction makes in-roads on real trials and places improper weights on
the scales of justice, upsetting their delicate balance.

In the interest of accuracy, telecasters are required to advise the
audience that the program it has just viewed was previously taped and

544   not a live telecast; or that it contained motion-picture film. Such precaution against deception, if it was logically extended to legal (or for that matter medical) dramas might very well contain the startling announcement:

"For reasons of time and production limitations, our presentation of the trials you have just seen has been partly symbolic, and not a faithful reproduction of the majesty of the judicial procedure which prevails in our country."

It Has Battered Its Rivals Out of Shape

By Martin Mayer

Nobody will ever be able to calculate the impact of television on the United States, because nobody can imagine what America would be like in the 1960's without television. Its influence reaches deep into the culture and spreads wide across the population. The influence has been most obvious, of course, on superficial levels, especially in the media marketplace, where television competes directly with older forms of organized entertainment and communication.

Radio broadcasting and periodical publishing have been battered completely out of shape by the power of a medium that within a few years of its introduction commanded the largest share of people's recreation time and industry's advertising dollar. Even where advertising plays no role, in movies, theater and book publishing, the rise of TV has changed the seller's attitude toward his work and the buyer's attitude toward his amusements.

Everything that happens in the world of human activity springs from many causes, and it is hard to say exactly how important television was in creating some of the recent changes in American entertainment and information habits. The light-romantic lending-library novel, for example, a staple of the 1920's and 1930's, has died the death in mid-century America, and presumably television killed it by offering great quantities of bland fantasy in the home, free of charge. But this same period saw an enormous expansion in magazine circulation, and the rise of the paperback publisher, nonexistent 30 years ago and now selling a million "pocketbooks" a day. With or without television, people have only so much time for reading. What killed the light-romantic lending-library novel?

Again, the big-city newspaper is in bad trouble, while small suburban papers flourish like radishes all across the country. Clearly television did it. Television can present national and big local news before the papers hit the streets; television competes with the city

545

546 papers for "national advertising" (advertising by manufacturers rather than by local stores). The suburban paper is free of these problems: it concentrates on the small, local story which television has no time to cover, and it lives off the storekeeper who cannot afford the cost or profitably employ the area-wide coverage of TV's advertising. But the move to the suburbs would have happened without television. Everybody likes to read about himself, a desire the suburban paper can most easily meet. Perhaps the crisis of the big-city papers would continue if all the TV stations shut down.

Elsewhere, the influence of television seems clearly paramount. Television can be credited with the virtual destruction of the very bottom layer of American popular culture—the comic book, the pulp magazine, the radio serial, the hillbilly movie. Newton Minow's wasteland has been in fact a flood over an abyss which used to be filled by garbage a good deal worse than the featureless rubble of routine television. Particularly in the hinterland, and in the city slums where residents had made almost no contact with the middle-class mainstream of American culture, TV has had an essentially civilizing effect.

The cold winds of competition from television were felt first, and most keenly, by what might be called "the majority media"— radio and movies, both of which aimed to sell their wares to most of the people. Both changed radically and rapidly. Driven from the living room to the kitchen, the bedroom and the car, radio after some floundering came to concentrate on reality, and on special products for minority markets. News, comments and interviews now alternate with the latest pop-music horrors for adolescents and with "good music," mostly on FM, for the more serious and literate minority of adults (whose patronage is sought by television only a few hours a week). Such programs are cheap to provide, and radio broadcasting equipment is cheap to operate. When TV stole most of their audience, radio stations were able to lower ad rates and still operate profitably.

Movies went the other way. For half-a-dozen years the movie companies battled television, refusing to sell their old films or to make new films for broadcast use. Finally, however, the assorted King Canutes of Hollywood realized that every time the tide came up they got wet. Theaters were closing by the thousands, the routine movie was losing money and the Eastern bankers and stockholders were becoming upset. Eventually, nearly all the film studios took on low-cost producing units to service the needs of television. Meanwhile, for theater use, much of the industry turned to the wide screen, the stereophonic sound track, the super-spectacular production which television could not hope to match. In movies as in radio, the adolescent market became more important, and a large number of well-developed juveniles were made into stars by the publicity departments of the studios. Probably because TV had spread the big-city culture more evenly through the country, movie makers were able to treat "controversial" and "unwholesome" subjects more honestly than they had in the 15 years before large-scale TV; and European producers suddenly found U.S. theaters ready to buy foreign films.

Movies, television and theaters all require similar talents, and the same people will operate in all three forms. Of the three, television needs the most, pays the lowest prices for top talent and (thanks to union rules) the highest prices for minor talent. Inevitably television has served as a training arena for gladiators who would later move to combat with the larger animals. The theater especially has been dominated of recent years by directors and producers who made their mark filling a small screen, and each Broadway season sees half-a-dozen plays by writers who began with television scripts. At the same time television made possible the growth of the off-Broadway theater. Occasional television appearances (at $320 and up) enable actors to work in the converted lofts and brownstones of Greenwich Village for $30 a week—and the chance of catching the eye of a television producer makes actors willing and eager to work at minimum rates under miserable conditions off-Broadway.

Network television's longest and bloodiest war, still continuing, has been with the magazines. Culturally and commercially, network television serves functions the magazine industry had arrogated to itself over the last two generations. For the first quarter of this century, magazines were a force uniting the widely scattered people of a single Nation—or, at least, uniting that social and educational level which reads magazines. Businessman, farmer, lawyer, teacher; residents in Chicago, Atlanta, Seattle—all read the same magazine every week. Manufacturers attempting to build national brands advertise nationally in magazines.

Radio broke the magazines' monopoly of national coverage, but people listen less carefully than they read (which is saying a good deal), and of course radio could have little influence on visual styles. Television struck the magazines where they lived: in what was looked at in middle-class households, nationwide. Consciously or unconsciously, the people who ran television centered their broadcast offerings at roughly the cultural and intellectual level of "the slicks" in the year 1950. But television also reached working-class households, as most of the "mass magazines" did not. With the rapid

548 rise in wages in postwar America, this added market was more attractive to advertisers.

Culturally and intellectually, the magazines found an answer: They moved up the scale. Like radio, they have come to concentrate more and more on reality, on relatively serious articles and opinion rather than cheerful short stories and abridgments of popular novels. A national community made more sophisticated by television could be sold more magazines than ever. Nearly every slick magazines published today sells two to five times as many copies as it did 20 years ago. But the economics of most magazines are such that each copy sold costs the publisher more than he ultimately receives from the purchaser, after the deduction of selling costs.[28] In their attempt to keep up with TV in sheer numbers of people reached, the magazines have placed themselves in a position where they need ever greater advertising revenue to stay afloat.

The relative effectiveness of magazine and television advertising is a matter of debate between the two industries; there is no simple answer. But in its war with the magazines, TV has had a simple weapon of enormous power, which even men in the business do not always understand.

Most people believe that "television has taken advertisers from magazines," a statement which conjures an image of advertisers like migratory birds flying from one perch to another. In fact, this mass movement has not occurred: Most companies that advertised in magazines a decade ago still advertise in magazines today. But they are less susceptible to the suggestion of the extra page, and it is the extra page that makes the difference between profit and loss.

A magazine may budget the sale of 60 advertising pages for a November issue, while a television network budgets the sale of 60 half hours of evening time in its fall schedule. Space salesmen for the magazine sell the first 50 pages easily, and time salesmen for the network quickly dispose of their first half hours. Thereafter, however, the going gets rough. And the magazine salesman must, by the rules of his business, sell his last 10 pages at the same price as the first 50—while the television salesman, by the laws of his business, is permitted to wheel and deal in program and perhaps even time prices to sell his last 10 half hours.[29] The undecided advertiser, then, can get a bargain from the network, while he must pay full price to the magazine; and soon he is no longer undecided.

Generally, the public benefits by fights between media, as the consumer benefits by real competition between producers of any goods or services. But the fight between television and the maga-

zines is something less than fair. At present, it appears that tele- 549
vision may kill the magazines, not because it is necessarily superior
as an entertainment or advertising medium, but because it operates
under more lenient rules. If the Federal Government is looking for a
sensible way to regulate the television networks, it could start in
this area. Under-the-table competition poisons relations among the
networks themselves almost as badly as it rigs the fight against the
magazines. By carrying over from Wall Street the key principle of full
disclosure—by requiring that all contracts for the purchase of programs
and network time be made a matter of public record—the FCC might
greatly reduce the negative impact of television upon at least one of
the other media.

Television is by its nature a greedy medium—it demands more
time from people than they really want to give it, more talent than the
world can supply, more money than advertisers can afford to spend,
more praise for accomplishments and forgiveness of sins than a reasonable critic can honestly offer. Yet the greed is at least partially
justified, for television is the central medium of entertainment and
information in American life, and the biggest bang in the mass-
producer's arsenal of selling-weapons.

Ultimately, in a market economy, questions of cultural influence
reduce to questions of dollars and cents. Media, like other economic
goods, compete in terms of value for money. But the market for media
is peculiar, because the consumers who enjoy the product pay only
part of the costs—and the advertisers who foot the big bills have no
very accurate way of judging the value of what they buy. Economic
competition is pretty irrational at best; media competition, even
further removed from reason, rapidly grows frantic: "When in trouble,/
When in doubt,/Run in circles,/Scream and shout."

The question: How large is the lion's share? And can't a civilized
community find an answer, without resorting to the law of the jungle?

Television's Impact on Our Civilization

By Louis Kronenberger

FEBRUARY 26, 1966

In approaching the theme of this series—the effects of television on our civilization—what I think must be said first is that television is not just a great new force in modern life, but that it virtually is modern life. What, one might ask, doesn't it do? It gives us—be we rich, poor, snowbound, bedridden or slow-witted—the time, the weather, the small news, big news, spot news: now in spoken headlines, now in pictured narrative, now at the very scene of the crime or the coronation itself. It plays, sings, whistles and dances for us; takes us to movies and theaters, concerts and operas, prize fights and ball games, ski jumps and tennis tournaments. It delivers babies, probes adolescents, psychoanalyzes adults. It dramatizes floods, fires, earthquakes; takes you to the top of an alp or the bottom of an ocean or whirling through space; lets you see a tiger killed or a tiger kill. It becomes a hustings or a house of worship; guesses your age, your weight, your job, your secret; guides you through prisons, orphan asylums, lunatic asylums; introduces you to Presidents, kings, emirs, sultans; lets you see a Winston Churchill buried or a Lee Oswald shot. It teaches you French, rope-dancing, bird calls and first aid; provides debates and seminars and symposiums, quizzes and contests; and it tells you jokes, gags, wheezes, wisecracks, jokes and jokes.

Television is thus a truly stupendous addition to American life—our supreme cultural opportunity. Nothing approaches it, either in the abundance, variety and immediacy of its offerings, or the vastness, heterogeneity and attendance-record of its audiences. It offers a mammoth handout of news, fun, art, sport, information; or of free refrigerators, cars, cruises, honeymoons, second honeymoons—all yours just for turning a knob, writing a letter, answering a phone.

Not too unnaturally, along with the handout there goes a sales talk. For this colossal addition of hours to American life, this supreme cultural opportunity, is also a tremendous segment of American business and our supreme cultural commodity. And not too surprisingly, what with Business paying the piper, Business calls—or cuts short, or calls off—the tune. And since television is Big Business operating with the help of Bigger Business, the two together constitute a form of Biggest Business—a fact we must face, since it makes any other fact about TV and its effect upon our civilization ultimately subsidiary and expendable.

It also tends to make any fresh insights and observations about the effect of TV on our civilization hard to come by. Before "we" can have any really new thoughts, TV must itself give proof of really new thinking; before we can find anything notably different to say, television must provide something notably different to say it about. To be sure, there are constantly new craft gadgets, seasonal fashions, technological wrinkles—and there is color television with its promise of greater audience pleasure and fiercer network rivalry. But though these are things that add considerably to our conversation, they add very little to our culture. In providing so vast a menu, television has also—barring lavish Christmas puddings and special treats—pretty much standardized the food, the preparation of it, and the after-dinner speeches as well.

A fair amount of the menu is unexceptionable; and a good deal more has given 100,000,000 people harmless enjoyment. A certain amount of TV is clearly good; a certain further amount—notably in Space-Age matters—is both good and unprecedented. But very much else is "not" good, and much beyond that is truly dreadful. Moreover, beyond what television has done, good "or" bad, there is the matter of just how television has done it. The particular nature of what is bad in what TV does, the particular nature of what is bad in the way it does it, indicate what seems to me the "outstanding" effect of TV upon our civilization—which is that it has made it less civilized. There is a decided exception to this, namely educational television; but educational television, for all the charity and technical help it receives from commercial broadcasting, exists in a condition of virtual poverty, which not only underlines the uncivilized effect elsewhere, it argues no very civilizing "intentions."

Let us gauge the effect in various ways. The "programs" themselves are predominantly geared to mediocre tastes and mass reactions—and geared, it would seem, in the hope that neither tastes nor reactions will improve. This doesn't just mean the proportion of sport to art on TV, or of broad comedy to adult humor; it means, even more, the proportion of trite formula to honest experiment, of glib comment to grown-up thinking. Further, the subject-matter of count-

552 less programs—sex, gossip, violence, material success, cash itself—
is uncivilized and uncivilizing both.

Take the most notorious example. The "technical" crime of the
big-money quizzes was their being rigged; the technical immorality,
that the networks could hardly not know it. But what was really degrading, indecent, uncivilizing was that, rigged or not, the quizzes
pandered to the venality of a whole nation, had multitudes glued to
their televisions not at all for the fun of the game, but for the size
of the stakes. Knowledge had become the grossest, the most un-
cultural, of commodities. (One can't help wandering whether, if
tomorrow playing Russian roulette for huge stakes on TV was declared
legal, it too wouldn't become the rage, with wildly mounting re-
muneration.)

Again, what is more uncivilizing, in fact brutalizing, than all the
violence that is offered on TV for sensational and not sociological
reasons? What could be less civilized than the endless cheap gags and
gossipy wisecracks; what less civilized than TV's flagrant invasion
of privacy—not just in terms of outright gossip, but in the way of
candid "discussion," or psychiatric "discovery," or photographs of
the sick, the unhappy, the doomed? And when the networks do
attempt a civilized subject (such as Michelangelo) all to often the
treatment makes civilized people squirm.

The "presentation" of the programs is worse, and far more uniform. Whatever the pros and cons for commercial television generally,
there can be no argument about how uncivilized, how rife with crudities, timidities, imbecilities, sponsored programs tend to be. The
stop-watch technique alone must make a sensitive viewer stop
watching. "Men," as Tyrone Guthrie has put it, "stand chalk-white
. . . on guard in the studio, charged with the single responsibility
of seeing that 'Othello' or Beethoven's 'Eroica' does not run one-tenth
of a second over, or under." If the esthetic distortions resulting from
this are often appalling, the grotesque and vulgar intrusions and
interpolations—the commercials—are worse. There are, to be sure,
exceptions; but for the most part the blatancy of the programs' com-
mercialized approach conveys the impression of a cash register in
the drawing room, and even right next to a deathbed.

As with programs and presentation, so with "procedure." The
"ratings" system, which computes not merit but mass popularity,
which queries not those best qualified to judge but those most apt to
judge routinely, is more than uncivilized: It is anticivilized. It turns
any illiterate into a critic; and entrepreneur into a craven; a defeated
contestant into a criminal (punishable by instant banishment).

For profits-seeker and pleasure-seeker alike, there might be point to 553 conducting polls with a view to correcting faults; but here improved quality is no more the issue than intrinsic quality.

Moreover, the general off-screen "atmosphere" of TV proclaims the lack of accident in how uncivilized the thing as a whole is. Everywhere cutthroat tensions seem mated with backstabbing tactics. The higher levels of the three great networks suggest a luxury-class Reign of Terror, where the people who live in glass doghouses and the limelighted shake-ups and feuds make TV's administrative life the gossip column's darling. TV doesn't even "wash" its dirty linen in public; it merely waves it. Perhaps the one sure news edge that the press still enjoys over television is the doings and misdoings, the firings and backfirings, of television itself. But though the power side of TV is always agitated and shifting, its money side is solid and stationary. In this, the Great Networks are splendidly assisted by the Great Artists' Representatives, so that the alluring daughters and nieces of art—Language and Laughter, Melody and Declamation and Dancing—are constantly bedded and wedded to the paunchy sons and nephews of Mammon. The general effect is often about as civilized as gluttony.

There is, finally, the cultural "irresponsibility" involved in all this. In an empire so vast as television's, in a network hierarchy so unfixed and collapsible, we must look to the very top for the policies that govern it and for the direction it takes. And there we find men known only for their immense wealth and their business power. Whatever their private enjoyments or hobbies, these are not men publicly identified with high culture; indeed, they have made everything in television that is so identified, everything that bespeaks artistic experiment, genuine enlightenment, pretty much shift for itself. Where important cultural events are not news already, these men seem to show small interest in making them so.

Without at all belittling TV's virtues, its triumphs of news coverage, its operas and concerts, its ability to inform or stimulate or amuse, its serviceability to the many millions of people who use it as a food and not a drug, the glaring fact remains that TV has consistently either imposed uncivilized elements on American life, or aggravated and intensified those it found there. It has helped destroy respect for privacy, it has helped foster a more rackety publicity. There has been nothing too elegant for it to coarsen, too artistic for it to vulgarize, too sacred for it to profane.

The Effects of Television

By Martin Maloney

MARCH 25, 1967

I guess I am just an old middle-of-the-roader at heart. On the one hand, I don't think I want to be an Oscar Mayer wiener, so everyone will be in love with me. On the other, or left, hand, I don't want to be a television mogul either. Oh, I know about their Countess Mara neckties and four-hour lunches with guinea hen under plastic and 75-to-1 martinis, and their Gotham hatcheries full of mini-skirted script girls and secretaries, but—well, I just don't want to be one.

The reason is that, sooner or later, to every television executive comes that moment of truth when he must justify the credit cards which have provided him with the above-named luxuries. He must emerge from his mink-lined foxhole and make a public statement, usually a pretty innocuous one, to the effect that there are worse things in this world than television, such as cancer and the napalm bomb. Then, according to time-honored ritual, he is clobbered with a barrage of charges and specifications so horrifying, all-encompassing and unprovable that the late Judge Jeffreys, the Hanging Judge, would have blushed to introduce them during the Bloody Assizes.

The charges inevitably have to do with the doleful effects of television on . . . oh, teen-age motorcycle buffs, redheaded divorcees under 35, Lithuanian numismatists in the middle-income bracket— you name it. The business of figuring out the horrid effects of TV is only one of the lesser American industries; there are few people who actually make a living at it. It is, however, a sort of addiction among intellectuals (an intellectual, in this context, is anyone who owns a typewriter and uses it for any purpose save writing personal letters). And the result is that the unfortunate TV titan, who is manifestly to blame for the medium as well as the message, is in pretty much the same position as was Mr. Sherlock Holmes at that point in his career when Col. Sebastian Moran was gunning for him with Von Herder's air rifle. All he had to do is let his shadow fall across the window blind, and zap!—he's ducking an expanding revolver bullet.

Practically speaking, for the panting and harried vice president,

there is no escape. No matter what he says or does, it always turns
out that he has very nearly wrecked the Republic. Consider, for instance, the matter of reporting the news. Back in 1956, the late
Columbia sociologist C. Wright Mills wrote a book called *The Power
Elite*,[30] in which he said that the mass media ("especially television")
served largely to distract the voters from thinking about their common
problems. When they ought by rights to have been brooding over
inflation or Ho Chi Minh, they were drooling over Elizabeth Taylor's
love life (hasn't she had a long one, though?) or watching a trained
seal act on *The Ed Sullivan Show*. Well, that seemed a reasonable
criticism to me, as I have always been fascinated by trained seals.

Then, in 1962, along came historian Daniel Boorstin, of the University of Chicago, with a book called *The Image,* which claimed that
the mass media were engaged mainly in the business of supplying
people with pseudo-news about nonhappenings, and thus getting
them out of touch with reality. I went right along with Boorstin, too;
as an occasional viewer of Los Angeles TV newscasts, I knew exactly
what he meant.

Recently, however, I did begin to think that television might just
have beaten the rap with its coverage of the war in Vietnam—
admittedly a dirty, painful, highly controversial affair about which the
television networks have told me, frankly, a great deal more than
I really wished to know. Apparently the broadcasters felt the same
way, for recently James C. Hagerty, once Mr. Eisenhower's press
secretary and now an ABC mogul, drew the black spot and subsequently turned up at a panel discussion of the International Writers
Guild with a few kind words about TV coverage of the Vietnamese
War. The war films run by the network news services, he said, show
"war as it is," and should do much to convince the fireside viewer
that war is "the least sensible way of settling disputes."

Hagerty was at once set upon by no less a pundit than Dr. Fredric
Wertham, in the pages of *The New York Times*. (Dr. Wertham, in case
you don't know, is an eminent psychiatrist and an implacable foe of
much pop culture—except, of course, for his own books.) In a signed
article entitled "Is TV Hardening Us to the War in Vietnam?"[31]
Dr. Wertham answered, with simple eloquence, and in about 1600
words, "Yes, it is."

An old hand at tracing the effects of symbolic violence on American society, Wertham notes that we begin by providing the nursery
with "kill toys" which "teach that it is fun to play killing. . . . The
education progresses to sadistic bubble-gum cards, violent crime
comic books, brutal movies and rough TV shows, crudely illustrated

556   booklets like "Sin and Pain" sold under the counter to teenagers (what kind of dime stores do they have in Wertham's home town, anyway?), gorily presented murder news, and so forth. The audience, so conditioned from childhood, finds Vietnam fighting pictures tame stuff. . . ."

The practice of relating all the ills of society, from mass murder to the seven-year itch, to whatever medium of public communication happens to be prominent at the time is by no means news. True, I haven't been able to locate any statements by eminent divines, circa 1500, on the subject "Is Movable Type Corrupting Our Youth?"— but I'm sure they were made, and may still survive, hidden somewhere in the junk-heap of history. As a matter of fact, some such statements—left atop the junk-heap of recent history—do survive; and if it's any comfort to James D. Hagerty and his colleagues in video, they have to do with one or other of the more antiquated media, such as movies. I cull the following testimony from a 1929 study—an alleged statement from a reformatory inmate on how he got there:

"Once I saw a movie, me and another guy. It was about a man who robbed a house. . . . He got in dat house and stole dis big roll (money). Me and dis guy, we said, 'Dat's easy, we kin do date.' So we lef' de show before it was over and here was a man's auto, an open car, parked. We went thu dis car . . ." But enough.

At least the recent testaments to the responsibility of TV for juvenile experiments in mopery, assault, and glue-sniffing, do not come couched in this sort of Happly Hooligan dialect. It's a small mercy, but a welcome one.

I do think that one of the happiest statements on the "effects" of a mass medium is also one of the earliest. Back in the days before the market crash, Herbert Hoover, then regnant in Washington, summoned to him a platoon of scholars and bade them survey recent social trends in the United States. When the survey was completed in 1932, one of the items noted was—well, guess!—"social effects of the radio." Now, in 1929, American radio broadcasting was about eight years old, and network radio hadn't quite reached its third anniversary. There were also no very good methods for establishing the effect of radio on anything. All the same, these good, gray scholars came up with a list of exactly 150 "effects," some of them quite charming. For instance, No. 7: "Illiterates find a new world opened to them"; or No. 20: "Revival of old songs, at least for a time"; No. 65: "Discouragement, it is said, of preachers of lesser abilities."

Of course, sooner or later the critic of mass-media critics has to face his own moment of truth: the question "Suppose they are right?"

My personal opinion, which is worth about $1.35 per cubic mile on the international market, is that nobody knows for sure. I have looked at all of the studies of mass media effects on everybody, but the ones I have looked at make me somewhat dubious of the claims of the more swinging critics.

Take, for instance, the celebrated "War of the Worlds" radio program which created a panic in the Eastern United States in October 1938. Here was a classic case of cause and effect. Whodunit? Orson Welles. What did he do? A scary radio show. What resulted? Panic. Yet when a covey of social scientists headed by Hadley Cantril investigated the phenomenon,[32] what did they find? Among other things, they found that a good many of the people who had been scared to death were deeply religious citizens, who somehow missed Welles' interplanetary fantasy altogether and thought that the end of the world had come. So if we don't want panic, maybe we should eliminate religion—or at least, the hard-core gospel, the sort of thing that makes people nervous? This is the sort of question that I should be glad to hand over to Dr. Wertham for investigation, if he hasn't anything else on hand.

I don't want anyone to get the impression from the foregoing that some of my friends are TV vice presidents. Excoriate them for spending millions on entertainments less entertaining than the annual St. Polycarp's Pageant at Simeon T. Garfunkel High School, if you will; pepper them with rock salt for their arrogance in supposing that their audiences are a clutch of faceless sub-morons, and I am with you. But if you really wonder why people beat children, or take heroin, or bomb civilians, or pollute the air they themselves must breathe . . . well, may heaven bless you, and I hope that you find a scapegoat a little more convincing than James C. Hagerty.

Notes to Chapter 5

1. The first article in the series referred to by Loevinger was by Arnold Toynbee and appeared in TV GUIDE, December 4, 1965. Other articles in the TV GUIDE series, "Effects of Television Upon Society," were by Louis Kronenberger (February 26, 1966), Eric Goldman (March 19, 1966), Benjamin Spock (May 28, 1966), Henry Commager (June 25, 1966) and Malcolm Muggeridge (July 23, 1966). The Toynbee (pp. 437-441), and Kronenberger (pp. 550-553) articles are included in this anthology.

2. Many of McLuhan's major theories regarding television may be found in: Marshall McLuhan, *Understanding Media: The Extensions of Man*, New York: McGraw-Hill, 1964.

3. William Stephenson, *The Play Theory of Mass Communications*, Chicago: University of Chicago Press, 1967.

558

4. For an elaboration of the theory which Loevinger is about to outline, see Lee Loevinger, "The Reflective-Projective Theory of Broadcasting and Mass Communication, *Journal of Broadcasting*, Spring 1968, pp. 97-116.

5. Leo Rosten, "What of Television's Effect in the Future?" TV GUIDE, October 6, 1962, pp. 6-8.

6. *Hullabaloo* was the name of a television series which appeared in 1964-66. The show featured music and dancing in a setting resembling that of a discotheque.

7. Daniel Boorstin, *The Image: or What Happened to the American Dream?* New York: Atheneum, 1962.

8. This article was printed in David Manning White and Richard Averson, *Sight, Sound, and Society*, Boston: Beacon Press, 1968. In that reprint the following footnote appeared after " . . . *The Beverly Hillbillies?*" "I would not exclude the possibility of achieving this result in part through a graduate system of federal subsidies, as proposed by broadcaster Stimson Bullitt, or through tax deductions for a portion of lost revenues, as proposed by former FCC Chairman E. William Henry; and I would support researcher Herbert Alexander's suggestion that Section 315 of the Communications Act be amended to permit a policy of 'differential equality of access'."

9. Of the $58.9 million of broadcast expenditures for 1968 primary and general elections, some $38 million or 64.5 percent, went to television; $20.9 million, 35.5 percent, went to radio; and presidential and vice-presidential campaigning accounted for nearly half of all radio and television budgets. Democratic presidential hopefuls outspent Republicans by 60 percent during the 1968 primaries, but Nixon-Agnew bought time at a 2-1 ratio over Humphrey-Muskie in the general elections.

10. In October 1969, a bill backed by thirty-eight Senators was introduced which would require broadcasters to provide each legally qualified Senate candidate with one-hundred-twenty minutes of prime television time and each House candidate with sixty minutes of prime time during the last five weeks before elections, at 70 percent off regular commercial rates. The measure would also permit candidates to purchase a thirty-minute block of program time or its equivalent at 80 percent off regular rates. Both time allotments would be distributed among districts that reached a substantial part of the regional or state population. ABC and NBC responded with concrete offers to give all political candidates a discount in 1970 and 1972. NBC said that if Section 315 were suspended in the next presidential campaign, it would offer four free prime-time half hours for appearances by the major candidates.

11. In testifying on the bill introduced in October 1969, to require broadcasters to give Senate and House candidates prime time at reduced rates, CBS president Dr. Frank Stanton said that passage of the bill would present a problem of overlapping jurisdiction, so that during election campaigns the viewing public would be deprived of the balanced programming to which it is entitled. Stanton maintained that CBS-TV covered at least thirty-eight congressional districts with one-hundred-four House candidates and five senatorial candidates in 1968. He calculated that if the bill were implemented and all local candidates used its provisions to the fullest advantage, by purchasing one-minute spots spread out evenly over the five weeks prior to the election, CBS-TV as well as the seven other New York City commercial stations would have to provide one-and-a-half hours of program time plus twenty-three minutes of political announcements each evening for thirty-five consecutive nights before the election.

12. Presidential candidates bought 183 network television spots in 1968. There are no local figures available because the FCC, in compiling the information, found that there were too many discrepancies.

13. Since this article was written the FCC has issued a Section 315 primer entitled "Use of Broadcast Facilities by Candidates for Public Office." The primer attempts to clarify some of the confusion regarding Section 315 by providing answers to more than one-hundred-fifty questions regarding the "equal-time" provisions. The NAB also has tried to clarify Section 315 for its member stations and it periodically issues a "Political Broadcast Catechism" for that purpose. The Catechisms also include interpretations of the FCC's Fairness Doctrine.

14. Section 18 of the Radio Act of 1927, Public Law 632, 69th Congress, February **559** 23, 1927.

15. Section 315 (a) of the Communications Act of 1934, amended on September 14, 1959 by 73 Statute 557.

16. As has been indicated, in October 1969 NBC said if Section 315 were suspended in 1972, it would offer four free prime-time half hours for appearances by the major candidates. This offer came at a time when the Senate was considering a bill to require broadcasters to give Senate and House candidates specified amounts of prime television time at specified reductions in commercial rates.

17. Among others: O. Ivar Lovaas, U. of Washington; Richard Walters, U. of Toronto; Paul Mussen, UCLA; Eldridge Rutherford, UCLA; Leonard Berkowitz, U. of Wisconsin.

18. Lovaas, O. Ivar, "Effect of exposure to Symbolic Aggression in Aggressive Behavior," *Child Development*, 1961.

19. Bandura, Ross & Ross, "Imitation of Film-Mediated Aggressive Models," *Journal of Abnormal and Social Psychology*, 1963.

20. Mussen & Rutherford, "Effects of Aggressive Cartoons on Children's Aggressive Play," *Journal of Abnormal and Social Psychology*, 1961.

21. Bandura, "Influence of Models' Reinforcement Contingencies on the Acquisition of Imitative Responses," *Journal of Personality and Social Psychology*, 1965.

22. Mussen & Rutherford, "Effects of Aggressive Cartoons on Children's Aggressive Play," *Journal of Abnormal and Social Psychology*, 1963.

23. Bandura, "Imitation of Film-Mediated Aggressive Models," *Journal of Abnormal and Social Psychology*, 1961.

24. Bandura and Huston, "Identification as a Process of Incidental Learning," *Journal of Abnormal and Social Psychology*, 1961.

25. Lovaas, O. Ivar. "Effect of Exposure to Symbolic Aggression in Aggressive Behavior," *Child Development*, 1961.

26. Berkowitz & Rawlings, "Effects of Film Violence on Inhibitions against Subsequent Aggression," *Journal of Abnormal and Social Psychology*, 1963; Walters & Thomas, "Enhancement of Punitiveness by Visual and Audiovisual Displays," *Canadian Journal of Psychology*, 1963.

27. Both the American Bar Association and the American Medical Association have managed to get the networks to agree to accept "guidance" with respect to scripts so that "reasonable accuracy" of portrayals of judicial and medical practices may be insured. Before their agreement with the networks, the ABA had threated to produce its own television series in order to present a "more accurate" picture of the Lawyer.

28. Most magazines are now sold at cut-rate subscriptions prices. Thus most magazine publishers no longer even receive their full subscription prices, let alone their newstand prices for a high percentage of the magazines they sell.

29. Since this article was written, both the concept of a "guaranteed cpm" (see note 2, p. 280) and official dual asking prices for the regular season and for summer re-run period have become more prevalent in television advertising. At the same time, national magazines have been encouraging regional advertising by permitting advertisers to buy only certain markets for reduced prices.

Some observers of the media might question the impression given by Mr. Mayer that magazines never practice rate cutting. Bryce W. Rucker, in *The First Freedom*, said: "magazines have been victimized to a much greater extent than have newspapers and broadcasting by unfair competition, chain domination, monopoly within specializations, subscription wars and advertising rate cutting."

30. C. Wright Mills, *The Power Elite*, New York: Oxford University Press, 1956.

31. *The New York Times*, December 4, 1966.

32. Hadley Cantril, *Invasion From Mars*, Princeton: Princeton University Press, 1940.

THE FUTURE

Chapter 6

The Future

In 1942, when there were five commercial television stations operating a few hours a week and less than ten thousand television receivers in the entire United States, Lee De Forest wrote in his book, *Television Today and Tomorrow*, "It would be difficult to overestimate the future importance of television in the home life of all who dwell within sure range of her transmitters." De Forest's statement is perhaps even more appropriate in 1970 than it was twenty-eight years earlier.

The following quotation appears in the first 1970 issue of TV GUIDE: "The mushrooming growth in available information and the demand for access to this information is bringing about a revolution in communications which will produce a profound change in the way society is structured and in the way we live." This revolution and the role television will play in it during the decade of the 1970s is outlined by Neil Hickey, Richard Doan, and David Lachenbruch (pp. 565–580). The authors suggest the vast potential of cable television and satellites for creating more and different types of television programming. These combined with other forms of "electronic gadgetry" will change the television receiver from an appliance into an elaborate two-way home communications center—a center which will be involved with everything from voting to grocery shopping. The authors then summarize the predictions of network executives regarding entertainment and news programming in the new decade. Hickey, Doan, and Lachenbruch foresee that the new technology of communications could change our entire life style, moving information rather than people and bringing every individual almost any type of entertainment, information or communication he might desire.

Cable television and international telecasting via satellite are discussed at greater length by Doan in the final two articles. Doan (pp. 581–585) maintains that up to now, CATV's threat to existing television is far more feared than real. But CATV operators are confident and broadcasters are buying into cable TV because of its great potential. Doan reviews some of the developments which observers

564 believe cable will induce, including a two-way phone-line service, a "wired city," a combination of domestic satellites for long distance program delivery and cable hookups for local distribution and a variety of home services, such as facsimile and computer access. He indicates, however, that many legal battles regarding CATV lay ahead.

Doan then describes the attitudes of network executives toward the possibilities of using satellites on a more regular basis (pp. 586–590) which suggest that some of the predictions regarding satellite usage during at least the early 1970s may be overly optimistic. This is because of time differences, the ability of jets to transport film with good pictures and sound within hours, the lack of sufficient satellite ground stations, international political considerations, costs and the fact that few human events, such as the Olympics, need satellite coverage. Doan maintains that perhaps another reason satellite coverage is infrequently used is a lack of interest in this country for events occurring overseas, except in Vietnam. In fact, foreign broadcasters, especially the Japanese, may soon be using satellites more often than do American networks.

Here Come the '70s!

By Neil Hickey
Richard K. Doan and David Lachenbruch

JANUARY 3, 1970

"Don't never prophesy," Josh Billings advised, "for if you prophesy wrong, nobody will forget it, and if you prophesy right, nobody will remember it." Nonetheless, we can't resist—as the Nation this week takes its first uncertain step toward 1980—venturing a few cautious predictions about life in the 1970s: about the so-called "communications revolution" and television's role in it. In preparation, the authors have quartered the terrain like eager bird dogs. We interviewed scores of broadcasters, legislators, scientists, Federal regulators and sociologists. One response was surprisingly common. After a slow, thoughtful shake of the head, the interviewee would say:

"The 1970s? That's a tough question. Ask me about the 1980s and I'll give you some hard answers that will hold up. But right now, we're at the foothills of a very, *very* high mountain and we're just testing our gear for the climb. In this decade we'll make slow and even painful progress, followed by a great leap forward in the 1980s."

What is involved here is nothing less than a new, emerging human right: The Right to Knowledge. There's simply more to know today than ever before in human history, and men are determined to possess it and to savor it. The electronics industry, in a recent report, stated: "The mushrooming growth in available information and the demand for access to this information is bringing about a revolution in communications which will produce a profound change in the way society is structured and in the way we live."

A vice president of the National Association of Broadcasters, William Carlisle, puts it this way: "Communications have progressed from evolution to revolution to explosion." It is now certain that the electronic gadgetry that will come into common use during the rest of this century will alter not merely our viewing habits, but the character and content of our lives.

But let's slow down to the 1970s and see if we can get a handle

565

566 on it. First of all, by 1979 there will be 225 million Americans, which is 22 million more than we have now. Forty-two million of those will be between the ages of 15 and 24.

We'll be richer: more than half of American households will have incomes of at least $15,500 a year. Seventy million homes will have TV sets instead of today's 59 million, and 80 per cent of those will be color. We'll be chiefly urbanized, with 80 per cent of our citizens living and working in metropolitan areas. A huge, 100 per cent increase—to $2 trillion—will be apparent in the Gross National Product.

In spite of the continuing youthquake, there will still be plenty of adults around—about 125 million, in fact, age 25 and over—and we'll all be looking for new ways to spend our added income and our added leisure time. The TV industry believes that viewing time will rise to 7 hours per household from its current 6; travel experts insist that Americans will be spending $12 billion for trips abroad (up from $4.7 billion in 1967); adult education will surely be on the rise; and our colleges will be groaning under a load of 10 million students, instead of the current 7 million.

But what about the shape of this modern phenomenon called television, which, since the 1940s, has insinuated itself so thoroughly into the very texture of American life? The seeds of drastic change—having been planted unobtrusively in the green acres of TV's outback —are showing their first few buds, which will doubtless prove to be hardy but slow-blooming perennials.

Potentially, the most colorful blossoms in this arbor are: 1. satellite transmission of TV signals, 2. cable television, 3. publicly supported, noncommercial television, and 4. TV-related gadgetry for home use. It's mostly the interrelationships among those elements that will determine what "television" will be like by 1979.

Consider: TV in America as currently constituted is principally a delivery system—something like an ICBM rocket—by which three giant broadcast companies (called networks) deliver a payload (large audiences) to a specific target (the advertiser). The bigger the payload, the bigger the pay-off.

Toward the end of the 1970s, that structure will already have started to erode into meaninglessness. Even now, technology has made it an anachronism, but the various guardians of the status quo are perpetuating and mumifying it until an orderly program for evolution can be agreed upon by all the interested parties. Nothing wrong with that. But the clock ticks on, and each day the possible gets one step closer to the probable.

"Why is television so banal so much of the time?" a high network
official is fond of saying. "Don't blame me. It's the fault of the system."
The sad part is that he's perfectly right. Fortunately, the system shows
signs of evolution.

Says the president of a cable television company in the Midwest:
"We've simply demanded too much of our commercial television in
this country. It can't be all things to all people, because the way it's
set up now, there just aren't enough commercial TV channels to satisfy
every taste. The combination of satellite transmission and cable television may change all that. Right now, it's as though we had this huge,
six-lane superhighway available to us, and we're all trundling down it
on a child's tricycle, trying to haul a load which rightly belongs to a
tractor trailer. How long we're destined to pedal along in this rather
foolish fashion is in the hands of our legislators, the FCC, the White
House, the courts, the Justice Department, the Communications
Satellite Corporation, the CATV entrepreneurs, the National Association of Broadcasters, and the American Telephone and Telegraph
Company."

What he means is that "the times they are a-changin'," and the
1970s are destined to be a decade of jockeying for position by a
panoply of vested interests, each of which has a big stake in the Communications Revolution and how it's going to alter life in America.

First, let's take a look at community antenna television, that
creeping vine which began 20 years ago as a scheme to bring better
reception to fringe areas and to import a few extra channels to homes
that were receiving only one or two. At this moment, about 2300 such
systems serve 3.6 million subscribers, but one reliable estimate has
it that by 1980 there will be 7500 systems wired into 30 million households; and revenues (mostly from monthly subscription fees) are expected to rise in that same period from today's $300 million to $3
billion a year.

That's big potatoes; but even so, the consensus is that by the end
of the 1970s CATV's potential will still be in its early adolescence.
The TV industry is "looking over its shoulder much as newspapers
and movie exhibitors did when radio and TV appeared," said Sol
Schildhause, the FCC's resident CATV expert, at a recent symposium.
"One might expect the TV industry to be self-assured. But it is not.
Instead, the mood seems to be one of anxiety and uncertainty about
the future."

Nobody doubts that commercial TV's collective brain trust will
find ways of adapting to the new technology. But it must look to the
day when most American homes will be wired for sight and sound,

568   receiving 50 or 75 TV channels, with the enormous potential which that capability implies for minority-interest programming: handling the family's varied needs via special hook-ups with stores, banks, airlines and post offices; plugging into college-credit courses for home study; reading the day's newspapers off the face of the tube and receiving automatic print-out copies of pages one wishes to preserve; tapping the almost infinite resources of computer-fed storage banks for data on every imaginable subject.

So far, the effect of FCC pronouncements on CATV has generally been to retard its growth in the big metropolitan areas of America, where an "adequate" measure of over-the-air service already exists. (A recent FCC ruling did, however, order cable operators to originate their own programming, starting in 1971, as well as retransmitting that of orthodox broadcasters.) This fact has induced a certain amount of understandable paranoia among cable entrepreneurs, who recently insisted in a published statement titled "The FCC and CATV: Overkill" that "the FCC has frozen CATV nearly to death."

Still, the infant cable industry has on its side a formidable array of distinguished partisans. For example:

A 15-man, blue-ribbon task force set up by former President Johnson reported in December 1968 that cable TV held out the promise of a new age of television "so structured that a wide variety of needs, interests and tastes can be achieved at low cost. . . . In the absence of restrictive Government policy, cable television will probably continue to grow rapidly. Those willing to pay will be able to enjoy the benefits, in terms of greater variety and diversity of programming. . . ."

The Justice Department's antitrust division last April laid down a few ground rules of its own which would, it said, "maximize competition" and "promote the ultimate goals of diversity, efficiency and innovation in communications." The goal, said Justice, was to help CATV become a "fertile source of original programming, and provide the diversity . . . that cannot be obtained over-the-air because of limited spectrum space."

A special task force appointed by New York's Mayor John V. Lindsay, and headed by the Ford Foundation's Fred Friendly, urged in September 1968 that New York establish a city-wide complex of cable systems "as rapidly as possible" in order to "help meet the expanding needs of a modern urban society. . . ."

Perhaps the most dramatic and detailed proposal for the future came from a pair of Rand Corporation consultants named Harold J.

Barnett and Edward Greenberg, whose 1967 paper called "A Proposal 569
for Wired City Television" envisioned a national system of wired
cities interconnected by satellite or some other inexpensive relay.

The most recent major testimonial to cable TV's bright future
came from the Electronic Industries Association, which, in an October
filing with the FCC, forecast that the 1980s would be the decade of
the "wired nation," when so-called broadband communications
would take over many services for homes, businesses, schools,
government and private institutions. John P. Thompson of the
Arthur D. Little, Inc. research organization, who was chairman of
the EIA committee, said he didn't foresee the disappearance of TV
and radio, as we now know them, before the turn of the century.
Commercial over-the-air broadcasters derived scant comfort from his
timetable.

"Cable television is where the action is," said Frederick Ford in
a recent interview in his Washington office. Ford is the former FCC
Chairman who until recently headed the National Cable Television
Association, and who has been plumping (as has another former FCC
Chairman, Rosel Hyde) for a cabinet-level Secretary of Telecommunications who would preside over the whole tangle of private and
governmental communications functions. "Nobody really knows
where it's all going," Ford says. "We don't yet know where the big
entrepreneurs will put their money. There's no prototype for what's
happening. It's a frontier. This is indeed a revolution in communications."

One of the most bullish prognosticators about CATV's role in the
1970s is Irving Kahn, whose TelePrompTer Corp. is one of the Nation's biggest cable systems. "Politicians will soon realize that
cable TV offers them the best means of reaching their constituencies,"
Kahn says, "since they can do it on almost a neighborhood-by-
neighborhood basis. And we in cable television believe that political
broadcasting should be free. Television until now has been predicated
on a scarcity of channels. But cable reverses that, and we now have an
economy of plenty instead of one of scarcity."

Kahn believes that in the 1970s communications will begin to
replace transportation. The time will come, he says, when people
will travel only for pleasure and rarely for business. There won't
be much reason to budge, once the "home communications center"
is in full operation and one can shop, study, conduct business and be
entertained without leaving the living room.

He's in agreement with most industry observers that pay television (with a per-program charge for individual attractions, rather

570   than a monthly maintenance charge) is not destined to burgeon in the
1970s, except as a "piggyback" service to cable subscribers. "It's
a combination of cable television and satellite relay that will under-
mine the old order," Kahn insists. "That's the big story of the 1970s."

"I foresee larger satellites over the Pacific, Atlantic and Indian
Oceans. As we get to the latter part of the 1970s, costs for satellite
usage will go down dramatically, and we'll be able to handle many
more channels of TV." The speaker was Dr. Joseph V. Charyk, president of the Communications Satellite Corporation.

"By the end of the 1970s, the networks will be distributing their
programs by satellite instead of by terrestrial lines. We'll have enough
channels so that we could broadcast every NFL and every AFL football game every Sunday to all parts of the country if we wanted to."
That's rotten news for the Nation's housewives, but it illustrates the
potential of satellite relay for expanding our choice of programming,
especially in conjunction with CATV. "A combination of satellites and
CATV could do some pretty dramatic things," Charyk said. "It will
be possible to interconnect all of the cable systems to present an almost unlimited number of programs."

It's nearly eight years now since the first live transatlantic television broadcast—a makeshift affair which endured (22 minutes)
only while the Telstar satellite was in range of a pair of earth stations,
one in Europe and one in the U.S. Now, we have progressed to a
full-scale international communications system with three synchronous satellites in fixed positions over the Atlantic, Pacific and
Indian Oceans and a large network of earth stations. By 1980, we'll
have vastly more powerful satellites and many times the number of
earth stations now operating.

So far, no domestic satellite hovers over the U.S. to cleanse and
clarify the country's communications problems. In 1965, ABC asked
permission to launch its own private satellite for the relay of its programs. Later, the Ford Foundation proposed a domestic satellite to
handle *all* network programs cheaply and educational programs free.
Only last October, CBS called for a three-network consortium to own a
satellite and thus beat AT&T out of a $20-million increase it was
asking for transmitting network programs. Then Comsat chimed in
and said it was ready and able to launch such a "bird" any time the
White House gave the OK.

But at this writing there's still no agreement among all the interested parties as to just how and when the U.S. will get its own
satellites for use here at home. President Nixon is known to have a
strong personal and political interest in the uses of satellite broad-

cast; his October message on U.S. Latin-American policy went to   *571*
Central and South America via satellite, and his Nov. 3 speech on
Vietnam had a vast international audience. Indeed, he is the first
President to have a resident expert in the White House on satellite
affairs: Dr. Clay T. Whitehead, who even now is busy writing a much-
awaited report for the President on satellites.

A few Washington insiders say that President Nixon is already
planning for the day when he can have a public exchange of views
via satellite with such figures as the Prime Minister of Great Britain,
the Chancellor of West Germany and even the Premier of the Soviet
Union. "The audiences for such confrontations, coming right into the
world's homes, would be *vast*," says one observer. "Think of the
interest in such a thing! Remember, in 1966, 400 million people
watched the World Cup soccer match between Great Britain and
West Germany; 300 million saw the opening and closing ceremonies
of the Olympics; and 500 million watched the Apollo 11 astronauts
on the moon."

Pondering the feasibility of such publicly distributed summit
meetings, we put the matter to James C. Hagerty, who was President
Eisenhower's press secretary and who now is a vice president of
ABC's parent company and thus privy to the network's thinking on the
usage of satellites. "Sooner or later it's bound to happen," Hagerty
said earnestly. "And it will be a great thing for world understanding
when it does. The belief here [at ABC] is that McLuhan is right in
saying the world is turning into a village. Things are moving and
they're moving fast—at a geometric rate. This is the age of the engineer."

Hagerty also sees the new satellite technology as a potentially
crucial instrument of peace-keeping and disarmament. "You can't
hide much these days," he says, hinting that spy satellites could easily
detect breaches in any disarmament agreement between the U.S.
and the Soviet Union. "You can't build missile bases overnight,
nor inconspicuously," Hagerty says.

One future development is sure to be the so-called "broadcast
type" of satellite capable of placing a television signal directly into
a home receiver or into a simple and inexpensive community "earth
station" atop an apartment building or in a village. Such satellite-
to-set transmissions will require more complex international agreements on global broadcasting than we have now. But already the first
application of that capability is in preparation: in 1972 the United
States and India will hoist a synchronous satellite which will hover
22,300 miles over the Indian subcontinent and be used to distribute
instructional television programs—on agriculture, hygiene, birth

572 control, among other subjects—to about 5000 villages. That startling collision of Space Age know-how and an illiterate Asian peasantry will dramatize some of the brilliant promise of satellite technology as a civilizing and unifying force.

"It's all accelerating like a snowball going downhill," says Comsat's Dan Karasik, who serves as that organization's manager for television development. "By the end of the 1970s, I can't think of an event of any importance that won't be on television world-wide. We'll see a world broadcasting union with operating centers going 24 hours a day, planning and sharing programs. We'll see a new welding of Asia, Eastern Europe, the United States, Latin America and Africa. Maybe we'll see a daily or twice-daily world-news roundup, with live reports from many parts of the globe—wherever news is happening. The world will be one big mixing pot. And culturally, we'll all be much richer people because of it." [A more conservative estimate of the use and importance of satellites appears in this section, pp. 586–590]

Next month, the 70 nations of the International Telecommunications Satellite Consortium (Intelsat) will meet in Washington to plan for the coming decade and beyond. In June 1971 scores of nations will meet in Geneva for the World Administrative Radio Conference, which will open up new frequencies for use by satellites. By 1975 a whole new generation of satellites—the Intelsat IV series—will be in operation. They'll be five times as powerful as the currently orbiting Intelsat III's, with an average capacity of 6000 circuits and 12 television channels. For the first time, the Satellite Age will be shedding its swaddling clothes.

A 1969 report by the Twentieth Century Fund on "Communicating by Satellite" hints at some of the possibilities for the 1970s. "The prospect of satellite broadcasting has stirred imaginations," it declares. "It has given rise to the hope, particularly in the United States, that it will permit a fresh start, providing an opportunity to break away from the economic structure—and cultural mediocrity—of present-day television broadcasting. It also has generated wishful visions of people all around the world witnessing major events as they happen, sharing cultural experiences, and learning about the ways in which all men live and work. And it holds out the promise that it can be utilized to help educate and inform the millions held back in the developing countries by illiteracy, by antiquated work practices, and by anachronistic traditions."

From today's role as a dispenser of entertainment, news and a little education, most experts fully expect your television set to evolve 573 into a tidy "communications center" for the home. The electronic circuitry and display screen of the TV set are capable of taking over many new duties, and by the end of the decade, the set should be well along in its journey from today's passive "appliance" to an active, multi-purpose electronic link between the home and the outside world.

As extra channels become available to viewers, the set will develop some fascinating new uses: it surely will become a two-way device, either in combination with the telephone or with a special talk-back circuit in the cable-connected TV set itself. You'll be able to shop without leaving home because several channels will be devoted entirely to displaying the wares of local merchants, which may be ordered either by phone or by pushing the proper talk-back button on your set. Billing will be handled automatically by computer.

A true democracy may be closer at hand because your TV set's two-way feature will allow drastically greater participation in local events, and the expressing of your opinion on local and national affairs. Watching a town meeting on TV, a viewer can participate in the discussion via telephone or vote by pressing a button.

The telephone itself will become a sight-and-sound device, with its own picture tube for two-way eyeball-to-eyeball conversations. Bell Telephone already has installed Picturephones in some business offices, and as one Bell official told us, "Picturephone will either be a large success, and growing, or it will have flopped" by the end of the decade. A few free-thinking engineers (not telephone-company employees) believe that the picture telephone ultimately will be part of your TV set, using the same picture tube, rather than being the property of the phone company. Whichever way it works out, extensions throughout the house and at the front door will give you complete closed-circuit baby-sitting and surveillance systems covering your entire home.

Early in the 1970s, your television set will be able to bring you a completely new kind of program: the video equivalent of your phonograph. CBS, RCA and Sony already have announced different systems, to go on the market within the next few years.

They operate in the same general manner: a program cartridge is inserted in a special player which is connected to any TV set through the antenna terminals. You pop in the cartridge and the program appears on your screen. CBS's system is called Electronic Video Recording (EVR), RCA's is dubbed SelectaVision (SV) and Sony calls its rig a Videoplayer. CBS hasn't given out any prices yet, but RCA

574   says its SV player will cost less than $400, and a half-hour color-program cartridge will be $10. Sony will be selling Videoplayers for around $350 and 90-minute color-program cassettes for $20. These video phonographs—and quite possibly other similar concepts—foreshadow major new uses for the home TV set. Eventually, TV cartridges may be sold as paperback books or phonograph records are sold today.

One company envisions introducing, in several years, "disposable" cartridges, which will be so inexpensive they can be viewed a few times and then thrown away—the action-and-sound equivalent of paperback books.

Later in the decade, possibly around 1975, popular-priced do-it-yourself camera-recorder units will be available widely. At least 50 companies are now at work developing them. With one of these video recorders you'll be able to make your own electronic home movies and show them back immediately through your TV set, or record one program (and save it for later) while watching another.

Do you find yourself short of reading matter? Soon your TV set will bring printed pages into your living room. Most scientists see this coming as a form of "facsimile," which already is in widespread business use. Systems which can transmit written material at rates of 15 to 30 pages per second were demonstrated experimentally more than 20 years ago.

A top RCA executive recently described the electronic "newspaper of the future": a print-out attachment to your TV set which, when produced in quantity, should cost between $200 and $400, and the paper a fraction of a cent a page. The Electronic Industries Association believes that such devices could be in widespread use by the late 1970s and also foresees an "electronic home library" in which "a reader can request a book or periodical from a large central library," using the telephone or TV talk-back device. "The desired book is then 'transmitted' . . . page by page" and received in the home for reading.

As the winds of change swirl about their skirts, television's network broadcasters continue to busy themselves "minding the store," much as they have for the last 25 years. There's little doubt that the traditional three-horse race between CBS, NBC and ABC will persist through the 1970s (nobody's talking about the 1980s) much as it has in the past, with the same scuffling for the largest chunk of the mass audience.

So-called "free TV" will continue to bring you half-hour comedies, variety shows, dramas, movies, sports and news. And what trends for the 1970s are discernible in those categories?

"The major changes in the surrounding social structure are coming from the young people," says Mike Dann, CBS's programming chief, "and they're going to have a profound influence on television. They're not interested in the traditional forms of TV. It's almost impossible to get today's young people to watch a situation comedy or a typical hour drama."

New program types will evolve as a result of these new tastes, says Dann. "We don't know yet what these will be, except that TV entertainment of the Seventies will have greater relevance to the real world. Young people are interested in the world around us and want to interpret it in their own way. Beyond that, all I'm sure of is that shows like *Laugh-In* and *The Smothers Brothers Comedy Hour* will look very traditional 10 years from now."

Prime-time movies may be in for a cut-back in the 1970s, dictated by a shortage of old Hollywood features. The programmers have been stoutly insisting they foresee no such pinch at least until the mid-Seventies, but privately some say the rash of sexually explicit, frank-talking and violent films currently in the theaters already is making it difficult for the networks to stock their movie shelves for future seasons.

TV programming is, as everybody knows, terribly cyclical as well as imitative. Right now variety shows and situation comedy are riding high and medical dramas are in revival, while Westerns, cops-and-robbers and other "action-adventure" dramas are at low ebb because of recent outcries over TV violence. But the common expectation is that crime shows, horse operas and other two-fisted fiction will return to favor in a few years.

Mort Werner, NBC's program chief, doubts that the level of violence ever will reach its former heights. "*No* chance," he says firmly. There seems little likelihood, also, that NBC or the other networks will bring themselves to adopt the BBC formula—long advocated by Werner—of running series in short stretches (say, six to 12 weeks), then taking them off for a few months, or forever. In the U.S. scheme of TV, if a series catches on, network management can't bear to shelve it until it has worn out its welcome.

Martin Starger, ABC's program boss, sees TV as "growing up, and I don't see why it shouldn't," with regard to its taboos. "I don't expect to see erotic films on TV," he says, "but the more adult ones will be shown. Just recently we've had *Tom Jones* and *A Man and*

576   *a Woman* on TV. Several years ago neither of these pictures would
have been shown."

Long-time TV observers are disturbed by growing signs of disaffection on, so to speak, both sides of the tube. Among viewers,
the young and the well-educated seem to have turned away from TV,
seeking other diversions. The Nielsen audience estimates have not
reflected any downturn in total viewing, but a widespread feeling
persists that the blandness of much TV entertainment ultimately is
going to drive a greater percentage of people to abandon the home
screen.

In a way, the real worry for TV's continued popularity is to be
found backstage. Although networks and stations are enjoying
phenomenal prosperty, the administrative and programming ranks
of the business are riddled with boredom and restlessness growing
out of a realization that the pattern of TV fare has become more or
less fixed and unchangeable. The broadcasters know what gets ratings,
and ratings are so vital to profits that they dare not dabble with programming that does not meet maximum-audience specifications.
The endless variations on tried-and-true "formats" have long since
ceased to excite anybody.

Sheer attrition will bring about some changes. The stars of TV's
first two decades—the Ed Sullivans, Red Skeltons, Lucille Balls—
will step aside for newer favorites. Can the *Bonanzas,* the *Gunsmokes*
and other durable series go on ad infinitum, perhaps with second-
generation casts? Who knows?

In the 1960s, network evening newscasts expanded from 15 to
30 minutes, and TV journalists are fondly hopeful that the 1970s will
bring a full hour of network news every weekday dinnertime. The
prospects are hazy; neither the networks nor their affiliated stations
are eager right now to surrender an additional half hour for news.

Richard S. Salant, CBS News president, has been most vocal
among the newsmen in advocating an hour of dinnertime news,
but he assumes, as do his counterparts, that he won't get it in the near
future. Elmer Lower, ABC's news boss, has advocated half an hour
of network news in the late evening—perhaps at 10:30—and he has
not given up hope of getting it.

Reuven Frank, president of NBC News, suggests that early evening is not the ideal time for the day's news roundup. "It grew out of
old radio patterns," he says. "Personally, I prefer the late evening
for network news. It's clearly an adult viewing time."

TV journalists universally are avid for at least a weekly hour of

prime time to toy with—to mount documentaries, investigative reports and political backgrounders. But inflationary tendencies in the
economy and a loss of revenue from cigarette advertising are two reasons given for not opening up a decent amount of prime time for such
programs—which inevitably lose money.

And besides, ever since the public outcry following TV's handling of the 1968 Democratic National Convention in Chicago, the
networks have been gun-shy of controversy. "Any hot issue worth
doing properly is bound to bring us a deluge of angry mail," says one
TV newsman. "And if there's one thing the networks don't want right
now—in the aftermath of charges about sex and violence and political
bias—it's another round of viewer anger over our practices." Thus,
no prognosticator is so bold as to predict that the networks will alter
their habit of playing it safe—both economically and politically—in
the treatment of news.

One thing that is sure is that the 1970s will see the passing of a
news team—Chet Huntley and David Brinkley—which for more than
a decade gave NBC dominance in the news ratings (Cronkite overtook
them in recent years). Huntley has served notice he wants to leave,
and Brinkley too has shown signs of tiring of the routine.

We can look forward, of course, to all the televised hurly-burly
of two Presidential Election years—in '72 and '76—and TV's newsmen are hoping they won't be as strewn with pitfalls as the events of
1968. Convention coverage may show some evolution. CBS's Salant,
while making no firm decision yet, still talks (as he did in 1968) of
abandoning gavel-to-gavel coverage in favor of a "selective" approach,
offering variety-show entertainment during lulls in convention proceedings.

Lower says firmly that ABC will stick to the late-evening roundup pattern which his network employed successfully in '68. Conversely, NBC's Frank is equally committed to airing conventions in
their entirety. But Frank thinks that election-year coverage may not
be the high points of news-department activity in the 1970s. "Instead, it may be the space story," he says.

And indeed, space is destined to be an ongoing preoccupation
of TV newsmen—since television has become so dramatic an adjunct
of America's lunar exploration program. The future of the program
seems secure, at least through Apollo 20, by which time the astronauts will be staying on the moon for days at a stretch, and chugging
over the lunar surface in vehicles.

Concurrently with the moon program, U.S. space officials will
be busy establishing mammoth space stations, which will be in orbit

578 around the earth late in the decade. According to Dr. Werner Von Braun, these stations will be large enough by 1980 to accommodate 50 astronauts working and living aboard them for months at a time.

Improved live television pictures of Mars and Venus, taken from unmanned space vessels, are a certainty. But our view of space will not end there. Among the "most fascinating and difficult proposals" for the 1970s, according to the British astronomer Sir Bernard Lovell, is for a "grand tour of the planets" by unmanned space craft, to be launched between 1976 and 1980, when several of the planets will be in a favorable conjunction which will not recur for another 179 years. "This strange journey would take about 10 years to complete," says Sir Bernard.

Money is the name of television's game: commercial broadcasters have it and "public" broadcasters don't. A couple of years ago, a Carnegie Commission study envisioned a network of 380 noncommercial TV stations by 1980, each offering a steady diet of quality programming as an alternative to the mass-appeal stuff aired by ABC, CBS and NBC. Then Congress passed a Public Broadcasting Act which set up a corporation to accomplish just that end. But so far, the funds voted for it have been so niggardly as to hamstring the whole idea.

Congress, and perhaps the White House, just aren't feeling very generous toward public television these days. The Ford Foundation is picking up a large part of the tab and seems willing to continue its support at least for the time being. But if public TV is to thrive in the 1970s, it will need the enthusiasm and the votes of legislators who aren't afraid to back it vocally.

John Macy, who heads the Federally created Corporation for Public Broadcasting, likes to imagine that by 1975 he'll have "a form of long-range Federal financing to provide a trust fund for the corporation which, together with contributions from private sources, would bring us to the level of $100-to-$130 million a year."

Given that kind of budget, he forsees "a full-fledged national network service with a capacity for live distribution of programs seven days a week, 14 hours a day." And if a domestic satellite with free channels for public TV is in orbit by then, it'll make things that much easier and cheaper.

Macy thinks the Carnegie Commission projection of 380 public-TV stations by 1980 is "somewhat excessive." It won't take that many, he says, to give public TV "total coverage" of the country's TV homes. In the news area, he sees public TV as a supplement to commercial

TV's coverage, particularly "providing depth and breadth" in the 579
handling of news. He'd like, for instance, to see Senate and House
sessions opened to public TV's cameras. Where is public TV going
in the 1970s? Not very far, unless somebody writes it a big check.

"Think about it this way," the FCC staffer was saying, pacing his
office in downtown Washington. "There's this wire leading out from
your television set, through a hole in the wall, and then down the
street to a building we'll call the neighborhood program-distribution
center—something like a telephone exchange. Inside the building are
some computers and a small receiving station capable of picking up
satellite signals.

"OK. I come home from work and I'm absolutely *dying* to see
Petticoat Junction. Do I sit around twiddling my thumbs until 8
o'clock when the program comes on? Nope. I pick up my program
catalogue, look up the code number, punch my touch-tone buttons,
and up pops the show on my TV screen. Suppose I want to read *Moby
Dick.* I just tap out the right code number and there it is, page by
page, on the screen.

"Maybe I want to take a college course, for credit; or settle an
argument about the Franco-Prussian War; or learn more about the
culture of India; or see a painting owned by the Louvre. It's all there,
waiting for me to summon it up—thousands and thousands of bits
of knowledge, guidance and entertainment, stored in computers,
awaiting my beck and call."

Those daydreams and many others are not mere fancy. They
are well within the bounds of engineering capabilities which we already have. And on the old assumption that "whatever *can* happen
will happen," they will continue their inexorable march from the
distant horizon to your own back yard.

At this moment, 80 per cent of Americans live on 10 per cent of
the land—an appalling and unnatural clustering (common to no other
vertebrate) which evolved spontaneously from the industrial revolution. The new technology will give us opportunity—if we choose to
take it—of spreading out without losing the capability of communicating with each other.

We now have the tools "not only to provide a means for new styles
in human settlements, but also to rebuild, in a sociological sense, the
crowded inner core of major cities," the Electronic Industries Association points out. Such systems are an "absolute necessity" by
the 1980s if the Nation is to find "real solutions to national pollution,
urban traffic, and inter-city transportation problems."

580   Up until now, we have been preoccupied with finding better ways of moving objects and people, and to that end have created highways, railroads, airports and subways. In the process, we've made a pretty snarl out of our cities, miring them in traffic congestion, toxic air and a bedlam of noise. The solution? Many informed people now are convinced it is to move information—instead of things and people.

Of all the "revolutions" facing us, says *Science and Technology* magazine, "communications has the most *potential* to produce something like the kind of revolution that came out of harnessing mechanical power.... It is technically possible to bring the mid-20th century, via wire and air waves, into the homes of the most remote and most backward people of the world."

A high United Nations official—a European career diplomat—mused about all this to TV GUIDE recently. "The most important thing is the right of individuals to choose for *themselves* what they will know and with whom they will communicate. Why must we accept the will of someone else in these matters: the directors of government TV services or the heads of commercial networks. The combination of international satellites and cable will provide the means of bringing to individuals all the information they need or want without interference or control."

Another UN official, Jean d'Arcy (formerly director of French television), says this: "In the same way that the railroad and the telegraph helped build the United States, communications satellites will fashion quite a different social structure of the world. We will see the formation of new communities quite different from the old."

Here in the United States, it appears inevitable that the 1970s will see the start of the process by which mass audiences will be pulverized into a million elite audiences, each liberated to pursue its own idiosyncratic tastes. Where once we bewailed conformity in American society, we may one day lament that we are too atomized, too disparate, too diverse to act together.

The prospects for enrichment are breathtaking. The best visionaries foresee the liberation of the individual through the new communications, and a better texture of life for all of us. The decade we are in can carry us far toward that goal, if we have the courage and the will to make the trip.

CATV—The Wave of TV's Future?

By Richard K. Doan

President-elect Richard M. Nixon and his staff, ensconced pending his inauguration in New York City's plush Hotel Pierre, have been watching TV on three receiving sets with extra channels showing United Press International news-ticker stories, continuously up-dated weather data, Broadway-theater news, and Wall Street developments.

Meanwhile, down in Greensboro, North Carolina, 6500 homes have access to a baby-sitting TV channel that plays animated cartoons continuously from 8 to 11 A.M. and from 3 to 6 P.M. Another channel these homes can watch prints out New York Stock Exchange quotations throughout market hours and reviews each day's trading up to 7 o'clock in the evening. A third channel televises Associated Press news all day. In Farmington, New Mexico, 4100 families can switch on their sets two evenings a week to a channel that runs a bingo game, with merchandise prizes offered to viewers playing along at home. And in Liberal, Kansas, the police can push a button in case of a town-wide emergency (say, an approaching tornado) and cut into every TV channel—and 12 of them, at that!—in 60 percent of the homes in town.

What these situations have in common is that they involve TV that you can't get by putting up an antenna. The pictures are piped into the receiving sets on wires. It's a service, already familiar to millions of Americans, known as community-antenna television, or CATV, or cable TV. Technology, it appears, is about to take a remarkable backward step: TV, born on the air waves, seems destined to become a sort of visual telegraphy. The TV of the future, if we can believe quite a few knowledgeable people in the communications world, will be a form of phone-line service—one-way at first, later two-way.

It's all part of a fanciful expectation widely bruited about by the

581

582 communications experts as a "wired-city concept." Truth is, it's already much more than a concept; it is a mushrooming service of such mind-boggling potential that a prominent veteran broadcaster, Roger Clipp of Philadelphia, predicted recently that "by 1985, using the most conservative figures, 46 million homes out of an estimated total of 10 million will be connected by wire to program-origination sources. For all practical purposes, most of the 800 or more TV transmitters (in the U.S.) can be padlocked."

Not surprisingly, such a prospect is giving the TV Establishment nightmares. Some observers even suspect that CBS's diversification into book publishing, toys, baseball and other fields[1] reflects in part an awareness that TV's status quo is of numbered days. In any case, CBS itself is already in wired TV, too, being owner of the world's biggest community-antenna system, with 100,000 subscribers, up in Vancouver, as well as having part interest in a San Francisco cable hookup.

Late last month CBS disclosed that it was seeking to acquire full ownership of two groups of CATV systems now operating in California and Washington.[2] NBC also is getting its feet wet in CATV, having five smallish systems scattered from upstate New York to California. Individual broadcasters as a group are even more involved in this seeming wave of the TV Future. One-third of some 3,600,000 homes served by more than 2300 CATV systems are the customers of broadcaster-owned CATV operations.

Around for about 15 years, CATV once was looked upon as a handy contrivance for enabling people to get better pictures in hilly areas or to see distant stations they couldn't otherwise receive. As such, the broadcasters naturally welcomed its existence (little dreaming CATV could turn out to be that old boogeyman Pay TV in a new guise).

Nowadays, CATV entrepreneurs, who've discovered that "cable-casting" programs of their own, along with relaying over-the-air shows, gives their service a double-barreled attraction, squirm uneasily when asked if they aren't indeed in the Pay-TV business. Not until they start charging per-program fees instead of a flat monthly rate (usually $5 or $6), they insist, they have no such plans as of now. Still, a U.S. circuit court, in upholding the Federal Communications Commission's right to govern CATV last August, cautioned that "indiscriminate CATV development feeding upon the broadcast service is capable of destroying large parts of it."[3]

Ironically, if CATV is on the way to putting broadcast TV out of business, it not only is biting the hand that feeds it, but devouring

it entirely. Cable TV's bread-and-butter is the distribution of "studio 583
quality" pictures from the on-air stations. Without them CATV would
have nothing but its own programming to offer. This is not to say, of
course, that a nation-wide network of cable systems might not some
day become a market for programs which at present only the big
TV networks can afford.[4] Indeed, just that kind of evolution is foreseen
by some observers, who believe the ultimate prevailing system will
be a combination of domestic satellites for long-distance program
delivery and cable hookups for distributing shows locally.[5]

Up to this point, CATV's impact is far more feared than real,
its inroads on viewing being a long way from denting the Nielsen
ratings. Starting with such a feeble "public service" gesture as televised time and weather reports, CATV operators went on to install
rotating "bicycle wheels" displaying community bulletin-board
announcements, and to transmit news (in printed form) and stock-
ticker quotations. Today, more and more CATV'ers are venturing out
with video cameras to cover local sports, school-board meetings and
graduation exercises, and more and more are dabbling in studio-
originated shows—kiddy entertainments, teen-talk sessions, game
shows and the like. Nothing elaborate yet, that is, but a few of the systems are beginning to show their own movies and to run commercials.

Movies and commercials on CATV are what really throw a scare
into a lot of people. In New York City, Manhattan Cable, franchised
to serve the affluent midtown and East Side areas (including the Hotel
Pierre), ran full-page newspaper ads last summer proclaiming plans
to show uncut, uninterrupted movie "classics" twice nightly. The
disclosure triggered howls of protest from movie exhibitors—in
claimed defense of "free TV"!—and forced a months-long postpone-
ment of the CATV movies while the city debated whether cable
systems should be allowed to run their own entertainments.

Apparently only about 10 percent of the existing cable systems
accept advertising, but prominent operators, such as Manhattan
Cable's Charles Dolan and TelePrompTer's Irving Kahn (who has
20 systems scattered from New York City to Hawaii), want the right
to air commercials even though they say they have no immediate
intention of soliciting them.

The FCC, for its part, seems unable yet to make up its mind
whether sales plugs should be *verboten* on CATV or not.[6] Last
summer the Federal agency told San Diego CATV systems they could
originate programming to their hearts' content, but not with commercials. A few weeks later the FCC slapped down a complaint from
North Carolina TV stations and ruled that a Greensboro cable system

584 could indeed carry both its own programs and commercials.

Then, last month [December, 1968], the FCC threw nearly everybody into confusion, if not dismay, by suddenly slapping a complicated series of proposed curbs on CATV.[7] One effect was virtually to bar cable systems from importing signals from distant stations until questions of copyright are resolved. These and other restrictions raised angry cries in some CATV quarters. Frederick W. Ford, president of the National Cable Television Association and himself a former FCC commissioner, charged the agency with trying to "eviscerate" the CATV industry. He also accused the FCC of "attempting to discredit" a Presidential task force on communications which had just urged a national policy of encouraging cable TV as the best means of diversifying the public's choice of programming.[8]

Some CATV interests felt, however, that the regulations were not too severe to live with and, indeed, in one respect removed cable from the role of a supplemental medium relaying other people's programs and conferred on it an identity of its own. The FCC said it not only approved of CATV originating programs, but would expect cable systems, to put something other than time-and-weather reports on at least one channel not used for relaying over-the-air programs.[9] Industry sources had to agree that this was more like a spur than a halter. It was clear, though, that legal battles lay ahead on many CATV fronts, with Congress certain to get into the scrap.

Three aspects basic to CATV give it its distinctly entrancing flavor: unlike advertiser-supported broadcast TV, it is a medium directly subservient to its consumers; whereas over-the-air TV is of necessity a mass medium and must cater to the broadest of tastes, CATV can be, is and will likely be highly local in its interests, even to catering to neighborhood needs; and while over-the-air TV operates in a scarcity of signal space—each of the big networks, for instance, having but one channel to program—CATV has almost an embarrassment of channels available, usually 12 to 18, in the future easily 50 to 75! Which means, of course, CATV can serve a multiplicity of minority interests, community by community, which over-the-air TV could never dream of.

At this point, to be sure, CATV is pretty small-town and small-potatoes. One of its achievements has been to deliver TV to countless remote hamlets, like Burns, Oregon; Moab, Utah; and Del Rio, Texas, which before had no TV at all. It frequently rewards small towns like these with more channels to watch than some major cities have: Tiny Thief Fall, Minnesota, for example, chooses from nine channels.

But big-time CATV also is on the move. New York City's two

initial CATV systems typify what is in the wind: In upper Manhattan, TelePrompTer is busy wiring up an area embracing the Harlem Negro and Puerto Rican ghettos. There are poor prospects for CATV service? Not so, says TPT's Irv Kahn. He points out that TV is the chief entertainment of the less affluent, who will sacrifice even some necessities for it. He is convinced they'll be eager CATV users, partly in this case because New York City has two Spanish-language UHF stations, hard to get over the air but picture-sharp on cable. Kahn pictures his uptown system as intent on strongly developing "people-to-people television," zeroed in on local concerns, another reason why the Harlem dwellers will buy the service.

Meanwhile, Manhattan Cable's enterprising "Chuck" Dolan has his eye on not one but two potential CATV gold mines: he is readying a 24-channel business-news service for corporate tenants of such office beehives as the Pan Am Building and Rockefeller Center; at the same time he is busily wiring up high-rise apartments and town-houses (11,000 by recent count) for piped-in programming which he hopes soon—given city blessing—will include not only movies, but live symphony concerts from Carnegie Hall and telecasts of Columbia University basketball games.

There are experts who feel such "exotic" CATV promises as facsimile newspapers, banking and computer services, meter-reading, police-fire protection and the like via cable are far, far down the pike. Even so, a leading radio-TV journal stewed editorially the other day that CATV proponents seem to have few inhibitions. They're acting, sniffed *Broadcasting* magazine, as though "tomorrow's cable operator would combine the functions (and the ownership) of the Bell system, the television networks, the independent television stations, the motion-picture theaters and who knows what other enterprises."

It's a heady dream, all right. And a lot of cable-TV people are as sure as they're breathing that they've got a head start in the Great Gold Rush of the 1970's.

Global Television—When?

By Richard K. Doan

JANUARY 27, 1968

Satellite TV, *si*. Global TV, not much. So far, anyway. And for reasons you might not readily guess. Take TV's coverage of the Vietnam war: Why not live TV via satellite out of Vietnam? Forget it! Hanoi, Saigon and Washington aren't about to arrange battle times and places to suit TV's prime time.

Well, then, how about lots of live-live TV news out of Europe? Nope, wouldn't work so well. Europe's in bed by the time we settle down for an evening of TV. Picking up news as it happens in Europe as likely as not would only cut in on *Treasure Isle* or *Everybody's Talking*. You sure the ladies would approve? Anyway, what's so big on the other side of the pond that we can't wait a couple of hours to see it? And what do we need satellites for if we can fly crisp, colorful film of it into New York in time for the evening news?

Besides, even though TV signals technically can circle the globe via satellite, it takes ground stations to pump the pictures up the bird and pick the returning pictures out of space; and earth stations, though growing in number every month, sometimes just aren't handy to an event somebody wants to televise.

Then, when it comes to getting satellite TV out of two big areas of the globe, there's the matter of a couple of curtains called Iron and Bamboo. The Russians don't choose to play in our satellite league. The Chinese have the A-bomb but no Early Bird, and presumably they wouldn't be speaking to us through it if they did.

And finally—or among the finallies—there's the cost. But a common assumption about satellite pickups being too expensive to permit frequent network newscast switches to Europe and Asia apparently is invalid. The TV networks, at any rate, insist the tab isn't all that prohibitive.

The charges levied by the Communications Satellite Corporation and foreign agencies operating earth stations are not exactly peanuts, it's true. A 10-minute color feed from London to New York even in so-called non-peak time can cost a network about $5375 [present

586

figure is $2490]. The Europeans have been slow in bringing down 587
rates in line with Comsat's and those charged by Japan for a New
York-Tokyo pickup. A similar feed over the longer distance to Asia
typically costs $4031 [$2520].

But expense is not the prime deterrent, say newsmen at ABC,
CBS and NBC. Clearing channels on the four man-made stars isn't
a major hurdle either, although in the recent past the networks were
inhibited in their use of the initial Pacific satellite because Comsat
sometimes couldn't get enough regular non-TV users to surrender
circuits, especially to feed color.

Exactly why there are such infrequent news pickups or special
programs piped via satellite seems to require other explanations.
Take Robert (Shad) Northshield's. He is executive producer of NBC's
Huntley-Brinkley Report, a program with anchor men in New York
and Washington, as anybody knows, but which, in the wake of initial
Early Bird excitement, was envisioned as soon to have a third anchor
man reporting nightly, and live, from London.

"Europe simply has been dullsville lately," Northshield observed. "The chief focus of our attention overseas is on Vietnam.
There just hasn't been much happening of consequence in Europe to
warrant satellite feeds. Anyway, most of the time we can shoot what
we want on color film over there and jet it to New York in time for
same-day use. The time differential (that is to say, when it's 9 P.M. in
London it's 4 P.M. in New York) works in our favor on European
coverage."

Sid Darion, Bob Young's news producer, points out that "the gimmick value of satellites is gone—we now use them just as though
we were switching to the West Coast." On the other hand, "Europe
is just so close by plane that there are few stories we can't fly back,
guaranteeing ourselves top picture quality and sound, at no risk to
poor transmission."

Walter Cronkite echoes these attitudes, but the CBS News star
says cost is a factor. "We could use a satellite feed nightly but something else would have to give, budget-wise. If we had a reasonably
priced Atlantic satellite, I think we'd use it every day."

Remarkably, there is no feverish agitation among TV newsmen for
facilities to feed live TV out of Saigon. As far back as October 1966,
Julian Goodman, news-trained president of NBC, predicted in a
speech: "Within a year it seems likely we will be transmitting directly
from Saigon. . . . Even live coverage from the battlefields of Vietnam
will be a technical possibility."

It isn't yet. There is still no Saigon earth station. The reasons

588 given are varied: The South Vietnamese government, which would have to authorize if not actually build such a facility, has no need or seeming desire to put one up. Besides, the U.S. military, while not censoring coverage of the war, apparently is not at all anxious to have live TV satellite-fed out of that zone.

In the same speech Goodman noted that "possibly within a year, portable ground stations will be available for shipment by plane to news spots anywhere in the world." Such gear exists—an ITT portable dish on shipboard has televised astronaut splashdowns from the mid-Atlantic—but thus far there has been no commercial use of it. One reason, it seems, is that a tab of somewhere around $300,000 would be incurred in flying this equipment to a remote locality and setting it up for a special feed.

. . . . .

In space, a third-generation satellite, the Intelsat III, [has been] positioned over the Atlantic, a second over the Pacific, and a third over the Indian Ocean. They [were] stationed in time to beam the Olympics from Mexico City to virtually every corner of the globe. A larger, more sophisticated bird than its forebears, Intelsat III [has] full-time video channels, elimating the necessity of blocking out telephone, telegraph, data and other users in order to clear a TV feed. Moreover, Intelsat IV is already in the works, targeted for lofting in 1970-72. Its capacity will exceed III's by five-fold. "As you can see," A Comsat official cited, "rates for TV use are simply bound to come down."

With bigger Intelsats, a proliferation of earth stations[10] and lower rates, won't satellite TV become commonplace on the U.S. networks? Surprisingly, not everybody in command thinks so. For instance, Richard S. Salant, CBS News president, comments, "The technological revolution has been way overplayed as to its influence on TV news coverage. I have long felt this. I see no marked step-up in our use of the satellites. I think it's unrealistic to expect it, partly because of time-zone differentials, partly because of costs." Satellites, he admitted, "are damned good" for covering "the great human events" like a Churchill funeral or the picking of a new Pope, but he thinks the networks on a day-to-day basis will continue to rely mainly on film flown in from abroad.

Actually, Comsat's records show there has been considerable escalation in use of the birds by TV. In 1965 TV systems abroad as well as in this country fed 33 hours, 30 minutes of programming via Early Bird. [In 1969 satellite usage totalled 779 hours of transmission and 1050 hours of receiving.] "Satellite use by TV has become a fever

chart of world events," Comsat's Dan Karasik noted. "The Arab-
Israeli war last June [1967] jumped the pickups to 50 hours. That was
not just incoming feeds from Rome (closest to the scene) and elsewhere, but included outgoing feeds to Europe and Asia of the United
Nation's deliberations in New York."

The U.S. networks, as a matter of fact, are by no means the only
TV users of Comsat's air-borne relays. Eurovision, Britain's BBC and
the Japanese commercial and viewer-supported networks are almost
as big Comsat customers as the Americans.

Looking down the TV pike three to five years, how much "via
satellite" news do the networks foresee? NBC's Reuven Frank
expresses a probably typical viewpoint: "In five years every place we
have a news bureau, around the world will be as close as Washington
and Chicago." But like other news executives, Frank see the birds
being employed largely to expedite filmed highlights of events. For
example, he thought that if the networks undertook live continuous
coverage of [a] summit meeting in the Pacific area between [the]
President and our Asian allies, "it could bore people to death." But
satellites would be needed to flash summarized coverage back home.

Says ABC's Sid Darion: "If there is real tragedy somewhere,
such as that cave-in in Wales, then of course all stops are pulled out
and there's no question about live coverage. Otherwise, we just use
satellites as a tool for possible competitive advantage." In five years
there will be lots of satellite-fed news on TV, thinks NBC producer
Shad Northshield, if only "because evening newscasts will be an
hour long by then."

News, naturally, is not the only fodder for satellite TV. Sports
events have been big features via Early Bird, especially on *ABC's
Wide World of Sports.* The only live telecast out of the Soviet to date
was ABC's of the Russian-American track meet at Kiev, ABC has on
occasion fed sports coverage live to three continents simultaneously.
One of the most ambitious programs for satellite use [was] ABC's
coverage of the Winter Olympics from Grenoble; [the] next fall [saw]
the greatest sports telecast—and biggest single satellite-TV event—in
history: the Olympics from Mexico, viewed live by upward of 400
million persons.

Roone Arledge, boss of ABC Sports, regards satellites as "a
neglected breakthrough in communications which ought to be in
routine use." At the same time he concedes not every foreign sports
event worth televising warrants satellite treatment. "There's not
much sense putting something on at 7 A.M. in the U.S., just so you can
say it's 'live via satellite,'" he observes. "Much depends on where

590 an event takes place and how important it is to show it while it's happening."

Entertainment via satellite is a potential novelty which has titillated the network programmers for several year, but thus far nothing of this kind has jelled. Both Thomas W. Moore, [former] president of ABC-TV, and Mort Werner, program chief of NBC-TV, have glibly proposed experimenting with a "Wide World of Entertainment" employing live satellite pickups from various foreign locales. Moore's idea is that late-night variety acts in European clubs could be beamed across the Atlantic during U.S. prime time. Werner has not divulged specifically what he has in mind except that it might involve Jack Paar as a roving emcee.

But very little—and that only for the novelty—has been attempted in non-news TV via satellite. The memorable demonstrations of Telstar's wonders, a few CBS: Town Meetings of the World," and the "Our World" telecast carried by U.S. educational stations last June [1967] remain, along with occasional sportscasts, the principal exhibits to date of the capabilities of satellite TV.

Comsat officials wouldn't be surprised to see foreign broadcasters, especially the Japanese, beginning to outdistance the U.S. networks in grasping opportunities for opening TV's windows on the world. The hang-up here at home, it seems, is a kind of parochial lack of interest in what's going on anywhere away from home shores except in that fought-over strip of land in Southeast Asia.

Notes to Chapter 6

1. In recent years, CBS has acquired Holt, Rinehart & Winston, Inc., publishers, Creative Playthings, Inc., and the Learning Center, Inc.– the country's largest producers of three dimensional educational systems and toys—and the New York Yankees. CBS also owns the largest mail-order record operation in the world and has made some very successful investments in the Broadway theater, including *My Fair Lady, Cabaret, Mame,* and *Sweet Charity.*

2. CBS, along with Time-Life, are also owners of Television Presentations Inc. which is offering CATV systems a program service (initially Madison Square Garden events, kiddie shows, movies, and so forth) taped on CBS's new EVR cartridges.

3. Black Hills Video Corporation *v.* FCC, No. 18, 052 (8th Cir., August 7, 1968).

4. The fear on the part of on-the-air broadcasters that CATV will someday be nationally connected led (in the Spring of 1969) to a proposed agreement between the NAB and the National Cable Television Association. Under the plan worked out by the staffs of these two organizations, broadcasters and cable operators would support legislation which would permit CATV to originate one channel of entertainment and one channel carrying advertising and to import distant signals to reach a total load of three network affiliates and three independents. But CATV would be made liable for

copyright payments, would respect the exclusivity provisions in contracts between stations and program suppliers, and CATV systems would be prohibited from interconnecting for entertainment programs. The NAB Board of Directors, however, refused to ratify the agreement.

5. In June 1969, following the NAB's announcement that its directors would not ratify the proposed NAB-NCTA agreement mentioned in note 4, National Cable Television Association President, Frederick Ford proposed a scheme to supply wired-television homes with a six channel feed via satellite for up to twenty-four hours daily by 1975. Two of the channels would be programmed by the Public Broadcasting System with educational and cultural fare, and one channel each would be alloted to weather reports, health and medical reports, Congressional hearings, and selected re-runs of commercial television's finest non-fiction. NCTA and Comsat officials estimated that, assuming thirty-nine million homes were linked by cable by that time, the cost could be as little as ninety cents a year per home.

6. In October 1969, the FCC promulgated rules permitting advertising by CATV systems, but only at the beginning or end of the cablecast program or "at natural intermissions or breaks within a cablecast" which are beyond the control of the CATV operator, as for example, a time-out in a sporting event or intermission in a concert.

7. For a discussion of the FCC rules and their possible implications, see *Broadcasting*, December 16, 1968.

8. The task force report was belatedly released in late May 1969 by the Nixon Administration, without comment. It is quite possible that President Nixon will set up his own communications task force.

9. In its October 1969 rule-making on CATV originations and commercials (First Report and Order Docket Number 8397 the FCC indicated that effective January 1, 1971, all CATV systems having 3500 or more subscribers must originate programming "to a significant extent."

10. Projections are that by 1972 there will be twenty-eight operational ground facilities located in fifty-three nations.

Index

Index

Index

A

ABC. *See* American Broadcasting Company
A. C. Nielsen Company, 122–125
  accuracy of rating, 388–397
  defense of ratings, 398–402
  See also Ratings
Ace, Goodman, 193
Ackerman, Harry, 198
Adams, Cindy, 66
Advertising, 230–251
  commercials
    effects on sales, 239–245
    mirrors of society, 236–238
    playlet, 233–235
    success factors, 246–248
    success of color, 249–251
Agnew, Spiro T., 6–9
Ahles, Richard, 424–426
Alcindor, Lew, 212
Alexander, Herbert E., 485–487
Allen, Roy, 71–72
Allen, Steve, 200
Amateau, Rod, 200
American Broadcasting Company Coverage of the 1968 Democratic Convention, 95–97
American Council for Better Broadcasts, 427
Ames, Louise, 501
Anderson, Donny, 212
Anderson, Jack, 91–92
Andrews, Peter, 231

Arledge, Roone, 589–590
Arlen, Michael, 5, 472
Ashley, Ted, 133
Asimov, Isaac, 502, 508
Aubrey, Jim, 392
Audiences, 412–445
  as pressure groups, 427–431
  attitudes toward television, 411–418
  intellects as, 442–445
  letters to networks from, 419–423
  raising the standards of, 437–441
  telephone calls to networks from, 424–426
  viewing, reasons for, 412–413
  wants and needs of, 434–436
  See also Ratings
Aurthur, Robert Allen, 174
Austin, Bud, 141–142

B

Bailey, Dick, 211
Bailey, John M., 94
Baker, Richard, 5
Bandura, Albert, 514–521
Bankson, Rodger R., 47, 48, 49
Banner, Bob, 198
Barrett, Dean, 5, 287–288
  on the Fairness Doctrine, 310–312
Barrett, Edward W., 21–22
Barron, James, 328
Barry, Bud, 140
Baseball. *See* Sports

596 Bell, Bert, Jr., 217
Bell, Howard, 351–352
Bell, William, 378
Bergin, John, 246–247
Berkowitz, Leonard, 518, 520, 524
Bertalanffy, Ludwig von, 522
Black, Shirley Temple, 14
Blacks and television, 252–264
limited progress of, 259–264
traditional roles of, 255–258
Bloom, Dan, 67–68
Bluel, Richard, 397
Bond, Julian, 98
Boorstein, David, 61
Brace, Clayton H., 22
Brelis, Dean, 44
Brinkley, David, 9, 93–94, 101, 305
Broadcast Rating Council, 386, 389
Browar, Herbert W., 198–199
Buckley, William, 95, 288
on the Fairness Doctrine, 316–318
Budd, Millie, 14
Bulletins, television news, 25–29
Burch, Dean, 491–492
Bureau of Applied Social Research, 409
Burns, George, 196
Burrington, David, 38, 39, 44
Busch, Gussie, 214
Bushnell, Asa, 217–218

C

Cable television (CATV), 299–301, 570–572
Caesar, Sid, 192
Callahan, Roger, 170, 172
Campaign costs and television, 484–487
Campbell, Eldon, 23
Cancellation of television shows, 122–126
Canned laughter, 194–200
Carmichael, Stokely, 61
Carroll, Walter, 260
Cash, Pete, 241
CATV (cable television), 299–301, 570–572
Cavanagh, Jerome, 70, 72

CBS. *See* Columbia Broadcasting System
CBS *Playhouse*, 188–191
Censorship, 285–337
corporate interests and, 323–339
effects on television of, 179–180
Fairness Doctrine
Barrett on, 310–312
Buckley on, 316–318
Pastore on, 313–315
problems raised by, 303–309
Schlesinger on, 319–321
FCC and, 290–302
See also "Permissiveness"
Charyk, Joseph V., 302
Chayefsky, Paddy, 174, 188–190
Chicago Democratic Convention. *See* Political Conventions
Child, Julia, 277
Children and television, 498-535
applying available knowledge, 528–533
ideal programming, 533–535
knowledge, television as a source of, 501–505
learning theory, 527–528
values disseminated by television, 505–510
violence
"Bandura" school of, 514–520
differing "schools" of, 520–526
sex, anti-social behavior and, 510–515
Cioffi, Lou, 38, 48, 50–51
Civil disorders. *See* Urban television coverage
Civil rights movement and television, 60–62, 65
Clark, Jim, 75
Clipp, Roger, 573
Code of the National Association of Broadcasters, 177, 345–349, 374, 515
Cohen, Joel, 10
Cole, Kathryn, 421, 422
Collingwood, Charles, 48
Colodny, Lester, 187
Color commercials, 249–251

Columbia Broadcasting System (CBS), 90
    corporate pressures and CBS news, 330–339
    coverage of the 1968 Democratic Convention, 95–97
    finalization of 1969–70 prime-time schedule, 127–134
Columbia University, 99
Comedy on television, 192–207
    canned laughter, 194–200
    laughter, causes of, 204–207
    writers for, 201–203
Commercials. *See* Advertising
Communications Act (1934), 285, 291, 295
    Section 315a of, 485–487, 490–499
    See also Fairness Doctrine
Community Relations Services (U. S. Department of Justice), 68
Compton, Neil, 474
Congressional Hearings, effects on tv drama of, 179–180
Conventions. *See* Political Conventions
Cooper, Jackie, 200
Cordova, Fred de, 203
Corporate pressure
    as a cause of censorship, 322-329
    CBS news and, 330–337
Corporon, John, 18
Cosby, Bill, 252, 260, 263–264
Cosell, Howard, 226–227, 229
Coss, Paul, 149
Cost factors of tv sports, 210–215
Cox, Kenneth A., 297–298, 301
Cronkite, Walter, 4–5, 17, 61, 94
Crouse, Jay, 11
Cunningham, Glenn, 307

D

Daley, Richard J., 87, 89–93, 95, 97–100, 103, 107, 108
Dann, Mike, 124, 127–134, 189-191, 256, 263, 361, 392, 575
Dantzler, Ray, 16
Darion, Sid, 587, 589

Davey, William, 209, 221
Day, Doris, 120
Daytime programming, 153–173
    soap operas, 156–168
    quiz shows, 169-173
DeForest, Lee, 563
Democratic National Convention. *See* Political Conventions
Demographics, ratings and, 393–395, 403–407
Detroit riots and television coverage, 70–77
Dewey, Thomas E., 83
Dichter, Ernest, 249
"Dimensions of Violence in Television Drama," 362–363, 364–370
Dingell, John, 102
Dirksen, Everett, 91
Doan, Richard K., 120–121, 175, 231, 338–339
Dodd, Thomas, 179–180
Dodd Committee hearings, 359, 511–515
Dodge, Frank, 160–161
Doefer, John C., 297
Dolan, Charles, 583, 585
Donkin, Paul, 395
Dortort, David, 120
Doubleday, Robert, 140
Douglas, Charley, 194–197
Drama on television, 174–191
    CBS *Playhouse*, 188–191
    Code of the NAB and, 177
    Congressional Hearings and, 179–180
    future of, 181–182
    network censorship and, 177–178
    plight of writers of, 183–187
    pressure groups and, 178–179
    self-censoring writers for, 181, 183–187
    "tyranny of the ratings" and, 180–181
Due to Circumstances Beyond Our Control (Friendly), 7, 324
Dunmore, Al, 71, 76
Dunne, John, 62
Dunphy, Don, 227
Durslag, Melvin, 209

598   Dylan, Bob, 328

E

Eckert, William, 220
Editorial policies of television news, 20–24
Edmondson, Ed, 90
Effects of television, 536–557
    defense of, 554–557
    on the English language, 538–540
    judicial proceedings, representations of, 541–544
    on other media, 545–549
    uncivilizing and anticivilizing, 550–553
    See also Role of television
Efron, Edith, 154–155, 174–175, 287, 411, 498–500
Eisenberg, Leon, 529–531
Eisenhower, Dwight D., 83–84
Eliasberg, Jay, 127, 131, 390–391
Ellison, Harlan, 183–184, 187
Elman, Irving, 270
English language, effect of tv on, 538–540
Ewbank, Weeb, 215

F

Fabray, Nanette, 192
Fairness Doctrine, 23, 286, 287, 288, 325, 328, 487
    Barrett on, 310–312
    Buckley on, 316–318
    Pastore on, 313–315
    problems raised by, 303–309
    Schlesinger on, 319–321
Federal Communications Commission (FCC), 23, 79, 87, 89, 95, 104, 371
    divergent opinions of functions, 295–302
    history and functions of, 290–295
    Section 315 rulings, 488–497
Felton, Norman, 270–271, 273–274
Feminine Mystique, The (Friedan), 161, 162, 268
Fern, Jack, 42, 45, 47, 51
Ferry, W. H., 75

Films. *See* Movies
Filmways Incorporated, 141
Finnigan, Joseph, 121
First, Freedom, The (Rucker), 325
Flynn, John, 37
Football. *See* Sports
Foote, Horton, 174
Ford, Frederick W., 295, 584
Foreman, Robert, 243–244
Frank, Reuven, 8, 16, 21, 79–80, 576–578, 589
Frank, Stanley, 208–209
Free speech. *See* Censorship
Freedman, Lawrence Zelic, 530
Freeman, Everett, 186
Friedan, Betty, 161–162, 265
Friendly, Fred, 3, 7, 20, 26–27, 150–152, 300
Friendly, Henry J., 291, 296
Fromson, Murray, 40, 48
Functions of television, *see* Role of television
Funny Men, The (Allen), 200
Funson, Gene, 22
Funt, Allen, 419, 420, 421
Furey, Ralph, 218
Future of television, 563–580
    CATV, 581–585
    satellite transmission, 570–572
Fyffe, Bill, 75

G

Galbraith, John Kenneth, 78, 230, 323
Gans, Herbert J., 336
Gardner, George E., 507
Garfinkle, Norton, 394–395
Garry, Ralph, 512
Geller, Bruce, 176–181
Gerbner, George, 362–363, 451
Gerhold, Paul, 240, 247
Girardin, Ray, 64, 75–76
Goelet, Peter, 429
Gold, Jack, 243
Goldberg, Arthur, 493–494
Goldberg, Leonard, 149, 150–151
Golden, Marc, 127
Goldenson, Leonard, 61, 139
Goodman, Julian, 8, 27–28, 65, 322, 361, 587–588

Goodson, Mark, 170, 420–422
Gould, Jack, 33, 475
Gowdy, Curt, 227, 229
Green, Gerald, 306
Greenwald, Harold, 161
Gregory, Karl T., 72–73
Groppi, James, 74
Grove, Bill, 22

H

Hagerty, James C., 10, 28, 65, 305, 555
Haley, William, 5
Hall, Durward, 303
Hall, Leonard 475
Halloran, James, 526
Harris Committee Hearings, 385–386
Harris, Oren, 304
Harris Survey, 3–4
Hartley, Ruth, 519–520, 525–526
Harlow, Harry F., 522
Healy, Jim, 228
Headford, Ron, 36–37, 44
Helffrich, Stockton, 339
    on the NAB Code, 345–349
Henry, Bill, 16
Henry, E. William, 299, 304, 308
Herford, Peter, 41, 44
Herzog, Herta, 153
Hewitt, Don, 306
Hickey, Neil, 9, 10, 34, 62, 79, 121, 477, 500
Hicks, Louise Day, 14
Hilgard, Ernest R., 529
Himmelweit, Hilde, 503–505
Hobson, Dick, 174–175, 192, 387
Hoffman, Nicholas, 511
Hoffman, Robert M., 249
House Committee on Un-American Activities, 88
House Interstate and Foreign Commerce Committee, 88
Howe, Quincy, 305
Howland, Jack, 420, 422
Hudson, Peggy, 339
Hughes, Howard, 211
Humphrey, Hal, 197
Humphrey, Hubert, 91, 92, 94
Huntley, Chet, 48, 98, 325

Hyde, Rosel H., 290, 294–295, 300–302, 377
Hyman, Herbert, 170

I

Image Candidates, The (Wyckoff), 473
Intellects as television audiences, 442–445
Intelligent Man's Guide to Broadcast Ratings, The (Mayer), 397
Interviews of television news, 13–16

J

Jaffe, Sam, 48
Jahncke, Ernest Lee, 356–358
Janowitz, Morris, 33
Jarriel, Tom, 67
Javits, Jacob, 473
Jencks, Richard W., 127
Jobin, Judy, 232, 498
Johnsen, Grace, 356–358, 513–514
Johnson, Lyndon B., 84, 85–86, 474
Johnson Nicolas, 288–289, 330–337
Jones, Jenkin Lloyd, 90
Judicial proceedings, effects of television representations on, 541–544
Julian, Artie, 199, 200

K

Kahn, Irving, 583, 585
Kalischer, Peter, 38, 47, 48
Kantor, Hal, 255–256
Karasik, Dan, 588–590
Karp, Nathan, 497
Keiter, Les, 227–228
Kemp, Frank, 247
Kennedy, Edward, 96, 98, 100
Kennedy, Florynce, 262
Kennedy, John F., 84, 474
Kennedy, Robert F., 6, 89
Kerner Commission (National Advisory Commission on Civil Disorders), 60, 61, 62, 73–77, 252
Kimball, Penn, 99–100, 102

600

King, Martin Luther, 6, 252
Kissinger, Henry, 8
Klapper, Joseph, 522
Klein, Barbara, 170, 172
Klein, Paul, 123–124, 395–396
Klein, Woody, 17–18
Knopf, Christopher, 176, 178, 180,
    181, 186, 187
Knowledge, television as a source of
    children's, 501–505
Koestler, Arthur, 523
Koslow, Marvin, 150, 151–152
Kronenberger, Louis, 537
Kubasik, Ben, 91, 430–431
Kubie, Lawrence S., 508
Kubrik, Stanley, 230
Kuhn, Bowie, 213, 214–215
Kulik, Buzz, 199

L

Lachenbruch, David, 563
Landis, James M., 293, 301
Lang, Kurt, 100–101, 104
Langhoff, Peter, 391
Language. *See* Effects of television
Laughter
    canned, 194–200
    causes of, 204–207
Laurence, John, 39, 67
Laurent, Lawrence, 475
Learning theory of children and
    television, 527–528
Lejins, Peter, 512
Leonard, Robert, 121
Leonard, Sheldon, 193, 197, 200
Lerner, Max, 65, 92–93
Lesser, Gerald, 533, 534
Letters, audience, 419–423
Lewis, Richard Warren, 120–121
Lindemann, Carl, 212, 214, 219
Lindsay, John, 99
Loevinger, Lee, 3, 104, 294, 297–298,
    451, 491
Logan, Clara, 513
Long, Russell B., 89, 103
Lower, Elmer W., 26, 305, 322
Ludden, Allen, 171, 172
Ludel, Susan, 498

Lumet, Sidney, 353–355
Lynes, Russell, 452, 509–510

M

McAndrew, William, 305
MacArthur, Douglas, 8
McCarthy, Eugene, 94
McClellan, John, 64
Maccoby, Eleanor, 503–504, 527
McCurdy, Gene, 149
McDermott, Thomas, 176, 181
MacDonald, Torbet, 64
McGee, Frank, 33
McGinniss, Joe, 472–473
McGovern, George, 94
McGuire, Don, 198, 200
McKinnon, Ellen, 420, 422
McLuhan, Marshall, 230, 250, 454
McNeil, Robert, 4, 34, 472
MacPhail, Bill, 211, 213–214, 222
Magazines, effects of television on,
    547–549
Magnuson, Warren G., 495
Mail, audience, 419–423
Mailer, Norman, 92
Makkay, Elizabeth, 507
Malcolm X, 61
Malone, Bill, 171, 172
Maloney, Martin, 35, 253, 363, 537
Maloney, Ray, 38
Mannes, Marya, 5, 154, 174, 265–266
Marks, Richard, 74, 76
Martin, Madelyn, 270, 274
Maschmeier, Howard, 149
Matney, Bill, 67
Mayer, Martin, 231, 286–287, 397,
    536–537
Menaker, William, 161
Menninger, Jean, 452
Menninger, Karl, 452
Meredith, James, 66
Metzger, Gail, 390
Midgley, Les, 8
Military criticism of television
    coverage of Vietnam, 36–49
Miller, Marvin, 215
Miller, Ray, 12, 18
Minow, Newton, 476–477
Mitchell, John H., 138–139

Moll, Alan, 14–15
Monash, Paul, 186–187
Monroe, William, 60
Moon, Henry Lee, 65
Moore, Thomas W., 139, 396, 590
Morgan, Edward P., 8
Morris, Howie, 192
Mosel, Tad, 174
Movies
  effects of television on, 545–549
  movie codes and television, 356–
    358
  sexy, 350–355
Mudd, Roger, 97

N

NAB Code (National Association of
    Broadcasters), 177, 345–349,
    367, 374
Nabors, Jim, 120
Nader, Ralph, 325, 332–333
Namath, Joe, 212
Napolitan, Joseph, 473
Nash, N. Richard, 174
National Advisory Commission on
    Civil Disorders (Kerner
    Commission), 60, 61, 62, 73–
    77
National Association for Better
    Broadcasting, 427, 428, 507
National Association of Broadcasters,
    Code of, 177, 345–349, 361,
    374
National Audience Board, 427, 429
National Broadcasting Company
    (NBC), coverage of the 1968
    Democratic Convention, 90,
    95–97, 107–111
National Citizens Committee for
    Broadcasting, 427–431
National Commission on the Causes
    and Prevention of Violence, 88,
    360–363, 451, 498, 508, 517–
    526, 534
Naylor, John, 150
NBC. *See* National Broadcasting
    Company
Negroes. *See* Blacks and television

Nessen, Ron, 39–40
Network censorship and drama, 177–
    178
Neuman, E. Jack, 176, 179, 507
Nevens, Joe, 17
New York Philharmonic, 432
New York Post, 91–92
New York Times, 472, 473
News, 3–32
  Agnew's criticism of tv, 6–9
  bulletins, 25–29
  challenges of tv, 30–32
  editorial policies of tv, 20–24
  interviews of tv, 13–16
  newspapers compared to tv, 3–5,
    11–12
  politics, television and, 477–483
  public reliance on tv, 9–10
  quality of tv, 12–19
  Survey of Broadcast Journalism
    criticism of tv, 5–6
  See also Political Conventions;
    Urban television coverage;
    Vietnam, television coverage of
Newsmen in Vietnam, 36–46
Newspapers
  compared to television news, 3–5,
    11–12
  effects of tv on, 545–549
Nielsen, A. C., Jr., 387, 389
Nielsen ratings. *See* A. C. Nielsen
    Company
Nixon, Richard M., 6, 84, 92, 472, 510
Nizer, Louis, 536
Norford, George, 259, 260, 263
Northshield, Robert (Shad), 34, 589
Norton, George, 190

O

O'Grady, Jack, 41
O'Hallaren, Bill, 193
Oliver, Don, 67
Opotowsky, Stan, 324
Orange, Aaron, 303
Orme, Frank, 428
Orr, William T., 145, 514
Overbay, Jim, 13–14

602 **P**

Paley, William S., 3, 127, 131, 432
Palmer, Edward L., 530–531
Pastore, John O., 89, 151, 288, 338,
    362, 496
  on "cleaning up" television, 340–
    344
  on the Fairness Doctrine, 313–315
Patrick, Van, 228–229
Pearson, Drew, 14, 91–92
Pell, Claiborne, 363
Pennington, Bob, 227
People Look at Television, The, 411–
    418
People Machine, The (McNeil), 4,
    34, 472
Perian, Carl, 512–514, 516
Permanent Subcommittee on
    Investigations, 64
"Permissiveness"
  "cleaning up tv," Pastore on, 340–
    344
  movie codes, 356–358
  NAB Code, Helffrich on, 345–349
  sexy movies on television, 350–355
  See also Violence and television
Perris, Don, 148
Peters, Art, 253–254
Petersmeyer, C. Wrede, 497
Peterson, Roger, 37, 39, 43–44
Peterson, Sheldon, 11–12
Pilot programs, 119–120
Pinkham, Richard A. R., 18, 144, 247
Political Conventions, 78–115
  Chicago Democratic Convention
    coverage
    by the networks, 95–98, 106–111
    complaints against, 87–88
    future effects of, 103–105
    investigations, letters and
      criticism of, 88–92
    objectivity of, 98–103
    opinion of academicians of, 98–
      101
    press and television antagonisms,
      92–95
    television and, 87–115

traditional role of television in, 81–
    86
Politics, 472–497
  campaign costs and television, 484–
    487
  criticism of Section 315a of the
    Communications Act, 488–493
  impact of television on, 477–483
  news coverage and, 477–483
Politics and Television (Lang), 100
Porter, Paul, 293–294
Powell, Tom, 15
Prange, Helen, 503
Preminger, Otto, 354
Pressman, Gabe, 12–13, 18
Pressure groups
  effects on television drama of, 178–
    179
  success of, 427–431
  See also Corporate pressure
Prime-time schedule, finalization of
    1969–70 CBS, 127–134
Programming, 119–152
  audience attitudes about, 414–418
  cancellation of shows, 122–126
  finalization of 1969–70 CBS
    prime-time schedule, 127–134
  obtaining sponsors for, 135–137
  selling of, 138–146
  Turn-On, 147–152
  See also Advertising; Blacks and
    television; Daytime programming;
    Drama on television; "Permissive-
    ness"; Sports on television; Wom-
    en and television
"Psy-Color-Gy" report, 249–251
Public Arts, The (Seldes), 192
Public Information Officers, 43–44, 51
Public reliance on television news, 3,
    9–10, 11–12
Publishing industry and television,
    545–549
Pucinski, Roman, 89–90

Q

Quality of television news, 12–19
Quiz shows, 169–173

R

Radio, effects of tv on, 545–549
Radio Act (1927), 285, 489
Rankin, Peter, 429
Rather, Dan, 39–40, 49, 94
Ratings, 122–126, 385–410
  demographics and, 393–395, 403–407
  difficulty obtaining accurate, 389–393
  methods of obtaining, 393–397
  Nielsen defends, 398–402
  "tyrany of," 180–181
  See also A. C. Nielsen Company; Audiences
Ray, William, 294
Rayburn, Gene, 170
Raymond, Charles K., 239
Read, A. Louis, 21
Reagan, Ronald, 14
Reasoner, Harry, 171
Reiner, Carl, 192
Renick, Ralph, 16
Reston, James, 18–19
Reynolds, Debbie, 120
Rich, John, 48
Rich, Lee, 191
Riots. *See* Urban television coverage
Robinson, Layhmond, 24
Rockefeller, Nelson, 474
Rodboon, Vallop, 39
Roddenberry, Gene, 176, 177, 180, 182, 185, 187
Role of television, 451–471
  actual and potential, 453–457
  as a form of communion, 458–460
  five functions of tv, 461–464
  for socially and culturally backward areas, 465–468
  senior citizens and, 469–471
  See also Children and television; Effects of television; Politics and television
Rolfe, Sam, 184–185
Roosevelt, Eleanor, 452
Roper survey, 3
Rose, Reginald, 174
Ross, Philip, 501

Rozelle, Pete, 210, 211, 213–214, 220
Rucker, Bryce, 325, 333
Rule, Elton, 148, 151

S

Salant, Richard S., 68, 105, 289, 305, 588
Sarnoff, David, 251, 494–495
Satellite transmissions, 586–590
Schickel, Richard, 459
Schlatter, George, 150–152, 200
Schlesinger, Arthur, Jr., 288, 474–475
  on the Fairness Doctrine, 319–321
Schneider, John A., 127, 131
Schneider, Paul, 184
Schramm, Wilbur, 503, 504, 505, 507–509, 516, 518–519, 521, 523, 526, 530–531, 532
Schwartz, Marvin, 354–355
Schwerin, Horace, 241–243, 247–248
Scott, Hugh, 64–65
Scott, Lloyd, 503
Screen Gems Incorporated, 138
Secondari, John, 306
Section 315a. *See* Communications Act (1934)
Seldes, Gilbert, 192, 433, 473
Selling of the President, The (McGinniss), 472–473
Senate Commerce Committee, 88, 91
Senate Communications Subcommittee, 64, 498
Senior citizens and television, 469–471
Serling, Rod, 174, 183
Sevareid, Eric, 5, 8, 48, 93, 98, 327, 336, 507
Sex on television. *See* "Permissiveness"
Shain, Percy, 12
Shapiro, Mike, 496
Shaw, David, 174
Shayon, Robert Lewis, 101, 253, 428
Sheehan, William, 65
Sidney, P. Jay, 260, 261, 264
Siepmann, Charles, 362
Silliphant, Stirling, 176–181, 183–185, 187
Simmons, Richard Alan, 176, 177, 181

604   Simpson, O. J., 212
Skornia, Harry, 4, 432–433
Smith, Howard K., 8, 48, 95, 98, 306
Snead, Sam, 221
Snell, David, 36–37
Soap operas, 153–154, 156–168
Society
   commercials as a mirror of,
     236–238
   effects of television on, 550–557
   role of television in, 451–471
Sommers, Jay, 199
Sonneborn, Harry, 18
Sorenson, Carl, 39
Sorenson, Theodore C., 446
Spence, Leslie, 428
Sponsors, 135–137
Sports Network Incorporated, 211
Sports on television, 208–229
   benefits of, 223–225
   corruption of sportscasters, 226–229
   cost factors in coverage of, 210–215
   detrimental influences of, 216–222
Sportscasters, corruption of, 226–229
Standards, raising of audience,
   437–441
Stanton, Frank, 7, 33, 61, 65, 94–95,
   127, 132, 322, 361, 387, 409,
   432, 433, 473
   Section 315, on, 494
Stein, Jess, 536
Steiner, Garry A., 244, 411–418
Steinman, Ron, 42
Stephenson, William, 454
Stewart, Bob, 169–170, 171–172
Stokes, Carl, 110
Stout, Bill, 36, 39–40
Supreme Court, 288
Surgeon-General's Scientific Advisory
   Committee on Television and
   Social Behavior, 362, 498,
   511–515
Survey of Broadcast Journalism
   (1968-69), 5–6
Sylvester, Arthur, 49, 51

T

Taft, Robert A., 83–84
Tankersley, William, 356–358

Tannenbaum, Percy, 362
Telephone calls, audience, 424–426
Television and Education in the
   United States (Siepmann),
   362
Television and Presidential Politics,
   473
Television Digest, 90
Television news. See News
Television News: A Critical Appraisal
   (Skornia), 4
Television Today and Tomorrow, 563
Thomas, Alan, 434–435
Thompson, Charles, 473
Thurmond, Strom, 83
Tinker, Grant, 198
Tors, Ivan, 508
Tower, Charles, 326–327
Toynbee, Arnold, 433
Treyz, Oliver, 138, 515
Truman, Harry S, 82–83
Tuckner, Howard, 36, 37–42
Turn-On, 147–152
TV—The Big Picture (Opotowsky),
   324

U

Unsafe at Any Speed (Nader), 325
Urban television coverage, 60–77
   civil rights movement, 60–62
   Detroit riot coverage, 70–77
   shaping of events by, 63–69

V

Valenti, Jack, 351
Values taught by television, 505–510
Vane, Ed, 170, 171
Variety, 156, 333
Vidal, Gore, 174
Vietnam, television coverage of, 33–59
   censorship and, 49–53
   as the first "television war," 55–59
   military criticism of, 36–49
   newsmen in, 36–46
Viewers. See Audiences
Viewing, reasons for, 412–413
Violence and television, 359–380

audience attitudes towards,
  416–417
children and, 510–528
"Dimension of Violence in
  Television Drama," 364–370
harmful effects of, 371–375

W

Walker report, 88–89, 94, 103
Wallace, Henry A., 83
Wallace, Mike, 94, 171
Walsh, Patrick, 231
Walters, Barbara, 421
Walters, Richard, 517, 521, 525
Wasilewski, Vincent T., 496–497
Watson, Carl, 351
Weinberg, George, 527–528
Werner, Mort, 394, 590
Wertham, Fredric, 526, 527, 555–556
Westfield, Wally, 8
Westin, Avram, 8
Wheeler, Harvey, 472
White, Larry, 170, 171
White, Phyllis, 184
White, Robert, 184
White, Sheldon, 533

White, Theodore, 472, 474
White, William S., 78–79
Williams, Mason, 327–328
Winick, Charles, 502, 504, 505, 523
Winsor, Roy, 156, 161
Wolfe, Digby, 150, 151
Women and television, 265–280
  lack of women newscasters,
    276–280
  traditional role of, 267–275
Wood, Robert D., 127, 133
Wood, William A., 13, 99
World Series, 212–213, 220
Writers
  comedy, 193, 201–203
  drama, 174–191
Wyckoff, Gene, 473

Y

Yankey, Tom, 227
Young, Whitney, 262–263
Young & Rubicam Incorporated, 140,
  141, 150
Younger, J. Arthur, 496

Z

Zousmer, Jesse 28